Hutterite Beginnings

Hutterite Beginnings

Communitarian Experiments
during the Reformation

Werner O. Packull

The Johns Hopkins University Press
Baltimore and London

Published in cooperation with the Center for American Places,
Harrisonburg, Virginia.

© 1995 The Johns Hopkins University Press
All rights reserved. Published 1995
Printed in the United States of America on acid-free paper

Johns Hopkins Paperbacks edition, 1999
2 4 6 8 9 7 5 3 1

The Johns Hopkins University Press
2715 North Charles Street
Baltimore, Maryland 21218-4363
www.press.jhu.edu

Library of Congress Cataloging-in-publication data will be
found at the end of this book.
A catalog record for this book is available from the
British Library.

ISBN 0-8018-6256-6 (pbk.)

Meiner Mutter, Leokadia (Seemann)
Packull (1905–94)

With gratitude to my life's companion,
Karen C. Fiebig-Packull

And to our children Christine and
Reinhold, to Kevin, to Lisa, to
Sara and Nicholas Packull-McCormick

Contents

Acknowledgments   ix

Introduction   1

Part One: The First Communitarian Experiments

One   At the Foundation: The New Testament
          Orientation of Swiss Anabaptist Biblicism   15
Two   The Oldest Anabaptist Congregational Orders:
          The Swiss Contribution   33
Three   In Search of the Promised Land   54
Four   The Philipites: Fugitives from Swabia,
          the Palatinate, and the Rhineland   77
Five   The Gabrielites: A *Volk* from Silesia   99
Six   Marpeck's Early Controversy with the
          Spiritualists: Expanding the Context   133

Part Two: The Emergence of the Hutterites

Seven   South Tyrol: In the Beginning, 1526–1529   161
Eight   Face to Face with the "Forces of Antichrist,"
          1529–1533   187
Nine   Dissension in the "Congregation of God":
          The Schisms of 1531 and 1533   214
Ten   The Return and Death of Jacob Hutter,
          1535–1536   236
Eleven Further Losses, 1536–1538   258
Twelve The Fate of the Philipites and the Gabrielites   283

Appendixes

A   Three Early Anabaptist Congregational Orders   303
B   The Pre-Hutterite Communities   316
C   Known Prisoners at Passau in 1535   318

Notes   323
Bibliography   403
Index   425

Acknowledgments

The Social Science and Humanities Research Council of Canada deserves first mention. Without the research grant and time stipend for 1987–88 as well as subsequent support this work would have been impossible. The original project envisioned a biography of Peter Riedemann, the "second founder" of the Hutterites. That biography still awaits completion, while the intended introduction to it ballooned into the present monograph.

Along the way it was my privilege to use the resources of a number of archives and libraries and to receive gracious assistance from many persons. I am most grateful to the Moravsky Zemsky Archiv, Statni Archiv Brno, and its most competent archivist Dr. M. Coupek; for help received at the Osterreichische Nationalbibliothek and its Handschriftenabteilung; the Diozesanarchiv in Vienna and its archivist, Dr. Johann Weissensteiner; the Archivio vescovile Bressanone (Hofarchiv Brixen) and its director, Dr. Karl Wolfsgruber and his extremely helpful assistant, Dr. Scheiber, who assisted also in the Bibliothek of the Brixner Priesterseminar; Prof. Dr. Noflatscher of Innsbruck who, as archivist in Bolzano, corresponded with me and provided me with literature and a copy of one of his as yet unpublished papers; the Tiroler Landesarchiv, Bibliothek des Fernandeums, and the Universitätsbibliothek in Innsbruck with its competent and extremely helpful staff; the Stadt- und Universitätsbibliothek Graz, and Prof. Dr. Karl Achem of Graz, for his personal interest in my work; the Generallandesarchiv Karlsruhe; the Württembergische Landesbibliothek Stuttgart; the Bayerische Staatsbibliothek and Universitätsbibliothek Munich; and the Universitätsbibliothek Basel.

Special thanks are due to Pfarrer Hans Wiedemann, former dean of the

Evangelische Lutherische Dekanat, Sulzbach-Rosenberg, Bavaria, who made copies of his archival transcriptions intended for a third volume of *Bayerische Täuferakten* available to me and to be placed at the Conrad Grebel College Archive; Magister Josef Franz Enzenberger, who made his exhaustive unpublished bibliography on Austrian Anabaptism and his private collection available to me; Dr. Karl Schwarz of Vienna, for a copy of Grete Mecenseffy's "Bibliographie"; Prof. Dr. Karl Vocelka, who made it possible for me to present parts of my findings at the Institut für die Erforschung der frühen Neuzeit, University of Vienna, July 6, 1992; and Prof. Dr. Gottfried Seebass at the Theologisch-Wissenschaftliche Institut, University Heidelberg, for his support and encouragement over the years.

Closer to home, I owe thanks to archivist Joe Springer of the Mennonite Historical Library and Dr. Leonard Gross, for providing me with photocopies of various materials; Prof. John Oyer and Prof. Walter Klaassen, who read the manuscript, provided valuable commentary, and recommended its publication; Dr. Heinold Fast, who was most encouraging after reading the manuscript; my colleague Prof. Arnold Snyder, for his positive comments; Prof. John Roth, who also read the manuscript and gave encouragement; above all, my "doctorfather" and friend, Prof. James Stayer, for his steady support, encouragement, and many editorial suggestions and for the exchange of ideas and information which make this a better book.

An early German version of parts of Chapters 3 and 7 appeared in *Wegscheiden der Reformation,* edited by Günter Vogler, 1993, and a much abbreviated part of Chapter 7 in the *Sixteenth-Century Journal,* 1991; a part on Clemens Adler of Chapter 5 appeared in the *Conrad Grebel Review.* Other materials in a different context were part of my published Thiessen Lectures. I am grateful for the permission to reuse these materials. Thanks are due to Prof. William Klassen; Prof. John H. Yoder; Prof. John Roth, editor of the *Mennonite Quarterly Review;* and Paul M. Schrock of Herald Press for permission to republish the church orders in Appendix A.

Thanks are also due to administrative assistants Eleanor Dueck, Katie Hamm, Chris Goertz, and Mary Lou Schwartzentruber; student assistants Lisa Schlegel, Rod Peters, Deborah Neill, and especially Dan Thut whose computer skills were extremely valuable in the last stages of the preparation of the manuscript; thanks to my former graduate students Prof. Douglas Shantz, Prof. Gary Waite, and Dr. Edmund Pries for intellectual stimulation. The maps are the work of Barry Levely, University of Waterloo; the sketches are gratis by my brother-in-law Leonard Gerbrandt. I am also grateful that so many of my colleagues at Conrad Grebel

College and the University of Waterloo have taken an interest in my work, especially Prof. John Miller, who sensitized me to the Hutterite perspective. Thanks also to the administrative staff of the college.

Finally, I must give special recognition to Karin, who spent many long hours transcribing my longhand into WordPerfect.

Hutterite Beginnings

Introduction

Introductions provide opportunities to stake a claim in the evolving historiography. Since this manuscript was completed during the anniversary year of Harold Bender's famous presidential address, it seemed appropriate to stake such a claim against the background of his Anabaptist vision statement.[1] Hans Hillerbrand described the statement as the "single most important interpretive piece of a whole generation of Anabaptist scholars."[2] It was, nevertheless, a partisan statement suggesting that the Anabaptists of Swiss origin constituted "the most nearly perfect embodiment of New Testament principles since the days of the Apostles."[3] Of course not everyone in Bender's generation followed this party line. George Williams's 1962 *Radical Reformation* provided a larger cast for the "more or less novel sixteenth-century experiments to reinstate the authentic Christian message." But even in its revised edition of 1992 Williams's encyclopedic work represented a harvest of midcentury studies rather than a harbinger of the new directions that came to the fore in the early 1970s and dominated the 1980s. According to Hillerbrand, a methodological gulf separated the Bender-Williams generation from the revisionists, among whom he listed Martin Haas, James Stayer, and Hans-Jürgen Goertz. These scholars allegedly treated the Reformation no longer as "a societal working out of theological issues" but as "the exact reverse"; that is, they considered theology as socially constructed and therefore, at best, one factor among others. Hillerbrand's observations provide a useful introduction to Anabaptist studies in the post-Bender generation, although they need careful testing.

By way of simplification it can be argued that the interpretation of the Reformation in German-speaking lands had separated into two main schools of thought by the time Bender began his studies in the 1920s and

1930s. On one side was Karl Holl, who in his person symbolized a return to a Luther-centered, religious-cultural interpretation of the Reformation. Coupled to German nationalism this interpretation influenced the likes of Gerhard Ritter and Emmanuel Hirsch.[4] Holl's contribution to Anabaptist studies came in his essay "Luther und die Schwärmer." Needless to say, Holl's negative views did not provide a good starting point for scholars in the free church tradition who were seeking to understand their forefathers. They naturally found greater affinity with the historiographic lineage that, through Ernst Troeltsch, reached back to Max Weber. Troeltsch's typological distinctions among church, sect, and mysticism as genuine expressions of the Christian faith seemed heuristically less prejudicial to the Anabaptists than Holl's "fanatics." But there were other reasons that made Troeltsch more attractive than Holl. Following Weber, Troeltsch held that the more progressive, democratic, and tolerant Anglo-American societies had been influenced positively by the "Reformed" and the nonconformist traditions of the Reformation. Such a reading of the Reformation legacy offered a more promising starting point for free-church historians than a theologically Luther-dominated interpretation. Alongside the Reformed, the Anabaptists could be viewed as progressives or as forerunners of the modern separation of state and church.[5]

As a student of Walter Koehler at Heidelberg, Bender was inducted into the Troeltsch-Weber interpretation of the Reformation. His own Swiss Mennonite background led naturally to a study of Anabaptist beginnings in the Swiss Reformed (Zwinglian) context. The results came to fruition in his published dissertation, *Conrad Grebel, 1498–1526: The Founder of the Swiss Brethren Sometimes Called Anabaptists*. Bender's opus represented church history in the tradition of the history of ideas, undergirded by an idealist philosophy of history. Accordingly, Anabaptism grew out of "things most surely believed." In the case of Grebel, the acknowledged leader of the first Swiss Brethren, personal and literary sources seemed worth considering for the things believed. Among the literary sources, the Bible in turn took prominence. The beginnings of adult baptism, January 21, 1525, were traceable to prayerful reflection on New Testament precedent and the desire to follow literally the Great Commission.[6] The search for the true Church and for pristine practice had led Grebel and his companions back to the New Testament. The implied biblical determinism assumed that wherever the sacred texts were read with sincerity and commitment the outcome would be the same: a return to a pre-Constantinian, New Testament church. Differences between Zwingli and the Anabaptists could be attributed to the latter's uncompromising adherence to New Testament principles and to Zwingli's deviation from them.[7] The possibility of a situational reading of the Scriptures played no significant role in this interpretive frame of reference. The dialectic between religious convictions and social situation had been decided in favor of the former. Hillerbrand's observation that Bender's generation saw the Reformation as a societal working out of theological principles seems partly correct.

The theological interpretation of the Reformation was, of course, in vogue among church historians of Bender's generation, a generation influenced by neo-orthodoxy in the related field of theology. This was true for both the Reformed and Lutheran traditions. Confessional yardsticks were invoked to delineate orthodox from heterodox movements. Bender's insistence on Anabaptist orthodoxy and his rejection of any humanist influence on Grebel are best understood in this context.[8] But it was already clear to Bender and his generation that an interpretive grid derived from the theology of the magisterial reformer's ill suited the more practical, ethical Anabaptists. It is a monument to Bender's historic astuteness that his vision statement condensed Anabaptist essence to discipleship, voluntarism, and nonresistant love. He thereby set Anabaptism and its heirs apart from those who sought their identity primarily in theological dogma.[9] It was the simplicity, clarity, and apparent historic authenticity of the vision statement which proved so persuasive and inspirational. With a stroke of genius Bender provided an alternative to the polarized liberal-conservative, modernist-fundamentalist debate that threatened to divide his own community of Mennonites. By focusing on practice and ethics while appealing to Reformation and New Testament precedent, Bender had found a potent usable past with normative contemporary relevance which would fuel a Renaissance in Anabaptist research.

What, then, led to the demise of Bender's normative vision? And why was that demise so readily accepted? These are separate, although related, questions without simple answers. For instance, it would be simplistic to argue that Bender's view of Anabaptism came under criticism primarily because of a shift in methodology from intellectual to social history.[10] Most scholars recognize that no single methodology is adequate to provide a definitive explanation of such a complex historic phenomenon.[11] True, key studies in the 1970s and 1980s revealed a shift to a more comprehensive social contextual reading of Anabaptist beginnings. But the history of ideas approach remains a necessary part of any attempt at understanding religious self-perceptions and the language of the period. Moreover, the methodological shift came only gradually and not in terms of either/or, religious or social explanation. Most of the so-called revisionists began with assumptions and methodologies not that different from those of Bender's generation.[12] They found fault not with Bender's methodology but with its selective and narrow focus in Swiss sources.

Problems arose when Bender's vision statement was turned on the past to sift true from false Anabaptists. What did not serve apologetic ends was pushed to the periphery as aberration, half-Anabaptist (*Halbtäufer*), or peripheral figures (*Randfiguren*). Such selectivity truncated and fragmented the Anabaptist movement, leaving scholars with too many anomalies. Balthasar Hubmaier, a key Anabaptist theologian who did not fit the sectarian, pacifist Bender model, had to be abandoned to Baptist scholars. The Hutterites, who insisted on the normativity of community of goods, did not entirely fit the original Anabaptist vision. More complicated was the case of Hans Hut, the most significant advocate of Anabaptism in South Germany and Austria. Hut explicitly rejected certain Swiss teachings and was compromised by his association with Thomas Müntzer. On Müntzer, Bender and his colleagues agreed with Holl, who considered him a religious fanatic and social revolutionary.[13] Attempts to rehabilitate Hut, therefore, postulated his conversion to an evangelical Anabaptism, but the results were unconvincing. The mystical Hans Denck and his controversial recantation also remained problematic. Similar observations were in order regarding Melchior Hoffman, the main link between Anabaptism in the South and in the North. His peculiar Christology and preoccupation with the Apocalypse did not fit an orthodox Anabaptism. And if Hoffman failed the litmus test of the Anabaptist vision, historic connections between true Anabaptists and the kingdom in Münster seemed out of the question altogether. But any attempt to link Swiss Anabaptism with the followers of Menno Simons without Melchior Hoffman left a major gap in the historic procession from pure Alpine springs.[14]

Hans-Jürgen Goertz, the revisionist perhaps most critical of Bender, complained that a version of Anabaptism—cleansed of spiritualistic, enthusiastic, apocalyptic, and revolutionary elements—was more myth than historic reality. According to Goertz, historic truth was better served by those who recognized Anabaptist diversity and sought a more comprehensive understanding of its social-religious manifestations, even if such a view created problems in terms of a usable past.[15] The historian's primary task was to be faithful to the sources and to aim at a comprehensive understanding of the past.

Of course, if we accept that Bender's contemporary commitments colored his vision, we must, in all fairness, entertain that possibility for the revisionists. In other words, did the revisionists have a different *Sitz im Leben* or write with a different audience in mind than did Bender and his colleagues? The answer seems to be a qualified yes. The so-called revisionists, by and large, wrote with less denominational commitment and primarily with the scholarly community in mind.[16] True, Bender was a skilled member of the scholarly fraternity, but as a leader in a community of faith he knew how to blend his scholarly interests and faith commitments in a way to serve that community. His critics, on the other hand, felt accountable primarily to the scholarly community that included "unbelievers." This is not to suggest that the revisionists were unsympathetic to church historians or insensitive to the depth of sixteenth-century religious commitments, but their social location was primarily in academia. They took for granted that Anabaptist studies had to be carried out in conscious dialogue with broader developments in the Reformation field. From the 1970s on these developments have been in the direction of detheologizing and rehistorizing the events collectively known as the Reformation. The Reformation has moved from the sacred realm into "the context of secular history."[17] Numerous studies on the Reformation in the cities have led the way, and a growing interest in the rural Reformation has followed.[18] During the 1970s and 1980s Anabaptist scholars began to interact with these historiographic developments. Influenced by the leading scholarship in the broader field, they sought a more comprehensive contextual, social-political understanding of the Anabaptist religious protest. This did not mean replacing the theological with a social explanation but rather an attempt to ground religious consciousness and meaning in the immediate historic circumstances.[19]

Without question the trend to rehistorize and detheologize combined with the recognition of Anabaptist diversity made it more difficult to identify a usable normative past.[20] As Goertz observed, "theology carries normative character and its normativity imbues history with normativity." A detheologized history correspondingly loses its normativity. Goertz cautioned against leaps over "historical distances" and counseled prudence in attempts to recover contemporary meaning from an unrepeatable past. He rejected an uncritical appropriation of the "great refusal," that is, of Anabaptist sectarian separation, and found it ironic that its descendants depended on the modern state for their preservation of a "toothless, anachronistic nonconformity." He criticized contemporary Mennonites for "accommodation with bourgeois capitalist society."[21] He sought contemporary relevance in Anabaptists siding with the forces of change in their own time. By way of modern analogy, this would mean an alliance with progressive contemporary social elements. For Goertz, these were to be found not in world-denying self-preservation but in social engagement. Social justice, not separation of state and church, seemed the crucial issue today. He believed that the Anabaptist communal and fraternal tradition could contribute toward a solution of the modern and postmodern human dilemma.

But any usable past presents the problem of intended constituency. The evident appeal of Bender's vision statement to members of the Mennonite and free church constituencies of North America suggests its usefulness to these communities. Goertz appears to have appealed to a different constituency. Reflecting on the demise of the normative vision and the acceptance of the pluralistic view of Anabaptism, Stayer surmised that the easy demise of Bender's view had as much to do with its limited appeal even among Mennonites.[22] By insisting on the normativity of the Swiss, Bender treated descendants of the northern branch like prodigals who could become true members of the Anabaptist family only by conformity to the ideal Swiss model, which had not been the case historically. Moreover, the post-Bender generation seemed more receptive to a radical social reading and more activist model of Anabaptism.[23] Whatever the merit of such an explanation, it highlights the problem with intentionally reconstructed usable pasts. Even the Mennonite constituency is becoming more rather than less diverse.

What dilemma may occur when a usable past becomes the primary interest in history may be illustrated with reference to a *Brief Summary of the History of the Swiss Anabaptists,* published in 1990 by the Eastern Pennsylvania Mennonite Church, a small conservative group. In a parody of Bender's labor this history considers as false teachers Hans Denck, Balthasar Hubmaier, and Melchior Hoffman, alongside the Münsterites. The truncated remnant is then invoked to condemn modern apostates, including Bender's own denomination, the (Old) Mennonite Church, as well as the General Conference Mennonites. Obviously, professional historians cannot be faulted if they lack enthusiasm for this kind of history or refuse to enter into disputes based on such selective uses of the past. Their priority, however problematic, must remain an approximation of the Rankean maxim: "Wie es eigentlich gewesen."

Turning to the post-Bender, revisionist scholarship, what then has changed? What has remained the same in our understanding of Anabaptism? One way to illustrate the changes is to highlight major revisionist landmarks. Admittedly, such an enterprise is selective, given the pluralistic state of present scholarship. But the selection proposed here can claim a certain consensus. With hindsight, 1972 and 1975 marked turning points in Anabaptist historiography. 1972 saw the publication of Claus-Peter Clasen's *Anabaptism: A Social History* and James Stayer's *The Anabaptists and the Sword.* It was also the year that Gottfried Seebass completed his "Habilitationsschrift" on Hans Hut, whom he described simply as "Thomas Müntzer's heir." Clasen's work has remained the most ambitious attempt at a social history of Anabaptism. At the time it provoked the criticism of traditionalists because it seemed to minimize the importance of religious or theological ideas. Equally provocative were his statistics that tended to reduce the significance of Anabaptism as a reform movement. Clasen argued against Marxist contentions of a connection to the Peasants' War. He considered the Anabaptists socially insignificant and culturally destructive. He distinguished a number of groups on the basis of geographic location and provided a description of practices and behavior which seemed at times incongruent with the traditional Anabaptist vision.

If Clasen's work could be written off as that of an unsympathetic outsider who lacked religious sensitivities, Stayer's study of political ethic proved more difficult to shrug off. His meticulous documentation revealed the existence of a variety of Anabaptist attitudes and positions on the sword, ranging from pacifist nonresistance to violent apocalyptic crusading. The broad sweep of his survey demonstrated the untenability of a homogeneous, nonresistant Anabaptism, while his detailed examination of Swiss beginnings illustrated how inextricably interwoven were religious and social-political issues. According to Stayer, even the founding members of Swiss Anabaptism initially oscillated between militance and pacifism. Nonresistance emerged as normative only after considerable ambivalence. Original intentions were not separatist but aimed at a radicalization and speeding up of the territorial reform process. In this scenario Hubmaier's magisterial Anabaptism at Waldshut did not represent an aberration but was part of the early Swiss Anabaptist experience.

Stayer's findings on the Swiss were supported by Martin Haas, who had come independently to a similar conclusion as he retraced the "path of the Anabaptists into separation" and illustrated the "interdependence of theology and social behavior."[24] According to Haas, nonresistance and separation emerged by trial and error out of a volatile situation in a struggle for religious and societal reform. Separation was as much a product of circumstances as it was the result of religious ideals. The Schleitheim Articles represented a crystallization of nonresistance and nonconformist tendencies latent earlier among some of Zwingli's radical followers. With it the idea of transforming the whole society had been given up.

The article by Haas appeared first in *Umstrittenes Täufertum*, edited by Hans-Jürgen Goertz and published in 1975. That same year saw the publication of "From Monogenesis to Polygenesis: The Historical Discussion of Anabaptist Origins," coauthored by James M. Stayer, Klaus Deppermann, and myself. This article attempted a new conceptualization of generic groupings in light of Anabaptist diversity revealed by the newer research.[25] Instead of postulating or fabricating a movement with a single tap root in Swiss soil and an assumed common vision, we proposed an interpretive paradigm that permitted heterogeneity in both roots and branches. Accordingly, a tripartite grouping into Swiss Brethren, South-German Austrian, and North-German Dutch Anabaptism seemed in order. *Umstrittenes Täufertum,* meanwhile, featured the clash between the traditionalist and revisionist interpretations. Theologically oriented articles appeared beside the newer, more contextually grounded histories such as the articles by Stayer and Haas.[26] Only with hindsight is it possible to argue that the polygenesis article and *Umstrittenes Täufertum* marked the passage to the post-Bender generation. The diversity of Anabaptism had entered the interpretive paradigm. The subjectively restrictive definition of *normative* Anabaptism had given way to a historically broader definition encompassing all who engaged in adult baptism. Gradually the new perspective brought other redefinitions. These were encouraged by yet another event in 1975, the anniversary celebrations of the Peasants' War, which placed this major social upheaval back on the research agenda from which it had been banned by a theologized Reformation.[27] Anniversary conferences commemorating 1525–26 accelerated the dialogue between East German Marxist scholarship and scholarship in the West, all with consequences for Anabaptist studies.[28]

After 1975 Anabaptist scholars found themselves increasingly engaged in dialogue with social historians who were in the vanguard of rehistoricizing the Reformation. As these scholars were drawn into a broader contextual consideration of their subject, the paradigmatic terminology in use since Bender's generation, including the labels *left wing* (Fast and Bainton) and *radical Reformation* (Williams), which subsumed the Anabaptists, gradually underwent redefinition.[29] If Williams thought of radical in a purely religious and literal sense of returning to New Testament roots, scholars of the late 1970s and 1980s focused on the interplay between religious perceptions and the social-political situation. They took note that the novel attempt to reinstitute the New Testament church was accompanied by anticlerical, antisacramental, antisacerdotal, and iconoclastic manifestations. To deny the objective validity of sacraments and to engage in ritual violence against sacred objects, such as crucifixes, shrines, images, and processions, had radical social significance. Refusal to give the oath or to participate in the defense of the existing order, when "Christian" Europe seemed threatened by the "infidel" Turks, had radical implications for sixteenth-century society. By depriving established customs, laws, and practices of their religious legitimacy in the name of a higher religious authority, the Gospel, Anabaptists in effect threatened the very foundation of existing society; or so it seemed to the authorities, who, not surprisingly, detected in Anabaptism echoes of the peasant rebellion.

True, traditional scholarship recognized the social radicality of some aspects of Anabaptism but considered these secondary or nonessential. Indeed, it could be argued that some of the radical features (e.g., iconoclasm) were not peculiarly Anabaptist but something they shared with others: Thomas Müntzer, Andreas Karlstadt, the "Zwickau Prophets," sacramentists, and in part the entire early Reformed movement. But this was precisely why revisionists took a broader view: "Both the isolation of the Anabaptist field and the idealization of the Anabaptists" had to be abandoned.[30]

On one front, however, revisionists agreed with the traditionalists, namely on the religious kinship of Anabaptists with the Reformed tradition, especially with regard to the Zwinglian understanding of the Lord's Supper. But the context in which the emergence of Anabaptism had to be understood was broadened from the city Reformation (Zurich) to the inclusion of Zurich's subject territory. If traditional scholarship saw Swiss Anabaptists as a radical wing of the Zwinglian Reformed party who pushed for speedier religious reforms, revisionists went further, noting that the future Anabaptists disagreed with Zwingli on the issue of tithe and the right of Zurich's villages to appoint their own preachers. Given the evident solidarity between early Anabaptists and the rural inhabitants on these issues, the inquiry broadened from a preoccupation with the religious disputes between Reformed theologians and Anabaptists to a consideration of the common aspirations of Anabaptists and peasants. Thus, ten years after Clasen formulated the thesis that the Anabaptists had no important connections to the Peasants' War of 1525, Stayer declared this connection in need of further clarification.[31] It was a task all the more urgent because Peter Blickle, a leading authority in peasant studies, suggested that peasant aspirations of reform should be considered under the rubric of Communal Reformation (*Gemeindereformation*).[32]

In contrast to the Princely Reformation, Communal Reformation presupposed the autonomy of the local community (village or town) or at least the right of the local parish to control its religious affairs, appoint and dismiss its spiritual leaders. These were to be preachers of the "pure Gospel": the Gospel understood as a blueprint for a more equitable fraternal society. The community or its discerning members assumed that they were qualified to judge whether or not the Gospel was being preached. In other words, the Communal Reformation was implicitly or explicitly premised on the notion that the local congregation constituted the hermeneutic community, qualified to discern the meaning of Scripture.[33] Obviously such assumptions, premised on a vernacular biblicism, had implications beyond purely ecclesiological matters and ran counter to the interests of established authorities, both spiritual and temporal. Not surprisingly, the Communal Reformation was brought to grief by the combined armies of princes, city magistrates, and in some cases bishops or abbots. Nevertheless, according to Blickle, a residual element of the Communal Reformation lived on in both the Reformed and Anabaptist traditions. Similar claims had been made earlier by East German Gerhard Zschäbitz but within a Marxist frame of reference of an overarching early bourgeois revolution. These claims had been largely ignored in the West.[34]

When Stayer reexamined these claims in his *The German Peasant's War and Anabaptist Community of Goods* (1991),[35] he found that in terms of economic attitudes Anabaptists owed "a crucial if indirect" debt to broader peasant aspirations. He was also able to document that a number of important early Anabaptists had been deeply involved in the peasants' uprising and undeniably influenced by it. These findings, "the tip of the iceberg," challenged not only Clasen's thesis of no connection between the populist and the separatist Anabaptist movements but also the traditional insistence on the categorical differences between the violent peasants and peaceful Anabaptists. And Stayer proposed yet another revision, namely that the Swiss initially aimed at the New Testament practice of community of goods based on Acts 2 and 4 but that circumstances forced them to settle for mutual aid. The South German and Austrian Anabaptists, under the influence of the "antimaterialist spirituality" of Thomas Müntzer, meanwhile, prepared the ideological ground for a more rigorous practice of community of goods, which eventually found its fullest expression in the Hutterite communities of Moravia. Stayer described the latter practice as the most radical social experiment of the day in which the "social radicalism of the early Reformation lived on unabated." In this view even the "war communism" of Münster seemed less of an aberration and a legitimate part of the Anabaptist story.

The point here is that Stayer's monograph illustrated not only a broadening of context but also an expanded definition of radicality, inclusive of social implications. In other words, Stayer was not only interested in the intellectual pedigree of ideas but in their social location and function.[36] Of course, if a social reading of radicality reveals commonalities between Anabaptists and other Reformation radicals, it does the same for the various Anabaptist groups. Stayer's attempt at history "from below," therefore, led him to soften the tripartite divisions postulated earlier in the polygenesis model, at least in regard to Anabaptist economic ethic. A similar tendency to soften distinctions among branches of Anabaptism, while emphasizing their commonalities with broader radical tendencies, may be found in Walter Klaassen's *Living at the End of the Ages: Apocalyptic Expectation in the Radical Reformation* (1992). Klaassen brought medieval depth as well as Reformation breadth to the topic. Thus, Anabaptist apocalyptic ideas were shown to be part of a rich medieval tapestry extending into the Reformation period. It was the climate of expectation, hope, and fear of change which gave apocalyptic ideas new potency during the Reformation. The sense of living at the end of time crossed the boundaries of various religious divisions while straddling elite and popular cultures. Differences among Anabaptist groups proved to be differences in degree of apocalyptic fervor rather than substance. Even some of the Swiss were caught in the end-time fever, a feature overlooked or minimized in earlier studies. By noting the apocalyptic "boulder" in the spiritual landscape of the Swiss while moderating the apocalyptic presence in the ideological landscape of other Anabaptist branches, Klaassen in effect played down a differentiation among branches of Anabaptism on the basis of eschatology or apocalyptic expectations. The Münsterites, depicted as extremists, were the exception.

My own research has led me to a similar softening of divisions among branches of Anabaptism. The effort to reconstruct the narrative of Anabaptist communitarian beginnings suggested that the Swiss, South German-Austrian, and Moravian Anabaptists sought to structure congregational life on the same New Testament models, foremost the apostolic church at Jerusalem with its practice of community of goods. The search for the oldest Anabaptist congregational order led back to Swiss sources, but attempts to identify a practicing congregation were not entirely successful. It appears that only Moravia provided the opportunity to actualize the Jerusalem model. The expulsions from Moravia in 1535, therefore, proved a major turning point for those affected, including the Austerlitz Brethren, Gabrielites, and Philipites. Marpeck and his urbanite followers turned consciously to a postdispersion, post-Jerusalem congregational model. The Swiss Brethren, as noted, settled for mutual aid earlier. Only the Hutterites retained and institutionalized the Jerusalem model, laying claim to the original communitarian vision.

Hutterites, unlike Mennonites, have not produced any academic historians from their midst, yet their history has been well served in our century by a number of competent and sympathetic scholars, among them Robert Friedmann, John Hostettler, and Leonard Gross. Although I cannot claim to write from an insider's perspective, I do not consider myself unsympathetic but decidedly on the side of the victims of sixteenth-century oppression. Nevertheless, I have been forewarned that members of the Hutterite community may find passages of this book less than flattering. I am expecting a similar reaction from some of my Austrian colleagues in regard to the description of Ferdinand's policy of suppression. In defense I plead a good conscience and honorable motives in terms of balancing the historic account. My aim, perhaps somewhat simplistically, has been to provide a sympathetic account of the incredible difficulties encountered and overcome by those valiant women and men seeking the kingdom of God in community.

Part One

The First Communitarian Experiments

Chapter One

At the Foundation

The New Testament Orientation
of Swiss Anabaptist Biblicism

This study, intended as a narrative history of early communitarian Anabaptism, took me back to the beginnings of Swiss Anabaptism. The evident importance of the *Swiss Congregational Order* for other branches of Anabaptism changed my opinion as to the significance of Swiss Anabaptism. Not that I want to revive a monogenetic interpretation of Anabaptism; the heterogeneity of Anabaptism is well documented. There can be no return to upholding Swiss Anabaptism as the normative model against which all other forms must be measured as derivative, deviations, or distortions. Nor is the purpose of this chapter to provide another account of Swiss beginnings.[1] The aim is rather more modest and specific: to reinvestigate the historic emergence of the New Testament orientation of Swiss Anabaptist biblicism which proved foundational for attempts to reinstitute the apostolic church. How did this orientation form, and how was it communicated and preserved?

The Formative Stage

According to scholarly consensus, the Swiss Anabaptists were radical biblicists who broke with Ulrich Zwingli because he reneged on the principle of *sola scriptura* when political push came to shove on practical reform issues. Harold Bender put it pointedly when he wrote that "the Anabaptists were biblicists and it was from the biblical fountains alone that they drank."[2] Bender exaggerated, because the founding fathers of Swiss Anabaptism were also avid readers of the contemporary press. But the label *biblicist* was justified not only because of the unflinching appeal to the Scriptures as final authority, but also because the Swiss Anabaptists declared their loyalty to the principle that only what was explicitly commanded in Scripture or demonstrated by its examples should be normative for the Christian congregation.[3]

It is clear that the narrow application of this criterion helped to shape the emerging Anabaptist community. But it was not the sole factor. The appeal to *sola scriptura,* never unambiguous in a society still predominantly illiterate, could serve a variety of ideological positions. Ideology was in part conditioned by the social-cultural situation (*der Sitz im Leben*). A situational reading of the Scriptures predisposed readers toward specific biblical texts or stories and influenced interpretation. The subjective factor helps to explain how the same texts could be interpreted differently and how qualitatively different forms of biblicism took shape.[4] The social reading of the Gospel as divine law to correct social and economic wrongs by those who led the peasants in 1525 illustrates this point.[5] To recognize the subjective-ideological factor at work in one "hermeneutic community"[6] but to deny it for another seems a prejudicial enterprise at best.

Swiss Anabaptist biblicism was no exception. In principle and fundamentally shaped by Zwingli's early position, it came to represent the dissenting community. That community, it can be argued, was born at the juncture of learneds' and commoners' Reformation and as a result of disagreements with Zwingli over reform polity. Consequently, the evangelical party separated into two hermeneutic communities with "very different . . . contextual readings of the same [scriptural] texts."[7] Zwingli consequently reserved control over the interpretation of Scripture for himself and his learned associates. The Bible "was to be interpreted, and events controlled, by an alliance of the power elite with the preaching intelligentsia."[8] This alliance, institutionalized in Zurich's Prophezei, left the interpretation of the meaning of the Scriptures in the hands of humanistically educated exegetes familiar with the original languages. The radicals, on the other hand, assumed a hermeneutic community with ongoing congregational conversations based on the vernacular Scriptures.[9] This view, written into the first Anabaptist congregational order,[10] ideally involved all members in the interpretation of the Scriptures and meant that ultimate interpretive authority rested not with a literate elite but with the believing, discerning community gathered to hear and obey God's Word. But such a view entailed bringing ordinary layman to the Bible "so that in fellowship with the brethren, he could form his own judgment." The implied "untiring occupation with the Bible by the whole congregation," in turn, explains the amazing knowledge of the Scriptures found among ordinary members.[11] Anabaptist biblicism, it can be argued, shaped and was shaped by the nature of the congregation, which functioned as a hermeneutic community.

No doubt, differences remained between ideal and reality. The ideal, in which all members were equal and the interpretation of the Scriptures was arrived at by consensus, would have proven difficult to achieve at the best of times. Even then, differences remained in matters of spiritual discernment and literary skills required for biblical exegesis.[12] Nevertheless, the attempt to practice the ideal may help to explain the New Testament orientation of Swiss Anabaptist biblicism. In the past, two hypotheses have been proposed to explain this orientation. In one line of argument, the New Testament emphasis arose out of the simple assumption that Christ constituted the final and full revelation of God's will to humankind.[13] Any serious desire to follow Christ's example and heed his teachings would obviously lead to the New Testament. The way of Christ as "hermeneutic formula" explains not only the New Testament orientation and selectivity toward the Old Testament but also the importance granted to the Sermon on the Mount and the sayings of Jesus within the New Testament.[14] In this view, an ethical epistemology determined the hermeneutic starting point.[15] Discipleship, the desire to follow the "rule of Christ," informed the content of Anabaptist biblicism and, in turn, called a New Testament community into being. According to this purely religious explanation, Anabaptist New Testament biblicism appears to have been shaped solely by an individual and collective desire to follow Christ.

The problem with such an explanation lies in its neglect of other factors. Hans-Jürgen Goertz's more contextual understanding of the origins of the New Testament orientation suggested that the Anabaptist position emerged in controversy with Zwingli who sought to transform Zurich into a theocracy.

Gradually they arrived at the discernment that it was not admissible at all to appeal to the Old Testament in matters pertaining to the Christian people of God. Only what is commanded in the New Testament could be normative. The more intensively Zwingli insisted on the Old Testament argument, the more compelled were the Anabaptists to let go of the Old Testament . . . [and because Zwingli] was on the way of reforming Zurich according to the pattern of an Old Testament theocracy, the Anabaptists, by way of reaction, had to found their reform alternative, the longer, the more, on the New Testament.[16]

This attempt at a historical contextual understanding seems preferable because it leaves room for external factors, ambivalence, inconsistencies, a gradual emergence, and dynamic development of Anabaptist biblicism under particular circumstances. These circumstances included Zwingli's own initial preoccupation with the New Testament.

Zwingli's Preoccupation with the New Testament, 1521–1525

When Zwingli took the stage as "people's priest" in Zurich during January 1519, he announced that he would preach *lectio continuo* directly from the Scriptures. He kept his promise and, during the next five years, preached his way through the New Testament. Not until April 1525 did he shift his emphasis to the Old Testament. The route through the New Testament began with the Gospel of Matthew and led Zwingli through Acts to Paul's first letter to Timothy, then to Galatians before he moved on to Second Timothy. This sequence made it possible to exegete the teachings of Jesus and the apostles and to contrast practices in the early church with contemporary abuses. Zwingli's early exegesis stood, no doubt, under the influence of the great Erasmus, whose second edition of the Greek New Testament, accompanied by his original Latin translation, came off Froben's press in 1519.[17] Like Erasmus, Zwingli was guided by humanist pedagogical concerns of appropriating the *philosophia Christi*, "the fullness of wisdom" revealed in Scriptures, as a rule of life which, if followed, would produce the truly virtuous, pious person. Erasmus himself had set the stage for a New Testament orientation in his preface (Paraclesus) when he wrote that "the pure and genuine philosophy of Christ is not to be drawn from any source more abundantly than from the evangelical books and from the apostolic letters. . . . The Jews saw and heard less than you see and hear in the books of the Gospels."[18]

It has been suggested that Zwingli's turn to Galatians coincided with a turn to the Reformation *sola gratia* debate. When opponents subsequently criticized his neo-Augustinian-Pauline positions as too one sided, Zwingli began an exegesis of the two Letters by Peter to show that in essentials Paul and Peter agreed. Sermons on the Letter to the Hebrews followed before Zwingli returned to the Gospels according to Luke and John as well as to the rest of Paul's Epistles.[19] And while Zwingli continued to develop as a theologian and reformer, it is also clear that his biblicism remained deeply indebted to the humanist pedagogical agenda that contrasted the pristine church with contemporary depravity and corruption. His biblicism was thus polemically directed against tradition, church hierarchy, and scholasticism. It was this polemical biblicism that roused popular support. But it should be noted that Zwingli, who took the Greek New Testament to the pulpit to ridicule opponents as unlearned *Pfaffen* because they could read the Scriptures only in Latin, never questioned the importance of humanistic linguistic skills for a study of the Scriptures.[20]

Nevertheless, assured of the singular clarity of the Gospel and with the Scriptures becoming available in the vernacular, Zwingli encouraged his supporters to follow his example in studying the New Testament. During the First Zurich Disputation in January 1523, Zwingli recommended that all priests in Zurich's territory buy "a New Testament in Latin or in German"[21] and that every "pious Christian who can read" begin as he had done with the Gospel according to Matthew, paying special attention to the Beatitudes. After Matthew, they should read Acts, Paul's Epistles, beginning with the Letter to the Galatians, and then the Epistles of Peter and the rest; only then should they study the Old Testament.[22] Later, during the October Disputation (1523), Zwingli commented that he had already preached his way through Matthew, Acts, the Epistles of Paul, including Galatians and Timothy 1 and 2, both Epistles of Peter, Hebrews, and most recently Luke.[23]

Without question, then, until the first sign of friction between him and his radical followers in the summer of 1523, Zwingli had been the trail blazer in New Testament studies. And although there are no studies of how many of Zurich's territorial clergy followed Zwingli's advice or example, evidence indicates that some of his lay supporters began studying the vernacular New Testament along the lines he recommended. During 1523, for instance, a Bible school formed around the book peddlar Andreas Castelberger. Two years later an investigation revealed that Castelberger and his group were reading the Letter to the Romans. We can assume that they had studied the Gospels, Acts, Galatians, and the other Epistles of Paul and Peter earlier. According to participants, topics discussed in the context of scriptural readings concerned, among other things, benefices, usury, provisions for the poor, tithes, rents, war, violence, pedobaptism, and drinking in public inns.[24] In other words, the New Testament was being read as a practical guide to the Christian life. The point here is that in a reply to the bishop of Constance, Zwingli himself initially encouraged such lay studies of the Scriptures. In 1522 Zwingli rejected the idea "that it was unlawful for laymen to know or read the Gospel" and that the interpretation of the Scriptures was to be left to the doctors of the church. According to Zwingli, "even the most ignorant, if they are pious," could with the aid of the Holy Spirit understand the Scriptures. He wrote that "it is not the function of one or two to expound passages of Scriptures, but of all who believe in Christ."[25] At the time, Zwingli failed to appreciate that such a view could support a dissenting hermeneutic community that would reject his own tutelage and consequently divide the reform party. The Word of God seemed so clear and certain in those early years that agreement on its meaning could be assumed. But once differences arose over the speed and nature of reform polity and the former students of Zwingli unlinked from the tutelage of the "learned heralds,"[26] different situational readings of the Scriptures emerged. Castelberger's Bible school for the commoners provided one of several settings for alternative interpretations; others existed in the villages with radical preachers such as Reublin and Brötli in Rüschlikon and Zollikon. During its formative stage, Anabaptist biblicism was shaped, on the one hand, by the nature and social-political situation of its hermeneutic community, and on the other by the vernacular Scriptures available to it. Within their community the Anabaptists retained the practice of "congregational conversations," whereas Zwingli eventually made scriptural exegesis the prerogative of a learned elite. Neither side appeared aware of a major turning point.[27] Each could claim to be true to original positions. Nevertheless, these positions polarized during debate on baptism.

Polarization on the Issue of Baptism

Although this is not the place to reiterate the complex issues leading to the separation of Zwingli from his former students, something must be said about the issue of baptism as a catalyst in polarizing the two hermeneutic communities. Conrad Grebel's letter of September 5, 1524, to Thomas Müntzer provides evidence that Grebel and his friends, including Castelberger, functioned as a group at odds with Zwingli.[28] The letter mentioned twenty like-minded believers "rejected by our learned shepherds."[29] The future Anabaptists, in turn, rejected the guidance of the learned and with it child baptism, calling for a radically reformed congregational celebration of the Lord's Supper. Unlike Zwingli, who attached relatively little congregational significance to the latter,[30] Grebel and friends considered the Lord's Supper a central congregational event to be "observed often," never alone or in "temples," because that led to false devotion and idolatry. The celebration need not be bound to a particular time, although they noted that Christ and his disciples celebrated it in the evening and that the church in Corinth did the same.[31] Ordinary bread and a "common cup" were to be used "with joy" to signify outwardly that the participants "are and want to be truly one loaf and body and true brethren to one another." The ceremony itself was to be simple, without vestments, with the presider reading or reciting either Matthew 26, Mark 14, Luke 22, or 1 Corinthians 11. These were to be words not of priestly consecration but of admonition to live in accordance with the rule of Christ in brotherly love and unity. By eating and drinking in faith and love the participants incorporated the body of Christ. Participation without intending "to live in a brotherly way" meant eating to one's condemnation. Public sins were to be subject to discipline in accordance with the rule of Christ, found in Matthew 18:15–20.[32] Anyone having been admonished in front of three witnesses and the congregation who persisted in living contrary to the Word of Christ was regarded "as a heathen and publican" and excluded.[33] Grebel and his friends believed that the true church could be restored "with the help of Christ's rule" and the examples of the apostolic church, particularly as described in 1 Corinthians 14 and Colossians 3.[34] Thus, even before adult baptism had become the sign of separation, Grebel and his friends acted as an independent congregation. This scenario is confirmed by Zwingli's complaints that Grebel and his group "want their own church" and that, on the basis of 1 John 10, they "greet no one." In his "Treatise on Baptism, Rebaptism and Infant Baptism," of May 27, 1525, Zwingli wrote that "those who initiated the strife over baptism had previously urged us often to begin a new church, that is, congregation or gathering, supposing they would gather a church that was without sin. But . . . we refused to agree to a separation."[35]

In his letter to Müntzer, Grebel also announced that he and his colleagues were searching the Scriptures to identify all abuses that had crept into the church since the time of the apostles.[36] The violation occupying Grebel's attention at the time was pedobaptism. He wrote that "if you or [Andreas] Carlstadt do not adequately write against infant baptism and all that pertains to it . . . I will try my hand at it and will finish what I have begun."[37] Two days earlier, September 3, 1524, he had informed Joachim Vadian of the same project, a collection of scriptural references under two general themes which, "unless someone else does it first," he would "thrust on the public."[38] The two themes were faith and baptism.

What scriptural references Grebel collected on the topics of faith and baptism can be surmised from the references found in his letter to Müntzer and in a topical concordance attributed to Grebel, although published under the name of Hans Krüsi in Augsburg.[39] Their main thrust was that, according to Christ's Great Commission (Mark 16:15–16), baptism should follow teaching and true faith. Both Old and New Testament passages were cited to support the view that children could not believe.[40] As beneficiaries of the universal redemption wrought by the second Adam, Christ, children remained innocent until they tasted of the tree of knowledge and were able to "discern between good and evil." Pedobaptism was, therefore, not only "senseless" but a "blasphemous abomination contrary to all Scripture."[41] The implied denial of the effects of original sin on children was to become a trademark of Swiss Anabaptists, but it was not the issue between Grebel's group and Zwingli.[42] Their differences on baptism would eventually focus the issue on the relationship of the two Testaments.

Turning to the Old Testament

Beginning in September 1524, disagreement between Zwingli and his former students centered on baptism. Discussions on December 6 and 13 of that year failed to bring reconciliation. Grebel and his friends insisted that what was not clearly taught or demonstrated in the Scriptures by means of example had no place in the church.[43] Studying the New Testament had convinced them that pedobaptism was not only wrong but "the chief abomination" invented by the Roman pontiff.[44] At the public disputation that followed on January 17, 1525 (the first on baptism), Grebel, Felix Mantz, and Wilhelm Reublin argued that children do not believe and do not understand the meaning of baptism. Baptism should be reserved, therefore, for believing adults "to whom the Gospel had been preached, who understand it, desired baptism, were willing to put the Old Adam to death, and wanted to walk in a new life."[45] But Zwingli, on the basis of the same hermeneutic principle, held that for practices such as pedobaptism, neither "commanded nor forbidden" in the New Testament, it was necessary to consult Old Testament precedent or parallel.[46] He claimed that circumcision provided an Old Testament analogy to New Testament baptism. The New Testament distinction between a circumcision of the heart and a mere outer one according to the flesh seemed analogous to the distinction between an inner spiritual baptism and an outer, symbolic water baptism.

Zurich's council sided with Zwingli, ordering the restoration of the baptismal font in Zollikon and the closure of the "special schools." Grebel and his friends, unconvinced by Zwingli's argumentation, decided that it was better to obey Christ's command and apostolic precedent than the council's judgment. On January 21, 1525, they took the step to adult baptism. The break with Zwingli and the magisterial reform party would prove irrevocable.[47]

The controversy over baptism, no doubt, provided part of the impetus for Zwingli's tactical shift to a study of the Old Testament and for his redefinition of the hermeneutic community.[48] The exegesis of the Scriptures became the prerogative of "prophets" skilled in the biblical languages, whose training became institutionalized in the Prophezei. The Prophezei, which opened June 1525, was, unlike Castelberger's Bible school, intended for an educated elite. Its public lectures were limited to former priests and others literate in Latin. Its curriculum centered on methodical studies of the Scriptures in the original languages. Public lectures opened with a prayer of invocation and proceeded to the reading of a scriptural text in the original language, which was then translated and interpreted. A discussion followed the exposition, and the lecture closed with an intercessory prayer. Beginning with the inaugural lecture on June 19, 1525, the studies in the Prophezei concentrated exclusively on the Old Testament.[49]

A few days before the Prophezei opened officially, Zwingli published his reflections, *Concerning the Office of Preaching*.[50] The reflections are of interest here because indirectly they shed some light on the emerging Anabaptist organization. Zwingli distinguished among prophets, evangelists, and apostles. The apostles were literally messengers sent to preach the Gospel where it had not been heard before. The task of prophets, on the other hand, was to expound and teach the Scriptures in existing congregations. Since apostles and evangelists were itinerants, it was best for them to be single and without possessions. Prophets, bishops, or pastors, by contrast, should be resident, married, good managers of their own households, and owners of property.[51] This meant that the "very poor and destitute" were less likely candidates for the office of prophet, bishop, pastor, or preacher because, according to Zwingli, the poor "usually manage their households poorly. For where one governs well, one becomes well-to-do."[52] And as if property qualifications were not sufficient, Zwingli defended the existing system of benefices. Benefices allegedly made prophets or pastors less dependent on contributions from members of the congregation, assuring greater freedom to expound the Scriptures without flattery. Clearly then, Zwingli justified and envisioned a leadership drawn from the well-to-do. Within the proposed church leadership structure, humanistically educated linguists would hold the highest office as prophet-exegetes. The planned Prophezei would train the reformed clergy needed in Zurich's territories to enforce and retain control over the reform movement. The Prophezei institutionalized the alliance between political and religious elite—"state" and church, *Polizei und Prophezei*. It was an alliance directed not only against the bishop of Constance but also the radical dissenters who, according to Zwingli, were stirring up the simple minded by arguing against benefices and claiming that pastors should live on voluntary contributions, not own houses, preferably be single, and should lodge with members of the congregation.[53]

Of special interest in this context is Zwingli's reinterpretation of 1 Corinthians 14:16–40. Three years earlier, Zwingli had appealed to this text to defend the congregation as a hermeneutic community against the bishop of Constance. He had written, "it is not the function of one or two to expound passages of Scripture, but of *all* who believe in Christ," although prophecy should be orderly so "that all may learn the truth, and all may be comforted."[54] Now, in early 1525, Zwingli's viewpoint was more qualified because Anabaptists, appealing to the same text, claimed that the proper order was not being followed.[55] Zwingli charged that the Anabaptists misunderstood the meaning of prophecy referred to in 1 Corinthians 14. He maintained that in the context of the apostolic church, *prophecy* meant primarily exegesis of the law and the prophets.

At the time of the apostles there were, however, also some who were called prophets and who proclaimed the meaning of Scripture to whole churches. For at that time there were as yet no New Testament Scriptures, and the apostles taught by mouth. . . . From this we learn that at the time of the apostles those too were called prophets who exposited the Old Testament Scriptures before the churches, as is well noted in 1 Corinthians 14:26–33.[56]

In contemporary terms, such a task required competence in classical languages, specifically Hebrew. In effect, this meant that prophecy was reserved for an educated elite with the necessary linguistic skills.[57] The necessary qualifications to be an exegete in turn imposed the restriction of a specific sequence on congregational conversations. Obviously, the educated elite interpreted the meaning of the Scriptures. Zwingli nevertheless wanted to maintain a role for the congregation as outlined in 1 Corinthians 14:26–37.[58] His comments on this important text, foundational for the first Anabaptist congregational orders, are worth citing in length.

The meaning of these words of Paul is this: When you meet to hear the Psalms or Scriptures, if there is one among you who is learned, who knows languages (especially if he speaks Hebrew), to whom God has given a special revelation, who can interpret and translate Hebrew words into Greek and the like, he shall take the matter in hand in order to edify with it. Those who can speak Hebrew . . . speak or read systematically in succession the passages of Scripture in which the prophets are speaking. Then one of them translates the same words into the ordinary language. And he who is not an interpreter or learned in languages should not speak before the exposition by the prophets, but be silent and speak only with himself and with God. Then when the Scripture has been read aloud in both languages, it is usually still not understood. Therefore the prophets now begin to explain the Scriptures and to reveal the will of God. Here the prophets must always likewise have been learned in languages, for all the other gifts serve the purpose of reaching to the highest, that is, to the prophets, which means to exposit (1 Corinthians 14:26–33).

Now when the prophets have spoken one after another in an orderly way, and . . . God has revealed the meaning of the Scriptures to someone sitting in the congregation, it would be proper [for him] to speak concerning the meaning of the Scriptures, but with such order and discipline that if someone else begins to speak, the former will be silent. Nor should still another begin to speak while the second is speaking, for it is fitting for them to speak in succession concerning the meaning of the Scripture while the congregation is assembled, yes, everyone in his own congregation and in succession in an orderly way, so that all may be comforted and taught the truth.[59]

Then, in a reference to the Anabaptists who cited the same text to justify the interruption of sermons, Zwingli wrote,

Note that although it is proper for all the men in the church to speak about the Scripture, it is proper only following the prophets and when the prophet has not understood or brought out the meaning. Therefore those who pretend to be apostles or prophets do not, in exposing the Scripture, act according to the practice of the apostles. They do not stay in their own churches but run to other churches and speak there without the prophets. And whereas they use this passage by Paul to prove that they may also interrupt by speaking from Scripture, they refuse to be interrupted themselves. I could mention examples when the trained prophets were coming to their sermon in which they [Anabaptists] read from the New Testament; and when the prophets requested permission to speak on the subject, they got the answer: it ill behooves them to speak on it. And when they [the prophets] have explained the real meaning, the Anabaptists did not accept it even though the rest of the church accepted it. And so they do not come into the church because they want to learn but because they want to teach and be taught by no one, although they claim . . . that they will accept teaching [instructions]. Paul says further (1 Corinthians 14:30–33): The prophets gladly listen to one another peaceably, also to those seated if they bring truth to light. For the spirits of the prophets are subject to the prophets; that is, if they are the prophets of God, they will gladly listen to those who reveal the hidden meaning of Scripture. And all of this will take place peacefully; for God is not a God of disorder and dissension but a God of peace.[60]

In essence, Paul's instructions to the Corinthians had become a law-and-order text. Zwingli considered none of the Anabaptists qualified to be prophets, for although they impressed the "simple folk," Zwingli maintained that "not one of them is learned."[61] Some had barely mastered the alphabet in the vernacular, much less classical languages.[62] Zwingli insisted that authorization for the prophetic or apostolic office came through existing parish structures. He noted that during the apostolic period leaders had been chosen in three different ways: (1) by the entire congregation; (2) by the collective leadership; or (3) by a single apostle. He preferred appointment through consultation between the congregation and the existing devout and educated leadership.[63] Individual claims of a special divine calling to the apostolic office needed authentication by supernatural signs and miracles, as had been the case at the time of the first apostles. Since Anabaptist leaders could demonstrate neither a special divine calling nor a legitimate calling from the local parish, they could not lay claim to the apostolic office. Besides, true apostles would take the Gospel to those who had never heard of Christ rather than create confusion among fellow believers.[64] Instead, Anabaptists, claiming apostolic authority, were running to congregations not their own, seeking to usurp the leadership there. It seemed to Zwingli that, unlike in Jerusalem where twelve apostles served a congregation of a thousand, in Zurich everyone wanted to be an apostle.[65]

Important here is that Zwingli's statements illustrate how the controversy over baptism had polarized points of view and forced a rereading of important New Testament texts pertinent to congregational order including 1 Corinthians 14. The reference to prophets in this text was now utilized by Zwingli to emphasize the leadership role of humanistically trained exegetes necessary to interpret the Old Testament. The tactical shift to the Old Testament on the basis of the Pauline text, as will be noted, left the Anabaptists at a disadvantage. Two hermeneutic communities had emerged with distinctly different biblicist orientations.

The Forgotten Factor

The Availability of the Vernacular Scriptures

Traditional scholarship on Swiss Anabaptism created a somewhat idealistic picture of congregations functioning as discerning hermeneutic communities that sought to arrive at consensus on the meaning of the Scriptures by congregational conversations. But such a congregational model assumes the availability of the Scriptures in the vernacular. Surprisingly, this availability and its relationship to the form and content of Anabaptist biblicism have received little attention.[66] Claims found in the older historiography that the Anabaptists emerged out of pre-Reformation conventicles with pre-Reformation vernacular Bibles can be dismissed as unsupported by evidence.[67] The historic facts point to the Reformation and the printing press as providing impetus and opportunity for lay studies of the Scriptures in the vernacular.[68] Luther's translation of the New Testament printed in 1522 led the way. Since Luther's cause and translation proved popular, numerous reprints appeared on a variety of presses, including those located in Basel and Zurich. These publications were eagerly awaited by Zwingli's supporters in Zurich. As early as November 21, 1522, Grebel reported that he anticipated receipt of a New Testament.[69] Although this could have referred to a Greek New Testament that he later studied with students whom he tutored, it was more likely a reference to the first reprint of Luther's New Testament which came off Adam Petri's press in Basel in December 1522. A few weeks later, January 1523, at the First Disputation in Zurich, concerning Scripture as the norm for reform, Zwingli drew attention to "the divine gospel and Scriptures" that had recently been "brought to light by means of print."[70] These references, shortly before and after the first printing of the New Testament in Basel, indicate how important Zwingli and his friends considered this publication. The printing press lifted the Scriptures from obscurity to the light of day, making available what had been inaccessible to ordinary people.

During the next two years, Zwingli preached his way through the New Testament, and literate laymen could test the truth of his claims on the basis of newly printed, vernacular New Testaments that were appearing in increasing numbers. In Basel eleven editions were printed between 1522 and 1525.[71] To help the native reader, a glossary of Swiss terms was added to Luther's translation, and eventually the whole New Testament was translated into the Swiss dialect. The first Zurich edition of the New Testament did not appear until August 1, 1524. One month later, on September 5, Grebel informed Müntzer that even though all could now read the Gospel for themselves, few did so and instead continued to depend on the learned pastors for biblical instructions. This was obviously not true of Grebel and his companions, who had come to differ with Zwingli on a number of issues and felt "rejected by our learned shepherds."[72] They had begun an intense study of the New Testament on the meaning of baptism, a study that convinced them that pedobaptism was against the teachings and practices of the New Testament. If Grebel and his friends, who began to function as an alternative hermeneutic community, were in need of further copies of the New Testament, these became readily available.[73]

The point here is that for local consumption in Zurich and its environs, the vernacular New Testament was readily available from August 1524 on. Before that, Castelberger appears to have supplied interested parties with printed materials from Basel and elsewhere, and his home had become a meeting place for lay studies of the New Testament. Evidently Castelberger and his friends had not read the Old Testament, although beginning in December 1523, the first installment of it came off Adam Petri's press in Basel. The second and third parts did not follow until a year later, September and December 1524, respectively. Not until 1525 did the first installment come off Froschauer's press in Zurich; a second edition had to wait until 1527, and the fourth and fifth parts did not appear until 1529.[74]

The printing of the Old Testament, like that of the New, followed Luther's lead. The Swiss, however, managed to publish the entire Bible in 1529, well before Luther completed his translation.[75] The celebrated *Zuricher Bibel* by Froschauer appeared in 1531. Credit for translating the Old Testament into readable Swiss must be given to Zwingli and his assistants at the grammar school and the Prophezei. The founding fathers of Swiss Anabaptism made no overt contributions to the translation project, nor did they sponsor their own independent translations, although Grebel, Mantz, and Balthasar Hubmaier certainly had the know-how to translate from the Latin or Greek. True, Anabaptists Hans Denck and Ludwig Hätzer made at least an indirect contribution to the translation of the Old Testament by their 1527 publication at Worms of the prophets.[76] However, the biblicism of Denck and Hätzer differed from that of the founding members of Swiss Anabaptism. Both wrestled with perceived contradictions within the Scriptures which could be overcome by emphasizing the spirit over the letter, the unmediated, inner word over the written witness or historical record.[77]

Perhaps more interesting and of greater historic import is the question of whether Swiss Anabaptist biblicism, which was in its formative stages during the period 1523 to 1527, was at all influenced by the sequence in which the vernacular Scriptures became available for local consumption. Did the vernacular biblicism of Swiss Anabaptism form without the benefit of the entire vernacular Bible? In other words, were the congregational conversations of the emerging dissenting hermeneutic community, which understood itself in terms of ultimate biblical truth,[78] restricted to the New Testament—that is, if one takes seriously that these conversations were premised on lay participation? The question of the availability of the Scriptures in the vernacular is certainly more than rhetorical. It raises the possibility that the New Testament orientation of early Swiss Anabaptism was influenced by particular historical circumstances that included the limited availability of the vernacular Scriptures.

The importance of the New Testament orientation for Swiss Anabaptism has long been noted. Harold Bender observed that the Swiss derived their faith "solely and directly from the New Testament." He considered it their genius that they returned "to the original idea of the New Testament."[79] A survey of important early Swiss documents supports such a view. The New Testament orientation of these documents is striking. For example, the December 1524 "Petition of Defense" by Felix Mantz contained references to the Gospels, Acts, and Paul's Epistles, but only one to the Old Testament.[80] Similar observations are in order for the concordance attributed to Conrad Grebel;[81] the Schleitheim Articles; Michael Sattler's letter to Wolfgang Capito and Martin Bucer;[82] the *Swiss Congregational Order;*[83] as well as the "Submission to the Diet [*Landestag*] of Grüningen," dated June 4, 1527. The "Submission," the work of ordinary laymen, maintained that the Old Testament ended with Christ, who "established another, a new one, in which we are from now on to be in a new life and no longer in the old."[84] Such statements prompted Zwingli to charge, "you have now at last come to the point that you can deny the whole Old Testament."[85] And although Zwingli's polemics must be taken with a grain of salt, the absence of Old Testament references or their minimal presence in early Swiss Anabaptist statements does suggest a New Testament-centered biblicism in which the Old Testament received a lesser status. This brought charges from other contemporaries that the Anabaptists were Marcionite *Neutestamentler.*[86]

The questions remain of whether the New Testament orientation emerged as a consciously, deliberately held principled position; and if so, when?[87] Unfortunately, no reflections on the process leading to this hermeneutically most significant position have survived from the early Swiss Anabaptist side. In their absence, the historian may be permitted to suggest that Zwingli's own public preoccupation with the New Testament from 1522 to 1525 and the easy accessibility of the vernacular New Testament from late 1522 on—in contrast to the piecemeal marketing of the Old Testament available in complete form for local consumption only from 1529 on—were influential factors. The paucity of references to the Old in contrast to the numerous references to the New Testament in early Swiss documents implies that during its formative stages Swiss Anabaptist biblicism was affected profoundly by the vernacular New Testament. When conservative impulses became dominant in subsequent generations, Swiss Anabaptists financed reprints of the early Froschauer New Testament rather than accept editions revised and improved by the learned. Such reprints became known as subversive "Anabaptist New Testaments" and were subject to confiscation.[88] By this stage, Swiss Anabaptists had not only locked into a New Testament biblicism but fixed on a particular vernacular edition.[89]

Returning to the separation of ways between Zwingli and his former supporters, the observation is in order that the two parties became only gradually conscious of different positions on the relationship of Old and New Testaments. Zwingli's own initial preoccupation with the New Testament masked potential differences. Besides, like all Christian students of the Scriptures, Zwingli read the Old Testament through the eyes of the New. Ultimately, this involved "spiritual expositions" based on distinctions between letter and spirit, even when in principle the two Testaments were considered of equal authority and import.[90] The Anabaptist New Testament orientation, on the other hand, had not been intentionally exclusive of the Old Testament. The Anabaptists shared Zwingli's radical *sola scriptura* position. Not surprisingly, then, awareness of different emphases dawned only slowly as a result of disagreements over reform polity and consequently different situational readings of the Scriptures.

The evangelical party had divided into two camps before the issue of baptism polarized the situation. Some of the radical evangelical preachers in the villages had suspended pedobaptism before Grebel and his friends undertook a serious study of the issue. It was probably no accident that this study commenced shortly after a vernacular New Testament came off Froschauer's press in August 1524. During the ensuing debate, Zwingli ridiculed the radicals for assuming that the early church premised its practices and ceremonies on the New Testament. The New Testament, claimed Zwingli, came into being after the fact. The biblicism of the apostolic church, he insisted, had been an Old Testament biblicism.[91] Zwingli's tactical shift to the Old Testament during the debate over baptism left ordinary members of the dissenting community at a disadvantage. Attempts by their own educated leadership to support their arguments with occasional references to the Old Testament met with Zwingli's scorn. In his

May 27, 1525 *Treatise on Baptism, Rebaptism and Infant Baptism,* Zwingli wrote that he heard "for a fact that some of them present some strange interpretations from the Old Testament to the simple people. I cannot understand how they dare to do this, for they never granted me the analogy to circumcision for which I had a clear word, indeed, not analogy but in the Old Testament it was precisely what baptism is in the New."[92]

Two years later, the "Joint Decree for the Suppression of the Anabaptists" echoed similar sentiments: the Anabaptists were so "impudent as to base and maintain" themselves by an appeal to "both Old and New Testaments."[93] Nevertheless, appeals to the Old Testament appear to have been the exception rather than the rule and were possibly solicited by Zwingli's polemical taunts. The New Testament provided the norms for all church ceremonies and doctrines, as far as the Anabaptists were concerned.

In what followed, the Anabaptists turned what Zwingli considered a defective, truncated biblicism into a virtue. They insisted on a clear distinction between the two Testaments, two covenants, two peoples of God, the old and the new. They charged that Zwingli's emphasis on the Old Testament "would make Jews out of us," that it led back to the servitude of the Old Testament instead of the "freedom of the spirit that comes with the new covenant pertaining unto the children of God through Christ."[94] Thus, between 1525 and 1527, hermeneutic fronts hardened. When in subsequent discussions with Anabaptists representatives of the magisterial reform party insisted on the use of both Testaments, the Anabaptists appear to have been at a disadvantage.[95] This was, of course, not the case for the educated leadership, as for example Grebel, Mantz, and Hubmaier. But this educated leadership was soon martyred or exiled. Before leaving the historic stage, however, they had managed to provide the fledgling movement with scriptural guides that would equip ordinary members with an impressive array of "proof texts" to defend the soundness of their positions. Scholars have long considered Hubmaier's treatise "On Christian Baptism of Believers" one of these highly influential apologies of the Anabaptist position.[96] Perhaps even more influential among ordinary lay members was a concordance attributed to Grebel. The latter will occupy the last pages of this chapter.

A Scriptural Guide

In September 1524 Grebel had announced that he would thrust on the public a study of faith and baptism. Heinold Fast convincingly argued that this work, a topical collection of Scriptural passages, appeared in print under the name of Hans Nagel von Klingnau. Fast identified Nagel with

Hans Krüsi, the popular Anabaptist preacher of Tablat near St. Gall, who was executed on July 27, 1525. Fast believed that the booklet appeared posthumously in Augsburg.[97] Prior to its publication, this collection of texts or concordance appears to have circulated in manuscript form on Swiss soil. Krüsi testified that he had received a handwritten manuscript from Grebel.[98] If this was the same in content as the published version, then it consisted of fifty-three scriptural references, forty-three to the New Testament, ten to the Old. Thirty-seven of these, with nine from the Old Testament, concerned faith; sixteen references, only one from the Old Testament, referred to baptism.[99] Krüsi himself belonged to the literate leadership of Swiss Anabaptism. Before his involvement with evangelical reform, he had been a teaching assistant at the Latin school at Wil, which presumably meant that he could read Latin. Krüsi is known to have purchased a vernacular New Testament and to have borrowed an Old Testament or part of it.[100] Witnesses testified that he read and taught from both Testaments.[101]

In the pamphlet attributed to Krüsi-Grebel the argument for adult baptism proceeded from the example of John the Baptist, the command of Jesus, the practice of the apostles as found in the Acts, the case of rebaptism in Ephesus, and from a more formal doctrine of believers' baptism drawn from the Epistles. Fast recognized a repetition of this pattern of argument in such diverse documents as Felix Mantz's "Petition of Defense" (1524), the "Appeal of the Prisoners of Grüningen" (1527), Georg Schnabel's "Questionnaire" in Hesse (1538), and Pilgram Marpeck's *Testamentläuterung* (1544).[102] The circulation of this selection of passages or miniature Bible, therefore, appears to have been very influential. It helps to explain how, at a time when both literacy and possession of Bibles were still rare among commoners, a relatively consistent and coherent argument supported by an impressive biblical learning spread rapidly among ordinary people. But did such preselected, predetermined guidance through the Bible not truncate the biblical witness and limit congregational discussions? Fast viewed scriptural aid in a positive light: "Here [in Krüsi's concordance] access to the Bible is made easy for the peasant. In a few hours he can learn what is necessary for him to know."[103] In other words, the miniature Bible concentrated the essentials of the scriptural message for the uneducated seeker. But it was more than an effective instrument for evangelizing. It was a genuine outgrowth of taking seriously the priesthood of all believers, of making biblical knowledge attainable for the laity, and closing the gap between ordinary lay persons and literate leaders.

Swiss Anabaptist biblicism took form in a particular historical milieu. Recent studies have focused and elaborated on the position of the emerging

Anabaptists in the social-political matrix that influenced their situational reading of the Scriptures. Accordingly, the Anabaptists had positioned themselves between the learned and popular culture and, as a hermeneutic community, nurtured a vernacular biblicism through congregational conversations. Such conversations tended to be dominated by practical concerns, a reading of the Scriptures for rules of life, the reform of abuses in church and society, and the proper reorganization of congregational life. But the Anabaptist leadership was also involved in conversation with other reformers, particularly Zwingli. Zwingli's reform agenda and his New Testament expositions decisively influenced the form and content of early Swiss Anabaptist biblicism. Zwingli's students proved, if anything, more stringent and consistent in the way they sought to eliminate abuses considered incongruent with the rule of Christ and the apostles. The parting of ways saw the emergence of two different hermeneutic communities and two different types of biblicism.

The sequence in which the vernacular Scriptures became available may have further encouraged a popular New Testament orientation among Zwingli's radical supporters. Evidence that the New Testament was readily available in the vernacular from late 1522 on, but that the Old Testament became available only piecemeal and the full Bible not until 1529, may go some way to explain the predominance of New Testament citations in early Swiss Anabaptist documents. Swiss Anabaptist vernacular biblicism, it can be argued, took shape before a wholistic reading of both Testaments was an option for a hermeneutic community that had rejected the tutelage of the learned. It was perhaps not coincidental that the break with the learned came at precisely the point when Zwingli and his colleagues shifted their attention to the Old Testament.[104] The breakaway community retained a biblicism focused on the New Testament; 1 Corinthians 14 provided their community model. Other texts, especially Acts 2 and 4, Ephesians 5, and Colossians 3, proved foundational for the prescribed congregational order.

Zwingli's shift to the Old Testament coincided with a firm assertion that the interpretation and exegesis of Scripture belonged to the learned, an assertion institutionalized in the Prophezei. This institution would serve the magisterial Reformation well. Paradoxically, the more open hermeneutic Anabaptist community with its consistent extension of authority to the laity, the priesthood of all believers, would function with a truncated biblicism, whereas the more elitist community installed by Zwingli operated on the assumption of the equal authority of the two Testaments.[105]

Chapter Two

The Oldest Anabaptist Congregational Orders

The Swiss Contribution

In his recent book (1991) James Stayer argued that Swiss Anabaptism pioneered the practice of community of goods in imitation of the apostolic church informed by a reading of Acts 2 and 4. Although the Swiss eventually abandoned this practice in favor of a watered-down version of mutual aid, Stayer believed that they did provide the inspiration and example for other Anabaptist groups. As in his 1972 treatment of the Anabaptist positions on the sword, so in his latest work Stayer carefully differentiated and nuanced a variety of teachings and practices with regard to community of goods. Among other things he traced the influence of Thomas Müntzer's "antimaterialist piety" to the first Moravian experiments with community of goods. But the center piece supporting Stayer's claims about early Swiss practice was the *Swiss Congregational Order,* which he described as a "rule of sharing and a rule against exploitation."

This study intersects with Stayer's work at several points and in some instances supplements his findings. That is the case in this chapter, which examines the oldest surviving Anabaptist congregational orders.

In Search of the Oldest Congregational Order

All historic inquiry depends for its accuracy on the reliability of its sources. The authenticity of the sources is a prerequisite to historic truthfulness. The study of Anabaptism is no exception. Students of Anabaptism encounter the problem of reliability in the form of internal versus external sources. External sources (*Täuferakten*), court records of statements made by Anabaptists under duress, torture, and threat of life tend to reflect the agenda and questionnaires of the prosecutors. They need constant testing and critical evaluation against internal evidence, documents that reflect the "real" opinions of the Anabaptists. The historian is thus confronted constantly by alternative interpretations. And even an a priori commitment to one side or the other does not always solve the dilemma. What is to be done, for instance, when time, place, and authorship of a crucial document remain controversial or contested? In such a case, the historian has no choice but to consider all of the options before drawing tentative conclusions. The search for the oldest Anabaptist congregational order illustrates this point. Three first-generation orders have survived: (1) *The Congregational Order,* found in the Bernese State Archive (hereafter designated as the *Swiss Order*); (2) *The Church Discipline,* found in Hutterite sources (hereafter referred to as the *Discipline*); and (3) *The Common Order,* found in the *Kunstbuch* (hereafter identified as the *Common Order*). Although conflicting opinions about their antiquity, place of origin, and authorship have been offered in the past, the relationship of these documents to each other, reproduced in Appendix A, has never been examined thoroughly. Since these are the key documents offering a window on early Anabaptist organizational structures, the circumstances of their origins are worthy of careful consideration. Such consideration must begin with a reexamination of previously proposed hypotheses as to the oldest Anabaptist church order, its time, and its place of origin.

The Church Discipline *(1529?)*

In 1955 Robert Friedmann published a translation of what he considered "the oldest church Discipline of the Anabaptists."[1] Although the *Discipline* was found in Hutterite codices, Friedmann believed it to be of pre-Hutterite origin because it appeared under the date 1529 and advocated a "community of charity," not a full-fledged Hutterite community of goods. At first Friedmann suggested Hans Schlaffer as the author of the *Discipline,* believing that it had been drafted as a congregational order for the Anabaptists at Rattenberg in the Inn Valley. In a correction three years later Friedmann proposed Leonhard Schiemer as the most likely author, because Schiemer assumed spiritual responsibility for the Rattenberg congregation.[2] Since Schiemer and Schlaffer suffered martyrdom in early 1528 (Schiemer, January 14; Schlaffer, February 1), the *Discipline* dated from 1527. Both Schiemer and Schlaffer were associated with Hans Hut's party, and, although Friedmann did not develop the argument, a case could have been made that the *Discipline* was associated with organizational efforts in the summer and fall of 1527. Evidence suggests that Hut and others met in Steyer at that time to give the fledgling movement in Austrian territories some organizational shape.[3] Later that fall, a number of leaders, including Hut and Schiemer, met at the Martyrs Synod in Augsburg for a similar purpose.

If Schiemer was the author of the *Discipline* and intended it for the Rattenberg congregation, as Friedmann suggested, a case could be made that he was influenced by deliberations at Steyer or Augsburg. Such a scenario finds support in Schiemer's epistle to the congregation in Rattenberg. Dated 1527, the epistle contained admonitions and language similar to those found in the *Discipline*. In this letter the former Franciscan wrote,

Keep brotherly love, do not forget prayer [the Lord's Prayer?]; watch the time so that you do not waste an hour unnecessarily. Meet often. If you cannot gather all at once, let half or a quarter of you come together. When you read, read mostly in the New Testament and in the Psalms. You should know that God has spoken to the Jews in a hidden way through Moses and the prophets; but when Christ himself came, then he and the apostles expressed all things with clear understanding. Christ proclaimed publicly that the law and the prophets hang on the two commandments, love God with all your heart and your neighbor as yourself. Whoever gives himself entirely to God with body and life, trusts him totally and calls on him in all need; whoever is patient in suffering and keeps brotherly love, has no need to go to a higher school. He finds [understanding] in his heart and in the witness of the Scriptures. Of this the Old and New Testament testify [and] even though it would be good to read in the Prophets, the books of Kings and Moses [the Pentateuch], that is not absolutely necessary [*so ist es doch nit vasst vonnöten*]. One finds everything in the New Testament. What is indicated [*angezaigt*] in the Old is clearly revealed in the New. And the Psalms are the quintessence [*ausszug*] of all prophets. Paul says: "we boast only in the cross of our Lord Jesus Christ; because he is our life and resurrection, through whom we are saved and redeemed."[4]

A comparison of Schiemer's statement with the *Discipline* reveals striking similarities, among them the admonition to meet frequently, to begin with prayer, to read the Scriptures, not to waste time with idle chatter, and to live fully surrendered to the will of God and in brotherly love. Very interesting is the conscious New Testament orientation coupled to the assumption that the Scriptures can be understood without higher schooling by obedient, believing hearts. Indeed, the whole tenor of the statement, with its admonition to read the Psalms, seems in concord with instructions found in the *Swiss Order*. The *Swiss Order* was the most likely basis for the *Discipline*.[5]

Returning to earlier conjectures about the *Discipline*, it should be noted that George Williams, followed by John A. Hostettler, had expanded on Friedmann's hypothesis by inferring that "one version of the Rattenberg regulations" was included in *The Chronicle of the Hutterian Brethren* (hereafter, *The Chronicle*) with the indication that it "became the constitution of the Austerlitz community in 1529."[6] This inference was supported by an entry in *The Chronicle* which read, "In the year 1529 the congregation [*gemain*] made the following Order as to how Christians, who stand in the apostolic faith, should live, be taught, be led and should agree to hold among each other."[7] The text of the *Discipline* follows. And although *The Chronicle* does not identify explicitly the congregation as that of the Brethren at Austerlitz, the context seems to imply as much. Moreover, in that year a number of future Hutterites joined the Austerlitz Brethren, and Jacob Hutter himself arrived to investigate the life and teaching of the community. His agreement reached with the Austerlitz leadership could explain how the congregational order of the Austerlitz Brethren entered Hutterite sources and was preserved under the date 1529. Hostettler's conjectures, therefore, made sense and could have become another link in the argument that ascribed the origin of the oldest Anabaptist order, the *Discipline*, to the Tyrol (Rattenberg) and/or Moravia (Austerlitz). This line of argument was taken up and expanded by Stephen Boyd in his study of Marpeck. According to Boyd, Marpeck carried the "communal order composed by Schiemer for the Rattenberg congregation in 1527" to Krumau (Cesky Krumlov) in Bohemia, from whence it allegedly traveled to Austerlitz. Marpeck then brought the *Discipline* to Strasbourg, where he used it as a guide in his attempt to "organize the Anabaptists there."[8] However, in all essentials the *Discipline* resembled the *Swiss Order,* suggesting dependence on the latter. This changes the transmission history of the oldest Anabaptist order.

My own search for the oldest Anabaptist congregational order initially followed conjectures derived from Friedmann's hypothesis as outlined above. In due course I discovered that the *Discipline* and the *Swiss Order* were generically related. Although Ernst Müller published an edition of the *Swiss Order* as early as 1895, neither Friedmann nor John H. Yoder, who, respectively, published translations of the *Discipline* and the *Swiss Order,*[9] compared the two documents or examined their relationship. The same had been true of a number of other scholars.[10] Yet even a cursory comparison reveals that the twelve-point *Discipline* constituted little more than a scrambled and somewhat expanded version of the seven-point *Swiss Order.* Thus Article 1 of the *Swiss Order* corresponded with Article 2 of the *Discipline;* Article 2 of the *Swiss Order* with Article 7 of the *Discipline;* Article 3 with 6; Article 4 with 3; Article 5 with 4; Article 6 with 8; and Article 7 with 11. Articles 1, 5, 9, 10, and 12 of the *Discipline* contained additional material or expanded on matters raised in the *Swiss Order*. Since living documents as a rule increase with time, the *Swiss Order* appears to be the older of the two documents. This discovery led me to conclude that in matters of congregational organization Swiss Anabaptism laid the foundation and developed the New Testament model emulated and adapted by other groups as far as Austerlitz, Moravia.[11]

The Swiss Order (1527?)

Origin and Dating

Scholarly consensus assigns the *Swiss Order,* preserved in the Bernese State Archive,[12] to Swiss origins. Supporting evidence is provided by the present location and language of the document. The manuscript appears to be in the Swiss or Upper Rhine (*Allemanisch*) dialect.[13] In other words, location and language identify it as a Swiss document. Müller, the first to publish the *Swiss Order,* had discovered the undated manuscript filed with other Anabaptist documents (*Täuferakten*).[14] Because one of these other documents, apparently by the same hand, consisted of the Schleitheim Articles, speculation grew that the two documents originated in tandem. Delbert Gratz, who advanced this line of argumentation in the 1950s, presumed the *Swiss Order* not only to be Swiss in origin but "to have been written during the decade of the 1520s."[15] With time, this hypothesis became more refined, each contributor gaining a stake in its correctness. Most recently Stayer used the *Swiss Order* to buttress his argument that early Swiss Anabaptists practiced community of goods based on their reading of Acts.[16]

Earlier, Yoder expressed an emerging consensus that the *Swiss Order* and the Schleitheim Articles[17] were linked in time and place of origin. He summarized the case for this conclusion as follows:

This set of instructions concerning congregational order and worship was circulating in April 17, 1527, together with the Schleitheim text, apparently in the same hand as the Bern text of the Brotherly Union. All must therefore have been seized at the same time in April, within six weeks of the Schleitheim gathering. It therefore has circumstantial grounds for being considered as linked with Schleitheim and with Sattler. It is the oldest known text on its subject, and has not previously been published in full.[18]

Yoder seemed more qualified in a footnote when he wrote that "it may be assumed" that the two documents "circulated together . . . and had been seized at the same time."[19] He failed to elaborate on the deductions that supported this hypothesis and did not explain how he arrived at the date of April 17, 1527. Some of this information was provided by Heinold

Fast.[20] Because of its importance for dating the *Swiss Order*, pertinent details are elaborated here. Fast established that the Bernese text of the Schleitheim Articles must have been one of four available to Zwingli when he refuted the same in his *Contra Catabaptistarum Strophas Elenchus*, published in late July 1527.[21] Zwingli had received copies of the Articles from Johannes Oecolampadius, the reformer of Basel, on April 24, 1527,[22] and from Berchtold Haller, the reformer of Bern, on April 25, 1527. Zwingli thanked Haller three days later, April 28. The Bernese text had been taken from Anabaptists who had only recently arrived from Basel.[23] Assuming that the copy of the Articles, presently in the Bernese State Archive, is the same as that taken from the Anabaptists in April 1527, it may also be assumed that the *Swiss Order*, in the same hand, dates from the same period—that is, from before April 25, 1527, when Haller sent a copy of the Articles to Zwingli.

Since linkage with the Schleitheim Articles sent to Zwingli from Bern has been used to establish the *Swiss Order*'s time and place of origin, the arguments for linkage must be weighed carefully. They involve three steps.

1. A copy of the *Swiss Order* and of the Schleitheim Articles exists in the same "unprofessional hand"[24] in the Bernese State Archive. It may be inferred, therefore, that the two documents came from the same source and fell into the hands of the authorities at the same time. A copy of the Schleitheim Articles is known to have fallen into the hands of the authorities of Bern before April 25, 1527.

2. Berchtold Haller sent a copy of the Articles to Zwingli on April 25, 1527, and Zwingli appears to have used a version of the Bernese text a little later that year in his refutation, the *Contra Catabaptistarum Strophas Elenchus*.

3. Deviations from the Bernese text by Zwingli may be explained as translator's license—the *Contra Catabaptistarum Strophas Elenchus* was in Latin—or as Zwingli's preference for one of the other texts of the Articles available to him.[25]

The above argument hinges of course on the basic assumption that the documents preserved in the Bernese State Archive date from early 1527.[26] The rest follows deductively. But some serious questions remain.

Residual Questions

For several reasons, doubts remain about the historic linkage between the *Swiss Order* and the Schleitheim Articles. First, the documents appear to advocate different leadership structures and different economic practices. Second, there is no confirmation that both were taken from the An-

abaptists in Bern or that both circulated together. Why, if both the Articles
and *Swiss Order* were taken at the same time in early 1527, did neither
Haller nor Zwingli mention the *Swiss Order?* Since the *Swiss Order* advocated community of goods, would not knowledge of it have provided
grist for Zwingli's criticisms?[27] Even more puzzling seems the evidence
that the very same Anabaptists, believed to have been the carriers of the
Swiss Order to Bern, "offered serious qualification to the principle of community of goods . . . at the very time the *Congregational Order* was upholding it."[28] Hans Hausmann (Seckler), when asked about community
of goods, replied that according to his understanding, 1 John 3:17 meant
having pity on one's brother who was starving or in need. It did not mean,
as some would have it, "that one should make or has made a rule that one
should throw all goods onto one heap."[29] Unfortunately he did not identify those who had made a rule that all goods should be thrown onto one
heap. To make his own position clear, Hausmann cited Acts 5:3–4, not
Acts 4, claiming that the denial of private property was against the testimony of Scripture (*es wer auch wider die geschrifft*). Had not Peter told
Ananias that it belonged to him "before and after it was sold?" Similar
interpretations were given by Hausmann's companions, Hans Träyer
(Dreier or Trayer) and Heinrich Seiler. Both repeated this interpretation
two years later.

   On the other hand, the statements by Hausmann and his companions
can be read as evidence that the subject of community of goods, Article 5
of the *Swiss Order,* did arise during the interrogation. Hausmann obviously answered questions on the subject. He also touched on another subject found in the *Swiss Order,* that of permitting all members the freedom
to speak in their meetings, Article 2 of the *Swiss Order.* Appealing to
1 Corinthians 14:26ff., Hausmann accused the established church of having abolished "the rule [or order] of holy Paul,"[30] which read, "When you
come together, everyone has a hymn, or a word of instruction, a revelation, [*einen psalmen oder ein ler oder ein offenbarung*], a tongue or an
interpretation. All of these must be done for the strengthening of the
church. If anyone speaks in a tongue, two—or at the most three—should
speak at a time.[31]

   At this point a caveat seems appropriate. Article 2 of the *Swiss Order*
called for daily reading of Psalms. Yoder considered this reference to the
Psalter "one of very rare early Anabaptist references to noncongregational
devotional exercise."[32] But such an exercise implied not only literacy but
also availability of the Psalter in the vernacular, neither of which, as
noted in the previous chapter, can be taken for granted.[33] And why did the
admonition to read the Psalms enter the *Swiss Order?* It was found at
the end of Article 2, which outlined a minimal procedure for congrega-

tional meetings, not noncongregational devotional exercises. Although no explicit scriptural reference was given, the *Order* clearly assumed 1 Corinthians 14:26 as a foundational text, the same Scripture to which Hausmann appealed to defend the participation of all members in congregational conversations.[34] In this text Paul referred to reading, chanting, or singing of the Psalms as a congregational exercise: "when you come together everyone should have a Psalm or song."[35] This was the text cited by a number of reformers who introduced singing or the chanting of Psalms—most notably Bucer in Strasbourg, followed later by Calvin.[36] Zwingli, in contrast, argued against music, singing, or chanting and desired that all "barbarous murmurs" and "worthless chanting" cease. He interpreted 1 Corinthians 14 in conjunction with Ephesians 5:19 and Colossians 3:16. Accordingly, Psalmody was to take place in the heart, not in the voice.[37] Zwingli believed that the Psalms were intended to teach women, considered intellectually inferior to men, how to praise God. Since women were not allowed to speak in the church, Zwingli inferred that they must have learned to recite Psalms at home.[38]

Grebel and his friends appear to have been of one mind with Zwingli in their attitude against singing or chanting. If anything, they took an even stricter line. In their letter to Müntzer they criticized liturgical chanting as against New Testament practice. "This cannot be good when we find in the New Testament no teaching on chanting, no example. Paul reproves the Corinthian learned more than he praises them for murmuring in their assemblies as if they were singing, as the Jews and Italians pronounce their rituals in the form of songs."[39] On the basis of the same scriptural texts cited by Zwingli, Ephesians 5 and Colossians 3, Grebel argued that in these passages "Paul distinctly forbids chanting" and that singing was to be strictly a matter of the heart. "Christ commanded his messengers to preach only the Word according to the Old as well as New Testament. Paul also says that we should let the Word of Christ, not chant, dwell in us."[40]

The manifest attitude in Grebel's circle against ceremonial singing and chanting does not, however, offer evidence that the daily reading of Psalms advocated in the *Swiss Order* referred to domestic rather than congregational exercises. Certainly in the context of 1 Corinthians 14, Psalms were to be part of congregational worship. The emphasis in the *Swiss Order* on reading rather than chanting or singing the Psalms, if such an emphasis was intended, could certainly provide further evidence that the *Swiss Order* reflected early Swiss Anabaptist attitudes. It is certainly curious that neither the *Discipline* nor the *Common Order* repeated the instruction regarding the daily reading of the Psalms, although both appealed to 1 Corinthians 14.

Returning to Hausmann's statement given in Bern, it may be reiterated that this statement implied knowledge or agreement in substance with Articles 2 and 5 of the *Swiss Order,* even though no overt reference was made to its existence as a document. The statement clearly implies that Hausmann and his friends, like the author(s) of the *Swiss Order,* considered 1 Corinthians 14 normative for congregational life. Unfortunately, Hausmann's statement does not offer unassailable proof for dating the *Swiss Order.* His confession, like the copy of the *Swiss Order,* carried no date, and Hausmann is known to have visited Bern at least three times, once in April 1527, once in January 1528, and again in the spring of 1529. He and two companions were executed in July 1529. But during which of the three visits did Hausmann make the above statement? The editors and translators of his statement have pointed to its strong anti-Catholic overtones as evidence for its 1527 origin. Hausmann rejected intercession for the dead, images, and the consecration of altars and church buildings. He described the last as mere "houses of stone," the "temple of the devil," and those who frequented such places as the "miserable assembly of the devil." He rejected every form of sacerdotalism and sacramentalism, attacking priests for usurping Christ's priestly office. Through their "collection of benefices" and their "idleness," they were exploiting "the sweat of the poor" and robbing the "living temple" of God. He complained that no one was permitted to "interpret the Scriptures without getting the mark of the beast." Then in one of the clearest Swiss Anabaptist statements on Christ's high priestly office, Hausmann offered a classical satisfaction theory: Christ's "holy blood" had been once and for all "shed and sacrificed" in his sinless humanity. He thereby "wiped out all our sins" and made us "pleasing before God . . . and is thus a priest in eternity to cleanse from their sins all men who consider him to be a fitting high priest according to the order of Melchisedek." Through faith one became a beneficiary of Christ's atoning work; among fellow members of the body of Christ there was therefore "neither Jew nor Greek, nor slave nor free man."[41] All those baptized "into Christ's death" had separated themselves from idolatry and were part of the true temple not made by human hands.

If this testimony, which identified Hausmann as New Testament literate and theologically astute, is seen primarily as anti-Catholic, then it does seem logical to assign it to 1527. In January 1528, the Council of Bern sided with the Reformation, and after that Hausmann's opposition would have been directed primarily against the Reformed party. As noted, he was put to death in 1529 by a Reformed council.[42] But whatever the dating of Hausmann's testimony, discrepancies remain between it and the *Swiss Order,* allegedly taken from him and his companions in 1527. As noted earlier, Stayer, who considered the *Swiss Order* evidence for an early Swiss community of goods, saw in Hausmann's testimony a softening attitude toward community of goods "in which property-holding Anabaptist groups would deemphasize their earlier position that Christians have no absolute right of possession. Instead they would insist that, just as Christian baptism must be voluntary, Christian mutual aid must come about as the result of the voluntary decision of property holders."[43] If Stayer was correct, then Hausmann and his companions were articulating economic practices at variance with the instructions of the *Swiss Order* at the very time when they were allegedly responsible for introducing it and the Schleitheim Articles to Bernese territory. How does one reconcile these discrepancies? One possibility is that Hausmann represented the original interpretation of the *Swiss Order*. Those who sought to make a hard and fast rule of community of goods were the innovators.[44] An alternative explanation would place the beginning of the practice of community of goods very early and as not lasting very long. This was indeed the view of a contemporary, the chronicler of St. Gall, Johann Kessler.[45] Such a view would imply that the *Swiss Order* originated very early, perhaps before the Schleitheim Articles. But other ambiguities remain in Hausmann's testimony. His political ethic seemed to lack Schleitheim's radicality. He believed that temporal authority could be Christian if its actions were Christian.[46]

If Hausmann and his companions were the carriers of the Schleitheim Articles and the *Swiss Order*, why are there discrepancies? And if these two documents originated at the same time in the same place by the same hands, why have they not been preserved in tandem more often? Why are the Bernese documents the exception rather than the rule? And what is one to make of the two different leadership principles implied in the two documents? Article 5, agreed upon at Schleitheim, seemed to call for a single leader to exercise the office of shepherd or bishop. It stated,

The shepherd in the church shall be a person according to the rule of Paul [1 Tim. 3:7], fully and completely, who has a good report of those who are outside the faith. The office of such a person shall be to read and exhort and teach, warn, admonish, or ban in the congregation, and properly to preside among the sisters and brothers in prayer, and in the breaking of bread, and in all things to take care of the body of Christ.[47]

The *Swiss Order*, on the other hand, granted no explicit disciplining or presiding authority to a shepherd, suggesting instead an ad hoc leadership. Its Article 2 stated simply, "When the brothers and sisters are together, they shall take up something to read together. The one to whom God has given the best understanding shall explain it."[48] Jean Seguenny interpreted these instructions to mean that whoever had the best understanding of a particular passage had the right to speak. The differences between the *Swiss Order* and the Schleitheim Articles suggested to him that the *Swiss Order* predated Schleitheim. The *Swiss Order* seemed to describe a congregational structure without "settled leadership."[49] According to Article 4 of the *Swiss Order,* responsibility for discipline was vested in members of the congregation. "Everyone is bound and obliged . . . out of love [to] admonish the erring brother." Neither transgressions, calling for discipline, nor the penalties imposed are spelled out further in the *Swiss Order.* But the point here is that it implied a relatively egalitarian community in which ideally all members exercised the same authority. If this interpretation is correct, it would give credence to the supposition that the *Swiss Order* predated Schleitheim and that by 1527 the need for a more clearly defined authority structure had become apparent at Schleitheim. Yet, if Marpeck's criticisms of brethren in Appenzell are taken seriously, the lack of shepherds with vested authority remained a trademark among some of the Swiss Anabaptists into the 1540s.

In any event, whether pre-Schleitheim or not, the omissions in the oldest Anabaptist congregational order are as interesting as the inclusions. Nothing was said about separation, the ban, or, most strikingly, about baptism. These omissions stand in stark contrast to specific directives that implied a closely knit community, encouraged to meet three to four times weekly for fellowship and common meals. The meals were to consist of soup, vegetables, meat, and beverages. A warning seemed necessary against gluttony and drunkenness (Articles 1 and 6), but nothing was said about excluding the noncommitted or nonbaptized. As already noted, the *Swiss Order* called also for community of goods. The fact that its author(s) concerned themselves with menu and community of goods says something about their practical priorities. Questions arise regarding when and where on Swiss soil conditions existed as implied in the *Swiss Order?* This is more than a rhetorical question unless the *Swiss Order* is to be considered a prescriptive, utopian statement.

In Search of Practicing Congregations

Unfortunately, the sources do not yield the identity of the author(s) of the *Swiss Order,* nor do they make it possible to identify practicing congregation(s). Nevertheless, a number of possibilities exist. For instance, it is possible that conditions assumed in the *Swiss Order* existed in Zollikon for a short period of time between January and June 1525. Evidence indicates that meetings took place every day during the week from January 22 to 29. These gatherings, held in homes, involved New Testament readings, discussions, common meals, celebrations of the Lord's Supper, and baptisms.[50] When the leader, Johannes Brötli, was driven from Zollikon in early February,[51] the local congregation continued on its own. During the week from March 8 to 15, eighty persons received baptism. These brothers and sisters apparently practiced a form of community of goods and celebrated the Lord's Supper at every gathering. They also exercised discipline in the congregation of baptized believers.[52] Kessler wrote about this first Anabaptist congregation,

Most of Zollikon was rebaptized and held that they were the true Christian church; they also undertook, like the early Christians, to practice community of temporal goods (as can be read in the Acts of the Apostles), broke the locks off their doors, chests, and cellars, and ate food and drink in good fellowship without discrimination. But as in the time of the apostles, it did not last long.[53]

This description of practices at Zollikon fits the instructions of the *Swiss Order* that the Lord's Supper should be celebrated as often as the brothers and sisters met. In this context it is interesting to note that the admonition against debauchery and drunkenness surfaced in a defense of Anabaptist gatherings in which these were compared with meetings of guild fraternities. Apparently the latter had a reputation for encouraging debauchery and drunkenness; not so with Anabaptist meetings, which furthered piety and holy living. Anabaptists also defended their unauthorized reading of the Scriptures, claiming that since the Scriptures were available in the vernacular, "bishops or preachers" were no longer needed.[54] Unfortunately, the Council of Zurich thought otherwise and decided to suppress the first Anabaptist congregational experiment.

However, Anabaptism was not easily extinguished. It had spread rapidly to territories beyond Zurich's control. If Kessler's reminiscences can be trusted, Anabaptists in the territory of St. Gall organized along lines similar to those in Zollikon. Central to the emergence of Anabaptism were meetings of layfolk to hear the Scriptures read. By early summer, a separation of ways had taken place, and the Anabaptists had emerged from the populist phase with an identity of their own. According to Kessler, there were almost "daily excommunications" by that time, because the brethren had adopted a "pious, holy and blameless" lifestyle that included avoidance of "costly clothing, food and drink." In other words, separation involved a different lifestyle that expressed itself in the wearing of clothes made from coarse materials and the wearing of broad-rimmed felt hats. In agreement with the ethics of the Sermon on the Mount, Anabaptists also refused to bear guns, swords, or daggers, carrying only "broken-off bread knives."[55]

But the rhythm of separation from the larger society appears to have been uneven. In areas in which Anabaptism achieved a populist following, the development of separated congregations was held back. In territories in which the evangelical movement was still in its infancy, whole parishes came under Anabaptist influence as roving apostles or evangelists spread its message. A case in point was Tablat, near St. Gall. Here, in the spring of 1525, Hans Krüsi managed to win almost the entire parish for Anabaptism. Evidence indicates that he held congregational meetings that included baptisms, reading of the Scriptures, and a simple commemorative celebration of the Lord's death. He is also known to have favored a form of community of goods. Supporters pledged to defend him against any attempts by the authorities to capture him and bring him to trial. And even after his execution, whole villages in his sphere of influence appear to have remained Anabaptist friendly.[56]

In some areas favorable conditions may have prevailed into a later period. A relatively secure zone appears to have existed around the village of Teuffen in the territory of Appenzell. In 1528–29 the Anabaptist congregation of Teuffen attracted visitors from as far away as Southern Tyrol and Augsburg, hosting a major gathering during Christmas 1528.[57] And as late as October/November 1529, a disputation took place between Reformed clergy and representatives of Anabaptism.[58] Unfortunately, little is known about the Anabaptist community at Teuffen, its structure, members, or leadership. Evidence indicates that Hans Töblinger (Töbler or Töbisch) baptized in the area around Christmas 1528.[59] Töblinger had been in the company of Jörg Blaurock and Hans Hausmann at the Bern disputation on January 22, 1528. Later that year, Blaurock appears to have been active in Appenzell, where Anabaptists were said to have been two thousand strong. Whether true or not, evidence indicates that in relatively independent areas organized congregations existed well beyond the founding years.[60] And although it cannot be proven, it seems likely that these congregations were organized along lines similar to those of the first community in Zollikon and in keeping with principles outlined in the *Swiss Order*. However, by the 1530s, a public congregational life had become the exception on Swiss soil. Instead, most meetings were held clandestinely in out-of-the-way places, woods, fields, or barns. A main concern of these underground fellowships was to remain undetected or at least not to draw the authority's attention to their meetings.[61] Under such circumstances, some of the *Order*'s instructions were not applicable. Gradually a natural leadership structure appears to have emerged. It included local "shepherds, pastors, or watchmen" who protected the congregation from false prophets and wrong influences, while leaving baptisms to itinerant apostles.[62] Even the celebration of the Lord's Supper became less frequent.

By way of summary, then, it may be argued that conditions existed in some Swiss areas, even if only temporarily or in limited locations, for a congregational development along the lines indicated in the *Swiss Order*. This oldest known Anabaptist congregational order may very well date from the earliest days of the movement and predate the Schleitheim Articles. A number of concerns registered in the *Swiss Order,* such as gluttony, suggest that members were still young in the faith and that gatherings, complete with common meals, were relatively public. The example of Zollikon comes to mind, although similar conditions may have existed well beyond 1527 in regions such as Appenzell or in out-of-the-way places.[63] The main point is that the *Swiss Order* originated not *ex nihilo* but in context. It consisted of instructions that grew out of a particular situational reading of the New Testament and embodied the radical view of the congregation as a hermeneutic community. As noted in the previous chapter, this view was first articulated by the Grebel group during the dissociation process from Zwingli and the unlinking from the magisterial Reformation.

Adaptations: The Significance of the Swiss Order

As noted earlier, revisionist scholarship, my own included, emphasized differences among the various Anabaptist groups. Hans-Jürgen Goertz challenged the assumed normative significance of the Schleitheim Articles for a broad spectrum of Anabaptism,[64] a challenge moderated but supported by Arnold Snyder.[65] Certainly, in the context here, claims made by Yoder that the *Swiss Order* circulated widely together with the Schleitheim Articles remain unsubstantiated. On the other hand, it must be granted that both the *Swiss Order* and the Schleitheim Articles were known in Moravia because they entered Hutterite codices. The *Swiss Order* was evidently also known in Marpeck's circle, permitting the inference that it had significance beyond Swiss borders.[66] This observation is supported by a comparison of the *Swiss Order* with the *Discipline* and the *Common Order.*

The Swiss Order *and the* Discipline

As demonstrated earlier, the *Discipline,* transmitted in Hutterite codices, constituted little more than a rewritten version of the *Swiss Order.* Although the history of transmission remains unclear, the *Discipline* appears to have been tailored to Moravian conditions. It called for an increase of meetings from three or four to four or five a week, "if possible . . . even midweek" (Article 2 of the *Discipline*). In some instances, the *Discipline* offered greater detail or simply spelled out what the *Swiss Order* implied. For example, the *Discipline* prescribed that all meet-

ings begin with an invocation and end with an intercession and thanksgiving. The *Discipline* seems to have implied a more developed congregational life in other respects as well. It referred to chosen leaders
(*Vorsteher*), preachers, and elders (Article 5). And although it did not distinguish between spiritual and temporal offices, the *Discipline* appears to
have assumed a common purse and relief for the poor presided over by
deacons or servants of temporal affairs. When compared with the *Swiss
Order*, the *Discipline*, therefore, assumed a more developed leadership
structure.

A subtle shift of emphasis seems noticeable in regard to the formulation
of the Lord's Supper. The *Swiss Order* Article 7 called for a commemorative meal, "proclaiming the death of the Lord, and thereby warning each
one to commemorate, how Christ gave his life for us, and shed his blood
for us, that we might also be willing to give our body and life for Christ's
sake, which means for the sake of all the brothers." According to the *Swiss
Order*, such a memorial ceremony should take place "as often as the
brothers are together." When combined with the admonition of Article 1,
this would have meant a celebration of the Lord's Supper at least three or
four times a week, presumably in conjunction with the common meal. The
corresponding article in the *Discipline* (Article 11) retained the memorial
aspects of the Lord's Supper and, if anything, heightened the sense of solidarity between the participating members and Christ,[67] but it did not repeat the call for a frequent celebration of the Lord's Supper.

New was Article 9, addressing the subject of good-hearted seekers. According to the *Discipline*, "good-hearted seekers" should receive instructions in the "Gospel in the Creatures." No doubt this was a reference to
the Gospel of all creatures in the writings of Leonhard Schiemer and Hans
Hut.[68] Accordingly, the order "in the creatures" gave witness to the need
for cathartic suffering in obedience and submission. Just as the creatures
found their fulfillment in submission to humankind, so humankind found
fulfillment in submission to God, the individual in submission to the community.[69] Once the seekers had understood this Gospel and were prepared
to make a commitment to the community, they were to be accepted as
fellow members (*mitglied*). Somewhat curious in this context is the admonition of the *Discipline* to keep the initiation of new members secret.
Acceptance was "not to be made public before the world in order to spare
the conscience and for the sake of the spouse." This surprising instruction
may have a number of possible explanations. Not only does it imply the
existence of mixed marriages between believers and unbelievers, but it
could express concern that the decision by a spouse could lead to separation. It could further imply that the group was not yet living in a closely
knit community. In the Hutterite context, such instructions would not

make sense unless the *Discipline* referred to spouses who had not yet made the trek to Moravia. It is of interest that mixed marriages would become an issue between the Swiss Brethren and the Hutterites, with the latter encouraging separation from the unbelieving, uncommitted spouse. The same confidentiality clause also instructed that "what is officially done among the brethren and sisters in the brotherhood shall not be made public before the world." Official business presumably included discipline (Article 3). In this regard the *Discipline* tended to be more detailed than the *Swiss Order*. Public sins, for example, were to be brought "before all the brethren"; private or secret ones would be handled in accordance to the rule of Christ (Matthew 18).

Article 12 of the *Discipline* struck an apocalyptic note, calling for readiness to join the returning Christ so as to escape the coming punishment. Although new, this article corresponded to sentiments expressed in the preamble of both the *Swiss Order* and the *Discipline,* which alluded to these "most dangerous" or "most perilous times." Within this end-time scenario, the Word of God was seen as having a last or final witness.

Apart from the variations documented above, there were notable differences in the language of the two documents. The *Swiss Order* seems to be in the imperative mood: "all brothers and sisters of the entire congregation[70] *should* agree to hold the articles that follow." The *Discipline* spoke of an agreement reached, past tense: "We have all in one another's presence openly agreed to regulate everything in the best possible way. . . . we have unanimously agreed that this *Ordnung* shall be kept among us by all the brethren and sisters." The tone of the *Discipline,* therefore, suggests an agreement reached or an extant document accepted by an existing congregation.

Perhaps it is wrong to attach too great a significance to the perceived differences between the two documents. The important point is that the *Discipline* must be considered an expanded version of the *Swiss Order*. The differences illustrate that the latter was still a living text and that congregational practice and life were still unfolding. Circumstances dictated deviations or changes in the organizational model. From its inclusion in *The Chronicle* under the date 1529, it may be inferred that the *Discipline* had been adopted as a kind of constitution by a pre-Hutterite congregation. The call for four or five weekly meetings with common meals suggests the kind of relative freedom and community possible only, with a few exceptions, in Moravia.

But how did the *Swiss Order* find its way to Moravia? As will be noted below, a Swiss influence reached South Tyrol in the spring/summer of 1527, North Tyrol and Austrian territories as well as Nicolsburg (Mikulov) in Moravia in the same year (see Chapter 3). Subsequently, groups of

Swiss Anabaptists arrived in search of a refuge in Moravia, among them the key figure of the first congregation in Zollikon, Johannes Brötli (Pretle), as well as Wolfgang Ulimann, who had propagated Anabaptism in Appenzell. Disaster struck a band from the Appenzell led by Ulimann when they were intercepted at Waldsee in Swabia in 1529. Ten men, including Ulimann, were beheaded, some women drowned, and those who recanted were sent back to Swiss territory.[71] Not clear is how Brötli's death related to these arrests and executions. He is said to have suffered martyrdom at the stake by fire.[72] Despite these setbacks, the Swiss Anabaptist presence in Moravia increased. Kessler wrote that a lord of the Bohemian Brethren faith (a Picardi) had made land available to the refugees where "they dwell and engage in agriculture. And many from other places, where they have no secure abode [because of their faith], are moving down as well. Here some of them lead a strict life which, if the doctrine were pure and sound, would be worth praise and fame."[73] The strict life, referred to by Kessler, seems to imply moral uprightness and discipline in community. Such a life would have entailed some form of congregational order similar to that outlined in the *Swiss Order* or the *Discipline.*[74]

The point here is that the *Discipline* most likely entered Hutterite sources through a Moravian-Swiss connection. As suggested earlier, this link could have been the congregation at Austerlitz, although Swiss Anabaptists appear to have created their own communities in Moravia, distinct from the Austerlitz Brethren, the Gabrielites, Philipites, and later Hutterites. Among Swiss distinctives were a less rigorous leadership style, retention of the household as the basic economic unit, and refusal to allow divorce on religious grounds. But whatever community the *Discipline* had been tailored to serve, one thing seems certain: it came from the same cloth as the *Swiss Order.* A similar observation seems in order for the *Common Order* nurtured in Pilgram Marpeck's circle.

The Common Order *(1540?)*

Jean Seguenny believed that the *Common Order* originated in Strasbourg in 1528.[75] This hypothesis was based on evidence that in late 1528 Marpeck participated in efforts to organize the Anabaptist refugee community in Strasbourg.[76] A main concern appears to have been to provide material support. Marpeck's collaborators, Wilhelm Reublin and Jacob Kautz, implied in their subsequent confession that they wanted congregational discipline that involved admonition (*manung*) and the ban.[77] With Reublin present, it does not seem farfetched to suggest that these early Strasbourg efforts at organization were guided by knowledge of the *Swiss Order.* Clear is that the *Common Order,* like the *Discipline,* represented an adapted version of the *Swiss Order*. In its present form, the *Common Order* carried Leupold Scharnschlager's name and originated, in all likelihood as Fast argued, in the early 1540s. The full title, *Common Order of the Members of Christ Set in Seven Articles*,[78] could suggest that the document was intended to provide a common organization for a number of Anabaptist groups. Marpeck is known to have traveled to Moravia in the early 1540s in efforts to sponsor cooperation and unity among various Anabaptist groups. And although his efforts were rebuffed by the Hutterites, surviving correspondence indicates that some communities in Moravia retained contact and remained in fellowship with Marpeck and his circle of friends. The *Common Order* presumably embodied the organizational principles of Marpeck's circle and perhaps those of the Moravian congregations in fellowship with him. A comparison of the *Common Order* with the *Swiss* demonstrates not only reliance on the Swiss model but also a creative reworking of the same.

William Klassen, the first to note the similarities, understated the case when he concluded that the two documents "bear a striking resemblance."[79] Among the most obvious similarities is that both documents were organized into seven articles. The preamble of both alluded to the Word of God as having been brought to light in these "last days." Articles 1 of the *Swiss* and 2 of the *Common Order* correspond in content; the same is true of Articles 5 and 7, respectively. Similarities exist between Articles 4 and 6 of the documents. Only two out of the seven articles in the *Common Order* have no apparent parallel in the *Swiss Order*. All of this strengthens the impression that the author(s) of the *Common Order* consciously reshaped the *Swiss Order* to fit the circumstances of their own group. But even on matters of agreement, the *Common Order* seems more reflective, detailed, and theologically substantive than the *Swiss* (see Appendix A).

From the historian's perspective, the evident differences between the two orders are even more interesting than the agreements. Unlike the *Swiss Order* and like the *Discipline* (Article 5), the *Common Order* (Article 3) implied a structured leadership.[80] The most striking difference concerns the *Common Order*'s rejection of community of goods, which was advocated in both the *Swiss Order* and the *Discipline*. According to the *Common Order* (Article 5), the example of the early church, described in Acts 2 and 4, was not binding for the contemporary situation. It was "misunderstood by some giving rise to error and contempt, special sects and the like, and some have made of this example a law, a coercive measure [*Zwang*], a fetter, almost a carnal righteousness and requirement [*Forderung*]."[81]

These comments indicate not only a distancing from the early Swiss position but imply overt criticism of Hutterite attitudes and practices. Marpeck's efforts at dialogue and concord in Moravia foundered on Hutterite intransigence regarding community of goods.[82] As will be noted in Chapter 6, during his early period in Strasbourg Marpeck himself had advocated community of goods. But by the 1540s he and his supporters took the view that sharing of goods had been a voluntary matter in the early Jerusalem church and that it had ceased after the dispersion from Jerusalem. The contemporary situation, according to the *Common Order*, was analogous to the postdispersion period rather than the situation of the church in Jerusalem.[83] Temporal concerns for members of the congregation, nevertheless, figured prominently in Articles 2, 3, and 5 of the *Common Order*. Assistance and relief for the poor were considered Christian duties and were signs of compassion and fraternal charity. A collection was to be taken at every congregational meeting, and one of the brothers was to be entrusted with the responsibility of dispensing aid according to need. These instructions fit the known facts of Marpeck's circle in the 1540s with its members dispersed or existing underground in Augsburg. It was a reality different from that assumed in the *Swiss Order* or the *Discipline*. The *Common Order* said nothing about meeting several times a week. Instead, it made allowances for distances to be traveled to meetings and the severity of persecution. True, the faithful were admonished not to neglect the fellowship, "be their number small or great, two or twenty,"[84] but it was apparently not incumbent to celebrate the Lord's Supper at every meeting but instead on "occasion, according to convenience before dispersing."

Curiously, some aspects of the *Common Order* seem closer to the *Discipline* than to the *Swiss Order*, among them a more clearly defined leadership structure. Leaders were mentioned in Articles 2 and 3, with the person appointed for poor relief being reminiscent of the "servants of temporal affairs," first designated by the Austerlitz Brethren and later by Hutterites. Reminiscent of Austerlitz practice and later adopted by the Hutterites was the admonition in Article 4 that "faithful workers in the Lord's vineyard" and "shepherds" should be considered "worthy of double honour" in keeping with Paul's instructions to Timothy (1 Timothy 5:17).[85] Respect for the leaders was considered essential to the well-being of the congregation. Nothing seemed more detrimental and threatening, according to the *Common Order*, than to be "scattered abroad without shepherds."

In this context it should be recalled that Marpeck criticized some Swiss Anabaptists for not bestowing on their leaders sufficient authority and respect. It seemed to him that in a reversal of proper order the sheep were disciplining the shepherd.[86] In contrast, the *Common Order*, like the

Schleitheim Articles, bestowed on leaders the power to discipline wayward members. On this score, the instructions were therefore also considerably more detailed than those of the *Swiss Order*. The nature of the discipline was to reflect the seriousness of the transgression; whether it had been "secret or open, large or small, in word or deed, a vice of the flesh, false teaching [or] a licentious life" (Article 6). As noted, the *Swiss Order* mentioned only gluttony (Article 4) and/or frivolity (Article 3).

Differences appear also in the format prescribed for congregational meetings. The *Common Order* called explicitly for a combination of preaching and admonition. Every congregational meeting was to open with a prayer of invocation and close with intercessory prayer (Article 2).[87] No mention was made of reading Psalms or of congregational singing. In the absence of a recognized leader[88] the congregation was to choose someone "competent from among them" to read or speak. Obviously then, circumstances had in part dictated changes from the *Swiss Order*. These same circumstances, the urban and scattered nature of Marpeck's circle, may also help to explain the eventual demise of this group.

Of the three documents providing a window into early Anabaptist congregational structure, the *Swiss Order* may be considered the oldest.[89] The *Discipline*, once attributed to Leonard Schiemer and considered the oldest Anabaptist church order by Robert Friedmann, in fact represents a revised version of the *Swiss Order*. And although the history of transmission remains obscure, the allusion to a Gospel of all creatures in the *Discipline* suggests that this document had indeed been in the possession of a group under Hans Hut's influence. It is possible that this was the group that established itself in Austerlitz during 1528.

The *Common Order* also indicates knowledge of and dependence on the *Swiss Order*. Differences between the two reveal deliberate changes and adaptations dictated by the social circumstances in which Pilgram Marpeck's urban group functioned. These adaptations indicate first-generation habits not yet restricted by the weight of tradition. Scripture, specifically the New Testament, provided the model organization to be imitated. The author(s) of the *Discipline* expressed this principle when they suggested that "if however, a brother or sister is able to produce a better *Ordnung*, it shall be accepted . . . any time" in accordance with 1 Corinthians 14.[90]

Some questions remain about the specific context in which the *Swiss Order* originated. Neither exact time nor location of origin can be established with certainty. Claims that it originated in tandem with the Schleitheim Articles are speculative. It is possible that the *Swiss Order* predated Schleitheim. Its call for three to four meetings a week, complete with a common meal and celebration of the Lord's Supper, implied a relatively public congregational life. If such existed on Swiss soil, its time was limited to the earliest period and/or specific locations. Persecution drove Swiss Anabaptism underground or into exile. Some Swiss Anabaptists moved to Moravia, where opportunities presented themselves to live in accordance with the instructions of the *Swiss Order*. Evidence that the *Swiss Order* was adapted and revised in Moravia and in Marpeck's circle argues for a significant Swiss influence stretching across Upper Germany and Austria into Moravia. This influence, documented in subsequent chapters as well, moderates distinctions between Swiss and South German-Austrian Anabaptism made in my earlier writings.[91]

Chapter Three

In Search of the Promised Land

The importance of Moravia for sixteenth-century Anabaptism was never in doubt. Scholars such as Robert Friedmann and Jarold Zeman had seen to that. Yet, in the minds of some of us, Moravia seemed significant only for the Hutterite narrative. Consequently, we underestimated the importance of Moravia for Anabaptism as a whole. The connections to the rest of Anabaptism suggest a broader significance for Moravia. From 1527 on Moravia became the "promised land" for persecuted Anabaptists from Switzerland, the Rhineland, Palatinate, Swabia, Hesse, Franconia, Bavaria, Upper and Lower Austria, the Tyrol, and Silesia. The resulting proliferation of sects bewildered contemporaries and amazed modern historians.[1]

Anabaptists were not the only "heretics" to seek residence in Moravia. Contemporaries catalogued forty different sects, among them Utraquists and Bohemian Brethren (divided into a Major and Minor Party), Catholics, Lutherans, Zwinglians, Schwenckfeldians, anti-Trinitarians, sabbatarians, Adamites, Josephites (who held that Christ descended from the house of David through Joseph as his biological father), spiritualists, a variety of Anabaptists, and even the odd agnostic.[2] To hostile observers it seemed as if all of the heresies of the past had come to life again and chosen sixteenth-century Moravia as their residence. Nothing like this existed in the rest of Europe. Nothing like it would be seen again until the nonconformists of Europe attempted to create a new brave world in North America.

Some contemporaries found the plethora of religious commitments and conflicting truth claims confusing. On a visit to Austerlitz, a town with a population of around three thousand, Venetian weaver Marcantonio Varotto encountered thirteen or fourteen different religious persuasions. "So many sects, the one contrary to the others and the one condemning the others . . . all wishing to be the true church" drove the bewildered weaver back into the Roman Catholic fold![3]

From 1526 on, the Anabaptists became major constituents of Moravia's religious mosaic. Sebastian Franck mused that the Anabaptists could not have been more divided even if God had so desired it.[4] As Caspar Schwenckfeld noted,

One could write a large chronicle about the many and manifold sects among the Anabaptists, each condemning the other and often for ridiculous [*liederlich*] reasons. Obviously it cannot be the spirit of unity. . . . I have informed myself of their opinions for the most part. There are Swiss, Hutterites, Gabrielites, Pilgramites, Netherlanders, Friesians, Mennonites, Hoffmanites, etc. . . . No soul agrees with the other in the faith.[5]

Without prejudging diversity as negative, twentieth-century researchers have largely substantiated Anabaptist variety. The diverse backgrounds of the religious refugees to Moravia, it can be argued, accounted in part for their divisions. Friedmann distinguished five major communities: Austerlitz Brethren, Gabrielites, Philipites, Swiss Brethren, and Hutterites, but he suggested that further research would identify other groups.[6] This was done by Jarold Zeman, who documented at least ten different groups without including the "spiritualizing Anabaptists," such as the group led by Christian Entfelder at Eibenschitz (Ivanice). Zeman described the "basic trend within Moravian Anabaptism" as "a process of splintering" and observed that most divisions occurred during the founding years, fewer in the second half of the century when the Anabaptists enjoyed relative security and prosperity.[7] Eventually only the Hutterites survived. Understandably, they have received most of the attention, the other groups far less.

The remainder of the first part of this book aims at balancing the historic account. After all, the Hutterites, whose story is told in detail in the second part, emerged as a distinct group only after 1533, whereas the Austerlitz Brethren, the Gabrielites, and the Philipites formed an essential part of the pre-Hutterite experiments in community building. In fact, the Austerlitz community became a model for the others.

Seeking a More Perfect Life: The Brethren at Austerlitz

The Hans Hut Connection

According to *The Chronicle,* the Brethren at Austerlitz had a reputation of living "as one heart, mind and soul, each caring faithfully for the other." So great was their reputation that other Anabaptists "seeking a more perfect life" flocked to Austerlitz.[8] But the reputation did not last long, and the Brethren at Austerlitz had emerged from disagreements among Anabaptists in Nicolsburg. The tensions feeding the Nicolsburg schism can be traced back to quarrels in early 1527 between Balthasar Hubmaier, a doctor of theology, and Hans Hut, a self-taught jack-of-all-trades and former sympathizer of Thomas Müntzer.

Hut was without question the most influential missionary of early Anabaptism in Central and South Germany. His travels took him from Thuringia through Franconia and Bavaria to Moravia and Austria. These missionary journeys assured him a prominent place in the spread of early Anabaptism and in the story of communitarian Anabaptism. Scholarship of the last two decades has revised the impression left by Hutterite sources that Hut belonged to those who "valiantly suffered for the nonresistance attitude of true discipleship." Traditional attempts to seal hermetically Anabaptism from any contamination with the Peasants' War or Hut from Müntzer's influence have proven untenable.[9] Hans-Dieter Schmid, as early as 1971, considered "Hut's Anabaptism" a partial extension of Müntzer's program,[10] suggesting that Hut inserted believers' baptism into Müntzer's apocalyptic frame of reference. Gottfried Seebass described Hut and his associates as "Müntzer's heirs"[11] and confirmed that a number of Hut's Franconian converts had been participants in the Peasants' War.[12] More recently, James Stayer, working on a broader scale, reached a similar conclusion.[13] Indeed, one can speak of a scholarly consensus that Hut's contact with Müntzer was more than casual.[14] His name appeared as Hans from Bibra among the signatories of the "eternal league" formed by Müntzer and Heinrich Pfeifer on September 19, 1524, in Mühlhausen.[15] After their expulsion from Mühlhausen in October, Müntzer and Pfeifer visited Hut in Bibra. Accompanied by Pfeifer, Hut took Müntzer's manuscript, the *Special Exposé* to the press of Hans Hergot in Nuremberg and likely also had a hand in the publication of Müntzer's *Vindication and Refutation* through Hieronymus Hötzel.[16] Until the "shooting became too thick" Hut was present at the fateful battle of Frankenhausen[17] and subsequently defended the peasants' cause in his home territory around Bibra, thereby supporting the efforts of the local peasant leader, Jörg Haug. He fled the area only when troops from the Swabian League approached.[18]

Hut's "conversion" to Anabaptism in the spring of 1526 apparently did not involve an entirely religious reorientation. It did, however, take account of the changed circumstances of crushed peasant hopes. It seems that with the defeat of the peasants died expectations of the transformation of the entire society. Nevertheless, Hut's volatile apocalyptic expectations held out hope for a cleansed Christendom. The Turks would function as the instrument of divine wrath. His "sheathed sword" permitted an almost seamless continuation of ideological-theological themes inherited from Müntzer. Nothing illustrates this more clearly than Hut's views on "true baptism."

Evidence indicates that Hut had come to question pedobaptism as early as 1524. He had refused to bring his newborn to baptism in that year. His own acceptance of baptism on May 26, 1526, at the hands of Hans Denck in Augsburg suggests a continuity between his earlier antipedobaptism stand and "believer's baptism."[19] Hut understood baptism as an apocalyptic sealing of the faithful remnant.[20] Along with his peculiar "Gospel of all creatures" tailored for the commoners,[21] the apocalyptic message became a trademark of Hut's influence. The Gospel of or in all creatures could be illustrated with examples from the daily routines of peasants and artisans, namely that the divinely ordained salvation process involved submission to the divine purpose of cleansing through suffering. Accordingly, true faith, born through the inner experience of the "bitter" Christ, stood at the center of the salvation experience. True baptism came to signify the painful process of dying to creatureliness; water baptism was the outer sign of the inner sealing of the elect experienced in the true faith—all of this in an apocalyptic context of living at the end of time, which would witness the punishment of the godless. It was presumably this end-time mood that attracted so many Peasants' War veterans to Hut's message.

Among Hut's closest travel companions and confidants were Eucharius Binder, Joachim Märtz, and Jörg Volck, also known as Georg or Kolerin Volckmer. Volck, besides Hut the most important Anabaptist leader in Franconia, boasted to converts that he had fled from the territory of Count Wilhelm of Henneberg after the rebellion.[22] Since then, "God had put it in his mind to preach the Gospel in villages and mills."[23] The gospel he preached was Hut's version of the Gospel of all creatures with apocalyptic overtones. It should be mentioned that Volck expected a new order based on the common use of all goods. Curiously, the sources for Hut's Franconian ministry yield the name of Kilian Volckhamer, who shared a number of commonalities with Volck(mer). Although they never appeared together, both turned up in Thuringian records;[24] both were apparently sextants;[25] both traveled with Hut's confidants, Binder and Märtz; and both disappeared without a trace at about the same time. It seems, then, that Kilian Volckhamer, a later leader in the Austerlitz congregation, was in fact Jörg Volck, Hut's companion.[26]

Both Volck and Hut received a favorable reception not only in mills, hamlets, and villages, but also in some cities. During the spring of 1527 Hut and his companions spread Anabaptism in the territories of Bamberg, Erlangen, Nuremberg, and Augsburg. Arrests and executions of their converts brought Hut and his confidants to Nicolsburg in Moravia. Presumably information had reached them that this town had become a haven for persecuted Anabaptists, including Balthasar Hubmaier. The quarrel that erupted between Hut and Hubmaier did not center on Hut's pacifism versus Hubmaier's defense of the sword, as Hutterite chroniclers would subsequently have it,[27] but rather, as Stayer has put it, Hubmaier's attempt at instituting a "magisterial" Anabaptism.[28] Hut's preaching, while the lords of Liechtenstein were absent at the meeting of the Estates, seemed at cross-purposes with Hubmaier's intentions. Volatile apocalyptic aspects of the message, although popular with uprooted refugees flocking to Nicolsburg, apparently disturbed others and threatened the social peace in the city, thereby jeopardizing Hubmaier's attempt at reforming the entire community with the cooperation of its local lords, the Liechtensteins. During the ensuing conflict, Hut appears to have received support from refugees who had been or were later influenced by Swiss pacifist ideas. This, plus the fact that Hut advocated a form of community of goods, may explain his retroactive rehabilitation into a proto-Hutterite.

The oldest sources about the Hubmaier-Hut clash—Hut's statement at his trial and the controversial Nicolsburg Articles—permit the inference that Hubmaier accused Hut of spreading sedition. Hut allegedly taught (1) that "the Gospel should not be preached in churches but secretly and clandestinely in houses"; (2) that there was no room for secular authority among true Christians; (3) that no secular ruler or government had recognized or would recognize and accept the truth; (4) that the established governments would forfeit their authority to the Anabaptists; (5) that the Anabaptists would judge the world; and (6) that the pending judgment of the existing order and major changes in that order could be expected in two years. Hubmaier appears to have taken particular offense at Hut's apocalyptic message. According to Hubmaier, Hut's timetable was based on an erroneous reading of the Scriptures. The effect of such teachings was that it encouraged people to neglect their social responsibilities, their homes, property, and even kin. Such persons, arriving in increasing numbers in Nicolsburg, were creating welfare problems. Hubmaier and his supporters, therefore, decided to put a halt to Hut's unauthorized ministry. He was imprisoned with Hubmaier now functioning as the inquisitor, a role not appreciated by everyone. Sympathizers aided Hut's escape.[29] His subsequent itinerary through Austrian territories has been described as a "victory march" (*Siegeszug*). Grete Mecenseffy, the most knowledgeable scholar of Austrian Anabaptism in our century, considered Hut the "Anabaptist apostle" of Upper Austria.[30] His influence has been traced to Eisenstadt, Freistadt, Wells, Linz, Steyer, and Passau. Everywhere local evangelicals, frustrated by stalled reforms, responded favorably to his message. Hut practically won the entire leadership of the Anabaptist movement in these territories. Among them were Jörg Krautschlegel,

Thomas Waldhauser, Leonhard Dorfbrunner, Hieronymus of Mansee, Jacob Porter, Philip Jäger, and Jacob Wiedemann, along with Joachim Märtz, Leonhard Schiemer, and Eucharius Binder.[31] With such a plethora of leaders, each interpreting Hut's message in the context of his own circumstances, it seems difficult to generalize about the nature of Hut's influence. Besides, a majority of these converts soon met with martyrdom. Binder, Märtz, and Mansee died at the stake in Salzburg, October 25, 1527.[32] Hut himself died later that year in Augsburg. Schiemer, Dorfbrunner, and Waldhauser died in early 1528.[33] Wiedemann survived until 1535 or 1536. Nevertheless, these early apostles, all in one way or other touched by Hut's ministry, assured the rapid spread of Anabaptism in Austria and Salzburg territories, not least through the stories of their martyrdom.

Sometime during the summer of 1527, Hut's brand of Anabaptism leapt from Upper Austria to the Inn Valley to the lordships of Kitzbühl,[34] Kufstein, Rattenberg,[35] and to Salzburg territory.[36] The rapid spread of the movement was, no doubt, due in part to the presence of former monks, priests, and schoolteachers in its leadership. Despite the prominence of a literate elite, the movement's message was radically anticlerical and depended on neither learned theologians nor magisterial support for its expansion, organization, or continued existence.

It is possible that Anabaptism entered the Inn Valley even before persons associated with Hut's party brought it to full bloom. At his trial Hut recalled that a certain Kaspar Färber (Ferber) told him, as early as May 1526, of brethren in the Inn Valley who were dedicated to the Christian life.[37] But so far these brethren remain unidentified,[38] although the available evidence suggests that the stimulus for the sudden growth of Anabaptism in North Tyrol emanated from Hut's circle. As noted, this circle was hardly homogeneous, even though Hut's influence is traceable through his concept of the Gospel of all creatures. Of special interest here is evidence of the movement's rudimentary organization in these territories. Besides empowering other itinerant apostles, Hut seems to have encouraged the creation of conventicles with a local spiritual leader and a treasurer (*Säckelmeister*).[39] The duty of the latter was to dispense aid to needy members from a common purse. As noted in the discussion of the oldest Anabaptist church order (Chapter 2), it is possible that this form of organization reflected Swiss influences. It should be noted, however, that Hut and his colleague Volck preached all along that "goods should be common, so that one may help the poor and those who cannot work because of sickness."[40] Wherever Hut's influence can be documented, similar attitudes appeared. Stayer has shown this in relation to Hans Weischenfelder, Ambrosius Spittelmaier, Marx Maier, and Jörg Nespitzer.[41]

Nespitzer had been baptized by Hut in Passau along with others when

Hut stopped there on his way to Nicolsburg during the spring of 1527. Later, on his return, Hut stayed at the home of Hermann Keil, the treasurer or dispenser of aid (*Austeiler*) for the local congregation that had formed. Because this congregation was strategically located on the way to Moravia and because the documents provide some insights into its early structure, the Passau congregation deserves special attention.[42] Interestingly, Keil's statements given after his arrest in January 1528 agree almost verbatim with statements about the practice of mutual aid made by Hut's and Volck's converts in Franconia. True Christians willingly shared with brothers and sisters. The common treasury had been created to help the unemployed and sick.[43] One of the early spiritual leaders in Passau was Wolfgang Brandhuber, who appears in documents as Wolfgang, schoolmaster of Burghausen. This identification provides new background information about this important early leader. Brandhuber had come to Passau because of persecution in Burghausen, Bavaria. In the past, scholars confused him with his brother, a tailor by trade, who lived in St. Niclas near Passau.[44] Brandhuber was out of town when the arrests began in Passau during late 1527 and early 1528. His wife testified that in January 1528 her husband had gone to Bohemia with some like-minded companions and that he intended to return in two weeks if all went well.[45] It is possible that Brandhuber planned to visit the Anabaptist community forming at Böhmisch (Bohemian) Krumau (Cesky Krumlov). Upon returning to Passau he must have learned of the arrests and fate that awaited key members of the congregation and decided to shift his residence to Linz. By moving to Linz, Brandhuber escaped certain death in Passau. Only in 1529 did the authorities in Linz discover his identity as an Anabaptist leader. An investigation revealed that the former schoolmaster practiced community of goods in his household; that is, he shared his food, belongings, and income with all members of the household, including the domestics. In letters to other Anabaptist congregations, Brandhuber had praised community of goods as the proper Christian order.[46] For this reason, modern scholarship generally pointed to Brandhuber's letters as the first clear elaboration of the principle of Christian communism, later practiced by the Hutterites.[47] It should not be forgotten, however, that the *Swiss Order* had advocated community of goods earlier and that since the spring of 1528 a form of community of goods was practiced among the Austerlitz Brethren. As noted, this community, which had emerged from the conflict in Nicolsburg between supporters of Hubmaier and Hut, exercised considerable attraction and influence. It became the model for other Anabaptist communities in Moravia and in 1529 attracted a good number from the Böhmisch Krumau group. It stands to reason that by 1529 Brandhuber had also come under the Austerlitz influence. He was, therefore, not so much the founding father of the practice of community of goods as a member and articulator of a form of Anabaptism under a mixed Swiss-Hut influence.[48]

The Nicolsburg Schism and the Founding of the Austerlitz Brethren

Although Hubmaier and Hut were both removed from center stage in 1527,[49] tension persisted between the local Reform Party, led by Hubmaier's successor, Hans (Johannes) Spittelmaier, and the refugees, led by one-eyed Jacob Wiedemann.[50] Concerned with the unity of the civic community of Nicolsburg, the local Reform Party continued the policy of magisterial reformation in cooperation with the lords of Liechtenstein, using the local parish facilities. The "pilgrims, strangers and guests," meanwhile, formed separate conventicles. Led by Wiedemann, the refugees introduced a self-administered mutual aid program and held separate house meetings, refusing to attend the local parish church.[51] Hans Spittelmaier felt it necessary to warn openly against the schismatics, deriding them as "little group makers and staff bearers" (*heüffler* and *stäbler*).[52] The reference to staff bearers suggests that the Wiedemann group, under a Swiss influence, assumed a nonresistant stance. This view seems supported by their refusal to pay taxes earmarked for war with the Turks, an issue that polarized the two camps further.[53] The position assumed by Wiedemann's group, therefore, represented a new synthesis between Hut's and Swiss ideas.

At the beginning of Lent 1528 and after fruitless attempts at mediating the dispute, the lords of Liechtenstein ordered the schismatics to leave Nicolsburg. A group of about two hundred, not numbering children, left the city in March, and "because of their immediate need and distress" decided to pool all their resources. Two "servants of temporal affairs," with an assistant each, were appointed. Wiedemann assumed or retained overall authority as "servant of the Word."[54] Thus was born the first historically identifiable Anabaptist congregation known to have practiced full community of goods in Moravia. The catalyst for this event and for organizing the leadership along clear lines was the emergency situation. Since disagreements on property, on taking oaths, and on the payment of taxes surfaced later in this community, it is unlikely that these issues were the principal reason for the exodus from Nicolsburg or that private property had been disowned in principle with all its implications thought out. The observation of Friedmann seems therefore quite apropos.

Compelled by the emergency situation, the need of taking care of the many indigent Brethren, they pooled all their possessions and money in the manner of the first church in Jerusalem. But this act was at first not understood as a definite step toward complete community of goods comprising both consumption and production. This [later] development came but slowly step by step. . . . The groups around 1529–33 lived by no means in brotherly harmony; local quarrels over leadership and form of community-life mar these first years in Moravia.[55]

Friedmann's interpretation of the road to Austerlitz event assumed, of course, that the Hutterites offered the true standard for complete community of goods based on Acts 2 and 4. Elsewhere, Friedmann contrasted the practice introduced in 1533 by the "truly charismatic and prophetic" leader Jacob Hutter with earlier "vague experimentation." Seeking to explain the changes or, better, improvements, introduced by Hutter, Friedmann accepted the internalist Hutterite view and shifted to a purely idealistic-religious explanation of the staying power of Hutterite practice. "Emergency motivation would never have produced survival for any protracted period of time," he claimed. Only the virtues of brotherly love, of sharing, of yielded self-will (*Gelassenheit*), and of self-denying obedience could ultimately explain the survival of the Hutterite community.[56]

Whatever the merits of such an explanation, the community organized on the road owed its immediate survival to the good graces of the lords of Austerlitz,[57] a town on the main trade route that led from Vienna via Nicolsburg and Brünn to Bohemia[58] (see Map 1). Thanks to the kind reception by the lords, the newcomers were able to establish themselves quickly, moving into town from the land first designated for them. Special concessions included a six-year rent exemption, building supplies, permission to locate near the potter's market, and encouragement to increase their numbers. The lords were willing to accept a thousand of them. Mindful of friends and relatives left behind, the settlers sponsored missions with tidings of their good fortune.[59] As a result, membership in the community tripled within a short time to six hundred adults. Among those who heard about the love and harmony among the Brethren at Austerlitz were the refugees at Böhmisch Krumau. A group of eighty to ninety of these, primarily from Upper Austria and North Tyrol, who had fled to Bohemia in the wake of the first persecution in late 1527 or early 1528, joined the Brethren at Austerlitz in 1529. One of their leaders was Virgil Plattner, a former priest and vicar from Rattenberg who was captured and executed at Schärding in the same year.[60] Among the new arrivees from Krumau were also the future Hutterite leaders Hans Amon, Christoph Gschäll, and Leonard Lanzenstiel.[61] Their group leader, Hans Fasser, returned to Bohemia and was subsequently excommunicated as a fornicator. Of importance here is the manifest appeal radiating from Austerlitz over the territories of Austria, the Tyrol, and beyond.

In the same year, 1529, Jacob Hutter, who had emerged as a leader in South Tyrol (see Chapter 8), arrived to investigate a report that at Auster-

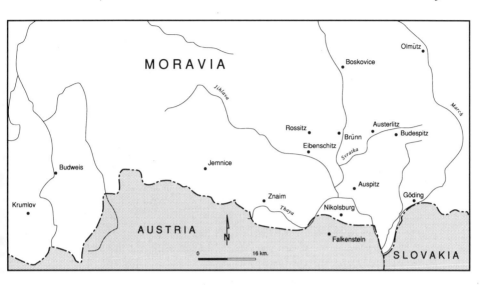

Map 1. Moravia

litz "God had gathered a people . . . to live as one heart, mind and soul, each caring faithfully for the other."[62] Discussions with the elders led to a uniting, meaning presumably an acceptance of Hutter as a representative of the Austerlitz community and Hutter's acceptance of the community as the model or mother congregation. Hutter returned to South Tyrol to report on "the community of saints he had seen and experienced at Austerlitz [and] how, in the name of them all, he had united with those at Austerlitz in peace and unity of soul and spirit and how they had sent him on his way home to the Tyrol in peace."[63] From this time on, Austerlitz provided a beacon of hope as a place of refuge and an organizational model worthy of imitation. Evidence indicates that Hutter began to organize the Anabaptists in South Tyrol according to the teachings, practices, and example he had witnessed in Austerlitz. A common treasury was introduced, servants of temporal affairs appointed, and a decision made to dispatch the first group to Austerlitz. This group was led by Jörg Zaunring, described in government search warrants as of "medium height, wearing a light brown coat, brown trousers, a rough hat, no beard and having a little [high-pitched] voice."[64] Despite government efforts to apprehend him, Zaunring and his band managed to make their way to a fraternal reception in Austerlitz during the early summer of 1530.

Unfortunately, fraternal feelings lasted only a few months. In January 1531 a major schism rocked the Austerlitz community. Although the details of that story, in which Zaunring played a prominent part, will appear in Chapter 9, it should be noted here that the community at Austerlitz was rapidly outgrowing its maximal size for sound group dynamics and easy administration. Among other things, it proved impossible to house six hundred adults in one place or even in the same part of the town. It was also impossible to find a meeting place large enough for a general assembly during the winter months. The community was, therefore, divided into three separate congregations, each meeting in different quarters and presumably still living in private dwellings. Wiedemann remained overall bishop, and three assistants—Kilian (Volckhamer), Jacob Mändel, and Franz Itzinger—led the respective groups.[65] A host of problems surfaced as these refugees attempted to build a new community, such as, for example, what to do with unbelieving spouses or brethren in need of wives while there was a shortage of women.

The sources are silent about solutions developed and provide few details about ordinary members who made up the rank and file of the community. Only about the leaders do we have some information. One-eyed Wiedemann was a Swabian from Memmingen, the birthplace of the peasant manifesto of 1525, the Twelve Articles. His relationship to the events of 1525 is unknown; perhaps a Swiss influence can be assumed on the basis of geography. It is not known when and by whom he was inducted into the Anabaptist movement. It is possible that he, like others, had come via Strasbourg. Like Hubmaier and Hut, he appears to have arrived in Nicolsburg as a refugee.[66] If he was already in Nicolsburg during the Hubmaier-Hut conflict, then he must have sided with Hut. It has been suggested that he and Philip Jäger were with Hut at Steyer in early July 1527.[67] In the fall of that year Wiedemann followed Hut to the Martyrs' Synod in Augsburg. Here he met, among others, Jacob Kautz, Hans Denck, and Ludwig Hätzer.[68] Later in Nicolsburg he became the leader of the separatist staff bearers and, as noted earlier, led the exodus of the schismatics from Nicolsburg in March 1528. His main collaborator at that point was Philip Jäger, about whose identity or background nothing is known.[69]

Among the first servants of temporal affairs in the Austerlitz community was Jacob Mändel, who had previously been treasurer to one of the lords of Liechtenstein.[70] For reasons no longer clear, Mändel left the employ of Liechtenstein and joined the schismatics, where his expertise must have been considered an asset. In Austerlitz he became the leader of one of the three congregations. More is known about Franz Itzinger, who had been chosen servant of temporal affairs alongside Mändel and led another group in Austerlitz. Evidence indicates that he had been a well-to-do citizen in the town of Leoben in Styria. Arrested in late 1527 or early 1528, Itzinger had somehow regained his freedom and fled to Nicolsburg where he joined the schismatics and the exodus to Austerlitz.[71] In early 1530 he led a group of fellow citizens from Styria to Austerlitz. Although his house and other property at Leoben had been confiscated, Itzinger as leader of one of the groups in Austerlitz allegedly cultivated the lifestyle of an aristocrat (see Chapter 9). Both Itzinger and Mändel knew Latin; both therefore belonged to the literate elite of sixteenth-century society before becoming Anabaptists. Their emergence as leaders seems to indicate that education and social status influenced leadership choices even though the Austerlitz group practiced community of goods.[72] The question arises of whether the practice of "special honors" for the leadership, a practice that created considerable dissent but was institutionalized by the later Hutterites, arose from a similar social deference rather than purely New Testament precedent.[73]

The third group leader among the Austerlitz Brethren, Kilian Volckhamer, may have been a former sexton and associate of Hans Hut.[74] As noted, Kilian Volckhamer and a Jörg Volck appeared in documents as members of Hut's inner circle. Previous scholarship assumed them to have been two separate persons. Both were considered principal leaders in Hut's circle. The question arises whether, given the state of the sources and the spelling of names based on oral statements made by converts in different regions, the two should not be considered one and the same person.[75] If true, then Kilian Volckhamer, a leader of the Austerlitz Brethren, was a former participant in the Peasants' War who, like Hut, was forced to flee his home territory when the rebellion was crushed.[76] Perhaps it was with Volckhamer's group that Hut's son found refuge after his father's death.

The point here is that the known leaders of the Anabaptist community established at Austerlitz appear to have come from the privileged literate of society.[77] Since they came from different regions—Swabia, Franconia, or Thuringia and Styria—one may speculate that ordinary members came from equally diverse regions. To mold such diversity into a cohesive functional community must have been a difficult task and may help explain the difficulties experienced in late 1530 and early 1531 (Chapter 9). These difficulties led to an exodus of disgruntled members and the establishment of another community at Auspitz. Here and in nearby Rossitz two other communities already existed under the leadership of Gabriel Ascherham and Philip Plener. Their neglected history will be the subject of the next two chapters.

But before the narrative of the communities established in Moravia can be continued, cognizance must be taken of the host society that offered the religious refugees protection and a niche in its economic culture. The communities cannot be treated as if they constituted autonomous islands unto themselves with little or no relationship to the larger society, although such a treatment has been encouraged by the internalist view that mirrors Anabaptist self-perceptions of separateness. *The Chronicle,* although the single most important historical source for the study of Anabaptist communities in Moravia, represents such an internalist Hutterocentric view. Consequently, it provides little or no information about the larger reality in which the Hutterite experience took shape. In light of centuries of defamation in the mainstream historiography, much can be said for this parochial perspective. And perhaps some experiences, such as the effects of persecution, can only be appreciated through the eyes of the victims.[78] Yet, a purely internalist point of view runs the risk of ignoring important historic factors that shaped the Anabaptist experience, threatening or securing its survival.[79] For this reason something must be said about the conditions that prevailed in the promised land to which the Anabaptists began to flock in increasing numbers from 1528 on.

Conditions in Moravia

Political Ecology

It is a common observation that the promised land for religious dissenters has been, more often than not, a frontier region. Here, for various reasons, they enjoyed opportunities to unfold a life in keeping with their convictions. In the case of Moravia, these opportunities were provided by feudal lordlings who offered the hunted heretics religious tolerance in return for economic benefits. This symbiotic trade-off was made possible by the history that had shaped the political-economic and cultural-religious conditions of Moravia.[80]

The margraviate of Moravia was part of the kingdom of Bohemia and, along with Bohemia, experienced the fifteenth-century turmoil that followed in the wake of John Huss. The outcome of the Hussite wars favored local aristocratic rather than royal central control, particularly in Moravia. The crown and church, to the extent that they represented universal religious or territorial temporal interests, emerged from the fifteenth-century conflict as losers, the magnates and the nobility of Moravia as winners. By 1470 the more powerful magnates "had taken control at the expense of the towns, peasants and king."[81] These magnates dominated regional defense as well as church patronage. Friedmann described the resulting realities in sixteenth-century Moravia as "thoroughly feudal."[82] In some cases Moravia presented an anomaly, perhaps even a feudal anachronism. While political developments in the rest of Europe seemed to be inexorably moving toward greater administrative cohesion and social control under monarchs, princes, or city councils, in Moravia the interests of local magnates prevailed into the seventeenth century against all attempts to increase central authority. Here, the "Spanish" policies of Ferdinand I foundered because of entrenched political and religious opposition.

Ferdinand I had inherited the crown of Bohemia and Hungary only on August 29, 1526. Attempts to enforce his will in matters of religion ran counter to a century of tradition in Moravia and met with the determined resistance of its nobility. Unlike the Bohemian Estates who, because of the peaceful coexistence between Utraquists and Catholics, were satisfied with guarantees of tolerance of the two confessions, the Moravian Estates, among whom there were also members of the Unity of Brethren, insisted that Ferdinand had no right to intervene on their lands in matters of religion.[83] In the resulting tug of war with Ferdinand, the lords of Moravia found unlikely allies in the Turks and in the religious nonconformists who streamed to their Estates from German-speaking territories. The Hussite religious legacy had prepared the lords to look upon religious dissenters as potential allies in the defense of their own liberties. The external Turkish threat, on the other hand, restricted Ferdinand's ability to pressure the magnates into following his policies. As a front-line monarch, Ferdinand considered it his religious duty to defend Christendom against the expansionist Ottoman Turks. But there were other reasons why the Turkish threat took priority. The Turks occupied parts of Ferdinand's inheritance and initially supported John Zapolya I, a rival claimant to the crown of St. Stephen.[84] To defend against the Turks and assert his claims in Hungary, Ferdinand needed the financial and military assistance of the Moravian Estates; to assure their cooperation, he was forced to make concessions as to their traditional rights. Such rights frustrated attempts to enforce religious conformity. Ferdinand's clout remained limited to the four "royal" cities of Moravia: Olmütz (Olomouc), Brünn (Brno), Iglau (Jihlava), and Znaim (Znojmo).[85] But these cities remained relatively weak, vis-à-vis the lords of Moravia. Olmütz was also the seat of the diocese, but attempts by Ferdinand to use the bishop of Olmütz or ecclesiastic channels to strengthen his authority encountered the same obstacles. Other towns, such as Nicolsburg, Eibenschitz, Austerlitz, Auspitz (Hustopece), Rossitz, and Schackowitz, in which Anabaptists initially established their communities, remained entirely subject to local lords.

By way of summary then, the political economy of Moravia was determined by the tug of war between Ferdinand and Moravia's powerful Estates. Religious toleration, for which Moravia became proverbial during the sixteenth century, was tied directly to the fortunes and interests of its feudal lords. These lords were inclined to expand their influence at the expense of both crown and church when the opportunities arose. Such opportunities were provided by the coming of the Reformation and the arrival of religious refugees. Ferdinand's dynastic connections and the Turkish threat, on the other hand, made his alliance with the Catholic Church a foregone conclusion. The young Hapsburg saw himself cast in the role of Christian monarch destined to defend Christendom against infidels without and heretics within. But Ferdinand's success was dependent not only on the good will of the Estates in his various territories, but also on his good fortunes in war on the new front in Hungary and on Hapsburg fortunes in general in the Holy Roman Empire of the German nation.[86]

The Martin Göschl affair illustrates how the Moravian Estates were inclined to take advantage of the coming of the Reformation to further their interests. When the evangelical movement entered Moravia, Göschl, then the provost of the rich convent Heavenly Rose and the coadjutor to the bishop of Olmütz, joined the ranks of would-be reformers. In 1525 he married a former nun and in his position as provost prepared to dissolve the convent and secularize its property. Early in 1526 the property was transferred into the common trust of the Moravian Estates, then presided over by Jan of Pernstein as governor of Moravia. Arkleb of Boskowitz (Boscovice) was appointed bailiff, ostensibly on behalf of the Estates. For his part in the transaction, Göschl received a hefty commission of one thousand gulden.[87] The case of Göschl demonstrates that motives for welcoming the Reformation into Moravia, as elsewhere, were mixed. Whatever Göschl's religious convictions, he appears to have gained a wife and a considerable sum of money by joining the Reform Party. The magnates were willing to support reform and to tolerate heretics for similarly mixed religious and political-economic reasons. Defrocked by the church and threatened by Ferdinand, Göschl found protection in Nicolsburg at about the same time that Balthasar Hubmaier arrived there. The politically astute Hubmaier seems to have gained a quick overview of the situation. He dedicated two of his publications to the supporters of Göschl—that is, to Lords Pernstein and Boskowitz.[88] With this gesture, Hubmaier, no doubt, sought to gain the good will of these powerful patrons for his brand of reform. He thereby also sought to endear Anabaptism to particular political interests in Moravia, a point not lost on Ferdinand and his advisors.

Moravia became the promised land for persecuted Anabaptists because some of its aristocrats could afford to defy Ferdinand. By permitting Anabaptist settlements on their land, the magnates hoped to increase their income. It was hardly accidental that the majority of Anabaptists settled in South Moravia where they may have constituted 10 percent of the population during their "golden years."[89] The Bohemian-Hungarian wars of the second half of the fifteenth century had left this part of Moravia depopulated. Many homesteads and villages had been abandoned.[90] These were made readily available to new settlers by the magnates who, unencumbered by precedent, defined their contractual relationships with the "foreigners" in ways that would profit their manorial economies. Agreements made with leaders, who acted on behalf of a whole group, rather than with individual leaseholders, simplified the procedure of administration and rent collection.[91] It was presumably simpler to collect rents from communities than from individual impoverished peasants who disappeared into the woods when the tax collector arrived. Frugality, honesty, hard work, and new skills made the Anabaptists desirable settlers. The Anabaptists, in turn, found religious freedom, protection, and economic opportunities that bordered on privileges. Most importantly, they were permitted to establish self-administered communities in accordance with their religious beliefs. These, then, were the mutual interests behind lordly patronage and Anabaptist resettlement on Moravian soil.

But political-economic interests were not the sole factors in the symbiotic relationship that developed. A magnanimous spirit of toleration motivated some of the magnates. By sixteenth- and even twentieth-century standards, Moravian lords proved to be an unusually broad-minded and tolerant lot. As noted, the Liechtensteins at Nicolsburg permitted a disputation between two rival Anabaptists, Hans Hut and Balthasar Hubmaier. Later they attempted to mediate the schism between the two parties. Ulrich of Kaunitz, Lord of Austerlitz, tolerated so many foreigners and sects in that town that it became known as a new Babel! In 1537, Johann of Lipa, Lord of Böhmisch Krumau, Eibenschitz, and Schackowitz, offered safety to the heretic Paracelsus. Heinrich of Lomnitz, Lord of Jamnitz (Jemnice), ransomed Anabaptists from the dungeon of Passau. Johanka of Boskowitz, an abbess and "the mistress of Auspitz," permitted the founding of Philipite and Hutterite communities on her lands. Another member of her family, Dobesch of Boskowitz, and his spouse, Bohunda of Pernstein, tolerated the Gabrielite community at Rossitz.[92] But why this religious broad-mindedness among these nobles? As Zeman noted, many of these nobles belonged themselves to the religious disestablishment. They were either neo-Utraquist, adherents of the Unity of Brethren, or pro-Reformed (Zwinglian) in their orientation. Some of them sponsored dialogue between the indigenous heirs of John Huss and the representatives of the new reform currents, including the Anabaptists.[93]

How appreciative were the Anabaptists of their protectors and their new surroundings? Curiously, internal sources such as *The Chronicle* hardly mentioned the patrons, although evidence from the later period suggested that Hutterites grew fond of their protectors.[94] Of the early Anabaptist leaders, Hubmaier certainly appreciated the importance of noble protectors. The dedications of his publications from the Nicolsburg period read like a "Who's Who" of Moravian magnates.[95] As will be noted in Chapter 5, Gabriel Ascherham, leader of the Anabaptist community at Rossitz, appears also to have nurtured positive feelings toward the lower magistrates who protected the Anabaptists. Nevertheless, the fact remains that Anabaptist sources reveal disappointingly little about day-to-day interactions with the landlords or the larger host society. Only when external factors such as the Thirty Years War threatened their existence did they receive attention and then, of course, from a Hutterocentric view with little appreciation of the larger context of the conflict.[96] A major factor determining the larger context of the founding years was the war with the Turks.

The Turkish Threat

It is one of the lesser ironies of history that the advance of the "infidels" and the reality of war repeatedly brought relief from persecution to pacifist Anabaptists in Moravia. In February 1528 at a meeting of the Bohemian Estates, Ferdinand demanded the expulsion of all Anabaptists, claiming that they were secretly plotting insurrection. He repeated the demand before the Moravian Estates with whom he met at Znaim. But the Moravian Estates proved reluctant; they agreed only to expel "seditious preachers" and curb public religious meetings. Nevertheless, this first major persecution took the lives of several Anabaptists mainly in the "royal" cities; three were burned at Brünn, five at Znaim, and four at Olmütz.[97] The most notable victim of this first campaign of suppression, Balthasar Hubmaier, died in Vienna on March 10, 1528.[98]

The lords of Moravia, meanwhile, refused to pass a common law for the expulsion of all Anabaptists and in other ways delayed and obstructed Ferdinand's measures against the heretics. In fact, as the example of the lords of Kaunitz illustrates, they protected not only those persecuted but encouraged new settlements on their Estates. It was during this period that the Brethren established a community at Austerlitz. If Ferdinand, who had taken possession of Moravia only two and a half years earlier, planned to force the magnates into line, his efforts were frustrated by the aggressive advance of the Turks. He was forced to concentrate his attention and resources on the threat of invasion. The Anabaptists in Moravia were thus the indirect beneficiaries of the Turkish threat. Ferdinand's pressure eased in the summer of 1529, which saw the establishment of the Philipites at Auspitz and the Gabrielites at Rossitz.

Only with the decline of the Turkish threat in 1534–35 was Ferdinand able to renew his pressure on the Moravian lords.[99] Horror stories of atrocities in Münster helped to emphasize the alleged sinister designs of all Anabaptists. To press his demands, Ferdinand attended the Diet of Moravia in person, and in a decree of February 18, 1535, again ordered the expulsion of all Anabaptists. But the lords knew their guests too well to be stampeded by the Münster scare. They appealed to their ancient liberties and to the century-old tradition that made religion a "matter of heart," not of decree. They presented persuasive practical and legal arguments against the expulsions. Such measures would lead to depopulation, weaken the tax base, and thereby reduce their future ability to defend the territories against the infidel.[100] Besides, contracts with Anabaptists were legally and morally binding and could not be broken without bad faith on the lords' part. In short, the Moravian lords refused to accept the blanket condemnation of their guests as Münsterites and declined to participate in their persecution.

Nevertheless, under continuing pressure from Ferdinand, the Estates agreed reluctantly to dissolve the most visible communities (*gemeinschaftlichen Häuser*) and to expel those who undermined or threatened lawful authority. It is to their credit, however, that the Moravian lords refused to execute the religious dissenters on their Estates[101] or to expel those who had "settled as subjects on deserted homesteads and accepted the obligations of subjects." Furthermore, they demanded exemption for those in the "immediate service of lords [*unmittelbar im Herrendienst*]" as well as for women in childbirth, children, and the infirm.[102] Once granted, these exemptions were applied liberally to provide alibis for Anabaptists to remain in Moravia. But Ferdinand and his advisors saw through the scheme. The governor of Moravia, John Kuna of Kunstadt, was ordered to submit the names of all lords who refused to comply with the expulsion order. Those named were ordered to appear at Ferdinand's court within eight days. The governor was instructed to pay special attention to Johann of Lipa, Hans of Liechtenstein, Johann of Zierotin from Strassnitz and Lundenburg, Dobesch and Wenzel of Boskowitz, and the abbess of the Queen's cloister at Brünn, landlord of Auspitz.[103] Lords who pleaded binding contracts or humanitarian grounds for the protection of women and children were to submit the names of all adults and the number of children remaining on their Estates. At the same time, Ferdinand warned his vassals and administrators in other territories not to accept any of the expellees from Moravia.[104]

The lords of Moravia did their best to defuse, delay, obstruct, or ignore the king's latest orders. Diversionary tactics included public relations exercises—token official expulsions with fanfare to appease Ferdinand. All to no avail. Ferdinand's pressure continued. Reluctantly, the lords complied and ordered the most visible Anabaptist presence, the communities in Austerlitz, Auspitz, and Rossitz, to be dismantled. At Schackowitz, the site chosen by Jacob Hutter for the establishment of his new community and for the construction of a large housing project, the local lord advised a temporary suspension of the project and the dispersion of the community into smaller groups until Ferdinand's attention would be occupied elsewhere. But despite the good will of several lords, this second wave of suppression from 1535 to 1537 brought incredible hardships and dealt a devastating blow to the fledgling Anabaptist communities in Moravia. In effect, the expulsions of 1535 initiated the demise of the Austerlitz Brethren, the Philipites, and the Gabrielites (see Chapter 8). The Hutterite community was also sorely tested. It lost its founder and leader Jacob Hutter, its first schoolmaster, and a number of other leaders (see Chapters 10, 11, and 12); nevertheless, it survived. The expulsions from Moravia were never complete, and certainly not to Ferdinand's satisfaction, as may be seen from the almost annual repetition of his orders and threats.[105] The followers of Hutter survived in Moravia even though they had been dispersed. For them the years 1535–37 had proven cathartic, eliminating the half-hearted and molding the survivors into a closely knit fellowship under the leadership of Hans Amon.

During the years of respite, 1537–45, numerous Hutterite communities sprang into existence. Then, in 1545, buoyed by victory over the Turks, a more powerful Ferdinand resumed the policy of repression and expulsion. The Moravian Estates once again went through the ritual of defending the beneficial presence of their guests; but with their own liberties and independence threatened, the noble patrons counseled the Anabaptists to divide once more into smaller cells of five to seven and to settle on the Estates as "subjects." Although a number appear to have chosen this option as the lesser evil, a core of Hutterites did not. Since they considered community of goods essential to a true Christian life, they refused to give it up. They also rejected as unacceptable the status of subjects. To refute accusations made against them, they drafted a lengthy apology to the Estates and published Peter Riedemann's "Account of our Faith."[106] But Ferdinand persisted. At the Moravian Diet in March 1546 he demanded once more the expulsion of all Anabaptists. July 25, 1546, was set as a deadline; but Anabaptists remained, and the deadline had to be extended to April 23, 1547. At this point a number of factors strengthened Ferdinand's hand. In that year he crushed a rebellion in Bohemia, and his brother, Emperor Charles V, gained the upper hand against the Protestants in the Empire. Ferdinand was in no mood for compromise, and the Moravian lords knew when to yield. These proved the most difficult of times for the Anabaptists, especially the Hutterites. Left without lordly protection, they were forced to abandon their communities and were driven from place to place, open to every insult, vexation, and exploitation. As outcasts on the fringes of society they were forced to survive in caves—sixteenth-century catacombs—on the borders between Slovakia and Hungary. Some found new opportunities in Hungary. The rest drifted back to the Estates of Anabaptist-friendly lords in Moravia as soon as conditions improved. New expulsion deadlines in 1550 and 1551 demonstrate their continued or renewed presence.[107]

Finally in the 1550s, the power constellation changed once more in favor of the lords. Ferdinand was forced to expend much of his energies on a renewed Turkish threat. His continuing missives against the Anabaptists were routinely ignored. The Hutterites had escaped near extinction; their comeback was nothing short of miraculous. Who in 1547 would have believed that the tattered little band living in caves would two decades later enter the golden years of their early history? Without question, much credit must go to their own unbreakable spirit that enabled them to begin again and again, circumstances permitting. These circumstances depended on the fortunes of Moravia's noble patrons. Indeed, with hindsight, it is possible to see that the origin, survival, and prosperity of the Anabaptist communities in Moravia coincided with the Indian summer of late feudal polity in Moravia.[108] Anabaptist fortunes vacillated inversely with the Turkish threat and in accordance with the tug of war between local noble interests and the strength of central authority. During the second half of the sixteenth century, Moravia's magnates maintained the upper hand, permitting the Anabaptist-Hutterite communities to flourish, rising perhaps to as many as twenty thousand members, including children.[109] When the armies of Ferdinand II crushed the nobility at the battle of the White Mountain in 1620, the Anabaptist-Hutterite communities lost their protection. Without it they faced the choice of dismemberment and assimilation or exodus in search of another promised land. The Anabaptist presence in Moravia had come to an end.

Relations with the Indigenous Population

Finally, a caveat seems in order on Anabaptist relations with the native Slavic population. Sixteenth-century Moravia, to which Anabaptists fled for refuge, had not been an empty land. It contained an indigenous population as well as other foreigners. Unfortunately, very little is known about Anabaptist interaction with their neighbors. Only the attempts at religious dialogue with Czech Brethren received attention, but these were of a different, more official, nature than day-to-day interactions of interest here. It seems that initially at least, the hunted heretics were greeted with sympathy. When the first Brethren arrived in Austerlitz, they were welcomed not only by the lords but also by the townspeople.[110] They quickly developed good relations with some of the lords. But good relations with powerful magnates were of a different order than good relations with commoners. Can it be assumed that the interests of Moravia's elite coincided with those of their indigenous subjects when they settled religious refugees on their lands? Evidence suggests that the local commoners eventually came to perceive the newcomers as rivals for their daily bread. Both internal and external sources recorded the existence of hostility between the local population and the Anabaptist communities from the 1530s on. From time to time the lords had to protect the newcomers against angry indigenous commoners. *The Chronicle* relates that when Jacob Hutter and his people were forced to leave Schackowitz in 1535, they marched through a "crowd of ungodly, villainous robbers, who ground their teeth in rage, full of lust to rob and attack." Armed protection, provided by the lords, prevented the evil designs of the crowd, a circumstance recorded as "in accordance with God's will."[111] During the notorious raid on the Hutterite community of Steinabrunn in 1539, a reckless local mob aided Ferdinand's henchmen in rounding up the Anabaptists. In this case the local lord, having to contend with Ferdinand's armed men, was powerless to help the Anabaptists. In another incident riots erupted among the local population when the Hutterites procrastinated on an order to leave their settlement at Kostel. The Hutterites also needed the protection of the local lord at Pulgram when they closed shop there.[112]

Internal sources provided no explanation for these manifestations of hostility, other than ascribing them to "godless villains and robbers." An external source, the testimony of Czech Brethren, although from a later period, proved far more lucid about possible reasons for friction between the Anabaptist communities and the local population.[113] Apparently the hostility was not due to purely religious or ethnic factors. Economic complaints seemed to top the list. The effects of the Anabaptist communities on the local economy, rightly or wrongly, were perceived to be negative. Indigenous artisans suffered while the Anabaptist-Hutterite communities prospered, especially during the second half of the sixteenth century. It seems that the production of ovens, knives, carriages, and ornamental roofs was taken out of the hands of local artisans, who found themselves unable to compete with the more advanced technology, greater resourcefulness, and collective resources of the Anabaptist-Hutterite communities that manufactured outside the local guild structure.[114] Bulk purchases of grain and raw materials by the communities raised prices and meant that local artisans had to compete on an unlevel playing field. In some instances, leasing of large tracts of land and whole vineyards may have led to the removal of small leaseholders or squatters from these properties. Complaints were lodged that Anabaptist-Hutterites used the common forests to their advantage. Given these complaints, manifestations of animosity toward the Anabaptist communities become explicable. It comes also as no surprise that the Hutterite missionary outreach to indigenous neighbors appears to have been nonexistent or ineffectual.[115]

The vagaries and fluctuations of Anabaptist fortunes in the promised land are best understood against the larger canvas of the political realities that prevailed in the host society. Whether the Anabaptists were conscious of it or not, their fragile fortunes clearly were linked to those of their patrons, the nobility of Moravia. Any history of Anabaptist communities in Moravia must take cognizance of this historic fact. For good or ill, the Anabaptist communities became part of the Moravian political-economic landscape. The symbiotic, mutually beneficial relationship established between noble patrons and Anabaptists did not necessarily prove beneficial for native neighbors. Economic rivalries and jealousies appear to have been inevitable.

A chronological overview of Anabaptist fortunes in Moravia reveals a striking pattern: Turkish aggression and war invariably relaxed Ferdinand's pressure on Moravia's nobility and indirectly on the Anabaptists. Conversely, whenever the Turkish threat receded, Ferdinand renewed his demands for suppression and expulsion. As a result three distinct periods of persecution may be discerned: (1) 1527–29; (2) 1535–37; and (3) 1547–51. "Good times" began only in the 1550s and the golden years only after Ferdinand's death in 1564. Survival proved untenable when Ferdinand II crushed the nobility in the 1620s.

The first part of this chapter served as an introduction to the founding of the Anabaptist community at Austerlitz. This community, led by Jacob Wiedemann, had its origin in a schism at Nicolsburg, the roots of which can be traced to the conflict between Hans Hut and Balthasar Hubmaier. The enigmatic Hut was, without doubt, one of the most influential early Anabaptist propagators, whose influence reached from Franconia through Bavaria, Upper Austria, and North Tyrol, all the way to Moravia. Elementary congregational structures introduced by him incorporated concerns of mutual aid and even voluntary common goods. A Swiss influence appears to have been present in the refugee community led by Wiedemann in Nicolsburg and later in Austerlitz. Such an influence explains why Hutterite chroniclers subsequently placed Hut in the staff-bearing tradition. His name is honored rightly in conjunction with events that led to the exodus from Nicolsburg and the formation of the first known congregation to practice community of goods in Moravia, the Austerlitz Brethren. These Brethren, as will be shown in subsequent chapters, exercised a strong influence and provided a model community to other Anabaptist groups including the Philipites, Gabrielites, and Hutterites.

Chapter Four

The Philipites

Fugitives from Swabia, the Palatinate, and the Rhineland

That the Philipites and Gabrielites have received relatively little attention is hardly surprising since they disappeared as distinct groups, and information about them is scarce. The Philipite story had to be painstakingly reconstructed from shattered shards, as it were, which made this chapter a particularly difficult assignment.[1] Some of those shards have gone through Hutterite hands—hands belonging to a rival group not interested in preserving the narrative of the Philipites and their leader, Philip Plener.[2] But Philip and his people were an important part of early community building in Moravia, and they bequeathed a lasting legacy.

Named after Philip Plener, the Philipites[3] constituted an identifiable community in Moravia from 1529 until their expulsion in 1535. Thereafter scattered pockets of Philipites continued to exist in Upper Austria, Swabia, the Palatinate, and the Rhineland. Within a decade of the expulsion, those who returned to German territories appear to have assimilated into the Swiss Brethren,[4] a label that originated in Moravia and came into use in the 1540s (see Chapter 12). The first Swiss Brethren songbook, a forerunner of the *Ausbund*, contained a number of songs written by Philipites.[5] This in itself gives the Philipites historic significance even though, apart from the songs, little of substance appears to have survived from their pen.

Swabia, the Palatinate, and the Rhineland

Claus-Peter Clasen was able to identify seven towns and villages in the Upper Rhine Valley, the Palatinate, and Speyer areas from which members joined Philip Plener's community in Auspitz, Moravia.[6] Philip himself, also known as Weber (weaver), Plaermel or Blauärmel (blue sleeve), because he wore blue sleeves that identified him as belonging to the weaver or dyers trade,[7] hailed from Blienschwiller, not far from Strasbourg.[8] Converts in Augsburg described him as a Rhinelander, whose accent they found difficult to understand, and they placed his origin near Strasbourg.[9] Philip appears to have known the Strasbourg area well. He returned there from Augsburg in 1528–29, and 1536, after years of absence, he planned a rendezvous with other leaders of his group at the Inn to the Plow (*Wirtshaus zum Pflug*) in the gardeners' quarters.[10] Court records agree that Philip was rather tall, slim, bearded, and of pale complexion. They disagree on the color of his beard: in Augsburg it was said to be black, in Strasbourg "red, but not exactly red." The same sources described him as wearing red pants, a gray riding coat with a blue sleeve, and a black beret or hat.[11]

Unfortunately, nothing is known about Philip's pre-Anabaptist biography. His preference for accommodation in Strasbourg's gardeners' quarters could suggest social and perhaps radical religious acquaintances in this group, which had played a prominent role in the coming of the Reformation to Strasbourg. Philip's part in these events was not recorded; neither was his conversion to Anabaptism. Circumstantial evidence suggests that he joined Anabaptism in the Strasbourg area as early as 1526 or 1527. If he is Philip Jäger, who joined Jacob Wiedemann on the trek from Nicolsburg to Austerlitz in the spring of 1528, then he must have made his way to Moravia as early as 1527–28.[12] As to what form of Anabaptism Philip embraced in Strasbourg, Klaus Deppermann believed that two distinct orientations existed there from 1526–27 on.[13] Hans Denck, Jacob Kautz, and Ludwig Hätzer represented a spiritualist orientation; Wilhelm Reublin and Michael Sattler, the Swiss. But evidence for tensions between the two groups comes primarily from Hätzer's dislike of Sattler, whom he considered "a deceitful evil misanthrope [*einen listingen bösen lauren*]."[14] It has been assumed that Sattler returned the compliment by registering Denck and Hätzer in the Schleitheim Articles as "the false brethren."[15] But uncertainty remains as to the identity of the false brethren, and members of different orientations proved capable of cooperation. Reublin and Kautz, for instance, submitted a common confession while they were fellow prisoners in Strasbourg.

Nevertheless, differences did exist.[16] Kautz maintained that the true church was to be "bound to no place, time or person" and "without human addition." It was to be gathered by "shepherds who had a heavenly, not an earthly, calling and were not tied to a place, person or elements"[17] but were willing to "go into all the world to gather the scattered sheep among Jews and Gentiles." Such shepherds were to awaken true faith in the hearts of listeners by preaching the Gospel. True faith had to precede outer baptism. Only in this way could the true church be gathered.

It has been assumed that in contrast to Kautz, Reublin, a founding member of Swiss Anabaptism and possible coauthor of the Schleitheim Articles, represented a less spiritualist form of Anabaptism.[18] True, Reublin appears to have advocated a congregational polity in keeping with the *Swiss Order,* but if this kind of congregational life was incompatible with Kautz's notion of charismatic leadership, Kautz and Reublin seemed unaware of it. In their collaborative statement to the Strasbourg reformers, they described the minimal program for the true church as requiring admonition, the breaking of bread, and the use of the ban. Entrance into this church was through believers' baptism. Where these ingredients were missing, there could be no true church. Instead, "Christ was turned into a liar, the apostles into deceivers, the Scriptures falsified and Christ's Commission torn up."[19] Reublin and Kautz believed the latter to be the case in Strasbourg. Yet, even though fellow prisoners Reublin and Kautz presented a united front in 1528–29, their supporters subsequently formed distinct conventicles.[20] Those influenced by Kautz developed congenial relations with followers of Melchior Hoffman, whereas Reublin's followers remained separate. Hans Frisch, a member of Reublin's party, testified in 1534 that "he and his group were of Reublin's opinion. Other than that, their sect was divided in three divisions, namely those of Hoffman's, Kautz's, and Reublin's persuasion."[21]

The collaboration of Kautz and Reublin on a common confession should caution against an all too modern penchant for separating spiritualists from biblicists on the basis of finely honed typologies. Differences were no doubt latent but perhaps not yet as pronounced as they would become during the early 1530s in the debate between Marpeck and the spiritualists. Moreover, during the formative stages, groupings appear to have formed around leaders as much as around theological differences[22]— a situation that makes definitive identification of Philip's early contacts in Strasbourg impossible. All that can be said is that Philip had become part of a heterogeneous movement that reached from Switzerland to Strasbourg, to Worms, and to Alzey and via Esslingen to Augsburg. That Philip boarded with the widow of the martyred Augsburg leader Hans Leupold in 1528 documents his contacts with that community, whereas his choice of the Inn to the Plow, which had served as a meeting place for Anabaptist refugees from Augsburg and Esslingen, could suggest contacts with Reublin's group in the latter city.[23]

Augsburg, more so than Esslingen, represented a kind of melting pot for Anabaptism. Here the apocalyptic message of Hans Hut coexisted in some minds with the Swiss orientation of Jacob Gross and the humanist spiritualism of Denck and Hätzer, who, along with a host of lesser known leaders, gathered in Augsburg for the Martyrs' Synod in the fall of 1527. Perhaps the very heterogeneity of Augsburg's Anabaptism explains its phenomenal growth. The authorities decided to crush the sect. Hut, who died under suspicious circumstances in prison before the year's end, was one of their first victims. Citizens were fined and forced to recant or be expelled along with noncitizens. By the late spring of 1528 more than one hundred refugees from Augsburg had moved to Strasbourg.[24] Eighty-eight persons were arrested in Augsburg on Easter Sunday, April 12, 1528. Hans Leupold was executed two weeks later on April 25.[25]

In late 1527 Leupold traveled with Christoph Freisleben to Esslingen. Reublin introduced Anabaptism to this city and its environs in the spring of 1527.[26] Lienhard Lutz, the first *Vorsteher* of the Esslingen congregation, testified that after Reublin's initial mission "they had stood still" and examined the Scriptures. It seems that the Scriptures examined dealt with the relationship of faith and baptism, as outlined in the concordance attributed to Hans Krüsi.[27] Later in 1528, under the acknowledged influence of Reublin, Freisleben published a treatise on baptism, which repeated arguments already made by Grebel and supported by the scriptural selection found in Krüsi's booklet.[28] Without question, Leupold and Freisleben had made contact with Reublin and through him with Swiss Anabaptist teachings and practices that clearly shaped the Esslingen congregation despite the penetration of a Hutian influence from Augsburg.[29] This seems borne out by the organizational structures that developed in Esslingen during 1528 and corresponded to the structure indicated in the Schleitheim Articles. Reublin was considered the bishop. A local *Vorsteher* (in the first instance, Lienhard Lutz) had the task of reading and expounding the Scriptures. He was also empowered to enforce brotherly discipline, which involved admonition and the ban. Poor members were supported through a common purse with the aid of a *Säckelmeister*.[30]

The Esslingen congregation had its problems. At times total strangers had to be called on to do the readings in the absence of the local literates. But unguided readings could have undesired results. Therefore, in 1528, Reublin, who continued to exercise considerable authority, forbade exiles in Reutlingen the reading of the Scripture without the proper guidance. He also found it necessary to ban *Vorsteher* Lutz. Differences had arisen as to whether Reublin's sister should be permitted to have her newborn infant baptized. Apparently the moderate Lutz held sincerely that in matters of faith nothing should be coerced, not even *Nicht-Taufe,* the rejection of pedobaptism. This would have led to a mixed practice of child and adult baptisms, something Reublin refused to accept.[31] Despite these difficulties, Anabaptism grew rapidly in Esslingen, alarming the authorities. In early 1528 suppression set in. Reublin moved to Ulm, and Freisleben and Leupold, to Worms.[32]

Leupold baptized sixteen persons near Worms.[33] Worms had been home to Denck, Hätzer, and Kautz; and Kautz is known to have baptized about twenty persons in Alzey, northwest of Worms. Future members of Philip's community in Moravia would come from the Neckar and Rhine areas, and some Philipites resettled near Worms after the 1535 expulsion. In total, an estimated twelve hundred Anabaptists from these regions moved to Moravia.[34] Many fled as the result of the first major persecution in 1528–29. Circumstantial evidence, then, suggests that Philip had contacts within the Worms group and that his and Leupold's paths may have crossed in 1527–28. At least this would explain Philip's stay with Leupold's widow later in 1528.

Philip himself may have been driven from his home territory by persecution. The suppression of the Anabaptists in the Palatinate escalated on March 3, 1528, when Elector Ludwig V set a bounty on the heretics. Among the charges against them was that they intended to destroy all authority. Fourteen Anabaptists were executed at Alzey: the men beheaded, the women drowned, a woman who had the audacity to comfort the victims was burned, and those who had provided shelter fined.[35] The vicious executions aroused the sympathies of outsiders, among them reformers Johann Odenbach of Obermoschel and Jacob Otter of Neckarsteinach. Both published pleas for leniency, but these fell on deaf ears. Before this first wave of executions subsided, 350 persons in the territories of Ludwig V had lost their lives.[36] Detailed accounts of these horrible events traveled to Moravia with those who fled, and Hutterite chroniclers commemorated the martyrs of Alzey.[37]

Philip was, without question, affected by the turmoil of early 1528 which saw some Anabaptists flee east, others west. While many Anabaptists from Augsburg moved to Strasbourg, Philip moved east. If he is to be identified with Philip Jäger, who participated in the exodus from Nicolsburg in the spring of 1528, then he must have gone as far as Austerlitz. In late June or early July 1528 he took up quarters with Leupold's widow in Augsburg,[38] marking the first time that Philip's name appeared in the documents. He was already exercising leadership authority. During the next two months he taught and baptized in the Augsburg area and was joined in this task by Hans Greuel of Geltersdorf, a former schoolmaster, and Jörg Schachner of Munich.[39] The climate of fear, created by the council's actions against the Anabaptists earlier that year, made it difficult for Philip to support himself. Because of arrests and expulsions, attendance at Anabaptist meetings dwindled to twenty or so, with most of these participants transient laborers or coming from the fringes of society. Neither size nor need of the congregation warranted the presence of three leaders. On August 30, 1528, the group decided to suspend further meetings, with the leaders explaining that "according to the prophets, the time to teach was past."[40] In other words, a kind of *Stillstand* was initiated as Philip and the other leaders took their leave. Philip's subsequent actions indicate that he considered the *Stillstand* to be regionally limited.

Philip's departure was timely. Shortly after the final meeting, a number of the participants were arrested. They told the authorities that Philip was on his way to the Strasbourg area where the Anabaptists numbered close to five hundred.[41] Evidence indicates that Philip traveled via Ulm and the Neckar Valley. A sparse paper trail of official documents placed him at Fürfeld near Bad Wimpfen and in the hamlets of Nussloch and Leinen near Heidelberg, where the Neckar Valley opens into the Rhineland.[42] On May 1, 1529, Anabaptists from Nussloch testified that they had been baptized by Philip and that no other leader had visited them since. This was the second arrest for these converts who had recanted but now relapsed. The time between Philip's visit and the first and second arrests could mean that Philip's visit occurred as early as the fall of 1528. When questioned about Philip's travels and whereabouts, the converts knew only that he had been at Fürfeld and there found the local lords of Gemmingen sympathetic. When asked where the large majority of their brethren resided, none seemed to know. One hazarded the guess that it was near Ulm.[43] He had heard that many had been executed.[44]

The statements of these converts reveal that Philip must have spent some time in the Heidelberg area. News of his activity had reached Jacob Otter, the evangelical preacher of Neckarsteinach, upstream from Heidelberg.[45] Otter was not unsympathetic to the plight of the Anabaptists and pleaded leniency for the prisoners at Alzey.[46] In his 1528 publication he described them as sincere, morally earnest, avoiding idle talk, stressing modesty in dress, and shunning certain occupations.[47] Otter criticized the bloodthirsty tyrants who, without "examination of the Scriptures, without spirit and conscience, drive them away, imprison them, torture them, strangle, and kill them with great fury." He testified that there were "many pious, honest people among them, who had come into the matter out of divine zeal, desiring [only] to walk uprightly and live a Christian life."[48] He argued that attempts to show them in error should proceed through persuasion in friendly tolerance and without prejudice. At the same time, Otter found it necessary to warn his parishioners against secretive corner preachers who spread distrust against evangelical reformers like himself, thereby creating divisions. He criticized Anabaptists for their low view of the Old Testament and for refusing the oath. He maintained that by withdrawing their support from all government they also weakened good government and set themselves above divinely ordained temporal authority by determining the "rules and limits in what matters and to what extent they should obey."[49]

When Otter learned of Philip's presence in his bailiwick, confrontation and mutual recriminations began. According to the surviving account, Philip told Otter that he considered him a "wolf" who was threatening his sheep. Otter appears to have replied in kind.[50] Unfortunately, nothing further is known about this face-to-face exchange, although presumably it hastened Philip's departure from the Heidelberg area. He left behind a small nucleus of converts who had accepted baptism as a "sign of the covenant" (*Bundzeichen*), which committed them to a holy life. As one convert expressed it, by receiving baptism he had covenanted to desist from sinning; prior to baptism he had found it impossible to live uprightly. Baptism was, therefore, a matter for adults only. Furthermore, Philip had admonished his converts to shun pubs, gambling, and blasphemy and told them that attendance at mass meant participation in idolatry. True service to God consisted of helping brethren and neighbors in need. The converts claimed that Philip had taught obedience to secular authority in all things except in matters that went against the Word of God. He admonished his converts to remain steadfast under persecution. As one testified, "Philip Weber . . . had commanded him, in case of imprisonment, not to fall away from his second baptism, but to accept death if needs be. For if he fell away and accepted again the first [child] baptism, he would be eternally lost and of the devil."[51]

Although sparse, the above statements illustrate the practical, moral bent of Philip's teachings as understood by common laymen. They reveal the contours of a minimal Anabaptist program which, besides rejecting the established religious order, called for a moral reformation of ordinary lives in everyday situations. With baptism came a pledge to desist from common social sins such as drunkenness and debauchery and with it a separation from the larger society. And even though this minimal program remains too vague for a classification of Philip's specific Anabaptist orientation, it, along with other circumstantial evidence, point to a Swiss influence.

After leaving the Heidelberg area, Philip must have continued in the direction of Strasbourg. Nothing is known about his visit there or whether he made a detour to Worms and Alzey, from which converts would later join his community. If he did make his way to Strasbourg, his visit would have coincided with Marpeck's arrival. But the climate grew increasingly hostile. Plans to organize relief efforts for Anabaptist refugees by means of a common purse met with the council's disapproval.[52] On October 22,

1528, Marpeck, Reublin, and Kautz, the other leaders in the area, were arrested. Whereas Marpeck's social standing, wealth, and professional skills secured him city employ and a favorable hearing, Reublin and Kautz remained in prison for months and were then expelled.[53] Marpeck remained and would emerge as the key Anabaptist spokesperson in a controversy with the spiritualists, who arrived from Moravia and Silesia in the persons of Hans Bünderlin, Christian Entfelder, and Caspar Schwenckfeld (see Chapter 6).

Philip was long gone when the first Marpeck-spiritualist debate unfolded. It appears that he moved to Bruchsal on the east side of the Rhine, where he may have won his future assistant, Blasius (Plass) Kuhn (Kumauff) for Anabaptism.[54] Unfortunately, documents about Anabaptism in Bruchsal have not survived. Claims that its congregation numbered as many as five hundred may have been exaggerated,[55] but Anabaptists did reside in Bruchsal by early 1529. The city was subject to the Cathedral Chapter of Speyer. The Edict of Speyer, April 23, 1529, which decreed capital punishment for Anabaptists in the Empire, was strictly and immediately enforced in the chapter's territory. On June 19, 1529, the bailiff (*Stiftsherr*) received instructions to interrogate Anabaptist prisoners. Neither names nor numbers have been preserved,[56] but a list of martyrs taken in April 1531 from Julius Lober, a former leader of the Bruchsal congregation, registered five persons as beheaded in Bruchsal.[57] Sources for Bruchsal's environs indicate that prosecutions continued into 1531. Not surprisingly, Anabaptists fled in considerable numbers to Moravia, where they joined the community founded by Philip in Auspitz.[58]

A connection between the Bruchsal congregation and Philip's community in Auspitz was documented by Julius Lober's statement given upon his arrest on April 8, 1531 in Ansbach near Nuremberg.[59]

A former priest-preacher in the Klettgau, who took up the tailor's trade after the Peasants' War, Lober was baptized by Reublin near Strasbourg in 1529–30[60] and subsequently functioned as leader of the Bruchsal congregation. He described his office as that of an itinerant apostle who had no specific residence. In 1530–31 Lober served as courier between the Bruchsal congregation and Moravia.[61] Although the statements about his travels are somewhat confusing, it is clear that he visited the Gabrielites at Rossitz and the Philipites and proto-Hutterites at Auspitz.[62] On his return, Lober carried Reublin's letter to Marpeck, written in January 1531. The letter is a significant source of information about the schism of early 1531 at Austerlitz. It was taken from Lober at the time of his arrest, April 1531. At that time Lober estimated the number of brethren in Moravia at two thousand but denied having baptized anyone himself, a claim that rightly met with some skepticism in Nuremberg where the Ansbach authorities sought advice on the prisoners.[63]

Lober's statements are of special interest here because they provide some glimpses into the Anabaptist organization of which he and presumably Philip were a part. Lober spoke of shepherds, teachers, preachers, and elders, but there was to be "no respecting" of persons. Community of goods was voluntary in his circle, instituted out of fraternal love to help members in need.[64] Lober held further that children should not be baptized because they remained innocent until they committed conscious sins. Christ was only spiritually present in the Lord's Supper; one could not eat his flesh and blood. In accordance with Romans 13, Christians should be obedient to temporal authority, pay levies, taxes, interest, and rents (*tribut, zins, gult*), but, according to Matthew 5, the swearing of oaths was forbidden. These statements reinforce the observation already made about Philip's minimal program that it was decidedly Swiss in orientation. That Lober had been baptized by Reublin obviously supports such a supposition. But the point is that members of the Bruchsal congregation, led by Lober, ended up in Philip's community at Auspitz. This surely permits the inference that Philip's teachings and practices in his community were not all that different.

Lober and his fellow prisoners in Ansbach were released and driven from the territory after several months of incarceration. In January 1532 Lober was rearrested in Windesheim. Since his release in Ansbach he had baptized at least five persons, including the ill-fated Claus Frey, later executed in Strasbourg for bigamy.[65] Lober was beaten with rods and driven out of Windesheim January 26, 1532.[66] His subsequent fate is unknown. According to statements by members of the Bruchsal congregation, he became unfaithful.[67] Remnants of the Bruchsal congregation, led by Blasius Kuhn, had joined Philip's community at Auspitz in 1531.

Before he settled in Auspitz, Philip's own ministry appears to have been that of an itinerant apostle, perhaps in the service of the Brethren at Austerlitz. Besides Augsburg he is known to have visited Fürfeld, Leinen, Nussloch, Strasbourg, and probably Bruchsal, Esslingen, and Ulm (see Map 2). From his Augsburg contacts, it may be inferred that he knew of Anabaptists in the Worms area and was probably informed of martyrs in Alzey-Worms. The territories thus circumscribed—Swabia, the Palatinate, and the Rhineland—would become the recruiting grounds for his community in Moravia. Philip most likely crossed paths with Leupold, Reublin, Kautz, and Marpeck. And although the evidence is too fragmentary

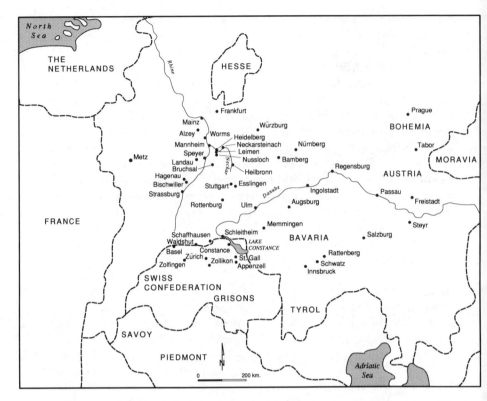

Map 2. South Central Europe

to classify his teachings, it seems safe to characterize them as more or less
Swiss. Accordingly, Philip taught that (1) traditional religious worship
amounted to idolatry; (2) Christ's presence in the Lord's Supper was not
bodily; (3) true Christians engaged in mutual aid; (4) true piety excluded
debauchery, drunkenness, and foul language; (5) baptism was for adults
and constituted a covenantal sign involving a commitment to live uprightly; (6) true discipleship involved separation from the world. Furthermore, if inferences may be permitted from beliefs and practices in the
Bruchsal congregation, then Philip and his group also rejected the oath
and accepted a leadership pattern that included teachers, elders, and traveling apostles. All of this seems congruent with the known facts of the
Austerlitz Brethren and of Swiss Anabaptism.[68] Or to put it in another
way, no evidence exists to suggest that Philip advocated a unique or different form of Anabaptism generically at variance with Swiss Anabaptism
spreading in these territories.

Philipites in Moravia: 1529–1535
Establishing Community

Philip and his Swabian band arrived in Moravia during 1529[69] and initially joined the Gabrielites at Rossitz. Considering Philip better qualified, Gabriel Ascherham entrusted Philip with the leadership of the joint communities. But differences soon led to an amiable parting of ways. Because accommodations at Rossitz were inadequate, Philip and his followers took up separate quarters at Auspitz.[70] *The Chronicle* recorded these events under the year 1528, although they must have taken place in 1529.

At that time several servants and their congregations settled in Moravia: in Znaim, Eibenschitz, Brünn and elsewhere.

A certain Gabriel Ascherham came . . . to Rossitz where he gathered the people and taught them.

Soon after this, Philip Blauärmel came to him from Swabia with several others. Gabriel took them into his community and laid down his service so as to give honor and precedence to Philip and his assistant. But soon Philip's actions no longer pleased Gabriel, so Gabriel assumed the leadership over his own people again and they continued living where they were. Philip moved away with his people and started another community. They still claimed to be brothers, but their hearts were disunited, and as a result two groups emerged, the Philipites and the Gabrielites.[71]

Written while Hutterites were still smarting from charges by Gabrielites and Philipites that they had broken unity, the account may have exaggerated differences between Gabrielites and Philipites. The events of the schism of 1533 (see Chapter 9) certainly demonstrate that Philip and Gabriel were still cooperating with each other and that their respective communities continued in fellowship until the 1535 expulsion from Moravia forced them to separate. Whether this means that in their teaching and organization the two communities were the same is not clear.[72] What is certain is that both communities experienced considerable growth over the next five years. The Philipites received a steady influx of refugees from Swabia, the Palatinate, the Rhineland, and elsewhere, increasing the size of the Auspitz community to about four hundred adults. Although ordinary members remain largely anonymous and faceless (see Appendix B), the names of some of the leading personalities appear in the sources. Besides Philip, these were Blasius Kuhn from Bruchsal, who became an associate servant of the Word (*Vorsteher*) alongside Philip; Burkhart Braun (Bämerle) of Ofen (Budapest); David the Bohemian from Schweidnitz in Silesia; and Adam Schlegel from Nuremberg. The last three had been itinerant apostles and members of the Austerlitz community before joining Reublin and Jörg Zaunring in the exodus to Auspitz. Because of continued tensions and quarrels in the proto-Hutterite community (see Chapter 9), all three appear to have moved into the Philipite congregation.

Schlegel's background illustrates what colorful characters were drawn into this experiment at apostolic community. A tailor from Nuremberg, Schlegel had been baptized in 1528 by the "son of a councilor" (*Ratsherr*), who had come to the metropolis from Moravia.[73] The mysterious son of the councilor must have been associated with the Brethren at Austerlitz because that was Schlegel's destination after his expulsion from Nuremberg.[74] Schlegel's associates in Nuremberg included, among others, the locksmith Beringer and Sixt Prunsterer, whose connections reached back to Hut's circle.[75] Schlegel was arrested along with others on January 22, 1529. Considered incorrigible, he was the only prisoner flogged and driven from the city. He subsequently moved to Austerlitz and led a number of other refugees to this community. As noted, in early 1531 Schlegel followed Reublin and Jörg Zaunring with other secessionists to Auspitz; and like Reublin, Schlegel was soon disgraced. According to Hutterite sources, Schlegel misled members of the community into "fleshly freedom." Presumably this meant that his views on community of goods were not as firm or strict as those of Zaunring, who had assumed leadership after Reublin's disgrace. Expelled by Zaunring, Schlegel joined the Philipites and became one of their itinerant missionaries, and in this capacity, he gathered converts from as far as Donauwörth and led them to Auspitz as late as 1534.[76]

The year 1534 appears to have been one of considerable growth for the Philipites and other communities in Moravia. Numerous Anabaptist families moved in small groups of ten to twenty from Swabia and other territories to Moravia, where they were allegedly already five thousand strong. Contemporary accounts provided vivid descriptions of the emigrants who rested in out-of-the-way places to escape attention. They considered the established churches to be temples of idols; they refused the oath, refused to defend themselves, rejected the real presence, oral confession, and the worship of saints, and they would not greet strangers. According to one report, they "greeted no one wherever they went, saying neither good morning nor good evening, as was otherwise customary."[77] And although it cannot be proven that all of these emigrants sought the Philipite community in Auspitz, Philipite recruiting grounds definitely included the Neckar Valley, Swabia, the Palatinate, and the Rhineland.

By the end of 1534, the Philipites at Auspitz had grown to the point where it became necessary to live in three separate households, led by Philip, Kuhn, and Schlegel. For reasons of employment, some Philipites lived in other locations as well.[78] Philip remained the spiritual leader with Kuhn as associate and Schlegel as assistant. The Philipites maintained fellowship with the Gabrielites and recognized Gabriel Ascherham as the senior bishop. All in all, evidence suggests that one year before their expulsion from Moravia, the Philipites were a dynamic, growing community, still drawing recruits from as far away as the Rhineland and Swabia. Yet within a few years of their expulsion the Philipites disappeared from the sources (Chapter 12)—but not without a trace. They left a legacy of song, to which we now turn.

The Philipite Legacy of Song

The First Swiss Brethren Songbook of 1564

Hutterite chroniclers reported that in 1535, "driven out of Auspitz into the fields, the Philipites reached the hill near Lassling, singing joyfully."[79] Four years later, a group, almost certainly former Philipites, was driven from Heilbronn. As they crossed the bridge, they reportedly sang "Psalms and songs of praise"[80] (Figure 1). Such penchant for song could support Friedmann's claim that Anabaptist hymnology was the "exclusive product of the Philipite genius."[81] The groundwork for Friedmann's claim came from Rudolf Wolkan's study of songs attributed to Anabaptist prisoners at Passau. Wolkan referred to these songs as "the trunk of Anabaptist poetry in Germany, specifically of the Swiss Brethren, that must have found their way out of the dungeon to the congregations in the same way as the many epistles and devotional writings of other Anabaptists, also in part composed in prison."[82] Wolkan observed that both Hutterites and Swiss Brethren initially shared the Passau repertoire.[83] As the Swiss Brethren developed lines of communications down the Rhine to the Netherlands, the musical heritage of the Philipites was supplemented by poetry and music from their northern cousins. By the time the Swiss poetic vein seemed to dry up, the Hutterites entered their most productive period, their golden age, the second half of the sixteenth century. As a result, the shared Passau trunk became quickly overgrown with new productions, and the two branches of Anabaptism shared fewer songs.[84]

None of this changes the fact that most of the hymns in the first printed Anabaptist songbook were the work of former Philipites. Published in 1564, this collection of fifty-three hymns, *Etliche Geseng,* claimed to be the work of Swiss Brethren[85] and indeed became the forerunner of the Swiss Anabaptist *Ausbund.* Curiously, two hymns that praised community of goods as the practice of the true church in its purest form were dropped from subsequent editions of the *Ausbund.*[86] According to these songs, community of goods, more than anything else, aroused Satan's fury against the true congregation of Christ.[87]

Unfortunately, nothing is known about the compiler or the community

Figure 1. Heilbronn circa 1550

that sponsored the 1564 collection of songs which presumably had been sung for some time. Some appear to have been used exclusively in Moravia,[88] suggesting a connection to a community there, as do the songs that extolled the virtues of living in community of goods. The songs later traveled west and became the property of the Swiss Brethren. The connecting link appears to have been former Philipites turned Swiss Brethren. This scenario seems confirmed by an examination of the known facts about the composers among the Passau prisoners.

Surviving sources shed some light on the Philipite connection of some of the songwriters. A tragic fate had befallen a number of former Philipites in 1535. After the expulsion orders, the community had been divided into small groups to return inconspicuously to their former home territories (see Chapter 12). For this purpose and in one of his last actions as leader of the entire community, Philip appointed a number of group leaders to guide these small bands. Among them was Michael Schneider (Yetelhauser), Hans Beck or Peck (Pfeifer), and possibly Dietrich of Heilbronn. These three leaders with approximately fifty ordinary members were apprehended near Passau and imprisoned at the forbidding fortress at Oberhaus, across from the city.[89] Some remained imprisoned for years, some died, some managed to escape, and others were eventually released.[90] Their statements, given upon arrest, provide one of the few sources about the Philipite community and its members and leaders and yield the names of the following baptizers: Lemlin of Sindelfingen, near Stuttgart, who was executed at Vaihingen;[91] Andre (Andreas) of Eysen, from Unteröwisheim, also described as from Berkheim near Heidelberg, who in 1532 was baptizing in the Palatinate and later was executed at Neuenburg on the Danube; Hans, presumably Hans from Schwaigern, who in 1530 baptized near Heilbronn and in 1533 at Neckarweihingen but had since become a "charlatan."[92] The same was said of Julius Lober, who had baptized members of the early Bruchsal congregation, including the wife of the songwriter Michael Schneider.[93] Schneider from Weil (der Stadt) or more likely from Weil (am Rhein), a few miles from Basel, had been appointed group leader by Philip.[94]

At least one other prisoner at Passau had connections to Basel. Hans Schluchtern had been baptized by Martin Wagner from Basel in 1531.[95] Schluchtern's wife had been baptized by Jörg Scherer of Ingersheim. This was no doubt Jörg Scherer who, along with Martin Fasser, baptized in the Esslingen-Stuttgart area in 1536–37. Anabaptism had been introduced to Esslingen by Reublin. Esslingen lay on the crossroads leading either to the Rhineland or to Switzerland. After 1535 former Philipites returned to the Esslingen area where Anabaptists, particularly in the Rems Valley, maintained themselves into the seventeenth century. These Anabaptists were clearly Swiss in orientation. One of their leaders, after 1536 and until his death in 1559, was Jörg Scherer.[96] Of special interest is that a Jörg from Ingersheim appears historically connected to the Passau songs. He and Schmidhans (Hans Schmid) are credited with having coauthored one of the hymns that made its way into the early Swiss collection.[97] If the song-writer Jörg of Ingersheim was Jörg Scherer of Ingersheim, who became a senior leader in the Esslingen area after 1536, then a link may have been established to the group that sponsored or utilized the first songbook. In that case, the first songbook originated at the crossroads of Philipite and Swiss influences to forge a common tradition.

But what of the authenticity of the songs attributed to the prisoners in Passau? Hostile contemporaries charged that ghostwriters put verses into the mouths of prisoners. Poets in Moravian communities allegedly began to write as soon as one of their members was imprisoned. Prisoners were said to have been too depressed and melancholy to engage in poetic crea-tivity as well as illiterate and therefore unable to commit songs to paper. But what really riled these gainsayers were the popular profane tunes sung by the Anabaptists.[98] Although claims made to discredit a powerful Ana-baptist medium must be taken with more than one grain of salt, there may have been truth in some of the charges. Anabaptists certainly used profane tunes, and sixteenth-century poets generally lacked inhibitions against borrowing of all sorts. Moreover, a sense of communitarian solidarity could blur the line between individual and collective authorship. Besides, there are reasons for skepticism about the authenticity of some songs at-tributed to early Swiss martyrs such as Mantz, Sattler, and Blaurock. A recent argument for the authenticity of the song attributed to Mantz en-countered difficulties and remained unconvincing.[99] However, to date there is no compelling evidence to question claims that the core of the songs published in 1564 originated in prison at Passau.[100]

The Songwriters

Problems arise with attempts to identify the prison composers and their Anabaptist affiliations. Not all of the contributors to the first songbook were Philipites. Prison eroded the ideological barriers between prisoners who had belonged to rival communities. Solidarity in suffering explains the mutual sharing of songs by Hutterites and Swiss Brethren which "be-lied the hostilities more frequently expressed."[101] Such were the songs of Hans Betz (Petz). The Chronicle recorded under the year 1537 that Hans Betz, a servant of the Gospel, and others died at Passau after "long suffer-ing and harsh treatment."[102] No doubt this was the same Hans Betz cred-ited with seventeen of the songs published in the first Swiss Brethren song-book.[103] Betz, a clothmaker from Eger (Cheb), had been baptized by a Jörg Haffner in 1530. He had joined a community at Znaim which was at odds with the community at Auspitz, but it is unclear whether the conflict was with the Philipites or the proto-Hutterites at Auspitz.[104] Little is known about the Znaim group. A group numbering about fifty was led

by Ulrich Stadler and Hans Kellermann in 1533. Stadler and some followers joined the Hutterites in 1537–38, but a community of those who refused to follow suit continued to exist at Znaim. In 1539 Christoph (Stoffel) Aschenberger, a leader of that community, traveled to Steinabrunn for
discussions with the Hutterites. While there, he and others were seized and
forced onto the notorious march to Triest to become galley slaves. Aschenberger's writings reflect a Swiss orientation, and a Swiss Brethren community remained at Znaim until 1591.[105]

In terms of our context, it seems reasonable to suggest that Betz's songs
entered the Hutterite tradition with former members of the Znaim community. At the same time, the remaining community of Swiss must have
continued to honor the memory of Betz as well, which would explain why
fourteen songs attributed to him have been preserved in the Hutterite repertoire and seventeen in the first Swiss Brethren songbook.[106] Hutterite
sources similarly honored another Passau prisoner and poet, brother
Bernhard Schneider, also believed to have died in the Passau prison.[107] He
appeared in official documents as a young person baptized in 1533 by
Hans of Schwaigern at Neckarweihingen.[108] Clearly then, both Hutterites
and Swiss Brethren considered Betz and Bernhard Schneider martyrs worthy of being remembered in song. But Hutterites seem to have been more
selective. They did not bestow the same honor on Michael Schneider, another Passau prisoner, with twelve songs to his credit in the 1564 songbook. Reasons for Schneider's exclusion from the Hutterite songwriters
are not hard to find. Michael Schneider did not die in prison; indeed, Hutterites may have known something about the circumstances of his escape.

Michael Schneider, also known as Yetelhauser, and not to be confused
with the young Bernhard Schneider, was the leader of a group of Philipites
imprisoned at Passau. Hans Beck or Peck (Pfeifer) from Grading near Hilpolstein was his assistant.[109] Both had been members of Philip's community at Auspitz. During their four-year ordeal as prisoners, these two were
befriended by Ruprecht Mosham, dean of the Passau cathedral. The
reform-minded Mosham believed that dialogue and improved prison conditions would be more effective than threats and torture in bringing the
misled heretics to their senses. But his leniency and unorthodox treatment
of heresy ran afoul of the cathedral canons. On November 14, 1538, they
complained to Duke Ernst, administrator of the diocese of Passau, that in
the presence of strangers and servants Mosham permitted one of the Anabaptist leaders, presumably Michael Schneider, to eat and drink at his
table like a guest.[110] Initially Duke Ernst supported Mosham's tactics because they seemed to bear fruit. He wrote back that the Anabaptist leader
in question had already made concessions on a number of points, and he
hoped that ordinary prisoners would do the same.[111] A six-point "recan-

tation" was drawn up and apparently agreed to by Schneider.[112] A request by Hans Beck for his freedom provides further evidence that he and Schneider were ready for compromise after more than three years of imprisonment.[113] By September 3, 1539, Mosham claimed to have won two of the leaders for his side and blamed Anabaptist alienation on the "heathenish, fleshly, unspiritual life of the clergy." By way of contrast he praised the Anabaptists for their upright life and considered them guilty only of having "sprinkled themselves a little with water out of ignorance and simplicity." But neither his success nor his criticism was received kindly by the local clergy, who now accused him of heresy. Fearing imprisonment himself, Mosham fled to Nuremberg.[114] Schneider and Beck seized their first opportunity to do the same. After cutting the prison lock out of its wooden frame, the two escaped and, on October 10, 1539, testified before the Nuremberg reformers in support of Mosham's claims that he had persuaded them to recant their Anabaptism. According to Beck, Mosham had convinced him that circumcision was the Old Testament equivalent of baptism. Just as no second circumcision was necessary in adulthood, so no second baptism was needed. The Spirit could work as well in children as in adults. Schneider admitted that he had considered children no different from Gentiles until they arrived at an understanding.[115]

But given this record, how did Schneider's songs come to appear in the Swiss Brethren songbook? What happened after Nuremberg? Thanks to the meticulous work of John Oyer, it is possible to trace some of the movements of Mosham and his two companions. By October 23, 1539, the threesome had arrived in Dinkelsbühl. Mosham apparently envisioned a grand scheme that would bring all of the various reform parties of the Empire back together in ecumenical unity. From Dinkelsbühl his steps led to Heidelberg for discussions with Elector Frederic of the Palatinate, and from there to Aschaffenburg for an audience with the Elector of Mainz, and on to similar stops in Trier and Cologne. In 1540 he participated in religious discussions at Hagenau and later in Worms, Basel, Bern, Zurich, Constance, Schaffhausen, Strasbourg, and Speyer.[116] It is not clear on how many of these engagements Mosham was accompanied by his two grateful converts. Quite likely they recognized before he did the impossibility of his undertaking and, having paid their dues for his kindness, returned to Anabaptism. Mosham, meanwhile, was incarcerated in the same dungeon at Oberhaus/Passau which for years had held his Philipite protégés. He died as the result of suicide in April or May 1543.[117]

More difficult to trace than Mosham's fate is that of Michael Schneider and Hans Beck. Oyer suggested that Schneider may have returned to Weil am Rhein, where Mosham spent some time in 1541 seeking dialogue with the reformers of Basel.[118] Since Schneider's songs, along with those of Hans Betz, were included in the 1564 collection, the inference is warranted that the two, like other Philipites, turned Swiss (see Chapter 12). Thus the songs of Philipites, Michael Schneider, and fellow prisoners became the common property of the Swiss Brethren scattered from Moravia to the Rhineland and to Switzerland.

In Search of the Philipite Spiritual Genius

Robert Friedmann suggested that Philipite teachings and practice expressed the "motley character of early Anabaptism." He described their economic practices as "a sort of emergency community of goods" and implied that a more principled community of goods as "brotherly love in action" was the achievement of Jacob Hutter and his supporters.[119] Friedmann based his assessment of Philipite teaching on what he believed to be the sole surviving treatise of the Philipites,[120] *Concerning a True Knight of Christ* (hereafter the *True Knight*). According to Friedmann, this treatise, a "high song" (*Hohe Lied*) on *Gelassenheit* could "not possibly be Hutterite in its thought and faith" despite its presence in one of the oldest Hutterite codices. He believed that its author, Hans Haffner, was the Philipite Hans Haffner, imprisoned at Passau. The latter Haffner was one of fourteen prisoners credited with a verse in a collective song.[121] A comparison of the verse attributed to him with the treatise on the *True Knight* convinced Friedmann of a spiritual kinship between the two. He therefore argued that the *True Knight* expressed a unique Philipite ethos. However, closer examination of official records indicates that the Hans Haffner imprisoned at Passau could neither read nor write. Prisoner Haffner came originally from Riblingen (Rüblingen) near Schwäbisch-Hall. He was an older person, married for forty years, who testified that he had worked as an ordinary laborer in fields and vineyards. After five years of imprisonment, Haffner and his wife Agnes (Engella) were released upon recantation.[122] Obviously he was not the author of the *True Knight*. Whether he had the poetic gift to compose the verse attributed to him remains an open question. There was at Passau another prisoner from Riblingen whose name is simply given as Hans the Younger. It has been suggested that he might have been the son of the senior Haffner,[123] but there is no evidence that he authored the treatise of the *True Knight*.

A search for other candidates who were named Haffner and capable of composing the work reveals that the name Haffner (potter) was not unusual among Anabaptists. Curiously, between 1536 and 1538—that is, after the return of the Philipites to the Rhineland—a Hans Haffner junior appears to have been active in Philip Plener's home area.[124] This Haffner apparently wrote an apologia in which he rejected pedobaptism and all other ceremonies not commanded in Scripture. But whether this Haffner was a Philipite or the author of the *True Knight* is unknown.[125] We must conclude that Friedmann's identification of the *True Knight* as the work of a Philipite remains unproven. The statements of the Philipite prisoners at Passau and their songs are still the primary source of Philipite teachings and practice.

An analysis of the songs, specifically those of Michael Schneider, reveals very common Anabaptist themes[126]—among them that of patient suffering. This is hardly surprising, especially if one accepts claims in the 1564 collection that these songs were composed in a "stinking, foul prison." But the theme of suffering, coupled to the emphasis on discipleship and obedience to Christ, is "standard Anabaptist" fare. The absence of vindictiveness against the persecutors, noted by Oyer, may reflect Schneider's relatively lenient treatment at the hands of Mosham rather than an Anabaptist norm. It certainly contrasts with some Hutterite songs that invoked and in some cases claimed to have called down divine vengeance on the persecutors.[127] Only one or two of Schneider's hymns are polemical against the established religion or Antichrist. Most songs were supported by a typically Swiss New Testament biblicism, although Old Testament stories were woven into some. These Old Testament stories may reflect an oral biblicism.[128] Surprisingly, the hymns said very little about the actual prison conditions under which they were composed, and it is not clear whether they originated during the early stages or near the end of Schneider's imprisonment in 1539.

As noted earlier, two of the songs in the 1564 collection extolled community of goods; one of these was a song by Schneider.[129] This song lamented the loss of communal living, of the practice of community of goods, and it contained clear reference to the expulsion from Moravia in 1535 and the dispersion of the community which followed. All of this suggests that it was written some time after these events with an appreciation of their consequences. It is therefore worth citing.

> Lord, your people are scattered now.
> Woe betide this greatest grief
> Do meet with us
> Oh God, let yourself be moved
> Your arm do stir again.
>
> Rescue your people from Satan's bondage
> and lead them again to your land
> that is our desire
> Oh God, grant it to us
> But your will be done.

> You have already promised us
> you will gather us again
> together out of all lands
> redeem us out of the bonds
> and lead us into your land.

The promised land to which Schneider wanted to return was no doubt Moravia. Schneider longed for the restoration of community life as it existed at Auspitz prior to the expulsion of 1535. The song depicted community of goods as the natural outgrowth of fraternal love and solidarity in fellowship one with the other. *Gelassenheit,* in this context, meant more than a mystical inner state of mind. It meant practical self-denial in terms of private possessions and mutual sharing. Whether Schneider and his companions were able to return to Moravia or to the practice of community of goods is unknown, but the song longing for a return to community life was dropped from subsequent editions of the *Ausbund.* That in itself raises interesting historic questions that go beyond this study (see Chapter 12).

One further observation remains: the legacy of song could be turned to polemical purposes. Usually the polemics were directed outward against the world and its persecutors. But sometimes, songs became pawns in inter-Anabaptist disputes. A story commemorated in later editions of the *Ausbund* is a case in point. The story, which has aroused considerable curiosity, describes a visit to Moravia by a delegation of Christian brothers from Thessalonica, present-day Greece.[130] The visit was apparently prompted by the request of Anabaptist galley slaves who touched shore in Turkish-controlled Thessalonica.[131] It has been assumed that these were Anabaptists taken prisoner at Steinabrunn and marched to the Adriatic in 1540. The transmission of the story of the visiting Thessalonians remains itself a historic problem. The story appeared first in the *Martyrs Mirror* and reached its editors through Hans Passiers van Wesbusch, who had moved from Moravia via Poland to the Netherlands in the early seventeenth century. Passiers heard the story from a "centenarian," Hans Knarr, the son of Hans Fuhrmann. Fuhrmann had been imprisoned for nine years with John (Hans) Peck (Beck or Petz?) and others at Passau. The good lord of Jamnitz was said to have traveled thirty-six leagues in person to bail out the prisoners, who subsequently took up residence at Popitz and Jamnitz in Moravia.[132] If Fuhrmann and Peck were fellow prisoners at Passau with the Philipites described above, then Fuhrmann gained his release in 1544.

In this case, the story in the *Martyrs Mirror* became the source for a song in subsequent editions of the *Ausbund,* rather than the other way around.[133] The song commemorated both the visit of the Thessalonian

Christians and the suffering of the prisoners in Passau. Thus two stories
were woven into one. The thrust of the song was overtly polemical and
anti-Hutterite in tone. After visiting the Hutterites first, these foreign
guests allegedly found that they had more in common with the Swiss
Brethren. The song gave as its source Lienhardt Knur (Knarr) "the old,"
who in turn had heard it from Hans Fuhrmann who, with Hans Brät (*sic*)
had been imprisoned with twelve others at Passau. These prisoners were
said to have been "members of the Swiss congregation." The reference to
the Passau imprisonment is of special interest here. If this imprisonment
referred to events that took place in the 1530s or 1540s, the story and
song could shed light on the fate of some of the survivors who had been
incarcerated for nine years. Hans Haffner senior and his wife were released in 1542 after almost seven years of imprisonment.[134] If some survived seven years, then it is possible that others, for example, Hans Fuhrmann, survived nine before being ransomed in 1544 by the lord of Jamnitz
to return to Moravia. It was presumably the congregation of Fuhrmann at
Popitz or Jamnitz, described as Swiss, which received a visit from the
Thessalonians between 1540 and 1544, hence the fusion of the two stories. Friedmann went so far as to suggest that members of this community
must be considered "the beginners of the *Ausbund*-hymn collection."[135] If
that is correct, songs were first collected and sung in Moravia. Their use
spread from there to the Neckar and Rhine basins. Whatever the case, the
Philipites, who disappeared from history as a distinct community, made
an important contribution to early Anabaptist hymnology and lived on
through their gift of song.

Philipite teaching and practice appear to have been akin to those of early
Swiss Anabaptism as reflected in the *Swiss Order*. An analysis of the limited sources reveals that Philipites rejected infant baptism and made similar arguments for believers' baptism found in Swiss Anabaptism. They
rejected the idea of the bodily presence and of any sacramental, sacerdotal
communication of grace. They placed the emphasis instead on faith commitment and discipleship (*Nachfolge*) as understood through a practical
reading of the New Testament. True faith expressed itself in moral uprightness, separation from the "world," and love for one's brothers and
sisters. Philipite congregational polity included an attempt to live out
Acts 2 and 4 similar to the instructions posited in the original *Swiss
Congregational Order*. Given these positions, Philipite transformation
into Swiss Brethren, a topic taken up in Chapter 12, would seem less
surprising.

Chapter Five

The Gabrielites

A *Volk* from Silesia

Silesian Anabaptism is an orphan in Anabaptist studies. Its beginnings are obscure, its generic peculiarities undifferentiated, its martyrs unclaimed and forgotten, its historic significance unexplained and unrecognized.

Reasons for this neglect are not hard to find. Silesian Anabaptism left no apparent heirs, no group to claim its name. Not surprisingly, then, the renaissance of Anabaptist studies, driven primarily by denominational concerns, passed the Silesians by. Scholars who initiated the renaissance tended to focus predominantly on the history of the three major groups that survived: the Swiss Brethren, the Hutterites, and Mennonites. Perhaps even more significant is the state of Silesian sources. No published edition of Anabaptist archival documents (*Täuferakten*) exists for Silesia. Archival holdings that once existed were lost or destroyed during World War II. Similarly, Silesian Anabaptism appears to have left no literature articulating its vision or describing its organization and practices. In short, the surviving evidence about this branch of Anabaptism seems too fragmentary to encourage scholarly inquiry.

Nevertheless, the goal of this chapter is to shed new light on Anabaptist beginnings in Silesia by focusing on three leaders involved in those beginnings: Oswald Glaidt, Clemens Adler, and Gabriel Ascherham. Of these, Adler, whose ministry in Silesia was previously unrecognized, authored the most substantive statement on the pacifism of early Anabaptism. Gabriel founded and led a community of Silesian Anabaptists more than one thousand strong in Moravia, with headquarters at Rossitz. For a while he functioned as overall bishop for two other communities, the Philipites and the proto-Hutterites at Auspitz. Glaidt, an important player in the beginnings of Anabaptism in Nicolsburg, went on to become a cofounder of sabbatarianism. All three were actively gathering "a people of God in Silesia" with their ministries overlapping. All three wrote treatises of significance for understanding Anabaptism in this region.

Gathering a People of God in Silesia

The Coming of Anabaptism

The duchy of Silesia was closely linked to the fate of Bohemia, Moravia, and Hungary. When Ferdinand I of Hapsburg became king of Bohemia on December 5, 1526, he also assumed authority in Silesia.[1] The Silesian cities of Breslau (Wroclaw), Schweidnitz, Jauer, Gross-Glogau, and their territories fell under Ferdinand's direct control. The territorial magnates, led by Duke Karl I of Münsterberg-Oels, Duke Frederic II of Liegnitz, and the bishop of Breslau, became Ferdinand's personal vassals. Unlike their counterparts in the Empire, these Silesian princes had no recourse to the Imperial Diet and lacked the tradition of relative independence enjoyed by their peers in Moravia. The Silesian Estates, therefore, tended to be more susceptible to Ferdinand's manipulations and pressures.

In the spring of 1527 Ferdinand came to Breslau for a meeting with the Silesian Estates. Here he made his religious preferences clear. A decree of May 17, 1527, ordered all church ceremonies restored to their traditional form. Clergy who had married were to be deprived of their income and stripped of all priestly functions. Karl I of Münsterberg-Oels was appointed governor of Silesia with orders to enforce Catholic orthodoxy and ceremony. An incident that occurred on the eve of Ferdinand's departure graphically demonstrated the attitude toward would-be reformers in his entourage. On May 20, 1527, members of Ferdinand's escort caught and stripped Johann Reichel, the reform preacher of Striegau, to his shirt, placed him on a horse, and hanged him from a "blooming pear tree."[2] Reichel's crime was the denial of the real presence in the sacrament of the altar.

Fortunately for Silesian reformers, many of the country gentry and a number of the cities resisted implementation of Ferdinand's mandate. Karl I lacked the resources to enforce Ferdinand's will. It became necessary to repeat Ferdinand's orders almost annually. An edict of August 1, 1528, to be read from all pulpits three Sundays in a row and thereafter every year at Easter and Christmas, prescribed the death penalty for anyone questioning the real presence. It ordered ruthless measures against those who rejected pedobaptism and engaged in rebaptism. Anabaptist meeting places were to be destroyed, persons unwilling to recant punished with death. No deviations from traditional ceremonies were permitted. Mary was to be revered as the mother of God, prayers to the saints were to be continued, oral confession made to local priests, the holidays of the church celebrated, the monstrance carried in procession. All holy artifacts, removed from churches or other sacred sites, were to be restored to their proper places; all church appointments would be reserved for traditionalists. Lords who refused to enforce the mandate in their territories or on their Estates would forfeit their privileges.[3]

Opposition to these policies crystallized around Frederic II of Liegnitz, who tolerated the indigenous reform efforts of the Liegnitz Brotherhood led by his courtier, Caspar Schwenckfeld, and humanist scholar Valentin Crautwald.[4] But protests in the name of ancient liberties against Ferdinand's policies fell on deaf ears, and Frederic found himself increasingly isolated. In search of political allies against Ferdinand's pressures, Frederic turned to the Lutheran princes of the Empire. In return for their support he opened his territories to the influence of the Lutheran reformers. Correspondingly, the influence of the indigenous Reform Party declined. Deprived of Frederic's confidence and protection, Schwenckfeld and the Liegnitz Brotherhood were pushed to the periphery. On April 19, 1529, Schwenckfeld resigned his position of councilor to Frederic and left for Strasbourg.[5]

While Schwenckfeld, the most visible member of the party, went into exile, other members, including the scholarly Crautwald, remained to form the spiritualist, sacramentist opposition against the new Lutheran orthodoxy. Having lost magisterial patronage, these Schwenckfeldians found themselves increasingly in competition with the Anabaptists, who seemed especially successful among the peasantry. An Anabaptist presence has been documented for the territories of Liegnitz, Glogau, Schweidnitz, Breslau, and Glatz (see Map 3). From these territories would come a number of important Anabaptist leaders, including David of Schweidnitz, also known as the Bohemian, and the later Hutterites, Bärtel Ridmaier, Welser the Silesian (Schlesinger), Peter Riedemann, and Caspar Braitmichel.[6] Before becoming Hutterites some of these men appear to have been associated with other communities in Moravia, for example the Gabrielites at Rossitz, the Philipites at Auspitz, or the Brethren at Austerlitz. All played prominent roles in establishing Anabaptist communities in Moravia.

Some histories have associated Anabaptist beginnings with the arrival of refugees from Thuringia in 1525. These fugitives, compromised by participation in the Peasants' War of 1525, allegedly brought Anabaptism to Silesia. But evidence for such claims is obscure.[7] More recently, Polish scholars suggested a connection between Anabaptist beginnings and peas-

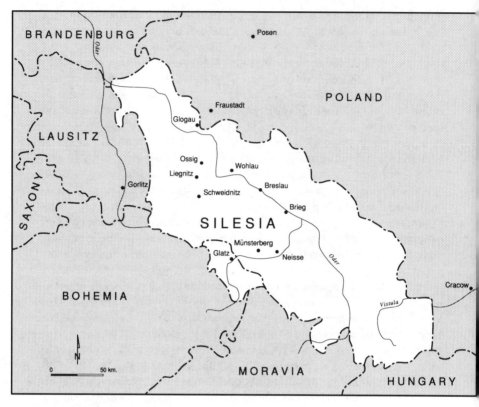

Map 3. Silesia

ant disturbances of 1526 in some Silesian territories.[8] As early as 1526, half of the village of Stolz near Frankenstein in the territory of Duke Karl was allegedly Anabaptist minded. The duke had these peasants flogged, their ears cut off, and the victims driven from his territories.[9] Only the dating of this event, not its actual occurrence, remains problematic.[10] Evidence of an Anabaptist presence in Silesia dates from 1527. By the end of that year the council of Breslau found it necessary to take measures against them. On January 2, 1528, the council forbade Anabaptists residence in Breslau and warned citizens not to provide lodging for them. It is possible that one of the Anabaptists of concern to Breslau was Oswald Glaidt.[11] Older scholarship alleged that Hans Hut, accompanied by Gabriel Ascherham, visited Silesia as early as 1526 or 1527. However, such a journey by Hut seems highly unlikely. More significant is that at his trial in late 1527 Hut stated that he knew of an Oswald and a Hess at Breslau. The reference to Oswald must have been to Glaidt. Hut, it seems, was informed of Glaidt's move to Silesia and his presence in Breslau during late 1527.[12] As for Gabriel, indirect evidence indicates that he became active in Silesia only after Hut's death. His history of the Brethren in Moravia began with the year 1528.[13]

Considering all of the available evidence, the best judgment appears to be that Anabaptists were present in Silesia by late 1527 and that it had been introduced from Moravia. As in Moravia, the Anabaptists in Silesia appear to have divided into different parties. Among the documented missionaries to Silesia was Oswald Glaidt, apparently accompanied by Andreas Fischer. Fischer and his supporters eventually would evolve into Old Testament sabbatarians and move to Slovakia. It was this group and its new Judaism, complete with Sabbath observance and circumcision, which roused the ire of Crautwald. Since that story has been told in a recent monograph, it needs no further attention here,[14] but Glaidt's involvement in the beginnings of Anabaptism in Silesia does.

Born at Cham in the Upper Palatinate, Oswald Glaidt had been a priest (most likely a Franciscan friar) before becoming involved on the side of reform at Leoben in Styria.[15] According to his own account, Glaidt was imprisoned and exiled from Austrian territory because of the Gospel.[16] Like many other religious refugees, he made his way to Nicolsburg where he was appointed assistant preacher by Lord Leonhard of Liechtenstein. On March 15, 1526, Glaidt represented Nicolsburg's evangelical party at an important synod at Austerlitz, sponsored by Moravian nobleman Jan Dubčanský. Those gathered sought to foster dialogue between native Bohemian Brethren, Utraquists, and members of the new reform movement. Several hundred religious leaders from both persuasions attended. Thanks to the account in seven articles (*Handlung*) published two weeks later by Glaidt, it is possible to determine his pre-Anabaptist religious stance.[17] Although previous scholarship classified his position as Lutheran, this seems warranted only in a very broad sense. Instead, the *Handlung* reveals Glaidt to be a member of a more radical Reform Party. Articles 2 and 4, concerned with the "table [*Tisch*] of the Lord," underscored the commemorative aspects of the Lord's Supper. Unlike the Bohemian Brethren who permitted children to partake of the elements, Glaidt believed participation should be restricted to adults who had experienced a spiritual rebirth. Other articles argued for clerical marriage and Christian freedom in matters of food. Striking was Glaidt's iconoclasm based on the principle that all things not expressly commanded in the Scriptures had to be abolished. This included the elevation of the host; lighting of candles; canonical singing, ringing of bells, or wearing of priestly robes; processions with the host; storage of the host in a tabernacle; masses for the dead; anniversary masses, special consecrations; and the use of holy oil, pastes (chrism), or holy water. Given these positions and assumptions, it must have been a relatively easy step to reject pedobaptism and to opt instead for the baptism of adult believers. This appears to have happened when Balthasar Hubmaier arrived in Nicolsburg. Evidence indicates that during July 1526 Glaidt collaborated with Hubmaier on *Old and New Teachers on Believers' Baptism*.[18] Hubmaier finished this work on July 21, 1526, in Glaidt's quarters. This soliciting of church fathers for the Anabaptist cause suggests that Glaidt's biblicism, like Hubmaier's, was not as radically primitivist to the exclusion of the church fathers and may help explain why he and other local clergy joined Hubmaier's efforts at installing a magisterial form of Anabaptism in Nicolsburg.

On January 26, 1527, Glaidt published an *Apologia* in defense of the Anabaptist direction he and Hubmaier had taken.[19] This publication was prompted by the personal attacks of Franciscans at Feldberg, perhaps former colleagues, who accused him of being a renegade monk who had run off with another man's wife and recanted his faith in prison at Vienna. Glaidt, the Franciscans alleged, had been driven out of Austrian territory because of his evil deeds. In reply, Glaidt insisted that these slanders were directed against him by the papal party to discredit his preaching of the Gospel. He appealed to his readers to judge for themselves whether Roman teachings on Mary, the saints, celibacy of priests, and a special spiritual estate within the church, the monastics, were scriptural. He went on to attack prayer to the saints as well as the use of images, altars, special feast days and seasons, and customs such as not eating meat on Friday. Traditional practices of fasting seemed to him sheer hypocrisy. In their place he advocated consistent moderation and sober avoidance of gluttony and drunkenness. Extreme unction and burial in consecrated soil seemed of no consequence. He held that there were no differences between Sunday and any other day. Alms and tithes were to be used for the local poor, the sick, and the old, not for begging friars. True preachers were to receive their due allowance, but the Scriptures said nothing about singers and chanters.[20]

Of special interest were Glaidt's brief reflections on baptism. Because children could not have faith and did not understand what it meant to follow Christ, they should not be baptized. It was necessary to follow the order of Christ's Great Commission; to do otherwise was to follow an anti-Christian order. Children who died without baptism were in "Christ's hand."[21] Glaidt wrote even less about the Lord's Supper, suggesting that too many booklets already existed on the subject. He believed that Christ was "eaten in faith" and that questions on how he was present in the elements were misplaced. Instead, believers were to rejoice in Christ's intercession at the right hand of God on their behalf.

Nothing in the *Apologia* suggested that in January 1527 Glaidt had espoused a separatist ecclesiology, although he did contrast the good fruit that came from true faith with the ways of the ungodly. The dominant theme of faith throughout the *Apologia* suggested that under Hubmaier's influence Glaidt had grafted the notion of believers' baptism onto his earlier reformed position. Yet, within four months of the *Apologia* publication, Glaidt found himself at odds with Hubmaier. The issue concerned, among other things, Hubmaier's treatment of Hans Hut (see Chapter 3). In June or July 1527, Glaidt left Nicolsburg and followed Hut to Vienna. Here he baptized the former Franciscan Leonhard Schiemer. It may be assumed that the two were acquainted or that Schiemer was familiar with Glaidt's *Apologia* directed against Franciscans.[22] Not clear is whether Glaidt followed Schiemer and Hut to Upper Austria. But in the fall of 1527 Glaidt must have taken the road to the territories of Frederic II of Liegnitz in Silesia.[23] Here he participated in amiable discussions with members of the indigenous Reform Party led by Schwenckfeld. These discussions were not yet strained by Glaidt's later adoption of sabbatarianism.[24] From Liegnitz Glaidt made his way to Breslau, where the authorities were trying to prevent Anabaptists from seeking residence. Nevertheless, Glaidt, assuming the role of an itinerant Anabaptist apostle, appears to have remained in Silesia for about two years.[25] Not until he and Fischer began to advocate antitrinitarian and/or sabbatarian ideas did the authorities act against them. The catalyst appears to have been Glaidt's tract *Concerning the Keeping of the Sabbath*, now lost, which must have appeared in 1530. It aroused concern in Liegnitz and later in Nicolsburg and Strasbourg.[26] Escalating controversy prompted Frederic of Liegnitz to take serious measures against the Anabaptists, and by 1531 most had been driven from his territories. But Glaidt had established a community of refugees in Moravia before then, and Fischer and some of his converts moved into Slovak territory.

This is not the place to recount the subsequent fate of sabbatarian Anabaptism in Slovakia or of Glaidt's eventual martyrdom in Vienna.[27] Of interest here are primarily his early teachings in Silesia. There are good reasons to believe that these, apart from the sabbatarian views, deviated little from the views expressed in the 1527 *Apologia*. From it and from refutations by Schwenckfeld and Crautwald of later developments of his thought, a partial reconstruction of Glaidt's Silesian teachings may be undertaken. These included a separatist ecclesiology. Glaidt apparently held that the church had fallen during the fourth century under Constantine and Pope Silvester (314–335). Restoration to pristine, pre-Constantinian purity involved a return to an assumed New Testament church model and apostolic teachings. According to Daniel Liechty's reconstruction of

Glaidt's teachings in Liegnitz, it appears that he and his group rejected the oath and chanted or recited psalms in their meetings.[28] If so, Glaidt must have softened his earlier position on chanting or "murmuring," possibly after an encounter with something like the *Swiss Order* or its supporting texts, specifically 1 Corinthians 14.

Glaidt's development from a New Testament ecclesiology to an Old Testament sabbatarianism, if such was the case, becomes explicable if one takes into account that from the beginning Glaidt's biblicism included the Old Testament. As noted in Chapters 1 and 6 of this book, the full hermeneutic implications of a two-Testament biblicism entered the debate between Anabaptists and spiritualists with full consciousness only in the 1530s. It is conceivable that someone with a flat biblicism, in which the two Testaments were granted equal authority, considered circumcision, the keeping of the Sabbath, and of the Ten Commandments of equal status to New Testament ordinances. Interestingly, some of the issues raised appeared on the agenda of another missionary to Silesia, whose ministry seems to have overlapped with Glaidt's, namely Clemens Adler.

Clemens Adler: A Swiss Connection?

Students of Anabaptism have known for some time that Clemens Adler authored one of the most significant early Anabaptist statements on nonresistance. But little or nothing was known about the author and the context out of which his treatise emerged. Rediscovered only in our century, the treatise was believed to be Swiss in origin. Scholars sought at first to discover Adler's identity in Swiss sources, whereas historians of the Silesian Reformation remained equally ignorant of Adler's role in Silesia. They had failed to recognize that the Clemens and the Adler who appeared in their sources were the same person.[29] It was my good fortune to make this identification and to discover a description of Adler's Silesian ministry in Hutterite sources.[30]

In 1946 Swiss scholar Samuel Geiser discovered an eighteenth-century Anabaptist codex in the attic of a Mennonite farmhouse in the Emmental, Canton Bern, Switzerland. Geiser's description of the codex was translated into English and published in 1951.[31] The treatise, dated April 12, 1529, carried the title, *The Judgment Concerning the Sword with Its Distinct Power in the Three Realms — the World [Gentiles], the Jews and the Christians — Including Other Concerns* (hereafter *Judgment*).[32] Geiser considered Adler's *Judgment* "an extraordinary testimony" of nonresistance in agreement with the Schleitheim Articles. The translators of Geiser's description of the codex shared this opinion, but their search for the author's identity and the context of his treatise remained fruitless. In

1956 they published the table of contents for the entire codex without any further information on Adler.[33] The discovery in 1961 of another codex containing Adler's treatise, this time in a former Hutterite dwelling at Sobotiste (Sabbatisch) in Slovakia, should have shifted attention from an assumed Swiss context to Moravia.[34] Two years earlier, Harold Bender speculated that Adler must have been a Moravian Anabaptist and assigned him to the Austerlitz "Stäbler party of Jacob Widemann, which later became the Hutterites."[35] But if that was the case, why did *The Chronicle* fail to mention Adler or his treatise? This is all the more puzzling because Adler's treatise was, as Bender put it, "a thoroughly non-resistant work . . . of high quality." James Stayer later agreed with this assessment and considered Adler's work "the first treatise in defense of the teachings of nonresistance."[36] As such it constitutes the most comprehensive and important early Anabaptist statement on nonresistance,[37] delineating positions on a number of other issues as well, including baptism, separation, discipline, temporal goods, the oath, litigation, and marriage. And while in agreement with the spirit of Schleitheim, the *Judgment* is unique in terms of the covenantal theology of history which undergirds its main arguments about the three realms of Christians, Jews, and Gentiles. Also unique is Adler's clear differentiation of his own position from that of Hubmaier's followers, the sword bearers and so-called *literalis*, a label apparently designating Lutheran neighbors. All of this adds significance to the treatise and raises the question of its historic context.

Adler in Silesia

Silesian sources reveal that Adler was active in the territories of Schweidnitz, Glatz, and Jauer. Contemporaries considered him among the noblest of the Anabaptist teachers in Silesia,[38] and subsequent histories claimed that he introduced Anabaptism to Schweidnitz as early as 1525.[39] But as noted earlier, such an early beginning seems highly unlikely. It is, of course, possible that Adler was active in Silesia before he became an Anabaptist. Circumstantial evidence suggests that he functioned as a missionary for a Moravian community in Silesia during the 1530s.

On October 13, 1533, the council of Breslau warned Frederic II of Liegnitz that Adler was proselytizing in the territory of Lord Bernstein near Glogau and that he persuaded many "poor people to move away with him." Frederic replied that Adler had been active previously in Liegnitz territory and that inhabitants of two villages moved away with him. He, Frederic, had imprisoned Adler for several weeks at Wohlau and then expelled him from his territories. From the above it may be inferred that Adler moved converts out of Silesia to Moravia. Since most Silesians appear to have joined the Gabrielites, it seems highly likely that Adler was associated with that community. The fact that *The Chronicle* makes no mention of his mission to Silesia, his martyrdom, or his treatise could support the hypothesis that he belonged to a rival community.

Some time after the above exchange between Breslau and Liegnitz, Adler and three companions were arrested at Glogau, tried, and beheaded.[40] Unfortunately a precise dating of the arrest and execution is no longer possible, but if the suggestion that it was not until after the expulsion of the Gabrielites from Moravia in 1535 is correct,[41] then Adler and his companions managed either to escape arrest in 1533 or spent an extended time in prison before their execution. Inasmuch as Glogau was a Gabrielite recruiting ground,[42] Adler's arrest there adds further weight to speculations that he was associated with that group.

The above information about Adler can be complemented by a marvelous account of his ministry in Glatz, Silesia (Figure 2), preserved in two of the oldest Hutterite codices.[43] The account, "A New Story That Occurred Recently at Glatz in Silesia" (hereafter "A New Story"), which up until now escaped scholarly scrutiny, must have entered the Hutterite codices through associates of Adler who joined the Hutterites. Because the account did not mention baptism but instead centered on the eucharistic controversy and in other ways communicated the excitement of the early phase of the Reformation, it is possible that the events it described preceded Adler's conversion to Anabaptism. A dating as early as 1525 cannot be excluded. As described in "A New Story," Adler's mission to the city of Glatz was inspired by a strong sense of living in the "last days." "Moved by the Lord to first preach repentance in Glatz," Adler entered "the temple of idols," interrupted mass, and ordered the priest to be silent. He then took the pulpit in a manner reminiscent of the early years of the Reformation and began to preach.[44] It took the opposition of priests and their assistants (*pfaffen und schuelern*) an hour to drown out Adler's preaching by chanting or singing. Unable to make himself heard, Adler moved outdoors where he continued his sermon. These unauthorized actions resulted in charges of public mischief and disturbing the peace. Imprisoned for the night, Adler was expelled from the city in the morning, but the incident became a *cause célèbre* among sections of the city's populace as well the local gentry. A "brother" led Adler to a nearby estate where the owner gathered his household, friends, and neighbors to hear him. Deeply moved, one of those present, a noble named Bannowitz, invited Adler to his estate for a similar service. News of Adler's presence at the Bannowitz Estate spread during the night, and early the next morning before breakfast a large crowd of peasants gathered. A delegation of about thirty entered the house, requesting that Adler "reveal the will of God" to them.

Figure 2. Glatz

Adler allegedly replied, "dear friends, look to it that you do not engage in monkey business [*Affenspiel*]. The will of the Lord is in you. Live according to it." But after further pleading, Adler consented to an open-air service under a large linden tree (*Lindenbaum*).

Beginning with the first Adam, Adler explained to the peasants the nature of the "Lord's covenant" (*Bund*) and the role of His commandments. When news of Adler's unauthorized preaching to peasants reached the authorities, territorial governor Count Johannes of Hartneck ordered the chancellor of Glatz to apprehend the preacher. Adler's arrest angered the peasants, and people ran angrily alongside the horsemen who formed the guard taking Adler back to Glatz. Upon arrival Adler was first placed into an ecclesiastical prison (*Pfaffenthurm*) and then transferred to the chancellery for an examination of his views. Here he told his interrogators that he thought as much of the eucharist "as of your priests!" It seems that this and other comments landed him in the councilors' tower (*Radtsherrn-turm*). Considerable sympathy for his cause in the city may explain why he was once more treated with mere exile and why he was hustled out of the city secretly at night. Four members of the gentry, imprisoned in connection with the affair, regained their freedom as well. According to the account, an undaunted Adler moved on to the town of Reichenbach.

Curiously, "A New Story" said nothing about Adler's subsequent martyrdom, offering instead an interesting epilogue that connected his ministry with that of the fifteenth-century Franciscan reform preacher, John Capistran. According to the epilogue, Capistran had prophesied that, as a sign of the end time, the Gospel would be preached under a linden tree. As a further sign, the person who cut down the tree would be smitten with blindness. When and if this tree produced new shoots, the day of the Lord would be at hand. At the time of the writing of the epilogue three parts of Capistran's prophecy had been fulfilled: Adler had preached under the linden tree; a man had cut down the tree and been smitten with blindness; the stump of the tree was sending up new shoots as a sign that the "true Gospel" had been preached. What remained was the coming judgment. The author noted correctly, no doubt, that at the time of the open-air service under the linden tree no one thought of Capistran's prophecy. The full significance of that event, it seems, had become evident only in light of subsequent reflections.

The account in "A New Story" presumably served a threefold purpose. First, it described the beginnings of Adler's reform ministry in Silesia. Second, it authenticated his ministry by an appeal to a late medieval prophecy attributed to a Franciscan reform preacher. And third, it impressed on the readers that the day of the Lord was imminent.[45] Still unanswered was the question of who made the connection to the fifteenth-century Franciscan reform preacher and why. Was Capistran's prophecy transmitted in the form of a popular Silesian legend, or had it been nurtured by reform-minded Franciscans? Was the hero of the account, Adler, like other early Anabaptist leaders, Glaidt and Schiemer, himself a former Franciscan, or was the author of "A New Story" a Franciscan? Capistran was identified as a monk whose preaching led to the burning of playing cards and gambling tables. The date of his death was given correctly as 1456.[46]

But playing cards and gambling had not been Capistran's sole concern. Dispatched as an apostolic nuncio to help eradicate heresy in Austria and adjacent territories, the popular preacher attracted great crowds by his denunciation of abuses within the church. Not surprisingly, his criticism of clerical abuses in turn aroused charges of heresy. Although influential from Italy to Poland and from France to Hungary, Capistran concentrated much of his efforts on territories under Hussite influence. Naturally he was also drawn into a response to a rising Turkish threat to these territories. At the Diet of Frankfurt in 1454, he became a main mover of a crusade

against the Turks and was present at the battle of Belgrade, allegedly leading the "left wing" (*sic*) of the "Christian" armies. These crusading credentials against internal and external heretics made him an unlikely
prophet to authenticate the beginnings of Anabaptism in Silesia. His militance and undeniable loyalty to Rome, charges of heresy notwithstanding, hardly recommended him as a spiritual progenitor of Anabaptism and
were in fact dissonant with Adler's celebrated treatise on biblical nonresistance and with Anabaptist refusal to pay war taxes for the conflict with
the Turks. The inclusion of Capistran's prophecy was therefore most likely
a case of selective, first-generation borrowing from a medieval Catholic—
or better, Franciscan—past. It came either out of the author's background
or was included because "A New Story" targeted a particular audience.

As for a possible connection between Franciscans and Silesian Anabaptism other than that of Glaidt and possibly Adler, it should be noted that
Bartel Werner and Michael Steinberg left the Franciscan establishment at
Schweidnitz in 1524 and distinguished themselves later as Schwenckfeldians in Glatz territories.[47] Along with Caspar Schwenckfeld and his colleagues at Liegnitz, they helped shape the peculiar spirituality of the indigenous Reform Party. In some Silesian territories Schwenckfeldians and
Anabaptists developed a most cordial coexistence.

Unfortunately, nothing is known about Adler's personal background
or possible connections with the Franciscans. He was obviously schooled
in Latin, so a formal education, as well as membership in one of the religious orders prior to his involvement on the side of the Anabaptists, cannot be ruled out. His treatise revealed considerable biblical erudition in
both Testaments. He also cited extrabiblical sources, among them the history of Flavius Josephus.[48] The treatise, it will be argued, represented a
unique covenantal theology that integrated common Anabaptist positions
with aspects of Silesian spiritualism.

Adler's Judgment Concerning the Sword

If Adler's ministry took place in Silesia and Moravia, then his treatise
must be read in that context. Was its purpose personal, or did it have a
collective, apologetic intention? The Silesian context could point to the
latter. Adler's treatise carried the date April 12, 1529. Perhaps it was coincidental, but one week later, Schwenckfeld left Silesia. The Lutheran
party had gained the ear of Frederic of Liegnitz, and the situation in Silesia
was becoming more and more difficult for the indigenous evangelical
party as well as for the Anabaptists. Some Anabaptists, nevertheless, still
hoped for toleration. On July 28, 1529, a group describing itself as faithful subjects and "obedient brethren, members drafted into the covenant
[*Bund*] of Christ," sent a petition to the Estates asking for safe conduct so

that they might present their beliefs.[49] It is possible that Adler and his group were behind the request. According to "A New Story," the notion of covenants figured prominently in Adler's preaching, and it was a central theme of the *Judgment*. It seems plausible that the *Judgment* originated as an apology to maintain the good will and protection of local lords in Silesia and perhaps Moravia.

Internal evidence points to a Silesian purpose. References to Lutherans suggest that they, rather than Catholics or Reformed, were perceived as main religious rivals, faulted primarily for lacking a spiritual understanding of the Scriptures. As scriptural literalists (*literalis*), they were contrasted with the *spiritualis* (*Geistlichen*). Adler cited Christ and Paul as teaching that "the letter killeth, the Spirit makes alive."[50] A literalist hermeneutic, according to Adler, belonged to the Old Testament (Jewish) dispensation rather then the New (the Christian realm).

In a similar vein, the *Judgment* criticized neighbors, referred to as sword bearers (*Schwärtler*), who failed to distinguish among the three different realms of the Gentiles, the Jews, and the Christians. Failure to make the distinction led to an indiscriminate reading of the Scriptures and a confusion as to which texts applied to which realm. According to Adler, the result was akin to mixing "cabbage with peas and turnips!"

Hours of World History and Three Lineages of Descent

The critical allusion to sword bearers implies Adler's familiarity with the rift among Anabaptists one year earlier at Nicolsburg. Adler consciously identified with the staff bearers (*Stäbler*). But his own biblical pacifism came with an interesting extrabiblical frame of reference, one informed by a spiritualism and a covenantal theology not found in the Schleitheim Articles or other early Anabaptist documents. Reminiscent of a Joachite or spiritual Franciscan eschatology, the *Judgment* distinguished twelve "hours" of world history.[51] Adam was identified with the first hour; Noah with the third; Abraham with the sixth; Moses with the ninth; and Christ, the "second Adam," with the eleventh. Three realms—those of the Gentiles, the Jews, and the Christians—each originating at a different point in time, were governed according to three different divinely ordained covenants and orders regarding the use of the sword. If Adler's oral presentation under the linden tree corresponded with his written work, then he outlined to the peasants God's grand scheme of salvation history which culminated in the new covenant offered through Christ. This covenant proved superior to those normative for Gentiles and Jews. A restorationist eschatology that aimed at the recovery of apostolic purity in the latter days served as a reference point to criticize contemporary abuses while interpreting contemporary events as signs of the end time. Scripture was assumed to provide the guidelines for all reforms, but a hermeneutic that distinguished "measure, goal and time" and was able to discern the biblical truth in three parts according to "lineage, hour, time and duration" was necessary to understand the nature, purpose, and applicability of its text.[52] Accordingly, Gentiles (the world), Jews, and Christians were subject to different divinely ordained orders—Christ's true followers to a superior spiritual order and law, the new covenant outlined in the New Testament.

But the main point of Adler's *Judgment* was to establish that the use of coercive force belonged to the realm of the Gentiles and Jews but had no role among the true followers of Christ. What distinguished Adler's argument from that found in the Schleitheim Articles was its historic attempt at explaining the origin of social-economic-political inequalities that initially made coercive authority necessary among humans. Thus, during the first hour, the Fall brought the subordination of woman to man, of wife to husband, and of child to father. "All power and authority began with the authority that included the disciplining of Eve and her children through Adam."[53] The resulting patriarchy, with its familial or clan discipline and with authority and power wielded by one human being over another, was the direct product of man's first disobedience or sin. Consequently, all temporal authority originated in the need to control the evil that had entered with the original sin.

A new form of authority and discipline became necessary during the second hour because of Cain's fratricide. This blood crime called for the appropriate response: capital punishment. Initially, the right to respond and avenge the shedding of blood seems to have been vested in blood relatives. But fratricide created special problems. God himself placed a sign on Cain lest he be slain.

God's covenant with Noah during the third hour ordained the emergence of nations or races through Noah's descendants as well as the emergence of suprafamilial and clan authority. The authority that "in the beginning had been common to all" could now be wielded only by "the properly ordained authority [*verordnete Oberkeit*] of every district, market town, and village."[54] But divinely ordained authority was perverted when "a few rich and powerful ones" from "the race of Cain," represented by Nimrod, usurped authority by force and introduced tyranny. "Out of this tyrannical and robbing race emerged the first magnates, princes, and kings." Thus began the subjugation of the poor, who were coerced to serve the rich and powerful. Typological and allegorical exegesis made it possible for Adler to identify the ruling race with the Gentiles or with the pre-Abrahamic generation—that is, with the "first lineage of descent." Jews and Christians, the physical and spiritual descendants of Abraham, could have nothing in common with the descendants of these usurpers. At best, the mighty of the world had a negative, punitive function in the divine, providential plan of salvation history.

They have and hold the scepter and regiment according to the order of this world. They are servants of God unto vengeance and punishment of evil, as were Emperor Augustus, Tiberius, Nero and others . . . to the present. All these, from the greatest to the least, are of one growth, one bread, and one soup.[55]

During the sixth hour God chose a "second lineage of descent," the "seed of Abraham." The covenant with Abraham stipulated that his descendants would be like the sand by the sea, a promise that would be fulfilled through his spiritual descendants, the Christians. Meanwhile, Abraham's biological offspring, the Jews, had been promised the territory of Canaan and given a physical sign in circumcision. The Abrahamic covenant and its covenantal sign were supplemented and reinforced during the ninth hour by the Mosaic law that intended to set the Israelites aside as a people distinct from all other nations.

Much of Adler's *Judgment* is taken up with an exposition of the Law of Moses in its moral, civil, criminal, and ceremonial aspects. These aspects are treated under three subheadings: (1) Concerning the first part of the Law, the Commandments; (2) Concerning the second part of the Law, the judgments and capital punishment; and (3) Concerning the third part of the Law, that is, of the Ceremonies.[56] The exposition of the Law of Moses, unique in early Anabaptism, with the possible exception of Melchior Hoffman's sermons on the furnishings of the Tabernacle, sought to demonstrate that Abrahamic covenant and Mosaic Law found their true fulfillment during the eleventh hour in Abraham's "promised seed," Christ. The Law of Moses had been unable to remove the effects of the Fall or the power of original sin, bringing at best the knowledge (*Erkantnus*) of sin. Christ, in contrast to Moses, offered not only true understanding of the Law but also the power to fulfill its demands. The old law had been external, written on stone; the new was imprinted on the heart by the Spirit. The sign of the Abrahamic covenant had been external; the sign of the New Testament, sealed by the blood of Christ, was internal, a circumcised heart. "For this reason it is also called a new spiritual law and worthier than the old, because just as spirit is worthier than body, and Christ more than Moses, so also is the new law superior to the old because the old was only a shadow and not the light."[57]

Christ had, therefore, revealed the "third lineage of descent"—that of the spiritual heirs of Abraham. These had been prefigured in the Old Testament, "the spiritual through the bodily." The Christian spiritual realm marked the third and highest stage in God's dealings with humankind. In the first stage, God had guided humankind through general and natural law; during the second, He had led the chosen people of Israel through Mosaic law; during the third, He guided the followers of Christ through the law of the Spirit. The new covenant given through Christ superseded the previous covenants because the new covenant of the Spirit made possible the attainment of a new order with greater perfection through the "true righteousness" revealed in Christ.[58]

Christ's Princely-Priestly Office

Having established the superiority of the new covenant, Adler attempted to demonstrate that in the "eternal principality of Jesus Christ" authority was wielded in a different manner than in the world or among Jews.[59] Drawing heavily on the book of Hebrews, especially Chapter 5, Adler argued that Christ's office of prince-priest, according to the order of Melchizedek, was qualitatively different and superior to all temporal authority. At the same time, Adler tried to show how Christ's high priestly office, which superseded the priestly lineage of Aaron, made the sacerdotalism and sacramentalism of the papal church redundant. In fact, the bulk of Adler's treatise discussed in detail Christ's high priestly office and the new covenant initiated by him and through him. The subtitles indicate the thrust of the argument.

1. The kingdom of Christ is spiritual, not worldly
2. Christ is not only king but also priest
3. Christ changed the temporal principality and priesthood into a spiritual one
4. The anointing of Christ Jesus over Judah and Israel
5. Concerning Mount Zion (as the Christian congregation (*Gemein*) in which Jews and Christians become one)
6. The kingdom of peace
7. Christ the king of peace
8. Christ the king of justice
9. Concerning the priesthood of Christ and its office
10. Christ's teachings
11. Christ the shepherd
12. Christ's sacrifice
13. Christ's prayer
14. Christ's burial
15. Christ's ascension

Unique in Anabaptist literature is Adler's exegesis of aspects of Mosaic ceremonial law, particularly its priestly office as fulfilled in Christ. Topics covered included the sacrifice of the high priest (according to the order of Aaron and Levi); the high priestly prayer or priestly intercession; the role of teaching or instruction; the temple built by Solomon as foreshadowing the Church of Christ; and the Sabbath.

Most likely none of this was original with Adler. His interpretation of the Old Testament certainly demonstrated familiarity with medieval allegorical and typological exegesis, allowing him to go beyond a literal historic understanding of Old Testament texts to their spiritual meaning. Accordingly, the daily sacrifice of the Old Testament foreshadowed the Christian's daily mortification of the flesh. The tabernacle or the temple as God's abode prefigured God's presence in the Christian's heart. The commandments preserved on tablets of stone in the Ark of the Covenant signified the law written in the heart and sealed by the Spirit. The manna stored in the Ark signified Christ, the "true bread," come from heaven to feed the inner spiritual man. The green rod of Aaron symbolized the Word of God which punishes sin in the congregation and identifies false prophets. The twelve show-breads, also signified by the twelve baskets of bread left over after the feeding of the five thousand, represented the "bread crumbs" or the "many pieces of the whole Scripture," which had been "carried together by the twelve apostles [*Bodten*] into the Twelve Articles [the Apostolic Creed] of the Christian Faith."[60] Therefore, feeding on Christ, the Word of God, and heavenly manna, by inference involved not only meditation on the Scriptures, but also contemplation of the Twelve Articles of the Christian Faith.[61]

Adler closed his *Judgment* with a prayer on "rightly keeping the Sabbath." He distinguished three types of Sabbath: literal, spiritual, and eternal. The eternal one prefigured in the year of Jubilee and seemed to await an eschatological, spiritual Sabbath. Presumably this would be a period when all would be taught directly by the Spirit. With other contemporaries Adler appears to have shared the expectations of an end-time conversion of the Jews. According to this scenario, Jews and Christians would be gathered into a united people "through the Word of God in the faith of Abraham and Christ."[62]

Curiously, a similar eschatological spiritualism appears to have inspired the sabbatarianism of Glaidt and Fischer. By 1530–31 Glaidt had turned to this subject, and both Glaidt and Fischer indicated a special interest in the Law of Moses and in Christ's high priestly office.[63] But Fischer, on the basis of eschatology and the equal authority of the two Testaments, went on to make Sabbath observation and circumcision obligatory for all true Christians, whereas Adler did not. Indeed, Adler's distinction between Old and New Testaments recalled Schwenckfeld's statements on the subject. According to Schwenckfeld, Glaidt, along with Jews and "chiliasts," awaited a temporal kingdom.[64] And although such polemical charges must be taken with a grain of salt, Schwenckfeld's differentiation between Old and New Testaments is most informative.

The Old had an external, bodily mediator, namely Moses; an external priesthood; external anointing; an external kingdom; an external sword; law and court. The New, however, has an inner, spiritual mediator, namely the man Jesus Christ. Christ has an inner kingdom and priesthood which he founded in justice, peace and joy in the spirit. He has an inner sword that cuts out the evil desires of the heart, divides and separates all that turns away from God. [He has] the sword of the Spirit, which is God's Word.

In the Old Testament there was a bodily authority which was part of the testament [covenant] and enforced the law of Moses with all that belonged to it, and served as a figure of God's dealings [with men]. In the New Testament there is a spiritual, divine authority, namely our Lord Jesus Christ. . . . He rules, protects, defends and represents his people and his doctrine (that is, the word of the cross and the Gospel of God in the Holy Spirit).[65]

Although Schwenckfeld penned these words with Glaidt in mind two or more years after Adler wrote the *Judgment,* his statement provided the context for a debate in Silesia which no doubt influenced Adler. Schwenckfeld argued that as far as "the outer man" was concerned, the Christian remained subject to temporal authority, but that temporal authority had no role in spiritual matters, although magistrates could belong to Christ's kingdom. "The worldly order," ordained by God for "temporal things," needed to be clearly distinguished from the spiritual regiment or kingdom of Christ.

Schwenckfeld's statements on the differences between the two Testaments and his insistence on a clear differentiation between the temporal and spiritual realms were similar to Adler's distinctions. Yet unlike Schwenckfeld's spiritualism, ultimately premised on a dualism of matter and spirit, Adler's New Testamentism was grounded in a theology of history. Adler rejected the use of the sword by Christians on the basis of three lineages of descent and three separate realms born at different stages of history, coexisting but qualitatively different. The sword was, above all, a Gentile institution ordained by God to keep law and order among the unredeemed. With time, tyrants usurped the power to wield the sword and establish princely and royal governments. Princely government was, by its very nature, a Gentile, non-Jewish, non-Christian institution. God had granted this Gentile institution to Israel only because the people of Israel lusted after it. He subsequently removed the temporal scepter from Judah and Israel to bring Abraham's descendants back to His original purpose, where He alone would be their Lord. Yet Jews, like Christians, were expected to pay tribute to Caesar.[66]

In the Christian realm, there would be neither force nor coercion. The Word of God was to be the sole instrument of discipline and persuasion.

The spiritual kingdom which is the Christian congregation [*Gemein*] cannot have a bodily king or stranger as hereditary lord, but only a spiritual one, who is Christ

Jesus alone, the living Son of God, our Lord. Since, however, the Lord and his kingdom are spiritual, how can the [spiritual] sword which is the Word of God, be temporal [*leiblich*] and kill? He who attempts to rule by force in this kingdom attempts to drive Christ out of His kingdom. But he who opposes Christ is an antichrist and will be consumed and destroyed by Christ through the word of His mouth at His coming.[67]

Adler's position was, therefore, decidedly that of a staff bearer. In short, the sword, ordained to punish evil, had no place among Christians. It belonged to the world or to the Jews. Capital punishment had been, at best, an Old Testament ordinance. The New Testament outlined a new ethic and a new order. Moses, the servant and the letter of the law, had been superseded by the son, the freedom of the spirit, and fraternal love. Christ, the prince of peace, according to the order of Melchizedek, the priest and king of Salem, had come to establish a spiritual, not a temporal, kingdom. "A spiritual kingdom could not wield a temporal sword."[68] Adler, therefore, clearly rejected the magisterial reform option or any aspiration for a territorial form of Anabaptism.

But how did this spiritual emphasis correspond with concrete aspirations to build communities? One possible explanation is that Adler conceived Anabaptist communities in traditional monastic elitist terms as islands within a larger society of nominal Christians. To be a true follower of Christ was a vocational calling to be *in* the world but not *of* it. New was the recruitment of the spiritual elite from among persons carrying on family and ordinary occupations. In a remarkable way, then, Adler integrated the Anabaptist message with a unique spiritualism. His views on the oath, baptism, and community of goods illustrate this point further.

Adler wrote that members of the spiritual realm and true followers of Christ could not swear in matters pertaining to civil-temporal affairs.[69] The only oaths permissible in the spiritual realm were those in the form of personal vows or promises to God, for example, the vows of baptism and marriage. Baptism with water was the outer sign of a covenant and pact, a promise in the name of the Father, Son, and Holy Spirit to live in accordance with God's will. It constituted a holy oath. By inference, baptism was for adults, not for children. Jesus' order not to swear applied to all civil oaths. It seems, then, as if Adler claimed traditional clerical exemptions and privileges for the Anabaptists.

Reminiscent of traditional claims on behalf of a spiritual estate seem statements in the section entitled "Judgment concerning temporal goods." Here Adler combined advocacy of community of goods with an argument that Christians should not take each other to court in matters relating to property or temporal things (*zeitliche ding*). Community of goods would further this end by eliminating litigation concerned with private property. He believed that true followers of Christ "do not quarrel, nor go to war, nor go to law, yea, none of them harm anyone in all Mount Zion."[70] It was their duty to abstain from revenge when wronged, "For a Christian must become conformed unto Christ, the lamb of God, in humility. He must also pick up his cross and follow Christ. Thus the lamb of God has been put to death from the beginning and is still daily being put to death."[71]

Among followers of Christ, therefore, a different attitude toward material possessions prevailed: an unselfish, mutual-aid ethic of sharing.

Among genuine Christians all possessions are common. None should seek sole ownership of property. Each should contribute according to his ability to the needs of the poor brothers or sisters. Where such [sharing] is not found among brothers and Christians, there is no genuine Christianity [*Christenheit*].[72]

True believers who treated material possessions with *Gelassenheit* and shared them with one another in fraternal love would have no need to take each other to court. A brother who failed to share offended the entire congregation. If wronged by outsiders, the brother should rather suffer injustice. To seek judgment in the courts of unbelievers concerned with temporal goods would mean submission to the judgment of a lower estate or realm. Members of Christ's kingdom needed to be mindful that God had chosen them to some day judge not only the world but even the angels. Should disputes regarding temporal goods arise in the Christian congregation, Adler counseled that the poorest and the least in the congregation, the "cast outs and unworthy," should be chosen to arbitrate the dispute to the "shame and embarrassment" of the entire congregation.

Adler's statements on community of possessions recall the instructions of the earliest Anabaptist church order and the practices of the earliest communities in Moravia, especially the Austerlitz Brethren, the Philipites, and the Gabrielites. They too advocated community of goods but did so without resorting to legalism or abolishing all households, private property, or inequalities. Above all, these communities were interested in establishing their separation and relative independence from the world. Paradoxically, this could be done only under the protection and tolerance of local lords. It is possible that Adler's treatise was addressed to potential noble patrons in Silesia or Moravia. His *Judgment* was one of the most substantial apologies for early Anabaptism in this region. A remarkably integrated statement, the *Judgment* had much in common with other early works that defied neat distinctions between Anabaptism and spiritualism[73] and seems reminiscent of the piety of the Silesian Anabaptists led by Gabriel Ascherham.

Gabrielite Leadership

Numerically the Gabrielites constituted the largest group of communitarians in the early Anabaptist settlements of Moravia. Gabriel Ascherham led not only a sizable community at Rossitz but, for a brief period, presided also as bishop over the associated communities of Philipites and proto-Hutterites at Auspitz. After the schism of 1533 (see Chapter 9), Jacob Hutter and his group went their own way while Gabriel continued to lead his community, consisting predominantly of Silesians.[74] These Gabrielites remained in fellowship with the Philipites until both were driven from their respective settlements in Rossitz and Auspitz in 1535.

Gabriel's chronicle of the beginnings of Anabaptism in Moravia from 1528 to 1541 is now lost,[75] and only one treatise from his pen has survived.

Gabriel Ascherham

Johann Loserth considered Gabriel "one of the most original figures among the separatists in Moravia" and used his surviving treatise as a model text for students of early-modern German paleography.[76] The semipopular studies by Wilhelm Wiswedel, published in the 1930s, are anachronistic and in need of correction at a number of points.[77]

Gabriel Ascherham, known also as Gabriel Kirschner or Kürschner because he was a furrier by occupation, was the son of Nuremberg furrier Paul Aschermann.[78] The name Aschermann became Ascherham in Hutterite codices and in Anabaptist studies. To avoid confusion the now familiar name of Ascherham has been retained, but since his followers became known as Gabrielites, it may be best to use Gabriel.

Nothing is known of Gabriel's childhood or education, but his excellent linguistic skills suggest at least an elementary education in one of Nuremberg's schools. At some point he learned his father's trade.

It is not clear when Gabriel became involved in the religious controversy of his day or how he made contact with Anabaptists. It is pure speculation that he may have been one of Hans Denck's students at St. Sebald in 1524–25. But if Gabriel was still in Nuremberg two years later he must have known about the execution of Wolfgang Vogel on March 26, 1527.[79] Gabriel later defended himself against accusations that he had been imprisoned in Nuremberg and recanted his faith, although this reference may have been to a later incident involving his expulsion from Nuremberg in 1535 (see Chapter 12). Claims in the older scholarship that Gabriel accompanied Hans Hut on a missionary journey to Silesia as early as 1526 or 1527 have not been substantiated.[80] *The Chronicle* stated tersely that Gabriel, a furrier born in Nuremberg, went to Silesia, taught and gathered a *Volk* there, and led them with him to Rossitz in Moravia.[81] After sifting through numerous Hutterite codices, Joseph Beck speculated that Gabriel had been won initially to Swiss Anabaptism, was appointed a shepherd, and was excluded before he became "the founder of independent congregations in Silesia."[82] Beck failed to give sources for these claims and most likely confused an account according to which Gabriel had problems with a Swiss in his community (see Chapter 4). Nevertheless, as noted in Chapter 3, Swiss Anabaptists took refuge in Moravia no later than 1528, and it is possible that Gabriel was associated with them.

The first mention of Gabriel in Hutterite sources placed him at Schärding on the Bavarian-Austrian border, not far from Passau.[83] On August 16, 1527, Leonhard Kaiser (Käser) was burned at Schärding; *The Chronicle* recorded his martyrdom beside that of Michael Sattler and Jörg Blaurock.[84] According to the account, a flower Kaiser kept in his hand refused to burn, the ordeal of fire thus proving him to have been innocent and truthful. Apparently the local magistrate responsible for his death suffered such pangs of conscience that he resigned and moved away. If Gabriel resided in Schärding then, he would have been affected by Kaiser's death and the events that followed. Early in 1528 thirty-five Anabaptists were arrested in nearby Passau, among them a Gabriel from Nuremberg, whose occupation was recorded as belt cutter (*Riemenschneider*), an occupation that would have obvious connections to furriers, tanners, and others in the leather trade. This Gabriel had been baptized by Wolfgang Schernegker from Burghausen,[85] who was none other than Wolfgang Brandhuber, schoolmaster from Burghausen. As noted in Chapter 3, because of a timely visit to Bohemia Brandhuber escaped the arrests in Passau and later settled in Linz.[86] Here he set up a model Anabaptist household in which all things were shared.

Curiously, the name of Gabriel does not appear among the recanters or those executed at Passau. If this Gabriel was Gabriel Ascherham, then we have found Gabriel's early link to Anabaptism. It was a link that connected him through Brandhuber with a movement that extended through Bavaria, Upper Austria, and Moravia to Hut's circle. Gabriel himself appears to have embraced a form of community of goods along lines similar to those practiced by Brandhuber in Linz. But he had been won to a heterogeneous movement, and it would be wrong to infer too much about his early Anabaptist beliefs from his having been a convert of Brandhuber. As noted in Chapter 3, Hutian and Swiss influences mingled in these territories with indigenous forms of sacramentarianism and spiritualism. Hans Bünderlin of Linz and Leonhard and Christoph Freisleben belonged to early Austrian Anabaptism. And as the Nicolsburg schism of 1527–28 illustrates, different orientations existed. It is possible that Gabriel's own orientation was from the beginning latently spiritualist, and it would be wrong to assume that the apparent spiritualism of his only surviving treatise marks a later deviation from an original Swiss New Testamentism.

Suppression most likely drove Gabriel from the Schärding-Passau area. Like others before him, he must have taken the road to Nicolsburg. From there, perhaps through contacts with Glaidt, Fischer, and Adler, he made his way to Silesia, where he unfolded a most successful ministry, winning many converts to Anabaptism. A hostile Silesian source alleged that Gabriel and Jacob Hutter led as many as two thousand persons from Silesia to Moravia.

These two leaders [Ascherham and Jacob Hutter], especially Gabriel, sent several of their assistants who led great numbers of people, after they sold their goods and left their dwellings, out of Silesia. They led them to Moravia as if it were the promised land. One group had over 2,000 people together; the larger number of these was from our fatherland Silesia. They had given up their belongings [property] for little money, collecting over 7,000 gulden, which they made available to Gabriel and his assistants as into faithful hands.[87]

The author of this 1535 report presumably meant that both communities—Gabrielites and Hutterites—contained Silesians by that time but that the greater share of these joined Gabriel, who established a community on the Estate of Bohunda of Pernstein at Rossitz.[88] Despite the large common fund, members of Gabriel's community eked out a living by hard, manual labor.[89] Yet the community grew rapidly over the next few years to an estimated twelve hundred adults.[90] From its inception in 1528 Gabriel's community represented an alternative community to that founded in Austerlitz during the same year.

In addition to Silesians, refugees from Swabia, the Palatinate, and Hesse eventually joined Gabriel. Among them were Philip Plener and his band. As noted in Chapter 4, Philip and his group left Rossitz to establish another community at Auspitz in 1529–30. Within a year they were joined by Austerlitz secessionists, led by Wilhelm Reublin and Jörg Zaunring. By mutual agreement among the leaders Gabriel was recognized as overall bishop (*Oberhirte*). This agreement would rupture during the major schism of 1533 which led to the founding of the Hutterites as a distinct group (see Chapter 9). But until that time, the three communities—Gabrielites, Philipites, and proto-Hutterites—lived in harmony, suggesting a similarity in practice and organization, if not teaching.

Evidence indicates that community life at Rossitz was similar to that of the Brethren at Austerlitz. Although no Gabrielite congregational order has survived, it is clear that Gabriel and his followers practiced a voluntary form of community of goods with a common treasury. Members of the community were divided into a number of households (*Haushaben*) led by deacons and elders. Gabriel, as recognized servant of the Word, was assisted by a number of itinerant apostles who continued to lead new converts to Rossitz from the mission fields. By inference it may be assumed that the appointment of the leaders involved consultation with the larger congregation as well as the drawing of lots.[91] The community quickly developed certain rituals and practices that involved, besides baptism and celebration of the Lord's Supper, weekly admonition services, greeting each other with the "brotherly kiss," banning as a disciplinary measure, and refusing to pay war taxes. These practices were given their ideological rationale by Gabriel who apparently also composed songs, carried on correspondence, wrote theological treatises, and kept a chronicle.[92] Only a fragment of this material has survived, including a letter reconstructed from a hostile Hutterite reply[93] and, thanks to Jesuit polemicist Christoph A. Fischer, a brief entry from Gabriel's chronicle. This leaves Gabriel's *On the Distinction between Divine and Human Wisdom* (hereafter the *Distinction*)[94] as the primary source from which to reconstruct his ideas. The *Distinction* covered a number of topics including an admonition to authority (*Obrigkeit*)[95] and discussions of the Lord's Supper[96] and baptism, which will be covered more fully in Chapter 12. The distinction between divine and human wisdom, which is of interest here, underlay the core for Gabriel's theology and piety. It is unique to early Anabaptist thought and was foundational to his plea for religious tolerance.

The Distinction

In its present form, the *Distinction* contains two introductions. The first, written by Gabriel himself, identified him as "servant of the Christian congregation" and as author.[97] Since he died in 1545, the introduction must have been written in 1544–45 at the latest. But some parts of the treatise may have been older. His discussion of the Lord's Supper, for instance, had its own introduction to all "good-hearted lovers of the truth" (*Gutherzigen Liebhabern der Wahrheit*), a form of address used also by Bernhard Rothmann, Pilgram Marpeck, and Caspar Schwenckfeld. Gabriel signed as "the least among the brethren and as nothing in the kingdom of heaven." A second major introduction, the work of "servants and assistants [*Mitgehilfen*] of the Christian congregation in Silesia and Moravia," indicated that the treatise was intended for circulation among the dispersed Gabrielites. It was presumably written in 1548, the date found on the codex, and suggests that the Gabrielites were still an identifiable group at that date and were distinct from four other groups: the sword bearers, the Austerlitz Brethren, the Swiss, and the Hutterites.[98]

The major theme of the *Distinction* concerned the differentiation between mere human or natural understanding versus that of the spiritual or divine. The two kinds of understanding separated those "sanctified through the spirit of divine discernment" (*Erkenntnis*) from those whose discernment remained literally elementary and preoccupied with temporal things. Central to this distinction was the quest for the nature of true faith. It was a quest that preoccupied a number of radical reformers, beginning with Thomas Müntzer, and had been of import in the discussions that led to the rejection of pedobaptism and the introduction of believers' baptism. Gabriel argued clearly that true saving faith was the work of the Spirit, but he defined such a faith as spiritual discernment and understanding.

Throughout his work, Gabriel engaged in hypothetical dialogues with Lutherans or fellow Anabaptists who failed to grasp the difference between divine and human discernment and were therefore unable to distinguish between true and false faith.[99] Among the Anabaptists, the followers of his erstwhile ally and then rival, Jacob Hutter, were most likely the main target of criticism, which echoed positions taken in the 1530s by spiritualists such as Christian Entfelder, Hans Bünderlin, and Schwenckfeld and had been opposed by Pilgram Marpeck (see Chapter 6). Gabriel sought an integration between subjective spiritualism that denied the need of externals[100] and a materialism that substituted ordinances and regulations for spirituality. According to Gabriel the "internal house of understanding" had to be set in order first. The external order would then follow naturally and unforcedly. Only divine discernment and wisdom would lead to the edification of Christ's body; mere human wisdom was responsible for its dismemberment.

Underwriting the differentiation between human and divine understanding and how these were attained was a scholastic distinction between two ordained orders: one natural, corporal, and created, the other spiritual and redemptive.[101] These orders entailed two kinds of perceptions: one natural, the other spiritual. Although all understanding of either order depended ultimately on God, a natural understanding of the corporal, created order was possible through sense perception; but even then, a true understanding that penetrated beyond appearances was possible only through the Spirit, present in all men as "a spark or a glowing wick."[102] In other words, the spiritual essence and meaning of the external world could be grasped only with the aid of divine illumination. All understanding that remained preoccupied with temporal things was bound to be superficial and incomplete. It followed that even in terms of the created order of things a mere natural understanding failed to grasp its divinely ordained purpose.

The ordained, redemptive, spiritual order could be understood only by the spiritual heirs of Abraham, that is, the heirs of the "special promise" or beneficiaries of the redemptive order brought by Christ. True divine understanding, unlike mere human understanding, was the work of the Spirit. Divine understanding and with it true faith were therefore the gifts of the Spirit.

Gabriel used the analogy of Hagar and Sarah to underline the contrast between human and divine understanding, between natural and special revelation, between once born and reborn, servants and children.

> It follows that all human wisdom is from God, and such wisdom is of God's Spirit. All men therefore have God's Spirit, but not all have the promised Spirit . . . which gives birth to sonship [and makes one] part of the kingdom of Christ.
>
> The Spirit of human wisdom gives birth to servanthood. These are the children of the temporal, namely Hagar. The children of divine wisdom are the legitimate ones and are accounted to Sarah.
>
> Human wisdom is inherited [*angeborne*] by all humans through a divine nature. Divine wisdom or the wisdom of the children of God, however, is received with the Spirit of promise through the new birth.[103]

Gabriel's chief concern, then, was with the nature of true faith, defined as spiritual understanding, and he focused on the epistemological problem of the reliability of spiritual truth claims and their origin. He retained an Augustinian-realist epistemology, which means that his distinction between natural-human and spiritual-divine wisdom was supported by a metaphysical, dualistic cosmology that postulated a physical and spiritual realm. Man's earthly abode stood in contrast with the superior heavenly dwelling place of spiritual beings and the divine.

> The wisdom of the children of God is heavenly, but the wisdom of the children of men is earthly. Both are from God because he is God of heaven and of earth; but just as heavenly things are superior to earthly things so is the wisdom of the children of God superior to the wisdom of the children of men. The children of men are made on earth and take their life out of water, fire, and light. Natural wisdom and natural reason are kindled in men by the planets, who are gods of the visible heaven, ordained by God so that men perceive the unity of all things which God has created for man's sake. But this wisdom serves only the earthly life because it is gleaned from the earthly heaven. God has commanded the gods of this heaven to remain in their order. And their time is in God's hands.[104]

Human understanding, therefore, could embrace only the created order of things, which, sustained by "the gods of the earthly heaven," would come to an end. An understanding of this passing reality remained merely an elementary wisdom (*elementische Weisheit*).

By way of contrast, divine wisdom, an essential understanding of spiritual-eternal things, originated in "the third [or] invisible heaven." It could come only through Christ because "no one ascended into heaven, except the son of man, who is from Heaven." Such understanding did not come through the senses but through being "raptured in the spirit" (*mit*

ihrem Gemüt entzückt), through being one with the mind of Christ"
(2 Corinthians 12). "Now the person that is one man, one body, one Spirit
with Christ, yes a son of God, will surely have his dwelling in heaven. As
Paul says: 'If you are then risen with Christ, seek that which is above.' "[105]
The manifest medieval assumption was that the knower had to be of at
least equal status to the thing to be known. A lesser could not know or
understand the greater. God revealed himself through Christ and could be
known only through Christ.

It is in its Christocentricism that Gabriel's epistemological concerns in-
tersected with Reformation soteriology. Gabriel accepted Luther's axiom
that man was justified by faith alone, but he defined faith as a spiritual,
cognitive gift or quality. Faith meant "to know him, whom to know is life
eternal." Although Gabriel did not develop an explicit Christology, his
emphasis, like that of Schwenckfeld and the spiritualists, leaned in a docetic direction, emphasizing the divine or spiritual nature of Christ.[106] Soteriological knowledge was by its very nature ontological and metaphysical. It originated in the spiritual union of the knower and the known.
Divine understanding, made possible through participation in the divine
nature of Christ, involved death to the creaturely self and a spiritual rebirth or resurrection to newness of life. It meant a literal becoming righteous or a being "made pious" (*fromm*).[107] With the majority of radical
reformers, Gabriel shared a concern that justifying faith involved more
than a mental state. It had to bring a real ontological change and express
itself in the life of the believer.

But how was true, justifying faith obtained? According to Gabriel, faith
could not be mediated through externals. "Faith with cognition [*Erkenntnis*] in the Holy Spirit is an inner working [*innerlich Wirkung*] from the
inside out. . . . As Christ says, the kingdom consists not in external man-
ners [*Gebarden*] but it is inward, in you" (Luke 17).[108] Gabriel shared this
emphasis on the inner with a number of other early Anabaptist leaders
including Glaidt, Adler, Schiemer, and Denck.[109] In words reminiscent of
Thomas Müntzer and Hans Hut, he argued that true faith began as a work
of the Spirit with the "pure and childlike fear of God."[110] As fear of God
increased, fear of man and of the creaturely diminished. But fear of
God included the "fear lest one neglect love of one's neighbor." True faith
was coupled to love. Gabriel described the preparation for the arrival of
faith and love in terms of

standing [before] the creator and savior totally free and *gelassen* without appropriating anything of one's own [*ihm selber nichts eignet*]; but to wait for the
promised childlike spirit through the grace and mercy of God, just as the apostles,
including those gathered with them at Jerusalem, waited in foresakenness [*Ver-
lassenheit*] upon the day of Pentecost.[111]

Because of Pentecost, the apostolic church had been a church of the spiritually illuminated and regenerate. Gabriel implied that subsequently a fall from divine to human wisdom had taken place and that in his own day the true church should be restored to its pristine spirituality. This renewed spiritual church would be a purified church, separated from the unregenerate "whores, thieves, robbers, liars, the proud, the stingy or those who sought their own gain [*eigenütizig*]." Gabriel's spiritualism, which distinguished between servants and children, between nominal and true Christians, supported separation from the ungodly, unspiritual, and unregenerate, and the establishment of a community of the regenerate.

His advocacy of believers' baptism must be seen in this context. Commenting on the controversy about whether children could have true faith, a prerequisite to baptism, Gabriel sought a mediating position. He wrote,

Now they want to attribute faith to minors, to children that cannot yet speak. By means of such immature faith they want to make children worthy of baptism; because one cannot receive baptism without faith. However, there are some who do not permit the minors any faith, yet do not want to reject Paul's saying, that without faith no one can please God.[112]

In other words, Gabriel implied that children were pleasing to God and therefore part of Christ's kingdom, but his description of faith as a spiritual cognitive quality supported the idea of baptism after the age of cognizance (see Chapter 12). Regarding baptism, Gabriel believed both the Lutheran and Hutterite views were wrong. But the polemical point of his spiritualism was directed primarily against the learned scribes who, because of their schooling, claimed a monopoly on the interpretation of the Scriptures. According to Gabriel, the Scriptures were sacred only in the context of the sanctified community. They could be understood only within the community of regenerates and spiritually endowed.

Therefore I ask you, you learned scribe, why is the biblical Scripture called a sacred scripture? Is it not because the Scriptures are separated and sanctified [*ausgesondert und geheiligt*]? Outside the Christian community the Scriptures cannot be holy. If they are not read by the sacred they are not understood. Because the sacred is understood and known only by the sacred.[113]

Since like could be known only by like, spiritual things were known only by those "anointed and sealed by the Spirit." Those who interpreted and preached without being anointed preached not the Word but the letter. They were comparable to Simon, the sorcerer (Acts 8), interested in the Scriptures only because they promised power and profits.

This is how it is now; the rich of this world send their children to the upper schools so that they [may] study and become knowledgeable in the Scriptures. Having received instructions in the letter, they go and make a business of it. They negotiate with people for a salary and sell continuously what they have bought for money, namely the letter.[114]

Such hirelings could never be true shepherds. As custodians and transmitters of human wisdom dealing in the dead letter, they had been the primary cause of the Church's corruption. But Gabriel did not stop with the criticism of the educated elite; he reserved his harshest criticism for unlearned literalists who considered their ignorance bliss and a primary qualification for understanding the Scriptures. These "peasants, cobblers, tailors and furriers . . . assumed that they had received a special revelation when they discovered something in the Scriptures not preserved or practiced by others." They considered themselves qualified for the apostolic office simply because they shared the same humble social origins of the first apostles. Directed against fellow Anabaptists, this criticism provided testimony about the antilearned prejudice in some Anabaptist circles expressed in the slogan *die Gelehrten die Verkehrten* or *gelehrter je verkehrter*. Presumably Gabriel's criticism was directed against the Hutterites. He had harsh words for those who "ran" to other Anabaptists "with great commotion [*Dröhnen*] proclaiming: you can't be saved with your property. You must sell it and leave it and move under the cross because without suffering and misery you cannot be saved!"[115] Not that Gabriel was against community of goods. His reproach was directed against what he considered a new legalism that made external conformity, rather than oneness in the Spirit, the organizational principle of community. Such legalism disturbed the tranquility of the brotherhood and created discontent.[116] Uniformity of practice, he insisted, should grow voluntarily out of oneness in spirit and *Gelassenheit* toward material things. It should not be solicited and extorted as a mandatory sacrifice. Community and fellowship (*Gemeinschaft*) were to be a spontaneous and voluntary outgrowth of the Spirit's inner moving in the heart (*Gemüt*).

Such was the case in the first church at Jerusalem; for the apostles had not preached anything about community of goods nor ordered any one to keep it. But as the Gospel was preached to them concerning the kingdom of God and Christ, those who believed received the same [kingdom] visibly, that is the Holy Spirit. He made them joyful and assured their hearts with heavenly blessings, so that they counted temporal property nothing in their relationship to their neighbor. Willingly of their own, without being told, solely out of the joy of the heart, they went and sold their property and brought the money and laid it at the feet of the apostles. And they gave to everyone according to their need. They began community of goods without being told, everyone gave out of his [own free will]. Community of goods, then, was an open witness of the kingdom of God that had already come to them. It was not something commanded by men for the sake of the kingdom of God.[117]

Gabriel contrasted this spontaneous apostolic congregation born out of joy and love in the Spirit with the community created and enforced by some in his own time. The coerced form of community of goods practiced by this group, presumably the Hutterites, violated the spirit of apostolic practice and amounted to a new form of simony.

Because now persons already accepted as brothers and Christians are admonished with special pleading to [practice] community of goods and are urged to give up their possessions with a heavy heart so that they might gain the kingdom of Christ. They are, therefore, not motivated to hold community of goods out of love by the Holy Spirit, but are urged to buy the kingdom of God by simony. And when they have given their property away with a heavy heart, they are [supposed to be] assured that they are God's children. Oh, the poor assurance that comes through elementary creatures [*elementische Kreaturen*], in that one seeks to buy the grace of God through money.

I tell you, if you can be saved only through community of goods, then you will never be saved. For salvation does not lie in good works but in the grace of God. And he who is blessed [*selig*] in him the [desire for] community of goods is uncoerced [*ungeheissen*]. It cannot be hidden because the heavenly mind [*Gemüt*] determines [*wirkt*] the temporal and natural one. Thus the whole human being, inner and outer, is one [*gemein*] with all that is its own.[118]

The citation above indicates that Gabriel advocated voluntary sharing and community of goods, a practice that had a spontaneous generation in early Anabaptism. It was presumably similar to the household sharing practiced by Brandhuber in Linz, only on a larger scale. From Gabriel's perspective, Hutterites were innovators and deviants from the voluntary original practice. By making community of goods mandatory, Hutter and his supporters had regressed from the freedom of the spirit to materialist bondage.

Gabriel criticized Hutterites also for making too much of their martyred leaders, especially of Hutter. By comparing him with Christ who, as "the true shepherd," had given his life for the sheep, they subtracted from the uniqueness of Christ's vicarious death, which alone made satisfaction for sins [*Genugtuung für die Sünde*]. The death of a mere mortal could have no such vicarious qualities, otherwise mortality would become the foundation of immortality. In what seems to be a dialogue with the ghost of his martyred rival, Gabriel wrote,

I know that you can answer hypocritically with the words: "I know well that I can save no one with my death. If, however, I seal with my blood what I have preached, then they [the brethren] are all the more comforted and assured." With such [words] you reveal clearly that your mission [*Sendung*] is not of God and that you did not receive the Spirit of promise; [indeed] you never tasted it. It is also revealed that you have neither scriptural nor spiritual understanding, and that those to whom you preached do not have the seal of promise, that is the Holy Spirit.[119]

According to Gabriel, Hutter and his supporters had fallen into a new bondage to literalism and legalism which resulted in fragmentation. Where once there had been unity of spirit, there now existed divisions. Where once there had been spontaneity, joy, love, and sharing in the spirit, there now were rules and regulations and coerced consciences. Reflecting on the state of affairs in the early 1540s, Gabriel was reminded of the tower of Babel. Selfish interests rather than spiritual priorities and God's honor had come to dominate the Anabaptist attempts at community building. Therefore, God had sent confusion, schism, and dispersion.

As they dispersed, however, every group [Volk] sought its own land. Every group wanted to have its own separate features, insisting on being the [only] true Christians. For these reasons they persecuted each other. Each group wanted to prove itself the [true] Christendom; some with Scripture, some with signs and wonders, some with suffering and death.[120]

These observations and Gabriel's dialogue with the ghost of Jacob Hutter gave evidence of the ongoing feud that had begun in 1533 and would continue for years (see Chapters 6, 9, and 12).

Before closing this chapter, some attention needs to be drawn to Gabriel's "Admonition to Authority," which shows some parallels to Adler's *Judgment Concerning the Sword*. Both use arguments of a spiritualist genre, but their focus is different. Adler developed an argument for Christian pacifism; Gabriel seemed more concerned with warning the authorities to exercise tolerance and permit pluralism. In that sense, his "Admonition" presents one of the finest sixteenth-century pleas for tolerance.[121] According to Gabriel, temporal authority should not seek to enforce true faith or eradicate error. Since faith was a matter of the heart and the work of the Spirit, it could not be imposed from outside by temporal means. Nevertheless, those wielding temporal authority could do so in a Christian manner on behalf of freedom of conscience. Gabriel grounded his plea for tolerance in a spiritualist eschatology reminiscent of Adler's *Judgment*. He alluded to three orders: one for the Gentiles, one for the Jews, and one for the Christians. Addressing Silesian, Moravian, and perhaps Polish lords as Christians, he argued that they could not appeal to precedent among Gentiles and that they had not been appointed "servants of wrath" in the Old Testament sense.

Should you seek to justify your role not from the [example] of the Gentiles but that of the Jews, that God has ordained you to [punish in matters of faith], then I say, "Christ has given his people a new commandment, also a new calling, that they should be children of peace and not servants of vengeance. God has forbidden them to eradicate evil [by means of force]."[122]

He interpreted the parable of the wheat and tares to mean that the two were to ripen together until divine judgment. The task of separating the wheat from the tares was to be left to angels, that is, divine agents, rather than to temporal authority. He dismissed fears that plurality of sects would jeopardize public order, saying that although unity of religion was desirable, consensus in true faith could come only through the work of the Spirit. Capital punishment for religious errors was to be rejected because God, the giver of life, was Himself patient with those in error. To kill a person for religious error meant interference in the divinely appointed time of grace permitted that person.[123] Only when religious error was advanced by force were temporal authorities justified to take defensive countermeasures. Gabriel testified to the peaceful intentions of the Anabaptists and considered their persecution entirely unjustified. Although he lamented internal schisms, he believed that these were also evidence of a spiritual awakening and a "hungering" for the "heavenly bread."[124] Such an awakening was bound to be accompanied by "immature zealousness." It would be wrong and against the moving of the Spirit to impose uniformity of religion. Unique was Gabriel's irenic tone. No mention was made of "prophets of Baal" or the "tyranny of Pharaoh," epithets that appeared in the literature of other Anabaptist groups. Gabriel seemed to have a more positive attitude toward authority than the early Swiss or Hutterites. At least he considered it worthwhile to admonish the authorities to exercise restraint and toleration. Presumably he appreciated the patronage granted his people by Silesian, Moravian, or Polish lords. One thing seems certain: like Adler and others, Gabriel recognized that without the good will and protection of at least the lower echelons of local authority, Anabaptists would find no refuge. In this case, he reached beyond the self-interest of his own group. His "Admonition" was an unusual defense of religious pluralism and plea for toleration grounded in the conviction that the kingdom of Christ could not be advanced by coercion.

There is new evidence on the activity of Clemens Adler which provides a new context for his *Judgment Concerning the Sword,* the most comprehensive and important early Anabaptist statement on nonresistance. Adler's theology of history shared some themes with those of two other missionaries to Silesia: Oswald Glaidt and Gabriel Ascherham. All three were also members of communities in Moravia, with the largest that of the Gabrielites.

Gabriel Ascherham reappeared at a number of strategic points in the narrative of Anabaptist communitarianism. His unique synthesis of spiritualism and Anabaptism, when viewed in the broader context of the Silesian mission of Glaidt and Adler, appears as less of an aberration. It is possible to argue that a special Silesian strain of Anabaptism, with spiritualist presuppositions, had a pedigree that reaches back via Glaidt and Adler, and perhaps even Hans Bünderlin, Christian Entfelder, and Leonhard Schiemer, to early Upper Austrian Anabaptism and beyond. This spiritualist strain would ultimately take Gabriel and his followers in a direction different from that of their fellow Anabaptists.

Chapter Six

Marpeck's Early Controversy with the Spiritualists

Expanding the Context

In 1959 William Klassen identified two anonymous tracts entitled *A Clear Refutation* (hereafter the *Refutation*) and *A Clear and Useful Instruction* (hereafter the *Instruction*) as being the work of Pilgram Marpeck.[1] External and internal evidence seemed to support Marpeck's authorship.[2] Klassen recognized in the *Refutation* a reply to spiritualist Hans Bünderlin, and he believed that the *Instruction* recorded Marpeck's disagreements with Caspar Schwenckfeld.[3] Since the two booklets dated back to 1531, Klassen concluded that Marpeck and Schwenckfeld clashed in principle as early as 1530–31.[4] Previously, scholars had believed that Marpeck and the Silesian spiritualist separated only later and that Marpeck's principal opponent in Strasbourg was Martin Bucer.[5]

Klassen's arguments for Marpeck's authorship of the *Refutation* and the *Instruction* are uncontested. If anything, they have been strengthened by the identification of Cammerlander of Strasbourg as the printer of the two pamphlets.[6] But was the context for the early Marpeck-spiritualist debate limited to Strasbourg, and was Marpeck's main protagonist Schwenckfeld? In his study on Marpeck's Christology,[7] Neal Blough suggested that Schwenckfeld initially influenced Marpeck's emphasis on the incarnation and also on a differentiation between the Old and New Testaments. Blough therefore muted the early clash between Schwenckfeld and Marpeck. My own research supports the view that Marpeck would have found Schwenckfeld's views congenial in his debate with the Strasbourg reformers. Later, driven by the controversy with the spiritualists,

Marpeck made the first studied Anabaptist "effort at relating the Old and New Covenants."[8] This effort would eventually bear fruit in the impressive *Testamentserleuterung.*[9]

Recent findings support the view that Schwenckfeld was not the primary target of Marpeck's early pamphlets. Heinold Fast drew attention to the fact that Marpeck's motto of the *Instruction,* "Not what, but that" (*Nicht was, sondern das*),[10] represents a response to the motto "Not who, but what" (*Nicht wer, sondern was*), found in a 1530 pamphlet written by Christian Entfelder.[11] For clues to understanding Marpeck's motto, Fast pointed to another pamphlet, *How the Scripture Should Be Distinguished and Explained*[12] (hereafter *Scripture Distinguished*), which sported a similar motto, "What—that." This undated, anonymous tract had been attributed to Michael Sattler, but evidence now points to Marpeck and Leupold Scharnschlager.[13] The motto "What—that" in *Scripture Distinguished* was intended to illustrate the relationship of the Old to the New Testament. The texts, under the respective columns of "What" and "That" differentiated the temporal and the heavenly Adam, walking in the flesh and walking in the spirit. The motto implies an almost spiritualist distinction between the Old and New Testaments, the Law and the Gospel. The same motto contrasting human effort with the work of the Spirit is also found in the *Kunstbuch.*[14] Fast, however, interpreted the motto, "Not what, but that," as directed against the spiritualists. He believed that Marpeck intended the motto against preoccupations with spiritual essence and that he pointed to the incarnation as God's revelation to humankind; in other words, his intention was primarily Christological. Unlike Schwenckfeld, whose emphasis on the glorified, ascended Christ ran the risk of docetism, Marpeck focused on the human Christ in whose suffering all true followers were invited to participate.[15] As a visible extension of the incarnation, the true church kept the teachings and order of Christ—the ordinances instituted by Christ and the apostles. The contrast, "Not what, but that," was intended as a nominalist critique of spiritualist tendencies to view externals as mere accidentals. Ultimately then, Marpeck's motto was directed against those seeking to avoid persecution by declaring externals adiaphora.

In a brief comparison of Marpeck's 1531 *Instruction* with Entfelder's 1530 *On Many Divisions in the Faith* Blough concluded that Marpeck's main antagonists in 1531 were Entfelder and Bünderlin, not Schwenckfeld.[16] Stephen Boyd, in his recent biography of Marpeck, seconded Blough.[17] These historiographic developments enlarged the textual context of the early Marpeck-spiritualist debate. The question arises as to whether the geographic context should be expanded as well. After all, four participants in the Strasbourg dialogue, Marpeck, Bünderlin, Entfelder, and Schwenckfeld, arrived in Strasbourg from Moravia or Silesia.[18] Their stay in Strasbourg was brief, and their debate produced echoes in Moravia. Perhaps that should not be surprising, since Entfelder's publications explicitly addressed issues current in Moravia, and spiritualist tendencies were present among Moravian Anabaptists from the beginning.[19] Previous studies failed to appreciate this larger context and, with it perhaps, some of the issues addressed in Marpeck's early writings.

A Reexamination of Marpeck's Contacts with Moravia

The work of Boyd shed considerable light on Marpeck's social and family background.[20] Accordingly, Marpeck hailed from a wealthy patrician family that held "mining and grazing rights" in the jurisdiction of Kitzbühl. Marpeck's father had been the city and district magistrate of Rattenberg on the Lower Inn. Pilgram Marpeck himself was appointed mining magistrate by Ferdinand I, a position he lost in 1528 because he found himself at odds with Ferdinand's policy of suppression directed against the evangelical movement, particularly the Anabaptists. Early that year Ferdinand ordered the creation of secret councils to deal with "heresy" in his hereditary lands, in the Tyrol, as well as in the duchy of Württemberg. Strategically placed inquisitors were appointed, and in some districts an itinerant police force (*streifende Rott*) was created to hunt down the heretics. The seventy-one executions in Marpeck's home town alone attested to the effectiveness of Ferdinand's measures.[21] The vicious campaign of suppression (see Chapter 8) drove many Anabaptists from the Inn valley to Moravia or Bohemia, where Ferdinand's authority was mitigated by the strength of the local Estates (see Chapter 3). One group of refugees, many from the Lower Inn region, settled in the mining town of Bohemian Krumau (Cesky Krumlov).[22] Relieved of his duty as mining magistrate on January 28, 1528, Marpeck soon followed his compatriots into exile to Krumau.[23] Indirect evidence suggests that he left the Rattenberg area in February or March 1528, about the same time as his fellow citizens Sigmund Schützinger and Melchior Schlosser.[24] Later, Schlosser probably functioned as a contact between Marpeck and the Anabaptist community at Austerlitz.[25] Schützinger became an itinerant leader in Upper Austria and North Tyrol. He and Jacob Hutter, the leader in South Tyrol, sided with the group that broke away from the Austerlitz Brethren in early 1531 and founded a new community at Auspitz (see Chapter 9). Among this breakaway group were eighty to ninety Tyrolese who, as noted in Chapter 3, had transferred from Krumau to Austerlitz in 1528.

It is possible that Marpeck first moved from Rattenberg to the Kitzbühl district, where Anabaptists found temporary protection at the castle of

Helena of Freyberg, near Münichau. Marpeck later corresponded with Freyberg through his friend and collaborator Leupold Scharnschlager, who was a native of Hopfgarten near Kitzbühl.[26] Hard evidence that Marpeck and his wife were in Krumau dates from July 2, 1528.[27] By that date Ferdinand's court had learned of Marpeck's presence in Krumau, and the duke's pressure may be why Marpeck could not remain there. His high profile as a former mining magistrate made his stay in any of Ferdinand's territories risky, and so he and his wife made their way to the distant metropolis on the Rhine. It is possible that Nuremberg served as way station (see Chapter 5).

The point is that Marpeck had followed his compatriots to the mining town of Krumau, which clearly means that he had some personal contacts among them. Indirect evidence indicates as well that Marpeck knew of the transfer of his kinsmen to the Austerlitz community. Melchior Schlosser,[28] Marpeck's contact at Austerlitz in the 1530s, would remain loyal to the Austerlitz Brethren during the schism of 1530–31.

In his biography of Marpeck, Boyd stated that "Marpeck came to Strasbourg a commissioned elder."[29] But commissioned by whom and by what group? According to Boyd, Marpeck associated with Reublin's followers in the Strasbourg area and identified generally with a Swiss orientation except for his position on the civil duties of a Christian and the oath. But the evidence is circumstantial; upon arriving in Strasbourg on September 19, 1528, Marpeck purchased citizenship, accepted civic employ, and therefore by implication gave the necessary oaths.[30] If true, this could mean that Marpeck held views similar to those attributed to a leader at Austerlitz who allegedly taught "that Christ had been a citizen of Capernaum and that therefore as citizens it was permissible to do civilian duties and swear the oath."[31] But even if this was Marpeck's attitude, he soon found himself at odds with the authorities in Strasbourg. At issue was an unauthorized relief effort for Anabaptist refugees in the city which, Boyd suggested, included an attempt at unifying and organizing the local congregation along lines outlined in the *Rattenberg Church Order.*[32] As discussed in Chapter 2, what Boyd considered the *Rattenberg Order,* also known as the *Discipline,* was an adapted version of the *Swiss Order* and most likely the order of the Brethren at Austerlitz. Both the *Swiss Order* and the *Discipline* advocated a voluntary form of community of goods, a practice explicitly rejected in the *Common Order,* which originated in the Marpeck-Scharnschlager circle. This *Common Order* also rejected the idea that practices of the Jerusalem Church were normative in the postdispersion era. Cumulative evidence now suggests that while he was in Strasbourg Marpeck wrote the anonymous pamphlet *Uncovering of the Babylonian Whore,* which advocated a form of community of goods and came off the same press as Marpeck's 1531 publications.[33] Does this mean that Marpeck advocated community of goods during the early period and changed his mind after the dispersion of 1535?

Curiously, the leader of the Austerlitz community, Jacob Wiedemann, appears to have visited Strasbourg in 1530 or 1531. Nothing is known about the purpose of this visit or Wiedemann's contacts in Strasbourg. But coming on the heels of publications by Bünderlin and Entfelder, with the latter explicitly critical of the Austerlitz community, Wiedemann's visit most likely was for the purpose of presenting the point of view of his community, perhaps in print. Wiedemann apparently was imprisoned during this visit. Refusing the oath, he was permitted to give his word of honor instead and was released upon his promise to leave Strasbourg territories.[34] Because Marpeck was in Strasbourg or the vicinity during 1530–31, he probably knew of Wiedemann's visit and arrest. The question arises as to whether the Austerlitz community, which had been joined by a number of Marpeck's compatriots from Krumau in 1528, was also the community that had commissioned Marpeck. Such a scenario would shed new light on Marpeck's *Refutation* and *Instruction* and his *Uncovering of the Babylonian Whore*. The writings could have been apologetic efforts on behalf of a larger Anabaptist community with members in Austerlitz as well as in Strasbourg, which would explain allusions to community of goods in the *Uncovering of the Babylonian Whore* as well as later distributions of Marpeck's Strasbourg publications from Austerlitz.[35] This hypothesis is also supported by Thomas Adolf of Speyer, who in January 1531 testified that no one had the right to baptize "unless he has been sent for that purpose by the congregation, which congregation is in Moravia." Marpeck was identified as one so commissioned.[36] Clearly, early members of Marpeck's circle looked to a congregation in Moravia for leadership. If this congregation was Austerlitz rather than Krumau, which was in Bohemia, then Marpeck's absence from the Rhineland in 1532 may have been because of a visit to Austerlitz.

One year earlier the Austerlitz community had been rent by schism, with some of Marpeck's acquaintances moving to Auspitz and others remaining at Austerlitz. The rival communities sent different versions of the schism to their contacts abroad, and it is likely that Marpeck, after his expulsion from Strasbourg in January 1532, traveled to Moravia to investigate the dispute.

The years from 1532 to 1544 remain obscure in Marpeck's biography. It has been assumed that he served as itinerant apostle for a Moravian church for part of this period.[37] And although that church cannot be identified with absolute certainty, indirect evidence indicates that by the early 1540s it had been dispersed and that Marpeck felt a sense of responsibility for the scattered remnant in Moravia. He visited Austerlitz in the spring of 1540 and Schackowitz in 1541. But his efforts at uniting the fragmented communities failed. Hutterite sources recorded the visits as follows:

A teacher named Cornelius [Veh] from the Austerlitz group came to Schackowitz with some of his followers, and in front of the gathered church they did all they could to slander its order and teaching. They hoped to weaken some of the believers and make them fall away. But the believers remained unswayed.

Similarly, a man by the name of N. Pilgram arrived soon afterward, full of guile and intrigue. He claimed he had come to the country to gather and unite all groups that had broken up over matters of faith, but he straightaway proved the opposite. His very presence seemed to cause disturbance and confusion, and his slanderous talk confirmed this. When the brothers and sisters met to seek comfort and strength in the Lord's Word and knelt with one accord to pray, this slanderer wanted to join them in prayer. The brothers and sisters did not permit this, because of his great lack of understanding—he had first poured contempt on them and now wished to pray with them. He talked on and on. The brothers and sisters did not react but continued in prayer. He then became incensed and said openly that he would rather unite with the Turks or the pope than with this church [Gemein], and he left in a rage.[38]

Although this account fails to elaborate on Marpeck's contempt and slander and lack of understanding in terms of Hutterite order and teaching, it may be surmised that the disturbance and confusion were caused by his arguments that community of goods was no longer an essential part of true discipleship and was no reason for remaining disunited. Cornelius Veh, Marpeck's contact at Austerlitz, was, like Marpeck, an urbanite who accepted private property and maintained a positive attitude toward civil authorities.[39] But Hans Amon, who at the time led the Hutterites from the community at Schackowitz, would have none of it. Under his leadership, community of goods hardened into an absolute essential of true apostolic practice. But by the early 1540s Marpeck had come to a different view. He believed that community of goods had been practiced in the Jerusalem Church only, not in those churches living in diaspora.[40] Static interpretations of Marpeck have failed to appreciate this evolution of his perspective between the 1530s and the 1540s.

Obviously some remaining Moravian Anabaptists felt a greater appreciation for Marpeck's evolution and his concern with unity than did the Hutterites. Three years before Marpeck's death in 1556, elders of five congregations in Moravia thanked him for the work he had done among them.[41] Presumably this work included teaching and nurturing along the lines found in his writings and in the Common Order current in his circle by that time. What is of interest here is that Marpeck's early debate with the spiritualists echoed into the 1540s.

Key Issues in the Bünderlin-Entfelder-Marpeck Debate

It is almost certain that Bünderlin and Entfelder came to Strasbourg in 1529–30, not only under the influence of recent developments in Moravia but possibly with manuscripts in hand. As discussed in Chapter 3, 1528 had witnessed a major schism between Anabaptists in Nicolsburg. One year later Bünderlin arrived in Strasbourg from Nicolsburg, apparently representing the spiritualizing orientation taken by Hubmaier's successor, the learned Hans Spittelmaier.[42] Spittelmaier had preached openly against the schismatics who established the new community at Austerlitz. The practices of this community appear to have created tensions in nearby Eibenschitz, where Entfelder led the evangelical Reform Party. The chief concern of Bünderlin and Entfelder was the unity of the fledgling movement in Moravia. In his tract *Of the Manifold Divisions in the Faith* (hereafter *Manifold Divisions*), Entfelder lamented that differences on baptism were creating divisions. He warned against narrow-minded, legalistic sectarianism that led to separation and fragmentation. In an apparent allusion to the neighbors at Austerlitz, Entfelder warned his constituents to "let others have all things in common, greet only their brothers, do good only to one another," although he hoped that his former charges would remain more inclusive and broad minded. In the same context he criticized the staff-bearing pacifists: "Whoever does harm to another is of no concern to them, [because] they consider them outsiders."[43] Thus Entfelder took the view of the sword bearers who, like Spittelmaier, sought to further nonsectarian local and territorial reform. At the same time, Entfelder appears to have sought rapport with the indigenous Bohemian and neo-Utraquist Brethren. Under his guidance, infant and adult baptism coexisted at Eibenschitz, and good relations prevailed between German Anabaptists and the local population. But all of this had been jeopardized by the "stricter Anabaptist party, which appears to have gained control in the early fall of 1528" under influences from Austerlitz. As a result, the dialogue between the German and indigenous population had been disrupted and the social peace broken.[44] Entfelder's disillusionment and disappointment are reflected in his *Manifold Divisions*. He found it scandalous that controversy over externals caused divisions.

At the heart of the debate were apostolic precedent and authority for the reform or reinstitution of external ordinances. Anabaptists appealed to the Great Commission and its sequence of teach, believe, and baptize as the basis for reinstituting believers' baptism and discarding pedobaptism. But Entfelder maintained that as recipients of the Great Commission, the apostles had a unique historic mission based on Christ's special command, authenticated by supernatural signs and miracles that accompanied their ministry. Shortly after the time of the apostles, externals had become more important than inner spiritual regeneration of which baptism was the outer sign. With the loss of true regenerative spirit baptism other corruptions had set in, among them the division of Christians into clergy and laity and with that patronage and simony.[45] External matters, once considered adiaphorous (for example, certain kinds of drink and food, and celibacy), had been elevated to religious essentials; spirituality was replaced by external ceremonies, rules, and regulations. Under the guise of external piety immorality had crept in; adultery, debauchery, and drunkenness had become the order of the day. Among the abused and misused externals was baptism. Entfelder traced the first signs of misuse to Paul's time, when divisions occurred because groups named themselves after their baptizers. He noted that for the sake of unity Paul suspended baptism (1 Corinthians 1:12–17). Entfelder's motto, "Not who, but what," takes on new meaning in this context. The essential question was not who performed or who received the external rite, but whether the spiritual, inner event to which the outer testified was properly experienced and understood. His point was that the proper understanding of true baptism, as the regenerative inner work of the Spirit, had been lost in the post-apostolic church because of quarrels over externals and accidentals—the who, how, and when. Given the divisions in Moravia and Strasbourg over outer ceremonies, it must have seemed to Entfelder as if history were repeating itself. So, although he agreed with his neighbors that apostolic ceremonies had been utterly corrupted by the "Son of Perdition," the papacy, Entfelder questioned the usefulness and wisdom of insisting on the reinstitution of pristine rites. More importantly, he questioned the apostolic authority of those who insisted on their reinstitution. For such a task a special divine mandate was needed, just as in the time of the apostles. It was not sufficient to appeal to apostolic precedent and practice on the basis of the Great Commission and Scripture, as the resulting divisions over externals made clear. These seemed hardly the fruits of the Spirit, nor did they give evidence of mature spiritual discernment. Entfelder, therefore, considered Paul's suspension of baptism worthy of emulation. A moratorium (*Stillstand*) on the performance of church ordinances seemed preferable to increased bickering and fragmentation.

Earlier, Hans Denck expressed similar concerns when he wrote in his so-called "Recantation": "Now let him who baptizes anew see that he does not serve before he is called. For he who is neither called nor sent to teach, ventures in vain to baptize. On this account, I would, God willing, cease baptizing altogether unless I receive another call from the Lord."[46] Significantly, Denck emphasized the teaching office rather than the rite of baptism. Confronted by the fragmentation of the Anabaptist movement,

Entfelder did the same. The spiritual meaning of baptism had to be taught and understood properly. Since Pentecost, it had been the work of the Spirit to lead all into truth. Only the Spirit could bring the immediacy and meaning of Christ's life and death to the believer. Entfelder, therefore, belonged to a group of evangelicals who considered it more important to "guard the internal house of understanding"[47] than to reinstitute divisive ceremonies. In language later echoed by Gabriel Ascherham, Entfelder argued that proper teaching was possible only as the result of proper spiritual discernment, one that distinguished between outer symbol and inner essence, letter, and spirit; human words and divine Word; human wisdom and divine wisdom; human understanding and spiritual understanding. A true understanding could come only from "the inner glimpse of the invisible being, made possible by the hidden goodness which shines brightly in the revealed reality of the incarnate Word."[48]

Turning to Bünderlin, it is striking that the issue of apostolic authority figures prominently in the title of his *Explanation Through Comparison of the Biblical Scripture, that the Water Baptism . . . Exercised in the Apostolic Church Is Being Reinstituted at the Present Time By Some Without God's Command and Witness of the Scripture.*[49] Like Entfelder, Bünderlin believed that water baptism and other New Testament ordinances had been corrupted right after the death of the apostles, but the corruption by Antichrist would last until the "end." Those seeking the reinstitution of pristine apostolic practices would need a special, direct, divine command to do so, just as the apostles had received a special mandate. Without this, efforts at restitution would produce divisions and sects rather than a purified, restored church. Bünderlin believed that no one had received such a new mandate. Indeed, he criticized the new literalism about restoring apostolic ordinances, emphasizing instead the inner Word or spiritual witness accessible to all through the *imago Dei*. He believed that baptism, the Lord's Supper, and even the preaching ministry could and should be suspended to further oneness in the Spirit.[50] After all, the end-time church was destined to be a truly spiritual one.

Marpeck's two pamphlets of 1531 engaged and refuted arguments found or implied in the publications of Bünderlin and Entfelder. Marpeck's *Refutation* specifically addressed the questions of whether corrupted ceremonies should be suspended or could be reformed and whether the apostolic mandate remained in effect and had been passed on after the apostles to other faithful church leaders.[51] The main points of the *Refutation* may be summarized as follows:

1. It was not true that the "children of God should no longer use baptism, the Lord's Supper, and the Scriptures" because these had been corrupted by Antichrist beyond reform. Nor was it permissible to leave

outer ceremonies behind and "leap" to their spiritual observance.[52] Christ's ordinances remained in effect until his return.

2. The commission to baptize had not been limited to the apostles. No special, new, divine command or authentication by miracles was needed for the restoration of New Testament ordinances and apostolic practice.[53] Philip, the deacon, had preached and baptized in the spirit of the Great Commission without a special direct command from Christ.[54]

3. Apostolic authority had been delegated to other leaders in the Church, among them missionary shepherds [*sammelbischoff, sammelboten*], whose role it was to gather the flock; and to congregational watchmen or shepherds [*affterhirten, hüter*] to "guard the property and sheep gathered for the Lord."[55]

Apart from the suggestion that a distinction was made in Marpeck's circle as early as 1530–31 as to different leadership roles,[56] the *Refutation*, written mostly in the first person, demonstrated that the main issue was the question of apostolicity and apostolic succession—not a new issue but one debated at length throughout the history of the church. In the late medieval period, defenders of Rome relied heavily on arguments of apostolic and Petrine succession to support papal authority. Others had argued for apostolicity through "obedience to the word of the apostles in scripture, not to the command of their successor in office."[57] During the Reformation the argument shifted. With institutional apostolicity and succession of personnel or office discredited because all Reformation parties postulated a fall of the church and its corruption for a duration of hundreds of years, apostolicity could be argued only in terms of the teaching office in conjunction with Scripture. But the question of apostolicity received another twist when differences arose in regard to church ordinances and practice. Anabaptists appealed to the New Testament, specifically the rule of Christ, the Great Commission, apostolic practice as precedent and authority to reinstitute believers' baptism, the Lord's Supper as a memorial meal, the ban, and in some cases footwashing and community of goods as the marks of the true church. Spiritualists such as Entfelder and Bünderlin objected and advocated at least a temporary *Stillstand* when differences over externals led to divisions. According to Marpeck they advocated "that the children of God should no longer use the ceremonies of the New Testament, such as baptism, the Lord's Supper, and the Scriptures," because these externals, like those of the Old Testament, had been abnegated in favor of their spiritual fulfillment.

These spirits speak with neither discernment nor the support of the Scriptures, and think that, because the ceremonies of the Old Testament have been abrogated (as for example, in Hebrews 7, 8, 9, 10; Galatians 5), the ceremonies of the New Testament have also been abrogated. They are mistaken. Note, however, that if they do regard as abrogated (which they cannot) the ceremonies of the New Testament, ceremonies like baptism and the Lord's Supper, it should follow that all Scriptures, external teaching, separation from the world, ban, rebuke, exhortation, prayer, kneeling, the example of the believers . . . and all ceremonies for improvement and corporate benefit are no longer valid. If one is invalid, all are invalid; if one remains valid, all remain valid.[58]

It should be noted that Marpeck's other 1531 publication, *Instruction,* read like a more elaborated defense against objections raised by the spiritualists. Perhaps meant more for internal consumption than apologetics, which had been the case with the *Refutation,* the *Instruction* addressed the office of the apostles and the bishops, the ordinances of Christ, the deity and the humanity of Christ, expectations of a new prophet, and the meaning of the prayers and good works of Cornelius. The first three items repeated earlier arguments of the *Refutation.* Accordingly, Marpeck refuted the notion that the apostles had a historically limited mandate as witnesses to Christ's bodily resurrection. The first witnesses to the resurrection, Marpeck noted, were not the apostles but women who broke the news to them.[59] The witness to Christ's resurrection was a universal mandate, not limited to the first apostles. The generation that followed had the same mandate to proclaim the resurrected Christ and also to continue with ordinances instituted by him. Entfelder's argument that external ceremonies causing division should have been suspended just as Paul suspended baptism was explicitly rejected by Marpeck. If true, Paul should have suspended the Lord's Supper in the congregation of Corinth.

The discussion of Christology contained the implicit accusation that Marpeck's antagonists tended toward a docetic Christology, neglecting the humanity and incarnation in favor of the heavenly, divinized Christ.[60] At the same time, they attributed too much to the image of man's godlikeness and to free volition.[61] Allegedly some were waiting for a special commission, for another coming of the Spirit and for a second Elijah. Until such time, having suspended outer ceremonies, they seemed content with penance and inner renewal. Melchior Hoffman suspended baptism for a while, and expectations of a new Elijah and Enoch were strong among his supporters and those in Schwenckfeld's circle. Hoffman published his own views on the nature of the apostolic office in *Das ware trostliche . . . Euangelion . . . zu dieser letsten zeit . . . fürgetragen . . . durch die waren Apostolischen geyster/und knecht dess Herrn Jesu Christi.*[62]

Curious was Marpeck's ad hominem against *Geister,* influenced by the figurative exegesis found in Jewish commentaries. Unfortunately, he failed to elaborate and identify the opponents so implicated, so it is not clear whether he responded to information reaching him about the evolution of Glaidt and Fischer or whether he responded to a Strasbourg situation.

Hoffman had some missionary contacts with Jews near Strasbourg, and Martin Bucer used rabbinical Bibles, commentaries, and concordances.[63]

Less obscure was the allusion to the good works of Cornelius. The case of Cornelius had been cited as primary evidence of the direct working of the Spirit,[64] apart from or prior to externals, even the preached Word, because Cornelius had been considered acceptable to God even before hearing the Gospel from Peter. Interestingly, as early as August 13, 1524, in a letter to Frederic the Wise, Thomas Müntzer alluded to the story of Cornelius in Acts 10, inferring that he would rather be judged by those who experienced the inner working of the Spirit than by the "scribes." But the contrast intended by Müntzer appears to have been letter versus Spirit and Scripture versus unmediated Word of God. The example of Cornelius provided proof that even Gentiles and Turks could experience the moving of the Spirit in the heart and could, therefore, testify to true faith.[65] Marpeck must have encountered a similar argument, but the issue concerned the keeping of outer ceremonies. Since the Spirit had fallen on Cornelius while Peter was still speaking and before he was baptized with water, baptism by the Spirit preceded and was independent of baptism with water.[66] The latter, only an external symbol of the former, could be suspended or forfeited without danger to personal salvation. It is striking that this so-called early Marpeck-spiritualist debate did not focus on Scripture versus Spirit but rather on the significance of church ordinances and ceremonies, on ecclesiology and practice rather than on the soteriological question of how one arrives at true faith.

In the name of rebuilding the true ecclesia, Marpeck rejected the arguments for suspending external ordinances. He also contested vigorously charges that divisions and dissension discredited Anabaptist claims to represent the reinstituted apostolic church.

The false prophets also base their argument upon various divisions, and contrast these dissensions to the glorious congregation at Jerusalem, where they were of one faith, heart, and soul, and where they lived in the unity of the Spirit. These false prophets say that if the recently established church were the church of Christ, it would remain constant in prayer and in the unity of the Spirit. I answer, did there not arise dissension in the Jerusalem Church because of the distribution of food and temporal goods (Acts 6:1–7).[67]

By inference then, the early discussion with the spiritualists centered on unity and the reason for the lack of it. Marpeck admitted that disagreements had arisen but claimed that these were over practical issues such as the distribution of food and temporal goods. It is unknown whether he was alluding to problems in Strasbourg or wider afield. What did he mean by the "recently established church of Christ," and who were "the false prophets?" Entfelder and Bünderlin come to mind, but what of their spiritual kinsman Schwenckfeld, who arrived in Strasbourg in 1529? In *Judicium de Anabaptistis,* tentatively dated July 1530, Schwenckfeld criticized the Anabaptists for their lack of "knowledge of Christ" (*Erkenntniss Christi*) and accused them of bringing "fleshly and temporal" concerns into the "kingdom of Christ."[68] He raised doubts about their "apostolic mission" and suggested that

it might be useful [for them] to give greater heed to the catechism, that is, to look at a *thorough instruction of the Christian faith* through which the church was previously gathered, that is through the ministry of the Holy Spirit. . . . Item that they think more thoroughly concerning the order of Christ and the sending of the Holy Spirit and the entire ministry of the apostles from the inner out, not from the outer in; so that the Spirit have his office restored to him and so that they should understand [*erkennten*] the work of Christ's redemption a little better and learn to distinguish [it, the inner from the outer].[69]

Schwenckfeld thought that the Anabaptists needed to distinguish more clearly between inner and outer baptism. Proper spiritual discernment and the seal of the Spirit were prerequisite to the apostolic teaching office. He warned that "without God's command and mission it was dangerous to be hasty in divine matters."[70] A year later Schwenckfeld elaborated on the nature of the apostolic office.[71] Commenting on Paul's statement in 1 Corinthians 1:17, "Christ did not send me to baptize but to preach the gospel," Schwenckfeld explained that Paul considered teaching more important than baptizing. It was not that Paul despised or rejected water baptism, but he objected to an unbecoming emphasis on human agency and external rite. Such an emphasis was responsible for divisions into parties, each honoring its baptizer, despising the other. Schwenckfeld noted that Anabaptists were divided into three such parties or sects,[72] and he believed that they had lost or had never attained a proper understanding of the inner work of the Spirit. To rectify perversion in his day and restore a "proper understanding of the sacrament," Paul had found it necessary to emphasize the prior and most edifying office (*vorderlichste ampt*) of sound teaching. Schwenckfeld thought that the same emphasis was necessary in the contemporary situation. Obviously, then, the same issues that occupied Entfelder, Bünderlin, and Marpeck occupied Schwenckfeld in 1530–31. However, Schwenckfeld's attitude toward the Anabaptists was not malevolent; he reserved his harshest criticism for those who persecuted them and other dissenters because of their nonconformity.[73]

But why did Schwenckfeld enter the debate? Had he been part of it from the beginning? Was it a debate that originated in Strasbourg, or was it of consequence in Silesia and Moravia? Did Schwenckfeld react against Marpeck, taking the side of Entfelder and Bünderlin, or did Marpeck respond to Schwenckfeld on behalf of the Anabaptists? Marpeck's *Instruc-*

tion certainly reads like a response to criticisms. Marpeck took seriously the admonition to pay greater attention to the teaching office and to begin with a thorough instruction of the Christian faith. It would be wrong, however, to infer that the fronts between Marpeck and Schwenckfeld had been drawn irretrievably in 1531 or that attitudes had polarized beyond dialogue. Schwenckfeld's own Christology was still developing as were Marpeck's views on a number of issues including the modality of the Jerusalem Church and the relationship of the Old and New Testaments. With regard to the latter he appears to have been, as Blough observed, the learner and Schwenckfeld the tutor. Surprisingly, not until the 1540s were the lines drawn more clearly in terms of biblicism versus spiritualism as understood in the traditional scholarship.[74] Marpeck's early writings were ambivalent in this regard. Thus, although the main body of the *Refutation* defended externals against the spiritualists, its introduction and conclusion appeared to give priority to internals. Similarly, although the *Instruction* stressed the importance of the outer, Marpeck's "Confession," submitted a little later, retained an emphasis on the superiority of the inner.[75] To this must be added that some of Schwenckfeld's early charges did not seem to apply to Marpeck's views, whereas some of the innuendos in Marpeck's tracts were misdirected if intended for Schwenckfeld. But Schwenckfeld was at best only one member in a dialogue which, by means of print, transcended the Strasbourg context.

Echoes of the Marpeck-Spiritualist Debate into the 1540s

In 1959 Hans Hillerbrand published an "Anabaptist Confession" found in the City Archive of Regensburg.[76] Although author, place, or date of origin were not given, the confession seemed to be the work of a prisoner who addressed the governor of Moravia, Lord Jan von Pernstein. An examination of its content led to the conclusion that the document originated in about 1540. Hillerbrand noted that the Christological statement of the confession seemed directed against Melchior Hoffman or Caspar Schwenckfeld, and he therefore surmised a connection to the Marpeck-Schwenckfeld debate of the 1540s. Indeed, the confession reverberated with echoes of the Marpeck-spiritualist debate, leading Stephen Boyd to go beyond Hillerbrand in claiming the confession as "the work of Marpeck."[77] Boyd believed that it represented Marpeck's defense before a "local representative of Pernstein" in Moravia. Building on Hillerbrand and on suggestions by Heinold Fast, Boyd argued that in both content and terminology the confession mirrored Marpeck's position against the spiritualists and consequently provided a documentary "bridge in the development of Marpeck's thought between his early work (Strasbourg) and later controversy with Schwenckfeld" (Augsburg).[78] Boyd agreed with Hillerbrand's tentative dating of the confession. As for the confession's location in the City Archive of Regensburg, Boyd speculated that the document had been carried there from Moravia, most likely by missionaries from a community at Znaim, where a group of Pilgramites resided from about 1535 on.

However, a careful consideration of the evidence points to another author and context of this remarkable confession, which the author himself described as *A Short Instruction of Some Points of Our Faith* (hereafter *Points of Faith*).[79]

Hans Umlauft as Author of Points of Faith

Karl Schornbaum, editor of the Regensburg *Täuferakten,* connected the document to persons arrested on November 6, 1539. Most of these prisoners were soon released. But two, the shoemaker Hans (Johannes) Umlauft and the bookbinder Gabriel Weinberger, remained in prison for several months.[80] Neither Umlauft nor Weinberger was native to Regensburg; Weinberger came from Bayreuth, and Umlauft gave his home as Raisenberg in Meichsen, Saxony. Of the two, Umlauft was the leader, with Weinberger deferring to him as to the one "who has a gift from God to speak."[81] Weinberger's deference is not a surprise, for Umlauft proved an exceptional shoemaker; he wrote Latin and knew Greek. He also kept abreast of current reform literature, all of which support Schornbaum's suggestion that before he pursued a career as shoemaker and married a wife Umlauft must have been a priest or monk.

November 1539 was not the first time Umlauft found himself at odds with the Regensburg authorities. Two years earlier, on June 26, 1537, he petitioned council for a letter of good standing to the effect that his exile was for reasons of conscience and that he had carried out his trade as shoemaker competently and honestly.[82] Yet two years later Umlauft was still or again residing in Regensburg. Only in the fall of 1539 did he join the Anabaptists, accepting baptism from Georg (Hueter), a missionary for a community at Austerlitz, Moravia.[83]

The council's awareness of the growing strength of the Anabaptists led to the arrests on November 6. Two weeks later, on November 21, Umlauft petitioned council for a hearing or disputation in its presence. Instead, the council commissioned theologian Erasmus Zellner, the chaplain of St. Georg, to examine Umlauft's views. To make his case, Umlauft requested a light and books. A letter from Umlauft to Zellner outlined Umlauft's understanding of the eucharist and also proves that he had indeed received ink and paper as requested.[84]

Meanwhile, the council asked for advice from Nuremberg on how to treat the prisoners. It did not want to shed blood but feared that Ferdinand might use the evidence of an Anabaptist presence as an excuse to impose an occupation force (*besatzung*) on Regensburg. Umlauft's case was particularly difficult because he had given a *widerruf* three years earlier, broken his promise, and secretly instructed others. To cover all its bases, the council also informed Franz Hombst, the emperor's governor (*Hauptmann*) in Regensburg, of the arrests. Hombst carried out his own investigation and was in all probability the *Gebietender Gnädiger Herr Haubtman* addressed in the introduction to the confession, which I argue was the work of Umlauft.[85] The introduction implies further that the author and a number of prisoners had met with the *Hauptmann*, who told them that he and Lord von Pernstein had been informed that the prisoners "denied Christ, our Savior." When the author protested that their views had been misrepresented, the *Hauptmann* requested a written statement, which he promised to forward to von Pernstein.[86] This scenario suggests that the confession had been solicited by Franz Hombst[87] and agrees with the dating of the confession, permitting us to narrow the time of its origin to between November 20, 1539, and July 1540.

Although it is not clear whether *Points of Faith* ever reached its destination or made its intended impact on Lord von Pernstein, it is clear that the council of Regensburg followed the advice received from Nuremberg, according to which Umlauft was either to be released only upon signing a written recantation or placed in the pillory, flogged, and exiled forever from the city. Weinberger, on the other hand, was to be kept in prison with routine visits a few times a year to see if he would recant. To forestall intervention by Ferdinand, Regensburg was to issue an anti-Anabaptist decree so as to leave the impression that council was taking firm and appropriate measures.[88] Not advisable was a general inquisition, which would have alienated many citizens. Regensburg's council followed this strategy, issued a public decree, and refused to release Umlauft without a written and public recantation. After eight months in prison, on July 16, 1540, Umlauft recanted before an estimated crowd of two thousand. But once released, he moved to Moravia and according to a hostile chronicler relapsed into Anabaptist errors "three times" as bad as those he had held previously.[89]

For purposes of identifying Umlauft's Anabaptist connections it would be helpful to know what community in Moravia he and his wife joined. His baptizer, Georg Hueter, lived in or near Austerlitz, and in May 1539 Umlauft corresponded with Wolfgang Lutz in Austerlitz.[90] A contemporary source suggests that Umlauft joined a community at Pudweis, which Schornbaum identified with Budwitz, just northwest of Znaim.[91] Znaim or its vicinity was the residence of Wilhelm Reublin and home to a settlement of Swiss at the time. Some of Marpeck's contacts may have resided there as well. Given the variations in sixteenth-century spelling, Umlauft may have moved to Pudespitz or Budespitz near Austerlitz. Unfortunately, even if it could be established that he moved to Pudespitz, it would not help in a definite identification of the community. Ulrich Stadler, a member of the Austerlitz Brethren who established a community at Pudespitz in 1536–37 and in 1538 united with the Hutterites, met with the wrath of those who remained separate. Umlauft could have joined either group.[92]

As Hillerbrand noted, the relatively positive attitude toward temporal authority in *Points of Faith,* which explicitly granted the unqualified payment of taxes, does not seem to fit the starker dualism of the Hutterites. Moreover, nothing was said about community of goods, a practice normative for Hutterites, all of which makes it more likely that Umlauft joined a less rigorous group.[93]

An Analysis of Umlauft's Writings

When assessing Umlauft's authorship of *Points of Faith,* a comparison with his lengthy letter to Stephan (Rauchenecker) is in order.[94] Schornbaum dated the letter from the end of October 1539 because it did not mention Umlauft's incarceration. But the letter may have stemmed from an earlier period inasmuch as Umlauft alluded to Paul's escape from Damascus. Like Paul, he had not waited for the "plot of the forty men" to kill him but had fled, in keeping with Christ's command in Matthew 10:23. His only desire had been "a fair hearing, trial, and judgment." He admonished Stephan not to participate in the shedding of blood. By inference, then, Umlauft had escaped from Regensburg, and his letter may therefore have originated in conjunction with his problems in 1537. If so, it would belong to his pre-Anabaptist period and would provide some insight into his pre-Anabaptist ideas,[95] which could be described as sacramentist.

The letter recorded Umlauft's response to charges that he was part of a "heretical, seductive, and insurrectionist" sect.[96] At issue was his view of the Lord's Supper. He rejected the "old and new papists" alike because they sought Christ in "water and bread" or in the "dead letter, which you call the Word of God, even though it is only a witness of his Word." Umlauft obviously identified with a Reform Party that was neither Catholic nor Lutheran but more radical. If his position on the eucharist qualified him as a sacramentist, his view on the Scriptures, according to modern typologies, would qualify him a spiritualist. He wrote:

If the Scriptures are the Word of God, as you say, then why did they become a rope and snare that recoiled on the Pharisees, Matthew 22? Moreover, would not all those who do not hear [the Scriptures] and all who lived three thousand years before the written law, from Adam to Moses, be damned? In that case the kingdom of God would have to come from the outside in [*von aussen an und hinein*]. But that would be a denial of the living Word, of the Spirit and work of God; because Christ says the kingdom of God does not consist of outward appearances [*geberden*], but is in you. So [says] also John 5:39: Search the Scriptures in which you think to have eternal life, they are they that witness of me. But if they are only a witness of the Word, then they are not God's Word in themselves. If that were not the case, then all the children deprived of the Word who do not hear it would be damned, even though Christ counts them blessed and upholds them as a model and example of innocence for us all, Matthew 18:3; 19:14. For that reason one should ascribe blessedness solely to the [work of] the inner living Word of God, which to the ancients was Christ, and not bind it all to the outer word or Scripture; however useful it may be to those to whom God reveals its meaning. The outer word has been given only as a witness for the sake of those who contradict, deny and do not want to know that they have the Word in them, Deuteronomy 30:14. But the one who pays attention to the inner word in his heart and to the light which has been set and is lit in him, see Matthew 6:23; Psalms 5:12; that person will leap up because of the joy in his heart and out of the inner give the outer a witness, so that no godless person can persist and continue to excuse himself further as Paul tells the first Christians, 1 Corinthians 11:1. The Scriptures and outer word, therefore, remain only a witness and lantern [housing] to the inner word of God.[97]

Then, without giving his source, Umlauft cited verbatim from Denck's "Recantation" that although he considered the Scriptures "higher than all human treasures, he did not consider them as high as the Word of God."[98] He likened the Scriptures to a sheath that holds the sword or to a lantern that houses the light but is not identical to it. The misplaced reverence for the letter by the "new papists" was analogous to the Mariolatry of the "old papists." The instrument or vessel received the honor due only to the living Word of God. The fruits of bibliolatry (*sic*) were "heresy, superstition, and sects." As proof that God did not bind his "grace and people to outer elements and ceremonies," Umlauft cited the examples of Nathaniel and Cornelius. Both were found worthy and had true faith, that is, circumcised hearts, before they had received baptism, the outer sign of the inner circumcision.[99]

Given the above statements, which could classify Umlauft as a spiritualist, it is interesting that he rejected charges that his group had "no faith, word, or sacrament." Unlike the new papists whose preaching brought no improvement and who refused to live according to Christ's command and the proper Christian order, Umlauft and his associates followed an order (*ordnung*) that involved separation from open transgressors by means of fraternal discipline (*straf*) and the ban. It was an order that, in keeping with 1 Corinthians 14:26, permitted members to speak "one after the other openly [in the meetings] and bring their gifts and revelations freely before the people for their edification."[100] In other words, Umlauft, a spiritualist, called for a congregational life and discipline not unlike that prescribed in the *Swiss* and other early Anabaptist orders.

Turning to *Points of Faith*, it becomes evident at once that Umlauft was not only biblically literate but also familiar with a number of contemporary authors, including Anabaptists. Besides the verbatim citation from Hans Denck's "Recantation" in "Concerning Holy Scriptures," Umlauft alluded to the motto, "truth is immortal," found in both Hätzer's and Hubmaier's publications, and he appeared to have been familiar with Marpeck's *Refutation* and/or *Instruction* as well as Sebastian Franck's *Chronica*.[101] Of interest here is evidence that some of Umlauft's reading materials may have come from Moravia. A report by Regensburg to Ferdinand's court included "two copies of several writings" of which "many were being sent from Moravia here and there into the Empire."[102] This evidence of literature being disseminated from Moravia documents how important "the promised land" had become for the Anabaptist movement by 1539. The process of duplicating and disseminating apologetic Anabaptist literature from Moravia had begun. Umlauft's own conversion to Anabaptism was a measure of its success.

A comparison of his letter to Stephan with *Points of Faith* reveals striking parallels. The author of *Points of Faith* apologized about giving a written account of the "simple cognizance of divine truth" he found "in him."[103] He wanted to witness to "the truth of God in us." Then in what seems like an allusion to Denck's motto, that those who want to know Christ must follow him in life, the author noted that only those willing to do the will of the Father "could understand his Word." He distinguished the Word of God from the Scriptures, referring to the latter as a "co-witness" to the witness of God's truth in us. This truth was Christ, the Word of God, apart from which there could be no true knowledge of God:

which knowledge [*erkanntnuss*], however, cannot be received through human study [*studieren*] nor searched or received in any [external] place. It can be received only by the one to whom God out of grace, in *Gelassenheit* of that person's soul, gives it to be recognized through the light of his Spirit's illumination [*einleuchten*] and to understand [*zuerkennen*].[104]

We suggest that this basically spiritualist epistemology together with the insistence that the true church is built by the Spirit reveals Umlauft's rather than Marpeck's signature. Yet *Points of Faith* is clearly an Anabaptist document. Like other confessions solicited from Anabaptist prisoners, it followed in outline the *Apostolic Creed*.[105] Accordingly, the author opened with a statement that defines God as an "eternal, united, indivisible, immeasurable, unchanging being—God Father, Son, and Holy Spirit, whom we call one undivided, undifferentiated, impersonal God, who constitutes the perfect, sufficient good of all things."[106] Man arrives at true cognition or knowledge (*erkanntnuss*) of this impersonal God only through the spiritual revelation of Christ in the soul that is in the state of *Gelassenheit*. In this revelatory process the Spirit is the active agent, the soul the recipient. True knowledge of God is "more easily felt than expressed in words" (*mer empfunden dann ausgesprochen*). It is a blessed secret or mystery carried in the heart that is united with God and participating in his divine nature (*verainiget und vernaturet*) through Christ.[107]

But if some of the language could identify Umlauft with Denck's or even Entfelder's spiritualism, his carefully defined statement on Christ's two natures is reminiscent of Marpeck.[108] Two factors help to explain this affinity to Marpeck: the author's apparent familiarity with Marpeck's *Instruction,* and the author's concern with refuting charges before Lord von Pernstein that he and fellow prisoners "deny Christ, our Savior." Indeed, the author took pains to explain that this was another group, one that denied that Christ had taken "our flesh" and argued instead that he brought "heavenly flesh into Mary." This denial that Christ was "the seed of Abraham," Umlauft agreed, amounted to a denial of Christ's messianic lordship and implied that one needed to wait for another Messiah, another "seed of promise," to bring salvation. Such a view turned Christ's death and suffering into a mere "*fantassma* or appearance."[109] It was a view from which Umlauft distanced himself clearly, and not surprisingly, because it was the view attributed to the Münsterites.[110] Against the Melchiorite Christology Umlauft confirmed both the humanity and divinity of Christ, because only through both natures could Christ's work on the cross have salvific merit. Then, in a typically Sacramentist-Anabaptist fashion Umlauft utilized the Christological discussion to insert his view on the Lord's Supper. He argued that since his ascension Christ was "bodily [*leiblich*] seated at the right hand of God" where he would remain until his return in judgment. This meant that any notion of a "bodily presence in the bread of the altar," just because the priests "muttered five words over it," was nothing short of "heathenish idolatry."[111]

Turning to the article on the Holy Spirit, Umlauft defined the same as divine wisdom and power and used the sun as an analogy to illustrate the three-in-one doctrine. The sun was at "once being but also light [*glantz*], emanating from the being [*ausfluss*], and finally it was the sustaining reality and power [*wurkligkait* and *krafft*] felt in all creatures."[112]

In this context *Points of Faith* distanced itself from another group that argued that the apostolic office had come to an end with the apostles. Here were echoes of Marpeck's earlier debate with the spiritualists. Umlauft insisted that the apostolic office (*Ampt*) continued after the apostles. The office included preaching, baptism, the Lord's Supper, and discipline or the ban. Umlauft explicitly rejected arguments that a new and special divine commission, authenticated by signs and wonders, was needed to initiate reform and restore apostolic practices.[113] He refuted "objections by some, namely, that God had nowhere promised that the fallen Church, made desolate by Antichrist, should be rebuilt again." Against such objections Umlauft insisted that the apostolic office and the powers of the keys—to include by baptism and exclude with the ban (*einzeschliessen, ausszeschliessen*)—were essential for the continued rebuilding of the true Church until the end.[114] The argument was apparently directed against two groups: one holding that the entire apostolic office of "preaching, baptism, the Lord's Supper, and discipline," was obsolete; the other, more moderate, that only "the preaching of the Gospel should continue" but that "water baptism was not necessary." The latter group appears to have internalized baptism and perhaps other ceremonies as well, insisting that such should continue "in the spirit" only. Umlauft suspected that these "former brethren" had become Nicodemites, seeking to avoid persecution. They were "the many who have gone out from us even though they were not of us."[115]

Finally, the author defined his attitude toward temporal authority (*obrigkeit*). He held that all magistrates had been ordained by God to punish evildoers and protect the good. He pledged to obey good government and, if need be, suffer under evil or bad authority; "yes, also to aid and help her with taxes, rents, and tithes." But magistrates should consider their office one of servanthood (*dienstschaft*) rather than lordship (*herrschaft*) and should not burden their subjects unnecessarily.[116] Temporal authority should stay out of matters of faith and conscience. Umlauft drew a clear distinction between the Israelites of the Old Testament, a "servant people" (*knechtisch volk*) in need of external guides, and "God's children" of the New Testament, among whom all things were to be done through the "free preaching of the Gospel."[117] Should temporal authority go against God's truth and conscience, "we will reject all obedience without regard to accusations that [we disturb] the peace [or plot] insurrection." Umlauft closed with a plea to Lord von Pernstein not to judge *Points of Faith* too hastily. Should he be found in error, he and his fellow prisoner(s) were prepared to receive instruction. He had found it "very difficult" to put his "simple understanding of divine truth" into words and feared that it would be misinterpreted by "our many detractors."[118]

Whether *Points of Faith* ever reached Pernstein is not known. Its survival in Regensburg suggests that it did not. Umlauft was forced to recant before he was permitted to leave for Moravia. One thing seems certain: *Points of Faith* demonstrated that the Anabaptist-spiritualist debate regarding the apostolic office was current into the 1540s. It also revealed further the fluidity of Anabaptist-spiritualist ideological boundaries—drawn all too clearly in modern typologies. The Anabaptist-spiritualist narrative ran parallel, dissected, intertwined, and separated at a number of points. The confession did not illustrate "the development of Marpeck's thought," as Boyd suggested, but at best Marpeck's influence via literature being disseminated from a community in Moravia. This spread of Marpeck's influence clarifies that Marpeck's 1531 debate with the spiritualists had an audience not only in Strasbourg but also in Regensburg and Moravia.

Echoes in Gabriel's Distinction

Of special interest here is that Gabriel Ascherham appeared to address the same issues that stirred Marpeck and Umlauft but from a different perspective. Gabriel's antagonists were not the spiritualists seeking to negate externals but rather the brethren who had introduced a new bondage to rules and regulations. By the 1540s Gabriel's position had become analogous to that of the spiritualists criticized by Marpeck in 1531. Gabriel described as fruitless "all studying, learning, preaching, baptizing, breaking of bread, and all human artistry" unless the Spirit was permitted free reign. But if the reign of the Spirit was paramount, it did not mean doing away with all ceremonies, preaching, and discipline. Gabriel lamented divisions resulting over externals and compared contemporary divisions among evangelicals with the episode of the tower of Babel. It too had been an attempt at building the kingdom by temporal means. Like the spiritualists, Gabriel dated the fall of the church as coming right after the apostles and equated it with a fall from spirituality to externality, from divine to human wisdom. But recognition that the corruption had taken place right after the apostles in itself did not provide a mandate to begin the restoration of apostolic ceremonies. Such an enterprise needed a special divine command and authentication. Engaging his antagonists in a rhetorical debate about the historic mandate of the Great Commission and apostolic office, Gabriel wrote, "And should some say, that which Christ and the apostles established [*aufgerichtet haben*] was corrupted [*verwüstet*] by Antichrist, I answer: How dare you without special command from God rebuild that which was destroyed [*zerbrochen*] and had come to its end?"[119]

In other words, an appeal to the Great Commission with its specific historic mandate would not justify the restoration of apostolic ordinances.

These had come to an end in an implied providential course of the church's history. To restore pristine practices a special or new divine mandate was necessary. Gabriel engaged a line of argumentation refuted by Marpeck in the early 1530s. Yet, as noted, Gabriel did not argue for the suspension of all ceremonies; rather his point appears to have been a philosophic realist one, that their externality belonged to material accidentals. His main concern was with their inner spiritual essence and meaning, the inner workings of the Spirit. Outer ceremonies took their validity from the eternal Word and the Spirit who had continued their work even after external corruption. "God's Word and work cannot be destroyed because it is the eternal and indestructible power of God. Even though the Christian church once fell away from the foundation of divine truth, God's Word has not fallen." [120] Thus, although as a result of Antichrist's inroads, "external walls had crumbled, the Holy Spirit, on which the Church is still built today, remained." According to Gabriel, a spiritual rebuilding through true spiritual instruction would need to continue until a spiritual understanding filled the whole earth.

From his spiritual vantage point, the historic mission of the apostles had been unique. Theirs had been a special "call and commission [*Berufung und Sendung*] orally from God." Especially chosen by Christ from among many others, they had received special powers—to heal the sick and raise the dead—as authentication of their mission. They had been entrusted with a very special historic task: to testify to Christ's resurrection. [121] One of the prerequisites for such a task was a close association and acquaintance with Christ during his earthly ministry. Only those familiar with him in life could qualify as witnesses to his resurrection. After the resurrection Christ had revealed himself especially to the twelve and commissioned them to witness to his resurrection. This unique role in salvation history had been divinely preordained, foretold by the prophets of the Old Testament, and clearly spelled out in the New Testament. And if the apostles' mission extended to the ends of the earth, their fame was to "last until the end of the earth." Apostolic office and authority were therefore limited to the original twelve and to Paul, the latter as an exception especially chosen to bring the Gospel to the Gentiles. The apostolic witness to the resurrected, ascended Christ stood at the foundation of the church. There could be no apostolic succession, no more than there could be a succession of founding fathers. But what of the disciples of the apostles, chosen by the apostles? Were they not successors with the same mission and office? Not according to Gabriel:

If you say however: the apostles did also elect apostles and called them apostles, I reply as follows: those are more rightly called apostles than you because they witnessed of Jesus of Nazareth through the Scripture and demonstrated that he is

Christ in those places where he was unknown. But you preach Christ in those places where he is previously known. But I know of no election of apostles, except the ones [elected] by Christ and only the twelve including Paul.[122]

Arguments that the seventy, to whom the resurrected Christ had also shown himself, were also given the apostolic task to witness to his resurrection were explicitly rejected by Gabriel. In his view, the ascent of Christ and the descent of the Spirit at Pentecost marked a spiritual watershed. After that, in the post-Pentecost era, the Spirit alone would lead into all truth. All calling and commissioning became a spiritual or inner matter. Echoing earlier concerns by Entfelder about guarding the "inner house" of understanding—that is, the true spiritual meaning of Christ's life, death, and resurrection—Gabriel emphasized the need for spiritual discernment to distinguish between human and divine wisdom. After Pentecost and the closing of the New Testament canon, the office of the spiritually endowed preacher and teacher-exegete became the primary office of the church. As he explained,

I have the authority of the office of preacher because of the discernment [*Erkenntnis*] granted by the Spirit in my heart. My office and authority [are] not [those] of the apostles; because I have not received an oral command from God to institute something new, [or] not instituted by Christ and his apostles. My mission [*Sendung*], therefore, is not like that of the apostles, because it lies in that which Christ and his apostles instituted. Through the Spirit of divine discernment I have received mercy to build on the foundation which Christ and his apostles laid.[123]

These statements by Gabriel provide evidence of a continuing debate into the 1540s about apostolicity and apostolic succession hinted at as early as 1531 in Marpeck's writings.[124] Indeed, Gabriel's statements enlarged the context of the debate. It seems that from his vantage point the issue concerned authority and leadership. Gabriel disputed with the ghost and legacy of his archrival Jacob Hutter (see Chapters 9 and 12). To the extent that this was an inter- Anabaptist dispute, Gabriel represented the spiritualist wing and sought to shore up his own support and authority with an appeal to the charismatic gift of spiritual discernment.

However, the controversy regarding apostolicity was not limited to inter-Anabaptist conversations or polemics. That it had an outward apologetic dimension is illustrated by a document from the 1550s, attributed to the Hutterite missionary Leonard Dax.[125] In this *Account of Faith*, written in the form of a dialogue between an Anabaptist prisoner and an inquisitor, the inquisitor charged that no one could exercise apostolic authority, change ceremonies, or found new churches without a special divine commission (*Sendung*). The prisoner countered by distinguishing two kinds of apostolic commissioning: one directly from God, the other indirectly through an existing congregation. The prisoner laid claim to the latter. Dax belonged, of course, to a second generation of leaders, and his answer, though not glib, skirted the original issue. No congregation had commissioned the founders. The first-generation issue of apostolicity and authority regarding the restitution of pristine practices thus proved less vexing for second-generation leaders who functioned in the context of already existing communities and leadership structures. The need for a special divine commission, authenticated by signs and wonders, could be put to rest through a sober, routinized elevation of leaders in the name of the congregation of God. For Hutterites the debate with the spiritualizers had ceased to be an inter-Anabaptist debate.

The Marpeck-spiritualist debate reverberating in the writings of Hans Umlauft, Gabriel Ascherham, and Leonard Dax illustrates the foundational and supraterritorial significance of that controversy. Marpeck's antagonists were originally Christian Entfelder, Hans Bünderlin, and to a lesser extent Caspar Schwenckfeld. Evidence that Marpeck and members of his circle looked to a congregation in Moravia for authorization to baptize could suggest that Marpeck saw himself as an apologist for such a congregation. His documented contacts with Austerlitz in 1530–31 suggest the Austerlitz Brethren as the most likely group with which Marpeck identified during this early period. An alleged visit to Strasbourg by Jacob Wiedemann, leader of the Austerlitz Brethren, during this same time period could provide further evidence that Marpeck was a defender against positions considered insidious in Moravia as well as in Strasbourg. After the breakup and dispersion of the Austerlitz Brethren in 1535–36, Marpeck's contacts extended to congregations from Austerlitz to Eibenschitz, Jamnitz, Popitz, Znaim, Vienna, and Am Wald.[126]

The key issues of the early debate concerned the meaning of the apostolic mandate and authority in reforming or reinstituting New Testament ceremonies, chief among them adult baptism. The spiritualists and Anabaptists agreed that the fall and corruption of the church began almost immediately after the apostles. The controversy focused on whether it was necessary to reinstitute New Testament ceremonies and apostolic practice and on what grounds and model. Spiritualists saw as a model the unity in spirit of the Jerusalem Church. They were willing to suspend external rites and practices for the sake of unity and harmony. Although deeply concerned with unity, Marpeck was not prepared to sacrifice New Testament ordinances.

Of historic interest is the evident evolution of the debate originating in disagreements over practice, leadership, organization, and unity into fully developed ideological-theological differences. As consciously held positions these became part of the Anabaptist self-definition, at least for Marpeck, who distanced himself from "certain spirits who went out from us but were not of us." These ideological-theological differences, no doubt latent from the beginning, extended from ecclesiology to Christology and to different ways of relating the New and Old Testaments. Spiritualists approached both the Old and New Testaments in terms of letter and spirit. In the name of New Testament sonship they emphasized the freedom of the spirit. Marpeck agreed with the suspension of Old Testament ceremonies and began a more systematic Anabaptist reflection on the relationship of the two Testaments, one that made allowance for the normativity of the New Testament without jettisoning the Old.

The fact that Umlauft could in 1539 use spiritualist language to extol the virtues of the inner experience while defending antispiritualist positions suggests that the ideological barriers between Anabaptists and spiritualists continued to be more porous than modern typologies permit or the modern rationalist mind can grasp. A similar observation seems in order regarding Gabriel. If nothing else, such overlap in language illustrates that mystical and spiritualist modes of thought were more widespread among early Anabaptists and of greater longevity than thought previously. It should also put us moderns on guard against reading back into sixteenth-century debate all too systematic distinctions between biblicists and spiritualists unless the sixteenth-century protagonists made those distinctions themselves.

Evidence from Umlauft's trial that by the late 1530s an Anabaptist community in Moravia was supplying and distributing Anabaptist literature in the Reich indicates the prominent role played by the Moravian communities in terms of the larger Anabaptist movement. That some of that literature must have included Marpeck's 1531 tracts against the spiritualists confirms our thesis that Marpeck had been or became a spokesperson for a community in Moravia. His efforts at unity in the 1540s and his continuing contacts with Anabaptists in Moravia until his death in 1556 provide further credence to such a view and justify the inclusion of this chapter in the narrative of Moravian Anabaptism.

Part Two

The Emergence of the Hutterites

Chapter Seven

South Tyrol

In the Beginning, 1526–1529

Scholars agree that Anabaptism in the Tyrol initially represented a popular grass-roots movement. Gretl Köfler believed that one could "speak in good conscience of a mass movement," and Wolfgang Lassmann wrote of "a regular people's heresy" that enjoyed the active and passive support of a "large section of the population." A more cautious Edward Widmoser estimated that 5 percent of the population may have been Anabaptist and up to twenty thousand compromised in one way or other by the heresy. Franz Kolb counted 125 communities affected by an Anabaptist presence.[1] My own research suggests that early on, Anabaptism enjoyed the sympathies of a relatively large section of the population. Unlike in other German-speaking territories Anabaptism in the Tyrol came to represent the major Reform orientation, and after its demise no popular alternative emerged.

The initial popularity of Anabaptism is documented indirectly in the clergy's complaints about sagging church attendance[2] and directly in the demonstrated sympathies of the populace. Even after ten years of vicious official suppression, many commoners refused to cooperate with the authorities in hunting the heretics. As late as 1539 the officials of the prince bishop of Brixen reported that

the common man is [favorably] inclined towards Anabaptists, gives them support [*unterhalt*], food and drink, permits them to come and go from his house. No one notifies the authorities [*Herrschaft*], and when the authorities learn of an Anabaptist meeting, they cannot expect the help or support of the subjects to raid the meeting and imprison them. Even if they [commoners] do go along, they give no hand [in apprehending] the Anabaptists, but permit them to run to and fro, even alongside them in the forests, claiming not to have seen any, and even warn them of possible raids.

If this is how those act who are not in the sect, how must those act who belong to the sect?[3]

Some localities seem to have been especially receptive to Anabaptists. At one point an estimated eight hundred out of twelve hundred inhabitants of the city of Schwaz in North Tyrol were suspected of Anabaptist sympathies.[4] In the South, the Etsch (Adige), Eisack (Isarco), and Puster valleys proved particularly hospitable, with the mining areas of Sterzing (Vipiteno) and Klausen-Gufidaun especially receptive.[5] The district of St. Michelsburg[6] in the Puster valley and places such as Lüsen, St. Georgen, Pflaurentz, Welsberg (Monguelfo), Niedervintl, and Tauffers contained high concentrations of Anabaptists or their sympathizers[7] (Map 4).

These territories produced a plethora of capable leaders and faithful martyrs,[8] among them Jacob Hutter,[9] who would bequeath his name to a group of "communistic" Anabaptists which has survived against incredible odds into the present. Hutter and his fellow Pusterers (from the Puster valley) enjoyed the reputation of being among the toughest, most dedicated, disciplined, and zealous of the Anabaptists as evidenced in a letter by Peter Riedemann, the "second founder" of the Hutterites. Riedemann considered the Pusterers model members of the Anabaptist communities in Moravia and hoped to convert the Hessian Anabaptists into Pusterers, that is to say, into South Tyrolese.[10]

Because of the importance of South Tyrol to the beginning of the Anabaptist-Hutterite story, this territory deserves special attention. But the advent of Anabaptism in South Tyrol raises a cluster of questions. Who introduced Anabaptism to the South?[11] What accounts for its initial popularity and rapid spread? What was the relationship between Anabaptism and the uprising led by Michael Gaismair? Is it possible to reconstruct a social-religious profile of the early Anabaptist converts? What was the nature of the original message? When did Jacob Hutter join, and when did he emerge as the leader? How does one explain the dedication, zeal, and discipline that gave the Pusterers a special reputation among the communitarian Anabaptists in Moravia? To answer some of these and other questions it seems necessary to begin with a broader contextual view of the region.

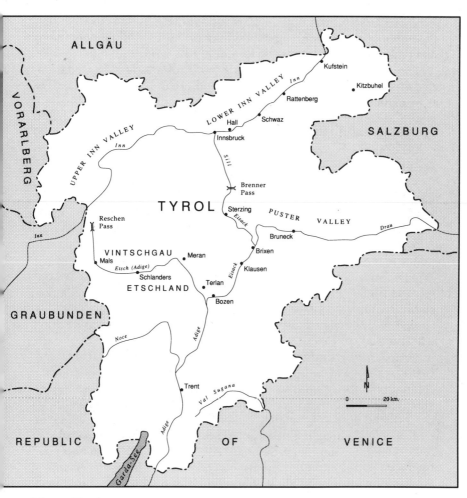

Map 4. Tyrol

Background and Context
Social and Political Economy

Some scholars have suggested that traits such as those admired by Peter Riedemann in the Pusterers were geographically conditioned and typical of "sturdy, forceful, and proud" mountain people. Others believe that the self-confidence, independence, and resourcefulness evident among the early Anabaptist-Hutterites were conditioned by the traditional freedoms and relative autonomy, particularly the "public" judiciary rights (*öffent-*

liche Rechtsfähigkeit) enjoyed by commoners in the Tyrol.[12] To appreciate these claims, a cursory background sketch of the social-political economy and religious geography of these territories may be helpful.

The landgravate (*Landgrafschaft*) of the Tyrol constituted a feudal mosaic of secular and ecclesiastical, rural and urban lordships interspersed with mining centers, all under the nominal sovereignty of Ferdinand I, whose administration and court for these territories presided at Innsbruck.[13] Included in the landgravate were parts of the ecclesiastical domains of the bishoprics (*Hochstifte*) of Brixen, Kitzbühl (Salzburg), and Freising. The subject territories were subdivided into administrative jurisdictions (*Gerichte*). Geographically, the Tyrol was divided into North and South, with the North subdivided into the Upper and Lower Inn regions. The South consisted of the Puster, Eisack, Jaufen, Etsch, and their various side valleys. The Inn valley, dotted with mines, included the cities of Hall, Schwaz, Rattenberg, Kufstein, and Innsbruck. The primary communication and transportation artery from Innsbruck to the South ran up the Wipp valley, over the Brenner Pass, and down the other side via Sterzing into the Jauffen, Puster, and Eisack valleys. The cities of Brixen, Klausen, and Bozen represented the major urban centers along the Eisack. The Puster valley, extending eastward above Brixen, had its own cluster of towns which included Brüneck, St. Lorenzen, and St. Georgen. Further south, just below Bozen, the Etsch valley opened west, extending through Meran to the Vintschgau (the Upper Etsch valley) and on to the Swiss Grisons.

The political-administrative developments in Tyrol's territories had favored the growing autonomy of commoners and their communities during the medieval period. Commoners gained at the expense of the feudal intermediaries, although "free lords" continued to exist into the sixteenth century and beyond. Since the fourteenth century, the commoners had been represented in the territorial diets (*Landtage*). This enfranchisement in tandem with relative local administrative autonomy could have contributed to the manifest self-reliance and independence of the Alpine population. But unlike their Swiss neighbors, the commoners of the Tyrol achieved their relative freedoms not against but in alliance with the territorial lords.[14] The mountainous terrain, the isolation of many hamlets, not to mention solitary homesteads, as well as the rudimentary nature of the administrative apparatus mitigated effective central control. Nevertheless, developments during the early modern period would strengthen central authority for reasons including the concerted effort of church and state against heresy.

Anabaptism appeared at a crucial juncture of social-political development. Coming in the wake of peasant unrest, Anabaptism represented a form of what Peter Blickle described as *Gemeindereformation,* or, to borrow Thomas Brady's phrase, an attempt at "turning Swiss." Anabaptism, by design or not, was nurtured in part by a desire for local autonomy. Yet, under suppression Anabaptism developed its own separatist, political subculture. The lack of intermediaries powerful enough to protect the dissenters forced them underground and ultimately into exile.[15] The successful suppression of the Anabaptists through close cooperation between temporal and spiritual authority, on the other hand, set the stage for the Catholic Reformation in the Tyrol.

The early modern administration of the Tyrol had been shaped by Maxmillian I, who assumed the office of landgrave in 1490. Nine years later, Maxmillian introduced a Territorial Order (*Landesordnung*), which included an attempt at codification of law and judiciary proceedings. But not until 1526 under Ferdinand I did this Territorial Order come into full effect. Among its purposes was to provide guidelines for civil and criminal justice,[16] the appointment of local officials, the selection and composition of local juries, court procedure, and payment of costs.[17]

Accordingly, each administrative district was to be staffed by a bailiff (*Pfleger*) and a magistrate (*Richter*). The bailiff's duties included the upkeep of a fortified place or castle to defend and protect the districts. In the jurisdiction of St. Michelsburg, this was the Michelsburg (castle) in whose shadow Jacob Hutter was born. The bailiff was also responsible for collecting rents, fines, and local tolls; communicating and enforcing regulations regarding forest and water rights and the mandates of the territorial lord; and maintaining or building bridges and roads. In other words, he was to preserve law and order and, in case of danger, mobilize and lead the local militia.

The responsibilities of the magistrate or judge included taking and enforcing the oath of fealty (*Huldigungsaid*) expected of all subjects sixteen years or older. In cooperation with the bailiff, the magistrate was to uphold territorial law and public order. In this capacity he resolved local disputes, enforced artisanal regulations, watched over commercial activity, protected the public against loan sharking or usury (interest more than 5 percent), and presided over all court cases in his jurisdiction.[18] Depending on the jurisdiction, the magistrate was assisted by a skeletal court staff that could include a solicitor (*Anwalt*), a court secretary (*Gerichtsschreiber*), and a court constable (*Gerichtsdiener*). Legal procedure, as defined in the Territorial Order, stipulated that the prosecution had the right to make its case first (*das erste recht*), and the defense could make a rejoinder (*das andre recht*). Both were then given an opportunity for summary arguments (*endrecht*). All serious cases involved judgment by jury. Both magistrate and jury were bound to render independent and fair judgment. The Territorial Order stipulated that each case was to be examined and weighed carefully and judgment rendered with due consideration to the circumstances. Traditionally, bailiff and magistrate were chosen from local notables; the same was true of the jury, which was sworn to render fair judgment without regard to the person's wealth or social status.[19] Only magistrates with special authority (*Malifizrecht*) could pronounce the death sentence, which could be carried out only by specially appointed, territorial executioners (*Scharfrichter*).[20] Depending on the nature of the crime, a death sentence varied from beheading to hanging, drowning, quartering, poling, breaking on the wheel, or burning. According to the Territorial Order, burning at the stake was to be reserved for arsonists, heretics (sorcerers, witches, and later primarily Anabaptists), coin forgers, and those convicted of sodomy.[21] Lesser punishments could lead to the loss of the tongue or oath fingers, floggings, or being dragged through the streets and having one's house demolished. Some crimes were punishable by imprisonment and/or fines.

During the sixteenth century the legal process was bent increasingly to serve central interests. Local resistance led by the lower echelon of magistrates could lead to their replacement, sometimes by "foreign" appointees.[22] No doubt the suppression of the Anabaptists furthered this development.

Special conditions prevailed in the Puster and Eisack valleys, much of which was subject to the prince bishop of Brixen, who exercised both secular and spiritual authority in his territories. The Puster valley, divided into four separate lordships (*Herrschaften*)—St. Michelsburg, Schöneck, Uttenheim, and Heunfels—had come into Hapsburg possession only under Maxmillian I. Because of his chronic financial needs, Maxmillian pawned these lordships to the bishop of Brixen on July 3, 1500, but retained sovereign rights (*Hoheitsrecht*), meaning that Innsbruck remained the final court of appeal for these territories. The possibility of playing off one authority against the other was not lost on the bishop's new subjects. Indeed, the subjects in the Schöneck and St. Michelsburg jurisdictions initially refused to recognize the prince bishop as their lawful lord. These two jurisdictions would subsequently hold high concentrations of Anabaptists.[23] The situation was complicated further by the existence of some local lords who remained directly responsible to Innsbruck and retained control in their own domains.

From 1525 to 1538 the bishop's seat at Brixen was occupied by George III, who had come to the office without religious training at the age of twenty-one by virtue of his being a bastard son of Maxmillian. George III treated the bishopric primarily as a source of income to promote his diplomatic career, which took him to various courts of Europe.[24]

Meanwhile, both spiritual and temporal administration were left to sub-alterns: a suffragan bishop, a governor (*Statthalter*), and councilors who administered the territories from the court at Brixen. These circumstances, as well as other factors discussed below, explain the evident alienation from both church and territorial lord by a good portion of the population in this region.[25]

The bailiffs and magistrates in the four major jurisdictions of the Puster valley, including Schöneck and St. Michelsburg, were appointees of the prince bishop of Brixen. Preferably, trustworthy persons (*Vertrauensmän-ner*) were chosen for such offices, although some offices were farmed out to the highest bidder. Understandably, potential buyers hoped to recoup their expenses and more.[26] The costs were, of course, ultimately borne by the local population.

Population and inflationary pressures during the first decades of the sixteenth century contributed to the economic insecurities in this area, in-cluding increasing indebtedness of peasant leaseholders, especially among the so-called free tenants (*Freistiftsbauern*) of the Puster valley. Lacking hereditary claims to their land, these tenants were subjected more and more to short-term leases or, in some instances, only yearly leases, which could be terminated on short notice by the landlord, the bishop of Brixen.[27] The resulting discontent explains in part why the Puster region with its heavy concentration of free tenants supported Gaismair in 1525–26 and later proved particularly susceptible to Anabaptism.

It would be simplistic, however, to assume that the peasant unrest and Anabaptism were the result of purely economic factors or the vexation of a particular social class. Ecclesiastical conditions contributed to the mal-aise that affected every social layer. Alienation cut diagonally across social class lines because the indigenous social structure was still organized around kinships, friendships, and dependencies that defied class analysis. Anabaptists were nobles,[28] former government administrators and clergy, as well as innkeepers and miners. The large majority, as was true for the society as a whole, were artisans and peasants. A good proportion of the peasants, especially in the Puster valley, seemed to come from the ranks of free tenants with temporary leases. On an even lower social niveau (*de-classiert*) were domestics, subject to the discipline of their domestic lord. Among the early Anabaptist converts, for instance, were a good number of young maids who served in households friendly to Anabaptists. But the leadership came predominately from literate artisan rank, well-to-do peasant proprietors, and former clergy or monks. In short, the educated and socially privileged tended to rise naturally to leadership positions in Anabaptism.[29] This makes it difficult to identify Anabaptism with a particular class or as a religion of the poor. Nonetheless, Anabaptism did appeal to those alienated—alienated by a number of factors, not the least of which were ecclesiastical conditions that prevailed in the Tyrol.

Ecclesiastical Geography

Historians seeking to understand the evident disillusionment with the traditional faith and practice which surfaced with the Reformation have pointed to a "crisis in the lower clergy."[30] This designation included the parish priest (*Pfarrherr*), journeyman priest (*Gesellenpriester*), and chaplain (*Hilfspriester*)—that is, the lower secular clergy who provided religious services for the general public. In the years before the Reformation neither the quantity nor quality of religious services met rising expectations. Religious fervor, not apathy or indifference, fueled alienation from the church, an observation supported by evidence of growing membership in religious lay fraternities and a "sacral construction" boom during the last decade of the fifteenth century.[31] For a variety of reasons, among them a decline in real income, the established church with its benefice and patronage system seemed unable to meet the growing spiritual need and religious fervor in the generation before the Reformation. Small hamlets and out-of-the-way places were served poorly, if at all. Journeymen priests or chaplains visited the less accessible places only five or six times a year.[32]

Increasingly this lower layer of the clergy was drawn from transient foreigners, often runaway monks, who for a variety of reasons preferred the road to monastic enclosure. These itinerants normally served only short periods of time in a parish[33] and supplemented their meager salaries by collecting fees for baptisms, marriages, burials, memorial masses, special dedications, or blessings. And although periodic concerns were raised about these vagrant priests, 75 percent of the lower clergy continued to be of foreign (non-Tyrolian) stock into the 1570s.[34] Unfamiliar with the native tongue, these foreigners added to the perceived neglect, antiforeign sentiment, and anticlericalism. Local peasants were reluctant to entrust their spiritual well-being to strangers.

As early as 1495 pressure arose for chaplains to read the Gospel in the vernacular.[35] At the same time, local communities sought control over clerical appointments and demanded that the tithe be used for local services. Thus, long before the Reformation debate entered these territories, the local population registered their desire for proper religious services and increased attention. Indeed, they were willing to protect the income of local chaplains or journeymen priests against the avarice of their superior, the parish priest (*Pfarrherr*). The more permanent parish priest or *Pfaffen,* more often than not, proved to be a *Konkubinarier*—that is, he lived in a commonlaw relationship and raised a family. Widespread into the 1570s, concubinage had become a status symbol of the economically more secure and settled parish priest. Those unhappy with transient chaplains or journeymen priests tended to be no less annoyed with *Konkubinarier,* who lived in contradiction to the church's ideal of celibacy and whose illegitimate family represented an added economic burden. Local sensitivities were ruffled further when priest and concubine aspired to prominent local social positions. *Pfaffen,* like lightning rods, drew economic, social, and moral religious resentment upon their heads.[36] Anabaptist anticlericalism resonated with and articulated popular sentiment. Jörg Zaunring, an early leader in South Tyrol, described parish priests as the most "godless people" under the sun, given to "all kinds of freedom and lasciviousness of the flesh, such as drunkenness, gluttony, whoring, and blasphemy." It seemed curious to him that one properly married to an "honest woman" could not serve as priest, while "one who lived in open adultery and whoredom, has a whore in his house and a number of others secretly, is considered a beloved servant of the sacrament of their mass . . . is held in high esteem, given a good parish or two, a canonry or prebend, yes, even a bishopric or two."[37]

According to Zaunring the discrepancy between celibacy prescribed for the priestly office and the actual nonpractice of it identified the traditional clergy not as servants of Christ but as prophets of Baal. The implied repetition of Christ's sacrifice in the mass and insistence on his bodily presence constituted the "abomination of desolation" predicted by Daniel.[38] Zaunring's evident anticlericalism and rejection of the mass were standard among Anabaptists and stood in continuity with the message of the radical evangelicals who formed the historic bridge between the Peasants' War and Anabaptism in South Tyrol.

Continuity with the Peasants' War

The Scholarly Debate

Interpretations that insisted on separating Anabaptism from the peasant uprisings because one was considered purely religious and pacifist, the other political-economic and violent, are no longer tenable.[39] An emerging consensus is that Anabaptism "began within the radical currents of the early Reformation and the Peasants' War."[40] This is true for German as well as Swiss and Tyrolian territories. Yet specific empirical evidence linking the Gaismair rebellion and Anabaptism in the Tyrol has been difficult to obtain.[41]

The suggestion of a connection is, of course, not new.[42] More than a century ago conservative historian Josef Jäkel, who considered Gaismair an evil, violent revolutionary and Anabaptism a social disease, argued for a direct link between the two.[43] Through guilt by association with Gaismair, Jäkel intended to discredit Anabaptists as social anarchists and religious fanatics. To make his case, he pointed to the geographic overlap between the two movements: districts that supported the Gaismair uprising later saw concentrations of Anabaptism. But the primary support for Jäkel's thesis came from the official reaction as recorded in government decrees. According to Ferdinand's mandate of August 20, 1527, "deceitful teachings and heretical sects" were spread by "some evil, capricious . . . persons, who did not get their fill from that immense and wretched blood-letting of the past years, but seek to revive new disobedience, insurrection and rebellion."[44] The same mandate blamed the Peasants' War on "false teachings of Christian freedom" and on subversive notions that "all things should be held in common, and that all authority [obrigkeit] should be abolished." Like Gaismair and his peasant supporters, the Anabaptists allegedly "disparaged all authority and lordship." Therefore they were charged not only with heresy but also with insurrection.[45]

But was there any truth to these charges? In response to conservative accusations, a more liberal Austrian scholarship, represented by Joseph Beck,[46] Johann Loserth, Rudolf Wolkan, Edward Widmoser, and Grete Mecenseffy, tended to emphasize the religious nature of the Anabaptist protest. In their noble attempt to revise centuries of official prejudicial historiography, these scholars underlined the pacifist, peaceful intentions of the religious nonconformists and with it their unjustified persecution. Committed to religious tolerance and cultural pluralism, they rejected the notion that any religious dissent, past or present, was subversive in principle. It was this liberal historiography, more congenial to North American values, which informed the Mennonite scholarly view of Austrian Anabaptism, primarily through Wolkan's student, Robert Friedmann, in his many contributions to the *Mennonite Encyclopedia* and *Mennonite Quarterly Review*. In this view Anabaptists were seen as purely religiously motivated; their suppression as entirely unjustified. A connection between pacifist, religious sectarians and armed rebels who attempted to transform the whole society seemed not at all obvious.

A very different view was presented by Marxist scholars who, unencumbered by apologetic religious sensitivities, readily agreed with conservatives about the subversive nature of Anabaptism. Czech historian Josef Macek saw in Anabaptism a continuation of Gaismair's assault on decaying feudal structures.[47] He wrote that "it is wrong and superficial to overemphasize the peaceful character of the Anabaptist movement, for by doing so one blurs its revolutionary effect."[48] Unfortunately Macek failed to make a convincing empirical case for his claims. Walter Klaassen, who considered Macek's general thesis as "quite likely correct," nevertheless found no convincing empirical evidence to support it.[49] A list of 113 Gaismair supporters yielded only two future Anabaptists.[50] James Stayer's investigation along the same lines fared little better. He raised the known number of Anabaptists who participated in the Gaismair affair to ten.[51] Yet both Klaassen and Stayer were inclined to believe that the Peasants' War created "indispensable preconditions" for Anabaptism.

This state of scholarly opinion invites another look at the Gaismair program in comparison with the original Anabaptist protest.

The Generic Argument: A Radical Anabaptist Profile

Gaismair's proposed Territorial Order of 1526 presented comprehensive reform proposals for the entire society.[52] The economic plan sought to secure the livelihood of the indigenous population. The sick and the poor were to receive aid according to their need, with special overseers appointed for this task. Community projects envisioned the clearing of swamps to increase the availability of arable land for growing agricultural demands. Local artisan industry was to be stimulated by the abolition of internal tariffs, with prices and salaries regulated for the benefit of commoners. The mining industry was to be placed under elected managers and operated for the common good. Foreign and usurious merchants were to be banned.

On the political front, Gaismair aimed at nothing less than an independent republic similar to some Swiss cantons. His Territorial Order called for an overhaul of the local judiciary system and administration. Equitable justice was to be furthered by annual elections of local magistrates and juries, corruption and conflict of interest avoided by set salaries, and the staff of the magistrate's court and the jury forbidden to accept gratuities. Social distinctions and privileges considered contrary to the Gospel were to be abolished, city and castle walls leveled. In short, society was to be restructured "so that no one would take advantage of the other."[53]

Concerning ecclesiastical matters, Gaismair's orientation was strikingly iconoclastic. He and his spiritual advisors considered the mass "an abomination before God and utterly unchristian." The reformed church would lose any claims to sacerdotal and sacramental powers, the clergy their privileged status. Priests were to be replaced with preachers, mass with sermon. The reformed pastor-preacher would hold his office by the grace of the community rather than an ecclesiastical hierarchy. Scripture was to be the sole guide for religious beliefs and practice. A special training school, similar to Zurich's Prophezei, was planned for the training of literate, reform-minded exegetes of the Scriptures. The church would come under lay control and lose its material wealth and power. Its monasteries would be dissolved, its hierarchy abolished. Local parishes would not only be empowered to choose but also to support their own pastors, who would receive fixed salaries from the tithe collected by representatives of the local community. Surplus funds would be reallocated for the care of the needy. All in all, Gaismair's program of 1526 envisioned "community reformation" (*Gemeindereformation*), a reformation that, in contradistinction to the princely or magisterial reformation, aimed at the relative autonomy of the local communities.[54] Anabaptism, it can be argued, embodied similar ideals.

A striking feature of Gaismair's religious program was its agitative tone.[55] Article 6 of the Territorial Order cited Deuteronomy 7:5 and 25 as divine mandates for the destruction, the "hacking down" and burning of idols. Images, shrines, crucifixes, and other "sacred" objects were to be removed; chalices and precious metals collected and minted into coins for the benefit of a stable territorial currency.[56]

When compared with Gaismair's religious program, Anabaptism displays many parallels, particularly its insurgent and anticlerical attitudes.[57] Of the early Anabaptists, Vintzentz Puchler had "broken a crucifix." Hans Grembser had kicked a statue he found "lying" by the road.[58] Balthasar Schneider and a certain Cristan were responsible for the destruction of an image at Vichter's place.[59] Hans Hueber engaged in "unseemly talk" to the effect that the local church bell should be thrown from the tower.[60] Valentin Schneider interrupted a procession with shouts that everything the priest said about the eucharist "stinks and is a lie." Jörg Parugkher, while in the churchyard, uttered invectives against "murder dens" in which no Christian order prevailed.[61] And Jacob Gasser, possibly the brother of peasant leader Hans Gasser, was questioned about a statue that had been "shot and hacked" to pieces.[62]

There were good reasons for questioning Jacob Gasser about the symbolic violence unleashed against "sacred objects." He had been guilty of one of the more spectacular sacrilegious acts.[63] On Saturday, January 27, 1532, rumors spread in St. Andreasberg (jurisdiction of Rodeneck) that something extraordinary would happen in church on Sunday. The next day Gasser interrupted the celebration of mass, tore from the priest's hand the plate containing the communion wafers, threw the wafers to the ground, and stamped on them. He then took the chalice from the altar and threw it against the church door. According to a report sent to Innsbruck, only the two priests and some of the women seemed shocked. Two men escorted Gasser outside, facilitating his escape through the crowd that was milling about in front of the church. One local supporter hailed Gasser's act as "a great miracle" and hoped that more would follow.[64]

No doubt Gasser's action was an usually bold demonstration of lay "enlightenment." Many shared his feeling of having been misled too long, but most expressed their disillusionment less explosively by simply shunning church services, some by joining the Anabaptists. Jacob Hutter, the undisputed Anabaptist leader in the region at the time of Gasser's action (see Chapter 8), presumably approved of Gasser's attitude, if not his action. He baptized Mrs. Gasser while she and her husband were running from the authorities. Moreover, judging from statements by others, Gasser's sentiments toward the mass was not uncommon among Anabaptists led by Hutter. Seventeen-year-old Katharina Tagwericher told her interrogators that "churches are damned temples of idols, whore-houses and murderers' dens in which priests [*Pfaffen*] murder souls." Hutter had taught that the Anabaptists were being persecuted "because emperor, king, and lords fear that if one permitted the [true] Christian [teaching] to continue, then their [the lords'] glory would diminish more and more." This had of course been the intention of the Gaismair project. It may be inferred therefore that Hutter and his converts approved aspects of that project. Asked about the sacrament of the altar, Katharina replied, "it is a damned, no good idol, invented by the priests for the sake of money." She held a similar opinion on pedobaptism, which she considered an "invention of priests for the sake of money."[65]

Many similar statements by other members of Hutter's network could be cited to demonstrate the same radical attitudes. Church buildings were considered mere stone piles (*stainhauffen*),[66] murderers' dens (*mördergrueben*), or temples of idols (*götzentempl*). "Only whores and pimps enter the stone piles."[67] Mass and the eucharist were seen as "an abomination and a stench before God"; pedobaptism "a dog's bath" (*ain sudlwesch*). Through pedobaptism the priest claimed to "drive demons out of the pure child while he, himself, is full of demons." In short, everything associated with traditional practices seemed utterly corrupt and anti-Christian. The clergy knew nothing of the Gospel and dealt in lies. They were selling the Lord like a piece of merchandise through the sacramental systems in order to support their whores and their own un-Christian life style. True followers of Christ could not participate in, attend to, or condone such ceremonies: "It was all idolatry and against God," from pedobaptism to extreme unction. It was more important to die in the true faith than to be buried in consecrated soil. The corpse might just as well decompose on the gravel heap by the mountain side. Contrary to its claim, the traditional church had no powers reaching into the next world and should have none in the present. Confession to priests was not only unnecessary but evil. No priestly consecration was needed for marriage.[68] The intercessory role of saints and with it the church calendar with all its saint days were rejected, as were rules and regulations concerning Lent, the eating of meat, and so on. All practices not found in the New Testament were dismissed as mere human inventions. In sum, "God the Almighty in heaven alone" was to be worshipped.[69]

Such radical immediacy without saints, priests, sacred objects, and sacraments meant that the Anabaptists recognized no religious authorities or spiritual guides other than their own.[70] They appealed to the New Testament as the source for true faith and practice. To grasp the full historic significance of the radicality of the Anabaptist protest, it must be recalled that both secular and spiritual authority in parts of South Tyrol were vested in one and the same person, the prince bishop of Brixen. The Anabaptist position, therefore, articulated more than purely religious grievances. From the perspective of traditionalists, criticism of the established church amounted to attacks on existing authority structures. Not surprisingly, from the vantage point of those who held power, Anabaptism stood in continuity with the Gaismair rebellion. Ideological parallels suggested a genetic relationship between the two.

But what of Anabaptist pacifism? Does it not, along with sectarian separation from the larger society, argue for drastic discontinuity with the Gaismair proposals? In 1527 Anabaptism was welcomed by evangelicals who, only a year earlier, threatened to defend the Gospel with force if need be. These evangelical sacramentists, who formed a loosely related network in the wake of Gaismair's aborted project, provided a historic link to Anabaptism. How quickly these sacramentists converted to a nonresistant position when they joined Anabaptism is difficult to ascertain, but allowance must be made for a transitional phase, including inconsistencies and ambivalences. Curiously, no pacifist statement survives from the first two years of Anabaptism in South Tyrol (1527–29). And the magistrate responsible for some of the first arrests in the Puster valley found "letters of threat and insult" (*Droh- und Schmähbriefe*) fastened to his dwelling as late as 1529.[71]

In that same year Hutter visited the community at Austerlitz and entered into an agreement that presumably included pacifism. Evidence that a nonresistant position had been clearly articulated and taught in South Tyrol by 1530–31 at the latest comes from statements by Anabaptists that they had been instructed to carry a staff only and not to resist arrest.[72] A report from early 1532 that Hutter himself carried a gun (*Büchse* or *Hake*) seems hardly believable, unless the informant remembered an earlier Hutter. If that was the case, then Hutter had at one point carried a

Hakenbüchse—a gun capable of penetrating thick knightly armor at seventy-five meters. Presumably such heavy gear was not part of Hutter's Anabaptist equipment but harkened back to his earlier period as a partisan of Gaismair.[73] In the fall of 1526 Hutter had exchanged such equipment (if the report is to be believed at all) for a New Testament, and in 1529 at the latest he joined the staff bearers.

The point here is that Anabaptists continued symbolic iconoclastic acts of violence even beyond 1529. These acts reveal a radical profile not unlike Gaismair's program, and the ideological overlap between the two reform movements is undeniable. This does not mean that all peasants who supported Gaismair became Anabaptists or that all Anabaptists had been Gaismair's retainers. Anabaptism emerged under changed circumstances and involved a shift to more religious-moral concerns. Above all, Anabaptists strove to reinstitute the apostolic church. Within the congregation of God they recognized no social privilege, only brothers and sisters in Christ.[74] Their meetings featured Bible readings, preaching, and discussions focusing not only on criticisms of traditional practices but also on how to institute the true Christian community with mutual aid and fraternal discipline. Compared with Gaismair's objectives, their expectations had been reduced with regard to the reformability of the larger society. With adult baptism a clear distinction emerged between insiders and outsiders. Relations to the larger society were governed by a new dignity as a new sense of identity as Christ's true followers took hold. Outsiders, whether emperor, king, or local lord, were considered Gentiles. "One should give rent to the authorities and nobles, but one should not do them any reverence or consider them higher than another simple lay person."[75]

This last statement echoes still with the defiance hurled against the prince bishop of Brixen and the Hapsburg authorities at Innsbruck in 1525–26, but it had been tempered by a new note of sectarian realism or *Gelassenheit* to give unto Caesar what belonged to him, but no more.

The Coming of Anabaptism

Pre-Anabaptist Evangelicals

Evangelical ideas entered South Tyrol through foreigners and in the form of "heretical" literature. Unfortunately, little is known about either of these transmitters. What is clear is that by 1524–25 a "radical" Reformation orientation had taken root in part of the population.[76] Gaismair's religious program can be considered Swiss Reformed, but conditions in the Tyrol were not Swiss. South Tyrol had territorial lords in Ferdinand and the prince bishop of Brixen. It lacked dominant urban centers with sufficient resources to support an independent city reformation. Consequently no dominant reformers emerged as had been the case in Zurich, Basel, Bern, or Geneva. In fact, no urban reformation with staying power crystallized. Lacking a dominant theologian-reformer as leader, evangelicals in South Tyrol remained unorganized, meeting in informal, largely lay-led conventicles that straddled the urban and rural worlds. And although towns—particularly Bozen, Klausen, and Sterzing on the major trade route—played important roles as marketplaces for the dissemination of Reformation ideas, no central focus or organization developed. The new ideas were simply carried into the countryside by itinerant preachers and colporteurs.

Among the early evangelical propagators in South Tyrol was a former Dominican from Ulm, Hans Vischer, who preached in the parish church of Sterzing as well as in the pubs and shops of its artisans. On Palm Sunday, March 15, 1526, Vischer explained to peasants gathered in Peter Kurssner's shop (*Stube*) that there was "nothing to mass" and that priests were engaging in idolatrous magic. He allegedly told his audience that their oaths as subjects meant nothing before God and that they should not support the landgrave's wars, which had no just cause. Instead, like the ancient Greeks and more recently the Swiss, they should drive out the nobles and princes and become masters in their own land. In short, Vischer incited urbanites and peasants alike to rebel against properly constituted authority, a charge he denied. Nevertheless, he was exiled.[77] He surfaced at the disputation between Catholics and Reformed at Baden in the Swiss Aargau, May 21 to June 8.[78] Nothing is known about his subsequent fate. What is important here is that already during his ministry at Sterzing Vischer advocated a Swiss style Reformation.

Indirect evidence suggests that Vischer's supporters in Sterzing had contacts with sacramentists further south in the Klausen-Gufidaun districts. A leading figure of these sacramentists was Mathias Messerschmied, a former canon (*Chorherr*) of Innichen in the Upper Puster valley, whose reform-mindedness can be traced back to 1524. In September of that year Messerschmied was imprisoned by the bishop of Brixen for spreading heretical ideas. Released on January 12, 1525,[79] the former canon made his way to Augsburg, where he honed his skills as a knifesmith.[80] He returned to the Tyrol late in 1525 or early in 1526 with literature and a literate wife. Evidence indicates that he was among the preachers who supported Gaismair.[81] In early 1526 he resided in Klausen. Here his home became a meeting place for a conventicle of sacramentists, his wife assisting in the meetings by reading the Scriptures or pamphlet literature. The fruits of the ensuing discussions in this conventicle became evident during Lent (February/March) 1526, when Messerschmied and his friends attained notoriety because they flouted church regulations concerning the eating of meats. In Klausen as in Zurich the coming of Anabaptism was furthered by the unseasonal eating of sausages! Known participants were Gilg Pader (Bader), Ulrich Müller, Hans Weber, Peter Pinter, Lantzinger, a former magistrate of Latzfons, and Wölfl (Wolfgang), a goatherd (*Geisshirt*). Practically all reappeared as Anabaptists in 1527.

Wölfl is the best known of these pre-Anabaptist evangelicals.[82] One of those novel lay preachers and colporteurs who made their appearance during the early Reformation, Wölfl, an uneducated shepherd, became the most effective propagator of radical religious ideas and was destined to play a crucial role in winning Hutter first for the evangelical party and then for Anabaptism.[83] Born in the Sarn valley, Wölfl had spent seven of his adolescent years herding livestock. During 1525 or 1526 he made his way first to the Vintschgau and from there to the Inn valley,[84] where he spent time in Inzing, Oberperfuss, Kematen, Füssen, Innsbruck, and Hall. At some point during these travels Wölfl was caught up in the Reformation debate and began to preach reform. A schoolmaster in Innsbruck taught him how to read print, and in the spring of 1526, the semiliterate Wölfl returned south, linking up with Messerschmied's conventicle in Klausen. Wölfl's unauthorized preaching soon ran afoul of a conservative priest named Steffan. During the ensuing conflict Wölfl received support from nearby miners who, along with members of Messerschmied's conventicle, pledged to "protect and defend" him with arms if necessary.[85] When a threatening letter against Steffan was nailed to the church door, the prince bishop's representative, Christof of Teutenhofen, vice captain (*Unterhauptmann*) in nearby Säben, intervened. Wölfl was taken into custody for questioning. Messerschmied and his supporters submitted a written appeal to the cathedral chapter's bailiff (*Stifts-verwalter*). The letter apparently bore fruit, for Wölfl regained his freedom with the proviso that he cease preaching.

Leaving Klausen, Wölfl moved to neighboring Gufidaun. Here the local bailiff, Hans Preu, heard him and seemed favorably impressed. Three years later Innsbruck demanded that the lord of Gufidaun, Georg von Firmian, replace Hans Preu because he proved delinquent in suppressing the Anabaptists.[86] Preu was not the only local official sympathetic to the evangelical message; Wölfl spent two weeks with the magistrate of Bozen, Jacob Huepher, and sold him a New Testament.[87] Huepher, too, was later reprimanded by Innsbruck for his lack of zeal in suppressing the Anabaptists.

Wölfl's mission to Gufidaun and Bozen was followed by an itinerary through to the Puster valley, with stops in Pflaurentz and Montal in the jurisdiction of St. Michelsburg (Map 5). His host in Pflaurentz, Gregor

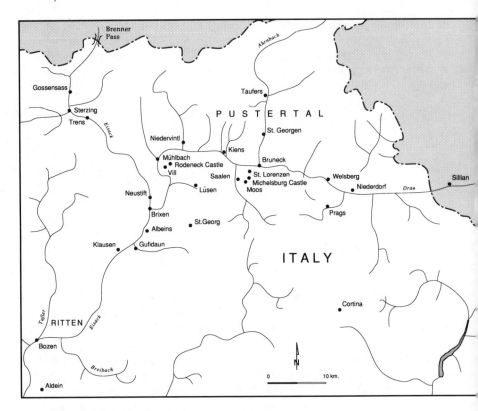

Map 5. South Tyrol

Weber, a friend and "teacher" of Hutter, was destined to become one of the first local Anabaptist martyrs.[88] Wölfl's unauthorized preaching received opposition from the parish priest in St. Lorenzen. Discussions with the priest in the presence of the magistrate apparently led to a further investigation before eight priests in Brüneck. Somehow Wölfl remained free and continued his preaching and discussions in private dwellings. Perhaps the most significant of these meetings took place at Stegen. According to his later account, "many people" attended in the home of the hatmaker, Caspar Hueter.[89] Among those present was Jacob Hutter. Ten years later Caspar Hueter testified that Wölfl influenced Hutter to travel all the way to Bozen in order to purchase a New Testament, which, upon returning, he read to members of Caspar's household. Shortly thereafter, Caspar and Hutter parted company, allegedly because Caspar had forbidden any further New Testament lectures in his home.[90]

Meanwhile, Wölfl continued his mission in the Puster. In St. Georgen he found a favorable reception among members of the Grembs family, whose name appeared later among the Anabaptists. Wölfl found a hearing as well at Tauffers in the Ahrn valley. Challenged at Sand by mining magistrate (*Bergrichter*) Hans Glögg, Wölfl warned that if he were silenced, five others would rise in his place; Wölfl again remained free. Local authorities seemed unsure of what to do with the popular lay preacher who also had some noble patrons. For instance, Wölfl spent eight days with Anton von Wolkenstein.[91] Later, von Wolkenstein was cited to Innsbruck, forbidden to host any more religious disputations, coaxed to reaffirm the doctrine of the real presence, and ordered to submit "all Lutheran books or books of the new sects" to the local priest. Yet von Wolkenstein's household later provided shelter to Anabaptists, and von Wolkenstein's wife Elsbeth and son Sigmund were implicated in the "sect."[92]

Clearly, then, Wölfl's itinerary of 1526 maps the existence of a network of evangelical sympathizers reaching from Bozen, Klausen, and Gufidaun to the Puster and its side valleys. Regardless of whether or not this network reached back to common sympathies with the Gaismair project, it certainly pointed forward to the coming of Anabaptism. Chronologically, geographically, and ideologically Wölfl's mission marked a transitional phase to Anabaptism. Gaismair's party had moved through the Puster region as late as July 1526, accompanied in some instances by raids on parsonages.[93] Gaismair's withdrawal no doubt left unfulfilled hopes and aspirations among his erstwhile supporters,[94] making it tempting to see Wölfl's ministry, which followed a few weeks later, as feeding on the residual resentment and the loss of faith in the religious establishment.

Wölfl's reception certainly suggests considerable interest in the evangelical message, and it would seem almost incredible if former supporters of Gaismair had not been among his well-wishers. The evident hesitation of local magistrates to prosecute the goatherd turned preacher obviously permitted the spread of evangelical ideas during this crucial and receptive stage. Nevertheless, complaints did reach Brixen and Innsbruck. On January 2, 1527, local authorities were ordered to be on the lookout for two "corner preachers" (*Winkelprediger*).[95] Within a week, Wölfl was under arrest in Brixen. His statement to the interrogators provided a glimpse into his religious views.[96] Wölfl considered the New Testament to be the final authority, and he drew his teachings specifically from the Gospel and the Epistles of Paul (*allain vom Evangeli und Epistl St. Pauls halt er*). He believed that the vernacular New Testament could be read and interpreted by ordinary lay persons as a guide to true faith and life. On this basis he held the mass to be idolatry. The sacrament of the eucharist had become "a piece of merchandise which the merchant locks up so that he may make some money on it."[97] In its place, Wölfl advocated the restitution of "our

Lord's evening meal" (*unsers herrn abendessen*). He told his interrogators that "pope, monks, and clergy [*Pfaffen*] are the Antichrist who mislead Christ's people." The corrupt church and its clergy could neither forgive sins nor dispense saving grace. Neither Mary, saints, nor priests could mediate between God and man.[98] Confession was at best a friendly consultation or a seeking of spiritual counsel. It was wrong to follow human inventions and regulations—such as clerical celibacy and avoidance of meat—contrary to apostolic practice. He was also highly critical of religious artifacts. Even a crucifix was nothing but wood, no more sacred than "sticks thrown at dogs or used to heat stoves!" He rejected holy water and the rite of *firmung* but said nothing as yet against pedobaptism. This suggests that as of January 1527 Wölfl and his friends had not yet imbibed any criticism of this rite. Neither had they relinquished the hope for the reform of the church and the entire society along New Testament norms, at least on the local level.

How did Wölfl come to these religious convictions? By his own admission, Wölfl had been exposed to Reformation pamphlets. In Hall he had heard a Landsbergin read "much about Lutheran matters,"[99] and he also heard Lutheran tracts being read at Inzing. In Innsbruck a schoolmaster had taught him to read print so that he "might defend himself with the Gospel and the Word of God." Once back across the Brenner, Wölfl had come under influences more radical than Luther, primary among them a booklet carried from Augsburg by Messerschmied. Making the rounds in Klausen, this booklet had been read in part by the city magistrate who discussed its content with Wölfl and Peter Binder (Pinter). Wölfl and Binder brought the same booklet to the Puster valley where it was read in many households and inns. Von Wolkenstein's "error" as to "the revered sacrament of the altar" suggests that he also had been exposed to the booklet, and Innsbruck subsequently ordered him to surrender all books and not to accept, order, or buy any heretical literature in the future.

Because of the unique impact of this booklet, it deserves special attention. Wölfl made the following statement about the booklet:

> He had read in a booklet, which Messerschmied brought from Augsburg, that the canon [of the mass] was nothing. And Messerschmied had also loaned the same booklet to Peter Binder at Klausen. He carried it with him into the Puster valley and let it be read in many places; especially at the new innkeeper's at St. Lorenzen and at Georg Weber's place in Pflaurentz; also at Anton von Wolkenstein's. And [Binder] had carried it into the houses at Klausen and let it be read everywhere by his son Hansl.[100]

But what booklet declaring the canon of the mass as nothing did Messerschmied bring from Augsburg? Titles published in Augsburg during

Messerschmied's stay there (1525) indicate that the mass and the nature of Christ's presence in it were the most hotly disputed topics in the press at the time. Philip Ulhart, Augsburg's "corner printer," published a series of pamphlets on the subject, among them Ulrich Zwingli's *Answer Against Hieronymous Emser, the Patron of the Canon or of the Stillmass.* He also published the bitter exchange between Luther and Karlstadt.[101] Karlstadtian arguments and vocabulary regarding images entered the Anabaptist discourse in South Tyrol;[102] and his *Chief Articles of Christian Doctrine,* a point-by-point refutation of Luther's *Against the Heavenly Prophets,*[103] fits the label "Lutheran and new sect literature" in the possession of Anton von Wolkenstein. *Chief Articles* reiterated Karlstadt's position on the sacrament of the altar and on images, a position that corresponded with Wölfl's teachings.

Unfortunately, the state of the evidence does not permit a definite identification of the publication so influential on the pre-Anabaptist circle of South Tyrol. As best as can be determined, it was Zwinglian or Karlstadtian, certainly not Lutheran in origin. This scenario helps to explain the receptivity to Anabaptism and its rapid spread once introduced into the evangelical network of South Tyrol. The ideological step from the sacramentist iconoclast orientation of Wölfl and his well-wishers to Anabaptism proved relatively small, as is borne out by the evidence that most of Wölfl's known contacts surfaced a few months later as Anabaptists. In Klausen these included Messerschmied, Ulrich Müller, Hans Weber, Peter Binder, Gilg Bader (Pader), Mrs. Bader (Pader), and Andrä Radler.[104] In the Puster valley they included Jacob Hutter, Georg Weber, Mair Paulle, and members of the Grembs and von Wolkenstein households. This brings us to the beginnings of Anabaptism in South Tyrol and to the role of Jörg Blaurock.

Jörg Blaurock: The Swiss Connection

Jörg (George) Blaurock's key role in the coming of Anabaptism to South Tyrol has been generally assumed, but there is some confusion as to timing. Johann Loserth, who considered Blaurock the initiator, knew only of his 1529 journey into these territories.[105] Yet there is evidence of an Anabaptist presence as early as 1527, and Hutterite sources place Blaurock in South Tyrol at the same time as Hubmaier's arrival in Nicolsburg, which would mean in 1526. The same sources list 1527 as the year of Blaurock's imprisonment and death.[106] But Blaurock died in 1529.

The discrepancies dissolve if one postulates two visits by Blaurock to South Tyrol: one in 1527, the other in 1529. Careful sifting of official documents supports such a view. A query from Innsbruck in January/February 1528 mentions a "Jörgen, the Anabaptist from Swiss territory," in connection with Ulrich Kobl. Innsbruck had learned that Kobl, a prominent former Gaismair supporter, was on his way up the Etsch valley to Bernese territory.[107] If Innsbruck's information was correct, then Kobl may have been on his way to a disputation scheduled for January 1528 in Bern. Blaurock attended the disputation between January 7 and 26, 1528.[108] It may be inferred, therefore, that Innsbruck reacted belatedly to information regarding Blaurock's presence in its territories because Blaurock was back on Swiss soil by September 24, 1527. On that day attempts were made to arrest him in St. Gall. Later in the year he was confined temporarily in Appenzell. His presence in South Tyrol, therefore, occurred prior to September 24, 1527, a scenario supported by other evidence, which indicates that an Anabaptist was proselytizing in the Vintschgau as early as the spring of 1527. On May 22, 1527, Innsbruck reprimanded the bailiff of Glurns and Mals, Jacob Trapp, for permitting a priest from the Engadin to speak regarding "rebaptism and other matters."[109] The time and location of the reported activity as well as the place of origin of the intruder seem to fit Blaurock, who appears to have come down the Etsch valley with the spring thaw of 1527.

Blaurock's whereabouts after attending the disputation of January 1528 in Bern remain unknown. During December 1528 he appears to have been near Tauffers in Appenzell, from which he traveled to Basel. Here he was imprisoned but released on February 14, 1529.[110] He was also detained upon returning to Appenzell during April 1529.[111] Blaurock returned to South Tyrol later that spring and was active in Vels, Tiers, Ab-Penon, Vils near Neumarkt (Egna), and Tramin on the Moos before being arrested in Gufidaun. His arrest has been recorded under July 14, 1529. He was burned in Klausen on September 6, 1529. According to Hutterite sources, one of the accusations against him was that "he had abandoned the priestly office he had held under the papacy." Peter Walpot, a future Hutterite leader, only eight years of age at the time, witnessed Blaurock's execution.[112]

The evidence, then, points to two visits by Blaurock to South Tyrol: one between May and September 1527, the other in the spring of 1529, leading to his martyrdom. Whether Blaurock's first visit followed contact with the Gaismair party is unclear, but such contact could explain why a number of Gaismair supporters were among the first converts. Blaurock's first mission reached down the Etsch valley to the Bozen-Klausen districts. The first arrests in these territories took place before the end of 1527. On January 29, 1528, Innsbruck reprimanded the magistrate of Bozen, Jacob Huepher, for failing to inform the court of Jörg's (Blaurock) whereabouts. The same communique demanded that Huepher follow the example of

Rattenberg and enforce the death penalty on two imprisoned Anabaptists. Huepher was to notify Innsbruck should the jury refuse.[113]

Jacob Huepher, who only a year earlier hosted Wölfl and purchased a New Testament, was delinquent in prosecuting the Anabaptists. This must have been all the more annoying to Innsbruck because prominent Gaismair supporters appeared among the earliest Anabaptists. In addition to Ulrich Kobl, these included also Hans Gasser, arrested before February 19, 1528.[114] Both Kobl and Gasser, local leaders in the Gaismair rebellion, hardly qualified as the *Stillen im Lande*.[115] But neither did Blaurock. Before venturing abroad, this impetuous founding member of Swiss Anabaptism had disrupted traditional church services, denounced spiritual and secular authorities alike, and gained a most favorable hearing among Zurich's rebellious subjects in the district of Grüningen.[116]

Gasser, who lived on the Ritten, a rather wild, inaccessible terrain (Einöde), had hosted an Anabaptist "synagogue" in his home—that is, religious discussions around scriptural readings. A certain Mairhofer had played a leading role in these discussions. The hospitality extended to Mairhofer by Gasser implies an acquaintanceship of the two preceding their involvement with Anabaptism. It is tempting to infer that this acquaintanceship reached back to participation in the Gaismair affair. Caspar Mairhofer had been Gaismair's messenger to the rebellious peasants in Salzburg with an offer of mutual "support and cooperation."[117] And in the fall of 1527, a Mairhofer accompanied Messerschmied from Klausen to Sterzing, where they organized a synagogue. According to an official report, this synagogue resulted in several conversions to "the sect of Anabaptism."[118] Of Messerschmied it was said that he had taken an "evil farewell from Klausen." He and other members of the sacramentist conventicle in Klausen had been implicated as Anabaptists before the end of 1527. In the following years Innsbruck ordered the confiscation of the properties of a number of fugitives, Messerschmied apparently among them.[119] Ulrich Müller, an original member of the Klausen sacramentists, died an Anabaptist martyr in November 1531.[120] Hutterite chroniclers remembered him as well liked by the people.[121] But not all of the original group became martyrs. Several recanted, among them Peter Pinter.[122] Wölfl, who, after regaining his freedom in 1527, had also become an Anabaptist, reappeared as a recanter in documents dated August 1534. But the recantation did not save him from the executioner. His influence as instigator of the sect was deemed so detrimental that he had to die.[123]

The Mairhofer associated with the original Anabaptists in Klausen appears to have been none other than Caspar Mairhofer from Niedervintl, who figured prominently among the early Anabaptists in the Puster valley and was probably a former confidant of Gaismair. Considering that

Bartlme Dill, arrested with other early Anabaptists in Bozen, was also a
Gaismair veteran, official fear of a connection between Anabaptism and
the previous uprising seems less paranoid. What is surprising is that these
former supporters of Gaismair remained free until involved with Anabaptism. This was true in the case of Hans Gasser, who regained his freedom
in 1528 even after having been implicated in the new heresy.[124] And when
Gasser was in trouble again, this time for breaking his oath (*Urgicht*) and
abetting the jailbreak of his brother, he remained on good terms with his
jailor, who, to the annoyance of Innsbruck, issued day passes to Gasser,
permitting his attendance at local social events (*sic*). On Innsbruck's orders Gasser was eventually transferred to Bozen, where he was executed
on March 9, 1529.[125]

A similar fate awaited Blaurock, who returned to South Tyrol two
months later. At the time of his arrest in early July 1529, Blaurock was
accompanied by Hans Langegger from the Ritten,[126] an indication of Blaurock's connection to Gasser's home territory. From the Ritten the Anabaptist network reached via Mairhofer to Klausen-Gufidaun, the Puster, and
Sterzing. Indirect evidence, therefore, supports the thesis that once introduced by Blaurock in 1527 Anabaptism had spread rapidly in South Tyrol
through the preexisting network of evangelicals. As will be noted in
Chapter 8, contacts were made with Anabaptists north of the Brenner in
1528, and in the same year a number of indigenous leaders emerged,
among them Jörg Zaunring, Michael Kürschner, and Jacob Hutter. When
Blaurock returned for his second missionary journey in 1529, he faced a
much expanded movement. Unfortunately, he returned also to vigilant attempts at snuffing out that movement and himself fell victim to Ferdinand's campaign of suppression.

Before closing this chapter, it may be useful to probe Blaurock's message in South Tyrol as understood by his converts. Statements by several
have been preserved in Hutterite sources and can be supplemented by others that survived in official archives.[127] Although some of these statements
represent responses to inquisitors, hence to a non-Anabaptist agenda, they
nevertheless reflect Anabaptist teachings.[128] When asked about Mary, her
state before and after conception, the prisoners unanimously expressed
their high regard for her, considering her to have been "a virgin before
and after birth." By inference, other questions concerned infant baptism,
the mass, oral confession, the keeping of Sunday and special holidays, and
the intercession of saints. All rejected the sacramental efficacy of pedobaptism in favor of a conscious commitment to discipleship as a prerequisite
to baptism. All rejected the bodily presence of Christ in the sacrament of
the altar. The ascended Christ was seated at the "right hand" of God, and
it was impossible for priests "to bring him down into the host, to handle

or transform him." The prisoners uniformly criticized the "gluttony and immorality" of priests and rejected confession to such persons. They claimed that "no day was more holy than another," although time should be set aside on Sunday for rest and meetings in which the Scriptures were read and discussed. Nothing was said about community of goods, the oath, or whether a Christian could wield the sword. These positions were either not generally held by the Anabaptists or not yet of concern to the inquisitors. Asked if they would coerce others to accept their faith, all answered in the negative. True faith was a matter of conscience. "God wants willing hearts." Yet "these true lovers of God," as *The Chronicle* called them, were executed.[129]

These earliest testimonials make it clear that whatever the social, economic, or political context of South Tyrol in which Anabaptism flourished, Anabaptism cannot be reduced to an ideological reflex conditioned by material circumstances. From its inception and at its core Anabaptism was a consciously religious movement premised on following Christ, on discipleship, and on attempts to reinstitute the New Testament church. Consequently Anabaptists became proverbial for their moral uprightness, modest lifestyle, and mutual care. The testimonial of a woman defending herself and her husband against suspicions of belonging to the Anabaptists illustrates contemporary conceptions. She pointed to her husband's alcoholic problems—he "filled himself with wine"—and her own penchant for profanities as evidence that she and her husband did not belong to the Anabaptists.[130] And although this evidence comes from a later date, it illustrates that moral earnestness characterized the Anabaptists from the beginning. Converts were expected to renounce profiteering, luxury, gluttony, debauchery, drunkenness, and immorality. An Anabaptist was expected to be virtuous and to give up pride. Baptism came with a moral imperative to mend one's ways, to live and behave differently from the "world."[131] Some converts expressed this commitment to Christlike conduct somewhat awkwardly in perfectionist terms: to become Anabaptist meant a commitment to sin no more. And although such a commitment seems presumptuous from a modern perspective, contemporaries had no difficulty in recognizing Anabaptist sobriety, honesty, uprightness of life, courage of conviction, and faithfulness in death. Even persecutors and executioners grudgingly acknowledged the saintliness of their victims. Without acknowledgment of these qualities the story of Anabaptist beginnings in South Tyrol would remain incomplete and distorted, Anabaptist perseverance in the face of vicious suppression incomprehensible.

The beginnings of Anabaptism in South Tyrol must be understood in their historic context, which included the Gaismair affair and the evangelical sacramentists. Ideological continuity between these earlier reform aspirations and Anabaptism can be argued on the basis of similar anticlerical and iconoclastic attitudes. Anabaptists rejected in principle the entire sacramental, sacerdotal, hierarchical church. In this, Anabaptism represented a movement of lay emancipation from clerical tutelage which concerned not only the salvation of souls but sought to rearrange existing religiously sanctioned power structures.

Introduced by Jörg Blaurock between June and August 1527, Anabaptism spread rapidly in the Etsch, Eisack, and Puster valleys, facilitated by the preexisting evangelical network with links to the Gaismair rebellion. This explains the presence of prominent Gaismair supporters among the early converts. The evangelical sacramentists who met in conventicles to study the New Testament and debate reform issues were probably influenced by Zwinglian and/or Karlstadtian literature. Their metamorphosis into Anabaptists can be seen as a natural ideological progression similar to that experienced elsewhere.

The conversion of boisterous radicals, who demonstrated their dislike for traditional religion by engaging in iconoclastic acts and threats against the opposition, into Anabaptist staff bearers took some time and involved a moral, ethical transformation that set the Anabaptists apart from the rest of society and distanced them also from their precursors. Although Anabaptists stressed the priesthood of all believers in their community, they also drew a clear distinction between outsiders and those fully committed to the Christlike life in the community. As the desire to transform the entire society gave way in favor of building separate communities guided by New Testament principles, the borders between Anabaptists and the rest of society became unmistakable. However, it would be wrong to think of Anabaptism in South Tyrol as socially and politically inconsequential. Its challenge of existing power structures was clearly recognized by the authorities who launched a vicious campaign of suppression, the topic of the next chapter.

Face to Face with the "Forces of Antichrist," 1529–1533

Because allusions to Ferdinand's policy of suppression are scattered throughout this narrative and because that policy was a most important shaper of the early Anabaptist-Hutterite experience, it seems appropriate to provide a brief summary of official policy and actions. Accordingly, the first part of this chapter attempts an overview of those assumptions and measures. The second concentrates on the Anabaptist struggle to survive. Jacob Hutter emerged from that struggle as the undisputed leader in South Tyrol and in his person came to personify this tough and dedicated branch of Anabaptism, baptized with fire and blood. No other branch, except perhaps the Melchiorites, would suffer on this magnitude. The survivors, who formed the inner core of the emerging Hutterites, found in this grisly depletion of their leaders and ranks the collective authentication that they constituted the "true congregation of God," the church under the cross, the "woman in the wilderness" pursued by the great dragon and forces of Antichrist. It is one of the ironies of history that the policies of Ferdinand left an indelible imprint on Anabaptist-Hutterite self-understanding.

How to Crush a "Damned Pernicious Sect": The Policy of Ferdinand I

The dubious claim to fame for having "smothered the . . . Tyrolean Anabaptist movement in its own blood"[1] goes to Archduke Ferdinand I (1503–64), who came into possession of the Austrian territories and the Tyrol in 1521. His domain eventually encompassed Hungary, Bohemia and Moravia, Silesia, Upper and Lower Austria, Styria, Carinthia, the Tyrol, Voralberg, the outlying (*Vorlande*) territories on the Upper Rhine, and, until 1534, the duchy of Württemberg. In his early twenties, educated in the Spanish tradition, Ferdinand was unfamiliar with the language and customs of his subjects and brought exaggerated notions of what constituted good government to his titles. In matters of religion he proved "an honest fanatic," without virtues of self-doubt.[2] As a Hapsburg he supported the Catholic faith and a united Christendom, considering it his God-given duty to eliminate heresy from his territories. To this end, Ferdinand issued no fewer than eleven decrees between August 20, 1527, and April 1534.[3] Some of these referred to Anabaptism as a "damned, seditious, pernicious, heretical sect and heresy,"[4] against which it was right and necessary to launch a bloody campaign of suppression.

The decree of August 20, 1527 (hereafter, the August decree), set the tone for subsequent policy toward religious dissenters and innovators, particularly Anabaptists. It therefore deserves special attention.[5] In essentials the August decree followed the imperial Edict of Worms (May 8, 1521); particulars were the work of Dr. Johan Fabri, a theologian, which may explain the less than lucid legal language.[6] A future bishop of Vienna, Fabri built a career on opposing religious innovators, first as a representative of the bishop of Constance and then in the service of Ferdinand. A former friend and fellow student of Balthasar Hubmaier, Fabri considered Hubmaier the "originator of Anabaptist doctrine,"[7] a consideration that left a mark on Ferdinand's policy during its crucial stage of formulation.

Hubmaier had been in conflict with authorities even before his involvement with the Reformation and Anabaptism. His popular preaching in Regensburg had unleashed anti-Semitic riots that led to the burning of the local synagogue and the expulsion of Jews from the city. Hubmaier himself became the spiritual custodian of a chapel built on the ashes of the former synagogue.[8] With the coming of the Reformation, Hubmaier turned pro-Lutheran, then Zwinglian, and finally Anabaptist. As city reformer of Waldshut, a Hapsburg possession on the Upper Rhine, Hubmaier in 1524–25 sponsored an alliance with peasants against the bishop of Constance and against the city's secular overlord, Ferdinand. To this end, Hubmaier encouraged the enlistment of Swiss volunteers, the traditional enemies of the Hapsburgs. At the same time, he introduced a form of magisterial-urban Anabaptism which featured mass baptisms of adults in Waldshut.[9] After the collapse of the rebellion, Hubmaier fled to Zurich, only to be imprisoned and forced to recant by his former protector, Ulrich Zwingli. Released, Hubmaier recanted his recantation and made his way to Moravia, a territory that, unfortunately for Hubmaier, would become another of Ferdinand's lordships in late 1526. Here, against the express orders and wishes of Ferdinand, Hubmaier encouraged the pro-Reformation lords of Liechtenstein to initiate the transformation of Nicolsburg into an Anabaptist haven. Thanks to this aristocratic protection and a printing press that published Hubmaier's writings, Nicolsburg became a Mecca for persecuted Anabaptists and a center for the dissemination of Anabaptist ideas. Considering Hubmaier's background, it should not surprise that Ferdinand charged him not only with heresy but also with sedition. Not even the powerful lords of Liechtenstein could save him. On March 10, 1528, Hubmaier was burned at the stake in Vienna and his wife drowned in the Danube (see Chapter 3), among the first victims of the August decree that had been shaped in part by a former friend, Johan Fabri.

In keeping with perceptions at Ferdinand's court, the charge of heresy and sedition was extended to all Anabaptists. After all, was not Hubmaier the leading Anabaptist theologian and its most learned apologist? Had he not supported rebellion in Waldshut and Nicolsburg? And did not the appearance of Anabaptism in the wake of the peasant uprisings provide proof that these heretics wanted to continue the rebellion in another form? To Ferdinand's advisors the answers seemed self-evident. They were enshrined in the August decree.[10]

The decree was directed not only against Anabaptists but also against Luther, Zwingli, Oecolampadius, and Karlstadt. Shortcircuiting the debate on the authority of tradition versus Scripture, the decree upheld the Apostlic Creed and the seven sacraments as a minimal standard of orthodoxy. All who deviated from this standard were to be punished in property, body, or with death. Detailed penalties for specific offenses were prescribed as follows:

1. All who questioned the divinity or humanity of Christ, his birth, suffering, resurrection, or ascension were to be burned.

2. All who despised Mary or suggested that she had not been a virgin before and after Christ's birth or held her to be a woman like other women should be punished in property or body or executed, in accordance with the degree of the blasphemy.

3. All who questioned the intercessory role of Mary, of the apostles, evangelists, martyrs, or saints were to be punished with imprisonment, exile, or other fitting penalties.

4. All who questioned and changed the ceremonies of the sacraments of baptism, mass, or extreme unction should be punished with imprisonment, exile, or other appropriate penalties.

5. All who shared bread and wine to celebrate the Lord's Supper in heretical fashion should be punished in property, body, or with death.

Houses wherein such meetings took place were to be confiscated and torn down as an "eternal remembrance."

6. All hamlets in which baptismal fonts, altars, or monstrances had been broken should lose their liberties and rebuild the sacred fixtures within a month.

7. All persons who dispensed the sacraments without being properly ordained should be executed by fire, water, or the sword.

8. All who despised oral confession and did not attend confession at least once a year or who tried to take the eucharist without first confessing to a priest should be punished with imprisonment, exile, or a monetary fine.

9. All priests and monks who had left their calling should be imprisoned and kept on bread and water for a month and then sent to their superiors for further penalties; if found guilty of additional heresy, they should be punished accordingly.

10. Those guilty of moral offenses, for example, illegal marriage or incestuous relationships, should be punished according to customary law.

11. Iconoclastic acts involving crucifixes, statues of Mary or saints, or the eating of meat during Lent or on Fridays and Saturdays should be punished with imprisonment.

12. All who taught that a Christian could not join in war against the Turks should be punished with imprisonment.

13. All who preached that good works had no meritorious value for the salvation of the soul should be exiled.

14. All those abetting or sympathizing with the heretics and providing support for them should be deprived of their civil rights.

15. The officials, officers, councilors, bailiffs, servants, or other officials delinquent in enforcing the decree should lose their office.

16. All printing and selling of heretical literature was forbidden; existing literature was to be turned over to the authorities within two months.

17. All who taught community of goods should be punished with beheading.

According to the authors of the decree, the last item had been on the agenda of the rebellious peasants, placed there by "false teachings of Christian freedom." The pertinent passage is worth citing:

Since a great insurrection and frightening bloodshed originated in the past among the commoners because of the spread of false teachings of Christian freedom, as if all things were to be common and there should be no authority, which teaching is in many places put anew into the imagination [*eingepilldet*] of the simple-minded poor [*armen unverständigen*]; we decree and desire that whoever is convicted of holding or teaching [the same] is to be executed with the sword.[11]

That the reference to community of goods in relation to the insurrection by the peasants was not without foundation has been demonstrated by James Stayer.[12] That it was an ideal practice preferred by Anabaptists should be clear from the earlier discussion of the oldest Anabaptist church orders (Chapter 2). Evidence indicates that it was an ideal espoused by early Anabaptists from Switzerland through German-speaking territories to Moravia, where the practice was institutionalized by the Austerlitz Brethren in early 1528 (Chapter 3).

Before that, the August decree had given Anabaptist teachings widespread publicity because, according to Ferdinand's instructions, the decree had to be read in all parish churches on Christmas Day 1527 and at Easter 1528. It was assumed that attendance would be highest on these most important church days. True, some administrators voiced skepticism about the wisdom of giving the decree this kind of publicity. Not only did inhabitants in out-of-the-way hamlets seldom attend church, but simple peasants could not be expected to understand the proclamation, even if they listened to it in its entirety, which, however, would be highly unlikely "because they do not remain that long in the church!"[13] But such objections were overruled. Ferdinand and his advisors would not be deterred. The new heresies had to be rooted out.

Reluctance by local magistrates to toe the official line could bring heavy-handed interference from Ferdinand's court. The trial of Anabaptists in Steyer during 1528 illustrates this point. The scholarly authority on these territories, Grete Mecenseffy, described the proceedings that evolved as an "early case of high-handed cabinet justice" (*Kabinettjustiz*).[14] The local magistrate (*Richter*) and jury had opted for temporary confinement in the hope of weaning the heretics from their errors.[15] But this leniency aroused the ire of Ferdinand and his advisors, who insisted on the "penalty of Horb," presumably the same treatment given earlier to Michael Sattler.[16] When members of the jury balked, Ferdinand demanded to know their names.[17] He also insisted on the most humiliating conditions for those willing to recant, thus making moderate attempts at compromise with the prisoners practically impossible. Ordered to march around the church on seven consecutive Sundays, bareheaded and barefooted, with the sign of a baptismal font on their penitential garb, a burning candle in their right hands, a rod in the left, the recanters were expected to kneel at the altar to receive three lashes from the presiding priest and then remain on their knees until the priest had completed the office of mass. A penitential garb was to be worn daily, and its bearers were excluded from all associations (*Gemeinschaften*). Except for a shortened bread knife, the men were forbidden to bear arms and could not change their place of residence. In other words, they were to lose their citizen status permanently and remain in Steyer as long as they lived.[18]

Faced with these conditions, potential recanters declared their intention to die rather than submit. Sympathies among the local population favored the prisoners, placing city council and local administrators on the horns of a dilemma. Ferdinand's special prosecutor, who had been sent to demand harsher sentences, feared for his safety and a general rebellion.[19] But pleas for moderation fell on deaf ears. Eventually seven of the prisoners were beheaded and their corpses burned. Ferdinand's wrath thus appeased, the city council mitigated some of the more onerous conditions for the recanters.[20]

The case of Steyer was not exceptional; the cities of Freistadt, Kitzbühl, and Linz experienced similar high-handed interventions. During a mass trial in Kitzbühl in May 1528, the magistrate and court secretary sympathized openly with the accused. As a result, 160 persons declared themselves willing to recant, but 36 of them subsequently changed their minds. The magistrate, like his colleague in Steyer, recommended temporary internment and proper religious instruction to sway these recalcitrants. But this arrangement displeased Ferdinand and his advisors. An outsider, Bartlme Angst, magistrate of Rattenberg, was ordered to preside over the final sentencing. When Angst procrastinated, he too came under criticism from Ferdinand's court. As in the case of Steyer, Ferdinand applied pressure on the jurors to ensure a correct outcome. The jurors bent; twelve Anabaptists were executed, some recanted, and others fled. As a result, fifty children were left orphaned or abandoned in the streets of Kitzbühl.[21]

The discovery of numerous other Anabaptist conventicles in Austria and the Tyrol appears to have fanned the hysteria at Ferdinand's court. In early 1528 rumors spread that the Anabaptists, four thousand strong, plotting "rebellion and insurrection," planned to unite during the coming summer.[22] To prepare for such an eventuality, Ferdinand created a secret council (*Ketzerkollegium*) to coordinate the suppression of the heretics. On March 22, 1528, four special commissioners were appointed for this task,[23] and six days later a general visitation and inquisition were instituted for Upper and Lower Austria, Styria, Carinthia, and Carniola.[24] Impatient with the inability of local officials to stop the spread of heresy, Ferdinand ordered the creation of "itinerant posses" (*streifende Rott*) to hunt down leading heretics.[25] The church was expected to serve as a local intelligence-gathering agency. Priests were ordered to keep lists of persons who did not participate in confession or mass.[26] In one instance, sealed lists were to be forwarded to Ferdinand's court by the local administrators. Such measures clearly furthered social control through the close cooperation between church and state, setting the stage for the Catholic Reformation and baroque absolutism.[27]

Ferdinand's policy and measures came in tandem with an ideological propaganda campaign that targeted the Anabaptists as scapegoats for contemporary misfortunes, war, famine, and other disasters. By their "dishonor, blasphemy of, and disrespect for the holy sacrament of divine office" they had offended God and brought His wrath on the land. "Christian king" Ferdinand called on his subjects to repent, weed out heresy, and return to the faith of their fathers. Only by "meditation, fasting, prayer, good works," and "solemn religious processions" could God's wrath be appeased. Gifted defenders of the old faith were ordered to preach in territories infected with the religious disease.[28] But maintenance of true religion and the eradication of heresy were not left to preaching. The traditional faith was to be shored up by the full force of the law and every other means available to the early modern state, including the use of children to flush out fugitive parents. Suspected hideouts or meeting places were raided or burned, the ruins left as stark warnings to would-be converts or sympathizers.[29] Innkeepers who harbored Anabaptists or served meat during Lent or other prohibited days could expect punishment "on body and property."[30] Informers were hired to infiltrate, to identify the leaders, and to discover the time and place of congregational meetings. Bounties were set on the heads of leaders. Small fortunes of thirty, forty, or up to one hundred gulden more than a day laborer could hope to save in a lifetime were offered for information leading to their arrest. In 1533, for instance, spies were hired to infiltrate the group led by Jacob Hutter.[31] So secret was the mission that the four undercover agents remained unaware of each other's identity. Among them was a mere sixteen year old who, while in prison, had been pressed into service with threats and promises in order to, among others, betray his own father.[32] Showing sympathy toward the heretics or providing them with food or shelter or having any commercial dealings with them was a crime. Those who refused to cooperate in the heretic hunt were threatened with fines, imprisonment, and torture.

Since the end justified the means, informers were permitted to accept adult baptism to gain the confidence of leaders who performed these rites. Some undercover operations produced results worthy of modern spy novels. In Hutter's home district of St. Michelsburg, Peter Lanntz (Lanz) played a double game so well that the authorities came to distrust him. Among other things he provided quarters for Anabaptist leader Hans Amon and gained the release of Mrs. Amon from prison. When called to task, Lanntz explained his double dealings as part of an elaborate scheme to gain the confidence of the Anabaptists. His real motive was greed. The

Anabaptists, in turn, had taken advantage of Lanntz's weakness; they bought his protection and made their escape.[33] An attempt to entice Amon back for a second visit failed.

Once arrested, Anabaptists could expect Ferdinand's full wrath, mitigated only by existing procedures and local sympathies. Fortunately for the victims, some local magistrates tended to be less zealous than their sovereign; a few were sympathetic, at least during the early stages (see Chapter 7). Most officials in the Tyrol, however, cooperated with the instructions from Innsbruck. Interrogations normally involved torture. Repeated torture left more than one steadfast victim broken in body if not in spirit. The documents reveal many gruesome examples, such as that of Hans Pürchner. While his interrogators took time out for lunch, Pürchner was left hanging in the torture chamber, all of his joints dislocated. He was unable to walk, stand, kneel, lift his arms, or feed himself, and on the day of his execution he had to be tied to a log to remain in a position appropriate for beheading.[34]

Sentences could range from fines, penances, floggings, or service as penal galley slaves, to the death penalty by drowning, beheading, or burning. Before the final sentence was carried out, efforts were made to save the souls of the condemned. Usually this meant visits by clergy qualified to dispute with the prisoners on the basis of Scripture. At times white magic was invoked, as in 1533 when the food of eleven prisoners was spiced with holy water and blessed salt in the hope of exorcising the demonic powers believed to hold sway over the prisoners.[35] In one instance priests were ordered to sprinkle holy water on two women who refused to recant. The results were not recorded. Floggings were usually considered more effective, especially for minors or females, who were deemed more pliable.[36] In the cases of women, a macabre code of chivalry was upheld in which the women were to be beaten only in "appropriate places" (*gepurlichen ortten*). At least one local magistrate found the task revolting and refused to carry it out.[37] Somewhat perverse from the modern perspective was the right-to-life policy extended to unborn fetuses, which meant that the death sentence against pregnant women was postponed until they had delivered.[38]

Anabaptist leaders who had baptized others could hope for no mercy, even if they recanted. Recantations were nevertheless considered desirable for propaganda purposes and could bring the less painful and more "honorable" death by beheading rather than burning.[39] Ordinary Anabaptists who recanted but became *relapsi* were generally executed without further trial. First recanters were subjected to humiliating public penance which, as noted earlier, could include the wearing of special garments of shame (*Schandkleider*).

When public executions stirred sympathies, the authorities changed customary procedures: the rights of the accused were curtailed, and jurors were instructed to deliberate behind closed doors. Secret justice (*Stillrecht*) was born.[40] Contact between jurors and accused was kept to a minimum, and the accused were deprived of a proper hearing and defense. The time and place of execution were kept confidential to avoid embarrassing last-minute public testimonials by victims to bystanders. Because such last-minute declarations of their innocence and faith left the "wrong" impression on spectators, those who did gather to witness the execution were kept far enough back so that they could not hear or understand the victim.[41] In other words, an attempt was made to contain negative publicity. To avoid challenges to specific charges at the time and place of execution, magistrates were encouraged to limit themselves to reading general passages from Ferdinand's decrees, thereby perverting customary procedures outlined in the Territorial Order. Thus the campaign of suppression impacted not only the fate of the victims but the evolution of judicial process itself. Established customs were perverted or ignored, with *Kabinettjustiz* imposed on procedure. The victims' options were death, recantation, or flight.

A sadistic aspect of the campaign of suppression was that the financial costs were borne largely by the victims; and the costs could be high. In June 1535, councilors of the prince bishop of Brixen complained to Innsbruck that they had spent six hundred gulden in the jurisdiction of St. Michelsburg alone.[42] To cover the costs, Anabaptist properties were confiscated and local stewards appointed to manage them.[43] Temptations to profit at the expense of the victims proved irresistible, and rumors soon spread that some local officials saw suppression as a lucrative business. It became necessary to decree the return of all confiscated property, minus court expenses, to rightful heirs.[44]

The heirs, alas, were more often than not orphaned or, in cases in which the parents had fled, abandoned children. When possible, parents made arrangements with friends or relatives and left trust funds behind. But at times circumstances made such arrangements impossible. For example, the arrest and flight of parents had left fifty children abandoned or orphaned in Kitzbühl.[45] If relatives or friends were unable, afraid, or unwilling to feed extra mouths, the abandoned minors were left begging in the streets. Some were placed in poorhouses (*Spitalpflege*); others became wardens of stewards appointed to look after confiscated properties. Some were farmed out to foster parents who received reimbursement from confiscated property.[46] Administrative disputes left children in limbo, without resources, protection, and totally at the mercy of their wardens or foster parents.[47] Older children (ages ten to sixteen) who shared the point of view of their parents could be interned and subjected to daily discipline—floggings—to correct their outlook.[48] Since they were not Anabaptists—baptism was reserved for adults from the age of sixteen on—it was left to local magistrates to see to it that their rehabilitation had progressed sufficiently before release.

To their credit, Anabaptists made every attempt to retrieve abandoned children, even though such missions meant great personal danger. Physically strong brethren were chosen to gather the children and lead them across the mountains to the community in Moravia. Despite government vigilance and against great odds, many children were thus transported safely via an underground network. The escape route from South Tyrol usually led north over the Brenner Pass down the Wipp valley to the Inn River and by boat downstream to the Danube. Before his arrest, one sturdy blacksmith carried fifteen children across the mountains.[49] No doubt, some children perished on the way, more died in Moravia, but parents and community cared for the children. It is beyond comprehension, therefore, that some twentieth-century scholars would still refer to these rescue missions as "kidnappings."[50]

Given Ferdinand's measures against them, it is surprising that Anabaptists survived at all. Even more surprising is their survival well into the 1530s, especially in the south. Without question, survival was the result of effective countermeasures, a supportive network, and intelligent leadership, which between 1529 and 1533 was in the hands of Jacob Hutter.

The Struggle to Survive

Countermeasures

The initial survival of the Anabaptists in Tyrol depended on the good will of relatives, friends, and the local population in general. However, Ferdinand's measures soon created difficulties for sympathizers and consequently inexorably drove the Anabaptists underground to inaccessible regions and eventually to the fringes of society. In their struggle to survive, they developed defensive techniques and organizational habits that left their mark on the nature and structure of the surviving community.

In the face of the "forces of Antichrist," an alliance of temporal and religious authority, the Anabaptists developed their own self-regulated, highly disciplined, closely knit brotherhood and network of supporters. Members were admonished not to divulge the names of their fellow believers or meeting places. As a precaution leaders kept their movements and destinations confidential. They traveled at night and hid in woods or pastures during the day. A network of the most trusted members organized larger congregational gatherings. Initially held in hamlets, villages, or towns, these meetings were shifted to outlying farmsteads, clearings, forests, mountain meadows, caves, and other less accessible terrain.[51] Rather astutely, the Anabaptists also learned to take advantage of "wind-still zones,"[52] border areas between jurisdictional or administrative districts whose magistrates were known for their rivalries and lack of cooperation.

Given limited resources, the Anabaptists proved capable organizers, overcame formidable logistical difficulties to hold congregational meetings, and facilitated the exodus of hundreds to Moravia. Congregational gatherings usually lasted several days with attendance ranging from 40 to 150 persons.[53] Keeping them secret was a major accomplishment. Preparations were made by the servant of temporal affairs in charge of the common purse. He would enlist able-bodied assistants to procure and transport the necessary provisions to the designated site.[54] Supplies for one occasion included fifty loaves of bread, half a bushel of nuts, two oxen, a cow, and at least one jug of wine. The oxen and cow were herded to the site, the former for slaughter, the cow presumably to provide milk.[55] It may be that the fellowship of several days in fraternal love increased the longing for life in a shared community such as was possible only in Moravia.[56]

With congregational meetings becoming increasingly difficult and the number of arrests and executions rising, more and more believers decided to leave for Moravia. To facilitate the exodus an underground railway was set up, with brethren or sympathizers placed at strategic points. Names of sympathetic innkeepers and boatmen were passed on as the fugitives traveled in small groups led by veteran guides. The preferred route across the Brenner and down the Inn included a number of Bavarian breweries.[57] All in all, the underground railway functioned amazingly well. Between 1528 and 1533 an estimated four to six hundred survived the trek from South Tyrol to Moravia. Unfortunately, not all succeeded in the great escape. A considerable number were caught and executed.[58]

The experience of Erhart Urscher and his family humanizes the traumatic dilemma of those caught in Ferdinand's dragnet. Urscher's involvement with radical causes reached back to the pre-Anabaptist period. During the Gaismair affair he and others raided the granary of a well-to-do proprietor. The booty was subsequently restored, but Urscher and his wife became involved with the Anabaptists.[59] At the time of their arrest in 1532–33 they were considered *relapsi*. During a previous imprisonment the Urschers had allegedly pledged to shun Anabaptism.[60] Yet in the spring of 1532 Urscher contributed the sizable sum of two hundred gulden to the Anabaptist treasury and later that year sheltered two Anabaptist fugitives in his hayloft. When those guests were arrested,[61] Urscher and his wife fled in panic, leaving their six children behind. While the hunt was on for the parents, the children were placed with a warden who sent the oldest, twelve-year-old Valentin, to herd livestock in mountain pastures. Valentine later testified that he and his siblings had been mistreated and gone hungry at the warden's house.[62]

The fugitive parents, meanwhile, had found shelter at the Peckelhaube (Pögglhaube), an inn near a hanging bridge on the Härscher. While Mrs. Urscher, who was pregnant, remained at the Peckelhaube, the father planned to retrieve his children. He made contact with his eldest in the pasture and briefed him on plans to fetch the siblings. One evening under the cover of darkness, the father and three brothers returned. The adults carried the little ones while Valentin ran alongside during the escape. Once reunited, the family fled to the mountains and spent the next three months in a hut. With the onset of winter and tiring of their isolated, fugitive existence, Urscher returned home to solicit the intercession of former neighbors and friends.[63] He was recognized and his presence reported to the local authorities by the local priest. Put on trial as *relapsi*, Urscher and his wife maintained that they had never abjured the true faith, would not do so now, but rather die "eight deaths." Their fate was sealed. Only the pleas of friends saved Urscher from execution by fire. He died by the sword.[64]

It says something about the thoroughness of the investigation that the innkeeper, "old and weak" Ulrich Peckelhaube, who had provided temporary shelter and employment for Urscher, was also hauled into court. The interrogation revealed that several Anabaptist leaders had been his guests and that Anabaptist meetings of up to seventy persons had taken place in the stable of his inn.[65] Ulrich pleaded ignorance of the religious affiliation of his guests, claiming that as innkeeper his had only been business interests. Apparently the explanation was accepted. Ulrich escaped with a monetary fine.

The Emergence of Jacob Hutter as Leader

One of the leaders who had frequented Peckelhaube's inn was Jacob Hutter, without question the key figure and organizer of Anabaptism in South Tyrol from 1528–29 on.[66] Born around 1500 in the hamlet of Moos, a stone's throw from St. Lorenzen in the Puster valley, Hutter came to personify the Pusterers. That he could read and write suggests some form of schooling, presumably in a church-related institution in nearby Brüneck. But instead of choosing the cloth, Hutter made hats for his livelihood. A statement by his former employer, hatmaker Caspar Hueter, remains the only source of information about Hutter's pre-Anabaptist years.[67] Explaining his relationship with Hutter ten years after the fact, Caspar recalled how one evening in 1526 he and Hutter gambled with Hutter's life savings at stake. Hutter lost but showed such suicidal remorse that Caspar felt compelled to return the gains even though he had won them fairly. Caspar's selective recollections were, no doubt, self-serving. Rumors told a different story: Caspar had attempted to cheat Hutter out of his savings, and Hutter had not suffered the attempt lightly. Since Caspar's statement had been solicited for Hutter's trial in Innsbruck, Caspar obviously intended to distance himself from the heretic while putting himself in the best light. Accordingly, he claimed that he had put a stop to Hutter's New Testament readings in his home and that Hutter left because he, Caspar, opposed his heretical views. Hutter had not returned in ten years.

Despite its self-serving bias, Caspar's statement nevertheless provided an authentic glimpse of Hutter's character. A stubborn persistence and temper that at times got the better of him appear to have been his trademark. But more important about Caspar's statement is the link it established between Hutter and the pre-Anabaptist network of evangelicals served by the goatherd Wölfl. As noted in the previous chapter, Wölfl's visit to Caspar Hueter's home in the fall of 1526 was instrumental in winning Hutter for the sacramentist cause. He had traveled to Bozen to obtain a New Testament which he studied avidly and explained to others from then on. In late 1526 or early 1527, perhaps prompted by Wölfl's arrest and his disagreement with Caspar Hueter, Hutter left the Puster region for the Drau valley and resided at Spital. He returned in 1528–29 to find that a number of his acquaintances and friends had become Anabaptists, among them Benedict (Gamperer), a former journeyman priest (*Gesellpriester*) of Brüneck. Gamperer, an early leader in the Puster region, was arrested along with Hutter's sister in 1529. Not clear is who baptized Hutter or chose and confirmed him in "the service of the Gospel."[68] It has been suggested that he threw himself almost immediately into organizing the Anabaptist congregation at Welsberg. The first arrests followed in March or April 1529. In all, fifteen prisoners were taken to Brixen, among them Hutter's teacher, Georg Weber, from Pflaurenz.[69] Weber and two others were burned at the stake; a fourth person was beheaded.[70] Also among the early local victims was Hutter's sister.[71]

From the very beginning, then, the vicious suppression touched Hutter personally. As early as December 1527, the bailiff of St. Michelsburg, Balthasar Gerhard, had been warned to be vigilant against the Anabaptists in his district[72] (see Figure 3). Brixen found it necessary to reprimand Gerhard because he "wished to deal leniently with the Anabaptists." It seems

Figure 3. St. Michelsburg

that Gerhard stirred himself to action only in early 1529 when he made a
number of arrests. The facilities at the Michelsburg soon proved inadequate to hold all of the prisoners; some prisoners were housed in Brüneck,
and the difficult cases were sent to Brixen. Gerhard favored financial fines
and leniency, whereas Brixen and Innsbruck agreed on the death penalty.
The prince bishop eventually found a more rigorous enforcer of his wishes
in Christoph Ochs, who became the magistrate of St. Michelsburg in
1531. Twenty-four executions were recorded for that district alone. Many
more believers recanted or fled.[73] The victims received at least passive sympathy from a broad section of the district's population, which alone explains the longevity of the underground network established by Hutter.
Among members of that network was also the widow of a former bailiff
of St. Michelsburg, Agnes von Waltenhofen, who fled to Moravia with her
daughter in 1539.[74]

   Hutter escaped the first arrests, but by late June 1529 Innsbruck had
identified him, along with Jörg Zaunring, as the principal leader in the
south. According to information received, Hutter baptized "for the sake
of money," meaning presumably that he collected funds for a common

purse, which had been established on the Ritten in the Puster valley and in other districts. Evidence suggests that Zaunring functioned as the primary treasurer (*Secklmeister*).[75] Congregational meetings were held which included the celebration of the Lord's Supper for all those baptized. In other words, by late 1529 an Anabaptist organization in South Tyrol had taken concrete shape. Without question that organization had been influenced by what Hutter had seen and heard on his visit to Austerlitz during that year (see Chapters 2 and 3). There is reason to believe that some of the money collected was used to facilitate the beginning of the exodus to Austerlitz. Zaunring himself would lead a contingent to Austerlitz in the spring of 1530.[76] Because of his leadership role in South Tyrol in 1529 and subsequent events that led to the formation of the proto-Hutterite community, Zaunring deserves special attention.

Like Marpeck, Jörg Zaunring hailed from Rattenberg. In early 1528 when other Rattenbergers, including Marpeck, fled to Bohemia, Zaunring moved south and proselytized for Anabaptism on the Ritten and the Schlern.[77] Unfortunately, little is known about his background, but a surviving letter[78] and treatise attributed to him give the impression that he was an educated, well-read person. The treatise, a "Short Prospectus on Christ's Last Supper" (hereafter "Prospectus")[79] in the form of a dialogue between the Christian and the world, may have influenced Hutter, who formed a special bond of friendship with Zaunring. The "Prospectus" rejected the argument of old and new papists alike. Luther, Osiander, and Hesius[80] are named among the latter as "eaters of idols" who misunderstood or deliberately perverted the meaning of the controversial statement, "this is my body." According to Zaunring, the scriptural meaning was to be attained by "interpreting the parts through the whole, [one] saying through other sayings." In keeping with this hermeneutic the New Testament revealed three meanings or definitions of Christ's body: (1) his the mortal body; (2) his clarified body, seated at the right hand of God; and (3) his body as the Christian congregation. To postulate the presence of Christ's mortal body in the bread was preposterous because Christ in his mortal body was seated at the table when he spoke the words, "this is my body." Furthermore, the Scriptures stated explicitly that "flesh profited nothing" (John 6:63). The clarified body could not be in the bread either because the ascended Christ was seated at the right hand of God as witnessed to by the martyr Stephen (Acts 9). There, in heaven, Christ would continue his work as mediator until his return on Judgment Day. Yet, according to 1 Corinthians the believers were to eat "until he comes." There remained only one possible correct meaning of the original statement "this is my body," namely "the congregation of God" (*Gemein Gottes*). It was the living temple of God through which Christ was present as the heavenly bread here on earth. Breaking the bread simulated (*asimuliert*) the broken body of Christ in the members. The symbolic breaking of the bread and drinking of the cup, therefore, indicated solidarity with Christ and one another in suffering as his body on earth. A false understanding of the bodily presence was at the heart of false religion. "Remove him from the baker's bread, and all monks, nuns, priests, bishops, cardinals, the pope, benefices, masses, processions, learning, hats and caps [*kappen und blatten*] collapse and are destroyed."[81]

False religion revealed itself through its evil fruits: "debauchery, drunkenness, adultery, blasphemy." These fruits seemed most evident among those who "ate daily" of what, according to Daniel 9, he identified as the "idol" (*Abgott*) that had made many Baalites fat (*feist*) "and even today brought enough into the kitchen." The body of the living God could not produce such fruits. Christ did not dwell in "stone piles" (*Steinhaufen*) and "temples of idols" but in his "holy congregation" (*Gemein*). "Yes, the congregation of God is the bread here on earth, . . . because we many are one body and bread, because we are partakers of one bread. Do you now see who is the bread? Namely his congregation here on earth, which like the bread was broken. Christ will live in his bread, . . . not in stone piles."[82] The ceremony of breaking the bread was, therefore, a remembrance and a sign (*zum Zeichen und Gedächtnis*) that the "Christian congregation, as Christ's body on earth, was of the same mind as Christ. The body was prepared to suffer innocently and permit itself to be broken like the bread for the Gospel."[83] Anyone unwilling to make the commitment to suffer with Christ in his body, the congregation, should therefore not participate in the symbolic breaking of the bread; for to do so would be to his or her own condemnation.

Although Zaunring may have written the "Prospectus" after his mission in South Tyrol, perhaps while serving as leader in Moravia or in prison in Franconia,[84] the arguments articulated in South Tyrol in 1528–29 must have been of a similar New Testament logic. Zaunring's views on the idolatry of the mass could expect a favorable reception, and Zaunring certainly continued the mission begun by Blaurock in 1527 among the radical evangelicals in South Tyrol. One of his prominent converts was Michael Kürschner (Klesinger), a former court clerk (*Gerichtsschreiber*).[85] Taught by Zaunring, Kürschner himself became a very effective missionary who, within a year, baptized an estimated one hundred persons in places throughout South Tyrol, including Gufidaun, Klausen, Völs, Karneid, Kurtasch, Kalten, and Leifers.[86] In the spring of 1529 Kürschner transferred north to the Lower Inn valley where, on April 26, 1529, Ferdinand's henchmen caught up with him near Kitzbühl. Taken to Innsbruck under heavy guard, he was burned on June 2, 1529.[87]

At about the time of Kürschner's arrest Blaurock returned to the South Tyrol. Whether he met with Hutter or Zaunring is unclear. It was sometime during 1529 that Hutter traveled to Moravia to investigate the community of Brethren which had formed at Austerlitz. According to *The Chronicle,* "the church" in the Tyrol, having learned that at Austerlitz "God had gathered a people in his name to live as one heart, mind and soul . . . sent Jakob Hutter with Simon Schützinger and some companions to the church at Austerlitz to make inquiries about all that had taken place."[88] While at Austerlitz, Hutter and Schützinger held discussions with the "elders of the church" and apparently came to an amicable agreement on teachings and practice—Hutter and his companions being "one heart and soul with those in Austerlitz." Presumably this meant that they agreed on something like the *Discipline* discussed in Chapter 2. It also implied that Hutter and Schützinger agreed with the Austerlitz Brethren on their staff-bearing position and on the practice of community of goods. Hutter returned to South Tyrol with a glowing report on what he had seen and heard at Austerlitz and "how in the name of them all, he had united with those at Austerlitz in peace and unity of soul and spirit."[89]

The loss of Kürschner, Blaurock, and others must have made the precarious position in which the Anabaptists found themselves very clear. Exodus to Austerlitz in Moravia presented itself as an escape from Ferdinand's henchmen and as an opportunity to build the new community. In the following year Zaunring led a contingent to Austerlitz, leaving Hutter the main leader in South Tyrol. A charismatic leader with "abundant gifts from God," Hutter proved a fine organizer and very persuasive New Testament exegete and preacher. As one of his converts testified, he "spoke not out of his own flesh but God was speaking through him."[90] Hutter used these gifts of divine discourse to build the congregation of God even in the face of "Antichrist."

The Pusterers

Despite Ferdinand's oppressive measures and the scattered nature of Anabaptist existence in South Tyrol, Hutter and his associates unfolded an amazing congregational life supported by a network of committed converts, dedicated supporters, and sympathizers. Although these were not drawn exclusively from the Puster valley, the inner core was; and before they became collectively known as Hutterites, they carried the designation Pusterers, with the connotation that they were particularly tough and dedicated. At least since 1529 these Pusterers belonged to the staff-bearing Anabaptists, who looked to Austerlitz as the model community. This meant that Hutter also taught the ideal of community of goods as the proper New Testament norm, although under the circumstances in South Tyrol a common purse had to suffice for the time being.[91] The common fund was used not only to support widows and children but also to finance provisions for meetings, to help those imprisoned or in hiding, and, as of 1530, to finance the exodus to Moravia. Under the circumstances this came to mean that converts were expected to surrender their surplus cash to the common treasury. Apparently this happened at baptism,[92] if not in reality, then in form of a pledge. Evidence indicates that the baptismal ritual or formula used by Hutter involved also a confession of faith by the candidate, who was asked: "Do you believe in God the Lord, in Jesus Christ and in the holy Christian Church?" Upon an affirmative answer, Hutter pronounced absolution: "Now your sins are forgiven by God." Then taking water, he baptized the candidate in the name of the Trinity, "the Father, Son, and Holy Ghost." At some point during the ceremony, Hutter also solicited a commitment to leave possessions, "yes, flesh and blood, wife and child," for the sake of Christ and his body on earth, the congregation of God.[93] To withhold even "a quarter" was seen as lack of commitment.[94] Since contributions were not returned if the contributor left Anabaptism, to join meant a serious, total commitment and acceptance of the persecution that could be expected. Anabaptism was not for the faint hearted. Turning over one's assets, in turn, strengthened interdependence and furthered group solidarity. At Hutter's last meeting before leaving for Moravia in 1533, for instance, all those present pooled their money in an action recalling the exodus of the staff bearers from Nicolsburg.[95] In this case, the "sweet offering" was carried out of the Tyrol to Auspitz by Hutter and his companions, to become an item of controversy in the quarrel that fueled the great schism (Chapter 9).

The first known treasurer of the common purse in the Puster valley was Hutter's close confidant, Hänsel or Hans Mair Paulle. Hänsel was possibly the son or brother of Caspar Mair Paulle, an early martyr in Hutter's home district.[96] Familiarity with the lay of the land and its population explains how Hänsel managed to outwit the authorities for years. As Hutter's key assistant, he assumed responsibility for organizing and provisioning congregational meetings as well as facilitating the exit of members to Moravia. He himself made frequent trips to Moravia and accompanied the returning Hutter in 1535 (Chapter 10).[97] Evidence indicates further that Hänsel concerned himself as much as possible with the well-being of those taken prisoner. Payments to jailors, even if indirectly, could improve prison conditions or even facilitate escape.[98] He served also as guide to other leaders. After Hutter's departure in 1533 he remained behind with Hans Amon and served as his guide and assistant. It was Hänsel who gained the release of Amon's wife from prison and secured lodging for Amon at Lanntz's home, all for a fee.[99] In 1534 he helped Amon lead the remnant to Moravia and one year later served as one of Hutter's most trusted couriers between the Tyrol and Moravia. He survived Hutter's arrest and death and served as guide to Onophrius Griesinger, who was sent to follow up on Hutter's last mission in South Tyrol.[100] Yet, despite his invaluable role in the beginning of the Anabaptist-Hutterite community, this Pusterer received no special mention in *The Chronicle;* his death was not recorded. A closer look at other Pusterers reveals a number of interesting relationships. Veronica Grembs, who served as a companion or midwife to Hans Mair Paulle's wife, was the daughter of well-to-do Hans Grembs and Elisabeth (Högerlin) of St. Georgen. One of Veronica's aunts was married to Balthasar Mairhofer of Lüsen, her other sister Margareth to Balthasar Mairhofer of Nidervintl.[101] In 1534 Veronica joined Amon on the trek to Moravia.[102] Others of this inner circle were less fortunate. Valentin Lukhner[103] and Paul Rumer were destined for martyrdom.[104] Like Veronica Grembs, Paul Rumer came from a notable family in St. Georgen. His father was a local pharmacist, his sister married to a physician. Another sister, Justina, was married to the well-heeled Paul Gall.[105] Leery of Anabaptism, Rumer initially warned his sisters against the heresy. Then, in 1530–31, his search for a leasehold (*Pachtgut*) brought him into contact with Balthasar Mairhofer of Nidervintl, whose wife, Margareth Grembs, was also a native of St. Georgen. It was Rumer's fortune or misfortune, depending on one's perspective, that he laid eyes on Mairhofer's daughter, Veronica. In his attempt to charm the young lady, Rumer apparently dressed too flamboyantly for Veronica's mother.[106] During one of the encounters Mrs. Mairhofer expressed disapproval of Rumer's apparel and asked him point blank "whether he did not desire to become godly and put aside his pride."[107]

Mrs. Mairhofer's admonition led to some reflection on Rumer's part. He subsequently attended Anabaptist meetings near Klausen at Mauls in the Jaufen valley and near Sterzing. At the latter place he was baptized by Hutter. In 1532 Rumer joined the trek to Auspitz to observe the truly Christian life in community there. He appears also to have honed his reading and writing skills while working in a mill and bakery in Moravia. Returning to South Tyrol in the company of Hans Amon, Rumer became an enthusiastic witness to the life in community possible in Moravia.[108] Arrested in the fall of 1533, Rumer gave one of the clearest statements of Anabaptist beliefs preserved in official records.[109] The stay in the community at Auspitz, plus his travels with leaders such as Amon and Christoph Gschäll, may partially explain the lucidity of his statement, but he had obviously studied some of the Anabaptist literature. His contrast between the traditional mass and the Anabaptist celebration of the Lord's Supper, as recorded by the court secretary, recalls Jörg Zaunring's "Prospectus."

When they break the bread, as Christ had instructed, they consent to die for the sake of God's word, just as Christ had given his body on the cross for them. And they receive the bread because, just as the bread consists of many grains, so many of them unite together into a Christian community [*gemeinschaft*]. The sacrament of the altar saves no one, because the priests devour it daily [*die pfaffen fressen von tag zw tagn*] and yet do not improve as a result but are the greatest whorers and adulterers.[110]

Unlike the priests, Anabaptists were serious in their quest for the godly life, ready to suffer for the true faith as had all the saints.[111] Here, in the statement of a young, simple layman, one encounters the view that the true church had its pedigree in the historic community of suffering saints, not in a hierarchy claiming apostolic succession or custodianship over orthodox dogma or orthodox rituals. According to the maxim, "by their fruits you shall know them," the contrast between true and false religion was unmistakable.

At the time of his arrest, Rumer was carrying a list of Anabaptist-friendly lodges in the route down the Inn to Moravia. Also in his possession were copies of letters by prisoners, the first such collection that we know of, indicating that prison letters were being gathered, preserved, and copied for wider circulation among the Anabaptists. But before turning to an examination of the prison letters a digression is in order about Balthasar Mairhofer of Nidervintl, whose name entered the narrative earlier.

Mairhofer's household in Nidervintl served as a link in the Anabaptist network, the Götzenberg above Nidervintl as a site for congregational meetings. Mrs. Mairhofer, as noted, had been instrumental in Paul Rumer's conversion, but her life touched others as well, among them Christoff Schuechknecht, another native of St. Georgen. In his statement to interrogators Christoff related how he, while working for Mrs. Mairhofer, surmised from her very behavior that she was an Anabaptist.[112] When he asked her whether she considered the teachings of the Anabaptists the "godly truth," she replied, "yes, if acted upon." Curious, the illiterate Schuechknecht found someone to read the New Testament to him. One of these readings was interrupted by the entry of Valentin Lukhner, who appears to have served as Balthasar Mairhofer's messenger at times. The newcomer greeted the reader with the "peace of God." When Schuechknecht puzzled about the meaning of the greeting, he was told that it was appropriate between true Christians only and that he, Schuechknecht, was "no Christian, and did not look like one!" When Schuechknecht responded that he wanted to live according to the "godly truth," Lukhner invited him to an Anabaptist meeting. Here Schuechknecht was baptized by Hutter. He understood this baptism to mean a commitment to the godly life, according to Acts 2 and 4, a life that would set him apart from behavior common in the larger society. As the interrogators recorded, "They [Anabaptists] hold all things in common, whatever God sends them, heavenly or earthly goods, and one possesses as much as the other. But among us the community is such that one is rich, the other poor and has to go begging. One cuts another's hands and feet off." [113]

Whatever the local interrogators may have thought about the virtues of the Anabaptists' communal ethics, they followed the orders of higher authorities. Shortly after the above statement, sometime in the fall of 1533, Schuechknecht became another victim of Ferdinand's policy of eradication. [114]

That the apostolic emphasis on sharing appealed not only to poor journeymen may be illustrated by the case of Balthasar Mairhofer from Nidervintl. A Balthasar Mairhofer served as Gaismair's messenger and appeared prominently among the first Anabaptists. [115] If he was Mairhofer from Nidervintl, then he belonged to the lower gentry and was a relatively wealthy landowner. Traditionally, the Mairhof (Mair Estate) had been a special fief (*Lehen*), held directly from the territorial lord with the proviso that its leaseholder owed special duties to the lord's court, including supplies for the lord's kitchen. In return, the leaseholder received privileges on his estate similar to those of the nobility. With time, tenure on the Mairhof had become hereditary, and the hereditary tenant had taken the name of the estate, Mairhofer. [116] Records for the year 1529 indicate that Mairhofer of Nidervintl was in dispute with the prince bishop of Brixen over refusal to pay estate rent (*Zinsen*). It seems that Balthasar, who had inherited the extensive estate from his father, Peter Mairhofer, considered himself the beneficiary of certain hereditary privileges, including exemption from land rent, which the bishop's administrators denied. Mairhofer's involvement with the Anabaptists may have provided the bishop with an opportunity to challenge his tenure and force payments of rent. Mairhofer was interned in Brixen during 1529–30. Implicated with him were his wife, their daughter Veronica, and one of their servants. The Mairhofers must have regained their freedom by means of a compromise, for on May 24, 1531, the bishop's court claimed that Mairhofer and his wife had violated an oath-bound pledge and rejoined the Anabaptists. An inventory of his assets was ordered. These measures notwithstanding, or because of them, Mairhofer made a substantial contribution to the common Anabaptist fund. [117] Arrested again in June 1533, Mairhofer regained his freedom by paying a hefty eight hundred gulden. His less fortunate servant was executed.[118] Even if wealth did not count among the Anabaptists, it still meant something at the bishop's court.

But Mairhofer's Anabaptist connection proved a major liability, and his troubles with the bishop's court continued. In January 1534, Mairhofer pleaded for the release of his son Hans on the grounds that as a minor he had joined the Anabaptists without understanding (*Verstand*). The son, imprisoned since the fall of 1533, was eventually released but only upon his promise that he would help ferret out fugitive Anabaptist leaders.[119] For this task Brixen enlisted also Peter Lanntz, who would eventually receive Mairhofer's estate, a property officially valued at 3,968 gulden, but according to popular opinion worth more than 10,000 gulden.[120] Lanntz also served his own interests by accepting money from those he was expected to betray; in 1534 he participated in a search action that netted Mrs. Mairhofer and led to her execution.[121] Balthasar Mairhofer escaped arrest and remained on the wanted list for years.[122] Evidence indicates that he escaped to Moravia where a Balthasar Mairhofer from Nidervintl in the Puster valley was chosen servant of temporal affairs in 1539 and confirmed in that office in 1544. It was a good choice; Mairhofer had contributed substantially to the common fund while he could. A key member of the Puster network from its inception, he had lost all—goods, kindred, wife. Mairhofer himself survived the onslaught of the "forces of Antichrist." Under the date 1552 *The Chronicle* recorded: "Brother Balthasar Mairhofer the older, a confirmed servant for temporal affairs, fell asleep in the Lord at Altenmarkt in Moravia and after bearing much tribulation went to those who are at rest."[123]

The case of the well-to-do Mairhofer, his relations through his wife to Anabaptists in St. Georgen, once more illustrates the impossibility of ascribing the spread of Anabaptism to some form of solidarity in terms of class interests. If anything, Anabaptism spread through clan, kin, and friendship connections. But entrance into Anabaptism eventually also led to a severance of family ties in the name of higher loyalty to Christ. Paradoxically the choice to join the new community, which placed family and individual second, was ultimately individual and in the final analysis cannot be explained by some extraneous cause. Simpler to fathom are the means utilized in the identity formation of the new community and the building of group solidarity as the congregation of God. One of these means was the growing collection of epistolary correspondence.

The Earliest Prison Epistles

Anabaptist scholars have long recognized the important part played by the Anabaptist-Hutterites in preserving the history of Anabaptist beginnings. Hutterite codices are without exaggeration the richest mine of information in the Anabaptist tradition, a monument to the vitality of the inner life of the community that created and preserved them. Besides *The Chronicle,* these codices contain a rich treasure of Anabaptist treatises and songs and a voluminous collection of epistolary correspondence unequaled by any other Anabaptist group.[124] An estimated four to five hundred of the letters by eighty or so authors have survived.[125] The prison epistles, alongside the martyr stories collected in song and prose, proved, no doubt, most important in shaping community identity as the church of the martyrs, the faithful remnant under the cross. In this context we deemed it appropriate to insert into the narrative a discussion of some of the earliest prison epistles and their authors.[126] A key concern will be to establish their historicity.

Among the earliest preserved prison communiqués are those attributed to Leonard Schiemer and Hans Schlaffer, dating from 1527–28.[127] The oldest prison epistles pertaining to South Tyrol are letters ascribed to six brethren apprehended in Sterzing in 1531–32.[128] The circumstances of the origin of the letters, their historicity, and authenticity can be established from official sources. The principal writer for the six prisoners was Lamprecht Gruber from Villnöss, whose first epistle must date from an even earlier imprisonment.[129] The earlier date is suggested by a reference in the first epistle to the gathering of God's children in the unity of the spirit at Austerlitz.[130] Gruber alluded to a circular reporting favorably on the situation in Austerlitz. Not clear is whether this circular was the work of Hutter after his visit to Austerlitz in 1529 or whether it came from Zaunring after his arrival in Austerlitz in 1530. Gruber wrote,

You have made known to us concerning those at Austerlitz, about whom we are overjoyed and commend and praise the Lord. We also want to pray to God without ceasing that the eternal father may, to his praise, bring to pass that his children be united and gathered in all places in the unity of the Holy Spirit. . . . It is a great joy to us that in all places the Lord so richly calls out his little children. As you then have written to us, the Lord permits his power to be seen in his people so that the world may be convinced thereby.[131]

Apparently at the time of writing Gruber knew nothing yet of the schisms of early 1531 which led to the establishment of a new settlement at Auspitz.[132] The very fact that the letter was preserved with the glowing praise of the Austerlitz Brethren indicates further that its content remains unedited and authentic.

Gruber's second letter was written in Sterzing in 1532.[133] By that time the prisoners obviously knew of the schism in Austerlitz because official records documented that they were on their way to Auspitz when arrested.[134] This second letter also recorded Gruber's personal trauma. He had weakened under torture, recanted, and been released. Seized by remorse, he rejoined his fellow prisoners voluntarily.

The third letter described visits by "conspirators of the serpent," that is, clergy who twisted the meaning of Scripture. Deeply devotional, this letter expressed gratitude for strength to remain calm and steadfast in the face of the coming execution scheduled for the following Wednesday. To this "wedding feast," which would unite them with Christ, the prisoners invited their brothers and sisters as witnesses.[135] Among those invited was Kuntz Füchter (Cunz Viechter or Fichter), a local treasurer of the common purse from the Jaufen valley. By April 6, 1532, at the latest, Füchter himself was behind bars in Sterzing. He remained there until his execution. Intercepted with others on his way to Moravia,[136] Füchter carried money donated by Balthasar Mairhofer of Nidervintl and contributed an interesting letter to the growing collection. Modeled on Gruber's earlier letters, Füchter's language and tone were less refined or restrained,[137] prompting modern scholars to speculate that his discourse came closer to that of the common people.[138] Füchter alluded to pedobaptism as a "damned dirty bath" (verfluchtes sudlbad) and referred to the prosecutors as "bloodhounds," to priests as "fathers of lies" from the "lineage of Cain"—the same as those who killed the prophets and Christ. Only God's long suffering prevented the earth from opening and swallowing this brood alive. Upon Christ's return in judgment, these "liars, blind leaders, and servants of Satan would inherit the fiery pool."[139] When priests led a procession past his prison window, Füchter interrupted and entertained by singing "German songs."[140] Presumably these were of a profane genre or in the form of mocking songs (Spottlieder). All of this seems supportive evidence that Füchter himself had a hand in the destruction of a sacred picture found torn near his dwelling.[141]

Füchter's letter indicated further that he had submitted a written account of his faith, something he lived to regret because it was used against him and apparently refuted with some success by clergy sent to dispute with the prisoners. Füchter reported that some prisoners had lent their "ears to the serpent" and fallen away, among them a certain Paul Gall, the brother-in-law of Paul Rumer.[142] By April 18, 1532, Gall and his wife, Justina, had indicated their willingness to recant. Conditions of release included a fine of five hundred gulden, payment of prison and court costs, as well as a public recantation from the pulpit of the parish church in Sterzing. The Galls were expected to indicate penance (pusswertigkeit) by standing on three consecutive Sundays behind the priests celebrating mass. But once free, Gall and his wife soon relapsed. Evidence indicates that Gall had joined the ranks of secondary leaders and become a local treasurer. Arrested again, he became another victim of Ferdinand's suppression.

Justina Gall fled to Moravia,[143] but before doing so she had also lost her brother Paul Rumer, who was executed at St. Michelsburg sometime before October 24, 1533.[144] At the time of his arrest in 1533, Paul Rumer had on his person a small codex (*büchel*) containing copies of several letters that he had transcribed. Among these was a letter by Hans Beck (Peckl) of Brixen, who had been a fellow prisoner with Lamprecht Gruber at Sterzing in early 1532. Beck, like Gall, must have avoided martyrdom in Sterzing by recantation but relapsed, for he and six others were later executed in Gufidaun.[145] The arrest of this group in Gufidaun triggered the flight of others from the area in July 1533. Incredible as it may seem, these refugees, including twenty-five children, managed the great escape to Moravia.[146] As will be noted in the next chapter, Hutter himself left for Moravia in late June 1533, leaving Amon behind as the main servant of the Word. Meanwhile, Beck's prison letter, addressed to Hutter and his inner circle—Amon, Valentin (Lukhner), Hans Meyer (Paulle), Bartle Schneider, and Paul Riemer (Rumer)—must have reached Amon.[147] Because a copy of the letter was taken from Rumer later in 1533—but another survived in Hutterite codices[148]—it may be inferred that Amon decided to have a copy made for local consumption before he sent the original to Moravia. The practice of employing copyists in so-called *Schreibstuben,* where all incoming and outgoing mail was copied, had not yet been institutionalized in the communities of Moravia.[149] Of historic interest is also that the authenticity and accurate transmission of the surviving text can be confirmed from official documents of Rumer's trial. During his interrogation Rumer was asked to explain an oblique reference by Beck concerning the escape of a squirrel. Rumer revealed that the reference in Beck's letter was to Simon Pänntzlen's house in Rattenberg. Pänntzlen kept a squirrel, which had escaped when a window was thoughtlessly opened.[150] The escape of the squirrel had become a code designating Pänntzlen's place as an Anabaptist shelter or meeting place for those on the trek to Moravia. Since the surviving copy of Beck's letter in Hutterite codices contained the reference to the squirrel, it provided proof that Hutterite scribes transmitted accurately even after the original meaning was no longer clear. The epistles are therefore a trustworthy historic source.

Very moving in Beck's letter was his report of the vacillations of his fellow prisoner, Wölfl from Götzenberg. Isolated and tortured, Wölfl recanted under oath but felt deep remorse after he had returned to the others. Fickle in spirit, Wölfl begged his fellow prisoners to pray for his steadfastness and asked to be reaccepted. Beck and the others were at a loss as to how to deal with Wölfl's weakness. They requested guidance from the outside leadership. Then, in allusion to Gruber's earlier letter, Beck and his companions closed with an invitation to their "wedding feast." *The Chronicle* confirmed that Beck and his fellow prisoners, including Wölfl, remained steadfast and suffered martyrdom.[151]

The impact of prison letters, such as those of Beck, Füchter, or Gruber, read to their fellow believers who were still free, can hardly be overestimated. An example is provided by Christoff Schuechknecht, mentioned earlier. Shortly before his arrest Schuechknecht had attended a meeting at which Hutter's first letters from Moravia and some prison letters were read.[152] The latter left such a deep impression that the illiterate Schuechknecht decided to have someone write a prison letter to his brother in the name of his imprisoned father, Andre Zimmermann. He hoped that the impact of such a letter would move his brother to repentance and win him for the Anabaptist cause. Obviously, Schuechknecht considered a letter in the name of his imprisoned father more effective than one in his own name. His arrest in the fall of 1533 put an end to any such endeavor. Both Schuechknecht and his father joined the lengthening list of martyrs.

The case of Schuechknecht illustrates that the epistles, particularly prison letters, proved a very effective means of communication to inoculate the fledgling congregation of God in South Tyrol, as well as in Moravia, against the terror unleashed by the powers of "Antichrist." No other Anabaptist group sponsored and produced an epistolary collection that was comparable either in quantity or existential, devotional quality. With time, these communiqués were standardized in spirit and style and patterned after the New Testament apostolic models, particularly those of Paul.[153] They served not only for the edification of the contemporary congregation but also as a rich source from which the first Hutterite historians reconstructed much of the early years of their community. As Friedmann already recognized, 20 percent of the "Great Chronicle" consists of "inserted epistles, while the great part of the text is made up of excerpts from such records."[154] In other words, in the beginning, before *The Chronicle,* was the epistolary collection. As the next chapters illustrate, inasmuch as possible and where appropriate, this study utilized the epistolary collection as the primary source. Here in a test case, a small sample of the oldest prison epistles was examined for its authenticity and historic veracity against the external official record. The procedure established that at every point at which internal and external documents overlapped, Hutterite sources proved historically reliable and at times filled gaps in official records. It goes without saying that the two kinds of document provide different perspectives on the events they recorded.

Ferdinand's measures to crush the Anabaptists in the Tyrol proved all too successful. For scholars to whom the history of the Tyrol seems unthinkable without the religious and cultural dominance of the Catholic Church, Ferdinand's policies secured these territories for the Catholic Reformation. From this perspective, Anabaptism had no lasting influence and contributed only by default to the growing cooperation between church and state which shaped Tyrol's history and culture into the present.

Viewed from the North American distance through the perspective of the victims, the effective suppression of Anabaptism seems less of a historic blessing. Ferdinand's measures perverted customary judicial process, coerced consciences, deprived subjects of individual and collective rights, drove the victims from home and friends, stole their property, destroyed families, and took innocent lives. Not surprisingly, in the Anabaptist discourse Ferdinand and his advisors represented the powers of evil. By 1533 Ferdinand's measures had made it extremely difficult, if not impossible, to maintain any kind of congregational life in South Tyrol. Arrests of key members of the network no doubt influenced Hutter's decision to move to Moravia in 1533. Having led the congregation of God for almost five years, he could not elude much longer the authorities who were on his trail. No stranger to Moravia, he had visited the promised land almost annually since 1529, and his joining the Pusterers already there must have seemed inevitable. Little could he know the consequences of that decision (Chapter 9). In 1534 Amon followed suit with the remnant. 1533–34, therefore, marked a watershed in relations between the leaders and community now in Moravia and those still in South Tyrol. Moravia became the home base, Tyrol an adjunct mission field. Even Hutter's return to South Tyrol in 1535 (Chapter 10) did not alter the new relationship. Home missions continued for years after Hutter's death, but they became carefully regulated. Unauthorized visits and unofficial contacts were discouraged and in the 1540s forbidden by the post-Hutter leadership.[155] The Anabaptist presence in the Puster and its side valleys had dwindled to missionary visits. Although martyr fires continued to flicker sporadically for another twenty years, Ferdinand's suppression had triumphed. The victims were either dead, muted by fear, or struggling to build new communities in exile.

Ferdinand's success raises one further point worthy of reflection. The Anabaptist experience in the Tyrol casts doubt on the hallowed belief that the blood of martyrs constitutes the seed of the true church. If the Anabaptist martyrs represented that seed, fire and blood led to the extinction of the Anabaptists in the Tyrol. Yet, somehow, strangely, the martyr seed did find new soil. The gates of hell did not prevail. The new communities in Moravia entered their golden years just as Anabaptism in the Tyrol was being snuffed out and Ferdinand went to his own reward.

Chapter Nine

Dissension in the "Congregation of God"

The Schisms of 1531 and 1533

Year after year, Jacob Hutter's tenure in South Tyrol had become increasingly more difficult. Ferdinand's unrelenting pursuit of the heretics tore at the fibers of the underground network. Because he was the leader and main culprit in the eyes of the authorities, each arrest with its accompanying torture put Hutter's survival at greater risk. No doubt these circumstances were part of the deliberations that made his departure for Moravia easier, especially when news arrived that he was needed to help lead the new community in Auspitz. The schism that followed set the stage for the emergence of the Hutterites as a distinct group. But the narrative of the schism of 1533 began with earlier tensions in the "congregation of God."

Chapter 3 documented how during the spring of 1528 differences between Hubmaier's successors and Jacob Wiedemann led to the establishment of the Brethren at Austerlitz. Premised on the apostolic precedent of sharing all things, the Austerlitz community became a beacon of hope and a model for persecuted Anabaptists far and wide, including South Tyrol. Flooded by refugees from diverse regions and social backgrounds, the Brethren at Austerlitz tripled their numbers within two years, but this rapid expansion brought growing pains and tensions that surfaced in late 1530. The stage was set for the schism of 1531 and the founding of a new community at Auspitz.

The Schism of 1531: New Beginnings at Auspitz

Among the disaffected in Austerlitz by late 1530 were members of the former congregation in Krumau, Bohemia. Only in 1529 had a large number from this congregation, many of them natives of North Tyrol, moved collectively to Austerlitz in search of "greater perfection." In the following year they had been reinforced by more Tyrolese, North and South, led by Jörg Zaunring, who assumed an unofficial leadership role among his fellow countrymen after Hans Fasser, who led the group from Krumau, returned to Bohemia as "a fornicator" (see Chapter 3). The newcomers soon found reasons to complain about life and teachings at Austerlitz.[1] It seems that the real and the ideal did not entirely coincide and that Jacob Wiedemann, who functioned as overall bishop, was either unable or unwilling to enforce homogeneity of practice. The catalyst for growing dissension was Wilhelm Reublin,[2] who arrived a haunted and sick man during the last months of 1530. His credentials were impressive. A founding member of Swiss Anabaptism, Reublin had been involved in its prehistory at Basel and Zurich. He had baptized Hubmaier at Waldshut and is believed to have been a main mover, along with Michael Sattler, in the composition of the Schleitheim Articles. It was Reublin who brought Sattler to the area of Rottenburg, where Reublin's wife and young son were arrested along with Sattler. The authorities considered Reublin, not Sattler, the "chief Anabaptist,"[3] and while Sattler's trial wound to its bitter end, Reublin was building the congregation in nearby Esslingen. He subsequently spread accounts of Sattler's martyrdom and himself suffered imprisonment in Strasbourg. "Eternally" exiled from Strasbourg in March 1529, with threat of drowning should he return, Reublin undauntedly propagated Anabaptism in the Rhineland before making his way to Moravia.[4] He arrived in Austerlitz sometime in October or November 1530 with a letter of introduction, it seems, from Pilgram Marpeck.[5]

Despite his impressive credentials, Reublin was not permitted to teach or preach in Austerlitz. Not surprisingly, he complained. In his letter to Marpeck, dated January 26, 1531,[6] Reublin alleged that at Austerlitz ordinary members—he was presumably among them—ate "peas and cabbage," while in separate dining rooms the leaders and their wives dined on "roasted meat, fish, poultry, and good wine!" One of the leaders cultivated an elegant lifestyle while little children were dying of malnutrition. Reublin counted twenty such victims during his stay. He was also appalled by the authoritarian style of leadership. Reublin felt that these evident imperfections in the congregation of God had deeper spiritual causes, and he was determined to address them.[7]

In the absence of Jacob Wiedemann, the main leader, Reublin took his concerns to Kilian Volckhamer, one of three group leaders, with the request that he be permitted to address the groups in a congregational meeting. After consultation with the other leaders, Volckhamer rejected the request.[8] *The Chronicle* recorded in some detail what happened next. Vexed by what he considered improper teachings and practices but muzzled by the leadership, Reublin, one evening in early 1531, "began reading rather loudly" from the Scriptures.⁹ Having thus gained the attention of those present, he used his chosen text, presumably 1 Corinthians 14, to criticize the order that prevailed at Austerlitz. His unauthorized exposition and criticism found a favorable reception among a number of malcontents, disillusioned with the Wiedemann regime, among them Jörg Zaunring. The Hutterite account of the events that led to the formation of a new community at Auspitz subsequently emphasized Zaunring's role. Nevertheless, Reublin's role needed explanation. Since he would be expelled from the new community as a charlatan and an Ananias and since the Hutterites themselves later placed the same strictures on unauthorized preaching as Reublin had faced at Austerlitz, the Hutterite endorsement of the 1531 schism and of Reublin's conspicuous role in it provided a problem for later Hutterite chroniclers. They had recourse to God's special providence, according to which God could use "unredeemed men" to correct "disorder in his church."¹⁰ This became a standard explanation for other equally difficult cases.

Volckhamer and the other leaders at Austerlitz no doubt agreed with the assessment that placed Reublin among the unredeemed, but they failed to see in him the divine instrument of correction. Messengers fetched Wiedemann, who attempted to discipline and silence Reublin. But the damage had been done. Wiedemann and his subalterns obviously underestimated the extent of disaffection. A number of secondary leaders or would-be leaders, each with his own cortege of followers, came to Reublin's support. Besides Zaunring, they included Burkhart (Braun) of Ofen, David of Schweidnitz (the Bohemian), Hans Amon, Christoph Gschäll, and Adam Schlegel. Emboldened by their support, Reublin sought to convince Wiedemann and the established leadership that according to Scripture "they were neither teaching nor standing rightly."

But Wiedemann had a different reading of the Scriptures. When private discussions failed, Wiedemann proceeded with a public ban against Reublin. Before an assembly of the entire congregation, Wiedemann explained "how, in his absence, Reublin had pushed himself forward, teaching things that were opposed to what [he] Jacob and his assistants taught." Such presumptuous usurpation of authority and the resulting confusion and dissension could not be of God and needed to be disciplined. Wiedemann then asked all who supported the ban against Reublin "to come and stand with him."

To Wiedemann's dismay a group of forty to fifty, led by Zaunring, refused to vote with their feet and remained on the side of Reublin. When Wiedemann queried why they sided with Reublin, Zaunring replied that no one should be condemned without a proper hearing and that Reublin should be given an opportunity to defend himself before the congregation. Instead of accepting the suggested procedure, Wiedemann decided to discipline Zaunring as well, but his measures proved counterproductive, as an increasing number now felt that Zaunring and Reublin were being treated unfairly. Wiedemann saw the polarization as proof that Reublin was a "false prophet and trouble maker [*aufruerer und unglucksmacher*]." The two ringleaders and their supporters were excluded from the tables of the community. Reublin played his part by going out from such "unclean, false, deceptive prophets and liars" and shaking the dust, or rather snow, from his feet.[11] It was not the most edifying episode in the early history of Anabaptism. Mature men and women, who had left goods, friends, kindred, and home under the death sentence to found "a more perfect" Christian order, pronounced anathemas on each other.

On January 8, 1531, in the dead of winter, Reublin and a group of 150 adults left Austerlitz for Auspitz.[12] The children and the infirm remained temporarily with sympathetic citizens in Austerlitz and with Burkhart of Ofen as their guardian. According to Reublin, Jews and Gentiles showed greater pity on the exiled than their former brothers and sisters, who turned them out without compensation for their contributions to the common treasury.[13] In his letter to Marpeck, Reublin charged that four hundred gulden had been added to the common coffers during the previous four weeks alone. Only 5 percent, twenty gulden, had been spent on grain during that period. Yet he and the others who were expelled were told that there was no money in the treasury. Where had it gone? Queries with local bankers revealed that the leaders of the community had exchanged "handfuls of gulden" for smaller currency—the kind used for everyday personal shopping—so much so that demand for change had outstripped supply. Reublin and his group, meanwhile, were sent packing in the midst of winter with no more than one kreutzer per person.[14]

The bitterness of Reublin's charge takes on weight only in light of contemporary exchange rates and wages. A gulden was worth sixty kreutzer.[15] Reublin and his group of 150 adults were allegedly sent out with approximately 150 kreutzer or about three gulden among them, when a domestic servant or day laborer could earn from three to five kreutzer a day.[16] Thus dealt the very brethren who had institutionalized community of goods as the ultimate expression of brotherly love and sharing with those who found fault with their practice or criticized their leadership.

Leaving Austerlitz "in great dread of highwaymen," Reublin and the impoverished band traveled in the direction of Auspitz, the home of the Philipite community. By January 26, 1531, about fifty adults had found shelter in an abandoned parsonage at Steurowitz near Auspitz. Others were housed near the horse market in Auspitz itself. Further hardships and disappointments awaited them as some found employment with another former disgruntled Austerlitzer, named Caspar.[17] *The Chronicle* recorded that "wishing to unite" with Zaunring and his people, Caspar "took the brothers into his home, pretending to be happy to give them lodging. He let them work in his vineyard with scarcely any food until the time the vintage was gathered in. Then he revealed his treachery, gave up the idea of brotherhood, and ordered them out of his house empty-handed."[18]

Fortunately for the newcomers, the mistress of Auspitz, Johanka of Boskowitz, abbess of the convent at Brünn, provided credit so that they were able to survive.[19] During the spring of 1531 it proved possible to transfer the children and the sick from Austerlitz to Auspitz. David of Schweidnitz, responsible for logistics, hired protection for the convoy, something later held against him by Jacob Hutter. Even so, the parsonage at Steurowitz, to which some of the children and sick were transferred, proved unsafe. Armed robbery, in which a brother lost his life, led to the transfer of all children to the house by the horse market. The new community, determined to treat the children with greater care than had been the case at Austerlitz, appointed a God-fearing brother and several sisters to educate the children "in the discipline and ways of the Lord."[20]

Evidence indicates that both the Austerlitz Brethren and the exiles newly established at Auspitz sent their version of events to the various home territories, including the Tyrol.[21] News of the schism created consternation among those looking to Austerlitz as the model congregation. In the spring of 1531 Hutter, representing South Tyrol, and Sigmund Schützinger, representing North Tyrol, arrived on a fact-finding mission. They found both parties at fault but assigned greater blame to Wiedemann and his assistants. A summary of their findings, as preserved in *The Chronicle,* stated that "in the first place, they [the Austerlitz Brethren] had acted unjustly in expelling the innocent; secondly, they had allowed freedom of the flesh, resulting in a return to private property; thirdly, there had been marriages with unbelievers; and there were many similar points,"[22] which may be reconstructed from other Hutterite sources and Reublin's letter.

A comparison of these two sources reveals differences in emphasis. Reublin, not surprisingly, placed himself center stage; Hutterite sources underlined Zaunring's role. In Reublin's account the authoritarian leadership structure in Austerlitz figured more prominently than the practice of community of goods. He complained that the rich had separate living quarters. The leaders allegedly wore upper-class shoes, shirts, overcoats, and furs, something common members could not afford and considered unbecoming. They also enjoyed a better diet. Reublin was appalled by the inadequate care given to children. Parents who had contributed as much as fifty gulden to the common treasury watched helplessly as their children died from the lack of proper provisions. Meanwhile the leaders were living in high style, showering gifts on each other. Coerced marriages of young sisters had led to four separations.

Then, extending his criticism to the teachings of the Austerlitz leadership, Reublin lamented that the Lord's Prayer had been discarded.[23] He found too much emphasis on the external act of water baptism and not enough on its inner meaning and complained that little children had been condemned "to hell," meaning presumably that he differed with the Austerlitz leadership on the question of children's innocence. Reublin considered the Austerlitz position on war taxes hypocritical—taxes were paid indirectly. He cited David of Schweidnitz as in agreement with him on this issue. But most disconcerting for Reublin was the fact that the Austerlitzers did not follow the rule of Paul as outlined in 1 Corinthians 14 and did not permit ordinary members to speak in the congregation. Thus the Spirit of God working through mutual admonition had been stifled.

Hutterite criticism generally agreed with the points made by Reublin. Wiedemann had pressured younger sisters into marriages with older men. Wiedemann allegedly also threatened marriages with unbelievers. For reasons no longer clear, the sisters had been screened according to their ability to recall certain texts and answer a number of questions. Those who passed this testing received high praise, but "simple, unassuming sisters, although faithful and devout, were ridiculed and put to shame." Hutterite sources repeated Reublin's charge that children were neglected. They also claimed that social distinctions were being perpetuated, that the leaders were arrogant. "Some of the servants who had learned more than one language—Franz Itzinger, Jakob Mändel, among others—came to think highly of themselves." Not surprisingly, Hutterite sources tended to make more of inconsistencies concerning the practice of community of goods. Some members at Austerlitz allegedly kept private purses. They "went to market to buy what they liked for themselves." Inconsistencies existed regarding the oath and nature of separation from the rest of society. One of the leaders at Austerlitz allegedly taught "that Christ had been a citizen of Capernaum and that therefore as citizens it was permissible to do civilian duties and swear oaths."[24] In all, Reublin and Hutterite criticisms agreed that the Brethren at Austerlitz failed to live up to expectations.

The schismatics hoped to do better at Auspitz. Alas, the task of building community proved difficult. United in opposition to the failings at Austerlitz, the secessionists soon discovered that agreement on what was wrong did not automatically convert into a harmoniously functioning community. Physical deprivation, separation from former friends, adjustment to new surroundings, inadequate accommodations, and different backgrounds taxed their tolerance levels and challenged the cohesiveness of the new community. New tensions and disagreements arose. Within a year the leaders of the exodus, Reublin and Zaunring, would be disgraced.

Reublin, who in his letter to Marpeck pictured himself as a new Moses or Joshua chosen to deliver the true followers of Christ from the bondage of one-eyed Wiedemann, became the first prominent casualty. He must have been particularly vulnerable because, unlike Zaunring, he lacked a sizable coterie of followers dedicated to his leadership. Reinforcements from the Rhine valley or Swabia, his sphere of influence, arrived belatedly or joined the sister community led by Philip Plener. Reublin's expected moral and financial support from Marpeck never materialized because his letter to Marpeck, carried by Julius Lober, was intercepted in Ansbach territory near Nuremberg. Besides, Marpeck appears to have retained friendly contacts with the Brethren at Austerlitz (see Chapter 4).

The first difficulties surfaced during the fall of 1531 when Caspar refused to pay those who had worked in his vineyard. At about that time the arrival of a Swabian leader and his small band revealed the existence of differences of opinion between Reublin and others in the community on an unidentified article of faith. According to *The Chronicle,*

At that time, because God wished to purify his people and because sinners cannot remain in the church of the righteous, it happened that a servant of a little group in Swabia arrived in Auspitz to inquire about the faith, Ordnung, and teaching of the church of God. He spoke with Wilhelm Reublin about various articles of faith, but as they could not agree on one point, this servant from Swabia did not want to stay. When he told them how Reublin had explained one of the articles, the elders said, "But that is not the position of the church," and suggested that perhaps he had misunderstood. But the man insisted that that was how he had heard it from their teacher Reublin. The elders asked Reublin, but he denied it. The man from Swabia, however, still insisted on what he had said before and called upon God as witness. Reublin was severely admonished, but he, too, called on God as his witness. Finally others who had also heard him proved him wrong, and he had to admit his guilt and confess that he had spoken as the man had testified. The elders told Reublin that the matter was too serious for them to close [solve].[25]

Unfortunately, the surviving sources failed to name the leader from Swabia or the article of disagreement,[26] but Reublin's leadership was now in trouble, with worse to come. While the elders waited for the arrival of Hutter and Schützinger, Reublin fell ill and confided the existence of a personal fund to an attending sister, who reported this to the elders, thereby sealing Reublin's fate. *The Chronicle* reported the affair as follows:

Without the knowledge of the elders and the church and regardless of the great hunger among the people, he had hidden twenty-four gulden that he had brought with him from his home.[27] In his illness he entrusted this money to a married sister named Katharina Loy, who immediately reported it. . . . Around this time Jakob Hutter and Simon Schützinger arrived from Tyrol. They examined Reublin's situation carefully and summoned him before the church. He was excluded as an unfaithful, malicious Ananias. He himself admitted that such a judgment was right.[28]

Reublin's movements after the expulsion are unclear. Evidence suggests that he was in the Esslingen-Horb area in midsummer 1531. If true, then he must have sought to collect members for a community in Moravia.[29] A Reublin faction continued to exist in Swabia and the Rhineland as late as 1534.[30] Reublin subsequently settled at Znaim, in Moravia, where a group of about fifty Swiss Brethren resided in 1533. His relationship to this group is unknown. In the midforties some members from this community merged with the Hutterites.[31] At about that time Reublin contacted Heinrich Bullinger in Zurich, and ten years later, in 1554, he sought shelter in Basel. Reublin spent his last years—he lived to be almost eighty—seeking to regain his inheritance.[32] One can only speculate that mergers between Swiss Brethren at Znaim and Hutterites excluded him.

Back in Auspitz in 1531, Hutter and Schützinger installed Jörg Zaunring as servant of the Word. Adam Schlegel, Burkhart of Ofen, and David of Schweidnitz became Zaunring's assistants.[33] Having thus put God's house in order, Hutter and Schützinger returned to their respective charges in the Tyrol. But the exclusion of Reublin did not remove all difficulties. Before year's end, Zaunring and Schlegel were at odds with each other. Zaunring discovered that Schlegel "behaved in a scandalous manner," leading brothers and sisters into "licentiousness." "As soon as this was revealed, [Schlegel] was disciplined, his service was taken from him, and he was forbidden to teach."[34] But Schlegel received support from Burkhart of Ofen, and the two now criticized Zaunring's leadership from the sidelines. Eventually both joined the neighboring Philipites. Before long, Zaunring was also at loggerheads with his remaining assistant, David of Schweidnitz. David, it was discovered, had been dishonest: without the knowledge of the brethren he had paid the magistrate of Nikoltschitz to provide a protective escort for the children against robbers on the way from Austerlitz to Auspitz.[35] David stubbornly refused to see this precautionary measure as a transgression of the ethic of nonresistance or separation of church and state and was stripped of his office. During this festering dispute, rumors spread that Zaunring himself had shielded the adultery of his wife from public exposure and been guilty of a coverup.[36] Zaunring and David had disciplined Mrs. Zaunring and the adulterous brother in private. As part of the discipline, Zaunring refrained from cohabitation with his wife. But he took her back as soon as she indicated proper remorse, and in another private ceremony lifted the restrictions placed on her. Information about the affair was leaked by David after he and Zaunring had fallen out. David was later brow-beaten by Hutter into admitting that his disclosure of Zaunring's marital problems had been motivated by envy and spite.[37] But by then the damage was done; Zaunring's leadership had been tarnished.

When the Zaunring affair became public, some members of the community felt that the discipline assigned to the guilty party had been too lenient. Leonard Schmerbacher, one of the "servants of temporal affairs,"[38] brought the case before the congregation. "The whole church agreed unanimously that members of Christ should not be members of a harlot, and therefore Zaunring and his wife should be excluded and separated from the church." News was dispatched to the Tyrol that the congregation, "zealous for the truth, punishing wrong without regard of persons," found itself once more without a servant of the Word.

Hutter and Schützinger returned to Auspitz for Easter 1532.[39] Although they found the congregation's zeal praiseworthy, Hutter "wished it had not been necessary" to deal so harshly with Zaunring. After public confession and collective intercession the disgraced leader was rehabilitated[40] and reassigned as itinerant servant of the Word to Franconia and Hesse.[41] The decision against David of Schweidnitz was upheld. Like Schlegel and Burkhart Braun before him, David joined the neighboring Philipites.[42]

The first year at Auspitz thus took its toll on leaders among the schismatics from Austerlitz. Reublin, Zaunring, Schlegel, Burkhart of Ofen, and David of Schweidnitz had all been discredited, and the lot fell on Sigmund Schützinger to assume the office of servant of the Word in place of Zaunring.[43]

Schützinger, a native of Rattenberg, belonged to the earliest Anabaptists in North Tyrol. Innsbruck had known his name since March 1528 and in May of that year gave specific orders for his arrest.[44] Schützinger fled his home town, but, unlike other members of the Rattenberg community, including Marpeck who fled to Krumau in Bohemia, Schützinger remained underground in his home territory, becoming the main Anabaptist leader in North Tyrol.[45] In this capacity he had baptized, among others, Jeronimus Käls, secretary of the governor (*Hauptmann*) at Kufstein. Jeronimus would become the first schoolmaster for the children of the community at Auspitz, a supporter of Hutter and fellow martyr (see Chapter 11). As leader of the Anabaptists in North Tyrol, Schützinger had traveled to Moravia with Hutter at least twice before and now on this third visit had been chosen leader by lot. Presumably Hutter had been one of the other candidates eliminated by this method.[46] Wilhelm Griesbacher and Leonhard Schmerbacher were chosen to be Schützinger's assistants, as servants of temporal affairs. Before Hutter returned to the Tyrol he and

Schützinger forged an alliance with the two neighboring communities, the Philipites and Gabrielites. Gabriel Ascherham became the recognized overseer of the three communities with the agreement that in difficult matters the three communities would "seek each other's counsel as befits a united people."[47] This most likely involved mutual aid in both spiritual and material matters.

The alliance was put to the test when in 1532 soldiers, sent to fight the Turks, decided to plunder heretics in Moravia instead. The struggling community led by Schützinger was particularly hard hit.[48] The servants of temporal affairs found it difficult to meet payments on the loan from their landlord, the abbess of the convent at Brünn. Gabriel and Philip were either unable or unwilling to help financially or materially,[49] and Schützinger failed to provide the dynamic leadership desired by some during the resulting crisis. Although the sequence of events is no longer entirely clear, indirect evidence suggests that Leonard Schmerbacher, the servant of temporal affairs who had functioned as interim leader after Zaunring's dismissal, in early 1533 sent news of financial difficulties and dissatisfaction with Schützinger's leadership to Hutter via Hans Amon. Amon, Hutter's confidant and later his hand-picked successor, had served a similar role in 1531 and 1532.[50] Clear is that after Amon's arrival in South Tyrol a decision was made that Hutter would transfer his leadership qualities and funds to Auspitz. Amon would remain in South Tyrol.[51] A letter by Amon to this effect was sent to Schmerbacher,[52] providing unequivocal evidence that Hutter and Amon were making plans without consulting Schützinger and that these plans assumed a leadership role for Hutter in Auspitz.[53] That Amon confidentially addressed Schmerbacher rather than Schützinger implies that Schmerbacher belonged to a pro-Hutter faction unhappy with Schützinger's leadership. Even more revealing was Amon's fear that Hutter's move to Auspitz could cause a schism. He implored Schmerbacher to do his best to preserve unity and avoid division. The passage is worth citing.

Dearly beloved brother, I write to you in confidence as a faithful warning, for the sake of the dear brothers and sisters. When brother Jacob comes down and assumes the leadership of the people of God and serves them [with the Word], which I hope, and the dear children of God develop a special trust toward him but others become vexed or annoyed thereby; I pray you, my dear brother, that in as much as God gives you grace and understanding, you will do your best to avoid a root of bitterness to come up among the servants of God, as did happen [previously], may it be lamented to God. I hope, however, to God, that it shall not happen.[54]

That Hutter's move to Auspitz in the summer of 1533 was intended to be permanent may be surmised further from the preparations made. Amon reported that he had been chosen servant of the Word to replace

Hutter in South Tyrol and that Onophrius Griesinger had been appointed his assistant in temporal affairs.[55] These appointments most likely took place at a three-day meeting on the Götzenberg,[56] although the "shortage of leaders in Moravia had been discussed" at an even earlier meeting in Gufidaun. Because they arrested some of the participants, the authorities too had wind of Hutter's travel plans. On June 4, a warning was sent to the governor of Steiermark to be on the lookout for Hutter and Amon in the Enns valley.[57] And on June 17, 1533, two prisoners at Brixen testified that Hutter planned to leave for Auspitz and that a number of small groups were to follow. They knew that the destination was Auspitz, a little marketplace belonging to the abbess of Brünn. Six hundred brothers and sisters (*Geschwistriget*) were there already. They knew also that the Anabaptist message had received a favorable response as far away as Hesse and Thuringia. Their apostle, Zaunring, had been sent there because many in this region "repented gladly."[58]

Statements from this period also provided a rare glimpse of Hutter and Amon. Hutter wore a short yellow leather kilt (*röckl*) over brown pants, a black overcoat (mantle) and a small black cap, Amon a gray armor coat (*Wappenrock*)[59] of long Munich cloth and a small black cap. The same sources told of money collected and sent to Moravia, some of it after Hutter left.[60] Despite this detailed information and government vigilance to apprehend him, Hutter managed to make his way safely to Moravia. He used the Inn, not the Enns valley, holding his last meeting on the Stainer (Stamser?) Joch on August 1, 1533, arriving in Auspitz ten days later.[61] Amon's premonition that Hutter's arrival in Auspitz could cause division proved correct.

The Great Schism of 1533

The schism of 1533 is by far the best documented in early Anabaptist history because it marked the genesis of the Hutterites as a distinct group. Beginning as a dispute over Hutter's leadership role in the Auspitz community, it led to the breakup of the alliance with the Philipites and Gabrielites. Mutual recriminations, anathemas, and excommunications on both sides generated such bitter feelings that members of the different communities, even though they worked on the same fields, refused to greet each other, sit, or break bread with each other.[62] Slanders festered on for decades, including open letters of accusation,[63] mocking songs, and even rival histories of events leading to the schism, all with the aim of setting the record straight and stealing each other's "sheep." Unfortunately, only the Hutterite account of this feud survived and now constitutes the oldest part of *The Chronicle* which it preceded.[64]

The author of the original account was Caspar Braitmichel, the first and perhaps ablest of Hutterite chroniclers.[65] Braitmichel, a Silesian who shifted his loyalty to Hutter's community,[66] may have been an eyewitness to some of the events; but like all good historians, he relied on written documents for his primary sources. These consisted chiefly of Hutter's epistolary correspondence with Amon during and immediately after the conflict.[67] Writing two to three decades after the events, Braitmichel's intentions were honorable enough: to write "a short but truthful record . . . of the great distress and hostility provoked by Satan which the congregation, named after its shepherd Jakob Hutter, had to suffer." More specifically, he tried to refute an account by Hutter's chief rival and antagonist, Gabriel Ascherham. Ascherham had written a history of Anabaptist beginnings in Moravia up to the year 1541,[68] and it seems hardly accidental that Braitmichel took his account to the year 1542, claiming "poor eyesight" for anything beyond that. At the time of writing Braitmichel was able to invite his readers to "judge for themselves how God separated the devout from the hypocrites"; he nevertheless felt it necessary to qualify his invitation, "take care lest reading of rebellion and false spirits becomes a stumbling block. . . . There must be stumbling blocks to reveal the chosen people who withstand the test, but woe to those who make stumbling blocks. As for you, innocent and honest reader, rejoice in the Lord your God."[69]

Strong in condemnation of Hutter's antagonists, Braitmichel's account was weak in explanation, and with Gabriel's side of the story lost, it is difficult for the historian to offer a balanced view or proffer a satisfactory explanation for the schism other than normal human leadership rivalries. Even Friedmann, sympathetic to the Hutterite point of view, was unable to discern major differences in either teaching or practice between the opposing parties. He therefore simply invoked the principle of the survival of the spiritually fittest to determine who was correct. "Looking back" he considered Hutter "doubtless spiritually the strongest of the three leaders." Hutter laid a "foundation so clear and strict that it has survived all vicissitudes of history."[70] But whatever the merits of such an argument, discerning spiritual correctness cannot be the historian's chief concern. The primary task is rather to "get the story straight," that is, to provide an overview of the sequence of events that unfolded with the arrival of Hutter in Auspitz.[71]

The Leadership Struggle: Hutter Versus Schützinger

After almost yearly visits since 1529 and after sending numerous converts to Moravia, Hutter arrived in Auspitz on Monday, August 11, 1533, with intentions of more permanent residence. As noted, he brought with him a "temporal gift, a sweet sacrifice, a small sum of money."[72] The reception was amicable. According to Braitmichel, the "entire holy congregation of God" received him "like the Lord himself."[73] Schützinger and his assistants invited Hutter "to help them care for the people," something Hutter proceeded to do without delay.[74] In the next few days he met with disgruntled supporters, who apparently hoped that he would establish a new community with them. Instead, Hutter declared his intentions to stay and correct the abuses in the "house of God." On Sunday, August 17, Hutter reported to the gathered congregation on what God had done through him and others in the Tyrol.

Then he announced publicly that he had heard there were some in Auspitz who hoped that when he came he would move with them to a different place. All of these whom he had known he had called to him and admonished them, making it clear that he had no such intentions, much less taught or said so. But he would help punish according to God's Word any fickle, selfish people who still wanted to go somewhere else. And since God had sent him to the church, he would put all his efforts into overcoming any faults he found in the house of God.[75]

The announcement within a week of his arrival that he would put his effort into overcoming the faults in the community amounted to a censure and challenge of Schützinger's leadership. At least this was how Schützinger perceived it because he attempted to restrain Hutter. Within two weeks of Hutter's arrival, the two were at loggerheads. Hutter offered to "move on and serve wherever the Lord led him, if he was not needed," but he wanted to know the mind of the congregation first. When Schützinger refused to put Hutter's future role on the agenda of the congregational meeting set for Sunday, August 24, Hutter complained to Gabriel Ascherham, the recognized bishop. Gabriel agreed that Hutter's case should be heard by the entire congregation but found it necessary to counsel that Hutter should proceed "humbly." A certain Kaspar (Braitmichel?) from Rossitz was sent along with Hutter to communicate Gabriel's opinion to Schützinger.

Meanwhile, Schützinger had discovered that the two servants of temporal affairs, Schmerbacher and Griesbacher, favored Hutter's continued presence in the community as associate leader. Overruled by Gabriel and undermined by his assistants, Schützinger agreed to Hutter's appearance before a general meeting of the congregation, but he insisted that through "the drawing of lots God had entrusted this people to him and made him their shepherd and [that he] therefore intended to continue in this service. If Jakob had anything to say, he should do so briefly for he could not allow him to speak very long . . . he insisted on being the one to teach the people."[76]

Because of the absence of a number of brothers at places of work, the congregational meeting was postponed until Sunday, September 7, a convenient delay that provided Schützinger with the opportunity to present his side to Gabriel and Philip. He explained that Hutter aimed at nothing less than sole control of his congregation. Acknowledging Hutter's charisma and superior gifts as a speaker, Schützinger feared that if given associate status Hutter would undermine his authority. In response to Schützinger's representation, Hutter was cited before the three leaders at the nearby Philipite commune and in so many words told to return to the Tyrol. He in turn asked how they would feel about having gathered a people only to be told that they could not serve them. As the discussion dragged on into the night, the respective assistants were called in to settle the issue.[77] Somehow financial considerations entered the discussion because in the heated exchanges that followed Hutter was accused of having advanced his own leadership aspirations with the "sweet sacrifice" he brought from the Tyrol, an accusation he rejected.[78] Against Schützinger's appointment by lot Hutter insisted on his sense of divine calling and on the right of the congregation to decide his role. After considerable debate, which included a consideration of joint leadership—an idea rejected by Gabriel, who feared that this would lead to confusion and division[79]—it was agreed to bring the question of Hutter's future role before the congregation. But Philip and Gabriel were now decidedly on Schützinger's side.

On September 7 Hutter was allowed to make his case. He spoke with restraint, explaining why he had come and how, since his arrival, he had been hindered from doing the work to which God had called him. Schützinger spoke next, defending his divine mandate to sole leadership decided by lot. Gabriel supported Schützinger and warned the congregation not to despise God's chosen, graphically illustrating the consequences of turning against God's anointed with a reference to the Old Testament story of Korah's rebellion. He suggested further that Hutter's "proud and arrogant" bearing made him a more suitable candidate to be an itinerant rather than a residential servant of the Word. He opposed any division of authority, claiming New Testament precedent, namely that James had been sole bishop in the church at Jerusalem. At that point Hutter interjected with an offer to prove from the New Testament that Gabriel was wrong in regard to its precedent.[80]

As a form of compromise, some of the other leaders proposed that for "the sake of peace, love, and unity" Schützinger be given precedence as leader and Hutter granted a supportive role.[81] To this the whole congregation responded with "yes, yes!" When asked by Gabriel whether he would abide by the congregational decision, Hutter replied that he needed to "first consider it before God, and take counsel with the elders and servants." Upon this Gabriel retorted, "I have nothing more to say to you. I will be on my way." This left the congregation divided and in great anguish. On the following day Hutter accepted the decision but not without protest. He claimed that he had been misunderstood, misrepresented, and mistreated. But Gabriel would have none of that, cutting him short with, "You claim that we misunderstand you, but we too speak German! There was no need for you to say anything at all."[82]

The result was that Schützinger retained the office of leading servant of the Word, and Hutter's position and role remained ill defined. He was still in the community two weeks later, when, according to *The Chronicle*, "the Lord struck Simon [Sigmund] Schützinger so severely that he lay seriously ill in bed." Since the congregation could not be left without spiritual nourishment, the secondary leadership invited Hutter to assume the role of servant of the Word. Without any waste of time, Hutter, in a special service of admonition on Sunday, September 28, assailed the lax discipline regarding community of goods which had been tolerated under Schützinger's regime. His criticism struck a responsive chord with the servants of temporal affairs but touched a raw nerve with some other members who began "to mutter against Jacob." Others took Hutter's admonition to heart, among them Jörg Fasser (Vasser), who brought his bed and chest to the communal storeroom to demonstrate full surrender of all temporal assets to the community.[83] His wife, however, was more reserved. She withheld some of her own and her children's inheritance without her husband's knowledge. Later unmasked as the new Sapphira, Mrs. Fasser was called before a disciplinary committee and placed under the ban, meaning that until her reinstatement she had to eat her meals in isolation.

A few days later, it occurred to Hutter, who, according to *The Chronicle*, was blessed with the divine "gift of discernment," that Schützinger's wife, too, might be a Sapphira.[84] He raised his suspicions with the elders, who, upon his urging, launched an investigation. Taking inventory first of Hutter's quarters, the search party proceeded to the unsuspecting Schützinger. Here they discovered an inordinate supply of linen, surplus shirts, and the equivalent of "four Bernese pounds" in small coins.[85] While this was shocking enough, Hutter must have suspected more. "In the name and power of the Lord" he admonished a shaken Schützinger to come clean. Had he known of the money and was there more? A conscience-stricken Schützinger pulled another forty gulden from a secret place in the ceiling. Hutter and the search party were devastated by the evidence of such faithless deceit. As servant of the Word, Schützinger had "taught full surrender and community [of goods] to others and yet did not hold to it himself."[86]

The magnitude of Schützinger's crime, especially given the strictures outlined by Hutter a few days earlier, and the resulting leadership crisis demanded urgent action. Had not a similar situation led to the expulsion of Reublin? Hutter immediately sent for Philip and dispatched two men to inform Gabriel at Rossitz. Philip was not at home, and Gabriel was apparently preoccupied temporarily with other matters. Since Hutter and the elders "could not postpone dealing" with the crisis, they called a congregational meeting for Sunday, October 5, and briefed those gathered on Schützinger's duplicity. In the presence of the whole congregation, Hutter denounced the "faithlessness, greed, and treachery of heart" of his rival and admonished him to repent. A crushed Schützinger "promised to do so with all his might," made a public confession of his sin, and pleaded for forgiveness. But given his position and the seriousness of his transgression, it was deemed necessary to excommunicate him and "give him over to Satan."

Hutter had been vindicated. Those who had preferred Schützinger were reminded of how shabbily they had treated Hutter. Obviously it had not been a decision guided by the Holy Spirit that, one month earlier, confirmed the "Ananias" Schützinger as leader of the community, with Hutter publicly censored by Gabriel as unfit for such an office. Hutter was now "no longer certain" that he could serve such a people. He therefore invited them "to pray earnestly and to call on God to raise up a faithful shepherd and servant for them."

In response to this admonition, the entire Sunday and the following week, "eight days and nights," were spent in "loud weeping, groaning," prayer and search for discernment. By week's end a consensus emerged that Hutter should be accepted "as a gift from God to be their shepherd." Sunday, October 12, saw the installation of Hutter as official servant of the Word. First, the former supporters of Schützinger made a public confession of their "sin of ignorance." Then it was Gabriel's turn to approve of Hutter's elevation. He had arrived belatedly to a fait accompli and, whatever his misgivings, tied Hutter and the congregation "together in great love."[87] The crisis seemed past. Divine intervention, Schützinger's illness, and Hutter's admonition and premonition had triggered a series of events which led to Schützinger's demotion and expulsion and to Hutter's assumption of the sole leadership.

Parting Ways with Gabriel and Philip

With Schützinger removed, Hutter concentrated on the abuses in the congregation. Among his priorities was the removal of unfaithful members who stood in the way of a new unity to be forged with stricter discipline. Soon a number of those expelled complained to Gabriel and Philip. Within two weeks of Hutter's assumption of leadership, Gabriel and Philip felt it necessary to intervene.

On Sunday, October 26, two hours before daybreak, as the congregation gathered for further admonition and Hutter was about to address them on the topic of marriage and family, Gabriel, Philip, and their assistants arrived unannounced. According to *The Chronicle*, "they had slipped in quietly before dawn, like wolves in sheep's clothing."[88] After formal greetings and protestations that they had come for the sake of peace and harmony, Gabriel raised a number of concerns. Why had Bernhard Glasser been excommunicated? Why had Hutter refused to take back David of Schweidnitz? And why did Hutter now claim that Schützinger's leadership had been wrong all along and not of God? It seemed that by retroactively rejecting Schützinger's election Hutter was casting doubt on the discernment, credibility, and authority of Gabriel and Philip. After all, they had supported Schützinger's claim to leadership by lot against Hutter's insistence for equal status.

During the ensuing debate, differences of opinion surfaced on issues reaching back to the Zaunring affair. Gabriel and Philip accused Hutter of having extorted a confession of impure motives from David of Schweidnitz, who had leaked the story of the Zaunring affair. From Gabriel's perspective, Zaunring had been guilty of fornication and a coverup; his punishment had been too lenient. "The name of God had been horribly blasphemed" by the affair. Zaunring deserved to be banned and should have been "given over to Satan," that is, expelled from the community. Schützinger's sin, on the other hand, had been of a lesser magnitude, his expulsion too harsh. He had been subjected to humiliation and slander. In other words, when it came to questions of judgment, Hutter's had been partial and unfair.

As tempers flared and "much was said for and against both sides," with each calling the other liars, ordinary members were demoralized, not knowing what to believe. *The Chronicle* reported that "many were heard to groan, and the faithful were shaken to the depths. No one knew . . . who was right or who was wrong, and which side was to blame. . . . The brotherhood was unable to arrive at any clarity or true judgment."[89] Philip, described in Hutterite sources as an "especially insolent man," accused Hutter of having manipulated his own promotion, of having excluded one scoundrel because of money (Schützinger) and having promoted another because of it (Fasser).[90] Hutter, in turn, represented Schützinger's ouster and his own elevation as the will of God, arrived at through much prayer and searching of soul by consensus of the entire community. Accusations directed against him were, therefore, directed against the congregation, against the Holy Spirit, and ultimately against God. When Philip accused the congregation collectively of idolizing Hutter, some members shouted, "that is a lie!" Although Philip subsequently apologized, the damage was done. *The Chronicle* recorded that "Philip told a lie in face of the whole brotherhood."[91]

With the exchanges deteriorating into mutual recriminations, Philip, Gabriel, and their assistants proposed the formation of an arbitration committee of an equal number of elders from each community. "These brothers should judge the matter among themselves," that is, without the leaders. When the proposal was met with silence, Philip and Gabriel left.[92]

What followed next is sketchy. Under Hutter's guidance his congregation took the initiative and, after Gabriel and Philip left, condemned them as liars. Gabriel complained later that he had been condemned in absentia, had received no notice of the proceedings, and was not given a chance to defend himself. He attributed Hutter's rash action to fear of another public confrontation with him and Philip and to the fear that they would excommunicate him (Hutter). In other words, Hutter had acted preemptively in taking action against Gabriel and Philip.[93]

On the following day, Monday, October 27, Hutter sent messengers to the other two communities to inform them that their leaders, Gabriel and Philip, had been found to be liars. Not surprisingly, the emissaries were given the cold shoulder. Neither Gabriel nor Philip accepted the letter carried by the delegates. Instead, they sent a joint mission of their own to Hutter's congregation, proposing a general assembly of all three communities to deal with the issues without the leaders. Hutter accepted on condition that the final judgment should be in harmony with "the Word of God and true testimony." His congregation agreed.

It seemed as if a way might be found out of the impasse when an incident proved these expectations unrealistic. As the messengers were leaving with "embraces and the kiss of peace," one of them, Hans of Strasbourg, asked whether it was true that Hutter and his group had already "excluded" Gabriel. When Hutter replied, "we do not regard him as a brother or as a servant of God," the messenger lost his temper and called Hutter a "liar and a false prophet."[94] Hutter turned this show of anger into proof that the delegates had come with malice of heart and dishonest intentions. Right then and there he called on the congregation to "pronounce judgment" on the "slanderers, revilers, and Judases." At least one supporter agreed that the delegates should be treated "the same as Gabriel and Philip," that is, banned from the true congregation of God. The majority, however, were less certain and were once more left "trembling and full of pain." "A few irresponsible souls" even made a commotion, blaming Hutter for derailing the attempt at reconciliation. According to Hutter's own account it took five days of deliberations and prayer to regain the proper consensus. Omens in the sky and the timely arrival of support from South Tyrol aided Hutter's efforts.[95]

Since his arrival in August, Hutter had remained in constant contact
with Amon in South Tyrol, briefing him on developments in Auspitz. The
de facto monopoly on communication with friends and relatives back
home could only strengthen Hutter's influence with the Pusterers in Auspitz.[96] It must have been literally a God-send as well when, on Friday,
October 31, the very same day that reinforcements arrived from the Tyrol,
Hutter and several of his supporters observed a special omen in the sky. In
his return mail to the Tyrol Hutter described the phenomenon as follows:

On Friday, we saw three suns in the sky for a good long time, about an hour, as
well as two rainbows. These had their arches turned toward each other, almost
touching in the middle, and their ends pointed away from each other. This I, Jakob, saw with my own eyes, and many brothers and sisters saw it with me. After
a while, the two suns and rainbows disappeared, and only the one sun remained.
Even though the other two suns were not as bright as the one, they were clearly
visible.

I feel this was no small miracle. It was a sign from God, and there was surely a
reason why he allowed it to appear. This much I am able to tell you, but the Lord
alone knows what he had in mind and wanted to show us by it.[97]

The sign in the sky and assurances of support from home base, read
aloud to the congregation by Hutter,[98] helped to produce the desired consensus. Two days later, on Sunday, November 2, Hutter and his congregation severed all ties with the neighboring communities, warning them
against their false, lying shepherds—the suns that no longer shone.[99] Since
the warning went unheeded, it became necessary to excommunicate the
rank and file of Gabrielites and Philipites along with their leaders. Members of these communities were no longer considered brothers or sisters,
and Hutter and his supporters laid sole claim to representing the "congregation of God" in Moravia. Reflecting on the series of events leading to
the rupture, Hutter put the blame squarely at the feet of those who had
opposed him. He wrote, "It started as soon as I arrived. In fact, without
any fear of God, they persecuted and slandered me and all of us more
terribly than any unbeliever or cruel tyrant, any false prophet or false
brother, has ever done. . . . They spread many horrible stories about me,
saying that no greater rogue has ever come into the land. They all clamor
for revenge and wish me evil, and their greatest longing is that God may
put me to shame."[100]

From Hutter's perspective, it seemed only just and right that Gabriel
and Philip, not to mention Schützinger, who prior to his arrival "had such
a good reputation with most people that no one could oppose them," had
now been unmasked "as liars, slanderers, false shepherds, and false
prophets."[101] As for his own role in the schism, Hutter pleaded a clean
conscience. "I am not guilty of anything, great or small. God knows I did

not come to break the peace and the unity but to increase them. This I began to do faithfully, as I can testify with many other honest witnesses. God has kept my heart pure and undefiled. In this whole matter there has never been any falsehood or deceit in my heart. All the things for which they hate and revile me have come through the Lord's great mercy. He alone is the cause, and I will let him alone answer for it." [102]

Needless to say, Hutter's perception that he had acted solely for the good of the congregation of God stood in sharp contrast to the opinions of those who opposed him. A passage that has survived from Gabriel's pen illustrates the bitter feelings that remained on the other side even after Hutter's martyrdom. Since this is the only surviving passage from Gabriel's history, which in effect prompted Braitmichel's reply, it is worth citing in full.

I will write what I myself have seen, heard, and learned from truthful witnesses, and can defend with my conscience [*und nichts uber mein Gewissen anzeigen*].

First of all, this Jacob Hutter was a puffed up, ambitious person. For this reason he back stabbed and pushed out [*verstach or verstuft*] Sigmund Schützinger and had himself chosen leader [*obrister*] in his place. But he was unable to disguise his ambition and intentions, for, before he was elected, he shot out with great anger against the people saying: "Am I not also an apostle and shepherd, must I be cast out from you in this fashion?" But the great fruit that followed in the wake of his assumption of office and his reform of the congregation was that he destroyed love and unity. He divided people previously united.

One may sing or say what one wants about this Jacob Hutter now. I say [judging by the fruit] that he was an evil person. Having recognized him for who he was, even if he [subsequently] permitted himself to be boiled and roasted, I know of nothing else to say about him, except that he did not prove such [saintliness while] in this land. Yes, he exercised vengeance over all those who took the side of or agreed in part with Schützinger. And in his mischievous manner he intimidated the congregation with great threats, saying: "Do you see now, whom you praised? You held this rogue [Schützinger] for pious, and humiliated me [holding me in lesser esteem]. You intended to keep Schützinger in his office, but you gave a false judgment therein. Therefore do penance for your failings."

Such a person who seeks his own honor is called a real blusterer [*Poltergeist*]. That is not the spirit of Paul. It is a spirit of Baalim's children, children of a buffoon. But while Jacob carried his own praises to the heavens, boasting that he had Paul's spirit, a woman said to him: "You have the spirit of the devil." [103]

The judgment attributed to a woman, which, in sixteenth-century parlance was intended as an insult—namely that even a child or woman could see through Hutter—illustrates graphically the acrimony and charged atmosphere left by the 1533 schism.

Hutter's third report to the Tyrol gave some indication of the immediate fallout. Schützinger, who at first indicated sorrow about his failings, hard-

ened his heart once he was expelled. According to Hutter, he was "malign-
ing and abusing us like a wicked demon, a raging lion, a bloated dog!"
Taking the same line were David of Schweidnitz, a certain Gilg, a Marx
and "many others."[104] Some of Hutter's gainsayers were apparently stirring up "unbelievers." As will be noted in Chapter 10, they complained to
local authorities, seeking a return of their contributions to the community
that had expelled them.

But not all those disciplined by Hutter became hardened. Hutter was
able to report that the wife of Georg Fasser and a certain Bärbel from
Jenbach had submitted obediently to the corrective discipline prescribed
for them and been restored to full fellowship. He was pleased to report
that ranks depleted by defections had been replenished. In the three to
four weeks since October 28, 1533, 120 to 130 new members had arrived.
More importantly, since the final parting with Philip and Gabriel, the congregation of God had experienced "great love, peace, and harmony."

Unfortunately for Hutter and his community, within a year and a half
of the new-found peace and harmony, measures taken by Ferdinand
threatened the entire communitarian experiment in Moravia. Hutter himself would embark on the fateful return to South Tyrol. Yet his supporters
survived and reemerged from the devastating blows of 1535–36 as sole
claimants to the early Anabaptist communitarian tradition. The rival
communities had been eclipsed. When Braitmichel wrote the account of
the 1533 schism, the omen of the three suns in the sky had a clear
meaning.

But why tell this tale of human conflict, leadership rivalries, and schisms
in all its disastrous detail? The most compelling reason is simple enough:
without it the narrative of the early Anabaptist communitarian experiments is incomplete. The events of 1533 were a vital part of first-
generation community building and stood at the beginnings of Hutterites
as an identifiable group. To exclude the events leading up to 1533 would
amount to a falsification of the historic record.

The congregation of God that took shape in Moravia, as a human enterprise, remained susceptible to human weaknesses, jealousies, person-
ality clashes, and leadership rivalries. And whatever the overt religious,
spiritual explanation proffered by the participants, these struggles had to
do with interhuman relations, leadership rivalries, and power. In this
realm human inventiveness has, since time immemorial, proven infinitely
creative—from the use of crude force and institutionalized shenanigans to
the most subtle psychological manipulations.

Robert Friedmann, the most knowledgeable scholar of Hutterite history, could find no principled reasons for the 1533 schism other than per-

sonality clashes. Our study suggests one further factor: the growing preponderance of the South Tyrolese in the community affected by the schism. Both numerically and in terms of financial resources, not to mention inner cohesiveness, the South Tyrolese had become a powerful group within the Auspitz community. By contrast, the core group that left Austerlitz for Auspitz in January 1531 had consisted for the most part of North Tyrolese. Depleted in numbers, financially destitute, numbed by the defection of its first leader, a "fornicator," the treatment received in Austerlitz, the Reublin scandal, the Zaunring affair, not to mention the forced resignations of a number of secondary leaders, the idealism of this threadbare band would have eroded steadily had it not been for a stream of newcomers from South Tyrol replenishing the first love and communal treasury. The Pusterers formed the backbone of these newcomers, and their undisputed leader was Jacob Hutter. Hutter could count on their full support and expected to lead them. When financial and leadership problems continued he arrived with a "temporal gift, a sweet sacrifice," determined to resolve both. The stage was set for a showdown with Simon Schützinger. Schützinger's refusal to share the leadership with Hutter because he feared Hutter's dominance in such an associate leadership arrangement led to the involvement of Gabriel and Philip on Schützinger's behalf. But Schützinger's illness and the revelation of his incontinence regarding private property gave Hutter the opportunity to assume leadership. Schützinger's subsequent ouster brought about the separation of ways with Gabriel and Philip.

But the schism involved other factors as well. The antagonists recognized one of these when they suggested that money from South Tyrol had strengthened Hutter's influence in the community. But that was hardly the main factor. Hutter's support came above all from those he had gathered and who considered him their natural leader. During his exchange with Gabriel and Philip, when it was suggested that he continue as itinerant servant, Hutter retorted, "how would you feel if you had gone on a journey, entrusting the people to someone else, and then had to stand back when you returned home?"[105]

Finally, history, to be true, must aim at an inclusive, wholistic understanding of the past. It must include both ideal and reality, light and shadow. If this chapter has cast shadows on the all too human face of early Anabaptism, it has done so not to minimize but to accentuate the intensity of commitment that motivated participants in the first communitarian experiments.

Chapter Ten

The Return and Death of Jacob Hutter,
1535–1536

When, in July 1533, Jacob Hutter left South Tyrol for Auspitz, he could hardly have imagined the twists and turns in the path ahead and that he would be back within two years. Ferdinand's pressure on the magnates of Moravia was the primary cause and the long shadow of Münster a secondary reason for Hutter's return. The Estates of Moravia had little choice but to obey the order of "his royal Grace" and formally expel the heretics.[1] By now several thousand strong, the Anabaptists were a very visible minority, difficult to hide, particularly those living in community. Even lords favorably inclined toward the Anabaptists had no alternative but to serve eviction notices. Some advised "temporary" dismantlement of the communities and dispersion of their members. Hutter's community followed this advice, and most of the members remained in Moravia. With hindsight this proved to be the correct strategy. Even though key members of the leadership, including Hutter, were lost before better times returned, Hutter's community, led by Hans Amon, survived.

Hutter's Return

Last Days in Moravia

The aftershock of the schism of 1533 was felt into 1534 and beyond. One of the chroniclers recorded that "Jacob Hutter and his congregation suffered great distress during the year 34 from the apostate."[2] The distress created by the apostate influenced the decision to relocate from Auspitz to Schackowitz.[3] Complaints had also been made by former members of the

Hutterite community to the abbess of the Queen's Cloister at Brünn, on whose land the Auspitz community was located. Whatever became of these complaints, the strained relations with the landlord worsened when the abbess asked Hutter's community for a loan. Hutter refused, claiming that the money was needed for his own people, whereupon the abbess imprisoned the three key leaders—Hutter, Amon, and Jeronimus Käls— and others of the community. Since Amon was included, the imprisonment must have taken place in the second half of 1534. Earlier that year Hutter encouraged Amon to bring the remnant from South Tyrol to Moravia.[4] Aided by Onophrius Griesinger, Amon successfully carried out this mission, so that after 1534 "not many brothers and sisters were left in the Tyrol."[5]

That the imprisonment of the leaders by the abbess involved a demand for money may be inferred from the community's plea that it was short on cash and unable to ransom its leaders. During this dispute with the abbess, if not before, Hutter and his associates concluded that it was morally wrong to pay rent to a monastic institution; for "pope, priests, monks, nuns, and all who preach for their belly's sake are the greatest cause of idolatry and of hypocritical, sinful and corrupt living." It was decided that henceforth members of Hutter's community would not work for, trade with, "or have anything at all to do" with church-related institutions "because all their profits come from and are used in the service of idolatry."[6] From then on accommodations were to be sought only on the lands of temporal lords. Yet Hutter and his people must have come to some agreement with the abbess because the leaders regained their freedom and were permitted to stay on her land. Not until Ascension Day, May 6, 1535, did Hutter and at least part of the congregation transfer residence to "the lands of the lord marshal of Lippe" at Schackowitz.[7]

Construction of a large communal dwelling, the first such "pigeon coop" documented, was in progress at Schackowitz when the new landlord, although he had considerable "affection for the Lord's people," was forced to comply with a decision reached by the Moravian Estates. One of Lord Lippe's officials brought the news to Hutter and his people with an "earnest request" that they should consider the landlord's predicament and "not bring disgrace on him, for he too could not oppose the higher authorities but had to be obedient to them."[8] Only the infirm could remain; the rest, including children, had to leave. In a public relations exercise "with drums beating, flags flying," the Hutterites were escorted through a hostile "crowd of ungodly, villainous robbers" off the land of Lord Lippe. At the same time Lord Lippe had instructed Hutter to "gather his people together again" as soon as "the troubles" were over. It was this promise that the expulsion and evacuation were temporary which buoyed hopes and influenced the decision to weather the eviction orders in Moravia. *The Chronicle* described the scene. With bundles on their backs Hutter and his assistants led the way to the desolate heath near Tracht (Strachotin) in the territories of the lords of Liechtenstein. Here under the open sky they camped, adults and children alike, numbering approximately seven hundred adults and three hundred children.[9] The logistics of providing a group that size with the necessities of life, even for a short time, proved daunting.[10] The pressure on those responsible for the flock was intense. Massing of so many people in the wilderness—the Philipites and some of the Gabrielites camped in the same area—created suspicions in the local population and fed rumors that the Anabaptists planned some form of insurrection. But when the governor of Moravia, John Kuna, sent a fact-finding mission, they found "many children and sick people" instead of rebels allegedly armed with muskets and spears.

A stern confrontation ensued between Hutter and the governor's investigators. When asked whether Hutter and his community would leave Moravia as ordered, the hard-pressed Hutter vented his anger against Ferdinand's policy of extermination.[11] He told the governor's officials in so many words that "if the bloodhound Ferdinand wants us out, let him come in person." He and his flock would not leave Moravia voluntarily. Taken aback by Hutter's reaction, the officials suggested that he submit a formal written grievance or reply. The resulting letter, addressed to the governor, presumably more measured than Hutter's initial verbal response, has survived. It became part of the earliest account of Hutterite beginnings, ostensibly to counter misrepresentations by Hutter's rival, Gabriel Ascherham, that "Jacob Hutter had called King Ferdinand a bloodhound and was put to death on this account and not for the sake of God's truth."[12] Since Gabriel and his people were affected by the same expulsion order and presumably dealt with the same officials, his description of the events and Hutter's role in them provides an alternative perspective worth citing.

At the time when the king wanted to drive the congregations [*gemeinen*] from Moravia, the Abbess of Brünn sent her servant to Auspitz and drove Jacob and his people out of the house. When, however, the governor [*Landshauptmann*] sent his servant to him and informed him of the king's orders, Jacob answered and said: "Ah, that bloodhound, that murderer. In the Upland [*Oberland*] he drove us from our houses and homesteads, took what was ours and murdered our [brethren]. Now he wants to drive us from here as well." And he said to the servant of the governor, "Tell your lord as follows: We will move nowhere. If the bloodhound likes to have our blood [*ein Lust zu unserm Blut*], so let him come, we will await him here." But the servant said, "We cannot communicate such a message orally," because there was so much talk and scolding on Jacob's part that they could not remember it all. Therefore they said, "Write it in a letter." [And he did] with much scolding and blasphemy concerning the king. The sum of it was as follows: "We will await the king here."

After the letter had been delivered, they searched for this Jacob. Not wanting to be found, he soon fled. It proved too much for him to wait for the king there. From his actions one can infer that he was only a man of words, and that there was nothing to him. Other people in the territory had to suffer for his blustering. Jacob meanwhile fled to South Tyrol [*Etschland*]. The king sent notification concerning him, and when he captured him he had him burned at Innsbruck.

Thus perished this Jacob, under the disguise as it were of suffering for the Gospel. However, that was not the cause. He died rather because of his insults. He would have died even if he had twenty lives.[13]

Testing Gabriel's accusation against Hutter's letter to the governor suggests that Hutter's written language was more measured. The letter did not refer to Ferdinand as a "bloodhound,"[14] but then, Gabriel placed that expression into the context of a "stern" oral exchange. Even so, the letter alluded to Ferdinand as "the prince of darkness, the godless tyrant, the enemy of divine truth and of righteousness."[15] Such expressions in an official submission to Ferdinand's representative, the governor of Moravia, were sufficiently caustic to qualify as "lese-majeste," while Hutter's stern warning, his three-fold woes, and his lecture that the lords of Moravia were "unworthy to have us among you any longer," were hardly designed to endear him to the governor or the Estates.

Threefold woe to you, Moravian lords, into all eternity! You have given in to Ferdinand, the awful tyrant and enemy of divine truth—you have agreed to drive those who love and fear God out of your lands. You fear a weak, mortal man more than the living, eternal, almighty God and are willing to expel and ruthlessly persecute the children of God, old and young, even the Lord's widows and orphans in their need and sorrow, and deliver them up to plunder, fear, great suffering, and extreme poverty. It is as if you strangled them with your own hands. We would rather be murdered for the Lord's sake than witness such misery inflicted on innocent, God-fearing hearts. You will have to pay dearly for it, and you will have no more excuse than Pilate, who also did not want to crucify and kill the Lord Jesus. Yet when the Jews threatened him (by God's plan), fear of the emperor made Pilate condemn an innocent man. You do the same, using the king as your excuse. But God has made it known through the mouth of his prophets that he will avenge innocent blood with terrible might on all who stain their hands with it.

Therefore you will earn great misfortune and distress, deep sorrow—indeed, eternal torment. They are ordained for you by God in heaven, in this life and forever. In the name of our Lord Jesus Christ, we declare that this will certainly happen, and you will soon see that what we have spoken is God's truth. This we declare to you and to all who sin against God.[16]

Hutter's response, no doubt courageous and justified, proved nevertheless politically unwise. The governor ordered Hutter's immediate arrest.

But, "thanks to the foresight and presence of mind of the faithful," Hutter and his assistants could not be found, either in Schackowitz or on the heath. The constables, sent to take Hutter into custody, had to be satisfied with arresting Wilhelm Griesbacher and Loy Salztrager. The two were taken to the royal city of Brünn for trial. Their arrest must have taken place in late May or early June, for by June 9, 1535, Ferdinand responded with instructions that the prisoners be questioned on why "in the reply to the governor, they so maliciously insulted the king as a tyrant, murderer, and shedder of blood [*Blutvergiesser*]." [17] He also wanted to know why Hutter's followers "thought nothing of the [established] authorities and wanted none, yet among themselves desired and had authorities [*obrigkeiten*]." By June 14 Ferdinand had a reply, and on July 9 instructions were sent for the use of torture and, in case of intransigence, the death sentence. Under torture Salztrager recanted, a "weakness" he later regretted. Griesbacher remained steadfast and was burned at the stake in Brünn. [18]

Griesbacher's arrest, torture, and burning were a stark reminder, if such were needed, of the fate that awaited the other leaders, especially Hutter. With enemies among former brethren and now also among the nobility, Hutter's chances of escaping detection in Moravia for any length of time were slim. His ability to lead the congregation openly had been crippled. Even his name had become a liability. It was therefore "unanimously" decided that "he should move for a time to the Tyrol." In the interim the less conspicuous Hans Amon would lead the congregation in Moravia with specific instructions from Hutter on how to proceed in case another "servant of the Word" should be needed. [19] These instructions and the transfer of leadership to Amon subsequently proved crucial in the survival of Hutter's followers as a cohesive group. They demonstrate Hutter's foresight as the organizer and true leader of his community.

Katherine Präst: Hutter's "Hausfrau"

When Hutter returned to South Tyrol in July 1535, he did not travel alone. [20] With him were Jeronimus Käls, the schoolmaster of the community and probable scribe of the letter to the governor, the guides, Michael Schuster, also known as Michael Walser, and Caspar Kräntzler, as well as one female companion, Hutter's bride, Katherine Präst or Prust.

Evidence indicates that Hutter entered the state of matrimony ten days after transferring the headquarters of his congregation from Auspitz to Schackowitz. On May 16, 1535, Amon performed a simple wedding ceremony. [21] Until that date Hutter appears to have led his community as a bachelor. By November the newlyweds were in search of a shelter and childbed for Katherine Hutter. Curiously, Hutterite sources mention neither Hutter's marriage nor Katherine's subsequent fate. But then silence as to the female companions who bore children, worked alongside their husbands, and, like them, suffered persecution and martyrdom, was the rule rather than the exception in Hutterite sources, although the names of women were included regularly in the greetings of letters.[22] Such was the case with Katherine. Only one of Hutter's surviving letters referred to his "matrimonial sister" nicknamed Treindle.[23] Fortunately, official documents provide a little more information about her background and fate as well as insights into the important role played by women.

Katherine came from Tauffers in the jurisdiction of St. Georgen. This little town, in one of the side valleys of the Puster, had been home to a number of early Anabaptists and their sympathizers.[24] From Katherine's service record as maid (*diern*) in a number of proevangelical households, it may be inferred that she was in her early twenties when she married Hutter and was familiar with the religious debate before meeting him. Like other young women in the region, she appears to have left home at the age of sixteen or seventeen to serve as a housemaid. Among her employers was Hannsen Man of Trens (Tryns) near Sterzing, who was subsequently punished for his association with Anabaptists. It was while in Man's service that Katherine was baptized by Hutter. According to her recollections she had been introduced to the sect by Paul Rumer (Rumbler) at Paul Gall's home in Trens.[25] Rumer himself had been baptized with three young maids in 1531 or early 1532 at Schäffler's home between Sterzing and Gossensass.[26] Katherine appears to have been one of the young maids baptized with Rumer because another participant from her home town, Valentin Lukhner, recalled that a maid named Katherine was baptized at Schäffler's.[27]

As noted in Chapter 8, Anabaptist activity in or near Sterzing, which was strategically located below the Brenner Pass, came to the authorities' attention in early 1532. As a result a number of Anabaptists were imprisoned, among them Paul Gall, Rumer's brother-in-law. Gall regained his freedom upon recantation but was rearrested at Rodeneck in the following year and executed.[28] Katherine was also imprisoned at Rodeneck, but her life was spared because she recanted. She was rearrested with three female companions on or before March 25, 1533, by the magistrate of Bozen.[29] The four had participated in a larger congregational meeting led by Hutter at Villnöss.[30] While Hutter was at large and preparing to leave for Moravia, Katherine remained in prison. In May Innsbruck ordered that she and her unrepentant companions be flogged, but the disciplinarian (*Züchtiger*) chosen for this task refused.[31] Katherine somehow regained her freedom and in 1534 caught up with one of the treks to Auspitz where she joined the inner core of Hutter's supporters from the Puster valley. Within a year she was married to the leader and was back in South Tyrol with him.

Reconstructing the Network

South Tyrol had been left without a servant of the Word and with very few Anabaptists after Amon's departure in 1534. Hutter's first and primary task, therefore, involved the reconstruction of a network that would sustain his presence. It was a delicate task that called for patience and great caution in finding new converts. An advance party prepared the way. In the spring of 1535 three scouts traveled through the Puster region and announced to interested parties that they would return with a leader qualified to teach and baptize. A few days before St. Jacob's day, July 25, 1535, two members of the same party, Michael Schuster (Walser) and Caspar Kräntzler, spread the news that two leaders, Hutter and Jeronimus, had arrived.[32] Official files described the two as they entered the Puster region: Hutter sported a trimmed beard and white cut-off trousers, a tanned leather coat with folds in front and back, and a black felt hat. Jeronimus was described as a tall person with a black beard. He wore a black herald's coat (*Wappenrock*) and a black cap (*Slepl*).[33]

The party of five had entered South Tyrol across the formidable Thauern mountain range. Among their first stops was Tauffers, Katherine's home town, with the main attention given to the Puster valley, whose terrain was most familiar to Hutter. Disappointments awaited them. Some converts and former sympathizers had turned their backs on Anabaptism.[34] But Hutter could soon report of new converts, among them "dear brother" (Hans) Obern of Hörschwang. Obern, his wife, their daughter, and one of their two servants were among those baptized soon after Hutter's return.[35] Obern's homestead in Hörschwang became a kind of base camp to which Hutter would return again and again. By its history and location Hörschwang was ideally suited for this role. Practically all of its inhabitants had ceased to attend traditional church services. At Christmas 1531, Hörschwang had been host to an interesting party. A major Anabaptist congregational gathering featuring the leaders Hutter, Amon, Christoph Gschäll, and Toman (Thomas) Lynnal (Lindl) with seventy persons met in Hörschwang.[36] The host, a Mair, under whose roof the meeting took place, had to be excluded from the celebration of the Lord's Supper because he had not been baptized.[37] And in a twist to the Christmas story he spent the night in an ox stall of his own stable to provide adequate accommodation for his guests. Appolina, the wife of another local notable, Georg Ebner, served soup and dessert to the Anabaptist guests. Her son, Michel Ebner, and servant Sigmund Kiens joined the Anabaptists. Ebner senior was subsequently executed, and Appolina escaped to Moravia.[38] Given this background it is not surprising that Hutter hoped to find support in Hörschwang.[39] His first letter after returning to the Puster region originated there.[40] In it Hutter reported that new converts were added daily and that more assistants were needed from Moravia.[41] He seemed optimistic about reestablishing some form of congregational life. To this end he and his companions had already undertaken a number of missionary journeys. They traveled at night on back trails and arranged larger meetings in secluded places. For their own safety Hutter and his party camped out in the mountains.

This first letter is of historic interest also because it documented how difficult the decision to leave Moravia had been. Hutter raised the subject several times, reminding his readers that it had not been his choice. He had taken leave reluctantly and with grief, driven by circumstances.

You know, my dearly beloved, how God directed it and how it happened, namely that they pursued me and you viciously and mercilessly for the Lord's sake. And for that reason you dispatched me and sent me from you and let me go; yes, with great and earnest prayer and crying to the Lord; in sum, with great solemnity before God as your beloved brother in the Lord, as your servant and shepherd, who has been given to you out of his divine grace and mercy.[42]

Yet, if Hutter entertained thoughts that the situation in Moravia would soon improve, enabling him to return, news received before he even wrote the first letter had been disappointing. The flock he had left behind had scattered. As the summer passed, hope of finding a place for collective settlement faded. The indigenous population proved uncooperative and hostile, refusing "provisions and even water." There was no alternative but to break up into smaller groups of eight to ten adults, each seeking work and accommodation wherever possible. So, like the Philipites, Gabrielites, and Austerlitzers, Hutter's community was forced to disband. *The Chronicle* recorded,

But, when they were refused all provisions and even water, they at last had to separate into groups of eight or ten! Each brother with the little group entrusted to him had it laid on his heart very earnestly that they should care for one another . . . and that no one should hold back from helping another. It was said in particular that nobody should leave Moravia without asking advice.[43]

Hutter was heartbroken by the news of the dispersion. "My distress and pain have been great since I heard that you are being scattered," he wrote. "I labored long and hard in love to gather you. I also suffered for you. And now the ravening wolves come to scatter, to crush with their claws, and what is left they trample underfoot."[44]

My little children, I can hardly write; my sorrow is so great. It is not because my conscience accuses me, as if the scattering were my fault. No, I am not to blame for this scattering. God knows, it never sat well with me. I always faithfully warned you of it and fought against it. What God ordains and permits the godless villains is not my fault. I have accepted it and endure it with patience and suffering.

Therefore, let no one condemn me, as if I am at fault. I am blameless in this regard. My heart is free of guilt. I am innocent of all blood. It is the devil's brood, who like ravens and wolves, as the Scriptures say, have done this. . . . Did I not warn you constantly for two years of what has now happened?[45]

Did Hutter protest too much? Had not Gabriel Ascherham judged him more suitable for the itinerant ministry than for the leadership of a settled community, and did he not blame him in part for the hostile climate in Moravia? These accusations stung and were obviously on Hutter's mind. He closed his first letter in a somber mood with allusions to the "terrible day of the Lord" and signed off "I, Jacob . . . a miserable worm of the Lord, nevertheless his servant . . . because of his great grace and mercy, your apostle, shepherd, beloved brother . . . and your companion in sorrow."[46]

Even given the discouraging news from Moravia, Hutter could take comfort in the receptivity exhibited to his message by seekers closer to home. Shortly after his return to the Puster he renewed contact with Niclas and Anna Niderhofer, who had shown interest in Anabaptism as early as 1532.[47] Anna was the daughter of the magistrate of Schöneck, Peter Troyer, and surprisingly attended the first meeting called by Hutter. The meeting was held in a clearing above Erenburg on Sunday, August 5, 1535. Anna arrived under cover of darkness with her seventeen-year-old maid, Katharina Tagwericher. Tagwericher and two other maids (*diernen*) were baptized by Hutter during that meeting.[48] Presumably Anna Niderhofer approved of her maid's baptism, for Hutter was invited to visit her home. A week later Hutter spent three days (August 11–13) with the Niderhofers, instructing the household in the "Gospel and the way of God." Anna Niderhofer herself received baptism on this occasion, and her husband, Niclas, did so at the next gathering above Erenburg (August 24–25).[49] Four weeks later (September 21–23) Hutter was back, nurturing the Niderhofer household in the faith.

The Niderhofers belonged to the "brothers and sisters growing in godly righteousness and flourishing like lovely tulips and sweet lilies" mentioned in Hutter's second letter.[50] But this letter also recorded some worrisome developments. Local priests had learned that "we are in the territory and up in the mountains." They were pressuring people to "attend their sacraments and to worship their idols" or else face the executioner. Particularly disturbing was news that two former members, Christoph Bühler (Phüller) and Martin Nieder (Nidrens), from the Sterzing area, were collaborating with the authorities in Innsbruck. The two had been "excluded from God and his people," but Hutter feared that they might return to Moravia with evil designs. Similar news of defections in Moravia appeared to Hutter as signs that the apocalyptic separation of "chaff from wheat" had begun. He admonished the true hearted to "pay no attention to the rebellious and unfaithful, however great their number" but "to remain faithful till death."

Foreboding about developments in the Puster proved well founded. Shortly after Hutter's last visit with the Niderhofers, Peter Troyer learned that they, his own daughter and son-in-law, had become Anabaptists. On September 29 the distraught father sought advice from his peer Christoph Ochs, the magistrate in the neighboring St. Michelsburg district.[51] With tears Troyer confided that Hutter had been in the area for a while and baptized twenty-five persons, including Troyer's daughter and son-in-law. Ochs advised Troyer to notify the bishop's court in Brixen. A few days later, October 3, Ochs informed Brixen of his conversation with Troyer, suggesting that both he and Troyer be cited to Brixen and ordered to hunt down Hutter.[52] Ochs requested that his communiqué be kept confidential. Apparently Brixen followed Ochs's advice. Troyer was ordered to arrest the Anabaptists in his jurisdiction. On October 15 Troyer reported that some of the Anabaptists had left his district.[53] According to this information the leaders, Hutter and Jeronimus and their companions, were in either the Sterzing or Bozen area. He had learned that Hutter's wife was looking for a childbed and suggested that a search be made for her—"a poor maid" near childbirth—in St. Leonhard, St. Andreasberg, Lüsen, Rodeneck, and Tauffers. Troyer was obviously well informed, using his daughter and son-in-law as sources. Before reporting to Brixen Troyer had put his daughter out of reach by housing her with her brother, Paul Troyer, at a place "where she would not give cause for scandal."[54]

The information provided to Brixen by Troyer about Hutter and his five companions was at once relayed to other district magistrates and to Innsbruck, thereby setting into motion a chain reaction that would eventually lead to Hutter's capture and death. Informed of Hutter's presence in the territories, Innsbruck urged concerted action. No costs should be spared. The magistrates and bailiffs of the various jurisdictions were ordered to coordinate their efforts and received permission to cross into each others' territories in hot pursuit, thus denying Hutter and his companions windstill zones that straddled the jurisdictions.[55] The knight Caspar Kunigl von Erenburg and Doctor Jacob Frankfurter were to draft a coordinated plan and see to its implementation. Communicated to all local administrators on November 20, the plan called for a simultaneous search action of all suspected Anabaptist hideouts in all districts on the day after St. Andrew's, December 1, 1535. All participants were sworn to absolute secrecy.[56]

Although unaware of the action planned against him and his companions, Hutter observed with growing concern the measures mounted against his converts, a concern expressed in his third letter.[57] Here he noted candidly that the authorities knew his contacts and that he had "no human explanation" why these persons had not been arrested. The letter confirms official sources that "the godless magistrate, Peter Mayer" (Troyer)[58] had imprisoned his own daughter, Anna, her maid (Katharina), and his son-in-law (Niclas). Hutter knew further that Anna had then been taken to Greifenwink (Greifenburg) in Carinthia (Kärnten) by her brother Paul.[59] Besides corroborating Troyer's official report to Brixen, Hutter's third letter provides evidence of Hutter's own impressive intelligence-gathering capacity. The greetings conveyed through this letter make it possible also to identify Hutter's closest collaborators: Caspar Kräntzler, Michael Walser, Stöffel (Christoph Schmidt), Hänsel Meyer (Hans Mair Paulle), and Jeronimus (Käls); exactly five as claimed in official communiqués.

The letter indicates further that at the time of writing, Anna's maid Katharina had escaped from her prison in Schöneck with "an unsoiled soul" and that another "dear sister," named Nändl, had also regained her freedom. Both had joined the household of Hans Obern in Hörschwang. Nändl can be identified from official sources as Anna Stainer, an acquaintance of Hutter's wife.[60] In his first letter Hutter had mentioned that "dear sister Nändl lies still imprisoned. . . . But we hope to God the Lord will shortly help her out." The Lord did just that with a little aid from Hutter and his assistant Michael Walser. Nändl had been confined to Toblach since 1533, but her confinement had been of a lenient sort; she was permitted to "walk about freely." Hutter dispatched Michael Walser, who simply led her to Hörschwang. From there she had traveled with Hutter and Katherine to Sterzing, back to Hörschwang, and then south to Klausen, where she was arrested with the Hutters.[61]

Anna's statement, given subsequent to her arrest, helps flesh out and confirm the historic accuracy of information contained in Hutter's third letter, as preserved in Hutterite codices. But it does more; it provides a retroactive glimpse into the clan and friendship connections that had supported Anabaptism from the beginning. Anna came from St. Georgen, the home of Paul Rumer, who had been responsible for bringing Katherine Hutter into the Anabaptist fold. Anna herself had been introduced to the sect by Veronica Grembs. Like Veronica and Paul, Anna came from a respected family. Her father, Hans Stainer, was related to Peter Troyer and Christoph Ochs, the magistrates of Schöneck and Michelsburg, respectively. Like Hutter's wife, Anna had served as a maid in a number of evangelical households.[62] Her sister Barbara had also become an Anabaptist and been imprisoned. The distraught father provided the Anabaptists with meat on the hoof in return for a promise that they would supply his imprisoned daughters with the necessities of life. When questioned about his dealings with the heretics, Stainer pleaded paternal responsibilities. He claimed to have enlisted Paul Rumer's non-Anabaptist brothers in an effort to deprogram his daughters, but his daughters had rebuffed these attempts with "harsh words." The Rumers had given up in "despair."[63] The point here is that Anna was so well known to the Pusterers, who made up the core of Hutter's supporters in Moravia, that a mere mention of her nickname Nändl in Hutter's letter sufficed for her identification to readers in Moravia, some of whom came from the same town of St. Georgen.[64] Her family connections to local notables such as Peter Troyer explain the reluctance with which some local magistrates prosecuted Anabaptists. These magistrates had known some of the Anabaptists since childhood and from close acquaintance. They surely knew that these victims of Ferdinand's suppression did not conform to the pernicious insurrectionist image propagated by Innsbruck.

Returning to the fate of Hutter, it seems clear that the arrests made by magistrate Peter Troyer prior to October 15 tore a hole into Hutter's painstakingly reconstructed network. It was best to leave the area until the full damage could be assessed. Consequently, Hutter and his companions moved to the Sterzing district. The district was familiar terrain to Hutter, who had held a number of meetings there. But Sterzing had also been the scene of several executions.[65] Extreme caution was in order. Upon arrival, the two women, Katherine and Anna, found temporary shelter at Trens, while Hutter and his companions fanned out to visit scattered homesteads and the nearby mining district. At a general meeting a few days later, Hutter was able to baptize seven or eight new converts.[66] These were promising beginnings. Kräntzler remained in the area to nurture the new believers while Hutter and the others returned to the Puster valley. Distressing news awaited them; further arrests had taken place. Most alarming were reports from Lüsen. According to Hutter's fourth and last letter, a "godless person" had betrayed the brothers and sisters in Lüsen. Five or six had been taken to Brixen. As yet Hutter had no specifics, but scouts had been "hastily dispatched" to gather more information.[67]

Hutter was fully aware of the great danger posed by the new arrests. Lüsen, in the mountains east above Brixen, had been of strategic importance to his network. He had visited the village six or more times since his return and had baptized at least eight persons. Hutter would usually leave the town before nightfall without divulging his destination. From subsequent statements by his wife it appears that Auers and Villnöss were usual places on his itinerary from Lüsen. Among his converts in Lüsen were Niclas Praun, the bathhouse operator, and his wife Appolonia.[68] Praun's bathhouse had served as the local meeting place, and Praun was a main contributor to the common treasury. He had carried bread, flour, sausages, cheese, and two pounds of lard to an Alpine hut for Hutter and his companions.[69]

After Praun's arrest there could be no question of wintering in the mountain huts. Hutter and his companions knew too well what secrets torture could pry from its victims. The decision was made to send Jeronimus back to Moravia as a "living letter." He would brief Amon on the seriousness of the situation and on Hutter's plans. Jeronimus left shortly after the "hastily dispatched" scouts returned with a report on the situation in Lüsen. Hutter's letter reads like an eyewitness account. According to it the local magistrate "rode into the village of Lüsen, summoned all the men, women, and children able to walk and read the cruel mandate to them, forbidding them to house or shelter any of us. Anyone who did not heed would be punished more severely than ever, and his house would be burned to the ground."[70] But having read the mandate, the magistrate took no further action; it seemed as if he deliberately looked the other way. However, some opposed to the Anabaptists left him no peace, urging him to carry out his duty and arrest the offenders, who were known to everyone. The magistrate was therefore obligated to act.

The events described in Hutter's last letter can be tested against official documents, thus permitting a dating of the letter. On November 6 the bishop's court had ordered Hans Sergant, the magistrate of Lüsen, to read out the "mandates pertaining to the Anabaptists" and to arrest those who disobeyed them.[71] Since the sequence of events described in Hutter's letter suggests some time lapse between the reading of the mandate and the arrests in Lüsen, the arrests must have taken place in the second or more likely in the third week of November, a dating supported by other indirect evidence.[72] With the arrests, Hutter's friends in Hörschwang were now also vulnerable. Ober's home was raided on Saturday night, November 20, and Katharina Tagwericher was imprisoned for a second time. She testified that Hutter had been at Hörschwang only a week previously, that is, from Thursday, November 11 to Saturday, November 13.[73] Her host, Hans Obern and his wife, had left on an errand to Lüsen on the morning of her arrest, November 20. Presumably Obern and his wife were the scouts sent by Hutter to investigate the situation there. By leaving in the morning they escaped the raid on their home later that day. It may be inferred, therefore, that Hutter's last letter was completed between November 20 and 25, about a week before his last farewell from the Puster valley. Jeronimus, who, accompanied by Hans Mair Paulle carried Hutter's last letter to Moravia, left the Puster region at the same time. The preservation of the letter in Hutterite codices is proof that Jeronimus reached Amon. As will be noted in the next chapter Jeronimus was on his way back to the Tyrol by the first week of January 1536.

Martyrdom in Innsbruck

Hutter's Arrest

Whatever Hutter's original intentions about wintering in the Puster valley may have been, the arrests in Lüsen and Hörschwang forced a change of plans.[74] His last letter was full of foreboding. The "raging dragon had opened its jaws wide to devour the woman robed with the sun, the church and bride of Christ." Night was approaching; "the cloud by day," symbolizing the servants of the word, would be taken away. The scattered remnant needed to rely on the pillar of "fire by night," that is, on "the radiance of the holy spirit."[75] He feared that "I and the other servants of God will not be able to speak to you again or set eyes on you in this life,"[76] a premonition that proved correct.[77]

With the situation in the Puster region visibly deteriorating, Hutter moved south. Accompanied only by his wife and Anna Stainer, hiding in the forests during the day, traveling at night, Hutter and his companions arrived in Klausen on St. Andrew's eve, Tuesday, November 30.[78] It was the very night before the planned action against Hutter. Shortly before midnight the fugitives crossed the bridge over the Eisack just above Klausen[79] and knocked on the door of a former sexton of Klausen, Jacob Stainer. The widow of the sexton, Anna Stainer, a namesake of Hutter's companion Anna Stainer, had joined the Anabaptists in 1533 but had recanted since then. Because of noisy, drunken revelers (*truncken rott*) who had passed her house earlier, the widow opened her door very reluctantly and only after persistent knocking and pleading by Hutter's female companions.[80] Although she recognized her guests as Anabaptists, she permitted them "out of pity" to warm themselves by her fire because of the "bitter cold," with an understanding that they would move on as soon as possible. In defending herself later, she claimed to have offered neither food nor shelter.

Shortly after midnight, Hutter and his companions were about to take their leave, when unexpectedly the city magistrate of Klausen and the lieutenant captain (*Unterhauptmann*) of Säben arrived.[81] These two zealots appeared to have been informed that Hutter was on his way through. They had already searched the city of Klausen without success and, as a last resort, decided to visit the house of the late sexton Stainer, even though it lay outside their jurisdiction in the bailiwick of Gufidaun. As noted, Innsbruck had urged such a pursuit across administrative boundaries, and it was that kind of action which sealed Hutter's fate.

Once arrested, Hutter and his two companions were taken not to Klausen but to the episcopal fortress of Branzoll above the city (Figure 4). News of the arrest traveled with amazing speed. By 7 o'clock next morning, December 1, the administrators of the prince bishop in Brixen had not only been informed but had already drafted a letter to the court at Innsbruck.[82] Another letter was sent to the bailiff of Gufidaun, Adam Preu, because Hutter had been taken in his bailiwick. The lieutenant captain of Säben was instructed to separate the prisoners and to interrogate them separately. Hutter was to be especially secured without the slightest chance of escape or suicide. Two days later, December 3, in a communiqué to the bishop of Trent, the administrators in Brixen bragged about their superior reconnaissance,[83] a boast partially substantiated in Hutterite sources, which suggest that Hutter had been betrayed.[84]

The response to Hutter's arrest from Innsbruck was swift. A letter dated December 2 expressed deep satisfaction and ordered the lieutenant marshal (*Untermarshall*) Erasmus Offenhauser to escort the prisoner to Innsbruck. Logistical support from Branzoll to Sterzing was to be provided by the prince bishop; from there on the administrator of Sterzing was to be responsible.[85] Hutter's female companions were considered less important; only their statements needed to be forwarded to Innsbruck. The bishop's administrators were instructed further to furnish a questionnaire to facilitate Hutter's interrogation. This task was passed on to George of Waltenhofen and Christoph Ochs, respectively the bailiff and the administrator of Hutter's home jurisdiction, St. Michelsburg. The resulting questionnaire is the only document, other than the statements of Hutter's female companions, to survive from Hutter's trial—a trial obviously considered of great importance.[86] Even before Hutter was moved from Branzoll, the bishop's court in Brixen had entrusted the magistrate of Brixen, Leonard Mair, and the magistrate of Lüsen, Hans Sergant, with interrogations of Hutter and his companions, "without and with torture." These interrogations took place on Saturday, December 4, at Branzoll in the presence of a jury of eight men including three magistrates.[87] Mair and Sergant had prepared themselves by first questioning the prisoners from Lüsen. In other words, they could ask specific questions and test whether Hutter and his companions answered truthfully or evasively. Of the Branzoll interrogations, only the statements given by Hutter's female companions have survived. These statements were sent to Innsbruck on Tuesday, December 7, along with letters written by Amon, which had been found on Hutter at the time of his arrest.[88] These documents traveled to Inns-

Figure 4. Branzoll

bruck with Hutter, who had been moved from Branzoll to Brixen on Monday, December 6. He arrived bound and gagged in Innsbruck three days later, on Thursday, December 9.[89]

Trial and Death

Upon arrival in Innsbruck, Hutter was placed in the Kräuterturm (herb tower), a dungeon on the northeast corner of the city wall, considered especially secure (Figure 5). Four days later, on December 13, Innsbruck reported to Ferdinand that Hutter had already undergone preliminary questioning with and without torture.[90] Copies of his statements would be sent later. If these did exist, they, along with other documents related to the trial, are no longer extant, and the report sent to Ferdinand provides only glimpses of the obvious. Accordingly, Hutter rejected "all Christian ordinances," including confession and the "holy sacrament" of the altar, but denied any subversive intentions or that the Anabaptists planned to establish their beliefs by force.

Although Hutter was a recognized bishop of the heretics and the death sentence was a foregone conclusion, it was deemed desirable to extract from him a recantation of his religious errors for propaganda purposes. To this end, a trained theologian, Dr. Gallus Müller, was brought in to refute Hutter's beliefs with the aid of holy Scripture. Within three days the eager Müller had visited Hutter three times, with little or the wrong effect. Hutter allegedly responded with "scolding and cursing" (*shelten und fluchen*).[91]

Although trial documents did not survive, indirect evidence suggests that Hutter's interrogation was severe and detailed. Only a day after his arrival in Innsbruck, Ferdinand's court instructed Brixen to investigate Caspar Hueter of Prags near Stegen, a suggestion that came, by inference, from the questionnaire prepared by the bailiff and administrator of St. Michelsburg.[92] Hutter had been in the service of Caspar Hueter in 1526 when he became involved with the radical sacramentists (see Chapter 7). Caspar's statement was forwarded to Innsbruck on December 17.[93] Not surprisingly it put Caspar in the best possible light while incriminating his cousin Jacob. Yet as late as December 24, Hutter had not been interrogated on the basis of Caspar's statement or the larger questionnaire pertaining to the St. Michelsburg district.[94] It seems that Innsbruck awaited specific instructions from Ferdinand himself, while gathering evidence on Hutter. Ferdinand's response did not arrive until Christmas Eve and was hardly in the form of a seasonal greeting. There was to be no mercy for Hutter even if he recanted. He was to be questioned under torture on "how he came into this sect, in which principalities and territories he had

Figure 5. Kräuterturm

traveled or resided during the past [8 or 9 years], what persons of the nobility he had baptized, who had given him shelter and provisions . . . [and] what the numbers in the letter from the Moravian Congregation meant."[95] The belated arrival of Ferdinand's instructions meant that Hutter's interrogation and trial proper had to be postponed until after the "holy days." His real trial, therefore, began only in the new year. On January 1, 1536, Innsbruck ordered the captain of Kufstein, Christoff Fuchs, to send two "constables of the territorial court" (*Landgerichts-knechte*) to flog Hutter. Hutter had been uncooperative in Dr. Müller's efforts, and lashings "had proven successful with other prisoners."[96] Official documents record nothing further about the floggings or their effect, but Hutterite sources do. According to these Hutter was subjected to especially cruel treatment, placed into ice-cold water until almost frozen, then thawed in a hot room before being beaten with rods. Then, his body lacerated, brandy was poured into the wounds and set on fire. These measures were supplemented with psychic tortures. Priests tested their spiritual prowess in seeking to exorcise the "demons" that "possessed" Hutter. Gagged and bound, a feathered cap on his head in scorn and derision, Hutter was led into church—presumably to make a public spectacle of him and to break the demonic spell—that is, his steadfast spirit. Such treatment could, of course, only reinforce Hutter's conviction that churches with their sacred objects were temples of idols, the mass an abomination. Despite all of the cruelties, both physical and mental, Hutter remained firm in his faith.[97]

However, he did not remain entirely silent under torture.[98] On May 15, 1536, Innsbruck sent a "copy of a statement" (*Geständnisses*) made by Hutter to assist in the interrogation of Caspar Kräntzler at Sterzing.[99] After Hutter's arrest, Kräntzler, one of his closest confidants, had remained in the Sterzing area, avoiding detection until May 1536.[100] He was subsequently executed. Hutter's host at Hörschwang, Hans Obern, managed to escape this fate even though the authorities were hard on his trail. Obern, his wife, and oldest daughter fled to Moravia.[101]

Meanwhile Hutter's trial and suffering had drawn to its bitter end. Sometime after the flogging, on January 26, 1536, the court ordered another interrogation. The proceedings were set to begin at 7 o'clock in the morning with a secretary in attendance "when the prisoner was still fresh."[102] Again, none of the minutes or particulars of the interrogation has survived, nor has the final sentencing or the date of execution. A hostile source from 1588 maintained that the charges against Hutter included adultery and the leading of subjects and money from the Tyrol.[103] Yet Hutter's death by burning leaves no doubt that the main charge remained heresy. Confusion surrounds the actual date of execution. Previous scholarship suggested February 25, 1536, but Hutter's jailor sought to collect for eighty-seven days, which would move the date of execution to the middle of March 1536.[104] Even the final act stirred disagreements. The executioner preferred to administer a quick death by beheading Hutter, before dawn, out of the public eye. Ferdinand thought otherwise. He insisted on a public burning in the market square. Hutterite sources cite eyewitness accounts that the execution drew a large crowd. The same accounts picture Hutter, despite all the pain inflicted on him, as unbroken in spirit, taunting his tormentors to test their own faith with him in the fire. "Come here now, you gainsayers! Let us test the faith in the fire. This fire harms my soul as little as the burning harmed Shadrach, Meshach, and Abednego."[105] Not surprisingly, none of the gainsayers was prepared to test his own faith by the ordeal of fire.

It seems only fitting, therefore, that as a memorial the final word on Hutter's martyrdom should belong not to his gainsayers but to the community that for almost half a millennium cherished his memory and has borne the name of this true son of the Puster and disciple of Christ.

He was deceived and betrayed at Klausen on the Eisack River in the Adige region. They tied a gag in his mouth and brought him to Innsbruck, the seat of Ferdinand's government. They tortured him and caused him great agony by all they did to him, yet they were not able to change his heart or make him deny the truth. Even when they tried to prove him wrong with Scripture, they could not stand up to him. Full of hatred and revenge, the priests imagined they would drive the devil out of him. They put him in ice-cold water and then took him into a warm room and had him beaten with rods. They lacerated his body, poured brandy into the wounds, and set it on fire. They tied his hands and again gagged him to prevent him from denouncing their wickedness. Putting a hat with a tuft of feathers on his head, they led him into the house of their idols and in every way made a laughing stock of him. After he had suffered all their cruelty and yet remained firm and upright, a Christian hero steadfast in faith, these wicked sons of Caiaphas and Pilate condemned him and burned him alive at the stake. A huge crowd was present and saw his steadfast witness.[106]

The memory of Hutter could not be erased. The martyrdom of this "faithful servant of Jesus Christ, a man tested in fire," burned itself into the consciousness of the community he led. None of those who had quarreled with him in 1533 left a testimony as clear and irrefutable.

The Fate of Companions and Converts

As noted below, arrests in Lüsen and Hörschwang had put the authorities on Hutter's trail, driving him from the Puster valley, accompanied only by his wife, Katherine, and her friend, Anna Stainer. Once arrested, Katherine and Anna provided the authorities with information about their earlier movements and contacts. The latter, if they were not known previously to the authorities, were now in mortal danger. Hutter's host at Hörschwang, Hans Obern and wife, escaped to Moravia. Caspar Kräntzler, less fortunate, was executed a few months later in Sterzing. Of the three women arrested with Hutter, Anna Stainer, senior, was released. Katherine was moved before Christmas 1535 from Branzoll into the custody of Adam Preu, bailiff of Gufidaun.[107] Whether she gave birth in prison and what happened to the child are unknown. Clear is that attempts were made to gain a recantation from her. Since she had recanted once before, this was a distinct possibility, and priests were to be brought in for the task.[108] The outcome of these efforts was not recorded. Sometime between May and August 1536 Katherine broke out of prison but remained in South Tyrol. Two years later she was rearrested in Schöneck and this time executed.[109] Thus ended a courageous and tragic young life. In six years as

an Anabaptist, Katherine had suffered at least four imprisonments—
Rodeneck, 1533; Bozen, 1533; Branzoll-Gufidaun, 1535–36; Schöneck,
1538—and finally martyrdom. The fate of Hutter's hausfrau illustrates
graphically the costs borne by Anabaptist women. Her escape to Moravia
in 1534 and her marriage to Hutter in 1535 brought at best only moments
of respite. News of her husband's cruel death no doubt reached her while
she was awaiting the same fate in prison. That she sought to escape that
fate seems only human. Like her husband, Katherine eventually paid the
supreme price, but unlike her husband she has remained an unsung hero-
ine even in her own community. Hutterite chroniclers registered neither
her marriage nor her death.

Anna Stainer, junior, fared little better. Still at Branzoll as late as August 1536, she was eventually transferred to Gufidaun. She, too, escaped
or was released but was back in prison by January 1537, this time in
Bozen. Evidence suggests that she had made contact with Onophrius Griesinger, who had been sent to South Tyrol to follow up on Hutter's last
mission (see Chapter 11). Most likely she planned to join a trek back to
Moravia, but renewed imprisonment thwarted such plans. Unfortunately
the paper trail disappears with this her third imprisonment. Nothing is
known about her subsequent fate.[110]

Of interest here is also the tragic fate of Niclas Niderhofer and his wife
Anna (Troyer). They were separated in early October 1535, Anna having
been sent to live with her brother, Paul Troyer. Niclas was still in prison
two months later, on November 27, 1535. On that day Brixen threatened the use of torture, which led to Niclas's public recantation. On December 20, Niclas petitioned Brixen to pardon his wife, a request granted
January 4, 1536.[111] Once back together, the two regretted his recantation
and resumed contact with the Anabaptists. By August 1536 Niclas and
Anna had rejoined the Anabaptists and gone underground.[112] Their property was confiscated and leased out to another tenant.[113] Anna was later
discovered ill in a hut on the Götzenberg. Her father, the magistrate of
Schöneck, took her back, pleading for a second pardon on grounds of her
"simplicity and stupidity" (blödigkeit und einfalt).[114] Shortly thereafter
her father died, and Paul Troyer, Anna's brother, became magistrate of
Schöneck. Under pressure from Brixen, Paul cooperated more fully than
his father had done in the suppression of the heretics. In the fall of 1539
he apprehended his brother-in-law.[115] Sent to Brixen, Niclas recanted a second time and, surprisingly, was granted another reprieve. Subsequently,
with tears of contrition he sought reacceptance into the Anabaptist fold,
but his overtures were rejected,[116] and he found himself stranded in a social and ideological no man's land. Dispossessed and impoverished, he
was forced to eke out a living as a shepherd.[117] His wife, meanwhile, had

reached Moravia where conditions for the Anabaptist communities were improving. On March 15, 1543, Niclas sought permission for travel to Moravia, ostensibly to bring back his wife. Permission was granted, but only with the proviso that he first confess to a priest, receive communion, and provide guarantors who would pay a hefty fine should he fail to return. Official suspicions about his real intent were borne out when Niclas did not return. Two years later, in 1545, his unfortunate guarantors sought permission to visit Moravia to collect the sum of two hundred gulden, which they were fined because Niclas had broken his pledge. Nothing is known about the success of their mission.

Niclas most likely died in Moravia.[118] Whether he had been reunited with his wife and restored into the Anabaptist fellowship are unknown. His all too human recantations, contrition, and pleas for restoration into the Anababptis fold illustrate the cost of discipleship for some of Hutter's converts. Hutter's last mission had changed the lives of Niclas and Anna Niderhofer forever, and without their story the narrative of Hutter's last mission would be incomplete.

The years 1535–36 proved extremely difficult for the community led by Hutter. Hutter himself had been forced to leave the promised land and return to South Tyrol. The congregation left behind under Hans Amon broke up into smaller groups and scattered. Hutter's attempt at reestablishing a network in South Tyrol, which would have sustained his presence at least temporarily, had come to grief. In the wake of his own arrest, sadistic torture, and martyrdom most of his companions and converts were either forced to flee or recant or were executed. Hutter's premonition, recorded in his last letter, was coming true: the raging dragon had opened its jaws wide to devour the woman robed with the sun, the bride of Christ. As the next chapter indicates, there would be further losses. Others would sail through bloody seas to celebrate the "wedding feast" with Christ at the gates of hell.

Chapter Eleven

Further Losses, 1536–1538

The death of Jacob Hutter in 1536 dealt a devastating blow to his fledgling community, with further losses to come. In the next three years the community also lost its first schoolmaster, Jeronimus Käls, and its gifted missionaries Onophrius Griesinger, Leonhard Lochmair, and Georg Fasser. The commemoration of their loss in prose and song proved foundational to the identity formation of Hutter's followers as the true congregation of God, baptized in fire and blood; and the prison epistles associated with the ordeal of these leaders added to a growing depository of spirituality, an epistolary literature unequaled in Anabaptist history.[1] Jeronimus Käls, more than any other of the prison authors, provided a model of style and content for this important communication genre and reservoir of community values.

Most significant from the purely historic point of view is that this rich primary source can be tested against the surviving official documents, thus establishing their veracity. No other Anabaptist group bequeathed richer historic sources.

The Loss of the First Schoolmaster, Jeronimus Käls

Born at Kufstein in North Tyrol, Jeronimus was one of the better educated early Hutterite leaders. After entering studies at the University of Vienna in preparation for the priesthood,[2] he took up the life of a traveling student, venturing to the University of Leipzig, where he dabbled in humanistic studies.[3] It is not clear whether he entered the Reformation debate while he was in Saxony or only after his return to Kufstein, where he assumed the position of secretary and tutor with Christoff Fuchs, governor

(Hauptmann) of Kufstein.[4] In the service of Fuchs he heard about Anabaptists and sought them out. His queries led to Sigmund Schützinger, who baptized him during a congregational meeting attended by more than one hundred persons in a forest outside Rattenberg.[5] This baptism most likely took place before 1532 and possibly as early as 1528–29.[6] Schützinger recognized Jeronimus's assets and took him on a visitation tour into the Ziller valley and to Kitzbühl. In 1532 Jeronimus joined the community at Auspitz which, by the drawing of lots, had come under Schützinger's leadership. The rapid growth of the community to seven hundred persons with about three hundred children led to Jeronimus's appointment as schoolmaster and disciplinarian (*schuel oder zuchtmaister*). He held this position for three years—from 1532 to 1535—apparently siding with Hutter when Schützinger was ousted during the quarrels of 1533. In 1534–35 Jeronimus was imprisoned along with Hutter and Amon by the mistress of Auspitz as one of the recognized leaders of the community. He accompanied Hutter to South Tyrol in July 1535 and returned to Moravia with Hutter's last letter in late November or early December of that year.

Jeronimus was on his way back to the Tyrol when he was arrested in Vienna on January 7, 1536. With him were Michael Seifensieder and Hans Oberecker. During the interrogation that followed Jeronimus made no mention of his recent mission to South Tyrol with Hutter and remained vague about his destination. He explained to the investigating magistrate that the breakup of the community in Moravia had made his task as schoolmaster superfluous and that he left his wife and child in Moravia so he could find work in the mines at Koestein (Kufstein) or the Thauerich mountains. He hoped to send for his family once he had secured a residence and livelihood. When asked about the number of brethren left in Moravia, Jeronimus replied that estimates were difficult because they were "no longer able to gather or remain together." As for his companion, Hans Oberecker (Zimmermann), a brother in the same faith and a carpenter from the South Tyrol, Jeronimus claimed to have met him on the road and to have taken him along in order to teach him how to work in the mines.[7]

If these statements are accurate transcriptions of Jeronimus's answers, then his mission was to find a livelihood in one of the mining districts. Somewhat casual seemed his choice of companions, both of whom were relatively recent, inexperienced converts. Michael Seifensieder, like Jeronimus, had been a traveling student (*den Schuellen nachzogen*).[8] In 1525–26 he had turned to the business of soap boiling, hence his name. In his spare time Seifensieder studied the Scriptures and "inspired by the Spirit, had received the faith." Then in 1534 following the "commandment of Christ," he received baptism during a visit to Schackowitz. Returning to

Bohemia, presumably after the expulsions from Moravia, he remained with his non-German wife and children. Early in November 1535 his landlord evicted him because of his faith. Moving to Moravia, he "accidentally" met Jeronimus and joined his expedition. He claimed to be in the market for knife blades and grain (*Traidt*).

Hans Oberecker, the other member in the party, described himself as the son of a peasant from Affers (Auers) in the jurisdiction of Rodeneck. He had turned to Anabaptism after reading martyr legends and the New Testament and finding remarkable similarities between the persecuted saints of the past and present. On St. Jacob's Day, July 25, 1535, he attended a meeting called by Hutter and was baptized along with eight others in a brook near Lisen (Lüsen).[9] When Oberecker subsequently refused to enter the "temple of idols" or to participate in "unrighteousness and idolatry," the local priest reported him. Learning that the local magistrate was looking for him, Oberecker left his wife and child with his father and fled to Moravia. He had been in Moravia only eight days before joining Jeronimus, allegedly to find work in the mines.

What seems surprising was the vague goal claimed by the trio. Was Jeronimus candid with his interrogators? Did he deliberately hide his mission as itinerant apostle? Did this mission have the sanction of Amon? Obviously, Jeronimus had delivered Hutter's last message to Amon, but did he know of Hutter's arrest? If so, were Jeronimus and his companions on a mission to learn more about Hutter's fate, or had the decision been to send someone else while Jeronimus was commissioned to Upper Austria and North Tyrol? Whatever the answers to these questions, it seems clear that another apostle, Onophrius Griesinger, had been or was to be dispatched to South Tyrol before or immediately after the arrest of Jeronimus and his companions.

Meanwhile, Jeronimus and his companions unfolded a most interesting correspondence with Amon and the scattered community in Moravia. Jeronimus wrote at least eleven letters, and his companions have been credited with two each.[10] Jeronimus also penned a statement of faith submitted on behalf of the three.[11] These documents narrated the prison experience of Jeronimus and his two companions. The three arrived in Vienna on the evening of January 7 and entered an inn where they aroused the curiosity and suspicion of patrons because they refused to participate in the customary lewd toasts. A Judas figure, sitting at the table with them, then wrote a note in Latin suggesting that the three were Anabaptists. Although Jeronimus deciphered the message, the three decided to wait and see what happened next. Two hours later a guard arrived to escort them to the local magistrate, who placed them in a common prison. In the next two days Jeronimus wrote three letters, only to have them confiscated. Their content, if nothing else, must have further incriminated him and his companions.[12] A week later the three prisoners were brought before a jury. The presiding magistrate urged them to recant but instead received a lecture from the New Testament and an admonition to change his own life. Unable to cope with the erudition of the prisoners, the magistrate called on the University of Vienna for help. During the week of January 22, three clergy, led by Dr. Ambrosius Salzer, the rector of the university, arrived.[13] In his letters Jeronimus described the visitors as "three snakes, select wicked scoundrels, scripturally learned Pfaffen."[14] They had barely announced their intention to lead the prisoners back to the true path, when Jeronimus interrupted, declaring that he and his brethren were already on the true path and would not listen to "an alien voice" or dialogue with servants of Antichrist. As far as he was concerned, there were no "greater scoundrels, fornicators, adulterers, deceivers, or corrupters" than the clergy.[15] When the magistrate interjected that Jeronimus should not make such rash judgments before he even knew "the lords," Jeronimus replied, "God is lord, but they not at all."[16]

Despite these rather unpromising beginnings, a serious discussion ensued on a number of topics, including original sin, infant baptism, mass, and Jeronimus's own sense of mission. According to Jeronimus's account, his junior partners were excluded lest they witness his unmasking of the "two-facedness" of the priests. In more than two hours of discussion the theologians did their best to persuade Jeronimus of his errors. They "begged" him to reconsider for the sake of his life, his wife, and child and to "ponder their request before God." They would do the same with arguments presented by him. But Jeronimus refused to yield any ground and rejected any hint at compromise.[17] In the hope that the younger partners would prove more pliable and cooperative, they were placed into separate cells.

Two weeks later the prisoners learned that some members of Vienna's city council were sympathetic and that the magistrate intended to sway them in a friendly way (*mit Guete und freindlich*) in the hope of a face-saving compromise. He obviously did not want their blood on his hands. But should he fail, Ferdinand's orders to deal "severely and sternly" would have to be applied. The magistrate failed, and the three remained unmovable.

Meanwhile, Jeronimus had found a way of communicating with his fellow prisoners by using a slate. He had also discovered that singing overcame the echo in the prison and made it possible to speak with Oberecker.[18] The ingenious prisoners had also opened lines of communication with the outside. A courageous brother provided them with ink and paper at the risk to his own life. This brother had once been at Auspitz with

Offrus (Onophrius) Griesinger but did not "walk according to the rule of Christ." His prison visits were nevertheless appreciated. Presumably he smuggled out some of the letters as well. Incoming mail had been baked into buns delivered by a charitable and courageous woman. She, too, may have taken messages out. A fellow prisoner who was released carried a slate with Jeronimus's letter to Amon.[19]

Besides witnessing to the devotion and commitment of the prisoners, the letters contained specific historic information of interest. One implied veiled criticism of Amon's style of leadership. Jeronimus remonstrated for the appointment of more servants of the Word and of temporal affairs and suggested that the leadership demands left Amon with little time for reading, reflection, prayer, and "apostolic exercises."[20] If Jeronimus may be believed, no officially appointed servants of temporal affairs were left, and Amon was simply overworked. Surely, God had preserved some capable, "pious, God-fearing men" from the "onslaught of Jezebel." He urged that two such men be appointed as itinerant servants to minister to the scattered saints.[21]

Significant also was a reference to the fate of the Austerlitz Brethren. Mutual prison walls lowered inter-Anabaptist fences. Jeronimus had learned of the execution of Jacob Wiedemann. Because his report to Amon constitutes the primary source on the fate of the Austerlitz leader, it is worth citing in full.

My dear brother Hans [Amon], I let you know in love that we have heard and learned of many pious Christian hearts who have here in Vienna bravely witnessed to the truth of the Lord—brethren and sisters who remained steadfast and undismayed in the greatest tribulation. Even though they, like we, were confronted several times by the evil snakes, with promises, threats, torture, and pain in order to make them recant, they remained faithful to the Lord and were executed, preferring the eternal reward of God and despising the temporal one. Yes, we hear only good of them. We testify of them that God did great signs through them. Of the one-eyed Jakob we know nothing to say. The magistrate tells us that he did not sentence him because of baptism. [He claims that Jacob] would have gladly recanted; but that [he was executed] because he was guilty of something else. We do not believe the magistrate. He could claim the same of us. He speaks through the spirit of lies. We think as much of his claims as of a sour smoke that blinds the eyes. We believe also that all these, who confess the Lord faithfully, will be in the kingdom of God on that great day. They are from the Austerlitz community.

My dear brother and faithful servant of Christ, Hans, I know the Austerlitz group very well and that they do not walk according to the rule of Christ as the pious should, which is also true of other congregations that boast of Christ and his [great] commission. I testify also and am well assured in my heart, that your holy gathering and Christian fellowship [*Versammlung und Christliche Gemeinschaft*] is of God. I desire to and will give witness in truth as the need requires as long as I live. Yes, I know that you are the true little Christian flock [*Heüfflen*] and that you are faithfully zealous for the Lord and his house. Nevertheless, dear brother Hans, I believe fully that there are many zealous and pious hearts scattered in the various congregations. I pray you, my brother, take care of the beloved brothers and sisters that no one sin with overly hasty judgment concerning [the others]. Consider that the tongue can bless or condemn. Oh, beloved brother, the day of the Lord will reveal it all through fire, whether it was wood, straw, gold or silver. . . . I do not want to be found as one who judged what God has not ordered me to. . . . Accept it from me, not as if I had become disappointed with you, or as if I feel you had acted wrongly in regard to the congregation. No, [let us be] quick [anxious] to hear, slow to speak. Some brethren speak quickly and cannot control their tongue. I spoke to some of them in accordance with the Christian order, disciplined and admonished them that they should look out and speak so that they will be able to give an account before God.[22]

Equally historically significant is Jeronimus's farewell letter to his former pupils.[23] It opens a window not only on the first known Anabaptist classroom for children but also on the pedagogical principles guiding its first schoolmaster. The motto was, "the fear of the Lord is the beginning of wisdom." Although rejection of pedobaptism implied a rejection of traditional notions of original sin,[24] as schoolmaster Jeronimus worked with the assumption that

the human heart was bent toward evil from its youth on, and that the old serpent, which misled and deceived the first human . . . does not rest but is extremely active day and night to bring man under its power. Therefore, dear children, think and consider what I often told you, how God from the beginning forbade sin and commended the good, how he loved the pious and hated the godless.[25]

The resulting educational effort was directed toward nurturing godliness and conduct befitting the children of the congregation of God. The curriculum involved catechetical exercises that included the learning by rote of the Lord's Prayer, Apostolic Creed, and the Ten Commandments. A morning, evening, and mealtime prayer for the children have been attributed to Jeronimus.[26] Presumably literacy was a major objective for Jeronimus as educator, but it was not an end in itself. His main aim was to build and nurture Christian character. It was an aim in tune with the pedagogy of contemporary Christian humanists, involving discipline along the lines of "spare the rod and spoil the child."

Oh, my dear children, for two years I have disciplined you with diligent watchfulness in all things which I perceived to be wrong in you—gentle and harsh, mild and severe—as the Almighty has ordered his people, how they should teach and discipline their children from childhood, so that they do not grow into the godless world and be damned with her.[27]

Those unwilling to be molded or to accept corrections received a stern warning: they would "burn in hell." Jeronimus's philosophy of education, therefore, seemed to differ little from that of other educators. Its primary concern was to prepare the second generation for life in community.[28] It was the nature of this community which gave the educational effort a different context and effectiveness. Loyalty in the name of Christ to the community overshadowed individual and even parental interests; indeed, these were brought into alignment with the collective will as interpreted by the leadership. This theme is illustrated in Jeronimus's praise of children who "feared and loved God more than humans" and resisted those who "furiously [*Ungestieme*] wanted to draw them away from God and his people."[29] Included in the latter could be parents and family members. The honor due father and mother was shifted to the "brothers and sisters who have been given to you by God and assigned to you."[30] Finally, Jeronimus admonished his former pupils to remain faithful even onto death, something he was preparing to do.

Jeronimus's preparations notwithstanding, the local judge still sought to avoid the execution of his prisoners. Another "friendly" discussion led to their submission of a written confession (*Rechenschaft*).[31] At least one scholar considered this confession of special significance as representing "the earliest testimony to Hutter's teaching."[32] However, it was most clearly the work of Jeronimus who remained the teacher in relation to others. An analysis reveals that he followed the outline of the Apostolic Creed, presumably because, in keeping with Ferdinand's decrees beginning in August 1527, the Apostolic Creed was to be the minimal standard of orthodoxy (see Chapter 8). But if the magistrate hoped that the commentary solicited on the creed would give him an excuse to release his prisoners, he proved mistaken. Jeronimus used the creed only as a sounding board for Anabaptist teachings. Thus the exposition of the first article, belief in God as creator of heaven and earth, led to criticism and rejection of all wooden, stone, silver, gold, or painted idols. The article on belief in Christ solicited confirmation of his virgin birth, but instead of entering upon a discussion of the union of the divine and human in Christ, Jeronimus went on to emphasize obedience to Christ's teachings and the need to follow his example. Here, too, he proved to be in the humanist *philosophy Christi* tradition, which opened an opportunity to argue for adult baptism as in accordance with Christ's last command (Matthew 28, Mark 16) and with apostolic precedent. Since pedobaptism was contrary to Christ's commandment and will, it was the sign of Antichrist.

The article on Christ's crucifixion, death, descent into hell, and resurrection led not to abstract reflections on satisfaction theories or the nature of atonement but to an observation on the exemplary nature of Christ's obedience to God's will. For the believer the cross symbolized self-denial and willingness to suffer persecution in conformity with Christ. Christ's resurrection and ascension into heaven with a clarified body, in turn, provided opportunity to argue for his location, in essence (*wesentlich*), at the right hand of the Father until the final judgment. It followed that the glorified Christ seated in heaven could not be present "in temples made with hands," leading to the admonition that the magistrate should "not uphold the bread-god, but help to exterminate him!"

Jeronimus's exposition, then, demonstrated a practical rather than scholastic bent even though the article on the third person of the Trinity solicited an orthodox Latin reflex, namely that the Holy Spirit proceeded from the Father through the Son. The Spirit's role was to provide comfort to the sorrowing heart. Again, Jeronimus avoided abstract speculations or epistemological applications.

The article on the holy Christian Church solicited the explanation that the true Christian fellowship (*gemeinschaft*) maintained proper discipline, including the ban. Only the holy church had the authority to wield "the key of David," that is, the power to bind and to loose, to accept or exclude. Inside the true Christian fellowship there could be no coercion, hence no need for the temporal sword. And while taxes should be paid, true followers of Christ could not contribute to taxes earmarked for war or used to inflict capital punishment. Furthermore, Jeronimus and his fellow prisoners reiterated their belief in the bodily resurrection and life everlasting. Depending on the final judgment, the afterlife would be spent in either the kingdom of God or the "fiery pool."

In essence Jeronimus had used the Apostolic Creed to put forward key Anabaptist views. He felt no need to reiterate his position on the blessedness of children, the authority of his apostolic mission (*Sendung*), the oath, or other articles because these had been explained in earlier discussions.[33] These other articles must have included the practice of community of goods, a subject not mentioned in the confession, which closed with the prisoners' declaration that they were prepared to die for their faith.

Official reaction to the confession was not recorded. If the magistrate sought the opinion of the university theologians, their opinion was in all likelihood negative. The last letters by the prisoners suggested that their hope of release had faded. Hans Oberecker, the youngest in the faith, had been strengthened for the inevitable by three visions of the last judgment.[34] Michael Seifensieder had been visited by his wife, who urged him to save his life by recanting; he refused. Instead, he wrote a farewell letter to her and his children in Bohemia.[35] Jeronimus did the same. Earlier he had requested that after his death his wife Treindl (Katherine) "be provided with a fine brother" because the Lord had given her a special feminine gift.[36]

He had already promised his New Testament to some other sisters. The greetings conveyed at the end of his letter provide a window into the inner circle of the post-Hutter leadership, led by Hans Amon. The list of names included Onophrius (Griesinger), Christoph (Gschäll), Leonhard Sailer (Lanzenstiel), his "beloved brother" Walser Mayer, Peter Veit, Bastel Glaser, Georg Fasser, Peter Schneider, Kuentz (Cunz) Maurer, Simon Wandl, Wölffl Reschl, and Georg Bader.[37]

Sometime after these formal farewells, the prisoners had an encounter with some monks, possibly brought in to prepare them spiritually for their last ordeal. When the monks entered Seifensieder's cell with the eucharist, Seifensieder made it clear that they need not bother him with their "idols." Hearing the ensuing commotion, Jeronimus shouted, "God comfort you, dear friend; send the monks and godless knaves from you and do not listen to them! At that a monk ran over to me and said: 'You are a knave and a heretic. You will be burned soon.' Then I said to him: 'You godless knave, throw your fool's cap away, take a hoe into your hand and work.' "[38]

On March 31, 1536, shortly after that exchange, the "valiant knights and lovers of God," as *The Chronicle* calls them, were burned at the stake in Vienna.[39] Thus, only a few days apart, the hard-pressed congregation of God lost two of its founding leaders, Jacob Hutter and Jeronimus Käls. Although Hutter left his mark on the structure and organization, Jeronimus had helped lay the foundation of the inner house of learning. Besides the prison epistles, model exposés of practical piety, the confession and prayers, Jeronimus bequeathed at least three songs to the Hutterite repertoire.[40] Two, like his epistoral monologues with God, were deeply devotional, encouraging the "little flock" to persevere in the face of brutal suppression.[41] The other commemorated the Puster experience where, in "rain and wind," on mountains and in valleys, among traitorous "children of Judas," the hunted flock and its shepherd Hutter attempted to build the congregation of God.[42] Because neither city, village, nor hamlet was safe, the "flock of Christ" gathered in the "green forest." The song is of special historic interest because it commemorated events reaching back to 1533 and remembered traitors rather than martyrs. Four specific names were mentioned as "children of the devil and of Judas": Praweiger (Prabeiger), in verse 4; Georg Frue, in verses 5–7; Peter Lentz (Lanntz), in verse 8; and Christel (Christian) Pranger (Prengger), in verse 8. Since these names were also included in official documents, it is possible to test the accusations made against them in the song.

Praweiger was guilty of betraying a congregational gathering on the promise of pay from the clergy. *The Chronicle* drew historic parallels to Judas, according to which Praweiger "hurried to the magistrates . . . bringing back constables and the children of Pilate with swords, spears and clubs, going in front of them just like the traitor Judas."[43] Similarly, Frue first negotiated "a substantial reward"; then, with tears of repentance, feigning to be a seeker, he searched the Puster valley to locate the leader. Finding him at a congregational meeting, he begged leave to fetch his wife and child.

The servant [shepherd] did have misgivings but told him that if he was false-hearted and was planning evil, God would certainly know it, and he would have to bear hard punishment. But he answered: "Oh no! May God protect me from any such thing. Come home with me to my house!" He left and hurried to the judge, priests, and magistrates, who came with swords and cudgels and took the brothers and sisters by force.[44]

The facts of the Frue case can be tested against official documents, where it is recorded that on June 3, 1533, Frue had been commissioned to infiltrate the Anabaptists to determine the whereabouts of Hutter and Amon. He found them at a congregational meeting on the Götzenberg. Frue took his leave two days later to inform the authorities, but the raid that followed netted only eight Anabaptists. Hutter and Amon had escaped.[45] It was to be Hutter's last congregational meeting in the Puster before leaving for Moravia. Frue's name reappeared in connection with the hunt for Hutter in 1535, and three years later he brought to Brixen the news of Onophrius Griesinger's arrest.[46] That the Pusterers who fled to Moravia would remember him as a traitor is not surprising.

Less transparent was the alleged treachery of Christel Pranger. Pranger's mill at Ellen had served as a supply depot for Hutter and his supporters. Pranger ground flour, baked or stored bread for and bought portable property, such as feather beds, from the fugitives.[47] These commercial dealings with the Anabaptists became known to the authorities. One night, during the fall of 1533, the court secretary of St. Michelsburg and two constables arrived at Pranger's mill, demanding to know the Anabaptist hiding and meeting places. At first Pranger feigned ignorance, but when the bailiff and magistrate arrived as well, fear gained the upper hand, and he led the search party "to the hut and to the congregation."[48] The action was apparently intended to net Amon who, nevertheless, escaped.[49] Once pressed into service, Pranger, according to Hutterite sources, went further. Pretending to be Anabaptists, he and others "carried staves and talked and acted like brothers." Knocking on doors at night to ferret out sympathizers, they greeted suspects with "Peace be with you" and reported to the authorities those who replied "Praise be to God."[50] How many Anabaptists and sympathizers were betrayed this way is unknown. Official documents imply that Pranger renewed his commercial relations with Anabaptists. In 1534 he was fined for permitting Anabaptists to build huts on his tenancy (*Zinsgut*).[51]

268 EMERGENCE OF THE HUTTERITES

The other traitor commemorated in Jeronimus's song, Peter Lanntz, has appeared in this narrative before (see Chapter 10). In October 1533 Lanntz received orders to keep a suspected Anabaptist meeting place under surveillance.[52] In that same month he stood guarantor (*Bürge*) for Veronica Grembs of St. Georgen.[53] Veronica subsequently made the trek to Moravia. Lanntz, meanwhile, helped Amon's wife out of prison and gave Amon shelter.[54] Yet, Lanntz knew how to remain in the good graces of the prince bishop's administrators. After Mairhofer's flight from Nidervintl, Lanntz took possession of Mairhofer's large estate. By 1537 he had been appointed magistrate of Lüsen and by 1543, of Nidervintl.[55]

But what is to be learned from Jeronimus's song? Apart from communicating historic anecdotes, the song demonstrates Jeronimus's close identification with the core of Hutter's supporters, the Pusterers. The traitors named would have been unknown outside Hutter's inner circle. By composing the song in 1533–34 Jeronimus signaled his alliance with Hutter, Amon, and the Pusterers. It is not clear whether the rhyme was intended for use in Moravia or the Puster but presumably the latter as a warning to be on guard against infiltrators and traitors. As such, the song with its character assassination of the Judases named was part of Anabaptist countermeasures against the official campaign of suppression. This genre of poetry and song, conceived to recall the names of perpetrators and their fate, became uniquely Hutterite and may have originated with Jeronimus, who must be numbered among the first poets of the community.

One further point is worth making. In this case, Jeronimus's song clearly preceded the corresponding account in *The Chronicle*. By the time that account was written some of the traitors, like the Judas of old, had received divine retribution, struck "with great terror and horrible death."[56] We conclude that *The Chronicle* built on earlier oral circulations in the form of stories and songs but above all on the epistolary literature to which Jeronimus was a major early contributor.[57] Jeronimus, therefore, deserves to be numbered with Hutter and Amon among the most important shapers of the emerging Hutterites.

The Martyrdom of Onophrius Griesinger and Leonhard Lochmair

With the martyrdom of Hutter and Jeronimus died the last two servants of the Word in South Tyrol. But the homeland of the Pusterers was too important to be left without a spiritual guide. Amon and the community in Moravia decided to send Onophrius Griesinger.[58] Onophrius, like Amon, a Bavarian, was a natural choice because his "gentle manner and speech" made him a most effective apostle.[59] With Hutter, Jeronimus, and

Amon, Onophrius was among the most gifted and experienced of the early leaders. Before joining the Anabaptists, he had served as a secretary to the mining magistrate in the archbishopric of Salzburg, and it is possible that Onophrius's interest in Anabaptism dated from the executions of Hans Hut's followers in Salzburg territory.[60] By 1532 Onophrius baptized alongside Hutter and Amon in South Tyrol.[61] Back on a mission in the archbishopric of Salzburg, he was detained at Hopfgarten, but a hole left in the prison wall by a thief provided his escape. He returned to the Puster region,[62] where with Hutter's departure in 1533 he became Amon's assistant and the servant of temporal affairs.[63] Official files described him as young, of medium height, without beard, wearing an open, gray, waterproof overcoat (*lodein*), white pants, and brown knee socks.[64] In 1534, Onophrius and Amon led the daring exodus from the Tyrol to Moravia. Upon the expulsion orders of 1535 Onophrius returned with a group of carpenters and miners to Bömisch Krumau. He functioned as spiritual leader of those at Krumau, Brimitz, and Heroltitz, near Tischlowitz. Recalled by Amon after Jeronimus's arrest, he was commissioned as servant of the Gospel to South Tyrol.[65]

Evidence suggests that he and his wife arrived in early February 1536. Presumably his mission included resumption of contacts with Hutter's last converts because Hutter's widow joined Onophrius's entourage after her escape from the Gufidaun prison.[66] Onophrius himself was temporarily confined in Bozen during April 1536, but he too managed to escape.[67] Appraised of his prison break, Innsbruck placed a high price on his head, but the elusive Onophrius continued with his mission, holding meetings that lasted up to three days with more than forty attending. It seems that he was guided and aided by the very capable Hans Mair Paulle, who must have also functioned as courier between Onophrius and Amon.

Among the new converts was Hans Grünfelder (Grienfelder) of Lüsen, who, appointed as local servant of temporal affairs, accompanied Onophrius on a mission into the Etsch valley.[68] With his help, Onophrius survived the winter of 1536–37 in South Tyrol. Onophrius's wife was arrested in January 1537,[69] and he narrowly escaped the same fate two months later.[70] In May 1537 two courageous brethren, using a beam, bent or broke the steel bars of the prison window in Bozen, thus releasing Onophrius's wife and five other women prisoners.[71] The number of prison breaks and Onophrius's ability to elude the authorities suggest that Anabaptists still encountered considerable sympathy among the population. The ecclesiastical authorities in Hutter's home district of St. Michelsburg were dismayed to find that church attendance during Lent 1537 had dwindled to a mere nine hundred from the two thousand of earlier years.[72] The magistrate of the district feared that the "Anabaptists would continue to thrive in valley and mountain" unless properly educated priests were appointed.[73] He was aware of Onophrius's presence in his jurisdiction and knew that many of Hans Grünfelder's family relations—said to be numerous in and around Lüsen—had joined the sect. However, neither Grünfelder nor Onophrius could be found, most likely because Grünfelder and Onophrius led a number of "devout brothers and sisters" to Moravia in 1537.[74] Later that year Grünfelder joined Bastel Glaser (Bastian Hub-Mair) on a mission to the Upper Inn valley. The two were apprehended at Imst in early December 1537, and after a short trial they were beheaded and their bodies burned.[75] According to Hutterite sources, one thousand spectators were deeply moved by the steadfastness and witness of the martyrs.[76]

Onophrius, meanwhile, returned to South Tyrol, accompanied by Leonhard Lochmair. Lochmair, a former priest and member of the Austerlitz Brethren, had joined the Hutterites only recently.[77] Although he should have been less recognizable than Onophrius, Lochmair was arrested in late April 1538 and taken to Brixen. Since he was a former priest and an Anabaptist leader, Lochmair's case received special attention.[78] Innsbruck dispatched the court preacher and theologian Dr. Gallus Müller, a one-man inquisition, to gain a recantation, but it was the suffragan bishop of Brixen, Albrecht Kraus, who succeeded where Müller had failed. After two months in prison, on July 18, 1538, Lochmair signaled his readiness to return to the Catholic faith. A little later he made a solemn declaration to this effect in the parish church at Brixen,[79] promising to cooperate with the established church in bringing Anabaptists back to the fold should he receive a pardon. It was a major success for the suffragan bishop. However, by the time Ferdinand's pardon arrived on September 4, Lochmair had had a change of heart.[80] He told the suffragan that his recantation was given "in fear and fright" and in a fit of temporary "insanity." He himself could not understand or explain why he had done it and upon reflection had regretted it "twice as often as the number of hairs on his head." He no longer wished the king's pardon and refused to participate in any effort to sway others from the true faith. Not that Lochmair relished continuing imprisonment or ultimate martyrdom; two days later the jailers found him filing away at his chains.

Lochmair's change of heart had, no doubt, been encouraged by the arrival of Onophrius at the same prison. After Lochmair's arrest Innsbruck had doubled its efforts to capture this elusive leader. On May 20, 1538, a posse, "fifteen strong, of good and reliable subjects," was ordered to hunt him down. All bridges and passes were to be guarded, an effort unequaled since the capture of Hutter. In June, reports placed Onophrius in the Puster valley, yet not until an infiltrator betrayed him could the magistrate of

Schöneck, Paul Troyer, apprehend him on August 28, 1538. Onophrius had just completed a three-day congregational meeting when Troyer arrived. Transferred immediately to the safer prison in Brixen, Onophrius was already subjected to interrogations with torture even before the pardon arrived for Lochmair.[81]

Once in prison, the resourceful Onophrius had established communications with Lochmair.[82] Feeling deep remorse for his earlier recantation, Lochmair, with "pain, sorrow, and distress," asked forgiveness and reacceptance. He scratched the request on the wooden food bowl that also served Onophrius. *The Chronicle* recorded, "Finally, on the bottom of his plate, he wrote his request for forgiveness. . . . Seeing his faithfulness and genuine repentance, Onophrius pronounced forgiveness of his sin in the name of the Lord, restored him to his faith by interceding to God, and accepted him as a brother and member of the church."[83] After this reconciliation Onophrius wrote a letter on behalf of Lochmair in which he asked forgiveness of the community leaders, Hans Amon and Ulrich Stadler.[84] How Onophrius managed to communicate with Moravia is still a secret.

His interrogators, unbelievable as it may sound, sought to establish whether the brethren and their sympathizers planned an insurrection among the commoners.[85] Presumably this line of questioning was dictated by Ferdinand's dated mandates or paranoia at the court rather than the realities of South Tyrol in 1538. Nevertheless, Onophrius was "pulled up" twice in the torture chamber within eight days.[86] Failing to elicit any evidence that would support insurrectionist charges, the authorities called on the spiritual estate to convict him of heresy. That task must have proven less difficult. Last-minute arguments by local officials for a quiet execution before dawn were rejected by Ferdinand's administrators, who dispatched a special prosecutor to expedite the trial and get a public burning.[87] Fully aware of what awaited him, Onophrius, in the language of his community, invited the brethren to witness his "marriage" with Christ. It was All Saints' Eve, October 31, 1538, when "the sons of Pilate" thrust Onophrius alive into the fire.[88] Just before the execution, Oswald Schuster, one of the brothers who had heeded the invitation, pushed himself forward and in an expression of solidarity shook Onophrius's hand. Schuster was promptly arrested, but in what followed he escaped and with Onophrius's widow managed the trek to Moravia. One year later he would accompany Leonhard Sailer to South Tyrol to resume Onophrius's mission.[89]

Onophrius's cruel death had turned into a public relations *gaffe* for the authorities. Even the hardened mercenaries, hired for crowd control, were upset with the method of execution as a heavy rain doused the fire and prolonged the agony. The captain of the mercenaries, Stoffl (Christoph) of

Villach, had demanded a more expeditious execution by beheading. But neither the magistrate nor the council of Brixen felt authorized to overrule Ferdinand's orders. Instead, dry wood was brought to make a quicker end of the terrible torture. In his report to Innsbruck, the city magistrate of Brixen claimed that "some of the mercenaries indicated their disapproval with unseemly [*unziemlichen*] words, praising Onophrius as a saintly man."[90] And according to Hutterite sources, even Ferdinand's provost, Berthold Aichelin, in charge of the execution, was deeply moved by Onophrius's "integrity and steadfastness." In the end Aichelin "raised his hand and swore that as long as he lived, he would never again condemn an [Anabaptist] brother."[91] The captain of the mercenaries was similarly affected and later joined the community in Moravia.[92]

In light of the problems caused by Onophrius's execution, Lochmair's had been postponed. Since he was an ordained priest, his case was the prerogative of the bishop's court in Brixen, and he had to be defrocked first.[93] In a letter after the death of Onophrius, Lochmair wrote, "Only God knows why I am imprisoned so long. I had consoled myself to die with pious Onophrius, but God the Lord has denied it to me; I am waiting every day like a poor lamb. But the preachers must have their proper way and take off my priestly robes and only then deliver me to the hangman."[94] Shortly after he wrote those words in early November 1538, Lochmair was beheaded rather than burned.[95] Obviously the authorities in Brixen were more sensitive to the unfavorable response evoked by Onophrius's earlier execution than the more distant councilors in Innsbruck.

With Onophrius and Lochmair the congregation of God lost another two of its educated leaders. Both contributed to the early epistolary and song collection of the community.[96] They also added their testimony of faithfulness to the growing list of martyrs.

But martyrdom was not everyone's calling, as one of Onophrius's converts demonstrated. The case of Gilg Schneider (Preindle) from Lüsen illustrates how torturous could be the path of following the dictates of conscience. Schneider came to the attention of the authorities as early as Lent 1536, not because he failed to attend the annual ritual of confession and communion, as was the case with most suspects, but because he attempted to participate and failed. Although he had advanced normally through confession and absolution, his jaws locked when he arrived at the altar in anticipation of receiving the Lord's "real body." Unable to open his mouth, he began to shake in terror with eyes bulging. After regaining his composure, he expressed regret, dismay, and embarrassment at what had happened before the priest and those gathered. But even though he called on God for help and forgiveness, a second attempt at receiving the sacrament ended with the same result; he was neither "able to receive nor par-

Figure 6. Lüsen Chapel

take of the revered sacrament of the tender corpse of Jesus Christ"[97] (Figure 6).

Schneider's lockjaw could not be ignored. He was sent to the bishop's court at Brixen for further investigation by suffragan Albert Kraus. During the examination it was revealed that Schneider had heard Hutter but did not become an Anabaptist. Indeed, Schneider claimed to have rebuked Hutter when he "reviled and slandered the priests and authorities, including all those who did not want to join his sect." Schneider further assured Kraus that he wanted to remain in the faith of his fathers and that he accepted none of the teachings of Luther, Zwingli, or the Anabaptists. He declared his agreement with the Apostolic Creed, accepted pedobaptism as proper, and answered questions concerning the humanity and divinity of Christ with reasonable orthodoxy. He considered the sacrament of the altar a sacrifice to God and a spiritual food unto the salvation of the soul. He believed that one received the "whole Christ" with the consecrated host. In short, after four hours of intensive investigation, Kraus found Schneider to be an orthodox layman.⁹⁸ Consequently, on the Saturday before Pentecost (June 4, 1536), Kraus accepted Schneider's private confession so he could clear his conscience in preparation for the reception of the sacrament next day. On Sunday Schneider received public absolution in the parish church of Brixen and came forward with other communicants to receive the consecrated host dispensed by the chaplain. Yet despite the careful preparations, Schneider's jaws locked again. Notified of the predicament, Kraus found Schneider still kneeling by the altar. After admonishing him to come clean and not to keep any secrets, lest God punish him further, the bishop asked the bystanders to intercede with him in a common prayer for Schneider. But two further attempts to administer the sacrament produced the same results. Schneider's jaws would not open. He began to shake and perspire; his eyes seemed to bulge out of their sockets, frightening the other worshippers. Unable to administer the sacrament, the bishop marched Schneider into the vestry and assigned five weeks of penance after which Schneider was to report back.⁹⁹ But the deadline passed without Schneider reporting. On August 17, 1536, the delinquent Schneider was caught in the company of eleven Anabaptists in the mountains near Sterzing.

At his arrest Schneider and those caught with him were taken to Sterzing, but Schneider managed to escape into the high pastures. Driven from the mountains by the onset of winter, the fugitive made contact with a sympathetic chaplain in whom he confided his predicament.¹⁰⁰ The chaplain counseled reconciliation with the church. On February 22, 1537, Schneider sent letters through his wife to the suffragan bishop and the bishop's governor (Statthalter), and by April 1537 he was back in Brixen.¹⁰¹ An investigation revealed that after three weeks on probation, Schneider had taken to the mountain pastures and joined the Anabaptists, receiving baptism from Onophrius.¹⁰² The same investigation also revealed the cause of Schneider's lockjaw. Schneider confessed to having heard Hutter explain that the consecrated host was not the body of Christ at all but rather an idol and that those who swallowed it sold their soul to the devil. Hutter's words, recalled at the sight of the wafer, had created such abhorrence and panic that he could not open his mouth. He maintained that since descending from the mountains in late 1536, he had shunned contact with the Anabaptists and been in conversation with the local chaplain. As a simple layman he had been misled by the Anabaptists who had advised him to break probation and flee. As proof that his return to the old faith had been genuine and complete, Schneider pointed to his voluntary participation in oral confession, acceptance of penance, and reception of the holy sacrament. A certificate of confession (*Beichtzettel*) from the local priest supported his claim. Yet, even now in prison, feeling weak and ill, Schneider had asked for and received the "holy sacrament" with "great devotion" and without recurrence of lockjaw.[103] In other words, he had recanted and been cured of his spiritual malaise that had prevented his partaking of the body of Christ.

Yet despite his demonstration of contrition and sound spirituality certified by the local priest and a jury of laymen on May 30, 1537, Schneider was held in prison for several more months.[104] Not until August 14, 1537, was he released and then only after a public recantation from pulpits in Brixen and Lüsen and the swearing of an oath (*Urphed*) not to deviate again from the established faith. Whether Schneider kept his promise is unknown. Sources are silent about his subsequent fate. If nothing else, his story illustrates the psychological struggle of a simple layman caught between competing truth claims and loyalties, resulting in an inner conflict rarely captured in either Anabaptist or official documents. Schneider's story demonstrates as well the thin line that separated the martyr from the no-good recanter.

The Death of Georg Fasser and the Emergence of Leonhard Sailer

The attrition rate of itinerant apostles between 1535 and 1538 was such that new ones had to be commissioned. Among these were Georg Fasser (Vasser) and Leonhard Sailer (Lanzenstiel). Both were members of the inner core of Hutter's supporters, and both were chosen with the approval of Amon, who provided continuity of leadership during this difficult time period. Like Amon and Onophrius, Sailer was a Bavarian and belonged to the original group of Anabaptists who in 1529 moved from Krumau to Austerlitz, only to join the exodus to Auspitz in 1531. During the schism of 1533 Sailer joined the supporters of Hutter, and during the dispersion of 1535, as one of the second-rank leaders, he took charge of a group that settled at Drasenhofen, just outside Steinabrunn in Lower Austria.[105] This

settlement proved one of the more successful, growing quickly in membership. With its success Sailer's name began to appear regularly among the
leaders to whom itinerant apostles sent their greetings.[106] Nothing is
known about Sailer's pre-Anabaptist background or how he received the
names Sailer (rope maker) or Lanzenstiel (lance shaft).[107] His literacy suggests some form of education and may explain his choice as assistant to
the illiterate Georg Fasser when Fasser was commissioned as itinerant
apostle.[108]

Fasser hailed from Rattenberg, and it is not entirely clear whether he
and Sailer were commissioned as itinerants to Upper Austria and North
Tyrol or to Hutter's traditional recruiting grounds.[109] Fasser's choice as
itinerant apostle, even though he was illiterate, must have seemed natural
enough. He had been a key supporter of Hutter at the time of Schützinger's
ouster in 1533.[110] His election or appointment by Amon took place at a
general congregational meeting of the scattered flock at Easter, April 16,
1536, in a pine forest between Nicolsburg and Pulgram. The meeting, the
first since Hutter's death and Amon's assumption of sole leadership, included the celebration of the Lord's Supper.[111] After their appointment
Fasser and Sailer returned first to Drasenhofen, presumably to brief Sailer's community and make the appropriate preparation for their mission.
They took their leave on April 25, 1536, but traveled only as far as Windorf in Lower Austria before being arrested.[112] Nine surviving letters
document their prison experience.[113] The first describes the circumstances
of their arrest and provides a fascinating insight into the moral culture of
a public inn.[114] Upon arrival Fasser and Sailer found the local inn filled
with "grossly immoral Sodomites." Seeking quieter quarters in the stable
where they hoped to converse with local contacts, Fasser and Sailer were
assaulted by the Sodomites who, among other things, raped one of the
women in their party.[115] When Fasser and Sailer rebuked the immorality
of the gang with warnings of divine wrath and raised the specter of punishment through the Turks,[116] the Sodomites recognized them as Anabaptists. Fasser and Sailer were taken into custody and placed into stocks. The
following day they were escorted to the nearby market town of Mödling
and imprisoned. Fasser's denunciation of the wickedness of the Sodomites
and his warnings of the approaching judgment apparently left a deep impression on the magistrate and his assistants. The magistrate and the
whole council of Mödling visited the prisoners and with gestures of good
will, sought to reassure them of their own sympathies.[117] They explained,
however, that proper procedure meant that Ferdinand's court had to be
notified, an act Fasser and Sailer could hardly find reassuring. Not surprisingly, they warned the magistrate not to follow the king's order and
remained highly suspicious of their "godless" jailers. They complained

about the common criminals and "blasphemous Sodomites" with whom they shared the prison.[118]

The third letter is of special interest because of its allusion to the schism of 1533, the effects of the dispersion of 1535, and the continuing tension between Hutter's supporters and their former allies.

Behold the severity of God toward those who have fallen and his goodness toward you who have remained. God did not spare the former Israelites who had been the natural olive branches. But they are cut out as an example to the descendants . . . as has also been the case in our time, which we have seen with our own eyes. May it be lamented to the Lord.

While Philipites and Gabrielites were united with us, the Lord's vineyard sprouted. And right when it was supposed to bring good fruit came the mildew and created severe damage. And all the grapes in the vineyard that had tasted the proper sap out of the vine [that is], Christ, were spoiled and brought a bad tasting fruit; yes sour, bitter grapes.

Yes, dear brothers and sisters, we have to let you know a little out of fear for your and our good or example, so that we may learn the fear of God. Where are Philip, Gabriel, and the Austerlitzers? Oh God of heaven, protect your pious and faithful servants and your little children from evil. Truly the saying has been fulfilled on them [may God have mercy], "my shepherds," says the Lord, "have become dumb dogs." They can no longer bark. Oh my God, how have the shepherds of Israel, while they could see, been smitten with such great blindness and been made desolate. Oh, how did they drive so visibly, with their horns into the flock. Yes, they were truly the Egyptian sorcerers, who for a while with their signs imitated the pious servant and misled the people. May God protect and preserve us from such deceitful hearts.

Oh, my God, redeem out of their hands also those who in simplicity are misled through them. Oh, how much blaspheme, disgrace, and shame [have] come to the name of God as a result of it. The unrighteous have viciously slandered and defamed the pious, so that it is to be feared that many of them will never more obtain God's favor. Because they have defamed God's tabernacle, God, the Almighty, will defame them too. But it is known to God, as it is to you, beloved pious children of God, be it far from us, that we rejoice in their terrible fall. We feel and carry heartfelt pain . . . concerning them. We commit it to God, he will reward everyone according to the labor of his hand.[119]

Although this statement is weak on particulars, its allusion to the mildew, to severe damage, to the shepherds who had become dumb dogs, and to Egyptian sorcerers indicates the chasm that opened among brethren in 1533. The allusion to the terrible fall of the Gabrielites and the Philipites presumably referred to the breakup of their communities, their return to private property, and the disappearance of some of their leaders. The statement documented that by early 1536 Hutterites laid claim to represent "the true Christian flock" and to be the sole heirs to the original communitarian Anabaptist vision.[120]

In terms of the more immediate situation, the letter informed Amon that his courier Klaus Müller had been imprisoned as well. Müller was being held in a "stinking hole" of an abandoned house where he "heard neither church bells nor the singing of birds." His contact was limited to the jailor who brought food once a day.[121] The isolation was intended to soften young Müller for instruction, but the priest enlisted for the task proved so incompetent that the magistrate literally ordered him to shut up. Meanwhile Fasser and Sailer managed to breach Müller's isolation using the jailor to carry messages back and forth on a slate.

The continuing correspondence with Amon and the community recorded the rise and fall of the prisoners' hopes and fears. The fourth and the seventh letters requested that Amon improve the letters' contents because they had been written in haste.[122] But if editorializing took place, it most likely occurred in regard to spiritual and moral exhortation rather than any embellishment of historic data.

The seventh and eighth letters, written during the last week of May 1536, conveyed a mood of impending martyrdom.[123] Fasser was ready to part with his most precious possession, a personal face cloth of Jacob Hutter. Sailer was prepared to send his New Testament.[124] The magistrate threatened torture and fire unless they recanted. In short, the prisoners feared that they would never see their brothers and sisters again.[125] Yet, only a week later, they struck a different note.[126] Details are vague, but the magistrate appears to have offered them a way of escape. The prisoners sought Amon's advice. Amon counseled abiding by promises (Gelübde) made. By inference this meant rejecting the offered route of escape,[127] leaving the magistrate on the horns of dilemma. His prisoners belonged to the supporters of Hutter who had been recently executed in Innsbruck. Jeronimus and his two companions had suffered the same fate in Vienna. "According to the king's orders" the magistrate of Mödling was obligated to follow the example of Innsbruck and Vienna, something he wanted to avoid. If the prisoners had any illusions about the pain that awaited them, a visiting merchant lady from Innsbruck gave them a tearful account of Hutter's death.[128] At about the same time a compassionate member of the council of Mödling implored the prisoners to soften their condemnation of all others as non-Christian. It is possible that such a concession was to be part of a face-saving device sought by magistrate and council to permit release. But Fasser and Sailer remained uncompromising, berating Ferdinand as a gruesome murderer. The dismayed councilor took his leave with gentleness (Sanftmut), ordering a good meal for the prisoners. Clerical inquisitors were expected from Vienna within a week, and Fasser and Sailer seemed resigned for the inevitable.

The last surviving letter from prison contained news that several fellow prisoners had been won for Anabaptism—no doubt a cause for rejoicing in Hutterite quarters but a further headache for the magistrate and councilors of Mödling. Of a more personal nature were hints about problems with Sailer's wife which preceded her husband's imprisonment. As early as January 11, 1536, Jeronimus, in a letter to Sailer, alluded to the problem: "Beloved brother Lienhart, I remember well your sorrow [*Truebsal*] which the godless wife has brought you [*auffhuet*]. Be of good cheer and let her go. Since she did not want to follow you, it is to her own detriment. In his own time, the Lord will come and deliver you and the other depressed souls; for time brings roses."[129]

Then in a letter to Sailer Amon reported that he had visited Sailer's wife but had not discussed with her her "falling away." He expressed the hope that Martha would be restored. Upon this, Sailer wrote a separate letter to Martha informing her of employment opportunities at the magistrate's vineyard at Mödling and requesting her presence for two weeks. The penance required of her before being reaccepted he left to Amon.[130] Unfortunately, Hutterite documents did not record how her case was resolved; but she later accompanied Sailer on a mission to South Tyrol, thus suggesting some form of reconciliation.

Not clear are the events that led to the release of Fasser and Sailer. Indirect evidence implies that the magistrate and council of Mödling procrastinated in carrying out the executions. The two remained in prison or under house arrest for several more months, but no correspondence survived from this later period. It is possible that relaxed conditions had made direct access to the prisoners possible, hence there was no need for written communiqués. *The Chronicle* reports simply that after nearly a year Fasser and Sailer were released by "God's special intervention" and that their "consciences [had been] wonderfully preserved from harm." They returned "joyfully" to the community at Drasenhofen where they were "received with great rejoicing as beloved and honored guests."[131] Accordingly, Fasser and Sailer returned to their community during the spring of 1537. Later that year Fasser, who had embarked on another mission, was rearrested at Pöggstall. The magistrate of this market town in Lower Austria proved less sympathetic; Fasser was tortured and beheaded for his faith.[132]

After the loss of Fasser and the death of Onophrius Griesinger one year later, Leonhard Sailer emerged as Amon's most trusted itinerant apostle. In this role Sailer succeeded Onophrius as servant of the Word to the Puster region of South Tyrol. He was active in the territories no later than April 16, 1539.[133] An official description from this period depicted him as being of medium height, wearing a steel gray herald's coat, cutoff white trousers, a black woolen cap, and a bit of a black beard.[134] Sailer arrived in time to harvest the seeds sown by Onophrius and to benefit from the sympathies aroused in the population by Onophrius's martyrdom. However, Innsbruck's pursuit of all Anabaptist leaders coming to the territories continued relentlessly. By September 15, 1539, the authorities had apprehended Mrs. Sailer in Lüsen.[135] Nevertheless, Sailer was successful in making new converts, baptizing them, and sending them in small groups to Moravia.[136] He was back in his community near Steinabrunn when, on that fateful December 6, 1539, 150 members were arrested. Most of the men were marched to Triest as galley slaves. The leadership, including Sailer, escaped.[137] Sailer resumed his mission as itinerant apostle but was back in Schackowitz when, on February 2, 1542, Amon died.[138] As the last itinerant servant of the Word in the Puster, Sailer was well positioned to assume Amon's office. But the leadership transition was not without difficulties. It led to a confrontation with Christoph Gschäll and eventually to the recall of Peter Riedemann.[139] At least since 1540 Sailer had carefully controlled all contact with South Tyrol. Only authorized personnel were allowed on return visits.[140]

Not all the new converts found satisfaction in the congregation of God in Moravia. Lienhart Arnold, baptized by Sailer in April 1540, apparently could not bear the tension among the various groups and returned with wife and children to the Tyrol. The disappointed tailor told his interrogators of "dissension, jealousies, hatreds, backstabbings, and pride among the brethren at Schackowitz."[141] Such stories contributed to the decline of the Puster as the main recruiting ground. Sailer had in effect been the last productive servant of the Word in the lineage of Hutter, Amon, Jeronimus, and Onophrius. By the time Sailer succeeded Amon as servant of the congregation of God in Moravia better times had returned. Already in 1540 half of the Hutterites, a community five hundred strong, had reunited at Schackowitz. In total Hutter's group was said to number one thousand adults.[142] The policy of surviving in Moravia had proven correct, although Hutter and many of his closest advisors did not live to see the day.

The years following the expulsion orders from Moravia in 1535 created incredible hardships for the emerging Hutterites and took their toll in terms of first-generation leadership personnel. In addition to Jacob Hutter the community lost Jeronimus Käls, Wilhelm Griesbacher, Onophrius Griesinger, and Georg Fasser, not to mention a host of secondary leaders including Bastel Glaser, Michael Seifensieder, Leonhard Lochmair, Hans Grünfelder, and others. Of the first-generation senior leaders, only Hans Amon, Christoph Gschäll, and Leonhard Sailer survived beyond the difficult years. Ordinary members had been forced to scatter in smaller groups. Some "wandered about the land in misery and suffering for almost a whole year."[143] Others found temporary quarters as members of larger groups. Onophrius had taken one such group back to Bömisch Krumau; an Oswald (Schuster?) settled with a group at Tischlowitz; Mathes (Legeden) at Rohrbach; Sailer at Drasenhofen; Ulrich Stadler at Austerlitz; Wolf Stroebel at Poppitz. Some members survived at Auspitz, Schackowitz, Rackwitz, Pulgram, Kostel, and Znaim.[144]

And although there were defections, the common hardships molded the group into a more uniform, cohesive community. Whenever possible, Amon sought to gather them for fellowship and for the ministry of the Word. *The Chronicle* recorded under the year 1536:

They came by day and night, walking many miles through wind, rain, snow, and mud to hear the Word of the Lord. Each cared for the other in a brotherly, Christian way, with warmth and tenderness, ready to serve each other in love. They had to make do with small, cramped dwellings, all moving closer together and putting up with many shortages and worries. Yet they wholeheartedly thanked and praised God for it all. They were all kind and patient, as befits the saints who say they are guests and sojourners on earth. They seek a better country, a heavenly one ruled by the Lord Jesus Christ, and that is why they bear with one another patiently, like guests in a foreign land.

Their children were brought up communally, entrusted to God-fearing sisters, who conscientiously took care of them and led them to the Lord through Christian discipline.[145]

Even if this account, filtered through a selective memory, omitted defections, bickerings, and other human foibles, it did describe accurately the hardships overcome by the faithful in Moravia.

But Hutter's supporters did more than survive. They emerged from the terrible blows of 1535 to 1538 with a clear leadership structure, a sense of identity, and purpose of mission as the reinstituted congregation of God. And although much credit must go to Amon who traveled tirelessly up and down the land to encourage and admonish the scattered flock, the martyred leaders, Hutter, Jeronimus, Fasser, Onophrius, and others, provided inspiring models of faithfulness onto death. The stories of their martyrdom, retold in prose and song, and the growing collection of prison epistles, copied, circulated, and read by the community as their collective story, proved instrumental in building consensus and a sense of identity. Foundational was the conviction that they, as a group, unlike the Philipites, Gabrielites, and Austerlitzers, represented the faithful remnant that had retained the apostolic ideal of community of goods, a practice considered an essential mark of the true apostolic church.

When the situation began to ease, the survivors regrouped in larger collectives. As early as Easter 1536, the Hutterites had met under the open sky as a general congregation to celebrate the Lord's Supper and fill the gaps of leaders lost.[146] And even though there were further losses, the Hutterites were never left leaderless. They emerged from the very difficult period more cohesive and resilient. By 1540 they had resumed the community project that had to be abandoned in 1535 at Schackowitz.

Chapter Twelve

The Fate of the Philipites
and the Gabrielites

This final chapter brings closure to the narrative of the Philipites, the Gabrielites, and the Austerlitzers, whose demise as distinct entities eventually left the Hutterites sole heirs to the early Anabaptist experiments with community of goods. With hindsight it seems obvious that the decision of these communities to obey the orders and leave Moravia in 1535 marked the beginning of the end. But the demise at first did not seem inevitable. Indeed, Hutterite survival appeared more precarious, for the core of Hutter's supporters could not return to their homeland, the Tyrol, because there, too, suppression reigned. Hutter's own return ended in martyrdom. His flock scattered over Moravia, Bohemia, and Lower Austria but managed to survive by the grace of God and the protection of aristocratic patrons willing to ignore Ferdinand's explicit orders. Amon did his share to shepherd the flock and keep it together.

The impact of the "first major persecution in Moravia"[1] on the other communities was initially similar. The Philipites were forced to abandon their settlement in Auspitz, the Gabrielites Rossitz, and the Austerlitz Brethren their dwellings in Austerlitz. Like the Hutterites the Brethren at Austerlitz lost their chief leader, Jacob Wiedemann, and other leaders as well. In search of new settlement opportunities some Austerlitzers moved as far east as Volynia and Ruthenia. The Gabrielites drifted back to Silesia or relocated with Gabriel in territory straddling the border of Silesia and Poland. Philipites trekked back to the "Reich," Swabia, the Palatinate, and the Rhineland. Their fate is best told first.

The Philipites

Returning to the Reich

At the time of their expulsion from Auspitz the Philipite community numbered approximately four hundred, not counting children. Like the Hutterites, the whole community at first took up temporary quarters on the desolate heath of the Liechtenstein domain.[2] Because the Philipites left no record of their experience, a Hutterite account will have to suffice.

[The Philipites] reached the hill near Lassling, singing joyfully, and set up camp there. Their leading servant, Philip [Plener or Blauärmel] and Blasius [Kuhn], mounted horses and set off from there, pretending to search for a place of shelter for their people. Not long after, a message came back that everyone should look out for himself and find a place to live as best as he could. These two are still searching to this day and have found no place. So they were like false shepherds and hirelings, who allowed the flock to be scattered among the wolves. Their judgment on Jakob Hutter, recorded earlier, now proved to be true for themselves. Their flock has indeed been scattered, and many have come to ruin. Some cannot return even today. In the beginning they surely followed God's command to leave country and family, but they looked back and loved the world again.

They separated into small groups, some to go to Würtemberg and others to the Palatinate, but a large group was captured at Wegscheid and at Ilzstadt near Passau. About sixty people in all were taken to Passau, and some were in prison there for up to five years suffering acute hunger and severe treatment besides. Many of them died while in prison. A few returned to the congregation of God after their release, but the rest went to utter ruin, their hearts perverted and bent on doing wrong.[3]

The negative view of Philip Plener as a leader, expressed in Hutterite sources, seems one-sided at best.[4] Philip, who outlived Hutter, gave a kinder assessment of his rival's fate, and his efforts to seek alternative places for settlement appear to have been genuine. Unable to find such alternatives in Moravia,[5] Philip and his associate, Blasius Kuhn, extended their search to the original home territories in Swabia and the Rhineland where persecution had tapered off. As discussed in Chapter 4, before leaving Moravia Philip and Blasius divided their people into smaller groups, appointed group leaders, and spread the children among them. One such group, led by Michael Schneider, had been arrested at Passau. Statements of the prisoners indicate that they were in search of a place where they could practice their faith and support themselves through honest labor.

It seems that Philip and Blasius themselves led groups through Swabia to the Rhineland or the Palatinate. Evidence indicates that former Philipites resettled in the Worms and Strasbourg areas.[6] Adam Schlegel accompanied a group to the Neckar valley near Heilbronn and Eppingen (see

Chapter 4). Other Philipites resettled near Ulm and in the Esslingen area.[7] Among their leaders were Hans Gentner and the veteran Burkhardt Braun of Ofen, both of whom later joined the Hutterites; others joined the Swiss.

The evident number of Philipites returning to Württemberg territory suggests that it was most likely a Philipite group that in the summer of 1535 requested official permission from Duke Ulrich of Württemberg to settle in his territories. The supplicants promised to be loyal subjects with body and goods.[8] The request was premised on the notion that Ulrich, himself a former fugitive and sworn enemy of Ferdinand I, might be sympathetic to refugees from Hapsburg persecution. But the supplication came at an inopportune time. Under the spell of events in Münster, Ulrich and his advisors on June 18, 1535, issued a decree against the Anabaptists.[9] Nevertheless, returning supplicants continued to enter Württemberg territory with appeals that their properties be restored to them.[10] Eventually Ulrich and his advisors learned to distinguish between Münsterites and those returning from Moravia. The territorial order of 1536 instructed local magistrates to question Anabaptists "whether they had been in Münster or Moravia and what had been their reason for moving there." It was still feared that these former "Swabians, Franconians, Bavarians, Hessians, Saxons, and other Upper Germans," who had first "run to Moravia" and were now returning, would create unrest.[11] Of course, nothing was further from the truth. The returning travelers longed only for a quiet place of refuge where they might earn a living peacefully without having to compromise their religious convictions. The point here is that official documents support the view that Anabaptists returned to Württemberg from Moravia in considerable numbers during 1535–36.

Philip and Blasius apparently continued to look for resettlement opportunities into the summer of 1536. The search extended into the Rhineland,[12] with a planned rendezvous of leaders in Strasbourg during the fall of 1536. The Inn to the Plow in the gardeners' quarters had been designated as the meeting place, but something went wrong. Adam Schlegel and three companions, including Hans from Heilbronn, were arrested when they arrived in Strasbourg.[13] Their statements of August 23, 1536, indicate that Philip and Blasius were traveling with part of the community's treasury.[14] The money was to be used for the purchase or rent of land. The purpose of the meeting in Strasbourg was for Philip and Blasius to give an account.[15] Because of the arrests and because Schlegel was still in prison four months later, nothing came of the rendezvous.[16] But Blasius had kept his promise and arrived in Strasbourg a few days before the arrests.[17] Whether Philip had done the same is unknown. He certainly knew Strasbourg well enough to note danger and avoid arrest. Indirect evidence suggests that he remained in touch with members of his community well into 1536 and perhaps beyond; apprised of Hutter's martyrdom, he had expressed his sympathy and admiration for Hutter's steadfastness, which was relayed to Hutter's supporters. Philip's sympathy was most likely communicated to the Hutterites by Blasius or by Hans Gentner. Evidence indicates that Blasius was back in Moravia during 1537–38, participating in discussions between former Philipites and Hutterites. Gentner, a junior leader among the Philipites, joined the Hutterites at about this time. Peter Riedemann, who joined the Hutterites in 1537 and was party to discussions with Philipites, claimed in a letter written that year that God had "exposed Philip as a thief."[18] From the historian's perspective it is unfortunate that Riedemann failed to elaborate on "how one thing led to another." He had obviously taken the Hutterite point of view, which, as early as May 1536, implied that Philip had been delinquent in his duties as leader and interpreted his subsequent disappearance with part of the community's treasury as deliberate thievery.[19] But were such accusations justified? The evidence does not permit an objective answer. It should be noted, however, that Hans Gentner, a Philipite leader turned Hutterite, was accused of the same crime by Philipites when he shifted his allegiance and apparently transferred some of their funds to the Hutterites. As for Philip, the only conclusion possible is that he disappeared with part of the community's treasury sometime between the abortive rendezvous in 1536 and mid 1537. Whether he absconded deliberately or was a victim of foul play is unknown. Blasius Kuhn, meanwhile, remained a leader among former Philipites scattered from Moravia[20] to the Rhineland,[21] the Palatinate, Württemberg, and Upper Austria.[22]

A group of Philipites returned to the area of Heilbronn, a traditional recruiting ground for Philipites, with Philip himself active in nearby Fürfeld during 1528. Before traveling to Strasbourg for his rendezvous with Philip in the summer of 1536 Schlegel had met with a group of thirty in a forest near Heilbronn. This was presumably the same group that caused repeated concern in Heilbronn between April 20, 1536, and December 17, 1539. During that time period the council warned its citizens and subjects repeatedly not to harbor Anabaptists. On June 9, 1537, Hans Schreiner (Gentner?) from Gmünd, a leader of the group, had been driven out of the gates.[23] Yet two years later a group of forty and their leader, who lodged at the Red Bridge, had to be driven out again.[24] These Anabaptists were, no doubt, the Philipites visited by Peter Riedemann on his way to Hesse in 1539–40.[25] At about this time or shortly thereafter these Philipites converted into Swiss Brethren, to whom they bequeathed their legacy of song (see Chapter 4). From the Hutterite perspective the transformation into Swiss Brethren was further proof that the Philipite leaders had been false shepherds who led their people not only out of Moravia but also back into private property. But not all Philipites followed this route. Hans Gentner, one of their leaders in the Neckar region, returned to Moravia and with others joined the Hutterites.

Becoming Swiss

At this point a digression seems in order regarding the origin and meaning of the label *Swiss Brethren*. John Horsch, a linchpin in the twentieth-century renaissance of Anabaptist studies, provided a simple explanation. Writing about events that occurred in St. Gall, he noted that "regular attendants . . . [at] Bible meetings called each other brothers and were commonly known as Brethren." Since these brethren were primarily Swiss and the meetings took place on Swiss soil, the label *Swiss Brethren* seemed justified.[26] Harold Bender provided this nomenclature with specific content, wider circulation, and respectability through his groundbreaking work on Conrad Grebel, subtitled "Founder of the Swiss Brethren, Sometimes Called Anabaptists." If taken seriously, Bender's title could suggest that the Swiss Brethren designation took priority over that of Anabaptist. Bender justified the use of the title with reference to the songbook of 1564 which contained songs "composed by the Swiss Brethren in the Passau prison [Schloss]." Although this seemed to be the first use of the label *Swiss* by the group itself, Bender noted that the "originators of this designation," the Hutterian Brethren, had "very early referred to the noncommunal Anabaptists of Switzerland, South Germany, and the Rhineland, who were all of Swiss origin, as Swiss Brethren."[27] This in turn justified Bender's retroactive designation of Grebel as the founder of Swiss Brethren, thus strengthening his contention that the Swiss Anabaptists, although stressing mutual aid, never adopted the Hutterite practice of community of goods. Bender's usage entered the scholarly discourse as specifying a particular Anabaptist orientation, "all who were direct successors of Conrad Grebel . . . and Sattler" whether in Swabia, Alsace, or Moravia.[28] However, James Stayer's reexamination of early Swiss Anabaptist attitudes on community of goods and my own work on the early church orders (see Chapter 2) suggest that Bender's label *Swiss* may have to be qualified.

The label appeared only in the late 1530s or early 1540s,[29] after the expulsions of 1535 and the return of Philipites from Moravia to Swabia, the Palatinate, and Rhineland. As noted in Chapter 4, the Passau songs, described in 1564 as the work of "Swiss Brethren," were largely composed by Philipites. Hutterites first used the label *Swiss* in 1542 in conjunction with former Philipites, who had returned to the Kreutznach area in the Palatinate and there "united with the Swiss."[30] The uniting of Philipites with Swiss in 1542 suggests that the Hutterites considered them distinct groups prior to that date. Not clear is what this uniting meant other than acceptance of private property. Some Philipites who left Moravia with those "who united with the Swiss" must have been uncomfortable with the transformation into Swiss and returned to Moravia where they joined the Hutterites. Among them was the veteran Burkhardt Bämerly (Braun) of Ofen, a servant of the Word among the Philipites, who by 1542 had joined the Hutterites.[31]

That the label as used by the Hutterites was not a badge of honor may be inferred from a list of Swiss shortcomings recorded in *The Chronicle* under the date 1543. The list was occasioned by the conversion of Hans Klopffer from the Swiss to the Hutterites. Klopffer, a Swiss leader from Feuerbach near Stuttgart,[32] cited the following reasons for breaking away from the Swiss: (1) the Swiss had left the true Christian community; (2) they paid war taxes; (3) several of their elders and teachers had questioned their own calling and left their offices (*ämpter*) but then resumed them and thereby made a mockery of the Lord's work; (4) the Swiss had become lax in discipline, permitting failings to be settled privately. This had led to the inclusion of persons with unclean hearts and minds.[33]

Of the allegations by Klopffer the one about some Swiss leaders laying down their offices but then resuming them is most interesting. The allegation appears to be confirmed by an experience reported by Peter Riedemann.[34] During a visit with brethren in Lauingen near Ulm in 1539–40 Riedemann found congregational life in total disarray. The local leaders had been challenged by a charismatic itinerant apostle to prove that their calling was of God and not of men. Unsure, they laid down their offices and with it admonition so that discipline had practically ceased.[35] At about this time, in the early 1540s, the designation *Swiss Brethren* appeared also in letters by Pilgram Marpeck,[36] and by the 1550s it had found its way into official documents.[37]

As best as can be determined the label *Swiss Brethren* was in use by the late 1530s as an inter-Anabaptist distinction. When used by Hutterites it denoted disobedience to apostolic practice of community of goods and a lack of clearly defined leadership structure and of discipline. Not clear is whether the negative baggage loaded onto the Swiss label by Hutterites grew out of the Moravian experience with Swiss communities or whether anti-Philipite feelings, reaching back to the schism of 1533, prejudiced the Hutterite view of the Swiss when they united with Philipites. In other words, was Hutterite prejudice against Philipites foisted on the Swiss? What is clear is that the Swiss label was not confined to those from the Swiss geographic region. Indeed, statistics indicate that by the late 1540s the majority of the so-called Swiss were Swabians, Rhinelanders, or Palatiners.[38] Without question Philipites-turned-Swiss reinforced the growing numeric strength of the Swiss in these regions. That strength helps explain why so many Swiss Brethren events—colloquia, conferences, and disputations—from the 1540s on took place outside Switzerland, in the Alsace, the Rhineland, and the Palatinate.[39] Above all, Philipites becoming Swiss explains why the first songbook of the Swiss Brethren contained the songs of the Philipite prisoners at Passau and why two songs extolling the virtues of community of goods found in the 1564 collection disappeared from subsequent editions (see Chapter 4). Hutterites, on the other hand, acclaimed the very practice of community of goods as the mark of the true congregation of God. It was a practice possible only for those who after 1538–39 were living once again in communities in Moravia. It proved impossible for those living in Diaspora.

The Gabrielites

Return to Silesia?

The fate of Gabrielites is difficult to trace. By all accounts the Gabrielites had formed one of the largest communities in Moravia with a majority of its members coming from Silesia. Since Gabriel's treatise dated 1544 addressed brethren in Moravia and Silesia, it may be assumed that his community had in part returned to Silesia by that date[40] while others survived in or had returned to Moravia. The latter is confirmed by evidence that small groups had found shelter at Butschowitz (Pudespitz), Jarochniewitz, Bisenz, and Wratzow and by the suggestion that Gabrielites participated in discussions with the indigenous Unitas Fratrum in 1543 near Auspitz and in 1559 at Eibenschitz and Znaim.[41] Until 1565, when they united with the Hutterites, Gabrielites also lived at Kreutz, west of Göding (Hudonia).[42] Nevertheless, the expulsion order of 1535 ultimately had a devastating impact on the Gabrielites as a community. Like the other communities the Gabrielites were forced to abandon their main settlement at Rossitz. Subdivided into smaller groups, some preferred internal migration, moving east in Moravia. Others returned to Silesia or sought settlement opportunities in Poland.[43]

In May 1535 an unidentified group of "Brothers and Sisters, baptized in Jesus Christ and persecuted by King Ferdinand because of their faith," sent a supplication to Duke Albrecht of Hohenzollern for asylum in the duchy of Prussia.[44] The group included a statement of faith which distinguished clearly between Old and New Testaments. From the Law of Moses they accepted the commandments and the notion of a coming judgment. They considered little children clean and without sin and hence not in need of baptism. They celebrated the Lord's Supper in both kinds but rejected the bodily presence of Christ. Christ would remain bodily in heaven at the right hand of God until the final judgment. The group leaders had been chosen on the basis of virtue (*tuglich*) and learnedness and appointed with the laying on of hands. These leaders exercised discipline in the name of the community. Unregenerate sinners were excommunicated. This group held further that temporal authorities had the right to punish evildoers but should have no say in the congregation of God. Nothing was said about community of goods, the oath, or other Anabaptist distinctives.

After consulting his prelates and preachers, Duke Albrecht of Hohenzollern replied on June 28, 1535. The theologians considered the denial of original sin, the rejection of pedobaptism, and the views on the Lord's Supper and on the Scriptures to be in error. Accordingly, the duke's reply admonished the supplicants to leave their errors; perhaps Ferdinand would then tolerate them in Moravia. Duke Albrecht would not condone their erroneous teaching and therefore would not provide them with a place of refuge in his duchy.[45]

The petition to the duke had been signed in the presence of Lord Tschernacher of Schertlin in the domain of the lords of Liechtenstein. As noted earlier, the expulsion orders forced Hutterites and Philipites to camp in the open on the Liechtenstein domain. Other groups were presumably forced to do the same. The statement of faith in the petition to Duke Albrecht did not permit easy identification of the group involved. It could have been a statement by sword bearers, Gabrielites, Philipites, Swiss, or Austerlitz Brethren. All communities were under extreme pressure at the time to disband and leave Moravia. The Hutterites decided to scatter and await better times in Moravia, while the Philipites began the trek back to home territories. Within a year the Austerlitz community lost its main leader, Jacob Wiedemann, and others through execution in Vienna.[46] Two of its secondary leaders, Ulrich Stadler and Leonhard Lochmair,[47] led a group to "Little Poland," seeking settlement opportunities as far east as the borders of Ruthenia and Volynia. It was near Krasnik, southwest of Lublin, where Stadler wrote "Of the true Community [*Gemeinschaft*] of the Saints."[48] But conditions in the east proved equally difficult; by 1537–38 Stadler and a small remnant including Lochmair had drifted back to Moravia, eventually uniting with the followers of Hutter.[49] In 1538 Lochmair accompanied Onophrius Griesinger on the fateful mission to South Tyrol (Chapter 11). A remnant of Austerlitz Brethren stayed in Moravia for some time.

Another group of Anabaptists, in all probability the same group that had petitioned Duke Albrecht in May, moved to Prussia in the summer of

1535. Their itinerary supports the suggestion that they were Gabrielites. About two hundred of them moved first to Silesia and from there diagonally through Poland toward Thorn (Torun), then via Graudentz (Grudziadz) to Marienwerder (Kwidzyn) and on to Garnsee in Prussian territory.[50] There they were investigated by Bishop Speratus of Pomesen, who sent the reformers John Briesmann and John Poliander to examine the teachings and practices of the new arrivals. On November 13, 1535, the two theologians reported that the group in question was willing to accept the teachings of the territorial church. It was soon revealed, however, that this was not entirely correct. Fearing expulsion, the group had promised outward conformity. Some were still in the area as late as November 30, 1535, when new discussions opened.[51] Their situation was desperate. A retreat back through Poland, with no place to go, was out of the question. Winter was approaching, and Sigismund I, king of Poland, alarmed by the number of heretics entering his territories, had warned his subjects on September 27, 1535, not to make any agreements with them and to refuse them "water and fire."[52]

The ultimate fate of the refugees in the duchy of Prussia is unknown, but some must have remained. It has been suggested that they were of South German or Swiss descent and that they became the first "German Mennonites" in Prussia and neighboring Polish territories.[53] The point here is that these Anabaptists came from Moravia and entered Poland through Silesia, which suggests a Gabrielite connection.[54] But whatever the affiliation of these former "Moravians," they were likely encouraged by rumors of Duke Albrecht's tolerant policy. That such rumors were not entirely unfounded may be surmised from the fact that the spiritualist Christian Entfelder, a former leader of brethren at Eibenschitz, assumed the position of councilor to Duke Albrecht in 1536. William Graphaeus had preceded Entfelder, and Gerhard Westerburg followed suit in 1542. Thus two former Anabaptists and a sacramentist came into positions of influence at the Prussian court. In the same year, 1536, Dutch settlers turned to Entfelder for advice about Anabaptists in their midst.[55] Entfelder's reply is unrecorded, but it is generally assumed that he was partly responsible for the moderate policy that permitted the settlement of the first Dutch or Frisian Anabaptists in the area.[56] As for Gabrielites returning to Silesia, Ferdinand warned the council of Breslau as early as June 6, 1535, not to accept them.[57] But despite his orders the next year saw a dramatic increase of Anabaptists in Silesia,[58] among them the veteran David of Schweidnitz, alias the "Bohemian." Hutter had expelled David from the Auspitz community in 1532 because of his role in the Zaunring affair. David subsequently joined the Gabrielites and after the expulsion of 1535 returned to Silesia. During the winter of 1535–36 he preached daily in

houses at Weizenrode, a village near his home town of Schweidnitz.[59] The
local cleric Peter Knott, himself a Schwenckfeldian, permitted a regular
Anabaptist congregation to develop. When these developments came to
the attention of Ferdinand's governor for the Schweidnitz-Jauer territory
in early June 1536, David was arrested,[60] but the sources are silent about
his trial or sentence. He was rearrested at Ottmachau in the fall of 1536.
On September 16, 1536, Ottmachau informed the council of Schweidnitz
of David's previous activity in Weizenrode. Only then did the council
make inquiries with the local pastor, asking him to submit a list of Anabaptist suspects and their sympathizers. Knott obliged only reluctantly,
asking for leniency on behalf of the suspects.[61] Unfortunately, nothing further is known about either the fate of the Anabaptists at Weizenrode or of
their leader, David.[62] It is possible that he found refuge with one of the
local lords who continued to flout Ferdinand's orders.[63]

One of the lords so inclined was Johann von Pernstein, the nominal lord
of the county of Glatz from 1537 on.[64] A Lutheran of sorts, Pernstein tolerated Schwenckfeldians and Anabaptists, an action that earned him the
reproach of Philip Melanchthon. The town of Habelschwerdt in Glatz
County had practically fallen into the hands of Schwenckfeldians and
Anabaptists. Located near the Neisse and Weistritz Rivers, where adult
baptisms by immersion had allegedly taken place as early as 1528, Habelschwerdt from 1535 on had become a haven for returning Gabrielites. The
returning groups and their supporters came to a mutually accommodating
arrangement with local Schwenckfeldians to whom they left the parish
church. The Gabrielites had no need of the church building because they
considered the whole town to be a temple and practiced mutual sharing.[65]
They met in houses, offered common prayers, chose preachers and teachers from their midst, and apparently continued to baptize adults. In the
1540s the group held discussions on Christology and eschatology with the
Schwenckfeldian leaders, Fabian Eckel and John Werner.[66] It is possible
that Gabriel Ascherham himself participated in these discussions and was
influenced by them. As suggested below, his treatise from this period indicates Schwenckfeldian influences.

Gaps in the sources make a reconstruction of Gabriel's movements after the expulsion orders of 1535 difficult. It seems that he visited his home
town of Nuremberg in late 1535 because on December 6, 1535, the council of Nuremberg expelled "the son of the Kürschner, Paul Ascherman." If
this was indeed Gabriel Ascherham,[67] then he must have returned briefly
to his home, perhaps for family reasons. By 1540 Gabriel resided in or
near the town of Fraustadt (Wschowa) on the Silesian-Polish border,
where he died in 1545. It was here that he reflected on and wrote a history

of Anabaptist beginnings in Moravia as well as his sole surviving treatise, *On the Distinction between Divine and Human Wisdom.* Curiously, "Wschowa would eventually become a center of the immersionist Polish Brethren."[68]

Toward "Silesian" Spirituality

Gabriel's *Distinction* contained statements on the Lord's Supper and baptism. An analysis of these statements, which at one time may have circulated separately among his followers, has been postponed until this chapter because they demonstrate Gabriel's evolution in the direction of what may be, for lack of a better term, labeled *Silesian* spiritualism. Gabriel's reinterpretation of church ceremonies was at least partly shaped by the geographic relocation of his community. At the time of writing Gabriel found himself off center stage on the Silesian-Polish border while his straggling sheep in Moravia were being enticed to join the revived Hutterite fold. The continuing conflict with Hutter's heirs had led to a certain fatigue and disillusionment registered in his criticism of the numerous schisms and of the church hoppers who "first look for truth in this group, then for a while in the next." They seemed forever in search of perfection: "my, this people leads a pure life. I must join them. Yes, we know that we are the right ones because our brothers have witnessed to it with their blood."[69] He recorded mood swings among the would-be community builders, "today happy and tomorrow sad . . . today assured and tomorrow in doubt." According to his own analysis, this manifest insecurity had spiritual roots; these unstable seekers had not anchored their faith in true knowledge of God.

For a while they are sword bearers [*Schwertler*], soon after Austerlitzer, shortly thereafter Swiss, next Hutterite. And there are great divisions and disunity, not only between the different groups, one people against the other; but each group [*Volk*] in itself is not united. One finds a variety of understanding and interpretation of Scripture among them so that it is often ridiculous to hear. There is no end to quarreling and disunity among them. Soon they run together and are glad that God has given them such peace and unity. Shortly after that peace is at an end, and they run from each other. Then follows such chiding and slander against each other that it is shameful to hear. Yes, they act in such a way that those who run away daily spread their slanders. If this be a people of God, then I must say that I cannot believe that God should heap such shame on his [own] name.

Neither do I believe that God permits the devil to have so much power for so much shame and depravity are to be found among them. Yet they claim all along to be spiritual and "the Lord is always with us," even though the devil has his game so openly and obviously [just] as he likes. Still they insist on being a people of God, even though the real basis [*Grund*] of truth is blasphemed by no one more than them. For it has come to the point that those who know them speak little good of them. But it is shrugged off with "the Lord be praised that all matter of evil is spoken against us for his sake."

Oh, you hypocrites, it does not happen to you for the Lord's sake but because of your adopted monkish sects and because of the shameful depravity found daily among you.[70]

It would be easy to write this indictment off as a case of sour grapes, bemoaning losses to the rival Hutterite community, were it not for Gabriel's fifteen years of experience as a key leader in early Moravian Anabaptism. Moreover, his observation about the many changes of affiliation in the early communities tends to be confirmed in other sources, including *The Chronicle*. It has a ring of historicity also because it has been a common observation that dissenters do not, overnight, good conformists make, even when ideology demands it. First-generation participants in the communitarian experiment confirmed the rule rather than the exception. The assets of these community builders included not only brotherly love and commitment to reinstitute the New Testament church, but also strong dissenting opinions, a dislike of the established order, strong anticlerical feelings, and a perception that the rest of society was depraved. Shaping a consensus and forming cohesive new communities out of uprooted fugitives would have been a most formidable task even under the best conditions at the best of times. Not surprisingly then, the early history of Anabaptist communitarianism is a story of sacrificial commitment and joy in newfound brotherhood as well as a story of disappointments, failings, quarrels, schisms, disillusionments, and tragic casualties. And although participants tended to explain, justify, or rationalize motivation, action, and behavior in religious terms, a variety of nonreligious factors obviously impinged and intruded on the attempts to reinstitute the apostolic church. It seems hardly accidental, for instance, that the initial division reflected geographic origins. The inner core of Hutter's supporters consisted of Pusterers from South Tyrol; Philipites came primarily from the Palatinate, Rhine, and Neckar valleys, and Gabrielites from Silesia. Diverse backgrounds, dialects, and customs were, no doubt, factors in the division and intergroup rivalries. Strong leadership personalities were another. Most groups assumed or were known by the name of their leader. The psychological cost of being hounded, uprooted, driven from family and friends, sojourning as pilgrims and strangers in a foreign land, must have been immense. Merging with those speaking the same dialect from the same region was natural.

Taking into account the difficulties the early divisions, the success and survival of the Hutterites become all the more amazing. But not all com-

munities evolved in a Hutterite direction. Gabriel moved in the direction
of spiritualism as his reflections on the Lord's Supper and on baptism
indicate.

The Lord's Supper

In his discussion on the Lord's Supper Gabriel distanced himself from
views held by the Hutterites and other Anabaptists as well. He criticized
as frivolous (*leichtsinnig*) the purely commemorative view that participants consumed nothing more than ordinary bread and natural wine. His
declared intentions were to correct this misunderstanding of a "main article of faith" and to bring about a renewal of the external ceremony (*äus-
serliche Erneuerung*).[71] The results baffled former allies and defy easy classification. Hutterites charged that he reinstituted a new form of mass and
idolatry. At issue was the use of a special ceremonial chalice. According to
the Hutterites, who used ordinary utensils and wooden cups without
pomp and ceremony, Gabriel and his people "observed the remembrance
of Christ" in a "false outward show." One of the elders would carry the
"cup in papist fashion, with a cloth wrapped around it as if it were holy
and could not be touched with bare hands, and gave it to each one to drink
from. He [Gabriel] even asserted that this bread and wine were spiritual
food and drink."[72] This accusation found support in Gabriel's insistence
on a solemn celebration, which modern scholars have viewed more kindly
than did the Hutterites. Rudolf Wolkan believed that Gabriel's views foreshadowed those of enlightened Catholics, whereas Wilhelm Wiswedel
suggested that they represented "brotherly warnings" or correctives
against subjectivist and profane tendencies in Anabaptism.[73] For a historic
understanding, Jarold Zeman's observation of parallels to the "basic
premises of Silesian spiritualism" is most useful.[74] These parallels are
worth testing because of evidence that Gabriel and part of his community
proved open to dialogue with other reform orientations and therefore also
more susceptible to influences from them. Indeed, Gabriel's views on the
Lord's Supper are better understood against the background of the teachings of his indigenous neighbors, the Schwenckfeldians in Silesia and
Czech Brethren in Moravia.[75]

Gabriel's understanding of the Lord's Supper was derived primarily
from John 6:35–36, which describes Christ as the "living bread come
from Heaven"—the Word that had taken flesh from Mary which alone
could nourish "the soul that searched after it in faith."[76] In John 6:51
when Christ spoke of "my flesh" as "the bread that I shall give for the life
of the world," he referred to his creaturely (natural) body, which was to
suffer and die on the cross. But this did not mean that he offered his crea-

turely, material body as food. True, in John 6:55 Christ stated "my flesh is food indeed, and my blood is drink indeed," but this needed to be interpreted in the light of John 6:63, where Jesus made it clear that "flesh is of no avail" but the "words that I have spoken to you are spirit and life."

The interpretation of the entire discourse in John 6 through verse 63 provoked the rhetorical question, "What then do the pope and Luther want to eat and drink, the dead flesh and blood, of which Christ says it is of no avail? Or do they want to eat and drink the transfigured [*verklärte*] flesh and blood which ascended into heaven?"[77] According to Gabriel it could be neither, for when Jesus spoke to his disciples of his body, he had spoken in the present, not the future tense. He was still alive, had not yet died or ascended into heaven. The reference to his body at the Last Supper was, therefore, neither to the dead nor the glorified body but instead to a third body. It was a reference to Christ's true followers who, as members of his body, in communion with their head and with each other, constituted an extension of his presence on earth.[78] In this context, Gabriel understood the words of institution (1 Corinthians 10:15–17) in a typically Anabaptist fashion as an invitation to share Christ's life in community with fellow believers. By way of analogy he argued that just as humans share the same nature because they share the same natural food, so those who by faith feast on the spiritual food, the Word of God, and drink of "the nature, strength and life" of Christ, share a common spiritual nature with each other through Christ. Those outside Christ share only in a common human nature, the nature of the first Adam. Only those who are one with the "second Adam, that is, in Christ, the promised seed of Abraham, separated from the world," share a second divine nature.[79] Partakers of Christ's nature, transformed into his image, constituted the spiritual heirs of Abraham. The Lord's Supper, as a symbolic celebration of participation in Christ's divine nature, was therefore not an ordinary meal,[80] but rather a special ceremony indicative of the "mystery [*Geheimnis*], how and why they have been separated [*ausgesondert*] from the world, and that they had become the beneficiaries of salvation through Christ's death."[81] It followed that the celebration of the Lord's Supper was for believers with spiritual understanding only. The elements were not ordinary bread or wine but a "sanctified and separated bread and wine" symbolic of the participants' separation from the world. The Lord's Supper was an extraordinary meal, a symbolic community event. To eat the symbolic elements as if they constituted just another meal would mean eating to one's condemnation.[82]

Drinking from the cup symbolizes a separated fellowship [*Gemeinschaft*] of the blood of Christ. And through an understanding in the Holy Ghost [they become] fellows [*Mitgenossen*] of the nature of the flesh of Christ. And therefore the understanding [*Verstand*] [of the mystery], which is the sacrament, sanctifies the bread and also wine, which are given to a grateful, praiseworthy [*löblichen*] remembrance of the death of Christ. And for this reason this bread and wine are holy and should be taken with high and great reverence [*Würdigkeit*], just as the children of Israel eat the Easter Lamb. Herewith Christ gave his disciples to understand that they were one bread and body with him; and should henceforth no longer celebrate . . . the blood of the Lamb [Passover] but his blood . . . namely the nature, power, and strength of [the risen Christ].[83]

Gabriel warned against those who were eating and drinking "without understanding the mystery of Christ," assuming that the Holy Spirit had revealed to them that they were eating common bread and drinking common wine. He summarized the mystery of Christ's presence as, "Not the body in the bread, but the bread in the body and not the blood in the wine, but the wine in the blood. As Paul says, 'the drink of the New Testament is in my blood.' "[84] It was the living Christ in his members which constituted the real presence. The community received its legitimacy not through a ceremony, but the ceremony received its validation and sacredness from the spiritually reborn gathered in community.[85] When all was said and done, Gabriel's understanding of the Lord's Supper was typically Anabaptist.

What, then, of the Hutterite charge that he instituted a new mass? An analysis of his surviving statement does not support such a view. Yet his criticism of those who treated the symbolic elements as ordinary bread and wine suggests that he favored a more solemn celebration. Moreover, his reflections have spiritualist overtones. Besides indicating a preference for Johannine texts, also favored by spiritualists, Gabriel spoke of "sacrament; knowledge of the mystery of Christ [*Erkenntnis des Geheimnis Christi*];[86] the hidden speech [*verborgene Rede*] of John 6" and of "understanding the mystery [*Verstand der Geheimnis*] of Christ's presence in his church [*Kirche*]."[87] Such terminology was foreign to the Hutterites. Coupled with a ceremonial reverence unfamiliar to them, Gabriel's teachings gave rise to the charge of a new idolatry even though his emphasis on the separated community was still typically Anabaptist. What was different was his spiritualist language of separateness with its emphasis on the mysterious presence of Christ through mystical union with his members.

Peculiar to Anabaptist literature and more akin to spiritualism was Gabriel's use of Old Testament typology to illustrate the separateness of the faithful. Old Testament priests, who alone ate from the shewbread and offerings in the temple, symbolized for him the community gathered around the table in communion with their Lord. Replacing the Passover with the Lord's Supper marked the "initiation [*Einleitung*] from the Old into the New Testament." The distinction between Old and New Testaments involved a differentiation between the physical and spiritual heirs of Abraham, between "servants and children of promise." The latter were endowed with a special spiritual understanding and with the promise of eternal inheritance.

Even if the language was obtuse, the spiritualist tendencies were easy enough to discern. The material elements, bread and wine, provided temporal nourishment only. Spiritual nourishment came only through the heavenly manna, through spiritual communion with Christ in faith.

Baptism

Gabriel's view on baptism was based on a similar distinction between an inner spiritual event and an outer symbol of it. He was critical of those who were preoccupied with the external symbol and thought that they had "need of nothing else" so long as "belief, baptism, community of goods [Gemeinschaft], and a separated life had been preached." Yet "they had never tasted the real thing. The Gospel through which [true] faith comes had never been preached to them." He accused these brethren of being too quick with water, baptizing seekers as soon as they agreed to the order as outlined in the Great Commission. But water baptism was not of the same import as the baptism of the Spirit. Gabriel cited the baptisms by Philip in Samaria (Acts 8 : 12 – 18) and by Apollos in Ephesus (Acts 18 : 24 and 19 : 1 – 7) as examples that water baptism and the gift of the Holy Spirit were separate events. In the first instance Philip had baptized Samaritans in the name of Jesus, but they received the Holy Spirit only after Peter and John had been dispatched to "pray for them that they might receive [it]." The Ephesians had been baptized by Apollos into "John's baptism" but had "not even heard of the Holy Spirit." Water baptism in itself added nothing intrinsically spiritual, and preoccupation with it could become idolatry. "Yes, I tell you that water neither gives nor takes anything from anyone. It hurts no one who uses it in ignorance [Einfalt]. If someone, however, places his salvation therein, that person engages in idolatry."[88] Spirit baptism could come before or after water baptism.[89] It was dependent not on water but on "the prayer of the saints in the Holy Spirit." It followed that only those who had experienced the baptism of the Spirit could guide others in things pertaining to the Spirit.

But what were the implications of this separation of inner and outer baptism? Closer inspection reveals that Gabriel advocated a kind of Stillstand on water baptism. He wrote that it was his "considered opinion that the papists and Lutherans and all supposed Brethren should not quarrel and bite each other concerning [external] baptism, because much innocent blood is spilled as the result of it. Yet, in truth, none is correct. If they would leave off baptizing, therefore, it would be much better."[90]

Clearly, by the 1540s, Gabriel's views were evolving in the direction of Silesian spiritualism. Dialogue with indigenous reform groups may have influenced this ideological development, and continuing persecution, no doubt, made suspension an attractive option. Gabriel observed that times were dangerous and that unnecessary martyrdom saved no one. To argue that "the Holy Spirit did not bind the church to any elemental creature" and that water baptism should therefore be optional would be a form of Nicodemism[91] and was perceived as such by contemporaries.[92]

Most shocking to Gabriel's former allies was his soft position on "the terrible blasphemy of infant baptism." Gabriel did not consider infant baptism intrinsically evil because all children were beneficiaries of Christ's atoning work. Addressing the second-generation issue of children nurtured in the community, Gabriel made allowance for those "raised in the Christian congregation [*Gemeinde*] and found obedient. Even if that person had no full understanding, that person could be baptized because salvation comes not from the order of baptism but through [obedient] faith. Baptism, however, should not be law but voluntary."

What, then, of child baptism? Did Gabriel condone it?

If one asks: Is child-baptism sin? I answer No, because . . . the symbol does no harm to that which it signifies, even though the symbol has not been commanded for its own sake. I believe that all children born into the world are grafted [*einverleibt*] into the Christian community through the death of Christ. However, for the sake of avoiding disorder, all kinds of superstition and abuses that originate with it, it is better to discontinue child baptism.[93]

In other words, because of the abuses associated with it, child baptism was best discontinued. And what of child baptism without abuses? Was it possible? Gabriel refused to answer his own rhetorical question "because some would immediately make a law out of it as happened under the papacy." In principle, then, although seeing no harm in the ceremony of pedobaptism, Gabriel argued for its suspension because of abuses associated with it and by inference preferred adult baptism. After all, church ordinances were intended for edification and improvement, never its opposite (*Besserung nicht Bösern*).

Although this is not the place to mount a comparative study of Gabriel's views with those of Schwenckfeld and the Czech Brethren, certain parallels are striking. Both of these groups preferred Johannine texts for their eucharistic theology. The fifteenth-century progenitor of the Czech Brethren, Petr Chelcicky, insisted that the eucharistic celebration was more than a commemorative occasion, the elements of the sacrament more than common bread and wine. Indeed, they constituted a mysterious union of material and spiritual substance, so that the communicant partook of both.[94]

The mysterious union of earthly and heavenly substance, of spiritual and temporal food, came apart for Schwenckfeld. According to his reading of John 6, "Only the Word of God, verbum incarnatum . . . feeds to life, whoever eats this bread will live in eternity."[95] Such eating could only be spiritual and was possible only through faith, a "lifting up of the heart." It was not a question of Christ coming down into the bread but rather of the believer ascending into heaven by partaking of Christ's essence.[96] Schwenckfeld's peculiar Christology with its insistence on the "closest union between Christ's two natures after the resurrection"[97] placed the emphasis on the nonmaterial, "noncreaturely," spiritual and heavenly nature of the postascension Christ.[98] Like Gabriel, Schwenckfeld held that the believer could become the beneficiary of Christ's redemptive work only through participation in his spiritual or divine nature. Such participation involved an inner feeding on Christ, the heavenly manna. Although Schwenckfeld was willing to suspend the outer symbol because it had become so divisive, the inner spiritual feasting on Christ remained crucial to his soteriology and Christology because his understanding of justification was above all transformationalist, spiritualist.[99] The eucharist remained absolutely central to his understanding of the communication of divine grace, *solus Christi.*

Gabriel's reflection on the Lord's Supper held a similar spiritualist orientation. However, Gabriel did not propose suspension, but rather a solemn celebration. His view was less individualistic; the external rite retained an important community function. Curiously, he seemed ready to suspend baptism or countenance both child and adult baptism. Here his view approximated the practice of the Czech Brethren.

The Hutterites, in seeking to refute Gabriel's view on baptism, cited verbatim a part of his statement found in his surviving treatise, thus providing proof of the authenticity of Gabriel's statement and treatise. It demonstrates further that Hutterite apologists were in the possession of Gabriel's work and were reading and responding to it. Thus under the date 1545 and in conjunction with an entry about some Gabrielites joining them, *The Chronicle* recorded that "Gabriel circulated a book among his people in which he wrote, 'If anyone asks me whether infant baptism is wrong, I will answer no. If he wants to know the reason, I say there is none.' He added that until the reason was known, infant baptism should be discontinued because of its misuse."[100]

The same source suggested that Gabriel's views in the "recently written" booklet, which he "sent around to be read in all places" where his people settled, deviated from the position he held earlier. Those Gabrielites joining the Hutterites had not given their agreement to the "terrible blasphemy of infant baptism" but remained steadfast in the "opinion that we all shared when we were still one people." And while the Hutterite interpretation of Gabriel's view may have been tendentious, it is clear that Gabriel had developed a position different from that of the Hutterites. This was not only true of the Lord's Supper and baptism, but also in regard to the practice of community of goods. If Hutterites had harsh words for him, he criticized them for what he considered their self-righteous, legalistic attitude: "I think simple-minded papists will some day judge those who have obstructed the grace of God . . . and think salvation consists of their readiness to repent, baptize, and [practice] community of goods." He was particularly incensed by their mission to other Anabaptist groups (*Völkern*): "you cannot be saved with property; you must sell all and move under the cross."[101] Obviously, Gabriel did not share this view. It seems that he and his supporters, like the Philipites, had abandoned community of goods after the expulsion of 1535 or were practicing it selectively where possible. A statement to this effect was made by the Hutterite missionary Hans Mändel.

In the beginning Gabriel wanted to imitate the pious even in matters of community of goods but, as I understand, in a lax fashion [*allein lässig*]. Where there was a *Haushabe,* they held community of goods with each other, but otherwise they carried on as before [*sonst ist es schlecht genug zugegangen*]. More and more they came from one thing into the next, but not out of the world but into it. They came also into unsound teachings until they all dissolved along with Gabriel.[102]

Mändel's suggestion that even in the beginning Gabriel and his followers did not practice community of goods with the same rigor and discipline, considered normative by Hutterites, is revealing. It seems that Gabrielites lived in *Haushaben* and practiced a voluntary form of community of goods. This practice, as described by Mändel, corresponds with other early experiments in community of goods, for example, Brandhuber's practice in Linz, the situation in Austerlitz, and perhaps the manner of the Philipites. These early voluntary, uncoerced experiments modeled on New Testament precedent and shaped by the refugee situation apparently left some room for individual choice and economic initiative. They may have also made allowance for seekers and uncommitted family members. All of this puts Hutter's own contribution into sharper focus. It was his legacy that community of goods became the quintessence of full discipleship in community. His Anabaptist vision assumed the primacy of the community over the individual and even over family and marital relationships[103] and found material expression in apartment-like dwellings dubbed "dove cotes" (*Taubenkobel*) by critical contemporaries.[104]

No easy historic lessons can to be drawn from the fate of the Philipites, the Gabrielites, and the Austerlitz Brethren. The expulsions from Moravia in 1535 certainly marked a turning point in these communities. All three eventually disappeared from the historic stage. The Philipites turned Swiss. Gabriel developed in a spiritualist direction that had been latent among certain Anabaptists from the beginning but was likely furthered by dialogue with Schwenckfeldians and or Czech Brethren. His synthesis of Anabaptism and irenic spiritualism, with its nostalgia for uncoerced first love and its evident disillusionment resulting from quarrels and schisms, betrays also certain Nicodemite tendencies. How much ordinary members understood of his finer distinctions between divine and human wisdom, his desire for a more liturgical celebration of the Lord's Supper, or his baptismology is unclear. Representative of the first-generation charismatic leadership, Gabriel may have become too dazzled by the inner light to lead the way to needed organizational structures that might have assured the survival of his people as a distinct group. No successors with the required leadership qualities emerged after his death. Even before his death in 1545 a number of his followers joined the Hutterites. A small remnant did so in 1565.[105] With them the Gabrielites, like the Philipites, the Austerlitz Brethren, and the Pilgramites, would disappear.

The followers of Hutter, on the other hand, survived. They too had been forced to disperse in 1535 and in number of martyrs outsuffered the other groups. Led by Hans Amon, they clung to Hutter's instructions and to Moravia in the hope of better times with the goal of reverting to communal living as soon as possible. This strategy, although severely tested not only in 1535–36 but again in the 1540s, proved correct. When conditions finally improved, the survivors rallied to live in strict community. By 1560 they stood on the threshold of their "golden years."

Three Early Anabaptist Congregational Orders

I	II	III
The Swiss Order [1527]	*The Discipline* [1529]	*The Scharnschlager Order*
or	or	[1540] or
The Congregational Order	*Discipline of the Believers: How a Christian Is to Live*	*A Church Order For Members Of Christ's Body Arranged in Seven Articles by Leopold Scharnschlager*
translated by John H. Yoder	translated by Robert Friedmann	translated by William Klassen

"Children, let all your works be done in order with good intent in the fear of God, and do nothing disorderly in scorn or out of its due season."—Testament of Naphtali II, 9

Paul says in 1 Corinthians 14:40, "Let all things be done decently and in order." Likewise, Colossians 2:5: "I rejoice when I see your order and the steadfastness of your faith in Christ." (Marginal glosses beside the quote from Naphtali read *yesterday,* beside the quote from Paul, *today.*)

Since the almighty eternal and merciful God has made His wonderful light break forth in this world and [in this] most dangerous time, we recognize the mystery of the divine will, that the Word is preached to us according to the proper ordering of the Lord, whereby we have been called into His fellowship. Therefore, according to the command of the Lord and the teachings of His apostles, in Christian order, we should observe the new commandment in love

Since the almighty God and heavenly Father is permitting His eternal and all-powerful Word to be proclaimed to all creatures in these most perilous times (Colossians 1) and has called us at this time out of pure grace into His marvelous light (1 Peter 3) to one body, one spirit, and one faith, united in the bonds of love (Ephesians 4; 1 Corinthians 1), to which we have all agred, in order that our calling be found worthy, not only with the word of the mouth but in the truth and power (2

Since our heavenly Father, to whom be eternal praise, honor, and thanksgiving, has in these last days called us from darkness into his marvellous light through knowledge of his holy truth, and since we are all baptized and have decided to become one body in Jesus Christ regardless of where we may be located in the world, therefore if we are to achieve our calling not only in words but also in deed and in truth, it is necessary that we follow the order through which

I	II	III
The Swiss Order [1527] or *The Congregational Order*	*The Discipline* [1529] or *Discipline of the Believers: How a Christian Is to Live*	*The Scharnschlager Order* [1540] or *A Church Order For Members Of Christ's Body Arranged in Seven Articles by Leopold Scharnschlager*
translated by John H. Yoder	translated by Robert Friedmann	translated by William Klassen

one toward another, so that love and unity may be maintained, which all brothers and sisters of the entire congregation [*Gemein* should agree to hold to as follows:

Thesalonians 1; 1 Thessalonians 1; 1 Corinthians 4; James 1), we have all in one another's presence openly agreed to regulate everything in the best possible way. For the improvement of our brotherhood [*Gemein*, so translated throughout], for the praise and honor of the Lord, and for the service of all the needy, we have unanimously agreed that this *Ordnung* shall be kept among us by all the brethren and sisters. When, however, a brother or sister is able to produce a better *Ordnung* it shall be accepted from him at any time (1 Corinthians 14).

we exist in love and can be exhorted and corrected, since indeed all things exist through order. In the following such an order is written down in articles. Nevertheless daily changes for improvement according to the nature and opportunities of the times we allow for.

1. The brothers and sisters should meet at least three or four times a week, to exercise themselves in the teaching of Christ and His apostles and heartily to exhort one another to remain faithful to the Lord as they have pledged.

2. In the second place: we shall sincerely and in a Christian spirit admonish one another in the Lord to remain constant (Hebrews 10:1; Acts 14, 15, 18; Colossians 1). To meet often, at least four or five times, and if possible . . . even at midweek (1 Corinthians 11, 14; Acts 1, 2, 9, 11, 20; Hebrews 10; 2 Corinthians 6; Matthew 18).

1. First: because manifold deceptions are everywhere making inroads it is necessary that the called, committed, and obligated members of Christ's body, wherever they may be in the world or in distress, insofar as it is possible, should not neglect the assemblies (Hebrews 10:25), but wherever and however they may, according to the place and the persecutions gather together for the sake of their love for Christ, be their number small or great, 2, 3, 4, 6, 10, 15, 20, more or less. Such meetings should take place with

I	II	III
The Swiss Order [1527] or *The Congregational Order*	*The Discipline* [1529] or *Discipline of the Believers: How a Christian Is to Live*	*The Scharnschlager Order* [1540] or *A Church Order For Members Of Christ's Body Arranged in Seven Articles by Leopold Scharnschlager*
translated by John H. Yoder	translated by Robert Friedmann	translated by William Klassen

wisdom, skill, reason, discipline, friendliness, and quiet demeanor especially since we see the day of the Lord drawing near. The Lord says: "Where two or three are gathered together in my name, there I am in the midst of them" (Matthew 18:20).

2. When the brothers and sisters are together, they shall take up something to read together. The one to whom God has given the best understanding shall explain it, the others should be still and listen, so that there are not two or three carrying on a private conversation, bothering the others. The Psalter shall be read daily at home.

7. In the seventh place: in the meeting one is to speak and the others listen and judge what is spoken, and not two or three stand together (1 Corinthians 14). No one shall curse or swear (Matthew 5; Romans 3; James 5) nor shall idle gossip be carried on, so that the weak may be spared (1 Corinthians 1; Ephesians 5; Colossians 3; 2 Timothy 2; Psalm 118). [*Geschichtbuch* here cites only Ecclesiasticus 23.]

2. Secondly: when they come together, they shall, where there is no special leader [*Vorsteher*], select someone competent from among them, and admonish him in a friendly and loving manner to read or speak to them according to the gift which he has received from God. Someone may also volunteer to serve out of love. One may follow another in speaking according to the way in which they receive, as Paul teaches (1 Corinthians 14), and thus exercise his gifts for the improvement of the members, so that our fellowship may not be the same as that of the falsely renowned, where only one and no one else can speak.

Before, however, they begin to speak let them fall on their knees (1 Timothy 2:1) and faithfully call upon God that he may add fruit to their speaking. After the talk

I	II	III
The Swiss Order [1527] or *The Congregational Order*	*The Discipline* [1529] or *Discipline of the Believers: How a Christian Is to Live*	*The Scharnschlager Order* [1540] or *A Church Order For Members Of Christ's Body* Arranged in Seven Articles by Leopold Scharnschlager
translated by John H. Yoder	translated by Robert Friedmann	translated by William Klassen

diligently admonish one another to walk according to the will of the Lord, to remain constantly in him, to watch faithfully and to wait for the Lord until he comes (Matthew 24:42; 26:41; Luke 12:35 ff.) that we may be found without blemish before him (Philippians 2:15) and that not only here but much more in the next world we may together be with the Lord and also may rejoice eternally (Isaiah 4:2f.). Furthermore, before dispersing call upon the Lord and intercede for all members, also for cases of special need, and for all men according to the directive of our beloved brother Paul (1 Timothy 2:1 ff.). Thanksgiving for all of God's gifts and good deeds (1 Thessalonians 5:17f.) should also be expressed and upon occasion according to convenience before dispersing, bread should be broken together in memory of the death of the Lord (1 Corinthians 11:24).

1. And beginning when the brethren are together they shall sincerely ask God for grace that He might reveal His divine will and help us to note it (Psalm 86, 118) and when the brethren

I	II	III
The Swiss Order [1527] or *The Congregational Order*	*The Discipline* [1529] or *Discipline of the Believers: How a Christian Is to Live*	*The Scharnschlager Order* [1540] or *A Church Order For Members Of Christ's Body* Arranged in Seven Articles by Leopold Scharnschlager
translated by John H. Yoder	translated by Robert Friedmann	translated by William Klassen

---

	part they shall thank God and pray for all the brethren and sisters of the entire brotherhood (1 Thessalonians 1, 5; 2 Thessalonians 1, 2; 2 Corinthians 1; Colossians 1, 3, 4).	
3. Let none be frivolous in the church of God, neither in words nor in actions. Good conduct shall be maintained by them all also before the heathen.	6. In the sixth place: decent conduct [*ehrbarer Wandel*] shall be kept among them (Romans 12, 13; Philippians 1, 2; 1 Peter, 2, 3; 1 Corinthians 1, 3; Galatians 5; Ephesians 5) before everyone (Titus 3; Matthew 5; 1 Peter 3) and no one shall carelessly conduct himself before the brotherhood either in words or deeds (Romans 1, 6; 2 Timothy 2), nor before those who are "outside" (1 Thessalonians 5; 1 Peter 3).	
4. When a brother sees his brother erring, he shall warn him according to the command of Christ, and shall admonish him in a Christian and brotherly way, as everyone is bound and obliged to do out of love.	3. In the third place: when a brother or sister leads a disorderly life it shall be punished: if he does so publicly [he] shall be kindly admonished before all the brethren (Galatians 2, 6; 1 Corinthians 5; 2 Thessalonians 3); if it is secret it shall be punished in secret, according to the command of Christ (Matthew 18).	6. Sixthly: when a brother or sister is overtaken by vices of the flesh, false teaching, licentious living and being, or in other cases of word or deed, there shall always be disciplined, modest, sincere admonition and correction from the leaders in trembling and fear of God, in love (Galatians 6:1; Matthew 18:15 ff.) Diligent attention is to be paid in each case of transgression be it secret or open, large or small, one warning or

I	II	III
The Swiss Order [1527] or *The Congregational Order*	*The Discipline* [1529] or *Discipline of the Believers: How a Christian Is to Live*	*The Scharnschlager Order* [1540] or *A Church Order For Members Of Christ's Body Arranged in Seven Articles by Leopold Scharnschlager*
translated by John H. Yoder	translated by Robert Friedmann	translated by William Klassen

more, how the person is dealt with according to gentleness and sharpness, patience and impatience. For correction and excommunication must be distinguished according to the actual circumstances and according to the witness of the Scriptures, so that everything take place according to the spirit of love and not according to the nature of the flesh (Titus 3:13; 1 Corinthians 5:1 ff.; Romans 2:1 f.; Ephesians 5: 11 f.; 1 Corinthians 6:5). The power of Christ is not a power to destroy or to exercise tyranny, but to improve, that also for Christ his bride may be kept pure, everywhere, both for those within as well as those outside the church so that an honorable, inoffensive walk may result and that no one block or make difficult the way and road to Christ and his kingdom.

5. Of all the brothers and sisters of this congregation none shall have anything of his own, but rather, as the Christians in the time of the apostles held all in common, and especially stored up a common fund, from which aid can be given to the poor, according as each will have need, and as in the

4. In the fourth place: every brother or sister shall yield himself in God to the brotherhood completely with body and life, and hold in common all gifts received of God (Acts 2 and 4; 1 Corinthians 11, 12; 2 Corinthians 8, 9), [and] contribute to the common need so that brethren and sisters will always be helped

5. Fifthly: since the example of the primitive church in Jerusalem (Acts 4:32–5:11) is misunderstood by some giving rise to error and contempt, special sects and the like, and some have made of this example a law, a requirement, a fetter, even almost a carnal righteousness, demand, and the like, therefore let us

I	II	III
The Swiss Order [1527] or *The Congregational Order*	*The Discipline* [1529] or *Discipline of the Believers: How a Christian Is to Live*	*The Scharnschlager Order* [1540] or *A Church Order For Members Of Christ's Body* Arranged in Seven Articles by Leopold Scharnschlager
translated by John H. Yoder	translated by Robert Friedmann	translated by William Klassen

apostles' time permit no brother to be in need.	(Romans 12); needy members shall receive from the brotherhood as among the Christians at the time of the apostles (Acts 2, 4, 5; 1 Corinthians 11, 12; Ephesians 4; Proverbs 5; Matthew 8, 15, 16, 17, 19; Luke 3, 6, 8, 9, 10, 12, 14, 18; 1 John 1, 2, 3, 4; Mark 3, 10, 12; Galatians 6; Hebrews 13; Daniel 4, 8; Luke 6, 8; 1 Timothy 1; 1 Corinthians 14, 16; Romans 6, 18; James 1; Philippians 2).	recognize that in the early church at Jerusalem the sharing of goods was a voluntary matter and further observe what took place after the dispersion of the church from there. Even Paul wrote about sharing material possessions and community of goods (Romans 15:25 ff.; 1 Corinthians 16:1 ff.; 2 Corinthians 9:1 ff.) and we likewise in true apostolic character are to pay heed that the bride and flock of Christ be not forced, but may be lead and fed voluntarily. Therefore the one who gathers funds [*Steuersammler*] is to pay heed, to accept the smallest gift without despising it, just as he does the greater (Luke 21:1–4) from both the rich and the poor, and faithfully thank both God and the giver. After that leave it to the Lord. For even though someone says, with worldly wisdom, "Ah, after all everyone has agreed to this and committed himself to it, why not diligently demand whatever is necessary?" we answer: The order of the Holy Spirit will not permit it. This work is not of man, just as it was not the flesh which initially promised or agreed. Therefore it must be

I	II	III
The Swiss Order [1527] or *The Congregational Order*	*The Discipline* [1529] or *Discipline of the Believers: How a Christian Is to Live*	*The Scharnschlager Order* [1540] or *A Church Order For Members Of Christ's Body Arranged in Seven Articles by Leopold Scharnschlager*
translated by John H. Yoder	translated by Robert Friedmann	translated by William Klassen

sought not in the fleshly nature but in the spiritual. Otherwise we disrupt the voluntary nature of God's relation to his people.

6. All gluttony shall be avoided among the brothers who are gathered in the congregation; serve a soup or a minimum of vegetable and meat, for eating and drinking are not the kingdom of heaven.

8. In the eighth place: when the brethren assemble they shall not fill up with eating and drinking, but avoid expenses [reduce expenditures] to the least, [eat] a soup and vegetable or whatever God gives (1 Corinthians 11; 1 Peter 4; Galatians 5; Romans 13; Ephesians 5; Ecclesiastes 37; Luke 21), and when they have eaten, all the food and drink shall again be removed [*Geschichtbuch:* "from the table"] (John 6; Matthew 4; Luke 9; Mark 6), for one should use with thanksgiving and moderation the creatures which God has created, pure and good, for our subsistence.

4. Fourthly: since there is a shortage of faithful workers who correctly, wisely and in good conscience faithfully seek for the lost and labor for the Lord in his vineyard (1 Thessalonians 5:12f.) and in turn daily causes much confusion, error and offense, there is an urgent need that when such a faithful worker is found and detected he be given due respect (Hebrews 13:7) and obeyed, for he is worthy of a double honor (according to the words of Paul, 1 Timothy 5:17). Share with him every good thing (Galatians 6:9f.) and all the support possible, as he may need in addition to work he is able to do on the side, so that he may not depreciate the messengers and workers of the Lord for whom we pray daily (Luke 10:2) lest the Lord allow us to be scattered abroad without shepherds. This applies not only for the sake of the ones who have seen the truth but also for the sake of the weak, milk-drinking vegetarians

I	II	III
The Swiss Order [1527] or *The Congregational Order*	*The Discipline* [1529] or *Discipline of the Believers: How a Christian Is to Live*	*The Scharnschlager Order* [1540] or *A Church Order For Members Of Christ's Body* Arranged in Seven Articles by Leopold Scharnschlager
translated by John H. Yoder	translated by Robert Friedmann	translated by William Klassen

| | | 1 Corinthians 3:2; Hebrews 5:12; Romans 14:2) and for the sake of those who in the future will be gathered to the Lord. |

| 7. The Lord's Supper shall be held as often as the brothers are together, thereby proclaiming the death of the Lord, and thereby warning each one to commemorate, how Christ gave His life for us, and shed His blood for us, that we might also be willing to give our body and life for Christ's sake, which means for the sake of all the brothers. | 11. When brethren and sisters are together, being one body and one bread in the Lord and of one mind, then they shall keep the Lord's Supper as a memorial of the Lord's death (Matthew 26; Mark 14; Luke 22; 1 Corinthians 11), whereby each one shall be admonished to become conformed to the Lord in the obedience of the Father (Philippians 2, 3; 1 Peter 2, 4; Romans 8; 1 John 2. Obedience: Romans 2; Philippians 2; 2 Corinthians 2, 10; 2 Thessalonians 1; 1 Peter 1). | 7. Seventhly: concerning teaching, baptizing, and the Lord's Supper, these are to be observed according to the content of the commission and practice of the Lord and his apostles, nor changed or perverted, nor anything to be added or taken from it (Deuteronomy 4:2; 12:32; Proverbs 30:6), as it happens among the antichrists and the falsely renowned. At all times each brother and sister is to be guided in all their actions by the secrets of the essential Christian faith, and whatever the Lord has entrusted to him to bear before the world with a clear conscience, to prevent the blasphemy of Christ's name, Word and honor. Whatever other matters and errors arise in daily life, they are to perceive them and act with godly fear according to the gospel of Christ (Philippians 1:27), corresponding to the faith and serving for the improvement and edification of everyone. We are to follow him faithfully and renounce |

I	II	III
The Swiss Order [1527]	*The Discipline* [1529]	*The Scharnschlager Order*
or	or	[1540] or
The Congregational Order	*Discipline of the Believers:*	*A Church Order For*
	How a Christian Is to Live	*Members Of Christ's Body*
		Arranged in Seven Articles
		by Leopold Scharnschlager
translated by John H. Yoder	translated by	translated by
	Robert Friedmann	William Klassen

all unrighteousness of words, works and manner of life, flee from it, abstain and separate ourselves from it (2 Corinthians 6:17). To the honor of God and of our bridegroom Jesus Christ in order that when he comes we may joyfully appear before him in holy adornment arrayed in the Holy Spirit (Matthew 24) so that he may fully possess what he acquired for us and prepared through his precious blood (John 14). Therefore we pray to our heavenly father that he may help us to accomplish this and achieve it through Jesus Christ his beloved son, our Lord, to whom be praise, honor, and majesty in the Holy Spirit from eternity to eternity. Amen.

In Christ the Lord, a brother by grace and a servant of the truth, also a partner in the tribulation which is in Christ, *Leupolt Scharnschlager.*

5. The elders [*Vorsteher*] and preachers chosen for the brotherhood shall with zeal look after the needs of the poor, and with zeal in the Lord according to the command of the Lord extend what is needed for the sake of and instead of the brotherhood (Galla-

3. Thirdly: when assembled in this manner, a leader if present (if not, any other elderly brother [1 Corinthians 14]) shall remember for the sake of the Lord the poor members with words that are wise, sincere, gentle, transparent, not pressuring and yet earnest, em-

I	II	III
The Swiss Order [1527] or *The Congregational Order*	*The Discipline* [1529] or *Discipline of the Believers: How a Christian Is to Live*	*The Scharnschlager Order* [1540] or *A Church Order For Members Of Christ's Body* Arranged in Seven Articles by Leopold Scharnschlager
translated by John H. Yoder	translated by Robert Friedmann	translated by William Klassen

	tians 2; 2 Corinthians 8, 9; Romans 15; Acts 6).	phatic words, that thereby hearts may be moved to a voluntary expression of compassion and grow into the nature and power of love which is genuine and pleasing in the sight of God. Above all, there should always be present a brother with a purse of money known to all the members of the church, so that each member either in the meeting or after, when the Lord admonishes him to, may know where to place his free-will offering and his gift of gratitude so that at all times when the need arises the poor can be assisted according to the amount available at the time. Then the brother who cares for the fund shall distribute it with a good conscience and in the fear of God, paying diligent heed, whether they are needy or not, whether greedy or not, not as the world deals with the poor without testing and inquiring about their manner of life and walk. For this is a holy commission (Acts 6:1 ff.).
	Additional Articles in the Discipline with no precise overlap. 9. In the ninth place: what is officially done	

I	II	III
The Swiss Order [1527] or *The Congregational Order*	*The Discipline* [1529] or *Discipline of the Believers: How a Christian Is to Live*	*The Scharnschlager Order* [1540] or *A Church Order For Members Of Christ's Body Arranged in Seven Articles* by Leopold Scharnschlager
translated by John H. Yoder	translated by Robert Friedmann	translated by William Klassen

among the brethren and sisters in the brother-hood [*Geschichtbuch:* "or is judged"] shall not be made public before the world. The good-hearted [an interested but not yet converted or committed] person, before he comes to the brethren in the broth-erhood shall be taught [*Geschichtbuch:* "the Gospel"] (Mark 16; Ro-mans 1; Colossians 1). When he has learned [*Geschichtbuch:* "under-stood"] and bears a sin-cere desire for it, and if he agrees to the content of the Gospel, he shall be received by the Christian brotherhood as a brother or a sister, that is, as a fellow member of Christ (Mattehew 7; Proverbs 19, 29; Colossians 4; Ro-mans 14; 2 Corinthians 6; 1 Corinthians 10; 1 Timothy 6; Matthew 10). But this shall not be made public before the world to spare the con-science and for the sake of the spouse (1 Cor-inthians 9, 10; Matthew 15).

10. In the tenth place: all the brethren and sisters after they have committed themselves, shall accept and bear with patience all that He sends us [*Geschichtbuch:*

I	II	III
The Swiss Order [1527] or *The Congregational Order*	*The Discipline* [1529] or *Discipline of the Believers: How a Christian Is to Live*	*The Scharnschlager Order* [1540] or *A Church Order For Members Of Christ's Body* Arranged in Seven Articles by Leopold Scharnschlager
translated by John H. Yoder	translated by Robert Friedmann	translated by William Klassen

	"accept with gratitude and bear with patience"] (Romans 6; John 13; Matthew 16; Luke 9; 1 Peter 4; 2 Corinthians 12), and [shall] not let themselves be easily frightened by every wind and cry.	
	12. In the twelfth place: as we have taught and admonished the brethren and sisters we shall always watch and wait for the Lord that we may be worthy to enter the kingdom with Him when He comes, and to escape or flee from the evil that will come to the world. Amen. (Matthew 25; Luke 21; 1 Thessalonians 5; 1 Peter 5; 2 Peter 3; Romans 2).	

Arranged by Werner O. Packull, using the *Swiss Order* as a reference point.

The Brethren at Austerlitz

Location
  Austerlitz (1528–35)
Leaders
  Jacob Wiedemann
  Philip Jäger [Plener?]
  Franz Itzinger
  Jacob Mändel
  Thoman Arbeiter
  Urban Bader
  Kilian Volckhaimer
  Kilian Auerbach
  Michael Kramer
  Ulrich Stadler, later a Hutterite
  Leonhard Lochmaier, later a Hutterite
Brethren from Krumau, Bohemia, who moved to Austerlitz in 1528–29
  Hans Fasser, leader of eighty to ninety persons; returned to Krumau and became
    unfaithful
  Hans Amon, Bavarian, cloth merchant, later a Hutterite leader
  Leonard Sailer Lanzenstiel, Bavarian, rope maker, later a Hutterite leader
  Christoph Gschäll, later a Hutterite leader
  Georg Fasser, later a Hutterite leader
  Bernhard Glasser, expelled by Hutter in 1533
  Hans from Strasbourg, later a pro-Gabrielite or pro-Philipite?
Secessionists from Austerlitz who in 1531 formed the proto-Hutterite community in
    Auspitz
  Adam Schlegel of Nuremberg, a later Philipite
  Burkhard Braun [Bämerli] of Ofen, a Philipite who later joined the Hutterites
  David the Bohemian of Schweidnitz, Silesia, later a Gabrielite or Philipite
  Wilhelm Reublin, the first leader of the Auspitz community, expelled
  Jorg Zaunring, the second leader dismissed, rehabilitated as an itinerary apostle
  Wilhelm Griesbacher, a servant of temporal affairs
  Leonard Schmerbacher, a servant of temporal affairs
Members of the Austerlitz community known through Reublin's correspondence with
    Marpeck
  Schlosser [Melchior], Marpeck's messenger to Austerlitz
  Kaspar Schueler, one of Reublin's messengers to Marpeck from Austerlitz.
  Kaspar, a former Austerlitz brother who had a vineyard in Auspitz
  Sebastian Thaurer
  Hans Eschlperger
  Hans Zuck of Altdorf

Reublin also mentioned the following

Martin Leopolden [Scharnschlager?]
Anderlin
Peter and Wolffen from Landau
Erhard Rosenstock from near Zurich

The Gabrielites

Locations identified in previous literature
  Rossitz (1529–35), the main community
  Kreuz, near Goding, joined the Hutterites in 1565
  Eibenschitz, Gabrielite resident, had debate in 1559 with Bohemian Brethren called
    Bunzlauer Brüder; cannot agree on baptism
  Butschowitz [Putschowitz] or Pudespitz in 1540s
  Jarchniewitz
  Bisenz
  Wratzow
  Fraustadt
Leaders
  Gabriel Ascherham [Kürschner] from Nurmberg
  Clemens Adler?
  Peter Hueter, who later joined the Hutterites
  Baclor der Tischler, leader at Eibenschitz in 1559
  Partl, presumably Bärtle Riedmair or Schlesinger [Silesian], who joined the Hutterites on
    January 16, 1545. Riedmair had been relieved of his leadership position by Gabriel
    because of a controversy involving a fur coat; his children Fabian Fitz, Merthin Voyt,
    and Jacob Heusler also joined the Hutterites in 1545

  Other Silesians who at one time were likely Gabrielites were Casper Braitmichel, Peter
    Riedemann, and David, the Bohemian, from Schweidnitz
Primary sources
  A chronicle: "Was sich verloffen hat unter den Brüdern" (1528–41)
  "Unterschied göttlicher und menschlicher Weisheit" (1544)
  Hutterite "Verantwortung d. Gabrielischen Briefs von uns der Gemeinde zu Schakkowitz"

The Philipites

Locations
  Auspitz
  Pulgram, transferred property to the Hutterites in 1538
  Znaim, Philipites or Swiss Brethren, who claimed to have "ihrer viele in Mähren,
    Böhmen, der Schweiz und in den Gebirgsländern"
Leaders
  Philip Plener [Blauärmel]
  Blasy Kuhn
  Adam Schlegel, from Nurmberg
  Burkhard Braun [Bämerli], of Ofen, joined the Hutterites in 1542 and died in 1567 at Tracht
  Michael Schneider, prisoner at Passau, songwriter
  Hans Gentner, joined the Hutterites in 1537
Early associates or leaders who baptized members of the Philipite community
  Julius Lober, a Swiss tailor and messenger between Reublin and Marpeck, fell away,
    became a charlatan [Schelm]
  Hans Greuel, a schoolmaster, associated with Philip in Augsburg in 1527–28
  Jorg Schachner, associated with Philip in Augsburg, left the movement
  Hans of Bibrach [Hut]
  Lemlin, Konrad of Sindelfingen
  Andreas, N. of Neiss [Unteröwisheim], was beheaded at Neuenburg on the Danube
  Wolf of Gritzingen [Grutzing, Grötzingen], was executed at Bretten on the Rhine
  Georg of Staffelstein [Jörg Nespitzer]; members did not know what had happened to him
  Hans of Schwaigern, became a charlatan [Scheln] and died

APPENDIX C
Known Prisoners at Passau in 1535

Group Investigated on August 23, 1535
A report by the Hofmarshall identifies Dietrich of Heilbronn as the leader.[1]

Name	Occupation	Place of Origin	Baptizer	Place	Time
Hans Haffner	Vineyard worker; illiterate	Rüblingen [Riblingen] near Oehringen	Adam Schlegel	Auspitz	1533
Katharina Haffner (married forty years)	Wife of Hans	Rüblingen	Adam Schlegel	Donauwörth	1534?
Michel	Ten-year-old boy entrusted to Haffner's by [Freundschaft]				
Jörg [Georg] Lang		Erzlinsweiler [Atzesweiler] near Oehringen	Adam Schlegel	Donauwörth	April 2, 1534
Eva Lang			Philip Plener	Auspitz	
Dietrich [of Heilbronn]	Leader of group; vineyard keeper	Heilbronn	Andre of Neiss	Heilbronn	1531
Kunegund	Wife of Dietrich	Waldenburg near Schwäbisch Hall	Adam Schlegel	Donauwörth	1534?
Hans Hoffman			Adam Schlegel	Auspitz	
Hans Hultzhoder	Peasant	Kupferzell near Oehringen	Adam Schlegel	Donauwörth	1534
Hans Lang	Son of Jörg Lang	Erzlinsweiler [Atzersweiler]	Philip Plener	Auspitz	1534
Amalie Lang	Wife of Hans		Adam Schlegel	Donanwörth	1534
A child of Lang family					
Hans the Younger [Haffner?]	Wife of Hans	Rüblingen [Riblingen]			
Engella Angela	Child entrusted to Hans and Angela		Philip	Auspitz	
Barbara					

Group Investigated on September 16, 1535.
Most acknowledged Michael Schneider as their leader [Vorsteher].

Name	Occupation	Place of Origin	Baptizer	Place	Time
Berhard Schrot	Glassmaker	Göbrichen [Gibichen] near Pforzheim	Andreas of Neiss		
Anna			Hans of Bibrach [Hut]		1527
Hans	Peasant	Schluchtern near Eppingen	Martin Wagner	Near Basel	
Margreth	Wife of Hans		Hans of Biberach [Hut] or Jörg of Ingersheim [Jörg Leserlin]		1527
Michel Schwister	Peasant	Seutern [Seytarn] near Bruchsal	Hans of Schwaizen [Schwaigern]	Near Heilbronn	
Conrad	Peasant	Züttlingen [Sitlins] near Neckarsulm	Julius Lober		
Barbara		Oettingen [Ottmis]	Philip Plener	Auspitz	
Georg	Fifteen years old	Heilbronn	Not baptized		
Margreth	Widow	Sternenfels [Maulbronn]	Hans [of Schwaigern]		1530
Ursula	Wife of Valtin	Bruchsal	Andreas of Neiss		
Barbara	Widow	Unteröwisheim near Maulbronn	Philip Plener	Unteröwisheim	
Apollonia	Wife of David of Innern Rusen		Adam Schlegel	Near Bruchsal	
Barbara	Ten years old				

Group Investigated on September 16, 1535

Seven of these named Michael Schneider as their leader; others seemed to consider Hans Peck as their group leader.

Name	Occupation	Place of Origin	Baptizer	Place	Time
Michel Kumbauf [Kuhn]	Relation to Blasy Kuhn?	Bruchsal	Philip Plener		
Anna					
Hans Peck [Beck, Pfeiffer]	Peasant arrested at Eggenburg with twenty others in 1534; burned through cheek	Greding near Hilpoltstein	Conrad Lemlin / Blasy Kumbauf [Kuhn]		
Elisabeth				Gemünt	
Oswald	Vineyard keeper	Ohrenberg [Augensperg] near Oehringen on Kocher	Jobst [Lober?] / Adam Schlegel		
Hans Fuchs	Sixteen years old	Bruchsal / Durlach / Durlach	Philip Plener / Conrad Lemlin / Hansen Kellner	Augsburg	1528?
Hans Steuber					
Anna (Steuber)				Heidlitzen near Bruchsal	
Bernhard Schneyder[2]	Young person; author of hymn	Fristlingen near Dillingen or Fristingen near Laubingen	Hans of Schwaigern		1533
Jacob		For time resident at Weil der Stadt; otherwise near Ulm	Philip Plener		
Margreth				Village of Eyssen	
Hans Kummich [Kimmich]	Vineyard worker, claimed there were fifty at a house in Bruchsal	Morsbach near Künzelsau	Blasius [Kuhn] / Blasius	Auspitz	
Judith			Wolf of Gritzing		

Name	Occupation	Place of Origin	Baptizer	Place	Time
Michel Schneyder	Leader of the group; appointed by Philip				
Gertraut Schneyder [Treytl]	Wife of Michel		Julius Lober	Bruchsal	1532
Apollonia			Philip Plener		
Barbara	Weaver; had two children with her	Bruchsal	Blasius Kuhn		
Anna	Daughter of Apollonia				
Anna	A young woman	Knittlingen [Khundlins]	Philip Plener	Auspitz	
Ursula	Fifteen-year-old youth	Baiertal [Peyrtl]	Blasius Kuhn	Auspitz	
		Künzelsau [Kuntzensee] near Wiesloch			
Anna		Füssbach [Kurzpach] near Oehringen	Philip Plener		

Group Investigated on September 24, 1535

These Anabaptists were arrested at Wegschaid. Because they seemed more willing to receive "divine instruction" and did not belong to the Auspitz group, they were given separate accommodations.

Name	Occupation	Place of Origin	Baptizer	Place	Time
Hans Petz [Betz]	Clothmaker; poet; songwriter	Eger	Jörg Haffner	Wörth Bavaria	1530
Peter Stumpheter		Schirling	Ulrich Stadler	Moravia [Austerlitz]	
Matheus[3]		Dorfdach near Hertzogburg	Andreas Vischer Georgen of Staffelstein		
Anna	Wife of Matheus				
Margareth	A young woman; the daughter of Lienharden Scheyers of Wuzierl				

Died in prison
  Bernhard Schneider, 1537
  Hans Betz [Petz], 1537
Escaped
  Michael Schneider [Yetelhauser], 1539
  Hans Beck [Pfeifer], 1539
Released
  Hans Haffner, 1541–42
  Katharina Haffner, 1541–42
  Appolonia; returned to the Bruchsal area by March 2, 1537, with two children (Krebs, TA Baden, 494–95).
Some were apparently released after nine years (1544) of imprisonment, when the Moravian lord Jamnitz took them under his wing as their bond and landlord.

[1] Friedmann's place identifications followed Wolkan and contained errors (Friedmann 1958b). I follow Bossert as given by him in the unpublished GLSSbt.S *Verein Für Reformationsgeschichte* (Täuferakten) 1974, Karlsruhe. 6 ff.

[2] A statement given under torture by Bernhard Schneider on September 18, 1535, has been preserved (Wiedmann Collection 96).

[3] Matheus lived in a community of about fifty at Znaim, led by Hans Kellermann. Matheus heard that those at Auspitz disagreed with them in a number of articles, but being a "simple man" he did not know what they were. He related further that in 1528–29 he and thirty-four others had been imprisoned at Empach [Taxenbach]. Seventeen had been executed. Under torture he and the other seventeen recanted and were released. Four weeks later he returned to the Anabaptist community in contrition and after a time had been reaccepted. No doubt he was part of the group caught by the provost of Lower Austria, Dietrich Hartitsch (Loserth 1956c).

Notes

Abbreviations

ARG	*Archiv für Reformationsgeschichte*
BQR	*Baptist Quarterly Review*
CE	*Catholic Encyclopedia* (1910–13)
CGR	*Conrad Grebel Review*
CS	*Corpus Schwenckfeldianorum*
JMS	*Journal for Mennonite Studies*
ME	*The Mennonite Encyclopedia*, vols. 1–5, 1955–90
MGB	*Mennonitische Geschichtsblätter*
MQR	*Mennonite Quarterly Review*
QGT	*Quellen zur Geschichte der Täufer*
Schlern	*Monatszeitschrift für Südtiroler Landeskunde*
SSA	*The Sources of Swiss Anabaptism*
WPM	*The Writings of Pilgram Marpeck*
ZHVSN	*Zeitschrift des hist. Vereins für Schwaben u. Neuburg*
ZKG	*Zeitschrift für Kirchengeschichte*

Introduction

1. Bender's address to the American Society of Church History was delivered in 1943 and published as "The Anabaptist Vision," *Church History* 13 (1944):3–24. I presented my reflections in a paper, "Interpretations of Anabaptism in 1993: The 'Anabaptist Vision' after Fifty Years," at an anniversary session in honor of Harold Bender at the meeting of the American Society of Church History at Oberlin College, Ohio, March 25, 1994. At the same conference Prof. A. Keim presented a paper contextualizing Bender's vision statement.

2. Hillerbrand 1993, especially 410.

3. Ibid., 418.

4. My colleague James Reimer examined the exchanges between Emanuel Hirsch and Paul Tillich (Reimer 1989).

5. I am indebted to Prof. James M. Stayer and his graduate student Sonia Riddock for their pointers regarding Holl and Troeltsch.

6. Bender 1950, 137.

7. Cf. the Yoder-Walton exchange on the turning point of the Zwinglian Reformation in Stayer and Packull 1980, 61–71.

8. John Oyer suggested that Robert Friedmann knew better but out of respect for Bender did not openly argue a humanist influence (Oyer 1990).

9. Oyer observed that to make Anabaptism respectable against Holl, Mennonite historiography "created in effect a free church confessionalism with orthopraxies replacing orthodoxy" (ibid.).

10. Regarding normative vision and historiographic developments, see my articles "Some Reflections on the State of Anabaptist History" (Packull 1979) and "Between Paradigms: Anabaptist Studies at the Crossroads" (Packull 1990a).

11. Thomas Brady's observation that Bender's agenda was "pulverized with the case shot of pluralistic analysis and social history" seems more appropriate than Hillerbrand's assessment (Brady 1988, 518).

12. My work followed the lead of Ken Davis and others in search for pre-Reformation antecedents rather than limiting intellectual influences to the reformers and the Bible (Packull 1977). More recently I traced Hoffman's exegesis of the Apocalypse to medieval roots (Packull 1986b).

13. Klaassen 1962; Seebass 1975.

14. Oyer included Hoffman alongside David Joris, the Münsterites, Hubmaier, and Hut as among those rehabilitated by the revisionists (Oyer 1990).

15. Goertz 1980, especially 144ff; Goertz 1992.

16. The possibility of membership in multiple communities militates against Karl Mannheim's classification of the intelligentsia or academics as *Freischwebende*.

17. Bernd Moeller's classic, first published in 1962, set the stage (Moeller 1972; see the Introduction by Eric Midelfort and Mark U. Edwards Jr.).

18. Cf. Brady 1982.

19. For example, Arnold Snyder's reconstruction of the intellectual and social context for understanding Michael Sattler (Snyder 1984).

20. Goertz 1980, especially 151ff.

21. Goertz 1992.

22. Stayer 1992.

23. Stayer speculated that the post-Bender Mennonite intelligentsia had greater exposure to problems in the developing world and was therefore open to a more activist model. Cf. Driedger and Kraybill 1994.

24. Haas 1980.

25. Besides Stayer, Haas, and Seebass, diversity has also been argued in John Oyer's *Lutheran Reformers against Anabaptist: Luther, Melanchthon, and Menius and the Anabaptists of Central Germany* (1964) and in the studies of numerous other scholars including Deppermann (1979) and myself (1977).

26. Stayer 1975; Haas 1975. Revisionist was also Seebass' treatment of Hans

Hut. See "Das Zeichen der Erwählten. Zum Verständnis der Taufe bei Hans Hut" (Goertz 1975, 138–64).

27. Ulrich Thomas (1977) listed more than five hundred publications from 1974 to 1977.

28. It can be argued that Rainer Wohlfeil's 1972 anthology marked the opening of serious dialogue: *Reformation oder frühbürgerliche Revolution?* Wohlfeil followed up with *Der Bauernkrieg 1524–26. Bauernkrieg und Reformation* (1975). English readers were introduced to the dialogue through *The German Peasant War of 1525*, edited by Janos Bak (1976) and *The German Peasant War 1525: New Viewpoint*, edited by Bob Scribner and Gerhard Benecke (1979).

29. On the meaning of *radical*, see the exchange between Adolf Laube (1988) and Hans Hillerbrand (1988).

30. Stayer 1982b. Bender and Friedmann attempted to separate the Anabaptists from any relationship with other dissenters, in particular Müntzer. Cf. Packull 1990d, 1990e.

31. Stayer 1982b. I have dabbled in this subject since 1977, inspired by Blickle's suggestion that the Peasants' War should be viewed as an attempt at revolution by the commoners (*Gemeine Mann*) and read a paper, "The Common Man in Early German Anabaptist Ideology" at the Sixteenth Century Studies Conference in October 1979 (Blickle 1981; Packull 1985, 1986a, 1989a).

32. Blickle 1992.

33. The Bible, it was believed, "was its own interpreter" (Blickle 1992, 42–43).

34. Zschäbitz 1980.

35. Stayer 1991, 148.

36. Stephen Boyd's biography of Pilgram Marpeck illustrates this point as well. Boyd spent considerable effort to unearth Marpeck's patrician background and the urban setting of the community he served. This urban context in turn helped explain Marpeck's social theology and his moderation and positive attitude toward civil government (Boyd 1992).

Chapter One. At the Foundation

1. Fritz Blanke, Harold Bender, John H. Yoder, J. F. G. Goeters, Heinold Fast, James M. Stayer, Martin Haas, Robert Walton, Arnold Snyder, Hans-Jürgen Goertz, Paul Peachy, and others have dedicated major studies to this subject. See also Packull 1985.

2. Bender 1950, 214.

3. There were some deviations. Christian Fessler of Zollikon wanted all books banned from discussions. Johann Kessler recorded that when some Anabaptists learned that the New Testament "was a matter of the spirit," they committed printed copies to the fire (Harder 1985, 435, 455; cf. also Gerber 1987, 291).

4. Gottfried Gerner, who examined the use of Scriptures by the Upper German Anabaptists, noted a preference for New Testament texts with moralistic or apocalyptic content (Gerner 1974).

5. Stayer called his second chapter "The Radicalization of the Social Gospel of the Reformation, 1524–27" in Stayer 1991, 45ff.

6. Yoder's phrase (Yoder 1967, 301ff.).

7. A case made by Arnold Snyder (Snyder 1990b, especially 278; also in Snyder 1991).

8. Snyder 1990b, 283.

9. Snyder argued that the Anabaptist continued an "early populist biblicism" that assumed the interpretive ability or at least the potential of all members of the congregation, whether educated or not (ibid., 271, 284).

10. See Chapter 2. Yoder argued that the abandonment of "the visible church" as "the hermeneutic community" led to a shift of "the locus of infallibility to the inspired text and technically qualified theological experts" (Yoder 1989, 26–27).

11. "Die täuferische Frage nach der Autorität der Schrift," in Fast 1959, 156ff. According to Fast, the Anabaptist position was one of simple obedience to the Scriptures. Similarly, Walter Klaassen wrote of "hermeneutic obedience" with the congregation as interpreter of the life and teachings of Jesus (Klaassen 1989a, 1–13).

12. In response to my arguments presented here, my colleague Arnold Snyder replied that he was not sure how the participatory congregational exegesis "actually worked—I am virtually certain that it was never as 'democratic' as it tends to appear in the descriptive literature in our century!" Letter dated November 30, 1992.

13. Clarence Bauman called it the *Grundgedanken* from which the distinction between the Old and New Testament was derived (Bauman 1968). See the discussion by Hans-Jürgen Goertz (1980, 58).

14. The *Swiss Order* invoked "the command of the Lord and the teachings of His apostles in Christian order." Friedmann (1980) argued that the Anabaptists were Gospel centered in their theology, whereas the magisterial reformers tended to have a Pauline emphasis.

15. A point also made by Ulrich Gerber (1987, 290).

16. Goertz 1980, 58, my translation. A similar argument was made by William Klassen (1959a).

17. The first edition appeared in 1516. "Some 3000 copies sold in the first two editions" (McConica 1991, 43ff.).

18. Cited by McConica 1991, 48.

19. Cf. Gäbler 1983, 45–46; Haas 1969, 88–89.

20. Zwingli's first principled defense, *On the Clarity and Certainty of God's Word,* was published in September 1522. Cf. Gäbler 1983, 58; Haas 1969, 93, 105.

21. Zwingli added, "For I also am not ashamed to read German at times, on account of easier presentation." The first New Testament in the vernacular had just come off the press in Basel (Harder 1985, 202).

22. Zwingli had learned that the Old Testament or part of it would soon appear in press. It was presumably a reference to the Pentateuch coming off Petri's press in Basel during December 1523.

23. Harder 1985, 236–37, 660 n. 14.

24. Ibid., 203–6; Packull 1990c.

25. Harder 1985, 185.

26. In his letter of December 18, 1523, to Joachim Vadian, Conrad Grebel expressed his disillusionment with the "learned heralds" who had overthrown the Word (ibid., 276).

27. Yoder 1980, 61–65; Walton 1980.

28. Kessler's report implied an organized congregation of sorts before the January 17, 1525, disputation on baptism (Harder 1985, 341).

29. Ibid., 289, 293.

30. Yoder 1958, especially 139. Gäbler wrote that Zwingli "beschränkte wie kein anderer Reformator den Gebrauch des Altarsakraments" and noted that its frequency of four times a year was in continuity with late medieval practice (Gäbler 1983, 98).

31. Here Grebel and his friends echoed Zwingli who, at the disputation in October 1523, argued that the ceremony should not be bound to any specific time and that details were to be left to the local congregation. He noted that the Philippians had the entire evening meal together but that Paul abolished the common evening meal when abuses arose (Harder 1985, 246, 377).

32. Specifically the rule of Christ, as per Matthew 18, referred to the procedure of excommunication. It should be noted that the *Swiss Order* invoked the "command or rule of the Lord" and the "teaching of his apostles" in a more general way as following their precepts.

33. Harder 1985, 289–90.

34. Ibid.

35. Ibid., 363.

36. Grebel himself could, of course, read the Latin Vulgate. He had a copy of Erasmus' *Annotations on the Greek New Testament*, which he read with some students (ibid., 286ff; 676 n. 17).

37. Ibid., 291; cf. 682 n. 85.

38. Ibid., 283.

39. Grebel's selection of texts on faith and baptism was to become a kind of miniature Anabaptist Bible with a wide range of influence.

40. Christoph Wiebe sought to demonstrate that Grebel's main point was that children have no faith and that Grebel did not argue for the natural blessedness of children. Wiebe claimed that Felix Mantz did not use the *Glaubensbegriff* in his *Protestation* but seemed more concerned with the *ordo salutis* (Wiebe 1989, especially 57–58).

41. See specifically the discussion of baptism in the letter to Müntzer. It included a reference to Deuteronomy 1:39 (Harder 1985, 290–91).

42. Zwingli himself was accused of holding that unbaptized children would not be damned (Haas 1969, 92, 150; cf. Klaassen 1989b).

43. Wiebe 1989, 56–57.

44. According to Zwingli, the Anabaptists claimed that Pope Nicholas II (1058–61) had made pedobaptism official.

45. Wiebe 1989, 56–57.

46. Zwingli cited the marriage ceremony and vows as other examples about which there was little in the New Testament (Zwingli, "Treatise on Rebels and Rebellions" in Harder 1985, 318–19).

47. Cf. Klaassen 1989b, 84–85; 1992a, especially 177.

48. Haas 1969, 89. The shift to the Old Testament coincided with Zwingli's rising interest and influence in the political arena that transcended Zurich.

49. At the same time Zwingli preached publicly on Old Testament books beginning with the Psalms and then going on to the Pentateuch. Oswald Myconius, schoolmaster at the Frauenmünster, held daily exegetical exercises on the New Testament beginning in 1524 (Gäbler 1983, 92–93; Potter 1976, 219–23).

50. June 3, 1525 (Harder 1985, 385ff.).

51. Zwingli cited 1 Timothy 3:5 (ibid., 394–95).

52. Zwingli qualified this to exclude candidates who were "sensual, bold, greedy, usurers or money grabbers."

53. At the same time Zwingli accused some "sectarian preachers" of having bestowed commissions on themselves and having consumed the meager resources of the poor while they had money in their own pockets (Harder 1985, 395, 397–98, 400).

54. See Zwingli, "Apologeticus Acheteles adpellatus," ibid., especially 185. The publication had a poem by Grebel attached to it.

55. Ibid., 395, 406.

56. Ibid., 392.

57. Zwingli cited the Anabaptists as claiming "One does not need a knowledge of languages. We understand the Scriptures as well as those who know many languages. It is a matter of the Spirit not of skill" (ibid., 402). Kessler reported that in St. Gall some Anabaptists "of the common . . . people, not much practiced in the Scripture . . . fell back on Matthew 11:25 "I thank thee, Father . . . that thou hast hidden these things from the wise and . . . revealed them to babes" (ibid., 381; also 369, 493).

58. Yoder argued that even at this stage Zwingli in theory supported "congregational conversation and decision making," and that he still hoped to convert the evangelical churches into New Testament congregations "in which every member would be free to speak and the others would judge" (Yoder 1969, especially 115–16).

59. Harder 1985, 392–93.

60. Ibid., 393.

61. A view expressed in December 1524 (ibid., 318).

62. Zwingli later told anecdotes about persons who stuttered in front of congregations, spelling out words they could not understand (cf. Snyder 1990b, 277–78).

63. Zwingli countered two specific arguments. One was based on John 3:34 and emphasized spiritual endowment. The other appealed to 1 Peter 2:5,9 and claimed that all members of the congregation had the right to prophetic office on the basis of the priesthood of all believers.

64. Zwingli accused his former followers of having used the tithe and interest issue to disturb the peace. They boasted of living in accordance with Acts 4 and holding all things in common (Harder 1985, 405–6, 409).

65. As will be noted in Chapter 6, the debate about apostolic authority remained alive for years.

66. The last one to examine this topic without testing the relationship to the nature of Anabaptist biblicism was Isaac Zürcher (Zürcher 1980–84).

67. Such claims had been made by Ludwig Keller, who wanted to connect the Anabaptists with conventicles of so called pre-Reformation evangelicals. It is true that at least eighteen pre-Lutheran Bible translations existed in Germany, but their circulation was limited.

68. Snyder emphasized the importance of "vernacular broadsheets and, especially, vernacular Bibles" and considered the latter "the undisputed textual focus" during the early period (Snyder 1993, 158–59).

69. Grebel in a letter to his brother-in-law Joachim (von Watt) Vadian (Harder 1985, 190, 640 n. 19).

70. Ibid., 202; cf. 646–47 ns. 27, 28; 659 n. 12.

71. The best source on the subject is still Mezger (1967). Besides Adam Petri's press, it was Thomas Wolff's press in Basel which produced New Testament editions.

72. Harder 1985, 289, 293.

73. Two further editions of the New Testament came off Zurich's presses in 1524 and one in 1525. Besides Froschauer, Johannes Hager published in Zurich (Mezger 1967, 43; Potter 1976, 128 n. 4; Locher 1981, 162–63, 574; Zürcher 1980, pt. 3, 55).

74. Froschauer published a six-part Bible in 1529 (Mezger 1967, 48–50; Zürcher 1980, pt. 3, 55).

75. Locher 1981, 162–3, 574. "Auch im Alten Testament schloss man sich an Luther an, war aber in Zürich eher fertig." Cf. Fluri 1956, 415–16.

76. It seems that Zwingli and his colleagues consulted this edition in their own work. A complete Bible containing a combination of Wittenberg-Zurich contributions appeared at Worms in 1529. Three editions of the entire Scriptures appeared also in Strasbourg between 1530 and 1535 (Zürcher 1984, pt. 3, 22, 55).

77. It has been suggested that between 1524 and 1527 Hätzer shifted from a "massive" biblicism to a spiritualism (Packull 1977, 56–57).

78. Phrases used by Snyder 1993, 173.

79. Bender 1950, 214.

80. That is, to Leviticus (Harder 1985, 313ff.).

81. Discussed in Chapter 2.

82. The entire letter with its twenty theses, upon closer inspection, consists of New Testament citations. Yoder's observation that "the preeminence of the New Testament within Scripture is taken for granted" seems like an understatement (Yoder 1973, 21ff.).

83. None of the biblical allusions in this oldest Anabaptist church order is to the Old Testament. I see this as evidence for its antiquity and authenticity. The later *Discipline,* with its more than one hundred Scriptural references, contains two references to Psalms, two to Proverbs, one to Ecclesiastics, and one to Daniel. Of more than forty references found in the *Common Order,* only three are to the Old Testament, with one of these to the apocryphal Naphtali. See the discussion in Chapter 2.

84. The "Submission" contains some forty references to the New Testament, none to the Old.

85. Zwingli, *Elenchus,* published at the end of July 1527, in Harder 1985, 486. Heinrich Bullinger later repeated this charge.

86. A charge made by Caspar Schwenckfeld.

87. In correspondence dated November 27, 1993, John Roth, editor of the *MQR,* suggested that Grebel, Mantz, and Hubmaier had a "theological bias toward the New Testament." The historic questions are, of course, how such a bias originated and why it was different from that of Catholics, Lutherans, or Reformed.

88. Reprints appeared in Basel in 1588, 1647, and in the eighteenth century. Cf. Zürcher 1980, pt. 3, 6ff.; Fluri 1956, 415–16; Yoder 1973, 25 n. 21.

89. In correspondence of November 27, 1993, John Roth proposed that the greater frequency of Old Testament references in the 1530s and 1540s suggests that Swiss biblicism was "still malleable." No doubt the availability of the vernacular Old Testament Scriptures and the polemics against the Anabaptists as Marcionites were factors for the greater number of Old Testament references. But whether there was a real substantive change from early biblicism would need further investigation.

90. A case can be made that medieval, typological, allegorical, tropological exegesis had been invented to harmonize the spirit or spirituality of the two Testaments, something more difficult to do with a literal or historic approach.

91. Zwingli, *Elenchus* in Harder 1985, 503.

92. Ibid., 366. The Old Testament references were in Grebel's collection of references on faith and baptism. One month earlier, Grebel wrote to Castelberger that he sent a copy of his assembled passages to Erasmus Ritter of Schaffhausen. Ritter apparently sent a copy to Zwingli (ibid., 426).

93. Dated September 9, 1527 (Harder 1985, 507–8).

94. Alleged accusations against which Zwingli defended in *Elenchus* in Harder 1985, 498–99.

95. The acceptance of this premise by Hans Pfistermeyer in 1531 at Bern contributed to his conversion to the Reformed position. See Yoder 1962, 133. The 1538 Bern disputation declared the full Bible as the basis for all discussions. Yet Anabaptist participants still cited 90 percent New Testament texts. One participant did not cite the Old Testament at all (Lavater 1989, especially 109-11, 113–14).

96. Hubmaier's tract carried the date June 11, 1525, and was a partial response to Zwingli's refutation of May (Pipkin and Yoder 1989, 95–149). In his response to Zwingli in 1526 Hubmaier wrote, "We have a clear word for baptizing believers and you have none for baptizing your children, except that you groundlessly drag in several shadows from the Old Testament" (ibid., 182).

97. Fast 1962a, 213–31; also *Ostschweiz* 2:265–73; *QGT;* Harder 1985, 425–26.

98. Grebel had also mentioned the collection of scriptural passages in a letter to Castelberger, dated April 25, 1525 (Harder 1985, 357–58, 427–28, 717 n. 25).

99. Of the Old Testament references three were to the Psalms, the others to the Pentateuch: five from Genesis, one from Exodus, and one from Deuteronomy.

100. Krüsi had bought the New Testament from a boy named Heini Locher for eight batzen. Alberli Schlumpf of St. Gall had lent him the copy of the Old Testament (*Ostschweiz* 2:262 n. 11, *QGT;* Harder 1985, 423–25).

101. Fast compared the Old Testament texts of Krüsi's booklet with Silvanus Othmar's 1518 Augsburg edition of the "Bibel teütsch" and the New Testament text with Adam Petri's 1523 Basel edition of "Das neu Testament." Fast concluded that the booklet deviated liberally from the texts to give a Swiss rendering. Cf. *Ostschweiz* 2:266 n. 5; 268 n. 7, *QGT.*

102. Fast 1962a, 225–29. Hubmaier's more substantive treatment on Christian baptism followed a similar pattern. So did an early work by Stoffel (Christoph) Eleutherobius (Freisleben), *Vom warhafftigen Tauf Joannis Christi und der Aposteln* (Frankfurt 1528). The author by his own admission had been influenced by Reublin.

103. Fast, 1962a, 225.

104. Of course not all Anabaptists were *Neutestamentler* in the Swiss sense. Hubmaier was well versed in both Testaments. Others, for example. Melchior Hoffman, were avid readers of the Old Testament. Bernhard Rothmann clearly distanced himself from the *Neutestamentler*. Echoing Zwingli, he wrote that "Christ and his apostles knew of no other scriptures from which to discern God and his will than what they took from the Old Testament, namely Moses and the Prophets." At the same time Rothmann did not "wish to diminish the importance of the New Testament" (Rothmann 1970, 225). But it was Marpeck who provided the most thorough treatment of the relationship of the two Testaments in his *Testamentserleuterung.*

105. The virtual identification of the two Testaments was more fully stated by Zwingli's successor, Heinrich Bullinger, in his *De testamentarum unitate sen uno testamento* of 1534. Cf. Klassen 1968, 21.

Chapter Two. The Oldest Anabaptist Congregational Orders

1. Friedmann 1955; reproduced in Friedmann 1961a.

2. Friedmann 1958a; cf. Friedmann 1959a, especially 34. Friedmann's thesis was most recently taken up by Boyd (1992).

3. Mecenseffy 1984, 78.

4. Schiemer, "Erstlich," especially 45.

5. The same letter, attributed to Schiemer, included an exposition of the Apostolic Creed and made reference to brethren from the *gemein* executed at Solothurn in Switzerland (ibid., 55). No martyrs from Solothurn are known from this early period, and it is not clear whom Schiemer had in mind. Cf. Geiser 1959a. The point is that he knew of Swiss Anabaptists.

6. Williams 1962, 232; Hostettler 1974, 17. Williams referred to the "twelve point program" as "the primitive constitution of the proto-Hutterites." He believed it "stressed the sharing of temporal goods somewhat more than the Swiss Brethren did." In his 1992 edition Williams noted its correspondence with the *Swiss Order* (Williams 1992, 353 n. 95).

7. *The Chronicle,* 77–79. Because of its greater accessibility and extensive footnotes, the English edition will be cited hereafter.

8. Boyd 1992, 52 n. 47; 54–55.

9. Müller 1972, 36–38; Yoder 1973, 34, 44–45.

10. Most recently the translators and editors of *The Chronicle,* 77–79.

11. I have come to this conclusion after careful consideration of the evidence with some nagging doubt that the oldest order may have originated in Moravia. Cf. Appendix A.

12. I would like to thank Dr. Heinold Fast who answered my questions regarding the *Swiss Order* in a letter dated October 8, 1988. He kindly sent me photocopies of the *Swiss Order* and the Schleitheim Articles in the same hand.

13. A linguistic comparison of the three documents still needs to be done. Linguistic experts could perhaps pinpoint the specific region of origin—Upper Rhine, Basel, Zurich, St. Gall, or Bern. In my view, expressions such as *siner* instead of *seiner, nütt* instead of *nit* or *nicht, kumen* instead of *kamen,* etc. indicate the Swiss or adjacent German vernacular.

14. Müller 1972, 36–38.

15. Gratz 1953, 25.

16. Stayer called Chapter 4 of his 1991 book, *The Swiss Brethren and Acts 4: A Rule of Sharing and a Rule against Exploitation,* 95–106, especially 105–6.

17. On the Schleitheim Articles, see Pletscher 1959, 460; Wenger 1955, 447ff.

18. Yoder 1973, 34.

19. Ibid., 53 n. 99.

20. *Ostschweiz* 2:26–36, QGT. Fast used the Bernese documents to establish a critical text of the Schleitheim Articles. He did not do the same for the *Swiss Order* because he could not substantiate that it originated at Schleitheim. In his letter to me, dated October 8, 1988, Fast wrote, "wenn wir wüssten, dass die Ordnung in Schleitheim entstanden ist, hätte ich sie aufnehmen müssen. Aber aus der Handschrift ist das nicht zu schliessen. Desshalb gehört sie dorthin, wo sie gefunden worden ist," that is, into the volume of Bernese documents.

21. The first part of the *Contra Catabaptistarum Strophas Elenchus (Refutation of the Tricks of the Anabaptists)* appears in English in Harder 1985, 478–505. The other two parts are in Jackson 1901, 177–219, 251–57.

22. Yoder 1962, 99 n. 18. Oecolampadius had received a copy of the Schleitheim Articles in mid March from Johann Grell, pastor in Kilchberg, a village in Basel territory. Oecolampadius also sent a booklet authored by Grebel which refuted Zwingli's position on baptism. Presumably this was the concordance on faith and baptism. See Chapter 1. Cf. Harder 1985, 476–77.

23. *Ostschweiz* 2:26 n. 3, QGT. Among eight Anabaptists involved were Hans Seckler (Johannes Hausmann) and Jacob Hochrütiner, son of Lorenz Hochrütiner, formerly from St. Gall. Two others were Hans Träyer (Dreier) and Heinrich Seiler from Arau. At the time of their arrest they allegedly had a following of twenty persons in Bern. E. Müller published Hans Seckler's statement that was given to the authorities (Müller 1972, 42–43. Cf. Yoder 1962, 99, 113).

24. A point made by Fast in his letter to me dated October 8, 1988.

25. According to Yoder, the Bernese text "does not always coincide with his [Zwingli's] Latin translation, and a few times the other reading reflected in his translation seems preferable" (Yoder 1973, 33).

26. In his letter to me, Fast wrote, "Es ist aber auch folgende Uberlegung möglich: Um Zwingli das Schleitheimer Bekenntnis zu schicken, muss Haller eine Kopie haben anfertigen lassen. Wenn er die Kopie geschickt hat, dann sind die in Bern vorhandenen Stücke diejenigen, die man bei den Täufern gefunden hat. Wenn Haller aber das Original geschickt hat, sind die Berner Ms nicht von Täufern sondern von Kopisten. Dann könnte die Ordnung später kopiert sein. Doch nehme ich an, das Original musste bei den amtlichen Akten bleiben. Das würde für das frühe Datum sprechen."

27. Zwingli criticized "some" Anabaptists on this matter in his "Treatise on Baptism, Rebaptism, and Infant Baptism" of May 27, 1525 (Harder 1985, 365).

28. An observation made by Stayer 1991, 104–5, 203 ns. 44–47.

29. The confession, believed to be Hausmann's, was translated and published by Springer and Springer 1986, especially 303.

30. As late as the spring of 1525 Zwingli spoke of 1 Corinthians 14 as the "rule of Paul." Yoder believed that even at that stage Zwingli still hoped to convert the evangelical churches into New Testament congregations "in which every member would be free to speak and the others would judge" (Yoder 1969, 115–16).

31. Springer and Springer 1986, 301. During discussions in Bern in 1531–32, Anabaptists defended, with an appeal to 1 Corinthians 14ff, the right of members to speak in meetings. "So einer also gesinnet und ein offenbarung hett, wie Paulus zum Corinth 14 . . . mag er harfürtragen mit ordnung nach der geschrifft, werdent wir im's lan galten, so wir doch all von gott gelert syn mussent" (Gerber 1987, especially 291).

32. Yoder took the liberty to translate "der psalter soll teglich by inen gelesen werden," as "shall be read daily in the home." He speculated that because of the high illiteracy rate and dearth of Bibles the reference may have alluded to rote recitations (Yoder 1973, 54 n. 102).

33. The first separate editions of the Psalter appeared in Basel and in Zurich in 1525; it did not appear in the Swiss dialect until 1527 (Mezger 1967, 49–50, 70). Separate editions had appeared in 1523 and 1524 in Augsburg: the first by Johani Boschenstein, the other by Othmar Nachtgal. Photocopies of the title pages were made available to me by the courtesy of the librarians Elizabeth Hart and Ruth Forrest of the Vancouver School of Theology. It should be noted that in 1525 Martin Bucer edited Johannes Bugenhagen's commentary on the Psalms, which was published in January 1526 in Basel (Hobbs 1991, 25ff., especially 34).

34. Yoder, who provided four New Testament references alluded to in the *Order,* did not list 1 Corinthians 14:26 or Colossians 3.

35. The Froschauer Bible of 1531 read, "wenn ir zusamen kommend, so hat ein yetlicher einen Psalmen / er hat ein leer / er hat ein zungen / er hat ein offenbarung."

36. It should be noted that the reformers of Ulm introduced a songbook and German Psalter in 1529, and in Rottweil members of the Reform Party sang or chanted Psalms in a street demonstration (Locher 1981, 437, 469–70). The first

evidence of an Anabaptist effort at putting a tune to the Psalms comes from a Hutterite codex of 1568. It is a "hymnic paraphrase of Psalm 111" (Oyer 1970).

37. Harder 1985, 229, 246. Gäbler claimed that Zwingli was against singing but accepted chanting (Gäbler 1983, 99).

38. This is Zwingli's interpretation of Philip's four daughters who prophesied. Since women were expressly forbidden to speak or exegete the Scriptures in the congregation, the meaning had to be that they "praised God in Psalms and other hymns" (Harder 1985, 401).

39. Ibid., 286.

40. Ibid., 287. It should be noted that practically everyone with a good Latin education would have known Latin Psalms by heart (Potter 1976, 221).

41. Springer and Springer 1986, 301. The statement on Christ's satisfaction could be seen as an elaboration of Article 7 of the *Swiss Order* which simply reads, Christ gave "his life for us, and shed his blood for us." Hausmann obviously cited the Epistle to the Hebrews.

42. Ibid., 289–91. Hausmann, Träyer and Heini Seiber (Heinrich Seiler) were drowned mid July 1529 in the Aare River.

43. Stayer 1991, 105.

44. This was a position held by Gabriel Ascherham.

45. Harder 1985, 344–45.

46. Springer and Springer 1986, 291, 303. The peculiarities prompted Springer to note that Hausmann's confession came closer in spirit to Hubmaier.

47. Yoder 1973, 39. Cf. Yoder's discussion, 52 n. 68. Cf. *Ostschweiz* 2:31, QGT. The "rule of Paul" was Zwingli's designation. Cf. n. 31.

48. Yoder 1973, 44.

49. This was Yoder's phrase in summarizing Seguenny's argument. Yoder suggested that the "one to whom God has given the best understanding" may be a code for spontaneously recognized leaders in the local group. It should be noted that the *Discipline* placed the emphasis on "one should speak and the other listen" lest there be "idle gossip and confusion." The translators of *The Chronicle* translated "only one at a time should speak." Cf. *The Chronicle*, 78 with Zieglschmid 1946, 84 (Jean Seguenny, cited in Yoder 1973, 54 n. 104).

50. The readings and discussions may have been guided by Grebel's concordance because of an evident emphasis on repentance, faith, and baptism. Cf. Blanke 1961, 21–42, 49–55.

51. In his letter of February 19 he asked his former congregation to send him a Bible (Harder 1985, 354). About Brötli, see Stayer 1977.

52. According to Blanke, they had the four marks of an independent church: preaching, baptism, the Lord's Supper, and discipline (Blanke 1961, 54).

53. Cited by Stayer 1991, 95–96. A slightly different translation appears in Harder 1985, 345; Zwingli related in connection to the June 12, 1525, incident, when the Anabaptists of Zollikon entered Zurich to prophesy its doom, that "they held all things in common" (ibid., 460).

54. This defense of their meetings has survived second hand through Zwingli's report of it. Cf. Yoder 1962, 94.

55. In their submission the Anabaptists of Grüningen declared that they had

laid off "pride, usury, hatred, anger, quarreling, fighting, sects, murder, drinking, gluttony, gambling, adultery, fornication, and all the lusts of the flesh" (*Schweiz* 1:234–38, especially 238, *QGT*).

56. Yoder 1962, 95–96; 117–18.

57. Augustin Bader came from Augsburg (Packull 1977, 134; Yoder 1962, 95 n. 5).

58. Cf. ibid., 96 n. 6, 114 n. 7, 118.

59. Earlier Krüsi and Wolfgang Ulimann appear to have been active here. Agatha Kamperer, an Anabaptist from the Southern Tyrol, testified that she had been baptized at Teuffen near St. Gall around Christmas 1528 by a brother Töbisch; probably Hans Töblinger of Freiburg in Uechtland (*Ostschweiz* 2:203, *QGT*). Joseph Beck gave the place as Tieffe and the translators of *The Chronicle* literally as "the hollow" near St. Gall instead of Teuffen (Beck 1967, 64; *The Chronicle*, 69, 72–73).

60. Yoder 1962, 117.

61. See the decree of suppression for Zurich territory of September 9, 1527 (Harder 1985, 508). For the later period, see Snyder 1990a, especially 355–57.

62. It seems that the function of the itinerant apostle "tied to no particular place" evolved for safety reasons; because the authorities were after the baptizers. For a view of the structure that had evolved by the nineteenth century, see Yoder 1962, 280ff.

63. In Bern territory or around Zoffingen similar conditions may have prevailed for a time. See Zürcher 1986.

64. Hans-Jürgen Goertz described the Schleitheim Articles as the "confession of an Anabaptist minority" (Goertz 1987, especially 23).

65. Snyder 1989. Snyder moderated Goertz's position.

66. As noted, Schiemer may have been familiar with its content.

67. It speaks of "one body, one bread, and one mind in the Lord." This had been Grebel's emphasis.

68. The passage reads, "Dem guethertzigen soll zum anfang das Euangelij Inn Creaturen fürgelegt und gepredigt werden." The translators of *The Chronicle* left out "in the creatures," and Friedmann too failed to translate it accurately (*The Chronicle*, 78). Cf. Zieglschmid 1946, 83–85. The accompanying reference to Colossians 1:16, Mark 6:15, and Romans 1 makes it clear that this is indeed an allusion to the Gospel of all creatures as preached in Hut's circle.

69. Packull 1977, 69–70. In Article 8 the *Discipline* urged that after the common meal, which, to reduce expenditures, should consist of soup and vegetables, "all the food and drink shall again be removed" because "one should use with thanksgiving and moderation the creatures which God has created, pure and good, for our subsistence."

70. Both the *Swiss Order* and the *Discipline* use the German *Gemein* or *Gemeinde*. Yoder translated *Gemeinde* as congregation; Friedmann, as brotherhood. I consider Yoder's translation closer to the original meaning, although *Gemeinde* can also designate a parish or a temporal community. Martin Luther had translated the New Testament word *ecclesia* as *Gemeinde* rather than *Kirche* (Midelfort 1990, 7ff., especially. 9). Midelfort has also drawn attention to the fact that

the word *family* became common only in the eighteenth century. Luther used *Gesinde, Haus,* and *Geschlecht* to translate the Latin *familia* or the Greek *oikos.* The basis of early modern economy (*oikonomia*) was the household.

71. It seems that Ulimann returned from Moravia to lead them. Cf. *The Chronicle,* 46, especially n. 3; Geiser 1959b; Ulimann, 787–88; *Ostschweiz* 2: 596, 604, 609, *QGT.*

72. Beck 1967, 20. Beck cited a communiqué by the Swiss that one of their preachers, Pretle (Brötli), had been burned at the stake.

73. *Ostschweiz* 2:636, *QGT.* The lord of Jamnitz (Jemnice) is known to have permitted a settlement on his estate and to have bailed some Swiss from prison at Passau.

74. The question must be raised whether the *Swiss Order* originated in Moravia. Some important documents believed to have been Swiss in origin upon closer inspection have proven otherwise. An example is the Cologne letter, written in response to queries about the beginnings of the Swiss Brethren and an important source on the beginnings of Swiss Anabaptism. Harder (1985) maintained that the information in the Cologne letter came from Swiss sources, but Fast and others took the view that the authors relied on a Hutterite account ("The First Believer's Baptism in Switzerland, Zurich, January 21, 1525" in Harder 1985, 338ff.; Fast 1978).

75. The editors of the *Elsass* 4:517–18, *QGT,* sided with Fast in moving the date for the *Common Order* found in *Das Kunstbuch* to the 1540s.

76. *Elsass* 1:185–86, *QGT.*

77. Ibid., 210–11.

78. "Gemeinsame Ordnung der Glieder Christi in sieben Artikeln gestellt (c. 1540)," published by Fast 1962b, 130–37. Translated by Klassen 1964. I want to thank Prof. Klassen for drawing my attention to this order and making an offprint of his translation available to me.

79. Klassen 1977, especially 2. I want to thank Prof. Klassen for making his unpublished paper available to me.

80. In correspondence with me, Stayer raised the question of whether the *Common Order* should not be seen as a modification of the *Discipline* rather than the *Swiss Order.* Marpeck's contacts with Moravia (see Chapter 6) could suggest transmission through Moravia. The fact that the *Common Order* retained the seven-point format, however, would imply a common source rather than a reworking of the *Discipline.*

81. My translation differs slightly with Klassen's. Cf. Klassen 1964. A similar point was made by Gabriel Ascherham in the 1540s. See Chapter 12.

82. See Chapter 6. After the Münster debacle and the expulsions from Moravia in 1535, a number of groups, including the Philipites and Gabrielites, also deliberately distanced themselves from this practice.

83. It is worth noting that Ulrich Stadler, a former member of the Anabaptists in Austerlitz, turned Hutterite, rejected six arguments against community of goods. The third of these was clearly directed against Marpeck's position. Cf. *Glaubenszeugnisse,* especially 225.

84. Klassen 1964.

85. It is worth noting that the Hutterite community in the early 1540s was rent by controversy on the double honor issue. Peter Riedemann wrote a letter defending the practice. Curiously, this same passage had been cited by Zwingli in defense of retaining benefices.

86. Klassen and Klaassen 1978, 361.

87. It should be noted that when Marpeck visited the Hutterites in 1541 he was not allowed to speak or join in prayer. Marpeck lost his temper and let it be known that he would rather unite with the Turks and the pope. *The Chronicle*, 210–11.

88. Marpeck appeared to have received his own authority originally from a congregation in Moravia. During his absence no one else baptized in his circle.

89. It is, of course, possible to see Hubmaier's liturgical efforts, his concern with catechism, and his "Form of the Supper of Christ" as the earliest attempts at structuring Anabaptist congregational life. Cf. "Form of the Supper of Christ" (1527) in Pipkin and Yoder 1989, 393ff.

90. Preamble, Friedmann, 1955; Appendix A. It should be noted that *The Chronicle* does not have the preamble.

91. Packull 1977; Stayer, Deppermann, and Packull 1975, 83-121.

Chapter Three. In Search of the Promised Land

1. Christoph Fischer, an early seventeenth-century Jesuit adversary of the Hutterites, wrote that missionaries enticed converts to emigrate with the slogan "Come to us in Moravia, to the promised land that is ours, and that God has given us. There you and your children don't have to suffer poverty and work hard as you do here. There you will certainly have food, clothing and shelter; your children will have training and schooling. You won't have to worry about anything. You women, when you're old, won't have anything to do but spin to avoid boredom and sit still. You men, you won't have to work hard anymore, only what you're able to do and as much as you want to" (translated and cited by Stayer 1991, 148). H. de Wind listed twenty sects in Austerlitz alone (de Wind 1955).

2. Urban 1986, 101ff.

3. Cited by Williams 1992, 1069–70.

4. Franck 1969, cxciii a–b.

5. *CS*, 17:218. Letter of April 30, 1560, to Daniel Groff.

6. Friedmann 1958b, 272–73.

7. Zeman 1969, 246–47 n. 25.

8. *The Chronicle*, 84–85.

9. Cf. Packull 1989a, 1990. The older view was represented by Harold S. Bender (1952, 262–78; 1953, 3–16). Similarly, see Friedmann 1956d, 1957b; Friesen 1984, 1986.

10. Schmid 1971, especially 329.

11. Seebass 1972.

12. Seebass 1974.

13. Stayer 1991, 61ff., especially 79–80.

14. Other known Anabaptists with connections to Müntzer were Hans

Römer, Heinz Kraut, Klaus Scharf of Mühlhausen, Balthasar Reif of Allstedt, Alexander Kirchner of Frankenhausen, Melchior Rinck, and in all probability also Hans Denck. Rinck's colleague, Heinrich Fuchs, lost his life in the battle of Frankenhausen.

15. Goertz 1989, 139–40.

16. English translation in Müntzer 1988, 253ff.

17. Meyer 1874, 241. Other later Anabaptists present were Klaus Scharf, Heinz Kraut, and Melchior Rinck.

18. Franz 1954, 265ff. Gottfried Seebass suggested that Hut brought Jörg Haug's *Christliche Ordnung eines wahrhaftigen Christen* to the press in Augsburg (Seebass, "Hut, Hans," 741–47).

19. Stayer argued for continuity between the antipedobaptism and the believers' baptism movement (Stayer 1993b).

20. Seebass 1975.

21. Packull 1986a.

22. Hut's birthplace Haina lay in Henneberg's territory. Under pressure Henneberg accepted the Twelve Articles but took vengeance as soon as circumstances permitted (Franz 1975, 238ff., especially 186, 243).

23. Berbig 1903. Cf. *Bayern* 1:199, *QGT;* Wappler 1913, 233–49; Bauer 1966, 27, 57, 60 n. 12.

24. With oral testimony and differing styles of written communication it is easy to explain the use of various names for the same person. Cf. *Bayern* 1:75–95, especially 80, 82, 94, *QGT;* Wappler 1913, 29, 32, 230–32, 234, 239, 244, 249, 280, 291, 306, 313, 323.

25. Stayer 1991, 167.

26. *The Chronicle,* 84. It is possible that Volckhamer traveled to Salzburg with Hut's companion Märtz and others. In early 1528 a number of Anabaptists seized in Auerbach, Bavaria, had fled from Salzburg. The leader among them was a former priest named Gilg, who had received his commission from Dorfbrunner. Kilian Auerbacher, a leader of the Austerlitz Brethren, wrote a letter in 1534–35 to Martin Bucer in which he criticized Bucer's participation in the persecution of Anabaptists (*Elsass* 2:401–11, *QGT;* Loserth 1959a).

27. *The Chronicle,* 80–81. See Stayer 1972, 141ff.; Packull 1977, 99ff. Williams repeated the view that Hut pressed a pacifist view in Nicolsburg (Williams 1992, 342).

28. Stayer 1991, 140ff.

29. Packull 1977, 99–106.

30. Mecenseffy 1984, 78.

31. It has been suggested that these were commissioned by Hut to baptize at a meeting in Steyer in the summer of 1527 (Mecenseffy 1964). For a good overview for these territories, see Lassmann 1980, 118ff.

32. In November 1527 in Salzburg twenty-five women and sixteen men did public penance with a cross on their foreheads and burning candles in their hands before receiving absolution (Dittrich 1990–91, 75).

33. Schiemer died January 14, 1528 (Packull 1977, 106ff.). Waldhauser was executed April 10, 1528, in Brünn, Moravia (*The Chronicle,* 59). A letter dated

the Saturday before Palm Sunday, 1528, written to those "who had been brethren in Brünn," has been preserved in Hutterite codices ("Thomas Walthauser, ein Sendbrief an die, so Brüder gewesen sind zu Brünn," *Episteln* 3 : 503–9).

34. Mecenseffy 1971, 155ff.

35. Widmoser claimed that Anabaptists were mentioned as early as March 1527 in relation to Rattenberg, but his source is vague (Widmoser 1951, 55).

36. For Salzburg, see the dated essay by Johann Loserth (1912).

37. Meyer 1874, 245.

38. Klaassen 1978, 106–7.

39. Cf. *Oesterreich* 1:42–45, *QGT*; Meyer 1874, 224–25. Augustin Bader and Gall Vischer, two followers of Hut from Augsburg, helped organize the congregation in Kaufbeuren along these lines in March 1528 (Packull 1977, 131–32).

40. Berbig 1903, 316; *Bayern* 1:95, *QGT*; Wappler 1913, 280.

41. Stayer 1991, 85–86, 114–15. It should be noted that Augustin Bader and Gall Vischer later established a commune that practiced community of goods in Lautern near Ulm. They were joined by Oswald Leber, a former preacher to rebellious peasants in the Odenwald area. See Packull 1986a, 51–67.

42. Wiedemann 1962, 262.

43. *Württemberg* 1 : 8, *QGT*. They also agreed with statements made by Augustin Würzlburger that "no one should have to beg and that those with surplus should place some of it into a common treasury." But anyone too lazy to work, anyone who sought to take advantage of the others, was expelled and considered a heathen. Asked about a rule or order concerning community of goods, Würzlburger knew of none except of what he had read in the New Testament. Of interest is also how Würzlburger, a schoolmaster in German (*teutscher schulmeister*), had become an Anabaptist apostle. Word had reached him that the congregation in Augsburg had elected him or another schoolmaster, Hans zur Weiden (Wiedemann?), for this task. The two let the lot decide between them. It fell on Würzlburger. The case of Würzlburger also suggested that the lines among various Anabaptist branches up and down the Danube were rather fluid. Würzlburger was baptized by Leonhard Freisleben on November 17, 1527, in Regensburg. His wife, Barbara, had been baptized by Burkhardt Braun of Ofen. *Bayern* 2:27–29, 31, 34, 38, *QGT*.

44. He lived in house number 7 at the Hofmarkt of St. Niclas (Wiedemann 1962, 268).

45. Margreth Schernegker from Vilshofen testified on February 6, 1528, that Wolfgang (Brandhuber), the schoolmaster of Burkhausen, was her husband (*eevogt*). He was the son of a Bader (Pader) from Obernberg. Of interest is that the Passau congregation had, presumably through Brandhuber, the following literature: "an old Latin Bible [*wibl*]; the New Testament; a booklet of Psalms [*psalmbuechel*]; the Prophets; and a book of theology (the *Theologia Deutsch*?).

46. *Glaubenszeugnisse* 1 : 137–43, especially 138.

47. Christian Hege wrote that he "laid the foundation for the practice of community of goods which was instituted among the Hutterian Brethren in 1528" (Hege 1955b).

48. Stayer placed Brandhuber in a line of influence emanating from Müntzer-

Hut (Stayer 1991, 122). But Brandhuber's position on not taking vengeance and not going to war indicated a Swiss influence and a new synthesis, which seems consistent with positions held by the Austerlitz Brethren.

49. Hut had returned to Augsburg where at the Martyrs' Synod—so called because most participants were soon apprehended and executed—his views stirred controversy. He was arrested around September 15 and died a few months later that year (Packull 1977, 118–21). The lords of Liechtenstein appear to have surrendered Hubmaier in July 1527 (Zeman 1969, 191 n. 64).

50. The religious leadership in the Liechtenstein domain appears to have remained almost entirely in the hands of former clergy. Besides Spittelmaier, the following belonged to the party opposed to Wiedemann: Oswald Glaidt, Christian Rodtmäntel (Entfelder?), Klein Utz, Gross Utz, Hans Werner, Andreas Mosel, and a Strützel (*The Chronicle*, 48). Ibid., 80–81, from its Huttero-centric perspective, named Hans Spittelmaier as the one who broke away.

51. Beck 1967, 72. "Haben in den Häussern hin und wider versamlung gehalten, die Pilgram, Gäst und Fremdling aus andern Ländern aufgenommen, die Gemeinschaft angenommen."

52. Ibid., 72; *The Chronicle*, 80.

53. Beck 1967, 50–51; Stayer 1991, 141. If this group was influenced by the Schleitheim Articles, it is also possible that it was familiar with the *Swiss Order*.

54. I am borrowing these designations from the translators of *The Chronicle*: servant of the Word = *Vorsteher* or *Diener des Worts;* servant of temporal affairs = *Diener der Notdurft;* instead of manager for *Haushalter* I prefer "assistants in temporal affairs." Not clear is whether these designations were used by Wiedemann's group and adopted by the Hutterites or whether they read them back into the beginnings.

55. Friedmann 1961c, 42.

56. Friedmann 1955a.

57. The lords were the Kaunitz (Kounice) brothers, Jan, Vaclav, Peter, and Oldrich (*The Chronicle*, 81–82 n. 2). Wiedemann had sent four men ahead to Austerlitz informing the lords of certain articles his group believed and practiced, among them an article that it was against their conscience to participate in war. The lords responded by sending them three wagons to speed up the trek to Austerlitz.

58. Jaroslav Panek noted that the first settlements including Nicolsburg, Austerlitz, and Rossitz all lay near this artery (Panek 1989, 656–57). Other early settlements were at Znaim, Brünn, and Eibenschitz.

59. *The Chronicle*, 82: "to other countries, especially the Tyrol."

60. He baptized in Rattenberg in the house of Hans Maurer and must have been an acquaintance of Marpeck. Cf. *Oesterreich* 2:111–287, *QGT; The Chronicle*, 59. A song in the form of a dialogue between God and man attributed to him is found in *Lieder*, 45–46. Panek described the Anabaptist congregation at Böhmisch Krumau as large (Panek 1989, 649–50).

61. *The Chronicle*, 85; Zeman 1969, 199 n. 96. "Haben sich auch dermassen aufgemacht und immer begert dem vollkommen nach zu jagen. Seindt irer bey achtzig Personen zu der gemain geen Austerlitz komen" (Beck 1967, 86ff.). A rem-

nant remained at Krumau because Hans Amon addressed them in two letters of
1537. Cf. Zeman 1969, 223.
    62. *The Chronicle*, 83–84 n. 1.
    63. Ibid., 84–85.
    64. *Oesterreich* 2:377, QGT.
    65. *The Chronicle*, 84; Beck 1967, 85.
    66. He does not appear in the records of fugitives involved in the peasants'
uprising or Anabaptists in Memmingen and surroundings. The information was
provided by Prof. Philip Kintner of Grinell College, Iowa.
    67. The claim was made by Alexander Nicoladoni but has been questioned
by Lassmann (Nicoladoni 1893; Lassmann 1980, 87).
    68. Beck 1967, 50 n. 2. Beck mentioned a Sigmund Hoffer and Hans Schlaf-
fer besides Kautz as Wiedemann's contacts in Augsburg.
    69. Curiously, Jäger does not appear among the names of Austerlitz leaders
after 1528. See Chapter 4.
    70. *The Chronicle*, 81.
    71. *Oesterreich* 1:175–76, 194, 211–12, QGT.
    72. The number of former schoolmasters who became leaders in the early
movement supports this view. To some extent the means of communication dictated that the leaders be literate.
    73. I deal with this subject in my forthcoming work on Peter Riedemann.
    74. *Bayern* 2:19–20, QGT.
    75. The distinction between Jörg Volck (also spelled Folcke, Volk, Volken,
Volcker, Volckmer) and Kilian Volckhamer (also spelled Volkhaimer, Volckmair,
Volkmair, Volkhaimer, Volckamer) was made by Wappler. Wappler's sources on
Thuringia referred to a Jörg Volcker and a Kilian. Wappler noticed that a Kilian
Volckhamer, a sextant at Grosswalba, appeared in sources relating to Hut's con-
verts at Königsberg. He inferred that Kilian Volckhamer of Grosswalba was the
same person as the Kilian mentioned in Thuringian sources. He concluded that
Kilian Volckhamer and Jörg Volck must have been two separate persons. Günther
Bauer, working with that assumption on Franconian sources, sought to uphold
the distinction between Volck and Volckhamer as two separate persons but felt it
necessary at one point to correct the sources. He suggested that where the name
Volckhamer appeared, the person in question was really Volck! There would have
been no need for this correction if Volck and Volkhamer were one and the same
person. Against such a conclusion seems the evidence that Kilian, the sextant, was
a little man (*ein klein mendlein*), whereas Volck was described as a thirty-year-old
Büttner (*puttner*) and relatively tall (*zimlich lang*). At the same time, a careful
reading of the statements made by Hut's followers left the impression that they
used the name Volck and Volckhamer interchangeably. Asked whether they knew
Hans Hut, Eucharius (Binder), Joachim (Märtz), Kilian Volkhamer, and Balthasar
Fridberger, the better informed seemed to know Hut and Volckhamer. The majority knew the latter as Volck. Thus Fritz and Hans Striegel of Uttenreut, named
Hans Hut, Volckhamer or Volkmair, and Balthasar (Hubmaier?) as principal
leaders. Most others named only Hut and Volck. One of Hut's converts gave Hut's
first name as Michel. *Bayern* 1:75–95, especially 80, 82, 94, QGT. Cf. Wappler

1913, 29, 32, 230–32, 234, 239, 244, 249, 280, 291, 306, 313, 323; Berbig 1903, 313; Bauer 1966, 27, 57, 60 n. 12.

76. Berbig, pp. 291-353, esp. 312. Cf. *Bayern* 1:199, *QGT;* Wappler 1913, 233–49. About Henneberg and the uprising in the Thuringian Forest area, see Franz 1975, 238ff., especially 186, 243.

77. As noted earlier, an "elect servant of the Lord Jesus Christ and a called shepherd of his holy congregation in Austerlitz," who signed himself as Kilian Auerbacher, chastised Martin Bucer in an eloquent letter for persecuting Anabaptists. *Elsass* 2:401–11, *QGT.* Cf. Note 26.

78. An example of good internal history and what it can contribute is that of Leonard Gross (1980).

79. Hruby (1935) and Zeman (1969) represent good attempts at utilizing external sources.

80. Panek considered the "unusually favorable social-economic and confessional-political circumstances determinants" for the establishment of the Anabaptist communities in Moravia (Panek 1989, 652).

81. John Klassen 1978, 138.

82. Friedmann 1957a; 1961b.

83. Panek 1989, 653.

84. John was crowned in September 1529, after the Turks took Ofen (Budapest). Cf. Barton 1985, 60ff.

85. Zeman 1969, 197. Friedmann listed only three. Friedmann 1957a, 748.

86. Panek 1989, 654.

87. Zeman 1969, 182 n. 24.

88. *Hubmaier* 328, 434, *QGT.*

89. Panek 1989, 658.

90. Zeman (1966) 40:266–78; ibid. 41:40–78, 116-60, especially 274.

91. Hruby noted that the Anabaptists were treated as foreigners well into the second half of the sixteenth century (1570), that the lords dealt with the leaders. Perhaps this aided the development of a clear authority structure in the communities (Hruby 1935, 71–72).

92. Points made by Friedmann 1957a.

93. Zeman 1969, 248ff.

94. Stayer wrote, "During the 'golden period' despite their ritual denunciations of the wicked world, Hutterite society was tied to the surrounding aristocracy by ties of interest, and even, it seems, of some mutual affection" (Stayer 1991, 154).

95. Simprecht Sorg, a nephew of Froschauer, printed sixteen of Hubmaier's works in Nicolsburg. Hubmaier dedicated his work "On the Sword" to Arkleb of Boskowitz, who had been governor of Moravia from 1519 on. *Hubmaier* 433, *QGT.* Cf. Zeman 1969, 165, 221. Hubmaier dedicated other writings to Burian Sobek who, in 1522–23, hosted Müntzer (Steinmetz 1971, 162). About Sobek, see Zeman 1969, 63, 64. About Jan Dubčanský to whom he had dedicated a tract on water baptism. Dubčanský was the main mover for colloquia between Utraquists and evangelicals at Austerlitz in 1526 and in February 1528 between rep-

resentatives of the Minor Party and Brethren on his Estate of Habrovany, near Austerlitz, see Zeman 1969, 69.

96. Panek suggested that the Hutterite experience of soldiers who raided their communities was no different from that of the rest of the population at the time and ought not to be exaggerated (Panek 1989, 656).

97. Hruby 1935, 198. Friedmann reported only one execution. Waldhauser died in Brünn on April 10, 1528 (Friedmann 1957a, 748).

98. Bergsten 1978, 379. The "Stäbler" left Nicolsburg nine days later.

99. Besides the Turks, Ferdinand faced Duke Ulrich of Württemberg, who was bent on getting his territory back. Ferdinand's troops were defeated on May 13, 1534, and he signed a treaty permitting Ulrich's return on June 29.

100. Whatever the Anabaptists' theoretical position may have been on not paying war taxes, it is clear that their payments contributed indirectly. Total separation from society did not exist.

101. Hruby 1935, 10.

102. As late as September, the Moravian Estates supported the request that the expulsions from Nicolsburg should be postponed until the Anabaptists there had been able to dispose of their property. Ferdinand refused (ibid., 13–14).

103. Ibid., 12–13.

104. By April 15, 1535, he had warned the governor of Upper Austria not to permit refugees from Moravia to settle there. He repeated these instructions on May 2 and June 30. *Oesterreich* 3:288, *QGT*. On June 6, 1535, he ordered the bishop of Breslau, Jacob of Salza, Duke Karl I of Münsterberg-Oels, and Duke Frederic II of Liegnitz, Brieg, and Wohlau not to tolerate the Anabaptists from Moravia on their Estates (Weigelt 1985, 80, 174 n. 33).

105. In 1538 Ferdinand imprisoned Lord Jan Dubčanský as a warning to others, and at the diet of 1540 he again demanded the expulsion of *all* Anabaptists.

106. I deal with these documents in my forthcoming work on Peter Riedemann.

107. Hruby 1935, 19. For the hardships during this period, see *The Chronicle,* 299–314.

108. Panek wrote of a late feudal "autonomously managed estate economy" (Panek 1989, 652).

109. Friedmann had estimated their membership at 25,000 with children (Friedmann 1955a, 198). Panek revised the figures downward. During the second half of the sixteenth century they made up perhaps 10 percent of the population in southeastern Moravia, with Neumühl (Nove Mlony) near Ludenburg (Breclav), their main community (Panek 1989, 657–58).

110. *The Chronicle,* 82. The townspeople may have been ethnic Germans, however, and the Brethren apparently were not too happy with the deserted farmsteads, which had been assigned to them first. They stayed only three weeks before seeking permission to move into town.

111. Ibid., 135.

112. Ibid., 188 190 n.

113. Zeman 1969, 266. The Brethren source probably dates from the 1570s.

114. Panek maintained that the complaints were in part justified. Integrated into the estate economy, the Anabaptists strengthened the feudal lordlings and weakened the cities (Panek 1989, 658–59).

115. *The Chronicle,* 160. The exception appears to have been a mission to Slovakia in 1536. It was sponsored by a local noble, who also donated land for a settlement, but the settlement lasted only four years.

Chapter Four. The Philipites: Fugitives from Swabia, the Palatinate, and the Rhineland

1. The most substantive previous treatments were those by Wilhelm Wiswedel (Wiswedel 1952a, 1952b; Friedmann 1959b, 1959c). See also Friedmann's more substantial article (1958b).

2. Wiswedel observed that Hutterite sources are "one-sided" against Plener and Ascherham (Wiswedel 1952a, 147).

3. Apparently so labeled by the Hutterites (*The Chronicle,* 79–80).

4. Wiswedel claimed that attempts of rapprochement with the Swiss on the Upper Rhine in 1539 failed but that they united a little later (Wiswedel 1952a, 148). Friedmann held that the Philipites, who returned to the Neckar-Kraichgau, Strasbourg-Worms areas after 1535, fused with the Swiss Brethren (Friedmann 1959b).

5. Friedmann 1955d.

6. Claus-Peter Clasen identified eighteen emigrants to Plener's community in Auspitz during the early 1530s (Clasen 1978, 17). For my own identification see Appendix B.

7. Bossert believed Philip went also by the name of Burner and Loyer, the latter a derivative of Löwe (lion). *Württemberg* 1:52, QGT.

8. This comes from a statement made on August 23, 1536, by Michel Gartner from Ettenheim, who had been baptized by Philip in Moravia four years earlier (1532). *Elsass* 3:39–40, QGT. The editors could not determine whether this meant Blienschwiller in Lower Elsass, Canton Barr, or a place near Colmar in the Upper Elsass, which has since disappeared. Or was it Bischwiller, not far from Hagenau?

9. Roth 1901, 126, 131: "sei nit ferr von Strassburg dahaim." This should correct previous guesses such as that of Bossert, who assumed that he came from Zaisersweiher, near Bruchsal. Wiswedel followed Bossert. Cf. Friedmann 1959c, 192.

10. *Elsass* 3:40, QGT. The Inn to the Plow, located on the Steinstrasse, had served as a meeting place for Anabaptists expelled from Augsburg and Esslingen in 1528 (ibid., 1:180 n. 3). For its location, see the map provided by Nelson and Rott 1984, 230–41.

11. Roth 1901, 128, 130. Cf. *Elsass* 3:40, QGT.

12. Williams claimed that Philip Jäger, a weaver (*Weber*) and Plener were identical. If Jäger and Plener were identical, the disappearance of Jäger from the Austerlitz leadership would be explained (Williams 1992, 352).

13. Deppermann 1979, 166.

14. *Elsass* 1:114, *QGT.*

15. Ibid., 197–99. The Strasbourg reformers who cited Hätzer thought better of Sattler. They also considered Kautz more dangerous than Reublin.

16. Deppermann wrote of "two distinctly different Anabaptist fellowships" (Deppermann 1979, 167). Is it possible that Deppermann read later distinctives back? But Gerhard Hein described the Anabaptists influenced by Kautz as "purely spiritualist in coloration" (Hein 1972–73, 105).

17. *Elsass* 1:203–4, *QGT.*

18. About Reublin, see Stayer 1982a; 1977, 83–102.

19. *Elsass* 1:205, *QGT.*

20. The reformers considered Kautz more learned in the Scriptures than Reublin. Reublin was not in agreement with Kautz in all points (ibid., 195–96).

21. Hans Frisch had been baptized by Reublin at Horb in 1527, later elected deacon, and appointed by the Vorsteher Adam Stumpffle. He described three orientations: "nemlich hoffmännisch, Kautzen und Reiblins meining" (*Elsass* 1:299; cf. pp. 288–89 of same, *QGT*).

22. Sebastian Franck exaggerated when he suggested that they had as many differences in teachings as they had leaders (Franck 1969, 193).

23. Landwehr 1986, especially 209. Hans Berlin from Esslingen moved to Strasbourg.

24. Among them was Ulrich Trechsel, who had been sent to Worms with a Peter Scheppach, who, like Philip, was a weaver by trade (*Elsass* 1:128–32, *QGT;* cf. Boyd 1992, 50 n. 42).

25. Roth 1901, 12–17.

26. Reublin accompanied Michael Sattler from Schleitheim to the area of Horb but managed to escape the arrest that led to Sattler's martyrdom. He had a sister in Esslingen, where he baptized around Pentecost (Landwehr 1986, 145).

27. Lutz and others testified that an understanding faith had to precede baptism.

28. Landwehr suggested that Reublin left for Ulm before arrests began in January 1528.

29. Landwehr saw a "Mischlehre" on certain issues such as the oath, permissibility to bear arms, an emphasis on spirit baptism, and apocalyptic expectations (Landwehr 1986, 167–69, 197).

30. According to Landwehr, leaders were acclaimed rather than elected and lacked a clear conception of their task. Most came from prominent social positions. The leaders after Lienhard Lutz were Bernhard Klein and Joachim Fleiner. Hans Bayerlin, Hans Fygenbutz, and Hans Utz served as *Säckelmeister.*

31. Landwehr 1986, 163, 169 n. 202.

32. Landwehr estimated that in early 1528 the Anabaptists in Esslingen and surroundings numbered about two hundred and made up 2.5 percent of the population (ibid., 114, 165).

33. The number of Anabaptists around Worms has been estimated at forty. They were led by a weaver and by a fisherman named Kraus. Cf. Hein 1972–73. Freisleben went on to Frankfurt (Packull 1977, 144–45).

34. Landwehr (1986, 210) cited Clasen.

35. *Baden und Pfalz* 4:125–26, *QGT*.

36. Beck 1967, 29–32; Krebs believed these figures were too high. *Baden und Pfalz* 4:141 n. 1, *QGT*. Deppermann noted that 41 percent of all executions between 1525 and 1618 in German territories took place during this first wave of suppression in 1528–29. Another 39 percent followed between 1529 and 1533 with only 20 percent in the 85 years after that (Deppermann 1979, 236).

37. Hutterite sources blamed the Burggraf Dietrich of Schönberg for the arrests and the blood council (Beck 1967, 311; Hege 1908, 58).

38. There is no evidence to place Philip in Augsburg as early as 1527 as Friedmann has done (Friedmann 1959c).

39. *CS* 17:338. By November 1530, Schachner had settled in Nuremberg. Thirty years later he had become a Schwenckfeldian who spoke negatively about the early Anabaptist leaders he had known in person, including Hut, Hätzer, Hubmaier, and Leupold (Packull 1977, 127–28).

40. Roth 1901, 126, 131. Some took advantage of the last chance to be baptized.

41. Ibid., 127.

42. *Baden und Pfalz* 4:138-40, *QGT*.

43. Ibid., 140. After leaving Esslingen, Reublin had been active in the Ulm area. The lords of Gemmingen reformed their territory of Fürfeld and Bonfeld with the aid of Martin Germanus. In 1530 Philip von Gemmingen of Fürfeld rejected claims that he had been a patron of Oswald Leber, a Peasants' War preacher and the companion of Augustin Bader. *Württemberg* 1:949, *QGT*.

44. *Baden und Pfalz* 4:140, *QGT*. An estimated 87 to 120 Anabaptists, or about 10 percent of the 1,200 evangelicals, including 40 preachers, whose deaths were blamed on the work of the notorious provost Bernhard Aichelin, were executed in Swabia (Landwehr 1986, 163, 199–200).

45. Hans of Landschad, a pro-Reformation noble and former Burggraf of Alzey, appointed Otter as preacher in Neckarsteinach but was pressured by Ludwig V to dismiss him. There is some confusion about the timing of Otter's dismissal. Wilhelm Diehl gave the date as 1527, but in the following year Hans of Landschad took measures to assure a better income for Otter and got him an assistant. As late as April 1528, Otter was still publishing from Steynach. In 1532 he accepted a position as Ambrosius Blarer's successor in Esslingen. Blarer had come from Ulm in the fall of 1531 (Maurer 1979, 344–48; Diehl 1917, 410–16).

46. *Baden und Pfalz* 4:127, 135, 141–47, *QGT*.

47. See his Introduction to Otter 1528; excerpt in *Baden und Pfalz* 4:127–30, *QGT*.

48. Ibid., 129. Otter had himself been driven from Kenzingen in the Breisgau in 1524–25 by the Austrian authorities. A number of his parishioners went into exile with him.

49. Ibid., 128–29.

50. Ibid., 140. Hege placed the accusation into Otter's mouth, but the original statement is clear: "daruf Philips Weber zum prediger gesogt: er, der prediger, sy ein wolf und sy ime under die schof komen, aber er, Philip, sy ein scheflein und heb ime als dem wolf die lemlein entzogen" (Hege 1908, 61).

51. Ibid., 139.
52. *Elsass* 1:185–86, QGT. Cf. Boyd 1992, 54ff.
53. Reublin was not released until March 1529.
54. Michael Jungmann testified in 1555 that he had been baptized about twenty years earlier (1535?) by a Blasius von Brussel (Bruchsal). *Baden und Pfalz* 4:352, 355, *QGT.*
55. Claims made by Friedmann (1959c) and by Hege (1955c). It is possible that this figure is derived from statements by converts in Augsburg that up to five hundred Anabaptists lived in the Strasbourg area.
56. *Baden und Pfalz* 4:477–78, *QGT;* Bossert 1904, 71–88.
57. Bruchsal appears as *brusel* in the list (*Bayern* 2:278–79, *QGT;* also printed by Beck 1967, 310–11).
58. *Baden und Pfalz* 4:479, 481, *QGT.*
59. Lober's wife had been arrested earlier with two other women and with Bernhard Weik of Bruchsal and Ulrich Hutscher of Oberntief near Windsheim. Cf. Schmid 1972, 68 n. 308.
60. Hege 1957c; *Elsass* 1:330–31, *QGT.* Cf. *Bayern* 1:217, *QGT.*
61. It seems that Lober wanted to return to Moravia at the time of his arrest. Ulrich Hutscher testified that Lober and Bernhard had visited him and that Lober had spoken of wanting to go to Moravia to "learn the order and nature" of the brotherhood there. Hutscher and Bernhard had apparently remained in the Nuremberg-Ansbach area. When asked about his plans, Lober gave his destination as Ulm, where he wanted to take a boat on the Danube. Presumably this meant he planned to return to Moravia after having visited the Bruchsal and Strasbourg areas. On his way back to Moravia he wanted to pick up his wife, who had lodged with Hutscher until her arrest. *Bayern* 1:243, 247, *QGT.*
62. He had been at the Estate of Dobitsch, presumably Tobitschau (Tovacov) near Prerau (Prerov) in the territory of Jan of Pernstein; or perhaps at the residence of Dobesch of Boskowitz (Boskovice), the husband of Bchunda of Pernstein, lord of Rossitz.
63. *Bayern* 1:217, *QGT.* It seems that Lober had also been in Bamberg.
64. Ibid., 219, 238.
65. Ibid., 2:186–87. Lober had moved to Windsheim with Hutscher. This corrected Hege's assertion that "What the Ansbach government finally did with Lober is not known" (Hege 1957c, 380). Frey testified that he had spent some time in prison with Lober at Windsheim. *Elsass* 2:92, *QGT.*
66. *Bayern* 2:187, *QGT.*
67. *Würtemberg* 2:3–7, *QGT:* "war zum Schelm geworden." Beck wrote that Lober had "left the Bruchsal congregation in the lurch" (Beck 1967, 71).
68. Goertz provided the following distinguishing features for Swiss Anabaptism: (1) no longer greeted outsiders; (2) called each other brethren; (3) emphasized simple dress; (4) shunned religious services; (5) emphasized mutual aid; (6) refused the oath; (7) refused office in the secular state; (8) refused to sue in court (Goertz 1987, especially 25).
69. Friedmann's belief that he arrived as early as 1527 does not seem warranted (Friedmann 1958b, 272; 1959c). Zeman believed that he was in Rossitz by

September 1528, but he assumed that he came straight from Augsburg (Zeman 1969, 228).

70. They settled on the lands of the Convent of Maria Sall of Brünn whose abbess, Johanka of Boskowitz, belonged to the same family as Dobesch of Boskowitz, the husband of Behunda of Pernstein on whose lands Gabriel's community settled. The Philipites resided just outside Auspitz on the road to Nicolsburg, whereas the proto-Hutterites, who arrived in January 1531 led by Reublin, moved into town (*The Chronicle*, 90).

71. Ibid., 79–80. The translators here took the liberty to translate what should read "Philip and his own moved to another house" as "moved away . . . and started another community" (cf. Beck 1967, 69).

72. A claim made by Beck: "In der Lehre und Organisation standen sie auf gleichem Boden" (ibid., 69).

73. Schlegel's statement given to authorities at Strasbourg in 1536. *Elsass* 3: 40, *QGT*.

74. Among possible baptizers from patrician background Marpeck comes to mind. Did Marpeck travel through Nuremberg in 1528?

75. Schmid 1972, 52–57, 62–63, 70–71. Beringer considered Wolfgang Vogel a genuine martyr. Schmid's distinction between an urban Anabaptism influenced from Moravia and an "older" rural form originating with Hut does not take account of the interaction between the two groups.

76. Georg Lang, who left Etzlinweiler in March, was baptized with his daughter-in-law April 2, 1534, by Schlegel at Donauwörth. Lang's wife and son were baptized upon arrival in Moravia by Philip. *Württemberg* [2]:5, 8, 20–21, *QGT*.

77. See the report by Bonifacius Wernitzer at Kirchberg on March 17, 1534 (ibid., 1, 7). Johann Herolt recorded in his chronicle for the year 1534, "In disem jar sein vil baurn mit weib und kind, in dem widertauf anhengig, hinweg in Merenland gezogen" (cited in ibid., section 6).

78. Tabisch, Kronau, and Güding are mentioned, the last under the lord Johann of Lipa. See the statement made by Dietrich of Heilbronn (ibid., 20–21).

79. *The Chronicle* 135–36.

80. That this group of about forty and their leader, who shook "the dust from their feet," were former Philipites is implied by the fact that nearby Fürfeld was the area of Philip's earliest ministry. In 1536 Schlegel met with a group of about thirty returnees from Moravia in a forest near Heilbronn. On June 9, 1537, a Hans Schreiner from Gmünd, a *Vorsteher,* was driven from Heilbronn. He is possibly the Philipite leader, Hans Gentner, who later turned Hutterite. On his recommendation, Peter Riedemann visited former Philipites in the Heilbronn region in 1539–40. For Heilbronn, see *Württemberg* [2]:56–63, *QGT*. See also Lichdi 1978, especially 27–28.

81. Friedmann 1958b, 294.

82. Wolkan 1965, 42.

83. A similar point was made by Liesenberg 1991, 71, 107–8. Other shared songs were about the martyrdom of Georg Wagner, about "seven brothers" who died in Schwäbisch Gmünd in 1529, and about the martyrs in Alzey. Wagner was

burned in Munich in 1527. Five pamphlets commemorated his martyrdom. One originating in Nuremberg became the basis of one of the first Anabaptist martyr songs that served as model and provided the tune for many others. Cf. *Ausbund* 11:60 and 20:12.

84. Wolkan 1965. Cf. Beck 1967, 132–33 ns. 2 and 3. Christoph Erhard, writing in 1588, claimed Hutterites had by then a "grossen mächtigen hauffen etlicher hundert geschribner Lieder" (Erhard 1588, 34a–34b.

85. *Etliche Geseng,* 1564. The first *Ausbund* of 1583 carried fifty-one of the fifty-three songs of 1564 (Bender 1929, 147–50). According to Friedmann, all subsequent seventeenth-century editions omitted three of the original songs, but one of these was retained by the Hutterites under the date September 5, 1539 (Friedmann 1958b, 29, n. 73; cf. Friedmann 1955d).

86. Ray Conrath, a friend of the Hutterites who believes that the Swiss deliberately attempted to hide their original commitment to community of goods, drew my attention to this editorializing.

87. One of Michael Schneider's hymns was dropped in the 1583 edition; the other by Hans Betz in the 1622 edition. Oyer, too, believed that the hymns were dropped because of their outspoken advocacy of community of goods (Oyer 1991, especially 278 n. 62).

88. For an examination of some of the lyrics and tunes cf. ibid., 282 n. 77. Tunes in the Meistersang tradition were popular from Augsburg, Nuremberg to Worms, Speyer and the Strasbourg area (ibid., 280).

89. For the sources on their experience see Packull 1989b. Some of these archival materials were previously utilized by Wolkan 1965; see also *Württemberg* [2], *QGT.*

90. For a list of their names and place of origin see Appendix B. Clasen noted that most were from Lower Swabia and northwest Württemberg (Clasen 1978, 22).

91. Bossert identified this as Vaihingen on the Enz, a tributary to the Neckar (statement by Hans Steuber; *Württemberg* [2]:17, *QGT*).

92. A Gewer Bauer from Schwaigern later accompanied Schlegel to Strasbourg.

93. Packull 1989b; *Württemberg* [2]:19, *QGT*. Cf. Oyer 1991, 262–63.

94. Wiswedel 1959; Oyer 1991, 258–59.

95. It seems that Schluchtern belonged to a Swiss group because he described them as living not in community but scattered "one here, the other there" (*Württemberg* [2]:16, *QGT*).

96. A Jörg Leserlin of Ingersheim recanted on September 5, 1533, at Stuttgart. His youth and simple-mindedness helped to give him a pardon (*Württemberg* 1:32, 71–72, 179, 197–98, 222–23, 1003, 1005, 1006, 1018, *QGT*). Bossert identified the later Jörg Scherer with Seelscherer, also known as Jerg Wernlin, who for a while served as bath master or doctor at Ulm's poor house (Seel or Armenhaus). Jörg Scherer had been imprisoned at Ulm in 1530. He knew Schwenckfeld and Marpeck. In 1532 he appeared under the name of Jerg Wernlin of Gunzenhofen (hausen). On October 27, 1537, he was exiled from Ulm for a second time. After that he spent time in the Rems valley and Esslingen area as well

as in Weiler zum Stein, Kirchenheim, and Stetten. He died in 1559 (*Würtemberg* [2]:952, *QGT*).

97. Wackernagel 1964, 5:1070; *Ausbund* 1981, 59:319. This Georg of Ingersheim is said to have died in prison.

98. Erhard 1588, Chapter 6. Wolkan believed that literacy was not necessary for writing songs (Wolkan 1965, 2–3).

99. Cf. Locher 1900, 271–84. The song appeared for the first time in the 1583 edition of the *Ausbund*.

100. Oyer accepted that these songs were composed and sung in prison (Oyer 1991, 282 n. 77).

101. Ibid., 282–83.

102. *The Chronicle*, 162 n. 2. Petz (Betz?) died in 1537 (Beck 1967, 132–33 n. 3).

103. Packull 1989b, 98, 99; *Württemberg* [2]:24, *QGT*; Wolkan 1965, 35–36; Hege 1955a. Peter Stumpfheter, a fellow prisoner of Betz at Passau, had been baptized by Ulrich (Stadler).

104. Matheus of Dornau, a prisoner at Passau and a member of the Znaim community, testified that "at Auspitz some of their sect were against them in some articles, but that he did not know in what articles because he was a simple person and not well informed." Matheus had been baptized in 1528 by Andre(as) Vischer, the later Sabbatarian. In 1529 he and thirty-five others were imprisoned at Empach (Taxenbach). Seventeen of his fellow prisoners had been executed. Matheus' wife, also an early convert, had been baptized by Georg from Staffelstein or Jörg Nespitzer, Hans Hut's brother-in-law (*Württemberg* [2]:24–25, *QGT*.

105. Aschenberger's letters to the elders and to his wife at Znaim were preserved in Hutterite codices. *Episteln* 2:105-111. Cf. Loserth 1959b; *The Chronicle*, 226. I am dealing with the details of the Steinabrunn affair in a planned second volume.

106. *Lieder,* 74–77. About Betz's songs in the *Ausbund*, see Schreiber 1979.

107. Beck 1967, 132 n. 2. Two verses of the song attributed to him were obviously added postmortem.

108. Packull, 1989b, 96. Bossert gave Schneider's home as near Dillingen, Friedmann's as near Lauingen in the Palatinate. Cf. *Württemberg* [2]:20–21, *QGT*.

109. Friedmann thought Beck was from Gerding near Eichstedt. In 1534 Beck had been imprisoned in Lower Austria and "burned through the cheek before release." He had been baptized by Blasius Kuhn; his wife Elisabeth by (Julius) Jobst in Gmünd. Cf. *Württemberg* [2]:2, *QGT*.

110. Packull 1989b, 100.

111. Letter by Duke Ernst of November 18, 1538 (Packull 1989b, 101). The Duke had been present during discussions with Schneider and Dietrich of Heilbronn (Oyer 1991, 264 n. 32).

112. Wiedemann 1965, 101 n. 30. Mosham later cited the recantation of Michael Yetelhauser (Jedelshauser) in his *Ain Christliche wahrhafftige, gründtliche Entschuldigung.*

113. The letter implied that Beck had written a previous one and that Michael (Schneider) had an audience with the duke. Beck admitted that he had been in error in some matters, without spelling them out (Packull 1989b, 105).

114. Oyer dated his arrival in Nuremberg at September 18, 1539 (Oyer 1991, 266).

115. Packull 1989b, 104, 107; Oyer 1991, 266–68. Not clear is whether he considered children lost until they had come to an understanding faith or whether he considered them innocent until they engaged in conscious disobedience.

116. Oyer 1991, 270–71.

117. Packull 1989b, 108.

118. Oyer 1991, 262–63.

119. Friedmann 1958b, 272–73 n. 2.

120. Friedmann 1931. Cf. Friedmann 1959b. The full title reads *Von einem Wahrhaften Ritter Christi, und womit er gewappnet muss sein, damit er überwinden möge die/welt, das/fleisch und den Teufel.* A typewritten copy with Friedmann's introduction, now in the Mennonite Archive in Goshen, Indiana, was made available to me by the courtesy of Dr. Leonard Gross.

121. Cf. *Ausbund,* 530–35. Friedmann 1958b, 291–92. The eleventh verse was attributed to Haffner, the first to Hans Betz, the third to Peter Strumpheter, the tenth to Hans Hoffmann, and the fourteenth to Bernhard Schneider. Friedmann could not identify the others. Their initials were given as M v.2; D v.4; J v.5; R v.6; D v.7; H v.8; B v.9; Til. v. 12; G v.13. Perhaps v.4 or v.7 was attributed to Dietrich of Heilbronn.

122. In 1540 or 1541. *Württemberg* [2]:3, 20, 28, *QGT.*

123. Oyer 1991, 261 n. 20.

124. Haffner's activity in Bischwiller prompted an attack by Johannes Schwebel, the reformer of Zweibrücken. See *Baden und Pfalz* 4:251, 510, 528–76, *QGT*; Jung 1910, 119–20, 204–5 ns. 56, 57.

125. A Jörg Haffner had baptized Hans Betz, a prisoner and poet at Passau. A Hans Haffner appears in Swiss sources as a subject of the Abbey of St. Gall along with a Martin of Teuffen (Harder 1985, 422).

126. Oyer analyzed the songs under the rubric of suffering, obedience, soteriology, *Gemein,* and biblicism.

127. Liesenberg drew attention to differences between the Hutterite and Swiss martyr songs on this score. Besides, Swiss songs tended to make statements of faith, whereas Hutterite songs recorded legendary miracles and tended to focus on the martyrs as steadfast heroes, capable of heroic self-sacrifice (Liesenberg 1991, 198, 216, 254).

128. Oyer drew attention to four of Schneider's songs as "only slightly expanded forms of straight Scripture" (Oyer 1991, 279).

129. "Wir schreien zu Dir Herre Gott," in *Etliche Geseng,* 28–30.

130. Braght 1951, 365–67.

131. Friedmann 1955b, 1956a. Friedmann speculated that they were members of the "Greek-Slavic Bogomile Church."

132. Oswald Glaidt led a community of "Jamnitzer" at the Bergstadt of Jam-

nitz until his death in 1545. The landlord of Jamnitz sent his Burggrafen, Heinrich of Lomnitz, to Passau to vouch for the costs (*Atzungskosten*) and to demand the release of the prisoners (Beck 1967, 152 n. 1).

133. This is my inference from the fact that the song, along with a cluster of others, appears only in later editions of the *Ausbund*, 892–95.

134. Packull 1989b, 110.

135. Friedmann 1955b, 63.

Chapter Five. The Gabrielites

1. Weigelt 1985, 49ff. McLaughlin 1986a, 3–21. King Louis of Bohemia died at the battle of Mohacs, August 26, 1526.

2. Hensel 1768, 159, 167–68.

3. Ibid., 169ff.

4. Shantz 1992.

5. McLaughlin 1986a, 114.

6. Cf. *The Chronicle*, 446–50. Gustav Koffmane also listed Ernst of Glatz and Veit Uhrmacher of Grünberg (Koffmane 1887, 39).

7. Hensel 1768, 196. Hensel cited Georg Aelurius (Aelurius 1625, 497).

8. Zeman 1969, 225 n. 204.

9. Weigelt 1987, 59, 167 n. 23; cited in Sommersberg 1729, 220.

10. Koffmane 1887, 38.

11. Weigelt 1987, 59, 167 n. 26.

12. A letter circulating among Hut's supporters in Augsburg may have originated in Breslau with a companion of Oswald Glaidt. The letter was dated January 1528. Cf. Packull 1977, 124–26. The identity of Hess is not known. An Anabaptist Hans Hess was arrested on November 26, 1530, in Nuremberg (Schmid 1972, 68). Wiswedel thought it was a Hans Hess who died in 1552 at the Hutterite community of Aexowitz (Wiswedel 1952b, 222). See *The Chronicle*, 317. The latter was a tailor; the one arrested in Nuremberg was a spoon maker.

13. Ascherham 1541: "Was sich verloffen hat unter den Brüdern . . . von dem 1528 bis auf das 1541 Jahr." Cf. Note 75 below.

14. Liechty 1988b, especially 40ff.; also Liechty 1987, 325–36. See also Weigelt 1985, 62–67; 1987, 361–69.

15. About Glaidt, see Loserth 1897, 70–73; Wiswedel, 1937a.

16. He made this claim in his 1526 *Handlung*. For a bibliography, see Liechty 1988a.

17. According to Williams, Glaidt's *Handlung* of 1526 was published in Nicolsburg, Zurich, and Worms, which suggests some connections with radicals in these territories (Williams 1992, 333–34).

18. Pipkin and Yoder 1989, 217ff., especially 249.

19. Glaidt 1527. For a summary of content, see Loserth and Friedmann 1956.

20. It is noteworthy that he cited 1 Timothy 5 in support of the claim that "true priests were worthy of double honor."

21. Liechty argued that a tripartite view of baptism indicated Hut's influence

on Glaidt (Liechty, 1988b, 49). But Hubmaier's influence makes more sense. Cf. Pipkin and Yoder 1989, especially 189.

22. Schiemer subsequently wrote an epistle on the tripartite aspects of true baptism, a concept first treated by Hubmaier but also developed by Glaidt and Hut (Schiemer, "dritt epistel," 77ff.).

23. Hubmaier dedicated his *Second Book on Free Will* to Frederic, perhaps in the hope that Frederic might be recruited as a patron for a magisterial form of Anabaptism. *Hubmaier,* 389, 400–31, *QGT.*

24. Schwenckfeld, "Vom Christlichen Sabbath," *CS* 4:452–518.

25. Simprecht Sorg, who had printed sixteen of Hubmaier's works as well as Glaidt's *Apology,* also moved to Liegnitz and began to print for Schwenckfeld (Weigelt 1985, 59, 167 n. 26).

26. Crautwald responded in 1531(?). Wolfgang Capito responded on the urging of the lords of Liechtenstein in late 1531, and Schwenckfeld's refutation dated from January 1, 1532 (Loserth and Friedmann 1956).

27. Glaidt was executed in 1546 and recognized as a martyr by the Hutterites for his courageous witness in the face of death. But this does not mean that he had joined the Hutterites. Cf. *The Chronicle,* 240–41.

28. Specifically Psalm 118 (Liechty 1988b, 49, 118).

29. Koffmane noted that a Clemens left Schweidnitz territory for Glogau in the company of Joachim Wittich from Breslau, who had joined him from Moravia. Koffmane implied that at Glogau the two were joined by an Adler. He was apparently unaware that Clemens's last name was Adler (Koffmane 1887, 43–44).

30. Packull 1991a. I had presented parts of my findings in a paper at an Anabaptist colloquium, Bluffton College, Bluffton, Ohio, April 16, 1988.

31. Geiser 1951. A typewritten copy of the entire codex is in the Mennonite Historical Library, Goshen College, Indiana (Adler 1529). Cornelius J. Dyck felt that the codex had not received the attention it deserved. According to Dyck, the "early treatise by Clemens Adler on biblical pacifism" merited special attention (Dyck 1990).

32. Adler 1529. Adler's treatise fills forty-one typewritten pages (pp. 69ff.) of the Geiser manuscript.

33. The translators of Geiser's initial report promised to search for Adler (Bender 1956, 72).

34. The codex or fragments of it were found in 1961 during renovations of a former Hutterite dwelling (Friedmann 1965, 35–37, 105).

35. Bender 1959. Bender knew from unidentified sources that Adler died in 1536. The source was presumably Friedmann, who through his extensive knowledge of Hutterite codices, must have encountered the story of Adler's ministry in one of them.

36. Stayer 1972, 169–70. Stayer followed Bender's suggestion that Adler was a member of Wiedemann's Stäbler group at Austerlitz.

37. Besides Adler's work, only the Schleitheim Articles and the *Aufdeckung der Babylonischen Hurn* dealt with this subject in any substance. According to Peter Brock, "neither work is especially distinguished either by its style or by the

effectiveness of its argument." Brock found "the most able presentation of that doctrine" in the writings of Marcin Czechowic (Brock 1991).

38. Koffmane 1887, especially 39.

39. Radler 1962, especially 41. Official correspondence referred to the Anabaptist called "Clement" as the originator and coauthor (*Ursacher . . . mit Anfenger*) of Anabaptism in the principality of Silesia.

40. Court records about him were destroyed during World War II. My queries at the Wroclav (Breslau) archive were answered to this effect on April 15, 1988, by the then director, Dr. Janina Pastawska.

41. Koffmane 1887, 43–45.

42. Weigelt 1985, 59.

43. "Ein Newe Geschichte" 1571 (hereafter "A New Story"). Under a slightly different title in Codex Montana 1565, Reel 22:263–64. The author wrote in the first person "out of love for his brethren." The question arises as to whether this story was copied from Gabriel Ascherham's history of Anabaptist beginnings, now lost.

44. Fast 1975.

45. Since "A New Story" disappeared from later codices, one wonders whether with time the predictions about the end lost some of their attraction.

46. He died on October 23, 1456. About him see *CE*, 452. Friedmann gave the date wrongly as 1556 and speculated that it referred to the time when the story was written or when it occurred (Friedmann 1965, 29).

47. Radler 1962, 45.

48. Adler 1529, 78. I am citing the pagination found penciled in on the upper left corner of each page of the typewritten copy.

49. Koffmane 1887, 41. The cathedral chapter concerned itself with the request on July 28, 1529.

50. Adler 1529, 85.

51. Cf. Packull 1986b.

52. Adler 1529, 69.

53. Ibid.

54. Ibid., 70.

55. Ibid., 71.

56. Ibid., 84ff.

57. Ibid., 76–77. Adler's distinction between Old and New Testament or covenant is reminiscent of Karlstadt's "Von dem Neuen und Alten Testament," which was written in the context of controversy concerning the sacrament of the altar. Karlstadt contrasted the Old Testament with its bodily sacrifices of blood with the once-for-all sacrifice brought by Christ, the ultimate intercessor and high priest (Barge 1905, 2:283ff.).

58. Adler 1529, 75.

59. Ibid., 79ff. "Von dem ewigen Fürstenthum Christi Jesu und von seinem Regement."

60. Ibid., 108ff.

61. Leonhard Schiemer wrote an exposition of the "Twelve Articles of the Christian Faith" because "these articles are a précis [*ausszug*] of the entire Scrip-

ture, the sense [of the Scriptures] is contained therein, whether they were composed by the apostles or other important [*fürneme*] Christians. There is nothing else found in the Scriptures according to our faith than is drawn [together] in these articles" (Schiemer, "Erstlich," 44ff., especially 47).

62. Adler 1529, 81. "aus zweien Volkern das ist aus Juden und Heiden durch das word Gottes in dem Glauben Aberham, Und Christi versamlet."

63. Liechty 1986.

64. "Wider den Alten uund Newen Abionitischen Irtum der Ihenigen / die Mosen mit dem Herren Christo / das gesetz mit dem Euangelio/ das Alt Testament mit dem Newen vermengen / und einen Zwang / des befreyten gewissens Im Christenthumb/ daneben anrichtenn" ("Auff Osswald Glaids buchlenn Vom Sabbath," CS 4:453ff., especially 489).

65. CS 4:474–75. Schwenckfeld wrote in 1531–32.

66. Adler 1529, 79. Missing are qualifications that no war tax or tax supporting the executioner should be paid.

67. Ibid., 76.

68. Ibid., 94. The similarities to Schwenckfeld's argumentation are again striking.

69. Ibid., 98ff.

70. The contrast here was between Mt. Zion and Mt. Sinai. CS 4:488–89.

71. Adler 1529, 82. Such an emphasis seemed not incongruent with the substitutionary notion, "but the Lord laid upon him all our sin" (101).

72. Ibid., 98ff.

73. Besides Glaidt's works, the writings of Leonhard Schiemer and Ulrich Stadler come to mind (*Glaubenszeugnisse* 1:58ff., 212ff.).

74. Maleczynska 1961.

75. Ascherham 1541. This work is not in the Oesterreichische Nationalbibliothek, Vienna, as Hans Hillerbrand (1991) claimed in *Anabaptist Bibliography 1520–1630* 1652:127. I have written to numerous archives in search of it, but so far without success.

76. Loserth 1894.

77. Ascherham (1544) published in Wiswedel in 1937b. The best works on Gabriel and his community are those of Robert Friedmann (1955c, 1956c).

78. Schmid 1972, 108–9 n. 481. Gabriel was also known by the name Gabriel Scherdinger or Schärdinger because he resided in Schärding before coming to Moravia.

79. Ibid., 15–25; Packull 1977, 90–91.

80. Repeated by Williams 1992, 629.

81. *The Chronicle*, 79–80.

82. Beck 1967, 69–71 n. 2.

83. *The Chronicle*, 79–80. Since Hutterites had access to Gabriel's chronicle and could use former Gabrielites as their source, they were well informed about Gabriel.

84. Ibid., 54–55. It also recorded the martyrdom of Virgil Plattner at Schärding under the date 1529 (ibid., 59–60; Beck 1967, 33).

85. *Oesterreich* 1:107, *QGT*. Another Anabaptist from Schärding, Brigitte,

daughter of Leonhard, recanted before April 2, 1528. She had been baptized by Hans Oeder of Passau. Oeder and his wife were arrested in Nuremberg before January 23, 1528. They had Hut's son with them. Oeder recanted one year later (Packull 1989b; Wiedemann 1962, 266, 274).

86. See *Oesterreich* 2:320, *QGT*. Brandhuber was the son of a Bader from Obernberg; his wife Margreth Schernegker came from Vilshofen. Brandhuber had a brother Jörg who was a tailor at St. Niclas, a suburb of Passau. See statements by Margreth Schernegker of February 5, 1528. She was in the same group of prisoners as Gabriel (Packull 1989b, 21, 22, 23).

87. "Wiedertäuferischen Gesindleins in Mähren und Schlesien seltsame Beschaffenheit" (1535 SA, Becksche Sammlung, G 10149, no. 68, fol. 22v, now in the State Archive at Brno, Slovakia). A microfilm copy of this text was made available to me by archivist Dr. M. Coupek.

88. Rossitz was also the residence of a group of Bohemian Brethren of the Minor Party, according to Zeman 1969, 238–41.

89. Hensel 1768, 196. Hensel repeated the figure of two thousand converts but gave 7,000 taler instead of gulden, cited in the source above.

90. Beck suggested that by 1535 the Haushaben at Auspitz contained two thousand adults. He estimated the Rossitz group at twelve hundred adults (Beck 1967, 69).

91. This emerges by inference from events discussed in Chapter 9.

92. See Note 75.

93. "Verantwortung d. Gabrielischen Briefs von uns der Gemeinde zu Schakkowitz mit unseren Aeltesten und allen Verklagten, verlesen vor etlichen mehr denn 100 Brüdern und mit der Bewilligung der ganzen Gemeinde überreicht." I used a microfilm copy of an 1572 codex in the Eastern European Anabaptist Collection, MIC A274, Reel 87, 31–33, Arts Library, University of Waterloo. Cf. Friedmann 1965, 14, 29, 54.

94. Williams was wrong when he thought this work to be lost (Williams 1992, 629). Beck was wrong when he thought it was published. It survives in manuscript form (Ascherham 1544).

95. "Eine Ermahnung an die Obrigkeit" in ibid., 251ff.

96. "Vom Abendmahl" in ibid., 255ff.

97. The work referred consistently to the "christliche Gemein" or "christliche Kirche." The designation seems to correspond to usage by Schwenckfeld, who emphasized the difference between it and Old Testament Israel.

98. Ascherham 1544, 10. Wiswedel wrongly considered the Austerlitz Brethren and Swordbearers as one and the same group.

99. Ibid., 18. He addressed their arguments directly with "So du aber willst beweisen . . . So du aber sagest: Die Apostel haben doch auch Apostel erwählt."

100. He rejected the notion of "some" that there were to be no externals (ibid., 23).

101. He wrote of "the order, which the maker of all things had ordained" (ibid., 19).

102. Ibid. Marpeck had warned that "some . . . attributed too much to this image of man's godlikeness, as they do, for instance, when, before the redemption

by Christ, they attribute all power and ability to man's free will" (Marpeck 1978, "Instruction," 79).

103. Ascherham 1544, 25. Gabriel obviously borrowed from a tradition that viewed wisdom in the feminine.

104. Ibid., 19.

105. Ibid., 20.

106. Throughout "A Clear and Useful Instruction," Marpeck argued against the docetic orientation of some. He insisted that "through Christ's humanity, the inward must be revealed and recognized" (Marpeck 1978, 76).

107. Ascherham 1544, 32.

108. Ibid., 17.

109. Schiemer translated "and dwelleth among us" as "in us." Adler told peasants that the "will of God is in you."

110. It should be noted that this was the motto on all of Entfelder's publications.

111. Ascherham 1544, 19–20.

112. Ibid., 33.

113. Ibid., 29.

114. Ibid., 13.

115. Ibid., 243.

116. Ibid., 14.

117. Ibid., 243.

118. Ibid., 243–44.

119. Ibid., 16–17. He went on to accuse them of superstition: "Erstlich, dass du sagst, sie werden durch deinen Tod versichert, das ist Zauberei."

120. Ibid., 11. In 1533 Hutter had seen three suns in the sky as divine portents that his separation from the Gabrielites and Philipites had divine approval. His followers considered his martyrdom another verification. Cf. Chapter 9.

121. A claim made by Wiswedel 1937b, 262.

122. Ascherham 1544, 253.

123. Ibid., 254.

124. He wrote of a "Wind der Sorgfältigkeit ausgegangen auf dass die Völker eifrig würden, nach seinem Willen zu fragen," or "Wind des Hungers" (ibid., 254).

Chapter Six. Marpeck's Early Controversy with the Spiritualists

1. "Clare Verantwurtung," English translation, Marpeck, "Refutation," in WPM 1978, 43–68; "Ain klarer vast nützlicher Unterricht," English translation, Marpeck, "Instruction," in ibid., 69–106; Klassen 1959a; see also Klassen 1968, 36–54.

2. The external evidence consists of a suspicion recorded by censors at Strasbourg that Marpeck published two booklets in 1531 and by a note attributed to Caspar Schwenckfeld, found in a copy of the "Instruction," suggesting that Marpeck must be its author. See Klassen 1968, 36–39, especially 37 n. 101; Klassen and Klaassen 1978, 43–44, 69–70; and Elsass 1:298, 335, QGT.

3. Bünderlin 1530; Klassen 1968, 41 n. 112. The strong internal evidence for this came from the rejection of "Stillstand" in the "Instruction" (Klassen 1968, 39).

4. Ibid., 43 n. 117. See Note 2 above.

5. Williams 1962, 274; Klassen 1968, 274.

6. An identification made by Dr. Helmut Claus, former director of the Research Library at Gotha, Germany. Dr. Claus made his findings available to me in a letter dated May 27, 1988. He also helped to identify the press for the anonymous tract *The Uncovering of the Babylonian Whore*. Cf. Packull 1993.

7. Blough 1984.

8. Klassen observed, "in the development of a 'Biblical' rather than a strictly New Testament theology . . . Marpeck's brotherhood took a leading role" (Klassen 1968, 106).

9. Marpeck used the 1536 Froschauer Bible and a 1529 Wormser edition. The preface of his "Explanation of the Testaments" (Testamentserläuterung) was translated by Klassen and Klaassen (1978, 555ff., especially 559). Walter Klaassen noted that Marpeck's "Concordance" of 1544 resembles unmistakably Schwenckfeld's work of 1532 (Klaassen 1986, 389ff., especially 394). Cf. *CS* 4:472–79.

10. Fast 1984, 66–74

11. Entfelder 1530. On Entfelder, see Seguenny 1980, 1:41–42; also Packull 1977, 163–75.

12. *Wie die Gschrifft verstendiglich soll underschieden / un erklärt werden / die vom Tauff sagest / wie der Hailig gaist mit seinen gaben vor und nach kumpt / un seine werck laistet / ernstlich durch der laer* (n.p., n.d.), translated by Yoder (1973, 171ff.).

13. I made this case in Packull 1993. Cf. Note 6.

14. Klassen had noted earlier the motto in the *Kunstbuch* (Klassen 1968, 38).

15. Cf. Boyd 1992, 69ff.

16. Blough 1987, 378.

17. Boyd added Sebastian Franck to those who followed the "spiritualist tendencies of Denck, Hätzer and Kautz" in Strasbourg. He maintained that the relations between Schwenckfeld and Marpeck remained cordial until their controversy in the 1540s (Boyd 1992, 59ff.; 104–7).

18. *Elsass* 1:225, 231–32, 252, *QGT*. Bünderlin came from Nicolsburg and Entfelder from Eibenschitz.

19. Zeman 1969, 240–41.

20. Boyd 1992, 5ff.

21. Ibid., 24. Eighteen persons were executed on May 9, 1529, in Rattenberg (Palme 1986, especially 72).

22. It should be noted that the lord of Krumau, Johann of Lipa, was also the landlord of Eibenschitz, the community served by Entfelder.

23. Boyd 1992, 52. This corrects Klassen and Klaassen (1978, 23), who assumed that Marpeck went directly to Strasbourg.

24. Schlosser's wife and Schützinger's wife are mentioned under March 30, 1528. Four children left behind by Schlosser, along with Schützinger's child and

Marpeck's three foster children, are mentioned under July 31, 1529. Cf. *Oesterreich* 2:99, 266, *QGT*. Also mentioned in this context were Paul Taurer, Konrad Streicher, and Wilhelm Dänkl.

25. I assume that the Schlosser mentioned in Reublin's letter was Melchior Schlosser of Rattenberg. According to Reublin, Schlosser was deceived by the Austerlitz group and remained there. *Elsass* 1:300–1, *QGT*. See Note 20.

26. Boyd 1992, 24. The preacher, active at the castle of Müchenau, known only as Paul, may have been Paul Taurer. See Note 24.

27. Zeman 1969, 199, 256 n. 57.

28. Reublin implied that he had sent an earlier letter to Marpeck and received a reply through Schlosser. The Hans Eschlperger mentioned in Reublin's letter was presumably Hans Aschlberger, one of the Aschlbergers who, with Andreas and Sebastian Taurer, belonged to the earliest Anabaptists in the Kitzbühl area (*Oesterreich* 2:96, 111, 151, 160–61, *QGT*).

29. Boyd 1992, 61.

30. Ibid., 52, 56, 58, 62, 136–37, 142. Against Boyd seems Martin Bucer's accusation that Marpeck taught "schweren und weren unruht sei." True, Marpeck's "Confession" makes no mention of or any objections to the oath. Boyd made a better case that by the late 1540s in Augsburg Maler and perhaps Marpeck had softened on the oath. But Boyd's use of the "Bekenntnis an Jan von Pernstein" as the work of Marpeck to buttress his argument regarding Marpeck's position in Strasbourg seems questionable. I argue below that this document was the work not of Marpeck but of Hans Umlauft (ibid., 97, 101). Cf. *Elsass* 1:350, *QGT*.

31. *The Chronicle*, 86.

32. Boyd 1992, 61–62.

33. Packull 1993. Boyd, following Klaassen, assumed Marpeck's authorship and cited the document as such (Boyd 1992, 73).

34. Beck 1967, 50 n. 2. It seems Beck had access to sources now lost.

35. In 1534–35 Scharnschlager's son-in-law, Hans Felix, and Felix' wife Ursula settled in Austerlitz (Boyd 1992, 99 n. 15). Cf. discussion below.

36. *Baden und Pfalz* 419–25, especially 422, *QGT*. Cf. *Elsass* 1:583 n. 1, *QGT*.

37. Klassen and Klaassen 1978, 37ff. Boyd believed that he visited Moravia several times during this period.

38. *The Chronicle*, 210–11. *Congregation* would have been a more consistent translation of *Gemein*.

39. Zeman 1969, 246. It may be assumed that Veh and his group were criticized in 1542 by Johann Kalenec, an elder of the Little Party of Czech Brethren, as being "Athanasians" and "tolerating harmful occupations . . . such as merchants, woodcarvers, painters, jewelers and innkeepers." Cf. Urban 1986, 27, 101.

40. Hutterite apologist Peter Walpot later cited Eusebius to refute this argument. He claimed that community of goods had been practiced in many places, not only in Jerusalem (Stayer 1991, 156–57).

41. Marpeck corresponded with elders in Austerlitz and other places. Cf. "The Servants and Service of the Church" in Klassen and Klaassen 1978, 549ff.

These associates of Marpeck remained visible until 1622 and, according to Ze-man, became identified as Swiss. But they "took part in municipal government, paid taxes, loaned money," etc. (Zeman 1969, 254–58 n. 75).

42. Spittelmaier's surviving treatise; Spittelmaier cited St. Jerome and Gerson.

43. Entfelder 1530, B vii r; A iii v; C v v; E vii v; E vii r.

44. Zeman 1969, 237, 239. In 1532 David Burda, a member of the Little Party, wanted fire to fall on the Austerlitz Brethren, an indication of the tensions between the two groups. Yet Schwenckfeldians, antitrinitarians, and Anabaptists coexisted at Eibenschitz into the seventeenth century (Waclaw 1986, 30–32).

45. Entfelder's anticlericalism is captured in the popular phrase cited by him: "priester, ye lenger ye wiester."

46. Bauman 1991, 257; Furcha 1975, 292.

47. See the discussion of Gabriel Ascherham's position in Chapter 5.

48. Entfelder 1533, B vi a–b. Although this statement comes from the 1533 pamphlet, it seems in harmony with Entfelder's earlier position.

49. Cf. Packull 1977, 155–63.

50. For a discussion of Bünderlin's other publications in Strasbourg, see Williams 1992, 381–83.

51. Klassen and Klaassen 1978, 43–44.

52. Klassen drew attention to the use of the term *Uebersprung* by Bünderlin (Klassen 1968, 43 n. 116).

53. Klassen and Klaassen 1978, 47.

54. Bünderlin implied that the apostolic office ceased with the apostles. As a result of the outpouring of the Spirit at Pentecost, the emphasis had shifted from externals to true inner spirituality. Pentecost had ushered in a dispensation of a direct relationship to God through the Spirit. This was to be the case until the end of time. He argued that Philip was an exception who had received a special commission through an angel to use water baptism on the eunuch (Bünderlin 1530, 33a–b, 34a, 35b).

55. The Klassen and Klaassen translation is not as accurate as it should be on this point. I therefore inserted the original concepts.

56. This could strengthen the argument that Marpeck assumed the role of an authorized "collecting shepherd" commissioned by a congregation in Moravia.

57. Jaroslav J. Pelikan cited Wycliffe and John Huss as representing this view (Pelikan 1984, 110–11).

58. Klassen and Klaassen 1978, 44, 52.

59. Ibid., 91–92; cf. Wiswedel, 1937b, 15.

60. Klassen and Klaassen 1978, 86–87, 94, 104. Williams suggested that Entfelder may have been "a proponent of some form of the doctrine of the celestial flesh of Christ . . . once condemned at Chalcedon" (Williams 1992, 465–67).

61. Klassen and Klaassen 1978, 79.

62. The tract appeared on the same press in the same year as Marpeck's tracts of 1531.

63. Klassen and Klaassen 1978, 89, 94; Hobbs 1991, 27.

64. Klassen and Klaassen 1978, 70, 101–4.

65. Friesen 1988, especially 68–69; 1990, 430–31.

66. The distinction between inner and outer baptism was common to many Anabaptists. See Chapter 1.

67. Klassen and Klaassen 1978, 103–4.

68. Schwenckfeld 1530, 831ff. Schwenckfeld's Anabaptist partner in dialogue appears to have been Jacob Kautz with whom he conversed in October 1529.

69. Words in brackets are mine (ibid., 832).

70. Ibid., 833.

71. Schwenckfeld 1531, 115ff.

72. Ibid., 129. The editors identified these somewhat awkwardly as "The Austrian Baptists, Nicolsburg; the South German, Augsburg; the North German Münster, n. 1. One could speculate that Schwenckfeld at this point knew Kautz, Reublin, Marpeck, Bünderlin, and Entfelder.

73. "so der Sacrament auff ihre weise nicht gebrauchen wollen" (Schwenckfeld 1531, 130).

74. In a letter dated February 21, 1544, Schwenckfeld wrote, "Sonst wisset ir zuvor langst . . . das ich von eueren tauf und lauf nichts halte darumb, das ihe euers ampts von gott keinen befelch weder sendung noch offenbarung habt, wie ihr auch der taufe Jesu Christi, die im hl. gaiste geschicht, keinen rechten verstand habt" (*CS* 8:865ff.).

75. An observation made by Dennis Martin (1988, 8 n. 9).

76. Hillerbrand 1959. "Ein kurtz unnderricht ettlich puncten unseres glauben."

77. Boyd 1992.

78. Ibid., 97–100. Boyd made repeated reference to it and lists it among "Marpeck's works." He indicated that Fast planned to publish it with his critical edition of the *Kunstbuch* (ibid., 162, 163, 165, 174).

79. "Hiemit gebietend Herr habt ir in kurtz underricht ettlich puncten unsers glaubens" (Hillerbrand 1959, 50).

80. This emerges by comparing *Bayern* 2:72 with 92–93; see also 78, 79, 82, 94–97, 109–14.

81. The council considered Umlauft *geschickt* (ibid., 93, 107–8).

82. The three days of grace to collect outstanding debts had been refused (ibid, 60–61).

83. Ibid., 75–76, 94–97. Georg and his travel companion, a Venzl (Wenzel or Fenzl), were described as *hutergesellen,* leading Schornbaum to infer that they were Hutterites. However, it seems more likely that they were literally journeymen hatmakers rather than members of the Hutterite community, an inference made by Claus-Peter Clasen (1978, 186).

84. *Bayern* 2:100–4, *QGT*.

85. Ibid., 92 n. 2. Hillerbrand 1959, 42.

86. Hillerbrand 1959, 42. The intended recipient was no doubt the same Pernstein who a few years earlier interceded on behalf of Anabaptist prisoners at Passau. The date for that intercession is given as 1532 (Zeman 1969, 80 n. 82; 221–23).

87. The appeal to Pernstein as "our rightful lord" (*Obrigkeit*) suggests that the prisoners appealed to him as if they were members of a community located in Moravia. Umlauft's wife's had moved there before he was released. On May 31, 1540, Umlauft petitioned council to permit him to join his wife (*Bayern* 2:109, *QGT*).

88. Ibid., 89, 92–93.

89. For his recantation, see ibid., 110–11, 114.

90. See Latin letter dated May 22, 1539, by Wolfgang Lutz from Kirchen (ibid., 62–63). Evidence indicates that there had been almost continuous contact with Moravia.

91. Leonard Widmann's *Chronik* recorded, "darnach di stat verpoten und gein dem merhischen Pudweis getan. Was er vor getan, tet er itzo dritopelt" (*Bayern* 2:114 n. 3, *QGT*).

92. Budespitz appears to be identical with Putschowitz or Budchowitz, a village about one mile northeast of Austerlitz. In 1537–38 six former elders of the Austerlitz congregation, among them Hans Hueter and Jörg Dräxler, began to live in community there. They, too, joined the Hutterites. Stadler died there in 1540 (*The Chronicle*, 160–61, 210).

93. Weinberger, who had been baptized by Onophrius Griesinger who became a Hutterite martyr, refused the oath. Yet Weinberger generally followed Umlauft's lead and recanted when Umlauft signaled his readiness to do so (*Bayern* 2: 66, 107, 110–11, *QGT*).

94. Schornbaum suggested that the recipient was Stephan Rauchenccker, a former priest who served the evangelical *Gemeinde* as deacon (*Bayern* 2:63–71, *QGT*).

95. This seems more likely than an October 1539 date or a date after exile in 1540.

96. Stephan had written to a Balthasar, presumably the Anabaptist carpenter, Walthasar Allewelt, a member of the Anabaptist congregation in Regensburg, who was exiled in 1539. *Bayern* 2:75, *QGT*.

97. Ibid., 67.

98. Cf. Umlauft's letter to Stephan (Rauchenecker) at the end of October or the beginning of November 1539 (*Bayern* 2:63–73, especially 67–68, *QGT*) with Denck's "Recantation" (in Bauman 1991, 247–50).

99. *Bayern* 2:69, *QGT*. He also cited Adam, Abel, and Enoch among others, as examples among the blessed without the benefits of outer letter or ceremony. He was answering charges "that we have no faith, word nor sacrament," a charge he rejected (*Bayern* 2:63–73, especially 67–69, *QGT*). The Cornelius story was a bone of contention between Marpeck and Spiritualists. Cf. Marpeck, "Instruction," 101–2. Umlauft's position here seems closer to that ascribed to Müntzer by Abraham Friesen (Friesen 1990, 5–22).

100. *Bayern* 2:66, *QGT*.

101. Hillerbrand 1959, 42, 47. The introduction also contained an allusion to Denck's motto that to know Christ one must follow him in life.

102. Schornbaum speculated that one of the items was a "Dialogue über die Kindertaufe" and the other a copy of *Points of Faith* (*Bayern* 2:97, 108, *QGT*). Weinberger testified that a certain brother Niclas had brought books for binding

from Bohemia. Among them was apparently a *Confession of Faith* by the Bohemian Brethren. It was presumably the German translation of the 1533 edition (Zeman 1969, 243–44).

103. "Wie wol unns seer schwer ist die ainfeltige erkenttnuss gottlicher warhait in unns in schrift Euch oder andern Zuezestellen" (Hillerbrand 1959, 42).

104. Ibid.

105. In his August Decree of 1527 Ferdinand II had made the Apostolic Creed the minimal standard of orthodoxy in his territories, hence responses to the creed were solicited from prisoners.

106. Hillerbrand 1959, 42.

107. Ibid.

108. Boyd 1992, 100–1.

109. Hillerbrand 1959, 40.

110. A chronicler in Regensburg, commenting on the arrest of Umlauft and others in November/December 1539, wrote, "I have left off here until one finds out what will come of it; because in Münster, Westphalia, it also began this way as it is all revealed in print" (*Bayern* 2:73, *QGT*).

111. Hillerbrand 1959, 44–45. This position is entirely consistent with Umlauft's statements on the subject in his letter to Stephan.

112. It is worth noting that this sun analogy appears in the song on the Trinity of the 1564 songbook of the Swiss Brethren. Psalm 54 and 126 were cited as the basis of the song.

113. Hillerbrand 1959, 46–47.

114. Even though it had been "darkened by the desolator."

115. Hillerbrand 1959, 46–47. Among persons so designated, Schwenckfeld, Bünderlin, and Entfelder come to mind.

116. Ibid., 49. Boyd argued that "the position taken . . . on civil authority is the same as that taken by Marpeck in the Strassburg *Confession* and letter of farewell to the council in 1532" (Boyd 1992, 101).

117. Among the servants "it was necessary to use force and beatings" (*da alles genött mit schlegen zueging*). Among children, by contrast, "all force ceases" (*aller Zwang aufgehört*) (Hillerbrand 1959, 49).

118. Ibid., 42.

119. Ascherham 1544, 20–22.

120. Ibid., 22.

121. Ibid., 15. Marpeck refuted this very argument in *A Clear and Useful Instruction* (1978, 91–92) by noting that women had testified to Christ's resurrection before the apostles.

122. Ascherham 1544, 18.

123. Ibid., 18, 24–25.

124. In 1538 a discussion took place between the Schwenckfeldian Fabian Eckel and Entfelder. It is possible that Gabriel was informed and involved. Boyd 1992, 92, 101).

125. The full title reads "Rechenschaft und Bekenntnuss des Christlichen Glaubens. Gestellt durch unsern lieben Brueder und diener Christy Leonard Dax in der Gefängnis." It carried the date 1556 in Codex Hab. 5. The date, as well as the catechismlike format, which suggests that it was used for pedagogical pur-

poses, cast doubt on the claim that it was written while Dax was in prison at Alzey in 1567–68, a claim made by Christian Hege (1957a, 21).

126. This emerges from Marpeck's "On the Inner Church" and "The Servants and Service of the Church" (Marpeck 1978, 418ff., 549ff.). Among Marpeck's later contacts in Austerlitz was Cornelius Veh, who distanced his group from the "pernicious sects" of the Swiss with their legalism and the Hutterites because of their community of goods (Boyd 1992, 103).

Chapter Seven. South Tyrol

1. Köfler 1983, especially 116; Lassmann 1987; Widmoser 1951, pt. 1, especially 84–85 and pt. 2; Kolb 1951, especially 10.

2. *Oesterreich* 2:382, *QGT*.

3. Ibid., 3:420–21, October 17, 1539.

4. See Loserth and Friedmann 1959.

5. In 1532 the magistrate of Sterzing complained that he needed forty, not two, constables to suppress the Anabaptists (*Oesterreich* 3:13, 34, *QGT*).

6. Ammann 1897.

7. Erika Prast considered St. Georgen and Pflaurentz pro-Anabaptist (Prast 1975, 191, 194).

8. Loserth described the Tyrol as "one of the strongest centers of Anabaptism during the sixteenth century and a fountainhead of great leaders of the movement" (Loserth and Friedmann 1959, 725). Of a total of 2,169 executions counted in Hutterite sources, 569 are listed as having taken place in Austrian territory, 349 of these in the Tyrol with 35 in the Puster Valley, 108 in the Etsch valley, and 206 in the Inn valley. Cf. Beck 1967, 277–80. These figures seem conservative, since Hutterites tended to be selective in their count.

9. Rudolf Palme listed Jörg Zaunried (Zaunring), Hans Amon (Tuchscherer), Hans Kräl, Niclas Geyerspühler, Jacob Portzner, Hans Mändel, and Onofrius Griesinger (Palme 1986–87, especially 52). Ulrich Stadler, Sigmund Schützinger, Pilgram Marpeck, Jeronimus Käls, Christoph Gschäll, Michael Kürschner, and others could be added.

10. Peter Riedemann wrote, "vermeine wol Pusterer zu haben" (Zieglschmid 1946, 197). The English translators missed the point with "I imagine some from the Puster valley might even return" (*The Chronicle*, 184–85).

11. Was it introduced from abroad as the government claimed? See *Oesterreich* 2:74–75, *QGT*.

12. Kolb 1951, 13ff.

13. Fichter 1982.

14. Meyer 1976, especially 188–89.

15. "Von keinem etablierten Stand verteidigt" (Palme 1986–87).

16. The specific title reads, "Gesatz und ordnungen der ynzichten, malefitz rechten und anderer notdurftigen henndeln des lannds der gravschaft Tyrol" (Moser 1982, 12).

17. It was to be revised once more in 1532 (ibid., 15). Divided into nine books, the eighth dealt with the *Strafrecht*.

18. Gruber 1977, 71.

19. Moser 1982, 14.

20. At the turn of the century, there were only two of these, one for the north, residing in Hall, the other for the south, residing at Meran. The ecclesiastical territories of Brixen and Trent had their own executioners (ibid., 14–15).

21. Ibid., 105.

22. Noflatscher 1994, 312–14.

23. Prast 1975.

24. Palme claimed "Er liess also sein Bistum total verkommen" (Palme 1986–87, 54). See also Loserth 1955; *Oesterreich* 3:29 n. 1, *QGT*.

25. Gelmi 1973, 60.

26. Lesser offices were those of game or fish warden. A study of thirty-eight officeholders indicates that twenty-one made profits and seventeen "claimed" losses and requested subsidies (Gruber 1977, 143).

27. Palme 1986, 69; Klaassen 1978, 6–8.

28. Among them were members of the von Wolkenstein clan. (*Oesterreich* 3: 156ff., 198ff., *QGT*).

29. Palme 1986–87.

30. Noflatscher 1989.

31. Extra buildings (*Sakralbauten*) included shrines (*Bildstöcke*) and chapels. Six out of ten parishes in the Sterzing area saw such construction (ibid., 111–12).

32. This was the case in the Jaufen valley served from Sterzing (ibid., 118).

33. According to studies provided by Noflatscher, chaplains served an average of 9.5 to 11.1 weeks (ibid., 92, 103).

34. In 1529 and again in 1540 the bishop of Brixen complained that the services for the common people were largely left to "run away monks, who today are here, tomorrow . . . somewhere else" (ibid., 94, 98, 99).

35. Ibid., 96–97.

36. Noflatscher argued that the resentment against parish priests was primarily social-economic in nature until post-Tridentine reform took place (ibid., 106–8).

37. Zaunring, in *Glaubenszeugnisse,* especially 146. On Zaunring see Chapter 8.

38. Zaunring cited Daniel 9. For other Anabaptist expressions of the same, cf. Klaassen, 1992b, 69ff.

39. Representing this view was Bender 1952 and 1953; see also the articles by Friedmann (1956d, 1957b).

40. Laube 1988, 9–33, especially 22. Cf. Stayer 1991.

41. Cf. Stayer 1991, 61–92, especially 86–89.

42. Arguments were made by Köfler (1983) and by Stella (1982a); see also Stella 1982b and 1983. Stella renewed claims that there were a number of baptizers in Gaismair's entourage (Stella 1990, especially 197).

43. Jäkel 1988.

44. *Oesterreich* 1:9, *QGT*.

45. A point made by Köfler about Leonard Schiemer's death (Köfler 1983, 114).

46. Beck 1967; Loserth 1892b; Wolkan 1923; Widmoser 1951. Besides her

many other contributions, Mecenseffy edited the three volumes of Austrian *Täuferakten* (*Oesterreich* 1–3, QGT).

47. Macek 1965, 468–73.

48. Ibid., 471 n. 217.

49. Klaassen found that the Anabaptists acknowledged "the rightness of peasant grievances and aims" but emphasized their nonviolent "mode of resistance." He suggested continuity with the peaceful intentions of the peasants and believed that the Anabaptist emphasis on mutual aid and sharing "bypassed and condemned the commercial enterprise and newly developing capitalism" (Klaassen 1978, 115).

50. They were Friedrich Brandenberger and Hans Gasser (ibid., 114–16).

51. Stayer 1991, 166.

52. On Gaismair's order, see Macek 1965, 370–79, and the English translation in Klaassen 1978, 131–36.

53. Macek 1965, 370.

54. Blickle 1992, 42–43.

55. For recent discussions of this subject, see the essays in Scribner 1990, especially Michalski, 69–124; Palmer, 125–42; Jezler, 143–74.

56. Klaassen 1978, 131–36. Gaismair and some of his advisors may have been influenced by Andreas Karlstadt's *Von abtuhung der Bylder, und das keyn Betdler unther den Christen seyn soll* (January 1522). The tract influenced events in Zurich. In 1523 Ludwig Hätzer published a kind of concordance with appropriate scriptural references on images. (Hätzer 1523). Simon Stumpf, Leo Jud, and Hätzer preached against images in Höng and Zurich, respectively. The second disputation in October 1523 dealt with the veneration of images and the mass. Cf. Eire 1990, 105–22.

57. Palme wrote, "Die Postulate der Wiedertäufer erwachsen aus einem radikalen Antiklerikalismus" (Palme 1986–87, 51–52).

58. He claimed to have done this before he joined the Anabaptists and "without much thought" (*Oesterreich* 3:93, 136–37, QGT).

59. Presumably this Bild was a sacred Bildstock. Cristan was executed at Rodeneck (ibid., 93).

60. Ibid., March 31, 1534, 237–38, 288, 314, 332. Hueber held nothing of church ceremonies and was an Anabaptist sympathizer, repeatedly in trouble because of it.

61. Ibid., June 1534, 258.

62. Ibid., 31. In 1529 near Welsberg, someone had torn down a statue (*Bildsäule*) of Mary and had hacked into the face of Mary (*durch das angesicht gehauen*) (*Oesterreich* 2:238, QGT).

63. Upon his arrest the government ordered that Gasser's *Urgichten* be obtained from Gufidaun, which means he had been imprisoned there previously (*Oesterreich* 3:35, QGT).

64. Ibid., 14–15, 49–50.

65. Ibid., 288–89.

66. The same derogatory description of churches as mere stone piles was current among Waldenses as early as 1398 (Müller 1895, 63).

67. In "On the Removal of Images," Andreas Karlstadt wrote that churches "might be rightly called murderers' caves, because in them our spirit is stricken and slain." Citing Ezekiel 6:9, Karlstadt argued that the use of images meant spiritual adultery and that "temples" with images were therefore "whorehouses" (Karlstadt 1522, 19–40; especially 20, 34–35).

68. Three pairs from the Sterzing area were married without a priest in late 1532 (*Oesterreich* 3:101–2, QGT).

69. Ibid., 20, 21, 72, 92, 101–2, 126–27, 135–37, 151, 287–89.

70. See statements by Valentein Fell (Föll) and Oswald Spiess, July 1532 (ibid., 72–73). Anabaptist leaders instructed their followers that in spiritual matters "they should be equal among themselves and obey no other spiritual or temporal authority except that of their leaders."

71. *Oesterreich* 2:331, QGT.

72. Ibid. 3:21. The first clear nonresistant statement appears to be that of Sigmund Kiens, February 11, 1532. Leaders forbade them "to carry any other weapon for defence except a staff, and if one wanted to arrest them, they should not resist."

73. Ibid., 29, 37; see the discussion by the editors of *The Chronicle*, 83 n. 1.

74. The principle prevailed, "sie sollen gleich sein" (*Oesterreich* 3:25, 73, QGT).

75. Ibid., 92.

76. In this the Tyrol was different from neighboring Carinthia (Kärnten), where Lutheran Estates assured a more moderate orientation. Cf. Loserth and Friedmann 1955.

77. Franz 1975, 335–37. The suggestion that Hans Vischer was Hans Bünderlin (Fischer) from Linz, an Anabaptist Spiritualist, seems now unlikely. Cf. Klaassen 1978, especially 33, 44, 131.

78. The disputation featured John Eck, Thomas Murner, and John Faber on the Catholic side and John Oecolampadius and Berchtold Haller on the Reformed side (Backus 1993).

79. Rastner 1974, 198ff.

80. It is possible that Messerschmied traveled to Augsburg because of Urbanus Rhegius or Jacob Strauss, both of whom had been active in North Tyrol.

81. Jürgen Bücking suggested that his brother, Paul Messerschmied, belonged to Gaismair's inner circle (Bücking 1972a, 342–44; cited in Stayer 1991, 87).

82. The most important source is Wölfl's statements of early 1527, partly transcribed in Rastner 1974, 199–201. Mathias Schmelzer has since reproduced Wölfl's entire statement in Schmelzer 1989, especially 615–18.

83. *Oesterreich* 3:262–63, QGT.

84. Schmelzer believed that Wölfl visited the Inn valley twice, preaching in Zirl (Schmelzer 1989, 615–18).

85. Ibid., 616. Apparently the city magistrate of Klausen was sympathetic to Wölfl and gave him a hat.

86. *Oesterreich* 2:199, QGT. In later documents, the bailiff's name was Adam Preu, and in 1533 seven Anabaptists were executed in Gufidaun.

87. "Der Landrichter zu Botzn hab Ime das new testament, von ime selber unbegert im markht khaufft." Mecenseffy interpreted wrongly as "Der Landrichter . . . hatte ihm ein neues Testament zugesteckt" (Mecenseffy 1984, 89). Wölfl had also been a guest of the city secretary and of a Peringer of Bozen.

88. Oesterreich 2:244 n. 2; 322, 323, QGT; Mecenseffy 1984, 89.

89. "Zu Stegen bey dem huetter hab er auch gepredigt und sey vil volks da gewesen" (Rastner 1994, 201).

90. See Chapter 10. Oesterreich 3:314, QGT; Mecenseffy 1985, 25ff.

91. Innerhofer 1980, 100.

92. Oesterreich 2:4–6; 3:221 n. 1; 244–45, 261, 264, QGT.

93. Cf. Trenkwalder 1968, 88.

94. Klaassen 1978, 63–64, especially n. 306; 116.

95. Oesterreich 2:1, QGT. Peter Pinter accompanied Wölfl. Pinter's son was later sent to fetch Wölfl back to Klausen (Schmelzer 1989, 615).

96. He was questioned on January 9, 16, and 18, 1527. Mecenseffy believed the records were lost but used them later without drawing out the implications (Oesterreich 2:2 n. 4, QGT; also Mecenseffy 1984, 89–90).

97. Schmelzer 1989, 616.

98. Yet, while awaiting trial and torture, Mary had appeared to him and told him to call on her and honor her, and she would protect him. Likewise St. Bernard had appeared to him in his sleep, an indication of his Catholic piety (ibid., 617).

99. A Christoff Landtsberger, preacher and "Pfarrer" in Hall, was used by Innsbruck in the 1530s to bring Anabaptists back to the old faith (Oesterreich 2: 82, 84, 99, 235, QGT).

100. Schmelzer 1989, 616.

101. Cf. "Ulhart im Dienste der Abendmahlslehre Karlstadts und Zwinglis" in Schottenloher 1967, 27–58. Ulhart printed three tracts by Karlstadt; cf. Schottenloher, nos. 91 and 92: 114–15; also 23–26; no. 94:115; also 30–31; nos. 104–6:118.

102. See Note 66. Karlstadt shared with later Anabaptists a concern for simple, plain dress. Austrian scholars have repeatedly claimed that Karlstadt visited South Tyrol during the fall of 1525. The claim is based on an entry under the date October 10, 1525 by Ludwig Emershofen, a canon and the administrator of the hospice (Spitalverwalter) at Klausen. Here it was claimed that Karlstadt preached in the village of Lüsen and traveled with miners to Klausen where he was asked to preach by local citizens. Cf. Rastner 1974, 198 n. 1; Gelmi 1973, 81; The Chronicle, 143 n. 1. But Karlstadt's known movements left no room for a visit to Klausen in the fall of 1525. By late June or early July of that year he was back in Saxony. Perhaps his presence in South Tyrol was of a spiritual nature or in the form of the printed page (Barge 1:306, 369, 371).

103. (Karlstadt 1525). Anzeyg etlicher Hauptartickeln Christlicher leere; the English translation is in Sider 1978, 127ff.; Barge 2:287ff., especially 294–95. Karlstadt composed the Articles in Rothenburg o.d. Tauber, conscious of the peasants' uprising. He accused Luther and his supporters of showing greater concern for registering and collecting rents and tithes than for the spiritual well-being of

the people. The booklet made positive references to good peasants and to a number of specific villages in which Karlstadt claimed to have good friends.

104. Müller and Mrs. Bader were imprisoned before the end of 1527. Müller was rearrested in September 1531 and beheaded on November 15, 1531. His wife remained in prison until March 1532. Their children inherited the property after a fine had been levied in 1535. Arrested also in the fall of 1531 were Hans Weber, Hans Schiesser, and Hans Feuchter (Feichter, Feuchtner, Feichtner). See Note 120; *Oesterreich* 2:42, 493–94; 3:74, 224–25, *QGT;* Rastner 1974, 201; Beck 1967, 105.

105. Johann Loserth postulated only one journey in 1529 (Loserth 1899, 1–29, especially 27. See also Neff 1955, especially 358–59).

106. *The Chronicle*, 47, 53; Beck 1967, 80–81.

107. Kobl and an Adam (Manngl) fled from Bozen with the son-in-law of the Gallpüchlerin. Blaurock traveled with his own wife and a daughter of the Gallpüchlerin. Blaurock's wife Elsbeth survived the death of her husband, remaining in her Swiss home area into the 1560s (*Ostschweiz*, 248, *QGT*).

108. Cf. ibid., 198–99, 434, 634.

109. As early as April 26, 1527, Ferdinand warned that a priest associated with Gaismair and Andre, a former priest of Lüsen and supporter of Gaismair, was later of the "new sect" (*Oesterreich* 2:3, *QGT;* Widmoser 1951, 56).

110. This information was passed on to me by Edmund Pries, Waterloo.

111. *Ostschweiz*, 203–4; *Schweiz* 1:301, 309, *QGT*.

112. *The Chronicle*, 53; Beck 1967, 80–81, 278; *Oesterreich* 2:274, 286, 290, *QGT*.

113. The two were Hans Schneider and Appolonia Niedermaier (from Landsperg). The Rattenberg precedent was the trial of Hans Schlaffer and Leonard Frick. Other early arrests in Bozen were those of Simon Treybenreif, the painter Bartlme Dill, his wife, brother-in-law and a maid (*dirn*), also Christian, the son of Jörgen Ballenberger (ibid., 66–67, 76, 80–81).

114. Ibid., 80–81.

115. Arrested before June 3, 1528, Kobl managed a prison break, thanks to his loyal maid who smuggled tools into prison (ibid., 144, 164, 175).

116. Hui 1989.

117. Macek 1965, 245.

118. *Oesterreich* 2:39–40, *QGT*. The government learned of the recent meeting before December 23, 1527. Mairhofer was described as having a long brown beard and wearing a gray military coat (*Wappenrock*).

119. A Messerschmied, who later resided in Bozen, was friendly to the Anabaptists (ibid. 3:176, 463, 467).

120. See Note 104. Listed in documents related to Müller in 1531 were Messerschmied and wife, Pinter from the Eisack bridge near Clausen, Hans Weber and Balthasar Mairhofer of Niedervintl. Others were Hans Schiesser, a baker; Hans Feuchter and his wife; Martin Tischler and a tall Kürschner, Caspar Schmid of Brüneck (*Oesterreich* 2:493–97, 3: 106, 121, 160, 169, *QGT*).

121. Beck 1967, 105; *The Chronicle*, 376 n. 1. Müller's widow fled, leaving two children behind (*Oesterreich* 3:43, 71, 224, *QGT*).

122. Schiesser, Feuchtner, and Weber apologized (*höchst entschuldigt*) (*Oesterreich* 2:497, 3:169, *QGT*).

123. Ibid. 3:262–63. Rastner believed wrongly that Wölfl was executed in 1527 (Rastner 1974, 201).

124. Others implicated besides Gasser and Kobl were Gasser's wife Anna and maid Lucia, Kobl's wife Margaret, Hans Portz, Anthon Mair and his wife, Christoph (Stoffel) Mair and his wife, Mathes Kerschpaumer and his wife, and Benedikt Sackmann and his wife. Of these, Christoph Mair was exiled from the Ritten because of his support of the Anabaptists; Anthon Mair sold his property and fled with his wife, sister, and a servant; Mathes Kerschpaumer and wife died at the stake; Gasser was beheaded; Sackmann and wife had their sentence commuted. Friedrich Brandenberger later named Hans Portz, Ulrich Kobl, and Peter Wirt (Pinter?) as having been of the Gaismair party. Cf. *Oesterreich* 2:78–79, 136, 175, 180, 188–89, 200, 203, 207, 213, 221–22 n. 1, 412, 466–67, *QGT*; and ibid. 3:75, 78, 159, 168, 169.

125. Gasser's daughter Barbara joined the Anabaptists (ibid., 81, 180, 194–95, 197, 217; and ibid. 3:116–17).

126. Langegger died with Blaurock (ibid. 2:274).

127. Hutterite sources preserve the statements of eight early martyrs. Four of these had been baptized by Blaurock: Thomas Inwald, Christina Döllingen (Töllingen), Elizabeth Kamperer (Gamper), and Mang Kager. The other four were Wolfgang from Moos, baptized by Michael Kürschner; Georg Frick, baptized by P. Benedict Kamperer (Gamper); Barbara of Tiers, baptized by Benedict; and Agatha Kamperer, baptized by a brother Tobisch near St. Gall. Benedict appears to have been the brother or husband of Agatha and/or Elizabeth Kamperer. Official documents dated October 9, 1529 mentioned five persons arrested in Bozen as either baptized by Blaurock or by Benedict Gamperer. This source identified a Rosina as a sister of Benedict and mentions a Jorgen Döllingen from Kärnten, possibly related to Christina Döllingen (*Oesterreich* 2:290, *QGT*; *Ostschweiz*, 203, *QGT*; Beck 1967, 89). Cf. *The Chronicle*, 53, 69–73.

128. The questions appear to have been drafted by the guardian of the Franciscans in Bozen for interrogations by the magistrate and a jury of nine. The Hutterites somehow gained possession of the official court records. The statements of the prisoners corresponded in content to that attributed to Blaurock himself in *The Chronicle*, 53, 69–73.

129. Ibid., 70–73.

130. Ibid., 556–57.

131. Ruprecht Hueber had been told to repent and mend his sinful ways. See also the story of Paul Rumer in Chapter 8. Cf. *Oesterreich* 3:176, *QGT*.

Chapter Eight. Face to Face with the "Forces of Antichrist"

1. A phrase borrowed from an unpublished essay by Wolfgang Lassmann (Lassmann 1985, 102ff.). For an overview of Ferdinand's policy, "Der Kampf Gegen das Täufertum" see Kuppelwieser 1949, 353ff. Ferdinand inherited the Tyrol after his brother Charles was elevated to holy Roman emperor (Brandi 1967, 135–39).

2. A point made by Lassmann. Ferdinand's neighbor, Count Wilhelm IV of Bavaria, was no better. Recanters were executed by beheading; those who refused were burned. The towerwatchmen of Burghausen, who "on the morning after" regretted his baptism and confessed to a priest that he had been under the influence of alcohol at the time, was ordered beheaded by his "gracious" lord, the count (Dittrich 1900–91, 75). The exception among territorial rulers was Philip of Hesse.

3. Lassmann 1985, 104.

4. *Oesterreich* 1:4, 9, *QGT:* "verfuerisch, kätzerisch secten"; 100: "verdambten Ketzereyen"; and ibid. 2:39.

5. Ibid. 1:3–12.

6. A point made by Mecenseffy (1964).

7. Neff and Loserth 1956.

8. On Hubmaier in Regensburg, see Obermann 1984, 77–78.

9. Cf. Stayer 1991, 63–72.

10. Hans Schiemer, executed before Hubmaier, was also charged with insurrection. Archbishop Lang in neighboring Salzburg had promulgated the first decree against the Anabaptists on July 3, 1527; a more explicit edict followed on October 18, 1527.

11. *Oesterreich* 1:8–9, *QGT.* The reference to previous disobedience and insurrection (*ungehorsam aufruer*) as having originated in false teachings appeared twice in the mandate.

12. Stayer 1991.

13. *Oesterreich* 2:74–75, *QGT.*

14. Mecenseffy 1964.

15. *Oesterreich* 1:93 n. 1, *QGT.*

16. About his cruel death see Snyder 1984, 100ff.

17. *Oesterreich* 1:93, 102, 105, *QGT.*

18. Ibid., 28–29. Mecenseffy 1984, 79–80. To bear arms was a symbol of citizen status.

19. *Oesterreich* 1:45-47, 53, *QGT.*

20. Ibid., 30–32.

21. Mecenseffy 1971, especially 156–59. Cf. *Oesterreich* 2:133–34, 149, 150, 177, *QGT.*

22. Ibid. 1:73.

23. Ibid., 94–96.

24. Lassmann 1985, 110; *Oesterreich* 1:100, *QGT*, mentions Lower Austria.

25. See the order of February 10, 1531 (*Oesterreich* 3:17–19, *QGT*).

26. Ibid. 2:178, 224.

27. Features of the later system included book visitations to enforce censorship and annual confession certificates for those who earned their bread in Protestant territory (Bücking 1972b, 63–98; 126–41, 175–89).

28. A Franciscan named Methardus was dispatched to preach in Sterzing, and in 1532 the preacher of Hall, Christoph Landsperg, was sent to Sterzing to help the local preacher, Leonard Ottentaler. Dr. Gallus Müller was used in impor-

tant cases such as Hutter's. In 1528 Müller was sent to preach in the Puster valley (Prast 1975, 200; *Oesterreich* 3:82, 84, 99, 235, *QGT*; Kuppelwieser 1949, 113).

29. *Oesterreich* 2:331, 383–88, *QGT*. See also the decree of August 20, 1533, in ibid. 3:143ff.

30. Mandate of February 10, 1532 (ibid., 17–19).

31. The suggestion to use spies was made as early as December 1529 by the captain (*Hauptmann*) of Rattenberg, Philipp von Liechtenstein (ibid. 2:320–21).

32. Ibid. 3:118, 274.

33. Kuppelwieser 1949, 181; Prast 1975, 175ff.

34. Packull 1990b.

35. *Oesterreich* 3:120–22, *QGT*.

36. Ibid. 2:230.

37. The *Züchtiger* of Meran refused to flog four women arrested April 4, 1533 (ibid. 3:110, 113).

38. As early as May 1528, Margaret Köblin, the wife of Ulrich Kobl, was given this treatment (ibid. 2:134–36; for others see 193, 214; also ibid. 3:110, 143).

39. In 1532 a number of Anabaptists were to be burned collectively along with their meeting place, all without much noise, lest adverse publicity should come from it (ibid., 86–87).

40. Ibid. 2:71.

41. Kuppelwieser 1949, 176.

42. *Oesterreich* 3:272, *QGT*.

43. Such property could be extensive. Balthasar Mairhofer of Niedervintl was rumored to be worth 10,000 gulden (ibid., 274).

44. Kuppelwieser 1949, 370.

45. *Oesterreich* 2:257, *QGT*.

46. For example, Heinrich Goldschmied of Sterzing left seven children behind. A warden was appointed for his property, worth 400 gulden. Some citizens offered to look after the children if they were given payment in the form of Goldschmied's movable property. The warden was instructed to see if these persons would not take the children without payment! Eventually Goldschmied's property was auctioned to the highest bidder. What happened to the children remains unknown (ibid., 72–88, 214, 216, 253, 302).

47. Widows with children were left without means of support while authorities squabbled over their inheritance. See the case of the widow of Oswald Hellrigel and her seven children (ibid. 3:114–15).

48. Cf. the government instructions of December 13, 1532 (ibid., 84ff.).

49. Confession of Rueprecht Hueber from Götzenberg in ibid., 183. Another who had accompanied children to Moravia was Hans Maurer (195).

50. Kuppelwieser referred to the collection of twenty-three such children in 1533 as "regelrechte Kinderentführung" (Kuppelwieser 1949, 198).

51. *Oesterreich* 3:323, *QGT*.

52. I am borrowing the term from a paper by Dr. Noflatscher.

53. On September 15, 1531, fifty attended a meeting near Villnös; at Christmas sixty to seventy at Hörschwang; eighty at Villnös in February 1532; forty later

that year near St. Michelsburg; ninety near the Brenner in 1532; seventy at the Pecklhaube, an inn near the Härscher. At Villnös the group received forty "gentile" visitors who mocked them (*Oesterreich* 3:167, *QGT*).

54. Ibid., 71, 159.

55. Ibid., 23, 71, 169, 198–99. A putrich of wine contained two to eight liters. In the early summer of 1532 Valtein Fell of Flaas drove two oxen to the Brenner where Hutter held a meeting with ninety persons. Hutter lived in an out-of-the-way hut (*abseits*).

56. A meeting in Gufidaun territory attended by eighty persons lasted eight days (ibid., 168).

57. Ibid., 163, 171.

58. Valentin Lukhner testified that most of the eighty who met at Villnös in early 1532 left for Moravia but that many were caught and executed (ibid., 167).

59. See Urscher's confession (ibid., 90–93). The victim of the raid was Wosstl Sallmann.

60. The Urschers were baptized by Blasius of Krossen in Leifers and imprisoned in Bozen. Blasius was executed before 1532 (ibid., 69, 93, 97–98).

61. They were Valtein Fell from Flaas and Oswald Spiess (Schuster) from Bozen. By August 10, 1532, Oswald had been released. He fled to Moravia. Frantz Käser, a master shoemaker, had guaranteed bail on his behalf (ibid., 74, 39, 99, 449).

62. Ibid., 95–96, 104–5.

63. Ibid., 97–98, 104–5.

64. The sources are silent about the fate of his wife and children (ibid., 135).

65. Ibid., 98–100, 175. Christoff Schumacher, the son of Andre Zimmermann of St. Georgen, made ten pairs of shoes for "the Salher ob der Pegglhauben" and others for the brothers and sisters. The leather came from Gaismair in Sterzing.

66. Gross 1982.

67. *Oesterreich* 3:314, *QGT*.

68. Documents referred to him as "hutter from Spital." Mecenseffy suggested that he returned an Anabaptist. If not, Gamperer seems the likely candidate to have baptized him (ibid. 2:263–65; Mecenseffy 1984, 82, 90).

69. Prast 1975, 188ff. Weber was arrested on April 27, 1529. See *Oesterreich* 2:244 n. 2, *QGT*.

70. Georg Weber, Katherine Rader, and Kaspar Mairpaul were burned; Wilhelm Samsfeuer was beheaded. Others received lesser sentences (Prast 1975, 190; *Oesterreich* 2:322–23, *QGT*).

71. Agnes Hutterin, identified as Hutter's sister by Mecenseffy, was executed in late 1529 or early 1530 (ibid., 311 n. 1; 312). Paul Dedic was wrong when he claimed that she recanted (Dedic 1957).

72. Gerhard resided at the castle which gave the jurisdiction its name (ibid.).

73. Recanters, besides paying fines, were required to make public confessions on three consecutive Sundays in the parish church of St. Lorenzen, whose priest was used by Brixen to instruct the prisoners.

74. *Oesterreich* 3:416, 456, *QGT*.

75. Cf. statement by Christoff Schaurer, arrested at Kufstein in 1529. Schaurer had been baptized by Wolfgang Brandhuber and represented, like Zaunring, a link between South and North Tyrol, evident since 1528 (ibid. 2: 319–20 n. 2).

76. He was active around Hall in the beginning of June 1530, moving onto the Zyller valley (*Oesterreich* 2:281–82, 363, 365, QGT). The Hutterocentric view makes Zaunring Hutter's assistant (*gehilffen*) sent to Moravia by Hutter with a group (*volk*) (Beck 1967, 39).

77. *Oesterreich* 2:263, QGT; Friedmann 1959e). Zaunring appeared in official documents as Zaunried.

78. Zaunring, "Eine schöne Epistel."

79. "Ain kurtze anzaignung des abentmals Christy" in *Glaubenszeugnisse* 1: 143ff. See also *Episteln* 3:510ff.

80. One Hutterite source gave the name as Hesus, meaning presumably the Erfurt humanist Eobanus Hesius (ibid., 512).

81. *Glaubenszeugnisse* 1:147; *Episteln* 3:514.

82. Ibid., 514.

83. Ibid., 515.

84. It is conceivable that Zaunring wrote the prospectus while in prison, after having been sent as an apostle to Franconia in 1532. Cf. Beck 1967, 39 ns. 1, 2.

85. Kürschner was baptized in June 1528 at Völs (Vells) on the Schlern.

86. Kuppelwieser 1949, 101ff.

87. The information in *The Chronicle* (69–73) that Kürschner was burned in Gufidaun is wrong. Cf. *Oesterreich* 2:248, QGT.

88. *The Chronicle,* 83–85.

89. Ibid.

90. Statement by Michael Ebner comes from 1531 (*Oesterreich* 3:22, QGT).

91. Lassmann was incorrect when he thought that community of goods and pacifism were only consolidated in Moravia and were not central to the grassroot level in the Tyrol (Lassmann 1987, 302).

92. Erhart Urscher donated 200 gulden. Paul Rumer surrendered 31 gulden of his inheritance according to the statement of September 19, 1533 (*Oesterreich* 3:92, 151–52, 157, QGT).

93. See the statement by Valentin Lukhner (ibid., 166).

94. Sigmund Kiens testified "Und welher . . . gelt oder anders hat, der mues sohls dem seklmaister erlegn . . . sy all und sey ir aller miteinander" (ibid., 25).

95. The meeting took place on the Brenner at the end of July 1533.

96. *Oesterreich* 2:244, QGT and ibid. 3:20–21.

97. In 1532 he visited the Niderhofers who hosted Hutter after his return in 1535. In 1531 he had been in Lüsen (ibid., 223, 237, 287, 299).

98. In January 1534 Hans was in Sterzing attempting to free Hans Maurer (ibid., 197).

99. It was Hans's wife, not Amon's, who lay in childbed at the von Wolkenstein's. Veronica Grembs and a Wincklerin from Sal waited on her (ibid., 195, 210, 219–20, 228, 332–34).

100. "Exkurs. Die Wiedertäufer," in Prast 1975, 175. Earlier Hans had been Jörg Vasser's guide (*Oesterreich* 3 : 292, 299, *QGT*).

101. Ibid., 274.

102. She communicated with her aunt from Moravia regarding her inheritance (ibid., 186, 201, 232).

103. Lukhner was executed before November 17, 1533. Hutter had entrusted him with 100 gulden so that he could support needy fugitives (ibid., 171, 180).

104. Lukhner and Rumer, like Hans Mair Paulle, Veronica Grembs, and others, had been guests at the von Wolkenstein's near Tauffers. In 1534 Sigmund von Wolkenstein, the son of Elsbeth, was brought to Brixen; he and three others, including the wife of Hans Mair Paulle, intended to move to Moravia. She recanted. Sigmund was placed in the care of Wilhelm Frh. von Wolkenstein at the Trostburg (Gruber 1977, 330).

105. *Oesterreich* 3 : 116, 138, 164, 403, 447, *QGT*. When Justina fled to Moravia in the summer of 1533, she left behind an estate worth 2,600 gulden.

106. About the concern with proper dress among contemporary young men, see Ozment 1990, especially 29.

107. *Oesterreich* 3 : 157, *QGT*. It should be noted that Karlstadt had written against expensive apparel. He wrote, "I well know that one deceives many simple people with costly clothes and that many fools judge one's person, knowledge and holiness on the basis of clothes. . . . Nevertheless it is not so incongruous with the example of Christ and the life of the apostles to wear a gray peasant's cloak as to wear things made of scarlet, satin, silk, camel's hair, velvet and gold" (Karlstadt 1525; English translation in Sider 1978, 134).

108. *Oesterreich* 3 : 158–59, 160, 178, 184, *QGT*. His brother Leonard was baptized by Amon shortly after the return. Leonard gave 7 of 10 gulden received from his father to the brotherhood. The rest was spent on clothing.

109. Friedmann considered Rumer's statement significant enough to transcribe. It was reproduced in *Episteln* 4 : 16–22.

110. *Oesterreich* 3 : 158, *QGT*.

111. Ibid., 161: "The saints in heaven were like the Anabaptists and had also suffered for the sake of the Word of God."

112. Ibid., 174, October 15, 1533. Christoff was the son of Andre Zimmermann, who also suffered martyrdom.

113. Ibid., 174.

114. Ibid., 173.

115. Balthasar and his wife were mentioned along with members of the original group in Klausen (ibid. 2 : 39–40, 80–81, 494).

116. Cf. the discussion in Prast 1975, 164ff.

117. Some of the money was destined for Moravia, but Kuntz Füchter, who carried it, was intercepted at Sterzing in 1532 (*Oesterreich* 3 : 170–71, *QGT*).

118. Ibid., 129, 131, 139.

119. Ibid., 214, 230.

120. Ibid., 188–89, November 1533. Lanntz was soon embroiled in a dispute over fishing and hunting rights, which he assumed came with the Mairhof. Cf. Prast 1975, 164, 175, 181ff; "Die Wiedertäufer" in Gruber 1977.

121. Her death was mentioned in a document dated July 8, 1535 (*Oesterreich* 3:189, 201, 259, 274, *QGT*).

122. Ibid., 189. Entries about him not edited by Mecenseffy are found in the Fürstliche Bischöfliche Hauptarchiv (FBHA), Brixen under H.A. 1104; 1533 X.2; 1536 X.24; 1537 VI.6.

123. *The Chronicle,* 186, 232, 317.

124. These codices also contained "the only independent account of the first believers' baptism in Zurich." Cf. Fast 1978, 22–31.

125. Robert Friedmann considered them "the richest sources for our understanding of the Anabaptists" (Friedmann 1956b). Most are accessible in the four-volume, uncritical edition published by the Hutterites between 1986 and 1991.

126. Friedmann estimated the prison epistles to number about 130 (ibid.).

127. *Glaubenszeugnisse* 1:43–125.

128. Friedmann 1965, 108; *The Chronicle,* 95; Beck 1967, 105–6. The prisoners were Lamprecht Gruber, Hans Beck, Lorentz Schuster, Peter Planer, Peter (Hungerl), and Hans Thaler (*Oesterreich* 3:25, *QGT*).

129. He had been arrested at Altrasen in 1530–31 and imprisoned with a Blasius of Krossen from Frankfurt on the Oder, Andre Schmaltz, and the widow of Jörg Weber, Hutter's close friend (ibid. 2:458–59).

130. *Episteln* 2:244–45.

131. Ibid., 244.

132. Gruber sent greetings to Jörg Zaunring and Zaunring's wife, to Leonhard (Schmerbacher), to his own wife Klärl (Klara), to "elders" in the Etsch valley, and to the church in Moravia (ibid., 244; *The Chronicle,* 93).

133. "Gesandt von Starzing in Tirol im Jahre 1532" (*Episteln* 2:246–47).

134. An analysis of the letters indicates that official records are incomplete. At least one of the prisoners, Lorentz Schuster, was executed before February 16, 1532. Peter Hungerl, Gruber's servant, was executed "with others." The fate of an imprisoned sister mentioned in the letter is unknown, but in September 1532 the authorities were looking for Gruber's widow, meaning that Gruber had also been executed. Cf. *Oesterreich* 3:24, 48, 97, *QGT*.

135. Indirect evidence suggests that the execution took place before February 16, 1532. "Lamprecht, samt seinen Mitgefangenen im Herrn–die dritte Epistel" in *Episteln* 2:274–76.

136. Johann Loserth's article needs updating (Loserth, *ME,* s.v. "Fichter, Konrad"; *Oesterreich* 3:48, 63, 171, 317–18, *QGT*). Implicated with Füchter was Erhard Gaismair, a relative of Michael Gaismair, also a Hueber from the Götzenberg.

137. The letter was dated 1532 and described as having originated in the Sterzing prison (*Episteln* 2:266ff.; Zieglschmid 1941, 16–23).

138. Friedmann 1929.

139. *Episteln* 2:269.

140. *Oesterreich* 3:59, *QGT; The Chronicle,* 95; Beck 1967, 106–7.

141. *Oesterreich* 3:93, *QGT.*

142. Ibid., 138. Not Dr. Gall Müller, sent to instruct the prisoners as Friedmann believed (*Episteln* 2:267, 271 n. 2).

143. Gall was executed before June 25, 1533 at Mühlbach (*Oesterreich* 3: 300, 315, 403, *QGT*).

144. Ibid., 185, 228.

145. Beck's letter originated in the Gufidaun prison. Fellow prisoners were Walser Schneider, Christian Allseider, Valentin Gsell (Gsäll), Hans Maurer of Flaas, Peter Krunewetter, and Wölfl from Götzenberg. The heading, "an die Gemeinde im Etschland und . . . in Mähren (und an Jakob Hutter)," may have been added later (*Episteln* 2:240–42; *The Chronicle*, 97; Beck 1967, 108–9).

146. *The Chronicle*, 98 n. 2.

147. Greetings were also sent to Justina Gall-Rumer. The surviving fragment of a second letter identifies her as the Gasserin (*Oesterreich* 3:48–52, 115–16, 138, *QGT*).

148. Friedmann 1965, 106, 108.

149. Friedmann 1956b.

150. *Oesterreich* 3:159, *QGT*.

151. *The Chronicle*, 98. This is another case in which official documents have not survived or have not recorded the executions, making a dating difficult. It suggests further that the Hutterite count of martyrs is more accurate than one based on official records (*The Martyrs' Mirror*, 444–45). The fragment of a second epistle attributed to Beck provided no further information and may be a corrupted text of the first letter. Noteworthy is that the greeting of all brethren with the "holy kiss many hundred-thousand times" became standard in many later epistles (*Episteln* 2:243).

152. According to Schuechknecht, the letters contained the Word of God and news that things were going well in Moravia. One of the carriers was Peter Hueter. Present at time of reading were Amon, Hänsel Mair Paulle, and twenty others (*Oesterreich* 3:175, 184, *QGT*).

153. A point made by Friedmann, who believed that "only epistles of the New Testament offer an adequate comparison to this unique literature which has the same spirit and in many cases even the same style as the apostolic model" (Friedmann 1956b).

154. Ibid.

155. Lienhard Raiffer-Schmidt testified on August 26, 1540, that Lanzenstiel would not permit anyone from Moravia to travel to the Tyrol (*Oesterreich* 3:449, 453, *QGT*).

Chapter Nine. Dissensions in the "Congregation of God"

1. *The Chronicle*, 87–88.

2. About Reublin see Stayer 1982a; see also Stayer 1977.

3. Snyder 1984, 77–79, 101.

4. He had baptized Julius Lober near Strasbourg in 1530. *Elsass* 1:227, *QGT*. See Chapter 4.

5. An exchange of messages between Reublin and Marpeck before the exodus in early 1531 suggests that Reublin remained in Austerlitz for several weeks. Beck's dating of the exodus as at the beginning of 1530 has misled others (Beck 1967, 49; Hostettler 1974, 19).

6. Reublin's letter is reproduced in Cornelius 1855, 253–59. The English translation is in Wenger 1949.

7. Cf. *The Chronicle*, 87–88.

8. The others were presumably Franz Inninger and Jacob Mändel.

9. The date "early 1530" given in *The Chronicle* is obviously wrong. A seventeenth-century codex more accurately gives early December 1530 as the time when Reublin began his readings (Dreller codex, at the Conrad Grebel College Archive, 45 verso). See Packull 1991b.

10. *The Chronicle*, 87.

11. Wenger 1949.

12. In his letter to Marpeck Reublin gave the number of adults as "drithalbert." This was also the number provided by *The Chronicle*, 88. Bossert believed the number to have been 300 (Bossert 1959, 307). Stayer numbered them at 250 (Stayer 1982a, 115). Hostettler believed that 350 went with Reublin, leaving 260 with Wiedemann in Austerlitz (Hostettler 1974, 19).

13. *The Chronicle*, 89.

14. Did Reublin stress the dire financial situation to solicit a contribution from Marpeck?

15. Barton 1985, 81. One gulden was 5 pounds Berner; one kreutzer was 12 pfennig.

16. Maids received two kreutzer a day. In the Sterzing area, a chaplain or journeyman priest received (in kreutzer) 4 for reading mass. A sheep cost 29 to 34; a pound of fish, 6 to 8; a hen, 4 to 5; one pound of cheese, 2; one measure of wine, 2; one measure (star) of salt, 18; thirty eggs, 5; one pair of shoes, 8; one blanket, 1 gulden; a hatchet, 10; a crock, 10; rustic linen cloth for a shirt, about 42; woolen cloth for an overcoat (*Loden*) 64 to 72. Cf. Noflatscher 1989, 83, 104–5, 109.

17. Was this Reublin's brother-in-law, Caspar Schüler? Schüler left the Esslingen-Stuttgart area in early 1530. His wife Barbara, Reublin's sister, gave the oath (*Urfede*) in Stuttgart on January 29, 1530. The Schülers made their way to Moravia. After his own arrival Reublin sent Schüler with a message to Marpeck. Schüler's Swabian origins could explain the purchase of a vineyard at Auspitz (*Württemberg* 1:16–17, QGT).

18. *The Chronicle*, 90. A more accurate source spoke of Caspar uniting with Zaunring and Reublin (Beck 1967, 97).

19. She also made a house at the horse market available (*The Chronicle*, 90).

20. It is not clear whether this was Jeronimus Käls, the first schoolmaster. Cf. Chapter 11.

21. Hans Amon and another brother (Christoph Gschäll?) represented the Auspitz case. The Austerlitz Brethren sent two of their own (*The Chronicle*, 90).

22. Ibid., 91.

23. Heinrich Bullinger later claimed that because of their perfectionism some Anabaptists felt no need to pray "and forgive us our trespasses" (Bullinger 1534, 23).

24. It is possible that this alluded to a later position (*The Chronicle*, 86).

25. *The Chronicle*, 91.

26. It is possible that it was Blasius Kuhn, who arrived with members of the Bruchsal congregation in 1530–31 (Beck 1967, 71 n.). See Chapter 4.

27. Beck had forty guilders (Beck 1967, 98; repeated by Bossert 1959, 307).

28. *The Chronicle*, 91.

29. Bossert claimed that he met with three hundred persons near Esslingen in July 1531. It is not clear whether this was before or after his disgrace (Bossert 1959, 307).

30. Hans Frisch, baptized by Reublin at Horb in 1527, had been appointed deacon by Adam Stumpffle (Schlegel?) to collect money for the needy (*Elsass* 1: 288–89, 299, *QGT*).

31. Some Swiss Brethren were still, or again, residents there in 1591 (*The Chronicle*, 226 n.; Loserth 1959b).

32. On February 8, 1559, Ferdinand replied positively to his requests (Bossert 1959, 307–8).

33. Beck 1967, 92 n.

34. *The Chronicle*, 92. On Schlegel, see Chapter 12.

35. *The Chronicle*, 92.

36. The brother involved was Thomas Lindl or Lindner of Schwaz. He was mentioned in Reublin's letter as one who had sided with him and Zaunring against Wiedemann. Lindl was among the earliest converts in the Tyrol (*Oesterreich* 2: 219, 227; 3:21, 26, *QGT*).

37. Gabriel Ascherham later maintained that "it was wrong for the brotherhood to have pressed him into confessing that it was envy that made him treat Georg Zaunring the way he did" (*The Chronicle*, 110).

38. Schmerbacher later also played an important role in the dispute between Schützinger and Hutter. Nothing more is heard of him after that. The other servant of temporal affairs, Wilhelm Griesbacher, was taken to Brünn in 1535 and burned there (ibid., 100–3). See also Chapter 10.

39. Beck dated it Easter 1531, correcting a codex that gave the date as 1533. But the date was 1532. By March 9, 1532, the authorities in Innsbruck knew that because of problems Hutter had been called to Moravia (Beck 1967, 101; *Oesterreich* 3:36, *QGT*).

40. *The Chronicle*, 93–94.

41. Ibid., 94 leaves the impression of a considerable time lapse "As his whole life continued upright, he was again entrusted with the service of the Gospel and later sent to Franconia." However, the time lapse was not more than two or three months because Zaunring's presence in Hesse was documented for the early summer of 1532.

42. Plener later held it against Hutter that he had expelled David of Schweidnitz and a Bernhard Glasser but accepted Georg Fasser because of his money, a charge Hutter denied (ibid., 105, 107).

43. The lot had been used as early as 1527 in Augsburg to determine leadership.

44. *Oesterreich* 2:99, 139, *QGT*. Jobst Schützinger, possibly a brother, was also to be arrested.

45. A report dated July 31, 1529, indicated that Anabaptists fleeing Ratten-

berg had left 131 children behind. Three of these were Marpeck's adopted children, one of them Schützinger's, four Melchior Schlosser's. It was feared that these children would die of "hunger and poverty and become beggars" unless the property of the fugitive parents was made available for their upkeep (*Oesterreich* 2: 266, *QGT*).

46. Hutterocentric is the claim that Schützinger had served as Hutter's assistant in the Tyrol (Friedmann 1959d).

47. *The Chronicle*, 93. The marginalia provided the Huttercentric view, "Gabriel and Philip united with us." A more accurate source recorded "Und seind drei grosse Gemainden worden, zwo zu Auspitz: die Philipper und Hueterischen genant; zu Rossitz der Gabriel mit seiner gemein . . . und haben in ainigkait und friden mit einander gehausset bis ums Jar 1533" (Beck 1967, 102).

48. *The Chronicle*, 94. The Gabrielites and proto-Hutterites had been the main targets; the Philipites escaped with less damage.

49. In their letter explaining the schism of 1533 Hutter's supporters later claimed that they had hoped the alliance would lead to a real union under single leadership. They accused Gabriel and Philip of jealously protecting their positions, concerned only with the interests of their own group and of having withheld aid from the proto-Hutterite community. Hutter had allegedly often sighed about the lack of unity. "Verantwortung des Gabrieler Briefs, Von uns Dienern der Gemein zu Schäkowitz . . . verlesen vor etzlichen mehr den hundert Brüdern" (Wolkan 1923, 197–200; I used Codex Hab. 5, 390ff.).

50. Hans Amon appeared in records dating from August 1529 as a cloth cutter (*Tuchscherer*) from Hall and an Anabaptist leader, "a tall person with a long red beard." His acquaintance with Hutter probably went back to Hutter's visit to Austerlitz in 1529 (*Oesterreich* 2:276, *QGT*).

51. This emerges from an entry that Hutter "brought a little temporal gift, a sweet sacrifice, yes a little provision, so that the debt incurred during the time of need [*Not*] and advanced by the abbess of Brünn and the Auspitzers be paid off" (Beck 1967, 103–4 n. 1).

52. Hutter and Amon had sent a letter in April, but the carriers were arrested at Kufstein before April 27, 1533 (*Oesterreich* 3:112, *QGT*).

53. The letter has been wrongly dated in Hutterite codices under the year 1536 ("Hans Amon, 1. Epistel gesendet aus der Grafschaft Tirol an Leonhard Schmerbacher in Auspitz" in *Episteln* 2:220–22). I compared Codex Hab. 17 and the Montana Codex for the proper text. It obviously dated from 1533.

54. The copy of the letter in *Episteln* 2: 221–22 contains an error. The passage reading "unser Widersacher heiratet nicht" should read "schläft nicht" and is a reference to Satan.

55. Griesinger had only recently escaped from the prison at Hopfgarten in the Archbishopric of Salzburg. Cf. Chapter 11.

56. See the confessions of Gertraud Pretz from Sterzing and her daughter Elisabeth. Gertraud had been baptized by Onophrius Griesinger a year before at Falkenhein (*Oesterreich* 3:126–27, *QGT*).

57. Ibid. 1:273.

58. Statement by Paul Rumer, September 19, 1533 (ibid. 3:157ff.).

59. *Wappenröcke,* short-sleeved overcoats, open at the sides, a socially distinguishing feature of *Fürstendiener,* were initially worn by nobles or knights (Noflatscher 1988, especially 326). I would like to thank Dr. Noflatscher for sending me a copy of the article as well another on the subject of *Wappenröcke.*

60. See statement by Vinzenz Puhl, July 11, 1533 (*Oesterreich* 3:135–36, QGT).

61. Kuppelwieser 1949, 203. Hutter traveled in the company of brothers and sisters from Schwaz and Rattenberg, Schützinger's home territory (*Oesterreich* 3: 150, QGT).

62. *The Chronicle,* 128.

63. Cf. "Verantwortung des Gabrieler Briefs," in Wolkan 1923, 197–200; Friedmann 1965, 14, 29, 54.

64. *The Chronicle,* 99ff.

65. Braitmichel, 371ff. This codex seems to contain the oldest copy of the above. For different titles of the original piece later incorporated into *The Chronicle,* cf. Friedmann 1965, 19, 25, 27, 29, 54, 89, 94, 175. Friedmann believed that the schism of 1533 and merger of 1545 provided the "external impulses for a more systematic history with its necessary substructure of a salvation history as its prehistory." Friedmann speculated that Braitmichel began *The Chronicle* during Peter Walpot's leadership, 1565 to 1573.

66. Braitmichel became the servant of temporal affairs under Amon's leadership at Schackowitz in 1538; servant of the Word at Holitsch in Hungary in 1548. He died in 1573 at Austerlitz. The report on the "Zerspaltung der Gemein" appears to have been written before the 1545 merger with some Gabrielites (Friedmann 1955e).

67. Braitmichel included almost verbatim Hutter's letter of November 22, 1533, and used the two previous letters as well (*The Chronicle,* 110–26).

68. Ascherham 1541, 55–57; English translation in Stayer 1991, 170–71.

69. *The Chronicle,* 99, 110.

70. Cf. Friedmann 1956e; 1958b; 1959c; 1964, especially 329–31;

71. The fullest previous discussion is by Loserth 1892b.

72. *The Chronicle,* 99; Beck 1967, 103. On October 6, 1533, Valentin Lukhner testified that Amon had sent brother Conntz (Kuntz Viechter?) with additional funds (*Oesterreich* 3:165ff., especially 171, QGT).

73. "Ien hat die ganze heilige Gemein gotes empfangen und aufgenommen, als den Herren selbs" (Braitmichel 1571).

74. *The Chronicle,* 99.

75. The English translation in *The Chronicle,* 99, is not quite accurate here. Cf. Zieglschmid 1946, 105ff.

76. *The Chronicle,* 100.

77. Schmerbacher, Griesbacher, and Kaspar from Rossitz are specifically mentioned, but Blasius Kuhn and Peter Hueter were presumably also present. Hueter was present at the Sunday meeting.

78. *The Chronicle,* 118–19.

79. Gabriel had had a bad experience with a Swiss leader (ibid., 101).

80. According to one version, the brethren found Gabriel's claims false (Braitmichel 1571).

81. The compromise proposal came from Schmerbacher after Peter Hueter, one of Gabriel's assistants, supported joint leadership.

82. *The Chronicle,* 101–3. It seems that Hutter had slipped into the dialect of his Tyrolese supporters, unless Gabriel meant his comment in a derogatory way, that Hutter could read the Scriptures only in the vernacular.

83. Fasser (Jörg Vasser) was from Kitzbühl (Mecenseffy 1971, 161; cf. Chapter 11).

84. *The Chronicle,* 103.

85. One pound was the equivalent of 20 groschen. One groschen equaled 10 kretuzer; 1 kreutzer equaled 12 pfennig (Barton 1985, 81).

86. *The Chronicle,* 104. In 1530–31 Schützinger, according to official documents, had 120 gulden in trust with a citizen of Rattenberg. His wife, Barbara, claimed 55 of these for her two young children. She also petitioned Innsbruck for the return of her confiscated property (*Oesterreich* 2:422, 480, *QGT*).

87. Some felt that they had been coerced by Gabriel's long speech and "threats" into preferring Schützinger. Cf. Braitmichel, 370ff.

88. *The Chronicle,* 105. In his letter to the brethren in the Tyrol, Hutter expressed relief that they had come before he began to speak on marriage because they would have attacked his words.

89. Ibid., 106.

90. Braitmichel 1571. The suggestion is that Fasser had been elevated to a leadership position.

91. See the margin in *The Chronicle,* 106.

92. The 1571 codex records that Philip Plener turned once more near the door and repeated, "I said that Jacob is your idol, and you worship him" (Braitmichel 1571, 394).

93. This is implied by the sequence of events given by the Braitmichel account (ibid.).

94. The 1571 codex puts Hans of Strasbourg in brackets: [Wie wir achten Hans von Strasburg] (Braitmichel 1571). It has been suggested that this was Leopold Scharnschlager's son-in-law, who in 1531 married Ursula Scharnschlager. Also known as Hans Felix, the clockmaker, Hans was ill and unemployed at Austerlitz in 1536. From 1547 to 1554 he resided at Znaim.

95. Although statistics are not available, it seems likely that by 1533 South Tyrolese had come to outnumber those from the North, who had dominated earlier. With contributors such as Mairhofer, Hutter and the Pusterers also brought greater assets to the community at Auspitz.

96. He sent a letter to Amon and Griesinger immediately after Schützinger's exposure and again within days after discussions with the other communities broke down. In a letter sent after October 31, 1533, Hutter wrote, "I have written this to you twice before; this is the third time and it will surely not be the last time." Kuntz Maurer and Michael Schuster were the carriers of the letter, dated October 30, 1533 (*The Chronicle,* 111, 124).

97. *The Chronicle,* 114.

98. This letter from Amon has not survived. As for the sightings, they were common in the sixteenth century as was the belief that they constituted divine omens. A year later (February 1534), Anabaptists in Münster witnessed a similar portent of three suns. They too considered it an omen of divine favor, but it turned out otherwise.

99. According to the oldest account, the messengers were sent to Philip's community on Sunday and to Gabriel's community on Thursday.

100. *The Chronicle,* 117–18.

101. Ibid., 120.

102. Ibid., 118.

103. Ascherham 1541, 55–57.

104. *The Chronicle,* 121.

105. Ibid., 101.

Chapter Ten. The Return and Death of Jacob Hutter

1. Cf. the mandate directed to the Estates of Moravia at a meeting at Znaim in the spring of 1535. The Estates complied on the first Sunday of Lent (Beck 1967, 117 n. 2).

2. Ibid., 114. The distress was largely the result of the strained relations with the neighboring community of Philipites, who refused any relations with the Hutterites, even greeting each other (*The Chronicle,* 128).

3. Hutter's supporters had purchased a house there as early as 1533. Schackowitz or Schakwitz was a half-mile (four British miles) south of Auspitz. It belonged to the lords of Lippe-Krumau (*The Chronicle,* 129, 132).

4. By March 1534 the authorities were aware that Amon was sending people across the Brenner and down the Inn River (*Oesterreich* 3:231, *QGT*).

5. Hutter made this observation in a letter to prisoners at Hohenwart after Onophrius Griesinger had arrived safely with a group (*Episteln* 1:37–44, especially 43; cf. *The Chronicle,* 131 n. 1).

6. Ibid., 134.

7. There is some confusion in the Hutterite records because they referred to expulsion from Auspitz and Schackowitz.

8. *The Chronicle,* 135; Beck 1967, 116–17. The marshall of Schackowitz became a central figure in a Hutterite song about the expulsion. The song recorded the decision of the Estates at Znaim that the Anabaptists were to be driven out, with force if necessary. The song was mentioned without the text in *Lieder,* 67.

9. The numbers come from a statement by Jeronimus Käls (Mais 1963, especially 92).

10. A group moved into the abandoned village of Starnitz (Starnice), eighteen miles south of Brünn.

11. The English translation "Jacob Hutter pleaded with the governor's servants" moderates the original, "Dieweil Jakob . . . ernstlich zusprach" (*The Chronicle,* 136; Zieglschmid 1946, 148).

12. The chronicler made the specific point of having copied Hutter's letter

from the original, the "first copy," presumably as proof that Ascherham's charges were untrue (*The Chronicle*, 137).

13. Ascherham 1541, 55–56. The Hutterite denial of the accusation is proof that Fischer's citation from Gabriel's lost account is authentic.

14. Zieglschmid 1946, 149–54. *The Chronicle*, 137–41. I compared these editions with that in the Montana Codex of 1566. Variations were minor.

15. *The Chronicle*, 137, 138, 140. Some editorializing in Hutterite codices over time is evident in the different renderings of the same passage. Where Codex Montana reads, "der gotloss Tyran und faindt," Zieglschmid has, "der grausam Tyrann and feind" (Zieglschmid 1946, 149).

16. *The Chronicle*, 140.

17. Beck 1967, 119 n. 1. An entry in archival documents suggests that Innsbruck received a report on Hutter's response as early as April 15, 1535. But this seems too early, unless there was a lapse in time between Hutter's oral and written response and the actual expulsions (*Oesterreich* 3:271, *QGT*).

18. *The Chronicle*, 141 n. 1; Salztrager was released after August 18, 1535 (Beck 1967, 118–20). Griesbacher's letter to the "True Pilgrims of the Lord in Moravia," sent through Hans Donner of Wals, is found in *Episteln* 2:180ff. Donner was beheaded in late 1538 at St. Veit in Carinthia. A letter by him is found in the same volume (120–22; cf. *The Chronicle*, 181).

19. Ibid., 142; Beck 1967, 117–18. Unfortunately details of these instructions have not survived. *The Chronicle* implied in another entry that the return to South Tyrol had been discussed earlier and that Amon "felt no special zeal" to go. Hutter did, however, and announced it "with many brethren present," but "they waited for the right time" (132).

20. Hutter was baptizing in the Puster region by July 25, 1535 (*Oesterreich* 3:297, *QGT*).

21. Ibid., 319.

22. Friedmann's claim that "the Hutterites have not a single letter written by women" is incorrect. At least four have survived (Friedmann 1956b, letter nos. 58, 61, 63, 91).

23. The reference is found in the greetings of Hutter's second letter from the Tyrol (Hutter 1979, 78 n. 1).

24. Katherine's father was Lorentz (Laurentzer) Präst (Prusst). Andle (Anne) Sackmannin from the Ritten was executed in Tauffers (Beck 1967, 278). As noted in Chapter 6, Wölfl had been at the von Wolkenstein residence near Tauffers in 1526.

25. *Oesterreich* 3:157, *QGT*. About Rumer and Gall from St. Georgen, see Chapter 8.

26. Gossensass was a mining center about three hours travel from the Brenner and one and a half hours from the Jaufen valley.

27. *Oesterreich* 3:168–70, *QGT*: "ain diern, Katarina geheissen." The other two were, respectively, the daughters of a man named Steger from Sterzing and Anna Stainer of St. Georgen. About thirty persons were present (ibid., 25, 53).

28. Ibid., 319. Gall was executed before May 16. His wife fled to Moravia (ibid., 92, 115–25).

29. Ibid., 110. With her were Clara Schneider and Elspet Lipp of Villnöss and Anna Gerber of Tisens.

30. Ibid., 106. Most of the seventy present were from the Puster valley; two daughters of Stainer from St. Georgen were among them.

31. Ibid., 113.

32. The third scout may have been Kuntz Maurer, who traveled with Michael Schuster as courier as early as 1533 (ibid., 290). About Jeronimus, see Chapter 11.

33. Ibid., 288, 298–99. A Slepl or Schläpple is better known as Schlapphut. Michael Schuster was also described as a tall person wearing a black herald's coat. Did the leaders exchange clothes as part of their disguise?

34. Michel Walder of Ellen near St. Lorenzen, baptized by Hutter two years earlier, had become a "no-good person." He was arrested in January 1534 and recanted (ibid., 207, 300; cf. 426, 436, 458).

35. Ibid., 300.

36. Ibid., 20. Jörg Vasser had baptized in the area during Easter 1531. Gschäll was later expelled for sexual promiscuity, and Lindl, as noted, was the brother involved in the Zaunring affair.

37. Ibid., 26–27.

38. George Ebner had been arrested and had given the oath to have no further dealings with Anabaptists. He broke the oath. On June 5, 1535, Appolina requested that she be released from the fine her husband had been condemned to pay. In 1553 her son Peter, as rightful heir, asked for her property (ibid., 199, 207, 211, 610).

39. As late as 1539 an Ebner gave shelter to Anabaptists (ibid., 429).

40. The letter dated from late July/early August 1535 and was carried by Michel (Michael) Walser (Schuster). It was wrongly listed under the date 1536 in *Episteln* 1:23–36 (*Oesterreich* 3:93–94, 298–99, *QGT; The Chronicle,* 111, 114).

41. Anyone coming without the permission of the leaders would not be welcome (*Episteln* 1:26).

42. Ibid., 28–29. A slightly different translation appeared in Hutter 1979, 75–101, especially 87, 88.

43. *The Chronicle,* 142.

44. Hutter 1979, 86–87.

45. He reminded them again that he had moved upon their "request and counsel . . . with much sorrow and many tears, a sorrow and pain still in his heart" (*Episteln* 1:25; Hutter 1979, 87, 90). And a little later in the same letter he wrote, "I could not prevent what has happened, nor can I change the situation we are in now, though it breaks my heart."

46. *Episteln* 1:35.

47. Hans Mair Paulle taught in his home, and Niderhofer was questioned by the authorities in March 1534 (*Oesterreich* 3:240, 287, *QGT*).

48. They were a Julia (Ulia), in the service of Sigmund Velser of Kiens, and a certain Rasstainerin (ibid., 287, 297, 301).

49. Niderhofer's statement agreed with that of Katharina Tagwericher on this date. Cf. ibid., 288, 290).

50. Hutter 1979, 103–18. Hutter wrote at least the greeting, if not the entire letter, in his own hand. The letter was written after Aug 24–25. *Episteln* 1 arranges letters 3 and 2 in the wrong sequence. Letter 2 is on pp. 55–63. At the time of its writing, Hutter was still anxious to hear whether his first letter, carried by Michel Walser, had arrived. Walser, on his way back with return mail, must have crossed paths with the carrier of the second letter

51. He was accompanied by the bailiff of Schöneck, Sigmund Hilber.

52. *Oesterreich* 3:276, *QGT*.

53. He mentioned Ulrich Häringin, the Rasstainerin, and Julia, the servant girl of Sigmund Velser (ibid., 277–78).

54. Ibid., 278.

55. Cf. ibid., 279–85.

56. Ibid., 285–86.

57. "Die 3 Epistel von Jacob Hutter an die Gemein Gottes in Mähren" in *Episteln* 1:46–47. Hutter 1979, 119–35, especially 134. The letter included greetings also from sisters Nändle (Anna Stainer), Klärle (Klara), and Hutter's wife Treindel, as well as from "the faithful members of this household" from which the letter originated. The household was, no doubt, that of Hans Obern at Hörschwang.

58. Presumably a copyist's error.

59. According to Hutter, Paul (Troyer) had become the bailiff (Pfleger) at Greifenwink (Greifenburg). After his father's death, Paul returned to assume his father's office as magistrate of Schöneck (*Episteln* 1:48–49).

60. Anna knew Hutter and his *hausfrau*, Christoph Schuster, and Hans Mair Paulle (*Oesterreich* 3:318, 299, *QGT*).

61. Ibid., 299. Approximately six weeks had passed between her leaving Toblach and the arrest in Klausen.

62. She served in the household of Hueber at Götzenberg, with a tailor at Vahrn, with the Gaysmairs near Sterzing, and with a Chonzen at Köfl (Cunz Kofler) near Stifles.

63. *Oesterreich* 3:223–26, 228–29, *QGT*. Besides Hutter, Anna knew the leaders Amon, Griesinger, Hans Mair Paulle, and Jörg Vasser.

64. Among her acquaintances in Moravia were Paul Rumer's sister Justina (the widow of Paul Gall), Veronica Grembs, and her former employers, the Huebers from Götzenberg (ibid., 228, 299).

65. According to Hutterite sources, thirty martyrs died in Sterzing (Beck 1967, 278).

66. The meeting took place in the basement of the home of the absent Schaffner (Schäfer?). Cf. statements by Katherine Hutter and Anna Stainer (*Oesterreich* 3:299–300, *QGT*).

67. *Episteln* 1:64–74; Hutter 1979, 137–57. The translation contains errors, for example, Lüfen instead of Lüsen.

68. They were baptized under a great pine tree at the edge of the forest (*Oesterreich* 3:297–99, 301, *QGT*).

69. Praun contributed 30 gulden to the treasury and estimated that he carried 50 gulden worth of provisions to a hut at Niderwies (ibid., 298, 301).

70. *Episteln* 1:73; Hutter 1979, 154–55.

71. *Oesterreich* 3:284, *QGT*.

72. Hutter's letter alluded to the arrest of a brother from Tauffers. Official documents listed a brother Martin, arrested on November 9. Martin had signaled willingness to recant (ibid., 285, 311–12).

73. This corresponds with Anna Stainer's statement that she had returned to the Puster valley with Hutter and had been in the area two weeks before they moved in the direction of Klausen.

74. Several mountain huts had been winterized with provisions. Two were located near Onach, between Hörschwang and St. Lorenzen (*Oesterreich* 3: 309–10, *QGT*).

75. The typological interpretation of clouds as teachers may have entered the Hutterite tradition through a study of Melchior Hoffmann's *Commentary on the Apocalypse* of 1530. The typology is also found in epistles by other leaders. See Chapter 11.

76. Hutter 1979, 147, 153–54; *Episteln* 1:69.

77. It is possible that the words *the other servants* were added by Amon. Hutter encouraged Amon to make necessary corrections or elaborations before circulating his letters.

78. The original destination had been Villnöss, northeast of Klausen. Contacts were a Georg Müller, his wife and a Mrs. Niclauer, but Müller had recanted and Mr. Niclauer was not a brother, so Hutter and his companions moved on (*Oesterreich* 3:301, *QGT*).

79. They crossed the bridge upstream near the safety shelter (*schutzhütten*). In 1533 Hutter stayed with Peter Pinter at Klausen and baptized in his house, located outside the city next to the bridge (ibid., 106, 160, 280–83, 285–87, 300–1).

80. Ibid., 130, 302.

81. Fischer confused some names. The bishop's bailiff (Pfleger) of Seber (Säben) was Riederer or Niederer. The magistrate of Klausen was Christoph Mairhofer. Anna junior, Hutter's companion, was not a daughter of the hostess, Anna Stainer senior. In fact, their relationship, if any, is not clear (Fischer 1956, 41ff.).

82. *Oesterreich* 3:292–93, *QGT*.

83. I checked the original document cited by Mecenseffy as 367 A, *Oesterreich* 3:295, *QGT*).

84. Beck 1967, 122: "Nicht lange darnach begab es sich . . . das . . . Jacob Hueter zu Clausen . . . (in ains alten Mans Hauss), durch Betrug und Verräterei . . . gefangen wardt." On November 27, Brixen instructed the bailiff of Schöneck to threaten his son-in-law, Niclas Niderhofer, with torture. It is possible that information given by Niderhofer put the authorities on Hutter's trail. Niderhofer was subsequently treated with disdain by some of Hutter's followers (*Oesterreich* 3:292, 295, *QGT*).

85. Ibid., 295.

86. Ibid., 294–95.

87. Ibid., 297–303. The names of those on the jury at Branzoll are listed under the date December 4, 1535.

88. This emerges from the accompanying letter sent along to Innsbruck with the women's statements. I consulted the original cited by Mecenseffy (ibid., 308, no. 371). Amon's letters taken from Hutter appear not to have survived.

89. Ibid., 306–11; Fischer 1956, 42.

90. "guettigen und peinlichen examination und frag" (ibid., 312–13).

91. Ibid., 313.

92. The list of names about which Hutter was to be questioned also included Grembs, Rumer, Zimmermann, and Schuster.

93. *Oesterreich* 3:314, *QGT*.

94. Ibid., 294–95.

95. Fischer 1956, 45 n. 89. Ferdinand and his advisors believed that the numbers concealed a coded message (*Oesterreich* 3:308–9, *QGT*).

96. Ibid., 317.

97. Beck 1967, 120–24.

98. Fischer wrote, "Huter aber bekannte gar nichts" (Fischer 1956, 45). Per Mecenseffy, "aber wir wissen, dass Huetter auf alle diese Fragen nicht geantwortet hat. Nie hat er einen seiner Brüder oder Schwestern verraten" (Mecenseffy 1985, 27).

99. *Oesterreich* 3:325, *QGT*.

100. Kräntzler was arrested on or before May 9, 1536, as was Gilg Lex and a fifteen-year-old boy. Arrested before January 3, 1536, were a Blasius Weyseyes, Mathias Lasacher, his wife Katharina Lasacherin, and Anna, the daughter of Connzen (Kuntz) Rayner (ibid., 317).

101. Obern left 100 gulden with Caspar Underainer for his immature children. A number of Underainers were Anabaptists; Hänsel Underainer was executed. Ochs, the magistrate of St. Michelsburg, managed to pocket 50 gulden of Obern's money (ibid., 321–34, 486–87).

102. Ibid., 319.

103. Erhard 1588, 19bff. One of the surviving questionnaires suggested that Hutter was questioned about cash and silver cutlery believed to be hidden (Fischer 1956, 45).

104. For a discussion of the date, see ibid., 48. An official communiqué spoke of February 25. Hutterite codices give the date as Friday before the first fast week, March 3, 1536 (Beck 1967, 123 n. 1). Yet, Friday after the first fast week, March 17, would explain why the jailer asked to be paid for 87 days.

105. Beck 1967, 122–24.

106. *The Chronicle*, 145; Beck 1967, 120–22.

107. *Oesterreich* 3:318, *QGT*.

108. A document dated February 5, 1536, and not edited by Mecenseffy, suggested that since Katherine had recanted in 1533 (at Rodeneck) she might do the same again (Tiroler Landes Archiv, Innsbruck, C.D. 1532–1536, Bl. 335). On April 28, Innsbruck ordered that learned priests be brought in to instruct her and Anna Stainer, who was to be moved to Gufidaun as well. But as of August 2, 1536, Anna was still in Branzoll.

109. *Oesterreich* 3:323–24 n. 1, *QGT*.

110. She had been arrested before January 27, 1537, along with the wife of

Onophrius; Pöchtin von Pinswang; Connz Kofler; and a Steinmetz of Sterzing (ibid., 342–43).

111. Ibid., 289, 290, 315, 317.

112. Hans Mair Paulle played a role in their return to Anabaptism (ibid., 332).

113. The Niderhofers left a boy behind; he was placed with foster parents in April 1538 (ibid., 375).

114. Other sources described her as "lacking common sense" (ibid., 333–35).

115. Niclas was caught around October 27, 1539. Leonard Sailer was in the area, presumably to lead some to Moravia (ibid., 378, 390, 419–20, 424).

116. Ibid., 470–72. Yet in 1540–41 Niderhofer gathered provisions for the Anabaptists leaving for Moravia. One of his suppliers was Mathies Ebner of Götzenberg.

117. Ibid., 450, 455, 472.

118. Ibid., 502, 555.

Chapter Eleven. Further Losses

1. The information in *The Chronicle* is based entirely on the prison correspondence. The pertinent letters were reproduced by Mais (Mais 1963, 87ff.; *The Chronicle*, 147–54).

2. *Oesterreich* 3:298, 303, *QGT;* Loserth 1957a.

3. Cf. the report by the city magistrate of Vienna sent to the governor of Lower Austria on January 15, 1536. A copy of this report is found along with other letters in the Archive of the Diocese of Vienna. It was used by Mais. I obtained photocopies of the pertinent documents for my own research (Mais 1963, 91 n. 13, 93).

4. Valentin Lukhner referred to Jeronimus as "schreiber zu Kopfstain" (Kufstein), suggesting that Jeronimus was the court secretary. Anabaptists were in Kufstein by December 1527. In April 1532 Jeronimus was described as a former servant of Christoff Fuchs. Jeronimus's mother became an Anabaptist, and her house was burned down as punishment. Jeronimus assumed a leadership position and began to baptize others (*Oesterreich* 3:52, 166, 298, *QGT*).

5. Hutter's wife claimed that Jeronimus had been baptized by her husband. If so, Hutter must have rebaptized Jeronimus because he considered Schützinger's baptism invalid (ibid., 300).

6. It is not clear when in his career Jeronimus moved to Augsburg where, according to his own account, he learned the carpet weaving trade before moving to Bohemia to work in mines. If this was after his baptism, then he may have been baptized as early as 1527–28, joining others in Böhmisch Krumau.

7. Mais 1963, 93.

8. He came from Stranstorff near Mistelbach (ibid., 93 n. 24).

9. Ibid., 94. On December 3, 1535, Niclas Praun testified that "young Oberegkh from Auers" had been baptized with him by Hutter in the brook under a fir tree. Oberegkh had helped Praun carry provisions to an Alpine hut (*Oesterreich* 3:297–98, *QGT*).

10. Mais (1963) listed them as numbers 4 to 18. The letters were printed out

of sequence in *Episteln* 2 and 3. Volume 2 includes two by Michael Seifensieder (63–68). A letter by Oberecker is included in practically identical editions in both 2:69–70 and 3:708–9.

11. *Episteln* 3, in two copies from two different codices, 128–40.

12. Jeronimus's first three letters date from January 11. None of these was addressed to Amon. Others were addressed to Leonard Sailer and to a sister Justina. These letters were included in Mais as numbers 4 to 6 (Mais 1963).

13. The visit by the rector suggests that either or both Jeronimus and Michael had previously been students at the University of Vienna.

14. "Do sassen 3 Schlangen . . . auserlösene arge Schälckh, schrifftgelerte Pfaffen" (Mais 1963, 108).

15. Ibid.; *The Chronicle*, 148.

16. I agree with Loserth, who described the judge's attitude as "outspokenly friendly," as giving the prisoners "kindly admonition"; and Loserth said that the prisoners "could not complain about the severity of the judge." The judge obviously sought to spare their lives (Loserth 1957a). This is not at all reflected in *The Chronicle*.

17. The claim in *The Chronicle* (148), that he was "tortured for two and a quarter hours," did not appear in Jeronimus's letter unless it was in a communiqué now lost (Mais 1963, 108).

18. Ibid., 112–14; *The Chronicle*, 149.

19. The carrier was to receive monetary reimbursement if he proved unfit to join the community. The baking woman was the wife of Leonhart Melmeser, a flour inspector or measurer.

20. It is possible that by *apostolic exercises* Jeronimus meant catechetical instructions.

21. Mais 1963, 117–18. It seems that Jeronimus's suggestion was accepted because Onophrius and Georg Fasser were appointed servants of the Gospel (*The Chronicle*, 152).

22. Mais 1963, 117–18, 144. That ecumenical solidarity in suffering had its limits is clear from the attitude of Hutterite prisoners ten years later. A Lutheran, who joined them in prison, was described as "stuck in the letter" and as "no better than the papal demons!"

23. Ibid., 101–5 (letter written during imprisonment at Auspitz in 1534).

24. For a discussion on where innocence ended, see Schwartz 1973.

25. Ibid., 102.

26. *The Chronicle*, 150–51.

27. Mais 1963, 102.

28. In some aspects, Hutterite education was less discriminatory and ahead of its time (Wiswedel 1940).

29. Mais 1963, 104.

30. The removal of children from parental care remained a problem for some parents. Michel Hornacker and Hans Braun and their wives testified in 1559 how the children had been taken from them and placed in schools six miles away. Three of Braun's four children died, the other apparently remained in the school. Hornacker's wife testified that she had experienced great sorrow, especially concerning

her children (*Württemberg* 1:185–86, *QGT*). For a similar experience see the story of Mrs. Pürchner (Packull 1990b).

31. Mais 1963, 131–35. Mais edited a copy believed to be in Michael Seifensieder's handwriting, now in the Vienna University Library. It compares favorably with the text given by Müller in *Glaubenszeugnisse* 1:205–10.

32. Loserth 1957a, 140.

33. Mais 1963, 133; *Glaubenszeugnisse* 1:209.

34. The confession closed on that topic (Mais 1963, 127ff.).

35. Apparently written in Czech (ibid., pp. 122ff.).

36. "mit einem feinen Br. versorget wurde. Ursach, der Herr geb ir die Gab der Beschneidung. Ich sag nit anders, dan das göttlich ist" (ibid., 119).

37. Mayer and Veit are described as "Seckler." Most of the others appear to have been leaders of smaller groups. Also mentioned were a Stoffel (Christoph) Schützinger; Jacob Stroschneider; Anthoni Kürschner; Andl, Amon's wife; Oswalt's wife Marthl; a Resl (Rosemary); and Treindl, Jeronimus's wife.

38. Mais 1963, 123.

39. According to *The Chronicle*, 150, they died on Friday, two weeks before Easter 1536. Easter was April 16.

40. These are found in *Lieder*, 67–71.

41. "In you, O Father, is my joy," translated in *The Chronicle*, 358–60; "Ich will dich, Herre . . . loben" in *Lieder* 67–71.

42. "Ich reu und klag den gantzen Tag" (*Lieder*, 68–69). Verse 1 ended with "Now note what happened in the last days" with the acrostic Jeronimus.

43. *The Chronicle*, 129–30.

44. Ibid., 130.

45. *Oesterreich* 3:122, 125, 131, *QGT*.

46. Ibid., 270, 419.

47. Ibid., 179–81, 198–99.

48. Ibid., 211. The incident is recorded under February 7, 1534, but must have taken place in the fall of 1533.

49. By the late fall of 1533 Amon and others had found refuge in the Mittenwalder Alps (ibid., 183).

50. *The Chronicle*, 130.

51. *Oesterreich* 3:412, 423, 426, 429, *QGT*.

52. It was the home of Kniepasser where Hutter's letters from Moravia were read (*Oesterreich* 3:173, *QGT*).

53. Veronica was the daughter of Hans Grembs and Elizabeth Höglerin of St. Georgen. A Hans Grembser had been baptized by Hutter in 1531 and visited Moravia. Veronica's aunt, Otilia, was married to Balthasar Mairhofer of Lüsen, her sister, Margareth, to Balthasar Mairhofer of Niedervintl. Margareth was executed before July 8, 1535. The Grembs had connections to the household of Anton von Wolkenstein, whose wife Elsbeth gave shelter to the pregnant Agnes, the wife of Andre Zimmermann of St. Georgen. Andre, an early martyr, appears to have been related to Erhard Zimmermann, the bailiff of the estate of Michel von Teutenhof at Neuhaus, which served Amon, Amon's wife, and others as a shelter. An attempt to trap Amon at Neuhaus failed when the bailiff of Tauffers arrested Zim-

mermann prematurely. Zimmermann's release left Amon suspicious. He did not return (*Oesterreich* 3:137, 186, 193, 198–99, 201, 219–20, 227–30, 231, 232, 274, 321, *QGT*).

54. Ibid., 189. An attempt to "entice Amon back" for arrest failed.

55. Ibid., 351–52, 506ff.

56. *The Chronicle*, 130. Praweiger had apparently already gone to his "just reward" at the time the poem was composed.

57. In another context, Tessa Watt observed that the shift from story in song to prosaic book version reflected growing literacy. Cheap print, so-called broadsheets, contained many songs or slanderous poems (Watt 1991, 4–6, 257).

58. *The Chronicle*, 152. Loserth 1956b.

59. *Oesterreich* 3:394, *QGT*.

60. Ibid., 128; Rischar 1968; Loserth 1959a.

61. *Oesterreich* 3:85, 126, 128, *QGT*.

62. His wife was helped by the cook (Beck 1967, 136 n. 1).

63. *The Chronicle*, 112, 126.

64. *Oesterreich* 3:128, 172–73, 328–29, *QGT*. Three years later, he was described as a tall person with a pointed beard, who spoke in a Bavarian dialect.

65. It is possible that he was commissioned to the south before Jeronimus's arrest and that Jeronimus aimed for a different destination in Upper Austria and North Tyrol (*The Chronicle*, 131 n. 1; 152).

66. She traveled with Mrs. Griesinger (*Oesterreich* 3:323, *QGT*).

67. Before April 26, 1536 (ibid., 324, 363). *The Chronicle*, 152, claimed that Griesinger had also been detained in Styria.

68. *Oesterreich* 3:328–32, 351, 371–74.

69. Her name was given as Anna Lentzin (Pöchtin of Pinswang). She appears to have suffered from epileptic seizures (*an dem fallenden sichtumb*) (ibid., 343, 398; cf. *The Chronicle*, 170 n.).

70. *Oesterreich* 3:346, *QGT*. Loserth wrongly dated this incident in 1536 (Loserth 1956b, 580). Beck claimed that Onophrius was arrested at Lüsen in April 1537 and transferred to Brixen, from whence he escaped (Beck 1967, 136 n. 1).

71. *Oesterreich* 3:364, 432, *QGT*. The two were an Aschperger and Hans Rainer. Rainer's brother Balthasar helped another person out in 1540.

72. Ibid., 355.

73. Ibid., 369.

74. *The Chronicle*, 168. The names of five persons sent down by Onophrius are included in *Oesterreich* 3:357, 364, *QGT*. On April 23, 1537, the authorities had placed 80 gulden on Onophrius's head if he were taken alive, 40 if brought in dead.

75. Ibid., 370–74. Glaser arrived in the area on September 29, 1537. In 1534 he and a small band had been intercepted at Hohenwart in Austria. He had been burned through the cheek, but his life was spared. He and Grünfelder were arrested before December 6, 1537, and executed in January 1538. Dr. Gallus Müller had been brought in to extract a recantation but without success (*The Chronicle*, 131, 162). Glaser left some songs. Cf. *Lieder*, 71–74.

76. The account in *The Chronicle*, 162, is based on Onophrius's letter. Cf. Beck 1967, 131–32 (Onophrius Griesinger, "Erster Sendbrief an die Gemeinde in Mähren," in *Episteln* 2:164–65).

77. *The Chronicle*, 169, states explicitly that Onophrius and Lochmair were sent out together (Beck 1967, 137ff.; Loserth 1957c).

78. *Oesterreich* 3:377, *QGT*.

79. A copy of his recantation dated before August 6, 1538, is included in ibid., 385–86.

80. Ibid., 384–85, 389–90; Beck 1967, 137–38.

81. Troyer arrived between 9 and 10 p.m. at Onophrius's mountain cabin. He found another thirty participants in other cabins. Arrested also was Michel Schneider, who had served as Onophrius's messenger to Moravia. In his last letter from the Puster valley Onophrius reported that Niclas Niderhofer was still in prison and faithful to the Lord. According to rumors he was to be executed secretly. This information should change the low opinion some had of Niderhofer (*Episteln* 2:165–68). The letter was carried by Jacob Zeugerlin (Zugerin).

82. *Oesterreich* 3:387–90, *QGT*.

83. The account in *The Chronicle*, 171, was based on Onophrius's third and fifth letters. Cf. *Episteln* 2:169–70, 176–79. Official documents also recorded the food bowl communication, thus providing independent confirmation of its veracity.

84. The letter, addressed to Lochmair's wife, contained greetings to Amon, Stadler, Peter (Riedemann?), Leonhard Sailer, and others (*Episteln* 2:102–4). Stadler led a remnant of Austerlitz Brethren into an alliance with the Hutterites (*The Chronicle*, 170 n.).

85. "pundtschuh ainer neuen empörung unter dem gemeinen Mann" (Beck 1967, 137 n.).

86. Cf. his fifth and last letter (*Episteln* 2:177).

87. *Oesterreich* 3:394–95, 397, *QGT*. Monks from Bozen, perhaps Franciscans, had visited him twice (*Episteln* 2:177). The special prosecutor was Dr. Schmotzer.

88. *Oesterreich* 3:395 n. 1, *QGT*; *The Chronicle*, 172; *Episteln* 2:175.

89. *Oesterreich* 3:399, *QGT*.

90. Beck 1967, 137 n.

91. *The Chronicle*, 172; Beck 1967, 140 n.

92. I assume that he was identical with Stoffel, the former captain from Villach, who joined before 1545. Cf. *The Chronicle*, 244.

93. Beck 1967, 138 n. Cf. Loserth 1957c, 382.

94. Ibid. It is also possible that the death of the suffragan bishop, Albrecht Kraus, between October 3 and 8, 1538, delayed Lochmair's execution.

95. *The Chronicle*, 172. A report in Beck 1967, 138 n., that he recanted a second time and was merely exiled seems incorrect, even though official documents do not record the execution.

96. Onophrius was credited with five letters and six hymns. Five are found in *Lieder*, 77–82. Lochmair left two letters and three songs (82–85).

97. "das hochwirdig sacrament des zarten froleichnams Jesus Christi nit nies-sen noch empfangen können, auch den mund nit eröffnen noch aufthun mögen" (*Oesterreich* 3:301, *QGT*).

98. Ibid., 326–27.

99. Added information not found in *Oesterreich* 3, *QGT,* is found in Del-monego 1974, 569–74.

100. The chaplain was presumably Paul Lueger of Lüsen.

101. It seems he had been arrested on April 4, 1537, and arrived in Brixen on April 8, 1537 (*Oesterreich* 3:349–50, *QGT*).

102. He had been baptized on or around July 13, 1536 (ibid., 328, 330, 350–52).

103. Ibid., 350, 352.

104. Ibid., 352–53. Innsbruck advised clemency on June 27, 1537.

105. A local noble named Sturtzhauser in the territories of Lord Hans von Fünfkirchen employed members of the group on his estate (*The Chronicle,* 142, 155, 162).

106. This is true of the letters of Jeronimus and Onophrius.

107. Loserth 1957b.

108. *The Chronicle,* 161–62.

109. See Chapter 9. A Fasser from Schwaz appeared in documents as early as 1527. He was a former monk who had married and worked in the mines as a water lifter. Presumably this was the Fasser active in the Puster region during 1528. It has been assumed that he was a different person from the Fasser discussed here (*Oesterreich* 2:30–31, 104, 106, 120, 126, 423; 3:20 n. 2, *QGT*).

110. (Jörg) Fasser (Vasser) had been an associate of Schützinger in Rattenberg as late as 1532 (ibid., 51; see also Chapter 9).

111. *The Chronicle,* 152.

112. *The Chronicle* (153) reported the place as Neudorf; Loserth as Windorf (Loserth 1957b, 292).

113. In addition to the nine letters by the prisoners, four responses by Amon have been preserved. Three of Amon's letters are in *Episteln* 1:85–95; letters by Lanzenstiel and Fasser in the same volume, 244–302; excerpts were translated in *The Chronicle,* 153 n. 1.

114. According to their first letter they had arrived at 2 p.m. and found the wife of Hans Schuster there. The letter, dated the Monday after St. Philip's and St. James' day, or May 2, 1536, was delivered by a paid courier, who received 12 kreuzer in advance and an unknown amount upon delivery (*Episteln* 1:244–48).

115. Ibid., 245: "namen sie uns auch ein einfältig Mensch mit Gewalt und haben also ihren Mutwillen mit ihr getrieben." *The Chronicle,* 152, translates this "a simple man," but the original in Zieglschmid is neutral, "ain ainfaltig mensch" (Zieglschmid 1946, 163).

116. *Episteln* 1:246. A partial translation appeared in *The Chronicle,* 153–54 n. 1. According to the letter they had warned the Sodomites with a story from the book of Judges according to which God had destroyed eighty thousand for such deeds.

117. *The Chronicle* did not mention the sympathetic treatment, remembering selectively the suffering of the prisoners.

118. The second letter was delivered by Klaus Müller, who had also carried Amon's letter to the prisoners (*Episteln* 1:249–54, especially 252). The letter warned that the "pillar of cloud" would no longer lead in the day. Everyone would have to live by their personal faith. The names of those with Amon (Blasi, Michel, Oswald, and Walser [Balthasar] Maier) are the same as those in Onophrius's letter, suggesting that they were part of a permanent staff with Amon. Cf. Amon's first response (ibid., 84–87; and excerpts in *The Chronicle*, 154 n.).

119. *Episteln* 1:258–59.

120. This statement seems to carry Amon's signature and contrasts with Jeronimus's warning made only a few weeks earlier against "overly hasty judgment concerning the others."

121. See the letter by Müller to his fellow prisoners (*Episteln* 1:266–67).

122. Ibid., 263, 279: "aber ich weiss dass du es fleissig bessern wirst denn ich schreib je einen kurzen Sinn." This increases the possibility that the passage on Gabrielites and Philipites had been added by Amon.

123. Letters six to nine were written May 13, 20, 27, and June 5, 1536, respectively.

124. *Episteln* 1:270–80. The seventh letter included greetings to Afruzen (Onophrius), and asked whether news had been received from Paul Fasser in the Adige valley. Sailer sent greetings to his wife Martl (Martha).

125. The eighth letter contained greetings to (Amon's) Andl, the Maierin, little Andl, Walser, Justina, Kurdl Fromdl, Blasy, Michl, Oswald, two Märtls (Martha), a Filga, Urschl (Ursula) Brälin, and another Andl (*Episteln* 1:281–84).

126. The ninth letter is in ibid., 285–91.

127. Ibid., 1:288: "möchten sonst vielleicht ausgegangen sein."

128. Ibid., 1:288–89.

129. Mais 1963, 98–99.

130. *Episteln* 1:286, 290. The passages are vague. Amon wrote about having to deal concerning "dem Abgefallenen," and Sailer wrote "wenn sie Buss sucht." Scholars who have sought evidence of autonomous behavior among Anabaptist women might have found examples among those who refused to follow their husbands into the Anabaptist faith.

131. *The Chronicle*, 154.

132. Ibid., 161–62. The entry of his death recorded that he did not know the alphabet "nevertheless preached the Gospel with power."

133. *Oesterreich* 3:449, *QGT*. With him were his wife, a Hans Mändl, Wölfl Röschl, and later Oswald Schuster.

134. Two accounts correspond (ibid., 411, 413–14, 453). Among Sailer's contacts were Niclas Niderhofer, who sought reacceptance with tears.

135. Ibid., 417. Kuppelwieser reported her name erroneously as Appollonia and claimed that she was drowned (Kuppelwieser 1949, 258, 267).

136. Among those who left for Moravia was Agnes von Waltenhofen, the sister of the countess of Neumarkt.

137. *The Chronicle*, 188.

138. Before his death Amon entrusted the congregation to Sailer (Beck 1967, 150–51). *The Chronicle* seems less decisive on this point (214).

139. I deal with the details of this affair in my study on Riedemann.

140. Leonhard Raiffer-Schmidt of Lüsen told interrogators that he had returned to pick up his family in June 1540 against the will of the brethren because Sailer "did not want anyone to travel from Moravia to the Tyrol" (*Oesterreich* 3: 449–50, *QGT*).

141. Ibid., 469.

142. Raiffer-Schmidt named Amon, Sailer, Gschäll, Peter Riedemann, and Hans Gentner as leaders (ibid., 454, 456–57).

143. *The Chronicle*, 142.

144. Cf. ibid., 155, 160, 162. Loserth also listed Nannsgarten and Waltersdorf (Loserth 1957c, 382).

145. *The Chronicle*, 155.

146. Ibid., 152.

Chapter Twelve. The Fate of the Philipites and the Gabrielites

1. Beck 1967, 116.

2. The Philipites located on a hill near Lassling, the Hutterites camped below it at "Stornitz [Starnice] under Lassling," an abandoned village near Tracht (Strachotin), about eighteen miles south of Brünn (Beck 1967, 116–17; Zeman 1966, 41:136; *The Chronicle*, 13, n. 2).

3. Ibid., 135–36.

4. Friedmann considered it "not quite just" (Friedmann 1958b, 275).

5. Loserth 1892b, especially 566. A settlement of Philipites remained at Pulgram. This group remained communal, and when it joined the Hutterites brought a bakery, the house of a charcoal burner, the house of the hatter, a school, and a large house (*The Chronicle*, 174).

6. Friedmann, 1958b, 284.

7. Jörg Scherer, along with Martin Fasser, baptized in the Esslingen-Stuttgart area by 1536–37. His group was visited by leaders from Switzerland, but former Philipites frequented the meetings as well. In the late 1530s the meetings held in forests attracted up to one hundred people. Some of these moved or returned to Moravia. As one of Amon's letters indicates, Hutterites had contact with this group. About Scherer see Chapter 4. Whether he was the Jörg Scherer who fell out with Hutter is not known (*The Chronicle*, 128–29).

8. Loserth 1892a, 123 n. 2; Bossert 1897, 92.

9. *Württemberg* 1:36–37, 41–44, *QGT*. Ulrich had taken the first measures on June 12, 1534.

10. Ibid., 39, 42–44, 46–47, 49, 52, 59, 62–63, 102, 997.

11. Ibid., 59.

12. In late 1535 Philip was in the area of Wangen (by inference from *Elsass* 4:549, *QGT*).

13. Ibid. 3:39–40; *Württemberg* 1:52, *QGT*. Was Hans from Oelbronn

(Heilbronn), presumably the Hans Schreiner driven out of Heilbronn in 1537, identical with Hans Gentner? The other two were Gewer Bauer from Swaigern (Schwaigern) and Michel Gartner of Ettenheim.

14. Schlegel testified that "there were about 200 of them to whom the money belonged" (*Elsass* 3:40, *QGT*).

15. Gewer Bauer stated that they had come to "take account, because the two [Philip and Kuhn] had promised to search for property [ein erdreich suchen] where they might settle" (ibid., 40).

16. Ibid., 52. Schlegel distinguished his group from staff bearers, sabbatarians, and Münsterites.

17. Kuhn was in Strasbourg on the Thursday before the arrests (ibid., 40).

18. Details are in my upcoming work on Peter Riedemann.

19. Cf. Fasser's and Sailer's letter; Chapter 11. This raises the question about the authenticity of this part of the letter, since Philipite leaders, Kuhn and Schlegel, still expected Philip to meet with them in Strasbourg in August 1536.

20. Besides Pulgram a settlement remained at Rayggen-Brunn. In 1543 this group participated in dialogue with the Unitas Fratrum (Zeman 1969, 248 n. 29).

21. Philipites were condemned along with Papists, Lutherans, and Zwinglians by Anabaptists meeting near Eckbolsheim, not far from Strasbourg in 1545. The editors of the *Täuferakten* believed the reference was intended for followers of Philip Plener, but perhaps it was intended for the followers of Philip Melanchthon (*Elsass* 4:144 n. 4, *QGT*).

22. Some Philipites settled in Steyer, Linz, and Gmünden and in the Attergau (Vöklabruck) (Friedmann 1958b, 279).

23. Schreiner, if identical with Hans of Oelbronn (Heilbronn), had been released from prison in Strasbourg earlier. I suggest he was identical with Hans Gentner. Cf. Note 13 above.

24. Bossert Collection, Württemberg [2]: 56–63.

25. For the relation of Riedemann and Hans Gentner to the Heilbronn group, see my upcoming work on Riedemann.

26. Horsch 1932, 243. Blanke (1961) used the title *Brothers in Christ*.

27. Bender 1950, x–xi.

28. Stayer 1991, 95.

29. Deppermann 1979, 160 n. 69. A distinction among "Schweizeranam," Hutterites, and Mennonites appears in Nicolaas Belsdijk's account of Hoffman's recantation and the disintegration of the Melchiorites as a distinct group in Strasbourg (*Elsass* 3:342, *QGT*).

30. Beck 1967, 152 n. 1. Beck suggested that Hutterites also used the label *Swiss* for Hubmaier's orphaned followers in Moravia, whose locations he gave as Bergen, Polau, Wisternitz, Voitsbrunn, Tasswitz, Urbau, Seletitz, and Jamnitz. He considered Oswald Glaidt a leader of the group at Jamnitz until 1545. In 1534 an Ulrich (Stadler?) led the group at Urbau. Hans Kellermann led fifty at Tasswitz. The *Grund- und Schirmherr* of Jamnitz was the *Landrichter* Heinrich von Lomnic, who sent his *Burgrafen* to Passau to obtain the release of some of the brethren.

31. *The Chronicle*, 224–27; Beck 1967, 151–53. According to the Hutterite

account, Bärml or Bämerle was imprisoned and tortured in 1557 and died in 1567 after having become a Hutterite servant of the Word.

32. Klopffer had been baptized by Martin Fesser (Fasser) in Esslingen (*Württemberg* 1:199, 497 n. 3, *QGT*).

33. Beck 1967, 153–54; *The Chronicle*, 225–26 n. 2. Klopffer had moved to a community at Pallau (Pavlov) in Moravia before joining the Hutterites at Schackowitz in 1543.

34. "Die 16. Epistel von Peter Rideman," in *Episteln* 1:179–82.

35. It seems that Riedemann's report captured the historic moment of disillusionment and confusion, when former Philipites under Swiss influence adopted a new leadership pattern. In 1540, Leonhard Roth wrote to Amon that Swiss influences in the Tyrol would lead to the "ruin and collapse" of proper congregational life (*The Chronicle*, 189 n. 3).

36. *Ostschweiz* 225–28, *QGT*; also Klassen and Klaassen 1987, 362 ff.).

37. Swiss Brethren are mentioned under the year 1559 (*Württemberg* 1:194, *QGT*): "ein sect und bruderschaft die Schweizer brueder genannt."

38. Clasen's statistics indicated that from 1530 to 1549 Germans outnumbered Swiss two to one and four to one between 1550 and 1618 (Clasen 1978, 9).

39. Conferences or disputations took place in 1555, 1557, 1568, 1571, and 1607. Of these, the best known are the disputation at Pfeddersheim in 1557 and the discussion at Frankenthal in 1571.

40. Beck wrote, "Gabriel's people [Völklein] in part withdrew to Silesia, intent on waiting out the storm there. They found here and there, e.g., at Rauden and Wohlau, an open reception" (Beck 1967, 70 n.).

41. Wiswedel 1937b, pt. 1:6, 10; Zeman 1969, 227 n. 214, 248 n. 29, 249ff.; Friedmann 1956c, 429. Urban claimed that they were also in the marketplace of Bucovice near Austerlitz (Urban 1986, 110).

42. *The Chronicle*, 238 n. 1.

43. Gabrielites settled at Gubrau and Jauer in Silesia and across the border in Polish territory at Meseritz (Miedzyrzecs) and near Posen (Poznaň). It is of interest that Marcin Czechowic, considered the formulator of the basic doctrines of Polish Anabaptism, studied in Posen during the late 1540s or early 1550s (Szczucki 1987).

44. Tschackert 1890, 314–15.

45. Ibid., 315.

46. Beck 1967, 50.

47. *The Chronicle*, 155–56 n.; 169–72.

48. Williams gives the place of settlement as around Krasnik Lubelski near Wlodzimierz (Williams 1992, 632; *Glaubenszeugnisse* 1:211–36).

49. An analysis of Stadler's spiritualist theology is found in Williams 1992, 1252–53.

50. According to Williams, the Gabrielites also settled on the Weichsel (Vistula) near Chelmna and Schwetz (Swiecie) (Williams 1992, 632; Wiswedel, 1937b, pt. 2:225).

51. Tschackert 1890, 998a: 326; 1003:327. Christoph Hartknoch reported of Bohemian Brethren seeking settlement in Prussia. He claimed that they sent a

Wilhelm Krineium, Baron of Ronau, to Duke Albrecht to arrange their first settle-ment in 1525. He wrote of "many hundreds," some settling at Thorn, with some in 1548–49 settling in Marienwerder, where their church, as late as 1686, was allegedly called the Bohemian Church. He listed Neidenburg, Garnsee, Hohen-stein, Gilgenburg, and Soldau as other places of settlement (Hartknoch 1686, 304–5).

52. Williams 1992, 633.

53. A claim made by Horst Quiring on the basis of Swiss or German names, for example, Kerwer (Gerber), Bolt, Baltzer, Funck (Quiring 1987, 337–42).

54. Beck suggested that the group that moved to Poland and Prussia was Ga-brielite (Beck 1967, 70 n.).

55. The letter was dated November 9, 1536 (Tschackert 1890, 1048:345). The mayor (Schulze) had ordered these Anabaptists to have their children bap-tized, but they demanded to see written orders, which he could not produce. If these were Dutch Anabaptists, then they began to arrive already in 1536.

56. Williams 1992, 614–16.

57. Koffmane 1887, 45.

58. Ibid.: "gerade in disem und dem folgenden Jahre muss das Taufertum in Schlesien seine grösste Ausdehnung erlangt haben. Von allen Seiten hören wir Kla-gen über das Anwachsen der Bewegung."

59. Radler 1962, especially 44, gave his name as David Behmisch, born in Schweidnitz, a tailor by trade. Some returnees had found employment as servants and maids with local artisans.

60. On June 12, 1536, the governor, Hans von Seidlitz, ordered an Anabap-tist to be kept in solitary confinement on a subsistence diet of water and bread at Schweidnitz. Two days later he ordered strict isolation with bread and water only every second or third day so that he might "come to his senses" (*besseren Geist*). The cost of imprisonment was to be paid by a nobleman's widow, Euphemia of Hochberg, who resided on a manor at Fürstein. On September 11, 1536, the gov-ernor complained that the cities, particularly Schweidnitz, had been uncooperative in his attempt to root out heresy.

61. Radler 1962.

62. In a missive dated August 5, 1536, Ferdinand demanded the expulsion of all Anabaptists from Silesia within two weeks (Koffmane 1887, 46).

63. Radler claimed that "David Behme wirkte dann noch ausserhalb Schle-siens als Wiedertäuferapostel" but gave no particulars (Radler 1962, 45).

64. He died on September 8, 1548, and Ferdinand passed over his heirs to give the territory to Duke Ernst of Bavaria (Weigelt 1985, 97, 100).

65. Williams believed that it was "more in the sense of fraternal sharing than common ownership" (Williams 1992, 629).

66. Weigelt 1985, 98.

67. The son and wife were to be imprisoned if they remained until morning (Schmid 1972, 108–190, especially n. 481).

68. Williams 1992, 632. Members of Gabriel's former community settled also at Gubrau and Jauer in Silesia and in Polish territory near Posen (Poznaň).

69. Wiswedel 1937b, pt. 1:35.

70. Ibid., 34–35.

71. Wiswedel 1937b, pt. 2:260, 262.

72. *The Chronicle*, 233. Not clear is whether Gabriel and his people kept to frequent celebrations as suggested in the early Anabaptist orders.

73. Ascherham 1544, 262.

74. Zeman recognized specific parallels to the 1520 pronouncements of Bishop Lukas of the Unity of Czech Brethren (Zeman 1969, 225–27).

75. A "hypothesis" put forth by Zeman (ibid., 227 n. 214).

76. Ascherham 1544, 255.

77. Ibid., 256.

78. As noted, Jörg Zaunring had emphasized this third meaning, the ecclesiological interpretation of the body.

79. Ascherham 1544, 257. Martin Brecht's observation about Bernhard Rothmann's view on the subject seems to fit Gabriel as well. "Die eigentliche Abendmahlsgabe ist die göttliche Natur Christi, mit der unsichtbar durch den Glauben die Seele erquickt wird im Gedächtnis an die Hingabe Christi" (Brecht 1987, especially 154).

80. Gabriel here refuted the argument that since to the believers all things were clean, they did not need to distinguish (*aussondern*) this meal (*Tischzeit*) from other meals.

81. Ascherham 1544, 257.

82. Ibid., 258. Here he came close to Hubmaier: "für war, wo wir nit underschayden das Nachtmal Christi vonn dem anderen essen unnd trinken, werdend wir unns selbs das gericht essen und trinken" (*Hubmaier*, 301. Cf. 103).

83. Ascherham 1544, 259–60.

84. Ibid., 258.

85. The position is reminiscent of that attributed to Zwingli; for whom "the body . . . is not localized in the bread but in the church gathered about the bread" (Courvoisier 1961, 76). Gäbler noted that for Zwingli the "Gemeinde" stood in the centre of the celebration. Its "believing remembrance" recognized the saving work of Christ behind the outer appearance (see also 121).

86. At the end of his treatise Gabriel hinted that the fall of the church coincided with the loss of the understanding of the mystery of the eucharist. This loss "lasted 1400 years. But God had preserved [the mystery] and revealed it in the 45th year, at a time when the error on the sacrament had been at its height." The question arises whether Gabriel was alluding to a date in the Hussite calendar or, like Adler, to a Franciscan one. Or was this a reference to his own discovery before his death in 1545? (Ascherham 1544, 260).

87. Cf. with the more common vocabulary used among Anabaptists (Klaassen 1981, 190–210).

88. Ascherham 1544, 237–38.

89. Cf. Freisleben's tract of 1528 in Chapter 6.

90. Ascherham 1544, 238.

91. Ibid., 239.

92. A contemporary Silesian source, hostile to Gabriel, suggested that he

"turned his coat in the wind" to disguise the fact that he and his followers were Anabaptists.

93. Ascherham 1544, 240–41.

94. Wagner 1983, 106, 108, 129.

95. *CS* 2:557ff., especially 576: "Folgt nun ein kurtze Erklerung des Texts im 6. Capitel Joannis."

96. Weigelt 1985, 53; McLaughlin 1986a, 72–73.

97. McLaughlin 1986a, 202.

98. Cf. Note 164 in Maier 1959, 49.

99. Cf. Weigelt 1985, 86ff., especially 88; Furcha 1970, 34; cf. 78, 79; Maier 1959, 49.

100. A comparison of the original German leaves no doubt that the chroniclers had Gabriel's statement on baptism in their possession (*The Chronicle*, 233, 235). Cf. Ascherham 1544, 240–41.

101. Cited by Fischer 1956, 67.

102. Mändel wrote in 1561. Beck 1967, 70 n.

103. A point made by Stayer 1991, 145–46.

104. The building of the first such structures at Schackowitz, begun by Hutter, was disrupted by the expulsions of 1535. It was apparently resumed and completed between 1537 and 1540, at which point Schackowitz housed a community of five hundred.

105. Beck 1967, 71 n. An official union took place on January 16, 1545, on the basis of five articles drafted by the Hutterites. The group that joined in 1565 resided at Kreutz near Göding.

Bibliography

Primary Sources

Adler, Clemens. 1529. Das Urteil von dem Schwert mit unterschidlichem gewalt dreier fürstenthum der Welt, Juden, und Christen, mit anderen Anligender sachen. Beschrieben durch Clemens Adler im Jahr MDXXIX (The Judgment Concerning the Sword). In Kopie eines Handschriftenbandes von Liedern und Glaubensartikel der Täufer, a typewritten transcription by Samuel Geiser, Mennonite Historical Library, Goshen College, Goshen, Ind. Made available by Joe Springer, curator of the Mennonite Historical Library.

Aelurius, Georg. 1625. *Glaciographia, oder Glätzische Chronica, das ist: Gründliche historische Beschreibung der berümbten und vornemen Stadt, ja gantzen Graffschafft Glatz, nach allen vornemsten Stücken.* Leipzig: n.p.

Ascherham, Gabriel. 1541. Was sich verloffen hat unter den Brüdern, die aus aller deutschen Nation vertrieben waren umb des Glaubens willen 1528–1541. In Fischer, Christoph Andreas. 1607. *Der Hutterischen Widertauffer Taubenkobel.* 55–57. Ingolstadt: A. Angermeyer.

———. 1544. Vom Unterschied göttlicher und menschlicher Weisheit (On the Distinction between Divine and Human Wisdom). In *Gabriel Ascherham und die nach ihm benannte Bewegung.* Edited by Wilhelm Wiswedel. *Archiv für Reformationsgeschichte* [ARG] 34: pt. 1, 1–35; pt. 2, 235–62. The original codex is at the Oesterreichische National Bibliothek, Vienna.

Aufdeckung der Babylonischen hürn/und Antichrists alten unnd newen geheymnuss greul (Uncovering of the Babylonian Whore). n.d. Strasbourg: Kammerlander. Transcribed by Hans Hillerbrand. 1958. In an early Anabaptist treatise on the Christian and the state. *Mennonite Quarterly Review* [MQR] 32:28–47.

Bauman, Clarence, ed. 1991. *The Spiritual Legacy of Hans Denck: Interpretation and Translation of Key Texts.* Leiden: E. J. Brill.

Bayern. 1934. Edited by Karl Schornbaum. vol. 1. QGT. Leipzig: M. Heinius Nachfolger.

Bayern. 1951. Edited by Karl Schornbaum. vol. 2. QGT. Gütersloh: Bertelsmann.

Beck, Joseph, ed. [1883] 1967. *Die Geschichtsbücher der Wiedertäufer in Oesterreich-Ungarn, 1526–1785*. Nieuwkoop: B. De Graaf

Beck, Sammlung. 1535. Wiedertäuferischen Gesindleins in Mähren und Schlesien seltsame Beschaffenheit. G 10149, no. 68, 22v. State Archive, Brno, Slovakia.

Berbig, Georg. 1903. Die Wiedertäufer im Amt Königsberg i. Fr. 1527–1528. *Deutsche Zeitschrift für Kirchenrecht* 35:291–353.

Braght, Thieleman J. van. 1951. *The Martyrs' Mirror*. Translated by Joseph Sohn. Scottdale, Pa.: Herald Press.

Braitmichel, Caspar. 1571. Von der Zerspaltung der Gemein. Sampt den Artikeln und Beschuldigungen, die wir wider den Philip und Gabriel haben. Codex Hab. 5, 371 MICA 274. Reel 87 of the Eastern European Anabaptist Collection. Waterloo, Ont.: Arts Library, University of Waterloo.

Bullinger, Heinrich. 1534. *De testamentarum unitate sen uno testamento*.

Bünderlin, Hans. 1530. *Erklärung durch vergleichung der Biblischen geschrifft, das der wassertauff sampt andern eusserlichen gebreuchen, in der Apostolischen kirchen geübet. On Gottes befelch und zeügniss der geschrifft, von etlichen diser zeit, wider eefert [eingeführt] wirt. Sintemalen der Antichrist dieselben all, zehend nach der Apostel abgang verwüst hat. Welche Verwüstung dann biss an das ende bleibt* (*Explanation through Comparison of the Biblical Scripture*). n.p.

The Chronicle of the Hutterian Brethren 1525–1665. 1987. vol. 1. Rifton, N.Y.: Plough Publishing House.

Corpus Schwenckfeldianorum [CS]. 1907–61. Edited by Chester Hartranft, Elmer E. Schultz Johnson, and Selina G. Schultz. 19 vols. Norristown, Pa.: Schwenckfelder Church.

Dax, Leonard. 1556. Rechenschaft und Bekenntnuss des Christlichen Glaubens. Gestellt durch unsern lieben Brueder und diener Christy Leonard Dax in der Gefängnis (Account of Faith). Codex Hab. 5, 233ff., 371 MICA 274. 1571. Bratislava City Archive. Reel 87 of the Eastern European Anabaptist Collection. Waterloo, Ont.: Arts Library, University of Waterloo.

Discipline: The Oldest Church Discipline of the Anabaptists. 1955. Translated by Robert Friedmann. *MQR* 29:162–66.

Ein Newe Geschichte Nemlich beschehen zue Glatz in der Schlesig (A New Story). 1571. Codex Hab. 5, 168–70ff., MICA 274. Bratislava City Archive. Reel 87 of the Eastern European Anabaptist Collection. Waterloo, Ont.: Arts Library, University of Waterloo.

Eleutherobius, Stoffel [Christoph Freisleben]. 1528. *Vom warhafftigen Tauf Joannis Christi und der Aposteln*. Worms: Peter Schöffer.

Elsass 1: Strasbourg, 1522–1532. 1959. Edited by Manfred Krebs and Jean-George Rott. QGT 7. Gütersloh: Mohn.

Elsass 2: Stadt Strasbourg, 1533–1535. 1960. Edited by Manfred Krebs and Jean-George Rott. QGT 8. Gütersloh: Mohn.

Elsass 3: Stadt Strasbourg, 1536–1542. 1986. Edited by Marc Lienhard, Stephen Nelson, and Hans-Georg Rott. QGT 15. Gütersloh: Mohn.

Elsass 4: Stadt Strasbourg, 1543–1552. 1988. Edited by Marc Lienhard, Stephen Nelson, and Hans-Georg Rott. QGT 16. Gütersloh: Mohn.

Entfelder, Christian. 1530. *Von den manigfaltigen im glauben zerspaltungen/dise jar erstanden. Inn sonderhait von der Tauff spaltung und iren urtail/Ain bedacht (Of the Manifold Divisions in the Faith).* 71/1:E7. Strasbourg: Microfiche BME.

————. 1533. *Von Gottes und Christi Jesus unsers Herr enerkandtnuss, ain bedacht / Allen schulern des hailigen gaists weiter zebendencken auffgezaichnet / mit freyem urthail.* Strasbourg: n.p.

Episteln 1527–1767. 1986–91. vols. 1–4. Elie, Man.: James Valley Book Center.

Erhard, Christoph. 1588. *Gründliche kurtz verfaste Historia von Münsterische Widertauffern.* Munich: Adam Berg.

Etliche schone Christliche Geseng, wie sie in der Gefengniss zu Passau im Schloss von den Schweitzer Brüdern durch Gottes gnad gedicht und gesungen worden. Psalm 139. 1564. The only copy is in the Mennonite Historical Library, Goshen College, Goshen, Ind.

Fast, Heinold. 1962b. *Der Linke Flügel der Reformation: Glaubenszeugnisse der Täufer, Spiritualisten, Schwärmer und Antitrinitarier.* Bremen: Carl Schünemann Verlag.

Fischer, Christoph Andreas. 1607. *Der Hutterischen Widertauffer Taubenkobel.* Ingolstadt: A. Angermeyer.

Fischer, Hans, G. 1956. *Jakob Huter: Leben, Frömmigkeit, Briefe.* Newton, Kan.: Mennonite Publication Office.

Franck, Sebastian. 1969. *Zeytbuch und geschichtbibel von anbegyn bisz inn disz gegenwertig M. D. xxxj. jar.* Darmstadt: Wissenschaftlicher Verlag.

Franz, Günther, ed. [1953] 1975. *Der Deutsche Bauernkrieg, Aktenband.* Munich. Reprint, Darmstadt: Wissenschaftliche Buchgesellschaft.

————. 1954. *Urkundliche Quellen zur hessischen Reformationsgeschichte.* vol. 4. *Wiedertäuferakten 1527–1626.* Marburg: Elwert.

Friedmann, Robert. 1955a. The Oldest Church Discipline of the Anabaptists. *MQR* 29:162–66.

Furcha, Edward J. [1975] 1989. *Selected Writings of Hans Denck 1500–1527.* Reprint, Queenston, Ont.: Edwin Mellen.

Glaidt, Oswald. 1526. *Handlung yetz den XIV tag Marcij dis XXVI jars, so zu Osterlitz in Merhern durch erforderte versammlung viles pfarrer und priesterschaften . . . in syben artickeln beschlossen.* Nicolsburg: Simprecht Sorg. Radical Reformation Microfiche Project, Section I Mennonite and Related Sources up to 1600, ID CAG Zug, Switzerland, at Conrad Grebel College Library.

————. 1527. *Enntschuldigung Osvaldi Glaidt von Chamb. Etwan zu Leybm in Oesterreich. Yetz predicannt zu Nicolspurg . . . etlicher Artickel Verklärung (Apology Oswaldt Glaidt).* Nicolsburg: Simprecht Sorg. Original at the State Archive, Brno, Slovakia. Made available by Dr. M. Coupek.

Haffner, Hans. n.d. *Von einem Wahrhaften Ritter Christi, und womit er gewappnet muss sein, damit er überwinden möge die / welt, das / fleisch und den Teufel* (Concerning a True Knight of Christ). A typewritten copy with introduction by Robert Friedmann. Mennonite Archive in Goshen, Ind. Made available by Dr. Leonard Gross.

Harder, Leland, ed. 1985. *The Sources of Swiss Anabaptism* [*SSA*]. Scottdale, Pa.: Herald Press.

Hätzer, Ludwig. 1523. *Ein urteil gottes . . . wie man sich mit allen götzen und bildnussen halten sol, uss der heiligen gschrifft gezogen durch Ludwig Hätzer.* Zurich: Froschauer.

Hesse: *Urkundliche Quellen zur hessischen Reformationsgeschichte.* vol. 4. *Wiedertäuferakten 1527–1626.* 1954. Edited by Günther Franz. Marburg: QGT.

Hillerbrand, Hans. 1958. An Early Anabaptist Treatise on the Christian and the State. *MQR* 32:28–47.

———. 1959. Ein Täuferbekenntnis aus dem 16. Jahrhundert. *ARG* 50:40–50.

Hoffmann, Melchior. 1531. *Das ware trostliche . . . Euangelion . . . zu dieser letsten zeit . . . fürgetragen . . . durch die waren Apostolischen geyster / und knecht dess Herrn Jesu Christi.* The tract appeared on the same press in the same year as Marpeck's tracts of 1531.

Hubmaier, Balthasar: Schriften. 1962. Edited by Torsten Bergsten and Gunnar Westin. *QGT* 9. Gütersloh: Mohn.

Hutter, Jacob. 1979. *Brotherly Faithfulness: Epistles from a Time of Persecution.* Translated by the Hutterian Society of Brothers. Rifton, N.Y.: Plough Publishing House.

Jackson, Samuel M., ed. 1901. *Selected Works of Huldrich Zwingli.* Philadelphia: University Press.

Karlstadt, Andreas. [1522] 1991. Von abtuhung der Bylder, und das keyn Betdler unther den Christen seyn soll (On the Removal of images). In *A Reformation Debate.* Translated by Bryan Mangrum and Giuseppe Scavizzi. Toronto, Ont.: The Centre for Reformation and Renaissance Studies, Victoria University.

———. 1525. *Anzeyg etlicher Hauptartickeln Christlicher leere.* Augsburg: Philipp Ulhart. English edition 1978. *Karlstadt's Battle with Luther.* Translated by Ronald J. Sider. 126–38. Philadephia: Fortress Press.

Klaassen, Walter. 1981. *Anabaptism in Outline: Selected Primary Sources.* Scottdale, Pa.: Herald Press.

Klassen, William. 1964. A Church Order for Members of Christ's Body. *MQR* 38:354–56, 386.

Klassen, William, and Walter Klaassen, eds. and trans. 1978. *The Writings of Pilgram Marpeck* [*WPM*]. Scottdale, Pa.: Herald Press.

Krebs, Manfred Krebs, ed. 1951. *Baden und Pfalz.* vol. 4. *Quellen zur Geschichte der Täufer* [*QGT*]. Gütersloh: Mohn.

Mais, Adolf. 1963. Gefängnis und Tod der in Wien hingerichteten Wiedertäufer in Ihren Briefen und Liedern. *Jahrbuch des Vereins für Geschichte der Stadt Wien* 19–20: 87–182.

Maler, Georg, ed. *Das Kunstbuch.* Sixteenth-century manuscript collection of Anabaptist tracts and letters at the Bürgerbibliothek in Bern, Switzerland. Typescript copy at the Mennonite Historical Library, Goshen, Ind.

Mantz, Felix. Petition of Defense. *SSA* 311ff.

Marpeck, Pilgram. 1551. Testamenterläuterung. Erleuterung durch ausszug/aus Heiliger Biblischer schrifft. Augsburg: n.p.

———. [1531] 1978. Ain klarer / vast nützlicher unterricht / wider ettlicher Trück

/ und schleichendt Geyster (A Clear and Useful Instruction). English translation in *WPM* 69–106.

———. [1531] 1978. Clare verantwurtung ettlicher Artickel / so jetzt durch jrrige geyster schrifflich unnd mündtlich aussschweben (A Clear Refutation). English translation in *WPM* 43–68.

Meyer, Christian, ed. 1874. Zur Geschichte der Wiedertäufer in Oberschwaben. Part 1. Die Anfänge des Wiedertäufertums in Augsburg. *Zeitschrift des historischen Vereins für Schwaben und Neuberg [ZHVSN]* 1:207–56.

Montana Codex [Braitmichel]. 1566. MICA 274. Reel 22 of the East European Anabaptist Collection. Waterloo, Ont.: Arts Library, University of Waterloo.

Mosham, Ruprecht. 1539. *Ain Christliche warhafftige, gründtliche Entschuldigung Herrn Rueprechten von Moshaim* [hereafter *Entschuldigung*]. Aschaffenburg: n.p.

Müller, Lydia, ed. [1938] 1971. *Glaubenszeugnisse der Oberdeutscher Taufgesinnter.* vol. 1. *QGT* 3. Leipzig: M. Heinius Nachfolger. New York: Johnson Reprint Corporation.

Müntzer, Thomas. 1968. *Thomas Müntzer: Schriften und Briefe.* Edited by Günther Franz. Gütersloh: Mohn.

———. 1988. *The Collected Works of Thomas Müntzer.* Edited and translated by Peter Matheson. Edinburgh: T. & T. Clark.

Oesterreich 1. 1964. Edited by Grete Mecenseffy. *QGT* 11. Gütersloh: Mohn.

Oesterreich 2. 1972. Edited by Grete Mecenseffy. *QGT* 13. Gütersloh: Mohn.

Oesterreich 3. 1983. Edited by Grete Mecenseffy. *QGT* 14. Gütersloh: Mohn.

Ostschweiz. 1973. Edited by Heinold Fast. *QGT* 2. Zurich: Theologischer Verlag.

Otter, Jacob. 1528. *Das erst buch Mosi, gepredigt durch Jacob Otthern zu Steynach.* Hagenau: n.p.

Pipkin, H. Wayne, and John H. Yoder, eds. and trans. 1989. *Balthasar Hubmaier: Theologian of Anabaptism.* Scottdale, Pa.: Herald Press.

Roth, Friedrich. 1901. Zur Geschichte der Wiedertäufer in Oberschwaben. Part 3. Der Höhepunkt der Bewegung in Augsburg und der Niedergang im Jahre 1528. *ZHVSN* 28:1–154.

Rothmann, Bernhard. 1970. Restitution rechter gesunder christlicher Lehre. In *Die Schriften Bernhard Rothmanns.* Edited by Robert Stupperich. 208–83. Münster: Aschendorfer Verlagsbuchhandlung.

Schiemer, Leonard. Die dritt epistel Leonhart Schiemers, darinnen wirt begriffen von dreyerley Tauf im Neuen Testament ganz clärlich entdeckt. *Glaubenszeugnisse* 1:77ff.

Schiemer, Leonard. Erstlich ein Epistl an die gemain zu Rottenburg [Rattenberg], darinnen hübsche erklärungen der 12 hauptstück unsers Christlichen Glaubens begriffen sein. *Glaubenszeugnisse* 1:44ff.

Schweiz 1: Zurich. 1952. Edited by Leonhard von Muralt and Walter Schmid. *QGT.* Zurich: Hirzel.

Schweiz 4: Drei Täufergespräche. 1974. Edited by Martin Haas. *QGT.* Zurich: Hirzel.

Schwenckfeld, Caspar. 1530. *Judicium de Anabaptistis.* CS 3.

———. 1531. *Der andre Sendbrieffe an alle Christgleubige geschrieben.* CS 4.

————. 1532. *Vom Christlichen Sabbath und Unterschaidt des alten und newen Testaments.* CS 4:452–518.

Wie die Gschrifft verstendiglich soll underschieden / un erklärt werden / die vom Tauff sagest (*How the Scriptures Are to Be Distinguished*). English edition 1978. *Legacy of Michael Sattler.* Translated by John H. Yoder. 150–77. Scottdale, Pa.: Herald Press.

Sider, Ronald J., ed. 1978. *Karlstadt's Battle with Luther.* Philadelphia: Fortress Press.

Spittelmaier, Johann. 1524. Entschuldigung Joannis Spitelmayer Prediger zu Nicolspurg von wegen etlichen artickeln, jne von de Clöster d'stat Veldsper sunnderlich feind, des creutz Christi on alle ursach zue gemessen. G10 Sbirken rukopisu 49, 1aa. State Archive, Brno, Slovakia. Made available by Dr. M. Coupek.

Springer, Nelson P., and Joe Springer. 1986. The Testimony of a Bernese Anabaptist. *MQR* 60:289–303.

Stadler, Ulrich. n.d. Von ordnungen der heiligen in irer gmainschaft und leben mit den güetern ires vaters alhie in dem Herren. *Glaubenszeugnisse* 1:222–27.

Swiss Order: A Congregational Order. 1973. In *The Legacy of Michael Sattler.* Edited and translated by John H. Yoder. Scottdale, Pa.: Herald Press.

Tschackert, Paul. [1890] 1965. *Urkundenbuch zur Reformationsgeschichte des Herzogthums Preussen.* vol. 1. Osnabrück: Otto Zeller.

Wappler, Paul, ed. 1913. *Die Täuferbewegung in Thüringen von 1529–1584.* Jena: G. Fischer.

Wenger, John C. 1949. Letter from Wilhelm Reublin to Pilgram Marpeck, 1531. *MQR* 23:67–75.

Württemberg, Herzogtum. 1930. Edited by Gustav Bossert Sr. and Gustav Bossert Jr. vol. 1. *QGT* 1. Leipzig: M. Heinius Nachfolger.

Württemberg. Manuscript collected by Gustav Bossert and Gustav Bossert Jr. intended as a future *QGT* vol. [2]. Karlsruhe Staatsarchiv, sig. GLA, Abt S, Verein für Reformationsgeschichte.

Yetelhauser, Michael [Jedelshauser]. 1539. Ain Christliche Bekhantnus unnd widerueff Michel Yetelhauser. *Entschuldigung.* Aschaffenburg: n.p.

Yoder, John H., ed. and trans. 1973. *The Legacy of Michael Sattler.* Scottdale, Pa.: Herald Press.

Zaunring, Jörg. n.d. Ain kurtze anzaignung des abentmals Christy. *Glaubenszeugnisse* 1:143ff.

————. Eine schöne Epistel. Codex Hab. 5, 334ff. Reel 87 of the Eastern European Anabaptist Collection. Waterloo, Ont.: Arts Library, University of Waterloo.

Zieglschmid, A. J. F. 1946. *Die älteste Chronik der Hutterischen Brüder.* (*Ein Sprachdenkmal aus frühdeutscher Zeit*). Ithaca: Cayugan Press.

Secondary Sources

Ammann, Hartmann. 1896–97. Die Wiedertäufer in Michelsburg im Pusterthale und deren Urgichten. *Programme des K.K. Gymnasiums zu Brixen* 46:1–52; 47:1–124.

Ausbund, das ist Etliche schöne Christliche Lieder. 1981. 13th edition. Lancaster: Verlag von den Amischen Gemeinden.

Backus, Irena. 1993. The Disputation of Baden, 1526 and Berne, 1528: Neutralizing the Early Church. *Studies in Reformed Theology and History* 1:1–130.

Bak, Janos, ed. 1976. *The German Peasant War of 1525.* London: Frank Cass.

Barge, Hermann. 1905. *Andreas Bodenstein von Karlstadt.* vols. 1 and 2. Leipzig: Friedrich Brandstetter.

Barton, Peter F. 1985. *Die Geschichte der Evangelischen in Oesterreich und Südostmitteleuropa.* Vienna: Verlag Herman Böhlaus.

Bauer, Günther. 1966. *Anfänge täuferischer Gemeindebildungen in Franken.* Nuremberg: Selbstverlag des Vereins für bayerische Kirchengeschichte.

Bauman, Clarence. 1968. *Gewaltlosigkeit im Täufertum: Eine Untersuchung zur theologischen Ethik des Oberdeutschen Täufertums der Reformationszeit.* Leiden: E. J. Brill.

Bender, Harold. 1929. The First Edition of the *Ausbund. MQR* 3:147–50.

———. 1944. The Anabaptist Vision. *Church History* 13:3–24.

———. [1950] 1971. *Conrad Grebel 1498–1526: The Founder of the Swiss Brethren Sometimes Called Anabaptists.* Scottdale, Pa.: Herald Press.

———. 1952. Die Zwickauer Propheten, Thomas Müntzer und die Täufer. *Theologische Zeitschrift* 8:262–78.

———. 1953. The Zwickau Prophets, Thomas Müntzer and the Anabaptists. *MQR* 27:3–16.

———. 1956. New Discoveries of Important Sixteenth-Century Anabaptist Codices. *MQR* 30:72–77.

———. 1959. Adler, Clemens. *Mennonite Encyclopedia* [ME] 4:1056.

Bergdolt, Johannes. 1920. *Die freie Reichstadt Windsheim im Zeitalter der Reformation (1520–1580).*

Bergsten, Torsten. 1978. *Balthasar Hubmaier: Anabaptist Theologian and Martyr.* Edited by W. R. Estep Jr. Valley Forge, Pa.: Judson Press.

Blanke, Fritz. 1961. *Brothers in Christ: The History of the Oldest Anabaptist Congregation, Zollikon, near Zurich, Switzerland.* Scottdale, Pa.: Herald Press.

Blickle, Peter. 1981. *The Revolution of 1525: The German Peasants' War from a New Perspective.* Translated by Thomas A. Brady Jr. and H. C. Erik Midelfort. Baltimore: Johns Hopkins University Press.

———. 1987. *Gemeindereformation: Die Menschen des 16. Jahrhunderts auf dem Weg zum Heil.* Munich: Oldenburg.

———. 1992. *Communal Reformation: The Quest for Salvation in Sixteenth-Century Germany.* Translated by Thomas Dunlop. Highlands, N.J.: Humanities Press.

Blough, Neal. 1984. *Christologie Anabaptiste: Pilgram Marpeck et l'Humanite du Christ.* Geneva: Labor et Fides.

———. 1987. Pilgram Marpeck and Caspar Schwenckfeld: The Strasbourg Years. In *Anabaptistes et Dissidentes.* Edited by Jean-George Rott and Simon L. Verheus. 371–80. Baden-Baden: Koerner.

Bossert, Gustav. 1897. Die Reformation in Kürnbach bei Eppingen. *Zeitschrift f. d. Geschichte d. Oberrheins* 51:92ff.

————. 1904. Beiträge zur badisch-pfälzischen Reformationsgeschichte. *Zeitschrift f. d. Geschichte d. Oberrheins* 61:71–88.

————. 1959. Reublin. *ME* 4:307–9.

Boyd, Stephen. 1984. Pilgram Marpeck and the Justice of Christ. Unpublished Th.D. dissertation, Harvard University.

————. 1992. *Pilgram Marpeck: His Life and Social Theology.* Durham, N.C.: Duke University Press.

Brady, Thomas, Jr. 1982. Social History. In *Reformation Europe: A Guide to Research.* Edited by Steven Ozment. 161–82. St. Louis: Center for Reformation Research.

————. 1985. *Turning Swiss: Cities and Empire, 1450–1550.* New York: Cambridge University Press.

————. 1988. Review of *Radical Tendencies in the Reformation: Divergent Perspectives. Sixteenth-Century Journal* 19:518.

Brandi, Karl. 1967. *The Emperor Charles V.* Norwich: Fletcher and Son.

Brecht, Martin. 1987. Die Theologie Bernhard Rothmanns. In *Anabaptistes et Dissidents.* Edited by Jean-George Rott and Simon L. Verheus. 149ff. Baden-Baden: Koerner.

Brief Summary of the History of the Swiss Anabaptists. 1990. A publication of the Eastern Pennsylvania Mennonite Church.

Brock, Peter. 1991. Marcian Czechowic in Defense of Nonresistance, 1575. *Conrad Grebel Review* [*CGR*] 9:251–58.

Buchholtz, Franz-Bernhard, ed. 1833. *Geschichte der Regierung Ferdinand des Ersten.* vol. 4. Vienna: Carl Schaumburg.

Bücking, Jürgen. 1972a. Mathias Messerschmieds reformatorische "Agitation" in Klausen (1527). *Monatszeitschrift für Südtiroler Landeskunde* [*Schlern*] 46: 342–44.

————. 1972b. *Frühabsolutismus und Kirchenreform in Tirol (1565–1665): Ein Beitrag zum Ringen zwischen "Staat" und "Kirche" in der frühen Neuzeit.* Wiesbaden: F. Steiner.

Clasen, Claus-Peter. 1972. *Anabaptism: A Social History, 1525–1618.* Ithaca: Cornell University Press.

————. 1978. The Anabaptists in South and Central Germany, Switzerland, and Austria: A Statistical Study. *MQR* 52.

Cornelius, C. A. 1855. *Geschichte des Münsterischen Aufruhrs.* vol. 2. Leipzig: n.p.

Courvoisier, Jacques. 1961. *Zwingli: A Reformed Theologian.* Richmond: John Knox Press.

de Wind, H. 1955. A Sixteenth-Century Description of Religious Sects in Austerlitz, Moravia. *MQR* 29:44–54.

Dedic, Paul. 1957. Michelsburg. *ME* 3:668–70.

Delmonego, Ernst. 1974. Das Stadtgericht Brixen. Die Gerichte Lüsen-Albeins und Pfeffersberg. 1500–1641. Unpublished Ph.D. dissertation, Leopold-Franzen University, Innsbruck.

Deppermann, Klaus. 1979. *Melchior Hoffmann. Soziale Unruhen und apokalyptische Visionen im Zeitalter der Reformation.* Göttingen: Vandenhoeck and Ruprecht.

Diehl, Wilhelm. 1917. *Reformationsbuch der evangelischen Pfarrerei des Gross-herzogtums Hessen*. Friedberg: n.p.

Dittrich, Christoph. 1990–91. Katholische Kontroverstheologen im Kampf gegen Reformation und Täufertum. *Mennonitische Geschichtsblätter* [*MGB*] 47/48: 71–88.

Driedger, Leo, and Donald B. Kraybill, eds. 1994. *Mennonite Peacemaking: From Quietism to Activism*. Scottdale, Pa.: Herald Press.

Dyck, Cornelius J. 1990. Research Notes: Topics for Research in Anabaptism. *MQR* 64:74–76.

Eire, Carlos M. 1990. *War against the Idols: The Reformation of Worship from Erasmus to Calvin*. New York: Cambridge University Press.

Enzenberger, Josef Franz. 1979. Das osterreichische Täufertum im Spiegel der modernen Historiographie. Essay, University of Vienna.

Fast, Heinold. 1959. *Heinrich Bullinger und die Täufer*. Weierhof: Mennonitischer Geschichts Verein.

———. 1962a. Hans Krüsis Büchlein über Glauben und Taufe: Ein Täuferdruck von 1525. In *The Heritage of Menno Simons: A Legacy of Faith*. Edited by C. J. Dyck. 213–31. Newton, Kan.: Mennonite Publication Office.

———. 1975. Reformation durch Provokation: Predigtstörung in den ersten Jahren der Reformation in der Schweiz. In *Umstrittenes Täufertum 1525–1975: Neue Forschungen*. Edited by Hans-Jürgen Goertz. 79–110. Göttingen: Vandenhoeck and Ruprecht.

———. 1978. Wie doopte Konrad Grebel? *Doopsgezinde Bijdragen. Nieuwe neeks* 4:22–31.

———. 1984. Nicht was sondern Das. Marpecks Motto wieder den Spiritualismus. *Ev. Glaube und G.: Grete Mecenseffy zum 85 Geburtstag*. 66–74. Vienna: Evangelischer Oberkirchenrat.

Fichter, Paula. 1982. *Ferdinand I of Austria: The Politics of Dynasticism in the Age of the Reformation*. Boulder, Colo.: East European Monographs.

Fluri, Adolf. 1956. Froschauer Bibles and Testaments. *ME* 2:415–16.

Franz, Günther. [1935] 1975. *Der Deutsche Bauernkrieg*. Darmstadt: Wissenschaftliche Buchgesellschaft.

Friedmann, Robert. 1929. Briefe der Wiedertäufer. *ARG* 26:68ff.

———. 1931. Concerning the True Soldier of Christ: A Hitherto Unknown Tract of the Philipite Brethren in Moravia. *MQR* 5:87–99.

———. 1955a. The Christian Communism of the Hutterian Brethren. *ARG* 52: 196–208.

———. 1955b. Christian Sectarians in Thessalonica and Their Relationship to Anabaptists. *MQR* 29:54–69.

———. 1955c. Ascherham, Gabriel. *ME* 1:174–76.

———. 1955d. *Ausbund. ME* 1:191–92.

———. 1955e. Chronicles, Hutterite. *ME* 1:589ff.

———. 1956a. Addenda and Corrections to Two Previously Published Articles by Robert Friedmann. *MQR* 30:78.

———. 1956b. Epistles, Anabapist. *ME* 2:230–33.

———. 1956c. Gabrielites. *ME* 2:429.

———. 1956d. Hut, Hans. *ME* 2:846–50.

———. 1956e. Hutter, Jacob. *ME* 2:851–54.

———. 1957a. Moravia. *ME* 3:747–50.

———. 1957b. Müntzer, Thomas. *ME* 3:785–89.

———. 1958a. Correction. *MQR* 32:236–37.

———. 1958b. The Philipite Brethren: A Chapter in Anabaptist History. *MQR* 32:272–97.

———. 1959a. Leonhard Schiemer and Hans Schlaffer: Two Tyrolean Anabaptist Martyr-Apostles of 1528. *MQR* 33:31–41.

———. 1959b. Philipites. *ME* 4:166–67.

———. 1959c. Plener, Philip. *ME* 4:192–93.

———. 1959d. Schützinger, Simon. *ME* 4:485.

———. 1959e. Zaunring, Georg. *ME* 4:1018–19.

———. 1961a. *Hutterite Studies: Essays by Robert Friedmann.* Edited by H. S. Bender. Goshen, Ind.: Mennonite Historical Society.

———. 1961b. Anabaptism in Moravia. In *Hutterite Studies: Essays by Robert Friedmann.* Edited by H. S. Bender. 58ff. Goshen, Ind.: Mennonite Historical Society.

———. 1961c. Hutterian Brethren. In *Hutterite Studies: Essays by Robert Friedmann.* Edited by H. S. Bender. 41ff. Goshen, Ind.: Mennonite Historical Society.

———. 1964. Jacob Hutter's Epistle Concerning Schism in Moravia in 1533. *MQR* 38:329–43.

———. 1965. *Die Schriften der Huterischen Täufergemeinschaften. Gesamtkatalog Ihrer Manuskriptbücher, Ihrer Schreiber und Ihrer Literatur, 1529–1667.* Vienna: Verlag Herman Böhlaus.

———. 1980. The Doctrine of the Two Worlds. In *The Anabaptists and Thomas Müntzer.* Edited by James M. Stayer and Werner O. Packull. 23–27. Dubuque, Iowa: Kendall/Hunt.

———. Translator. 1955. The Oldest Church Discipline of the Anabaptists. *MQR* 29:162–66.

Friesen, Abraham. 1984. The Radical Reformation Revisited. *Journal for Mennonite Studies [JMS]* 2:124–76.

———. 1986. Thomas Müntzer and the Anabaptists. *JMS* 4:143–61.

———. 1988. Thomas Müntzer and Martin Luther. *ARG* 79:59ff.

———. 1990. Acts 10: The Baptism of Cornelius as Interpreted by Thomas Müntzer and Felix Manz. *MQR* 64:5–22.

Furcha, Edward J. 1970. *Schwenckfeld's Concept of the New Man.* Pennsburg, Pa.: Schwenckfelder Library.

Gäbler, Ulrich. 1983. *Huldrych Zwingli: Leben und Werk.* Munich: Beck.

Geiser, Samuel. 1951. An Ancient Anabaptist Witness for Nonresistance. *MQR* 25:66–69, 72.

———. 1959a. Solothurn. *ME* 4:570–72.

———. 1959b. Ulimann, Wolfgang. *ME* 4:787–88.

Gelmi, Josef. 1973. *Kirchengeschichte Tirols.* Innsbruck: Tyrolia Verlag.

Gerber, Ulrich. 1987. Berner Täufertum: Gemeinsames und Trennendes. In *Anabaptistes et Dissidents.* Edited by Jean-George Rott and Simon L. Verheus. 285–96. Baden-Baden: Koerner.

Gerner, Gottfried. 1974. Folgerungen aus dem täuferischen Gebrauch der Heiligen Schrift. *MGB* 31:25ff.

Goertz, Hans-Jürgen. 1975. *Umstrittenes Täufertum, 1525–1975. Neue Forschungen.* Göttingen: Vandenhoeck and Ruprecht.

———. 1980. *Die Täufer, Geschichte und Deutung.* Munich: C. H. Beck.

———. 1987. Zwischen Zwietracht und Eintracht. Zur Zweideutigkeit täuferischer und mennonitischer Bekenntnisse. *MGB* 42/43:16–46.

———. 1988. The Confessional Heritage in Its New Mold: What Is Mennonite Self-understanding Today. In *Mennonite Identity, Historical and Contemporary Perspectives.* Edited by Calvin W. Redekop and Samuel J. Steiner. 109ff. Lanham, Md.: University Press of America.

———. 1989. *Thomas Müntzer: Mystiker, Apokalyptiker, Revolutionär.* Munich: C. H. Beck.

Goertz, Hans-Jürgen, ed. 1982. *Profiles of Radical Reformers: Biographical Sketches from Thomas Müntzer to Paracelsus.* Scottdale, Pa: Herald Press.

Gratz, Delbert. 1953. *Bernese Anabaptists.* Scottdale, Pa.: Herald Press.

Gross, Leonard. 1980. *The Golden Years of the Hutterites.* Scottdale, Pa.: Herald Press.

———. 1982. Jakob Hutter: A Christian Communist. In *Profiles of Radical Reformers.* Edited by Hans-Jürgen Goertz. 158ff. Scottdale, Pa.: Herald Press.

Gruber, Paul. 1977. Die Geschichte Niedervintl und Salern. Das Gebiet Spinges 1500–1641. Unpublished Ph.D. dissertation, Leopold-Franzen University, Innsbruck.

Haas, Martin. 1969. *Huldrich Zwingli und Seine Zeit.* Zurich: Theologischer Verlag.

———. 1975. Der Weg der Täufer in die Absonderung. In *Umstrittenes Täufertum.* Edited by Hans-Jürgen Goertz. 50–78. Göttingen: Vandenhoeck and Ruprecht.

———. 1980. The Path of Anabaptists into Separation: The Interdependence of Theology and Social Behavior. In *The Anabaptists and Thomas Müntzer.* Edited by James M. Stayer and Werner O. Packull. 72ff. Dubuque, Iowa: Kendall/Hunt.

Hartknoch, Christoph. 1686. *Preussische Kirchen-Historia.* Frankfurt am Main und Leipzig: n.p.

Hege, Christian. 1908. *Die Täufer in der Kurpfalz. Ein Beitrag zur badisch-pfälzischen Reformationsgeschichte.* Frankfurt: Hermann Minjon.

———. 1955a. Betz, Hans. *ME* 1:319.

———. 1955b. Brandhuber. *ME* 1:405.

———. 1955c. Bruchsal. *ME* 1:444.

———. 1957a. Dax, Leonard. *ME* 2:21.

———. 1957b. Lober, Julius. *ME* 3:379–81.

Hein, Gerhard. 1972–73. Die Täuferbewegung im Mittel-Rheinischen Raum von der Reformation bis zum Dreissigjährigen Krieg. *Ebernburg-Hefte* 6/7:97–115.

Hensel, Johann Adam. 1768. *Protestantische Kirchen-Geschichte der Gemeinen in Schlesien.* Leipzig and Liegnitz: n.p.

Hillerbrand, Hans. 1988. Radicalism in the Early Reformation. In *Radical Tendencies in the Reformation: Divergent Perspectives.* Edited by Hans Hillerbrand. 7–42. Kirksville, Mo.: Sixteenth-Century Journal Publishers.

——. 1991. *Anabaptist Bibliography 1520–1630.* St. Louis: Center for Reformation Research.

——. 1993. The Radical Reformation: Reflections on the Occasion of an Anniversary. *MQR* 58:408–20.

Hobbs, Gerald. 1991. Martin Bucer et la Bible. *Martin Bucer Strasbourg et l'Europe, 500e Anniversaire.* 25ff. Strasbourg: Eglise Saint-Thomas.

Holl, Karl. 1923. Luther und die Schwärmer. In *Gesammelte Aufsätze zur Kirchengeschichte.* vol. 1. *Luther.* Tübingen: Mohr Verlag.

Horsch, John. 1932. The Rise and Early History of the Swiss Brethren Church. *MQR* 6:243ff.

Hostettler, John A. 1974. *Hutterite Society.* Baltimore: Johns Hopkins University Press.

Hruby, Frantisek. 1935. *Die Wiedertäufer in Mähren.* Separatdruck, Leipzig. Previously published 1933 in *ARG* 30:1–36, 170–211 and in 1935 *ARG* 32:1–40.

Hui, Mathias. 1989. Vom Bauernaufstand zur Täuferbewegung. Entwicklung in der ländlichen Reformation am Beispiel des züricherischen Grüninger Amtes. *MGB* 46:113–44.

Innerhofer, Josef. 1980. *Taufers, Ahrn, Prettau. Die Geschichte eines Tales.* Bozen: Verlagsanstalt Athesia.

Jäkel, Josef. 1989. Zur Geschichte der Wiedertäufer in Oberoesterreich und Speziell in Freistadt. *Bericht über das Museum Fancisco-Carolinum* 47:1–82.

Jezler, Peter. 1990. Ettappen des Züricher Bildersturms. Ein Beitrag zur soziologischen Differenzierung ikonoklastischer Vorgänge in der Reformation. In *Bilder und Bildersturm im Spätmittelalter und in der frühen Neuzeit.* Edited by Bob Scribner. 143–74. Wiesbaden: Otto Harrassowitz.

Jung, Fritz. 1910. *Johannes Schwebel der Reformer von Zweibrücken.* Kaiserslautern: Hermann Kayser.

Klaassen, Walter. 1962. Hans Hut and Thomas Müntzer. *Baptist Quarterly Review [BQR]* 19:207–27.

——. 1978. *Michael Gaismair: Revolutionary and Reformer.* Leiden: E. J. Brill.

——. 1986. Schwenckfeldt and the Anabaptists. In *Schwenckfeld and Early Schwenckfeldianism.* Edited by Peter Erb. 389ff. Pennsburg, Pa.: Schwenckfelder Library.

——. 1987. Investigation into the Authorship and the Historical Background of the Anabaptist Tract "Aufdeckung der Babylonischen Hurn." *MQR* 61:251–61.

——. 1989a. Anabaptist Hermeneutics: Presuppositions, Principles, and Practice. In *Essays in Biblical Interpretation.* Edited by Willard Swartley. 1–13. Elkhart, Ind.: Institute of Mennonite Studies.

——. 1989b. Die Taufe im Schweizer Täufertum. *MGB* 46:75–89.

——. 1992a. Of Divine and Human Justice: The Early Swiss Brethren and Government. *CGR* 10:169–86.

————. 1992b. *Living at the End of the Ages: Apocalyptic Expectation in the Radical Reformation.* New York: University Press of America.

Klassen, John. 1978. *The Nobility and the Making of the Hussite Revolution.* New York: Columbia University Press.

Klassen, William. 1959a. Old Testament. *ME* 4:49ff.

————. 1959b. Pilgram Marpeck's Two Books of 1531. *MQR* 33:18–30.

————. 1968. *Covenant and Community: The Life, Writings, and Hermeneutics of Pilgram Marpeck.* Grand Rapids: Erdman Publishing.

————. 1977. Schleitheim and the Marpeck Brotherhood. Typewritten manuscript. 1–14. Made available by the author.

Koffmane, Gustav. 1887. Die Wiedertäufer in Schlesien. *Korrespondenzblatt des Vereins für Geschichte der evangelischen Kirche Schlesiens* 3:34–55.

Köfler, Gretl. 1983. Täufertum in Tirol. In *Michael Gaismair und Seine Zeit.* Edited by Christoph von Hartungen and Günther Pallaver. 112–22. Verona: Cierre Editrice Nuova Grafica.

Kolb, Franz. 1951. Die Wiedertäufer im Wipptal. *Schlern* 74:1–103.

Kuppelwieser, Karl. 1949. Die Wiedertäufer im Eisacktal. Unpublished Ph.D. dissertation, Leopold-Franzen University, Innsbruck.

Landwehr, Arthur. 1986. Die Wiedertäufer in der Reichstadt Esslingen von 1527–1618. *Esslinger Studien* 25:133–214.

Lassmann, Wolfgang. 1980. Die Frühphase der Süddeutsch-Oesterreichischen Täuferbewegung: Unter Besonderer Berücksichtigung von Salzburg, Niederoesterreich und Oberoesterreich. Unpublished paper, University of Vienna.

————. 1985. Exkursus: Zur Täuferpolitik Ferdinand I. Unpublished paper, University of Vienna.

————. 1987. Möglichkeiten einer Modellbildung zur Verlaufstruktur des Tirolischen Anabaptismus. In *Anabaptistes et Dissidents.* Edited by Jean-George Rott and Simon L. Verheus. 297–310. Baden-Baden: Koerner.

Laube, Adolf. 1988. Radicalism as a Research Problem in the History of Early Reformation. In *Radical Tendencies in the Reformation: Divergent Perspectives.* Edited by Hans Hillerbrand. 7–42. Kirksville, Mo.: Sixteenth-Century Journal Publishers.

Lavater, Hans Rudolf. 1989. Berner Täuferdisputation 1538. Funktion, Gesprächsführung, Argumentation, Schriftgebrauch. In *Lebenn Nach der Ler Jhesu . . . Das Sind Aber Wir. Berner Täufer und Prädikanten im Gespräch 1538–1988.* Edited by Schweizerischen Verein für Täuferg. 83–123. Bern: Stämpfli.

Lichdi, Elfriede. 1978. Die Täufer in Heilbronn 1528–1529. *MGB* 35:7–61.

Liebmann, Maxmilian. 1980. *Urbanus Rhegius und die Anfänge der Reformation.* Münster: Aschendorfer Verlagbuchhandlung.

Liechty, Daniel. 1986. Schwenckfelders and Sabbatarian Anabaptists: A Tragedy of the Early Reformation. In *Schwenckfeld and Early Schwenckfeldianism.* Edited by Peter Erb. 135ff. Pennsburg, Pa.: Schwenckfelder Library.

————. 1987. The Origins of Sabbatarianism among East Central European Anabaptists in the Sixteenth Century. In *Anabaptistes et Dissidentes.* Edited by Jean-George Rott and Simon L. Verheus. 361–69. Baden-Baden: Koerner.

———. 1988a. Oswald Glaidt, Simone Simoni, and Juan de Valdes. In *Bibliotheca Dissidentium*. Edited by André Séquenny. vol. 9. Baden-Baden: Koerner.

———. 1988b. *Andreas Fischer and the Sabbatarian Anabaptists: An Early Reformation Episode in East Central Europe*. Scottdale, Pa.: Herald Press.

Lieder der Hutterischen Brüder. 1983. 5th edition. Cayley, Alberta: Macmillan Colony.

Lienhard, Marc, ed. 1977. *The Origins and Characteristics of Anabaptism*. The Hague: Martinus Nijhoff.

Liesenberg, Ursula. 1991. *Studien zum Märtyrerlied der Täufer im 16. Jahrhundert*. Frankfurt: Peter Lang.

Locher, Gottfried. 1981. *Zwingli's Thought: New Perspectives*. Leiden: E. J. Brill.

———. 1987. Felix Manzs Abschiedsworte an seine Mitbrüder vor der Hinrichtung 1527. In *Anabaptistes et Dissidentes*. Edited by Jean-George Rott and Simon L. Verheus. 271–84. Baden-Baden: Koerner.

Loserth, Johann. 1897. Oswald Glaydt. *Zeitschrift des Vereins für die Geschichte Mährens und Schlesien* 1:70–73.

———. 1892a. Der Anabaptismus in Tirol. Von Seinen Anfängen bis zum Tode Jacob Huters (1526–1536). Aus den hinterlassenen Papieren des Hofraths Dr. Josef Beck. Vienna.

———. 1892b. Der Anabaptismus in Tirol von seinen Anfängen bis zum Tode Jacob Huters. *Archiv für Oesterreichische Geschichte* 78:430–604.

———. 1893. Der Anabaptismus in Tirol vom Jahre 1536 bis zu seinem Erlöschen. *Archiv für Oesterreichische Geschichte* 79:127–276.

———. 1894. Der Communismus der Mährischen Wiedertäufer im 16 und 17 Jahrhundert. *Archiv für Oesterreichische Geschichte* 81:135–322.

———. 1899. Georg Blaurock und die Anfänge des Anabaptismus in Graubünden und Tirol. *Vorträge und Aufsätze aus der Comenius-Gesellschaft* 7:1–30.

———. 1912. Zur Geschichte der Wiedertäufer in Salzburg. *Mitteilungen der Gesellschaft für Salzburger Landeskunde* 52:35–60.

———. 1955. Brixen. *ME* 1:431–32.

———. 1956a. Fichter, Konrad. *ME* 2:327.

———. 1956b. Griesinger, Onophrius. *ME* 2:579–80.

———. 1956c. Hartitsch, Dietrich von. *ME* 2:667–68.

———. 1957a. Käls, Hieronymus. *ME* 3:139–40.

———. 1957b. Lanzenstiel, Leonhard. *ME* 3:292ff.

———. 1957c. Lochmair, Leonhard. *ME* 3:381ff.

———. 1959a. Salzburg. *ME* 4:409–11.

———. 1959b. Znaim. *ME* 4:1034.

Loserth, Johann, and Robert Friedmann. 1955. Carinthia. *ME* 1:517–19.

———. 1956. Glaidt, Oswald. *ME* 2:522–23.

———. 1959. Tirol. *ME* 4:724–28.

Macek, Josef. 1965. *Der Tiroler Bauern-Krieg und Michael Gaismair*. Berlin: Deutscher Verlag der Wissenschaft.

Maier, Paul L. 1959. *Caspar Schwenckfeld on the Person and Work of Christ: A Study of Schwenckfeldian Theology at Its Core*. Assen: Van Gorcum.

Maleczynska, E. 1961. Gabrielowcy Slascy. *Odrodzenie i Reformacja w Polsce* 6:17–28.

Martin, Dennis. 1988. Catholic Spirituality and Anabaptist and Mennonite Discipleship. *MQR* 62:5–25.

Maurer, Justus. 1979. *Prediger im Bauernkrieg.* Stuttgart: Calver.

McConica, James. 1991. *Erasmus.* New York: Oxford University Press.

McLaughlin, Emmet. 1986a. *Caspar Schwenckfeld, Reluctant Radical: His Life to 1540.* New Haven: Yale University Press.

———. 1986b. Schwenckfeld and the South German Eucharist Controversy, 1526–1529. In *Schwenckfeld and Early Schwenckfeldianism.* Edited by Peter Erb. 181–210. Pennsburg, Pa.: Schwenckfelder Library.

Mecenseffy, Grete. 1964. Ein Früher Fall von Kabinettsjustiz. *Mitteilungen des Oberoesterreichischen Landesarchivs* 8:259–66.

———. 1971. Wiedertäufer in Kitzbühl. In *Stadtbuch Kitzbühl.* vol. 4. Edited by Eduard Widmoser. 155ff.

———. 1980. The Origin of Upper Austrian Anabaptism. In *The Anabaptists and Thomas Müntzer.* Edited by James M. Stayer and Werner O. Packull. 152–54. Dubuque, Iowa: Kendall/Hunt.

———. 1984. Ursprünge und Strömungen des Täufertums in Oesterreich. *Mitteilungen des Oberoesterreichischen Landesarchivs* 14:77–94.

———. 1985. Wer war Jacob Hueter? In *Die Hutterischen Täufer: Geschichtlicher Hintergrund und handwerkliche Leistung.* Edited by Ingolf Bauer and Christa Zimmermann. 25–28. Weierhof-Münich: Bavarian National Museum and Mennonitischer Geschichtsverein.

Meyer, Theodor. 1976. Ueber die Freiheit der Bauern in Tirol und in der Schweizer Eidgenossenschaft. In *Deutsches Bauerntum im Mittelalter.* Edited by Günther Franz. 177ff. Darmstadt: Wissenschaftliche Buchgesellschaft.

Mezger, J. J. [1876] 1967. *Geschichte der deutschen Bibelbübersetzungen in der schweizerisch-reformierten Kirche.* Nieukoop: B. De Graaf.

Michalski, Sergiusz. 1990. Die protestantischen Bilderstürme. Versuch einer Uebersicht. In *Bilder und Bildersturm im Spätmittelalter und in der frühen Neuzeit.* Edited by Bob Scribner. 69–124. Wiesbaden: Otto Harrassowitz.

Midelfort, Eric. 1990. Social History and Biblical Exegesis: Community, Family, and Witchcraft in Sixteenth-Century Germany. In *The Bible in the Sixteenth Century.* Edited by David Steinmetz. 7ff. Durham, N.C.: Duke University Press.

Moeller, Bernd. 1972. *Imperial Cities and the Reformation.* Philadelphia: Fortress Press.

Moser, Heinz. 1982. *Die Scharfrichter von Tirol. Ein Beitrag zur Geschichte des Strafvollzuges in Tirol von 1497–1787.* Innsbruck: Steiger.

Müller, Ernst. [1895] 1972. *Geschichte der Bernischen Täufer.* Nieuwkoop: B. De Graaf.

Neff, Christian. 1955. Blaurock, Georg. *ME* 1:354ff.

Neff, Christian, and Johann Loserth. 1956. Faber, Johann. *ME* 2:285–86.

Nelson, Stephen, and Jean Rott. 1984. Strasbourg: The Anabaptist City in the Sixteenth Century. *MQR* 58:230–41.

Nicoladoni, Alexander. 1893. *Johannes Bünderlin von Linz und die Oberoesterreichischen Täufergemeinden in den Jahren 1525–1531.* Berlin: R. Gärtners Verlag.

Noflatscher, Heinz. 1988. Alltag des Kanonikus. *Quellen zur historischen Wohnkultur, Denkmalpflege in Südtirol.* 325–36. Bozen: Landesdenkmalamt.

———. 1989. Gesellpriester and Kapläne in der Reformation. Das Deutsche Haus in Sterzing. In *St. Elisabeth in Deutschhaus zu Sterzing.* 81–120. Edited by Karl Gruber, et al. Innsbruck: Tyrolia Verlag.

———. 1994. *Heresy and Revolt: The Early Anabaptists in the Tyrol and in Zurich.* MQR 68:291–317.

Obermann, Heiko. 1984. *The Roots of Antisemitism in the Age of Renaissance and Reformation.* Translated by James Porter. Philadelphia: Fortress Press.

Oyer, John. 1990. Historiography, Anabaptist. *ME* 5:378–82.

———. 1964. *Lutheran Reformers against Anabaptist: Luther, Melanchthon, and Menius and the Anabaptists of Central Germany.* The Hague: Martinus Nijhoff.

———. 1970. A Newly Discovered Hutterite Codex at Copenhagen. *MQR* 44: 122–25.

———. 1991. Michael Schneider: Anabaptist Leader, Hymnist, Recanter. *MQR* 65:256–86.

Ozment, Steven. 1990. *Three Behaim Boys: Growing Up in Early Modern Germany.* New Haven: Yale University Press.

Packull, Werner O. 1977. *Mysticism and the Early South German-Austrian Anabaptist Movement, 1525–1531.* Scottdale, Pa: Herald Press.

———. 1979. Some Reflections on the State of Anabaptist History: The Demise of a Normative Vision. *Studies in Religion* 8:313–23.

———. 1981. Denck, Hans (ca. 1490–1527). *Theologische Realenzyklopädie* 8: 488–90.

———. 1985. Swiss Anabaptism in the Context of the Reformation of the Common Man. *JMS* 3:36–59.

———. 1986a. In Search of the "Common Man" in Early German Anabaptist Ideology. *Sixteenth-Century Journal* 18:51–68.

———. 1986b. A Reinterpretation of Melchior Hoffman's *Exposition* against the Background of Spiritualist-Franciscan Eschatology with Special Reference to Peter John Olivi. In *The Dutch Dissenters: Contributions to a Reassessment of Their History and Ideas.* Edited by Irvin Horst. 32–61. Leiden: E. J. Brill.

———. 1989a. Thomas Müntzer and das Hutsche Täufertum. *MGB* 46:30–42.

———. 1989b. An Inventory of the Hans Wiedemann Collection of Bavarian Anabaptist Documents. *MQR* 68:297–305.

———. 1990a. Between Paradigms: Anabaptist Studies at the Crossroads. *CGR* 8:1–22.

———. 1990b. Trial and Martyrdom of the Hutterite Hans Pürchner. *Fides et Historia* 22:18–24.

———. 1990c. Castelberger, Andreas. *ME* 5:128.

———. 1990d. Hut, Hans. *ME* 5:404–6.

———. 1990e. Müntzer, Thomas. *ME* 5:607–9.

———. 1991a. Clemens Adler's Judgment Concerning the Sword: A Swiss Connection to Silesian Anabaptism? *CGR* 9:243–50.

———. 1991b. A Seventeenth-Century Hutterite Codex: A Description. *Canadian Journal of History* 65:373–78.

————. 1991c. *Rereading Anabaptist Beginnings.* J. J. Thiessen Lectures. Winnipeg: CMBC Publications.

————. 1991d. The Beginning of Anabaptism in Southern Tyrol. *Sixteenth-Century Journal* 21:717–26.

————. 1993. Research Note: Pilgram Marpeck's *Uncovering of the Babylonian Whore* and Other Anonymous Anabaptist Tracts. *MQR* 67:351–55.

————. 1994. Die Anfänge des Täufertums im Tirol. In *Wegscheiden der Reformation: Vom 16. bis zum 18 Jahrhundert.* Edited by Günter Volger. 179–209. Weimar: Bohlaus.

Palme, Rudolph. 1986. Zur Täuferbewegung in Tirol. *Die Täuferbewegung. Tagung zum 450. Todestag Jakob Huters (1536–1986).* Edited by Christoph von Hartungen and Günther Pallaver. 66–81. Bolzano: Collana di Documentazione.

————. 1986–87. Zur Täuferbewegung in Tirol. *MGB* 43/44:47–61.

Palmer, Lee. 1990. Iconoclasts in Zurich. In *Bilder und Bildersturm im Spätmittelalter und in der frühen Neuzeit.* Edited by Bob Scribner. 125–42. Wiesbaden: Otto Harrassowitz.

Panek, Jaroslav. 1989. Die Täufer in den böhmischen Ländern, insbesondere in Mähren im 16. und 17. Jahrhundert. *Schlern* 63:648–61.

Pelikan, Jaroslav J. 1984. *The Christian Tradition: A History of the Development of Doctrine.* vol. 4. *Reformation of Church and Dogma.* Chicago: University of Chicago Press.

Pletscher, Werner. 1959. Schleitheim. *ME* 4:460.

Potter, G. R. 1976. *Zwingli.* New York: Cambridge University Press.

Prast, Erika. 1975. Die Vier Pustertaler Herrschaften—St. Michelsburg, Schöneck, Uttenheim und Heunfels—Unter Brixner Pfandherrschaft 1500–1570. Unpublished Ph.D. dissertation, Leopold-Franzen University, Innsbruck.

Quiring, Horst. 1987. Die Ausprägung der westpreussischen Mennoniten im 16 Jahrhundert. In *Anabaptistes et Dissidentes.* Edited by Jean-George Rott and Simon L. Verheus. 337–42. Baden-Baden: Koerner.

Radler, Leonhart. 1962/1970. Wiedertäufer und Schwenckfelder im Schweidnitzer Land. *Jahrbuch für schlesische Kirchengeschichte* 41:40–45; 49:31–35.

Rastner, Alois. 1974. Die Hauptmannschaft Säben. Das Stadtgericht Klausen. Die Gerichte Lantzfons und Verding 1500-1641. Unpublished Ph.D. dissertation, Leopold-Franzen University, Innsbruck.

Reimer, James. 1989. *The Emanuel Hirsch and Paul Tillich Debate.* Queenston, Ont.: Edwin Mellen.

Rischar, Klaus. 1968. Das Leben und Sterben der Wiedertäufer in Salzburg und Süddeutschland. Nach einem Brief des Prof. Johannes Eck an Herzog Georg von Sachsen aus dem Jahre 1527. *Mitteilungen der Gesellschaft für Salzburger Landeskunde* 108:197–207.

Schmelzer, Mathias. 1989. Jakob Huters Wirken im Lichte von Bekenntnissen gefangener Täufer. *Schlern* 58:596–618.

Schmid, Hans-Dieter. 1971. Das Hutsche Täufertum. Ein Beitrag zur Charakterisierung einer täuferischen Richtung aus der Frühzeit der Täuferbewegung. *Historischer Jahrbuch* 16:328–44.

————. 1972. *Täufertum und Obrigkeit in Nürnberg.* Erlangen: Dissertation-Druckerei Hogel.

Schottenloher, Karl. [1921] 1967. *Philip Ulhart: Ein Augsburger Winkeldrucker und Helfershelfer der "Schwärmer" und "Wiedertäufer" (1523–1529).* Nieuwkoop: B. De Graaf.

Schreiber, William I. 1979. Hans Betz: Poet of the *Ausbund. MQR* 53:131–33.

Schwartz, Hillel. 1973. Early Anabaptist Ideas about the Nature of Children. *MQR* 47:102–14.

Scribner, Bob, ed. 1990. *Bilder und Bildersturm im Spätmittelalter und in der frühen Neuzeit.* Wiesbaden: Otto Harrassowitz.

Scribner, Bob, and Gerhard Benecke, eds. 1979. *The German Peasant War 1525: New Viewpoint.* London: George Allen and Unwin.

Seebass, Gottfried. 1972. Müntzers Erbe. Werk, Leben und Theologie des Hans Hut (gestorben 1527). Unpublished Habilitationsschrift, Friedrich-Alexander University, Erlangen.

————. 1974. Bauernkrieg und Täufertum in Franken. *Zeitschrift für Kirchengeschichte* [*ZKG*] 85:284–300.

————. 1975. Das Zeichen der Erwählten. Zum Verständnis der Taufe bei Hans Hut. In *Umstrittenes Täufertum, 1525–1975. Neue Forschungen.* Edited by Hans-Jürgen Goertz. 138–64. Göttingen: Vandenhoeck and Ruprecht.

————. Hut, Hans (ca. 1490–1527). *Theologische Realenzyklopädie* 15:169–73, in press.

Sequenny, Andre, ed. 1980. *Bibliotheca dissidentium; repertoire des nonconformiste religieuxe des seizieme et dixseptieme siecles.* I. Baden-Baden: Koerner.

Shantz, Douglas. 1992. *Crautwald and Erasmus: A Study in Humanism and Radical Reform in Sixteenth-Century Silesia.* Baden-Baden: Koerner.

Snyder, Arnold. 1984. *The Life and Thought of Michael Sattler.* Scottdale, Pa.: Herald Press.

————. 1989. The Influence of the Schleitheim Articles on the Anabaptist Movement: A Historical Evaluation. *MQR* 58:323–34.

————. 1990a. Konrad Winckler: An Early Swiss Anabaptist Missionary, Pastor and Martyr. *MQR* 64:352–61.

————. 1990b. Word and Power in Reformation Zurich. *ARG* 81:263–85.

————. 1991. Biblical Text and Social Context: Anabaptist Anticlericalism in Reformation Zurich. *MQR* 65:169–91.

————. 1993. Communication and the People: The Case of Reformation St. Gall. *MQR* 67:152–73.

Sommersberg, Friedrich Wilhelm von. 1729. *Silesiacarum rerum scriptores.* vol. 1. Leipzig: n.p.

Stayer, James M. 1972. *Anabaptists and the Sword.* Lawrence, Kan.: Coronado.

————. 1975. Die Anfänge des Schweizerischen Täufertums im Kongregationalismus. In *Umstrittenes Täufertum, 1525–1975. Neue Forschungen.* Edited by Hans-Jürgen Goertz. 19–49. Göttingen: Vandenhoeck and Ruprecht.

————. 1977. Reublin and Brötli: The Revolutionary Beginnings of Swiss Anabaptism. In *The Origins and Characteristics of Anabaptism.* Edited by M. Lienhard. 83–102. The Hague: Martinus Nijhoff.

————. 1982a. Wilhelm Reublin: A Picaresque Journey through Early Anabaptism. In *Profiles of Radical Reformers: Biographical Sketches from Thomas Müntzer to Paracelus*. Edited by Hans-Jürgen Goertz and translated by Walter Klaassen. 107–17. Scottdale, Pa.: Herald Press.

————. 1982b. The Anabaptists. In *Reformation Europe: A Guide to Research*. Edited by Steven Ozment. 135–59. St. Louis: Center for Reformation Research.

————. 1988. Anabaptists and Future Anabaptists in the Peasants' War. *MQR* 62:98–139.

————. 1991. *German Peasants' War and Anabaptist Community of Goods*. Montreal: McGill/Queen's University Press.

————. 1992. The Easy Demise of a Normative Vision of Anabaptism. In *Mennonite Identity: Historical and Contemporary Perspectives*. Edited by Calvin W. Redekop and Samuel J. Steiner. 109ff. Lanham, Md.: University Press of America.

————. 1993a. The Radical Reformation. Typewritten manuscript.

————. 1993b. Saxon Radicalism and Swiss Anabaptism: The Return of the Repressed. *MQR* 67:5–30.

Stayer, James M., and Werner O. Packull, eds. 1980. *The Anabaptists and Thomas Müntzer*. Dubuque, Iowa: Kendall/Hunt.

Stayer, James M., Klaus Deppermann, and Werner O. Packull. 1975. From Monogenesis to Polygenesis: The Historical Discussion of Anabaptist Origins. *MQR* 49:83–121.

Steinmetz, Max. 1971. *Das Müntzerbild von Martin Luther bis Friedrich Engels*. Berlin: Deutscher Verlag der Wissenschaft.

Stella, Aldo. 1982a. Il "Sozialevangelismus" di Michael Gaismayr e le Origini dell Anabattismo Hutterita. *I. Valdesi e l'Europa*. 245–63. Torre Pellice edition, Tomin: Claudiana.

————. 1982b. *Rivolte Contadine Trentino-Tirolesi e Genesi del Comunismo Evangelico Dei Fratelli Hutterite*. Padova: Societa Cooperativa Tipografica.

————. 1983. Genesi del Comunismo evangelico hutterita: Storiografia e nuove interpretazioni. *L'uomo e la storia: Studi storici in onore di Massimo Petrocchi*. 207–28. Rome.

————. 1990. Hutterite Influence on Italian Nonconformist Conventicles and Subsequent Developments. *MQR* 64:195ff.

Szczucki, Lech. 1987. The Beginnings of Antitrinitarian Anabaptism in Lithuania and Poland in the Light of a So-far Unknown Source. In *Anabaptistes et Dissidentes*. Edited by Jean-George Rott and Simon L. Verheus. 343–57. Baden-Baden: Koerner.

Thomas, Ulrich. 1977. *Bibliographie zum deutschen Bauernkrieg*. Stuttgart: Dokumentationsstelle Universität Hohenheim.

Trenkwalder, Elias. 1968. Geschichte der Pfarrei Toblach. Unpublished dissertation, University of Salzburg.

Urban, Waclaw. 1986. *Der Antitrinitarismus in den böhmischen Ländern und in der Slowakei im 16 und 17 Jahrhundert*. Translated by Kordula Zubrzycka. *Bibliotheca Dissidentium*. Baden-Baden: Koerner.

Wackernagel, Philip. [1864-77] 1964. *Das Deutsche Kirchenlied.* vols. 1 and 5. Hildesheim: C. J. Olms.

Wagner, Murray L. 1983. *Petr Chelcicky: A Radical Separatist in Hussite Bohemia.* Scottdale, Pa.: Herald Press.

Waite, Gary K. 1990. *David Joris and Dutch Anabaptism, 1524–1543.* Waterloo, Ont.: Wilfrid Laurier University Press.

Walton, Robert C. 1980. Was There a Turning Point of the Zwinglian Reformation? In *The Anabaptists and Thomas Müntzer.* Edited by James M. Stayer and Werner O. Packull. 66–71. Dubuque, Iowa: Kendall/Hunt.

Watt, Tessa. 1991. *Cheap Print and Popular Piety, 1550–1660.* New York: Cambridge University Press.

Weigelt, Horst. 1985. *The Schwenckfelders in Silesia.* Translated by Peter Erb. Pennsburg, Pa.: Schwenckfelder Library.

———. 1987. Die Auseinandersetzung Valentin Krautwalds mit dem sabbatistischen Täufertum in Schlesien. In *Anabaptistes et Dissidents.* Edited by Jean-George Rott and Simon L. Verheus. 361–70. Baden-Baden: Koerner.

Wenger, John C. 1955. Brüderliche Vereinigung. *ME* 1:447ff.

Widmoser, Eduard. 1951. Das Tiroler Täufertum. *Tiroler Heimat. Jahrbuch für Geschichte und Volkskunde* 15: pt. 1, 45–89; pt. 2, 103–28.

Wiebe, Christoph. 1989. Konrad Grebels Ausführungen über Glaube und Taufe: Ein Versuch mit Thomas Müntzer ins Gespräch zu kommen. *MGB* 46:43ff.

Wiedemann, Hans. 1962. Die Widertäufergemeinde in Passau 1527–1535. *Ostbairische Grenzmarken. Passauer Jahrbuch für Geschichte, Kunst und Volkskunde* 6:262–76.

———. 1965. The Story of the Anabaptists in Passau, 1527–1535. *MQR* 39:91–103.

Williams, George. 1962. *The Radical Reformation.* Philadelphia: Westminster Press.

———. 1992. *The Radical Reformation.* Kirksville, Mo.: Sixteenth-Century Journal Publishers.

Wiswedel, Wilhelm. 1937a. Oswald Glaidt von Jamnitz. *ZKG* 55:550–64.

———. 1937b. Gabriel Ascherham und die nach ihm benannte Bewegung. *ARG* 34: pt. 1, 1–35; pt. 2, 235–62.

———. 1940. Das Schulwesen der Hutterischen Brüder. *ARG* 38:38–60.

———. 1952a. Philipp Plener und die "Philippischen." *Bilder und Führergestalten aus dem Täufertum.* vol. 3, 146–48. Kassel: Oncken.

———. 1952b. Die Täufer in Schlesien und Preussen. *Bilder und Führergestalten aus dem Täufertum.* vol. 3, 222–28. Kassel: Oncken.

———. 1959. Yetelhauser [Yedelhauser, Jedelhaus], Michael. *ME* 4:1003–4.

Wohlfeil, Rainer. 1972. *Reformation oder frühbürgerliche Revolution?* Munich: Nymphenburger.

———. 1975. *Der Bauernkrieg 1524–26. Bauernkrieg und Reformation.* Munich: Nymphenburger.

Wolkan, Rudolf. [1923] 1974. *Geschichtsbuch der Hutterischen Brüder.* Cayley, Alberta: Macmillan Colony.

————. 1965. *Die Lieder der Wiedertäufer. Ein Beitrag zur deutschen und niederländischen Literatur- und Kirchengeschichte.* Nieuwkoop: B. De Graaf.

Yoder, John H. 1958. The turning point in the Zwinglian Reformation. *MQR* 32: 128–40.

————. 1962. *Täufertum und Reformation in der Schweiz. Die Gespräche zwischen Täufern und Reformatoren 1523–1538.* Karlsruhe: Schneider.

————. 1967. Hermeneutics of the Anabaptists. *MQR* 41:291–308.

————. 1969. The evolution of the Zwinglian Reformation. *MQR* 43:95–122.

————. 1980. The turning point in the Zwinglian Reformation. In *The Anabaptists and Thomas Müntzer.* Edited by James M. Stayer and Werner O. Packull. 61–65. Dubuque, Iowa: Kendall/Hunt.

————. 1989. Hermeneutics of the Anabaptists. In *Essays in biblical interpretation.* Edited by Willard Swartley. Elkhart, Ind.: Institute of Mennonite Studies.

Yoder, Paton. 1987. The structure of the Amish ministry in the nineteenth century. *MQR* 61:280ff.

Zeman, Jarold. 1966/1967. Historical topography of Moravian Anabaptism. *MQR* 40:266–78; 41:40–78.

————. 1969. *The Anabaptists and the Czech brethren in Moravia, 1526–1628: A study of origin and contacts.* The Hague: Mouton.

Zieglschmid, A. J. F. 1941. Unpublished sixteenth-century letters of the Hutterian brethren. *MQR* 15:16–23.

Zschäbitz, Gerhard. 1980. The position of Anabaptism on the continuum of the early bourgeois revolution in Germany. In *The Anabaptists and Thomas Müntzer.* Edited by James M. Stayer and Werner O. Packull. 28–32. Dubuque, Iowa: Kendall/Hunt.

Zürcher, Isaac. 1980–1984. Die Täuferbibeln. *Information Blätter* (Schweizerischer Verein für Täufergeschichte). 4: 10–44; 6: 13–56; 7: 6ff.

————. 1986. *Die Täufer um Bern in den ersten Jahrhunderten nach der Reformation und die Toleranz. Sonderdruck Informationsblätter* (Schweizerischen Vereins für Täufergeschichte). 9.

Index

Aare River, 334
Aargau, 176
Abbess of the Queen's Cloister at Brünn.
    See Boskowitz, Johanka of
Ab-Penon, 182
Adam (Manng), 369
Adler, Clemens, 99, 106–20, 122, 126,
    130–32, 353–55, 400
Adolf, Thomas, 137
Aelurius, Georg, 352
Aexowitz, 352
Ahrn Valley, 179
Aichelin, Bernhard, 272, 346
Albrecht, Duke of Hohenzollern, 289–91,
    399
Allewelt, Walthasar, 362
Allseider, Christian, 377
Alsace, 287, 289
Altenmarkt, Moravia, 208
Altrasen, 376
Alzey, 79, 81–83, 348, 364
Ammann, Hartmann, 364
Amon, Hans (Tuchscherer), 62, 72, 138,
    193–94, 205, 211, 216, 223–25, 231,
    236–37, 240, 242–43, 248–50, 257,
    259–61, 266–69, 271, 275–76, 278–
    81, 302, 341, 364, 375, 377–78, 380–
    84, 386–88, 390–96, 398; wife Andl,
    193, 205, 268, 391, 395
Am Wald, 157
Andre, priest at Lüsen, 369

Andre (Andreas) of Eysen, 91
Angst, Bartlme, 192
Ansbach, 84, 85, 220, 347
Appenzell, 43–46, 49, 182
Arau, 332
Arkleb of Boskowitz. *See* Boskowitz
Arnold, Lienhart, 280
Aschaffenburg, 94
Aschenberger, Christoph (Stoffel), 93, 350
Ascherham (Kirschner, Kürschner, Scher-
    dinger, Schärdinger), Gabriel, 65, 70,
    87, 89, 99, 102, 120–32, 141, 154–58,
    223, 225–35, 238–39, 244, 277, 283,
    292, 293–302, 334, 336, 344, 352–57,
    363, 379–84, 400–401
Aschermann, Paul, 120, 292
Aschlperger (Aschlberger, Eschlperger),
    Hans, 359, 392
Attergau (Vöklabruck), 397
Auerbach, 338
Auerbacher, Kilian, 338, 342
Auers (Affers), 247, 260
Augsburg, 21, 31, 35, 45, 51, 57, 64, 78–
    81, 147, 176, 180, 330, 333, 335,
    338–41, 344–48, 352, 367, 389
Auspitz (Hustopece), 65, 67, 70, 72, 84–
    92, 99, 135, 137, 147, 204–5, 209,
    214, 217–25, 232, 235–38, 240, 259,
    261, 281, 283, 289, 291, 344, 348
Austerlitz (Slavkov), 36–37, 49, 52, 54–
    57, 62–67, 72, 74–75, 78, 81, 107,

Austerlitz (*continued*)
   148, 157, 174, 201, 203, 209, 215–35,
   275, 281, 283, 336–37, 340, 342, 350,
   353, 359, 364, 377, 378, 381–83

Backus, Irena, 367
Bader, Augustin, 335, 339, 346
Bader, Georg, 266
Bader (Pader), Gilg, 177, 181; wife, 181,
   369
Bad Wimpfen, 82
Bainton, Roland, 8
Ballenberger, Christian, 369
Ballenberger, Jörgen, 369
Balthasar of Nidervintl. *See* Maierhofer
Bamberg, 57, 347
Bannowitz, 108
Barbara of Tiers, 370
Bärbel of Jenbach, 234
Barge, Hermann, 354, 368
Bärml (Bämerle), 398
Barton, Peter, 342, 378, 382
Basel, 26–27, 38, 91, 94–95, 176, 182,
   215, 221, 326, 329–33
Bauer, Gewer, of Schwaigern, 349, 397
Bauer, Günther, 338, 341–42
Baumann, Clarence, 326, 360, 362
Bavaria, 54, 56, 60, 75
Bayerlin, Hans, 345
Bayreuth, 147
Beck (Peck, Pfeifer), Hans, 91, 93–94, 97,
   211–12, 351, 376–77
Beck, Joseph, 121, 179, 335–36, 340–41,
   346–50, 352, 355–56, 359, 364–65,
   369, 374, 376–81, 383–84, 386, 388,
   392–93, 396–98
Belgrade, 111
Bender, Harold, 1–8, 15, 28, 107, 287,
   323, 325, 329, 337, 349, 353, 365, 397
Benecke, Gerhard, 325
Berbig, Georg, 338–39, 342
Bergen, Moravia, 397
Bergstadt of Jamnitz, 351
Bergsten, Torsten, 343
Beringer, locksmith, 88, 348
Berkheim, 91
Berlin, Hans, 345
Bern, 37–41, 45, 94, 176, 182, 330, 332–
   33, 335
Bernstein, Lord, 107

Betz (Petz), Hans, 92, 95, 349–51
Bibra, 56
Binder, Eucharius, 57, 59, 341
Binder (Pinter), Peter, 180–81
Bischwiller, 344, 351
Bisenz, 289
Blanke, Fritz, 325, 334, 397
Blarer, Ambrosius, 346
Blasi, 395
Blasius. *See* Kuhn
Blasius of Brussel, 347
Blasius of Krossen, 373, 376
Blauärmel. *See* Plener, Philip
Blaurock, Elsbeth, 369
Blaurock, Jörg (George), 45, 92, 121,
   181–86, 202–3, 369–70
Blesdijk, Nicolaas, 397
Blickle, Peter, 9, 164, 325, 366
Blienschwiller, 78, 344
Blough, Neal, 133–34, 146, 358
Bohemia, 36, 60, 62, 66–67, 100, 187,
   201, 215, 260, 283, 363, 389
Bohemian (Böhmisch) Krumau (Cesky
   Krumlov), 36, 60, 62, 135–37, 214–
   15, 222, 269, 275, 281, 340–41
Bömish Krumau. *See* Bohemian Krumau
Bonfeld, 346
Boschenstein, Johani, 333
Boskowitz (Boscovice), Arkleb of, gover-
   nor of Moravia, 68, 342
Boskowitz, Dobesch of, 69, 71, 347–48
Boskowitz, Johanka of, abbess, 69, 218,
   223–24, 237–38, 380
Boskowitz, Wenzel of, 71
Bossert, Gustav, Sr., and Jr., 344, 349–
   50, 378–79
Boyd, Stephen, 36, 134–36, 146–47,
   154, 325, 332, 345, 347, 358–59, 361,
   363–64
Bozen (Bolzano), 164, 176–79, 184, 199,
   241, 245, 256, 269, 369–70, 373, 393
Brady, Thomas, 165, 324
Braght, Thieleman J. van, 351
Braitmichel, Caspar, 101, 225–26, 233–
   34, 381–82
Brälin, Urschl (Ursula), 395
Brandenberger, Friedrich, 366, 370
Brandhuber, Jörg, 356
Brandhuber, Wolfgang, of Burkhausen,
   60, 121, 129, 301, 339–40, 356, 374

Branzoll, 250, 252, 255–56, 387–88
Braun (Bämerle), Burkhart, of Ofen, 87, 216, 221–22, 285, 288, 339
Braun, Hans, 390
Brecht, Martin, 400
Breisgau, 346
Brenner, 164, 180, 196–97, 241, 373–74, 383
Breslau (Wroclaw), 100–103, 105–8, 291, 352, 354
Breslau, Bishop of, Jacob of Salza, 100, 343
Briesmann, John, 291
Brigitte (Goltperg), 355–56
Brimitz, 269
Brixen (Bressanone), 164, 179, 199–200, 207–8, 211, 224, 247, 252, 256, 267, 270–71, 274–75, 365, 373, 375, 392, 394
Brixen, Bishop of, 161, 166–67, 174–76, 200, 207, 245–46, 250, 273, 365
Brock, Peter, 353–54
Brötli (Pretle), Johannes, 20, 44, 49, 336
Bruchsal, 84–85, 91, 344, 378
Brüneck (Brunico), 164, 178, 199–200
Brünn (Brno), 62, 67, 70, 87, 218, 240, 338–40, 343, 396
Bucer, Martin, 28, 40, 133, 144, 338, 342, 359
Bücking, Jürgen, 367, 371
Bucovice, 398
Budespitz (Pudespitz, Butschowitz), 149, 289, 362
Budwitz (Budespitz, Pudweis), 149
Bugenhagen, Johannes, 333
Bühler (Phüller), Christoph, 244
Bullinger, Heinrich, 221, 330–31, 378
Bünderlin, Hans, 84, 121, 124, 132–34, 137, 139–46, 157, 358, 360–61, 363, 367
Burda, David, 360
Burghausen, Bavaria, 60, 121, 371
Burkhart of Ofen. *See* Braun

Calvin, John, 40
Cammerlander, 133
Capistran, John, 110–11
Capito, Wolfgang, 28, 353
Carinthia (Kärnten), 188, 192, 246, 367
Carniola, 192

Caspar (Schüler?), 218, 220
Castelberger, Andreas, 19–22, 27, 330
Cham, 103
Charles V, Emperor, 72, 370
Chelcicky, Petr, 299
Chelmna, 398
Christof of Teutenhofen, 177
Clasen, Claus-Peter, 6–10, 77, 344–45, 349, 361, 398
Claus, Helmut, 358
Colmar, 344
Cologne, 94, 336
Conrath, Ray, 349
Constance, Bishop of, 19, 23, 188
Constantine, 105
Cornelius, C. A., 378
Coupek, M., 356
Crautwald, Valentin, 101, 103, 105, 353
Czech Brethren, 299–300
Czechowic, Marcin, 354, 398

Dänkl, Wilhelm, 358
Danube River, 189, 196, 339
David the Bohemian of Schweidnitz, 87, 101, 216–19, 221–22, 230, 234, 291–92, 379, 399
Davis, Ken, 324
Dax, Leonard, 156–57, 363–64
Dedic, Paul, 373
Delmonego, Ernst, 394
Denck, Hans, 4, 27, 57, 64, 78, 80–81, 120, 126, 140, 150–52, 338, 362
Deppermann, Klaus, 7, 78, 324, 337, 344, 346, 397
De Wind, H., 337
Diehl, Wilhelm, 346
Dietrich of Heilbronn, 91, 348, 350–51
Dietrich of Schönberg, 346
Dill, Bartlme, 184, 369
Dillingen, 350
Dinkelsbühl, 94
Dittrich, Christoph, 338, 371
Dobitsch (Tobitschau) near Prerau, 347
Döllingen (Dollinger, Töllingen), Christina, 370
Döllingen, Jorgen, 370
Donauwörth, 88, 348
Donner, Hans, of Wals, 384
Dorfbrunner, Leonhard, 59, 338
Drasenhofen, 275–76, 279, 281

Drau Valley, 199
Dräxler, Jörg, 362
Dreier (Träyer, Trayer), Hans, 39, 332, 334
Driedger, Leo, 324
Dubcansky, Jan, of Habrovany, 103, 342–44
Dyck, Cornelius J., 353

Ebner, Appolina, 242, 385
Ebner, Georg, 242, 385
Ebner, Mathias, of Götzenberg, 389
Ebner, Michel, 242, 374
Ebner, Peter, 385
Eck, John, 367
Eckbolsheim, 397
Eckel, Fabian, 292, 363
Edwards, Mark, 324
Eger (Cheb), 92
Eibenschitz (Ivancice), 55, 67, 69, 87, 139, 157, 289, 291, 340, 358, 360
Eichstedt, 350
Eire, Carlos M., 366
Eisack (Isarco) Valley, 162, 164, 166, 186; River, 249, 255
Eisenstadt, 58
Elector of Mainz, 94
Ellen, 267
Emershofen, Ludwig, 368
Emmental, 106
Empach (Taxenbach), 350
Engadin, 182
Enns Valley, 224
Entfelder, Christian, 55, 84, 124, 132, 134, 137, 139–46, 152, 156–57, 291, 357–58, 360–61, 363
Enz River, 349
Erasmus of Rotterdam, 18, 327
Erenburg, 244
Erhard, Christoph, 349–50, 388
Erlangen, 57
Ernst, Duke of Bavaria, 93, 350, 399
Ernst of Glatz, 352
Eschlperger, Hans. *See* Aschlperger
Esslingen, 79–80, 85, 91–92, 215, 221, 285, 344–46, 349, 379, 398
Etsch (Adige) Valley, 162, 164, 182, 186, 269, 364, 376, 395
Etzlinweiler, 348
Euphemia of Hochberg, 399

Faber, John, 367
Fabri, Dr. Johan, 188–89
Falkenstein, 380
Färber (Ferber), Kaspar, 59
Fasser, former monk, 394
Fasser (Vasser), Georg (Jörg), 228, 230, 234, 258, 266, 275–81, 375, 379, 382, 385–86, 390, 394, 397
Fasser, Hans, 62, 215
Fasser (Fesser), Martin, 91, 396, 398
Fasser, Paul, 395
Fast, Heinold, 8, 30–31, 38, 50, 133, 146, 325–26, 330–33, 336, 354, 358, 361
Feldberg, 104
Felix, Hans, 359
Felix, Ursula, 359
Fell (Föll), Valentein (Valtein), 367, 373
Ferdinand I, 11, 67–75, 100, 135, 148, 151, 164–65, 184, 187–98, 212–14, 234, 236, 238–40, 247, 252–55, 261, 264, 270–72, 276, 278, 283, 285, 289–92, 343, 369–70, 388, 399
Ferdinand II, 73, 75, 363
Fessler, Christian, 325
Feuchter (Fichter, Feuchtner, Feichtner, Feichter), 172, 369–70. *See also* Füchter
Feuerbach, 288
Fichter, Konrad, 376
Fichter, Paula, 364
Filga, 395
Fischer, A. Christoph, 123, 337, 386–88
Fischer, Andreas, 103, 105, 116, 121, 143
Fischer, Hans G., 401
Flass, 373
Fleiner, Joachim, 345
Fluri, 329–30
Forrest, Ruth, 333
Franciscan(s), 104–5, 110–11, 370, 393
Franck, Sebastian, 54, 151, 337, 345, 358
Franconia, 54–57, 60, 65, 75, 202, 222, 379
Frankenhausen, 338
Frankenstein, 102
Frankfurt, 345
Frankfurt on the Oder, 376
Frankfurter, Dr. Jacob, 245
Franz, Günther, 338, 342, 367
Frauenstadt (Wschowa), 292

Frederic of the Palatinate, 94
Frederic II, Duke of Liegnitz, 100–101,
    105, 107, 111, 343, 353
Frederic the Wise, 144
Freiburg, 335
Freising, 164
Freisleben, Christoph, 80–81, 121, 331,
    345, 400
Freisleben, Leonhard, 121, 339
Freistadt, 58, 192
Frey, Claus, 85, 347
Freyberg, Helena of, 136
Frick, Georg, 370
Frick, Leonard, 369
Fridberger, Balthasar, 341
Friedmann, Robert, 11, 34–36, 52, 54–
    55, 61, 66, 89, 95, 98, 170, 212, 225,
    234, 303–15, 324–26, 331, 335, 337,
    340, 342–49, 351–56, 364–67, 375–
    77, 380–81, 384, 396
Friesen, Abraham, 337, 360, 362
Frisch, Hans, 79, 345, 379
Froben, press, 18
Fromdl, Kurdl, 395
Froschauer, press, 27, 29, 329
Frue, Georg, 266–67
Fuchs, Christoff, 253, 258–59, 389
Fuchs, Heinrich, 338
Füchter (Fichter, Vichter, Veichter),
    Kuntzen (Cunz), 210, 212, 375–76,
    381. *See also* Feuchter
Fuhrmann, Hans, 97–98
Fünfkirchen, Hans of, 394
Furcha, Edward J., 360, 401
Fürfeld, 82, 85, 286, 346, 348
Fürstein, 399
Füssen, 177
Fygenbutz, Hans, 345

Gäbler, Ulrich, 326–28, 333, 400
Gabriel. *See* Ascherham
Gaismair, Erhard, 376
Gaismair, Michael, 162, 167, 170–75,
    179, 182–83, 197, 366, 369, 373, 376
Gall (Gasserin), Justina, 210–11, 377,
    384
Gall, Paul, 205, 210, 241, 377, 384
Gallpüchlerin, 369
Gamper. *See* Kamperer, Elizabeth
Garnsee, 291, 399

Gartner, Michel, of Ettenheim, 344, 397
Gasser, Anna, 370
Gasser, Barbara, 370
Gasser, Hans, 172, 183–84, 366, 370
Gasser, Jacob, 172–73
Geiser, Samuel, 106, 331, 336, 353
Gelmi, Josef, 365, 368
Geltersdorf, 81
Gemmingen, 82, 346
Gemmingen, Philip von, 346
Geneva, 176
Gentner (Genntner), Hans, 285–87, 348,
    396–97
Georg of Firmian, 177
Georg III, Bishop of Brixen, 166
Gerber, Anna, of Tisen, 385
Gerber, Ulrich, 326, 333
Gerding, 350
Gerhard, Balthasar, 199–200, 373
Germanus, Martin, 346
Gerner, Gottfried, 325
Gerson, Jean, 360
Geyerspühler, Niclas, 364
Gilg, 234, 338
Gilgenburg, 399
Glaidt, Oswald, 99–106, 110–11, 116,
    121, 131–32, 143, 340, 351–53, 397
Glaser, Bastel (Bastien Hubmaier), 266,
    270, 280, 392
Glasser, Bernhard, 230, 379
Glatz, 101, 107–9, 292
Glogau, 101, 108, 353
Glögg, Hans, 179
Glurns, 182
Gmünd (Schwäbisch), 286, 348
Gmünden (Austria), 397
Göding, 401
Goertz, Hans-Jürgen, 1, 4–7, 17, 46,
    324–26, 335, 338, 347
Goeters, J. F. G., 325
Goldschmied, Heinrich, 372
Göschl, Martin, 68
Gossensass, 241, 384
Götzenberg, 206, 224, 256, 267, 372
Grading, 93
Graphaeus, William, 291
Gratz, Delbert, 332
Graudentz (Grudziadz), 291
Grebel, Conrad, 2–3, 20–22, 26–31, 40,
    46, 80, 287, 327–30, 332, 334–35

Greifenwink (Greifenburg), 246, 386
Grell, Johann, 332
Grembs (Grembser), Hans, 172, 205, 388, 391
Grembs, Margareth, 205
Grembs, Veronica, 205, 246, 268, 374–75, 386, 391
Greuel, Hans, of Geltersdorf, 81
Griesbacher, Wilhelm, 222, 240, 280, 379, 381, 384
Griesinger, Onophrius (Onofrius, Offrus, Afruzen), 205, 224, 237, 256, 258, 260, 262, 266–81, 290, 362, 364, 380, 383, 386, 389–90, 392–93; wife, 392, 394
Groff, Daniel, 337
Gross, Jacob, 80
Gross, Leonard, 11, 342, 351
Gross-Glogau, 100
Grosswalba, 341
Gruber, Lamprecht, 209–12, 376
Gruber, Paul, 364–65, 375
Grünfelder (Grienfelder), Hans, 269–70, 280, 392
Grüningen, 183, 334
Gschäll, Christoph, 62, 205, 216, 242, 266, 280, 364, 385, 396
Gsell (Gäsl), Valentin, 377
Gubrau, 398–99
Güding, 348
Gufidaun (Gudon), 172, 176–77, 179, 182, 202, 211, 224, 250, 256, 269, 366–67, 373–74, 388
Gunzenhofen (Gunzenhausen), 349

Haas, Martin, 1, 7–8, 324–28
Habelschwerdt, 292
Haffner, Agnes (Engella), 95, 98
Haffner, Hans, 95, 98, 351
Haffner, Jörg, 92, 351
Hagenau, 94, 344
Hager, Johannes, 329
Haina, 338
Hall, 177, 180, 364, 368, 374
Haller, Berchtold, 38–39, 333, 367
Hans (Schreiner) of Oelbronn (Heilbronn), 285, 397. *See also* Schreiner
Hans of Schwaigern, 91, 93
Hans of Strasbourg (Hans Felix), 231, 382

Hapsburg, 68, 175, 285
Harder, Leland, 327–34, 336
Häringin, Ulrich, 386
Härscher, 198, 372
Hart, Elizabeth, 333
Hartitsch, Dietrich von, 322
Hartknoch, Christoph, 398
Hätzer, Ludwig, 27, 64, 78, 80–81, 151, 329, 345–46, 366
Haug, Jörg, 56, 338
Hausmann, Johannes (Hans Seckler), 39–42, 45, 332
Hege, Christian, 339, 346–47, 364
Heidelberg, 2, 82–83, 94
Heilbronn, 89, 91, 284, 286, 348
Hein, Gerhard, 345
Heinrich of Lomnitz, Lord of Jamnitz (Jemnice), 336
Hellrigel, Oswald, 372
Henneberg, Lord, 338
Hensel, Johann, 352, 356
Hergot, Hans, 56
Herolt, Johann, 348
Heroltitz, 269
Hesius, Eobanus, 201, 374
Hess, Hans, 352
Hesse, 54, 122, 222, 224, 286, 379
Heunfels, 166
Heupher, Jacob, 182
Hilber, Sigmund, 386
Hillerbrand, Hans, 1–2, 146–47, 149, 323–25, 355, 361–63
Hilpolstein, 93
Hirsch, Emmanuel, 2, 323
Hobbs, Gerald, 333, 360
Hochrütiner, Jacob, 332
Hoffer, Sigmund, 341
Hoffman, Melchior, 4, 6, 79, 114, 143–44, 146, 324, 331, 387, 397
Hoffmanites, 55
Hoffmann, Hans, 351
Höglerlin, Elizabeth, 205, 391
Hohenstein, 398
Hohenwart, 392
Holitsch, 381
Holl, Karl, 2, 4, 324
Hombst, Franz, Emperor's governor, 148
Höng, 366
Hopfgarten, 136, 269, 380
Horb, 191, 345, 379

Hornacker, Michel, and wife, 390
Horsch, John, 287, 397
Hörschwang, 242–43, 246, 248–49,
    254–55, 372
Hostettler, John A., 11, 36, 331, 377–78
Hötzel, Hieronymus, 56
Hruby, Frantisek, 342–43
Hubmaier, Balthasar, 4, 6–7, 27, 30, 56,
    58, 60–61, 64, 68–70, 75, 104–7,
    139, 151, 181, 188, 214–15, 324,
    330–31, 334, 336, 340, 342, 346, 352,
    371, 397, 400
Hueber, Hans, 172, 366
Hueber, Ruprecht, 370, 372
Hueber of Götzenberg, 386
Huepher, Jacob, 177, 182–83
Hueter, Caspar, 178, 198–99, 252
Hueter, Georg, 147, 148
Hueter, Hans, 362
Hueter, Peter, 377, 381–82
Hui, Mathias, 369
Hungary, 67, 68, 73, 187
Hungerl, Peter, 376
Huss, John, 66, 69, 360
Hut, Hans (Hans of Bibra), 4, 6, 34–35,
    47, 52, 56–61, 64–65, 69, 75, 79–80,
    102, 105, 120, 126, 269, 324, 335,
    338, 340–41, 346, 350, 352
Hutscher, Ulrich, of Oberntief, 347
Hutter, Jacob, 36, 62–63, 72, 74, 95,
    120, 124, 129–30, 156, 162, 165,
    173–78, 184, 187, 193, 196, 198–213,
    214–60, 264, 266–70, 273–78, 280–
    84, 286, 291, 302, 357, 372–74, 377,
    379–88, 391, 401
Hutter, Katherine (Treindle), 240–47,
    249, 255, 384, 386, 388–89
Hutterin, Agnes, 373

Iglau (Jihlava), 67
Ilzstadt, 84
Imst, 270
Ingersheim, 349
Innerhofer, Josef, 367
Innichen, 176
Inninger, Franz, 378
Inn River, 135, 196–97, 383
Innsbruck, 164, 166, 175, 177, 179–81,
    183, 195, 199–200, 202, 222, 239,
    241, 244–45, 247, 250, 252, 254,
    269–70, 272, 278, 280, 368, 379, 382,
    388, 394
Inn Valley, 34, 59, 135, 164, 177, 202,
    206, 224, 270, 364
Inwald, Thomas, 370
Inzing, 177, 180
Itzinger, Franz, 64–65, 219

Jackson, Samuel M., 332
Jäger, Philip, 59, 64, 78, 81, 341, 344
Jäkel, Josef, 170, 365
Jamnitz (Jemnice), 69, 97–98, 157, 397;
    Lord of, 97, 336, 352
Jarochniewitz, 289
Jauer, 100, 107, 398–99
Jaufen Valley, 164, 205, 365, 384
Jeronimus. *See* Käls
Jezler, Peter, 366
Jobst, (Julius), of Gmünd, 350
Johannes, Count of Hartneck, 109
Jörg of Ingersheim. *See* Leserlin
Joris, David, 324
Josephus, Flavius, 111
Jud, Leo, 366
Jungmann, Michael, 347
Justina, 395

Kager, Mang, 370
Kaiser (Käser), Leonhard, 121
Kalenec, Johann, 359
Käls, Jeronimus, 222, 237, 240, 246–49,
    258–68, 278–81, 364, 378, 383, 389–
    90, 392, 394–95
Käls, Treindl (Katherine), 265, 391
Kalten, 202
Kamperer, Agatha, 335, 370
Kamperer (Gamperer, Gamper), Eliza-
    beth, 370
Kamperer (Gamper), P. Benedict, 199,
    370, 373
Kamperer, Rosina, 370
Karl I, Duke of Münsterberg-Oels, 100,
    343
Karlstadt, Andreas-Bodenstein von, 9, 21,
    181, 189, 354, 366–69, 375
Karneid, 202
Käser, Frantz, 373
Kaufbeuren, 339
Kaunitz, Jan, 340
Kaunitz, Peter, 340

Kaunitz, Ulrich (Oldrich), 69, 340
Kaunitz, Vaclav, 340
Kautz, Jacob, 49, 64, 78–85, 341, 345, 361
Keil, Hermann, 60
Keim, A., 323
Keller, Ludwig, 329
Kellermann, Hans, 93, 397
Kematen, 177
Kenzingen, 346
Kerschpaumer, Mathes, and wife, 370
Kessler, Johann, 42, 44, 49, 325, 327–28
Kiens, Sigmund, 242, 367
Kilchberg, 332
Kintner, Philip, 341
Kirchberg, 348
Kirchen, 362
Kirchenheim, 350
Kirchner, Alexander, of Frankenhausen, 338
Kitzbühl, 59, 135, 164, 192, 195, 202, 259, 382
Klaassen, Walter, 10–11, 171, 324, 326–27, 337, 339, 357–61, 365–68, 398, 400
Klassen, John, 342
Klassen, William, 50, 133, 303–15, 326, 331, 336–37, 357–61, 398
Klausen (Chinsa), 162, 164, 176–83, 202, 205, 246, 249, 255, 367–68, 375, 386–87
Klein, Bernhard, 345
Klein, Utz, 340
Klettgau, 84
Klopffer, Hans, 288, 398
Knarr, Hans, 97
Kniepasser, 391
Knott, Peter, 292
Knur (Knarr), Lienhardt, 98
Kobl (Köblin), Margaret, 370, 372
Kobl, Ulrich, 182–83, 369–70
Koehler, Walter, 2
Köffler (Kofler, Köfl), Cunz (Connz, Chonzen), 386, 389
Koffmane, Gustav, 352–54, 399
Köfler, Gretl, 161, 364–65
Kolb, Franz, 161, 364
Königsberg, 341
Kostel, 74, 281
Kräl, Hans, 364

Kräntzler, (Caspar), 240, 242, 246–47, 254–55, 388
Krasnik (Lubelski), 290, 398
Kraus, Albrecht, 270, 273–74, 393
Kraus, fisherman, 345
Kraut, Heinz, 338
Krautschlegel, Jörg, 58
Kraybill, Donald B., 324
Krebs, Manfred, 346
Kreutz, 289, 401
Kreutznach, 287
Krineium, Wilhelm, Baron of Ronau, 399
Kronau, 348
Krumau. *See* Bohemian Krumau
Krunewetter, Peter, 377
Krüsi, Hans, 21, 31, 45, 80, 331, 335
Kufstein, 59, 164, 222, 258–59, 374, 380, 389
Kuhn (Kumauff), Blasius (Plass), 84–88, 284–86, 350, 378, 381, 397
Kuhn, Elisabeth, 350
Kuna, John, of Kunstadt, 71, 238
Kunigl, Caspar, von Erenburg, 245
Kuppelwieser, Karl, 370, 372, 374, 381, 395
Kürschner, Anthoni, 391
Kürschner (Klesinger), Michael, 184, 202–3, 364, 370, 374
Kurssner, Peter, 176
Kurtasch, 202

Landsbergin, 180
Landschad, Hans of, 346
Landtsberger (Landsperg), Christoff, 368, 371
Landwehr, Arthur, 345
Lang, Archbishop of Salzburg, 371
Lang, Georg, 348
Langegger, Hans, 184, 370
Lanntz (Lanz, Lantz), Peter, 193–94, 205, 208, 266, 268, 375
Lantzinger, 177
Lanzenstiel, Leonard. *See* Sailer
Lasacher, Mathias, 388
Lasacherin, Katharina, 388
Lassling, 89, 284, 396
Lassmann, Wolfgang, 161, 338, 341, 364, 370–71, 374
Latzfons, 177
Laube, Adolf, 325, 365

Lauingen, 288, 350
Lautern, 339
Lavater, Hans Rudolf, 330
Leber, Oswald, 339, 346
Leifers, 202, 373
Leinen, 82, 85
Leipzig, 258
Lemlin of Sindelfingen, 91
Lentzin, Anna (Pöchtin of Pinswang), 392
Leoben, 64, 65, 103
Leonhard (Goltperg), 355–56
Leserlin, Jörg. *See* Scherer
Leupold, Hans, 79–81, 85, 346
Lex, Gilg, 388
Liechtenstein, Hans of, 71
Liechtenstein, Leonhard of, 103
Liechtenstein, lords of, 58, 61, 64, 69, 189, 238, 284, 290, 340, 353
Liechtenstein, Philip of, 372
Liechty, Daniel, 105, 352–53, 355
Liegnitz, 100, 106, 108, 111, 353
Liesenberg, Ursula, 348, 351
Lindl (Lynnal, Lidner, Lynngal), Thomas (Thoman), of Schwaz, 242, 379, 385
Linz, 58, 60, 121, 192, 301, 367, 397
Lipa, Johann of, 69, 71, 348, 358
Lipp, Elspet, of Villnöss, 385
Lippe, Lord Marshal of, 237
Lober, Julius, 84, 85, 91, 220, 347, 377
Locher, Gottfried, 329, 333, 350
Locher, Heini, 331
Lochmair, Leonhard, 258, 270–72, 280, 290, 393; wife, 393
Lomnitz (Lomnic), Heinrich of, 69, 352
Loserth, Johann, 120, 170, 181, 338–39, 352–53, 355, 364–65, 367, 369, 371, 376, 379, 381, 389–90, 392–94, 396
Louis, King of Bohemia, 352
Loy, Katharina, 221
Lublin (Lubelski), 290, 398
Ludenburg (Breclav), 343
Ludwig V, 81, 346
Lueger, Paul, 394
Lukhner, Valentin, 205–7, 211, 241, 373–75, 381, 389
Lundenburg, 71
Lüsen (Lisen), 162, 245, 247–50, 255, 260, 268, 270, 275, 374, 386, 392
Luther, Martin, 26–27, 181, 189, 201, 274, 335–36

Lutz, Lienhard, 80, 345
Lutz, Wolfgang, 148, 362

Macek, Josef, 170–71, 366, 369
Maier (Meier), Marx, 59
Maier, Paul L., 401
Maier (Mayer), Walser (Balthasar?), 395; wife, 395
Mair, Anthon, 370
Mair, Christoph (Stoffel), and wife, 370
Mair, Leonhard, magistrate of Brixen, 250
Mairhofer, Balthasar, of Lüsen, 205; Otilia, wife of, 391
Mairhofer, Balthasar, of Nidervintl, 205–8, 210, 268, 369, 372, 375, 382
Mairhofer, Caspar, of Nidervintl, 183, 205
Mairhofer, Christoph, magistrate of Klausen, 387
Mairhofer, Hans, 208
Mairhofer (Grembs), Margreth, 205–6
Mairhofer, Peter, 207
Mairhofer, Veronica, 205, 207
Mais, Adolf, 389–91, 395
Maleczynska, E., 355
Maler, Georg, 359
Man, Hannsen, of Trens (Tryns), 241
Mändel (Mändl), Hans, 301, 364, 395, 401
Mändel, Jacob, 64–65, 219, 378
Mannheim, Karl, 324
Mansee, Hieronymus of, 59
Mantz, Felix, 22, 27–31, 92, 327, 330
Marienwerder (Kwidzyn), 291, 399
Marpeck, Pilgram, 31, 36, 43, 46, 49, 50–53, 79, 83, 85, 123–24, 133–58, 201, 215, 217, 220, 222, 288, 325, 331, 336–37, 340, 348–49, 356–64, 377–79
Martin, Dennis, 361
Märtz, Joachim, 57, 59, 338, 341
Marx, 234
Mathes (Legeden), 281
Matheus of Dornau, 350
Mauls, 205
Maurer, Hans, 340, 346, 372, 374, 377
Maurer, Kuntz (Cuntz, Contz, Conntz), 266, 382, 385
Maxmillian I, 165, 166

Mayer, Walser, 266, 391
McConica, James, 326
McLaughlin, Emmet, 352, 401
Mecenseffy, Grete, 58, 170, 191, 331,
  338–39, 366, 368, 371, 373, 376, 382,
  387–88
Meichsen, 147
Melanchthon, Philip, 292, 397
Melmeser, Leonhart, wife of, 390
Memmingen, 64, 341
Meran (Merano), 164, 372
Meseritz (Miedzyrzecs), 398
Messerschmied, Mathias, 176–77, 180–
  83, 367, 369
Messerschmied, Paul, 367
Meyer, Christian, 339
Meyer, Theodor, 364
Mezger, J. J., 329
Michalski, Sergiusz, 366
Michelsburg, 165
Midelfort, Eric, 324, 335
Mistelbach, 389
Mödling, 276–79
Moeller, Ernst, 324
Montal, 177
Moos, 198
Mosel, Andreas, 340
Moser, Heinz, 365
Mosham, Ruprecht, 93–96, 350
Mühlbach, 377
Mühlhausen, 56
Müller, Ernst, 36–37, 332
Müller, Dr. (Gallus), 252–53, 270, 371,
  376, 392
Müller, Georg, 387
Müller, Klaus, 278, 395
Müller, Lydia, 391
Müller, Ulrich, 177, 181, 183, 369, 372
Münchenau, 136
Munich, 81, 349
Münster, 4, 10, 70, 236, 285, 336, 363,
  382
Müntzer, Thomas, 4–10, 20–21, 27, 33,
  40, 56–57, 124, 126, 144, 325, 327,
  337–39, 342, 362
Murner, Thomas, 367
Myconius, Oswald, 328

Nachtgal, Othmar, 333
Nagel, Hans, von Klingnau, 30
Nannsgarten, 396

Neckar Valley, 81–82, 88, 284, 294
Neckarsteinach, 82
Neckarweihingen, 91
Neff, Christian, 369, 371
Neidenburg, 398
Neisse River, 292
Nelson, Stephen, 344
Nespitzer, Jörg (Georg of Staffelstein,
  Jörg of Passau), 59, 350
Neudorf, 394
Neuenburg, 91
Neuhaus, 391
Neumarkt (Egna), 182, 395
Neumühl (Nove Mlony), 343
Nicholas II, Pope, 327
Niclauer, husband and wife, 387
Nicoladoni, Alexander, 341
Nicolsburg (Mikulov), 48, 56–64, 67–
  70, 75–78, 81, 100, 103–5, 112, 139,
  181, 189, 204, 276, 338, 340, 342–43,
  348, 352, 358
Niderhofer, Anna, 244–45, 256
Niderhofer, Niclas, 244–45, 256–57,
  374, 385, 387, 389, 393, 395
Nidervintl (Niedervintl), 162, 268
Niderwies, 386
Nieder (Nidrens), Martin, 244
Niedermaier, Appolonia, 369
Noflatscher, Heinz, 365, 372, 378, 381
Nuremberg, 56–57, 84–85, 94, 120,
  136, 148, 220, 292, 346–47, 349, 352
Nussloch, 82, 85

Oberecker (Zimmermann), Hans, 259–
  61, 265
Oberegkh of Auers, 389
Oberhaus, 91, 94
Obermann, Heiko, 371
Obern, (Hans and Dorothea), 242, 246,
  248, 254–55, 386, 388
Obernberg, 339, 355
Oberntief, 347
Oberperfuss, 177
Ochs, Christoph, 200, 245–46, 250, 388
Odenbach, Johann, of Obermoschel, 81
Odenwald, 339
Oecolampadius, Johannes, 38, 189, 332,
  367
Oeder, Hans, 356
Ofen (Budapest), 342
Offenhauser, Erasmus, 250

Olmütz (Olomouc), 67, 70
Olmütz, Bishop of, 68
Onach, 387
Onophrius. *See* Griesinger
Osiander, Andrew, 201
Othmar, Silvanus, 331
Ottentaler, Leonard, 371
Otter, Jacob, of Neckarsteinach, 81–83, 346
Ottmachau, 292
Oyer, John, 94, 96, 324, 334, 349–51
Ozment, Steven, 375

Packull, Werner, 7, 325, 329, 335–40, 345–46, 349–56, 358–60, 372, 391
Pader. *See* Bader, Gilg
Palatinate, 54, 77, 87–88, 122, 283–89, 294
Pallau (Pavlov), 398
Palme, Rudolph, 358, 364–66
Palmer, Lee, 366
Panek, Jaroslav, 340, 342–44
Pänntzlen, Simon, 211
Paracelsus, 18, 69
Parugkher, Jörg, 172
Passau, 58–60, 69, 89, 91–98, 284, 287, 289, 336, 339, 350–52, 361, 397
Passiers, Hans, van Wesbusch, 97
Pastawska, Janina, 354
Paulle, Caspar Mair, 204
Paulle, Hans (Hänsel) Mair, and wife, 181, 204–5, 211, 246, 248, 269, 374–75, 377, 385–86, 389
Peachy, Paul, 325
Peckelhaube, Ulrich, 198, 373
Pelikan, Jaroslav J., 360
Pernstein, Behunda of, 69, 122, 347–48
Pernstein, Lord Jan (Johan) of, 68, 146, 148, 152–53, 292, 347, 359, 361–62
Petri, Adam, 26–27, 326, 331
Pfeddersheim, 398
Pfeifer, Heinrich, 56
Pfistermeyer, Hans, 330
Pflaurentz, 162, 177, 180, 199, 364
Philip. *See* Plener
Philip of Hesse, 371
Pilgramites, 55, 147
Pinter, Peter, 177, 183, 368–69, 387
Pipkin, Wayne H., 330, 336, 352
Planer, Peter, 376
Plattner, Virgil, 62, 355
Plener (Blauärmel, Plaermel, Weber),

Philip, 65, 77–98, 122, 220, 223, 226–35, 277, 284–85, 344, 346, 348, 379–80, 382–83, 396–97
Pletscher, Werner, 332
Pöchtin von Pinswang, 389
Pöggstall, 279
Poland, 283, 289–90
Polau, 397
Poliander, John, 291
Popitz (Poppitz), 97–98, 157, 281
Porter, Jacob, 59
Portnzer, Jacob, 364
Portz, Hans, 370
Posen (Poznan), 398–99
Potter, G. R., 328–29, 334
Prags, 252
Pranger (Prengger), Christel (Christan), 266–67
Prast, Erika, 364–65, 372–73, 375
Präst (Prust), Katherine, 240. *See also* Hutter
Präst (Prusst), Lorentz (Laurentzer), 384
Praun, Appolonia, 247–48
Praun, Niclas, 247, 389
Praweiger (Prabeiger), 266–67, 392
Prerau (Prerov), 347
Pretz, Elizabeth, 380
Pretz, Gertraud, 380
Preu, Adam, 250, 255, 367
Preu, Hans, 177
Pries, Edmund, 369
Prunsterer, Sixt, 88
Puchler, Vintzentz, 172
Puhl, Vinzenz, 381
Pulgram, 74, 276, 281, 396–97
Pürchner, Hans, 194; wife, 391
Puster Valley, 162, 164–67, 174, 177, 179–81, 186, 198, 201, 203, 213, 241–45, 247–49, 255, 266, 269–70, 279–80, 364, 384–85, 387, 393
Pusterer(s), 162–63, 198, 203, 213, 232, 235, 247, 267–68, 294, 382

Quiring, Horst, 399

Rackwitz, 281
Rader, Katherine, 373
Radler, Andrä, 181
Radler, Leonhart, 181, 354, 399
Raiffer-Schmidt, Lienhard (Leonhard), 377, 396

Rainer, Balthasar, 392
Rainer, Hans, 392
Raisenberg, 147
Rasstainerin, 385–86
Rastner, Alois, 367–70
Rattenberg, 34–36, 59, 62, 135, 164,
183, 201, 211, 222, 259, 276, 339–40,
358, 369, 379, 381–82
Rauden, 398
Rayggen-Brunn, 397
Rayner, Anna, 388
Rayner, Connzen (Kuntz), 388
Regensburg, 146–49, 151–54, 188, 339,
362–63, 371
Reichel, Johann, 100
Reichenbach, 110
Reif, Balthasar, of Allstedt, 338
Reimer, James, 324
Rems Valley, 91, 349
Reschl, Wölffl, 266
Resl, (Rosemary), 391
Reublin, Wilhelm, 20, 22, 49, 78–81,
84–88, 91, 122, 149, 215–21, 235,
345–48, 359–60, 377–79
Rhegius, Urbanus, 367
Rhineland, 54, 79, 87–88, 215, 221,
283–87, 289, 332
Rhine Valley, 81, 220, 294
Riblingen (Rüblingen), 95
Ridmaier, Bärtel, 101
Riedemann (Ridemann), Peter, 72, 101,
162–63, 280, 286, 288, 337, 343, 348,
364, 393, 396
Rinck, Melchior, 338
Rischar, Klaus, 392
Ritten, 183–84, 201, 384
Ritter, Erasmus, of Schaffhausen, 330
Ritter, Gerhard, 2
Rodeneck, 172, 241, 245, 256, 260
Rodtmäntel, Christian, 340
Rohrbach, 281
Römer, Hans, 338
Röschl, Wölfl, 395
Rossitz (Rosice), 65–72, 84, 87, 99–132,
226, 228, 283, 289, 340, 356
Roth, John, 330, 344–46
Roth, Leonhard, 398
Rothenburg o.d. Tauber, 368
Rothmann, Bernhard, 123, 331, 400
Rott, Jean-George, 344

Rottenburg, 215
Rottweil, 333
Rumer, Justina, 205, 375, 386
Rumer, Leonard, 375
Rumer (Riemer, Rumbler), Paul, 205–11,
241, 246–47, 370, 374–75, 381, 384,
388
Rüschlikon, 20
Ruthenia, 283, 290

Säben, 177
Sackmann, Benedikt, and wife (Sackman-
nin, Andle [Anne]), 370, 384
Sailer, Leonard (Lanzenstiel), 62, 266,
271, 275–81, 377, 389, 393, 394–97
Sailer, Martha, 279–80, 395
St. Andreasberg, 172, 245
St. Gall, 31, 42–45, 182, 287, 328, 332,
335
St. Georgen, 162, 164, 178, 205, 208,
241, 246, 268, 364, 373
St. Leonhard, 245
St. Lorenzen, 164, 178, 198, 373
St. Michelsburg, 162–67, 177, 193, 200,
211, 245, 252, 267, 269, 373
St. Niclas, 60, 339
St. Sebald, 120
St. Stephen, 67
St. Veit, 384
Sallmann, Wosstl, 373
Salzburg, 59, 164, 183, 269, 338–39
Salzer, Dr. Ambrosius, 261
Salztrager, Loy, 240, 384
Samsfeuer, Wilhelm, 373
Sand, 179
Sarn Valley, 177
Sattler, Michael, 28, 37, 78, 92, 121, 134,
191, 215, 287, 324
Saxony, 147, 258, 358
Schachner, Jörg, of Munich, 81, 346
Schackowitz (Schäkwitz, Sakvice), 67–
71, 74, 138, 236–37, 240, 259, 280–
82, 381, 383, 398, 401
Schaffhausen, 94
Schäffler (Schaffner, Schäfer), 241, 386
Schärding, 62, 121, 355
Scharf, Klaus, of Mühlhausen, 338
Scharnschlager, Leupold, 50, 134, 136,
303–15, 359, 382
Scharnschlager, Ursula, 382

Schaurer, Christoff, 374
Scheppach, Peter, 345
Scherdinger. *See* Ascherham
Scherer, Jörg, of Ingersheim (Leserlin, Seelscherer, Jerg Wernlin), 91–92, 349–50, 396
Schernegker, Margreth, 339, 356
Schernegker, Wolfgang, 121
Schiemer, Leonhard, 34–36, 47, 52, 59, 105, 110, 126, 132, 209, 331, 335, 338, 352, 354–55, 357, 365, 371
Schiesser, Hans, 369–70
Schlaffer, Hans, 34, 209, 341, 369
Schlegel, Adam, 87–88, 216, 221–22, 284–86, 348–49, 397
Schleitheim, 345
Schlern, 201, 374
Schlosser, Melchior, 135–36, 359, 380
Schluchtern, Hans, 91, 349
Schlumpf, Alberli, 331
Schmaltz, Andre, 376
Schmelzer, Mathias, 367–68
Schmerbacher, Leonard, 222–23, 376, 379–82
Schmid, Caspar, 369
Schmid, Hans-Dieter, 56, 337, 348, 352, 355
Schmidhans (Schmid, Hans), 91
Schmidt, Christoph (Stoffel), 246
Schmotzer, Dr., 393
Schnabel, Georg, 31
Schneider, Balthasar, 172
Schneider, Bartle, 211
Schneider, Bernhard, 93, 351
Schneider, Clara, 385
Schneider (Preindle), Gilg, 272–75
Schneider, Hans, 369
Schneider (Yetelhauser, Jedelshauser), Michael, 91, 93–97, 284, 349–51
Schneider, Michel, 394–95
Schneider, Peter, 266
Schneider, Valentin, 172
Schneider, Walser, 377
Schöneck, 166–67, 246, 255–56
Schornbaum, Karl, 147, 149, 361–62
Schottenloher, Karl, 368
Schreiber, William, 350
Schreiner, Hans, of Gmünd, 286, 348
Schuechknecht, Christoff, 206–7, 212, 377

Schüler, Barbara, 378
Schüler, Caspar, 378
Schumacher, Christoff, 373
Schuster, Christoph, 386
Schuster, Hans, 394
Schuster, Lorentz, 375
Schuster, Michael (Walser), 240, 242, 246, 382, 385
Schuster, Oswald, 271, 281, 395; wife Marthl, 391
Schützinger, Jobst, 379
Schützinger, Sigmund (Simon), 135, 203, 218–30, 232–35, 259, 276, 364, 379–82, 389, 394; wife Barbara, 382
Schützinger, (Christoph) Stoffel, 391
Schwäbisch-Hall, 95
Schwaigern (Swaigern), 397
Schwartz, Hillel, 390
Schwaz, 162, 164, 381
Schwebel, Johannes, 351
Schweidnitz, 87, 100–101, 107, 111, 292, 353, 399
Schwenckfeld, Caspar, 54–55, 84, 101, 105, 111, 116–17, 123–26, 133–34, 143–47, 157, 299–300, 330, 345, 349, 354–58, 361, 363
Schwetz (Swiecie), 398
Scribner, Robert, 325, 366
Seckler, Hans, 39–40, 333, 334. *See also* Hausmann
Seebass, Gottfried, 6, 56, 324, 337–38
Seguenny, Jean, 42, 49, 334, 358
Seidlitz, Hans von, 399
Seifensieder, Michael (Michel), 259–60, 264, 266, 280, 390–91
Seiler (Seiber), Heinrich (Heini), 332, 334
Seletitz, 397
Sergant, Hans, 248, 250
Shantz, Douglas, 352
Sider, Ronald J., 375
Sigismund I, King of Poland, 291
Sigmund of Kiens, 374
Silesia, 54, 84, 99–132, 145–88, 283, 289, 291, 294, 354, 398
Silvester, Pope, 105
Simon, the sorcerer, 127
Simons, Menno, 4
Slovakia, 73, 103, 105, 107, 344
Snyder, Arnold, 46, 324–29, 335, 371, 377

Sobek, Burian, 342
Sobotiste (Sabbatisch), 107
Soldau, 398
Solothurn, 331
Sommersberg, Friedrich W., 352
Sorg, Simprecht, 342, 353
Speratus, Bishop of Pomesen, 291
Speyer, 77, 94
Spiess (Schuster), Oswald, 367
Spital, 199
Spittelmaier, Ambrosius, 59, 340
Spittelmaier, Hans (Johannes), 61, 139,
     340, 360
Springer, Joe and Nelson, 333–34
Stadler, Ulrich, 93, 149, 271, 281, 290,
     336, 350, 354, 362, 364, 393, 397–98
Staffelstein, Georg of. *See* Nespitzer
Stainer, Anna (Nändl), 246–49, 255–56,
     384, 386–88
Stainer, Anna, widow of sexton, 249, 255
Stainer, Barbara, 246
Stainer, Hans, 246–47, 385
Stainer, Jacob, 249
Stainer Joch, 224
Starnitz (Stornitz, Starnice), 383, 396
Stayer, James, 1, 6–10, 33, 37, 41–42,
     56–59, 107, 191, 287, 324–26, 332–
     40, 342, 345, 353, 359, 365–67, 371,
     377–78, 397, 401
Steffan, priest, 177
Stegen, 178, 252, 368
Steger of Sterzing, 384
Steiermark, 224
Steinabrunn, 74, 93, 97, 275, 280
Steinberg, Michael, 111
Steinmetz of Sterzing, 389
Stella, Aldo, 365
Stephan (Rauchenecker), 149, 151, 362
Sterzing (Vipiteno), 162, 164, 176, 183,
     205, 209, 211, 241, 244–47, 250,
     254–55, 274, 364–65, 367, 371, 373,
     375, 378, 386
Stetten, 350
Steuber, Hans, 349
Steurowitz, 217–18
Steyer, 35, 58, 64, 191–92, 338, 397
Stifles, 386
Stoffel (Christoph) of Villach, 271–72,
     393
Stolz, 102

Stranstorff, 389
Strasbourg (Strassburg), 36, 40, 49, 51,
     64, 78–85, 94, 133, 136, 139–40, 154,
     157, 284–86, 329, 344–45, 347, 349,
     357, 360, 397
Strassnitz (Strasnits), 71
Strauss, Jacob, 367
Streicher, Konrad, 359
Striegau, 100
Striegel, Fritz, 341
Striegel, Hans, 341
Stroebel, Wolf, 281
Stroschneider, Jacob, 391
Strützel, 340
Stumpf, Simon, 366
Stumpffle, Adam, 345
Stumpfheter, Peter, 350
Sturtzhauser, 394
Stuttgart, 91, 288
Styria, 64, 65, 188, 392
Swabia, 49, 54, 65, 79, 87–88, 122, 220–
     21, 283–84, 287, 346, 349
Swiss Grisons, 164
Switzerland, 54, 79, 289, 331, 336
Szczucki, Lech, 398

Tabisch, 348
Tablat, 31, 45
Tagwericher, Katharina, 173, 244, 246,
     385
Tasswitz, 397
Tauffers (Taufers), 162, 179, 182, 241–
     42, 245, 375, 384, 387
Taurer, Andreas, 359
Taurer, Paul, 359
Taurer, Sebastian, 359
Taxenbach. *See* Empach
Teuffen, 45, 335, 351
Teutenhof, Michel von, 391
Thaler, Hans, 376
Thessalonica, 97
Thomas, Ulrich, 325
Thorn (Torun), 291, 398
Thuringia, 56, 65, 101, 224, 342
Tiers, 182
Tillich, Paul, 324
Tischlawitz (Tischlowitz), 269, 281
Tischler, Martin, 369
Tobitschau (Tovacov), 347
Toblach, 246, 386

Töblinger (Töbler, Töbisch), Hans, 45, 335
Tracht (Strachotin), 238, 396
Tramin, 182
Trapp, Jacob, 182
Träyer (Trayer). *See* Dreier
Trechsel, Ulrich, 345
Trenkwalder, Elias, 368
Trens (Tryns), 241, 247
Trent, 365
Treybenrief, Simon, 369
Trier, 94
Triest, 93, 280
Troeltsch, Ernst, 2, 324
Troyer, Anna, 246
Troyer, Paul, 245–46, 256, 271, 386, 393
Troyer, Peter, of Niedervintl, 244–47
Tschackert, Paul, 398–99
Tschernacher, Lord of Schertlin, 290
Turks, 56, 61, 67, 70–75, 111, 144, 223, 276, 337, 342–43

Uechtland, 335
Uhrmacher, Veit, of Grünberg, 352
Ulhart, Philip, 181, 368
Ulimann, Wolfgang, 49, 335–36
Ulm, 81–82, 85, 176, 285, 288, 333, 339, 345–47, 349
Ulrich, Duke of Württemberg, 285, 343, 396
Umlauft, Hans (Johannes), 147–54, 157–58, 359, 361–62
Underainer, Hänsel, 388
Unteröwisheim, 91
Urban, Waclaw, 337, 359, 398, 421
Urbau, 397
Urscher, Erhart, 197–98, 373–74
Uttenheim, 166
Uttenreuth, 341
Utz, Hans, 345

Vadian (von Watt), Joachim, 21, 327, 329
Vahrn, 386
Vaihingen, 91, 349
Varotto, Marcantonio, 54
Vasser, Jörg. *See* Fasser, Georg
Veh, Cornelius, 138, 363
Veit, Peter, 266, 391
Vels. *See* Völs
Velser, Sigmund, of Kiens, 385–86

Venzl (Fenzl, Wenzel), 361
Vichter, 172. *See also* Feuchter
Vienna, 62, 70, 104–5, 157, 189, 258–62, 266, 278, 290, 355, 390
Villnöss (Villness, Philnes, Vilnes, Wilness), 209, 241, 247, 372–73, 387
Vils, 182
Vilshofen, 339, 356
Vintschgau, 164, 177, 182
Vischer, Andre(as), 350. *See also* Fischer
Vischer, Gall, 339
Vischer, Hans, 176, 367
Vogel, Wolfgang, 20, 348
Voitsbrunn, 397
Volck, Jörg (Georg), 57–60, 65, 341
Volckhamer, Kilian, 57, 64–65, 215–16, 338, 341
Volckmer, Kolerin. *See* Volck
Völs (Vels, Vells), 21, 182, 374
Volynia, 283, 290
Voralberg, 188

Wackernagel, Philip, 350
Wagner, Georg, 348–49
Wagner, Martin, 91
Wagner, Murray, 401
Waldenses, 366
Walder, (Michel), 385
Waldhauser, Thomas, 59, 338–39, 343
Waldsee, 49
Waldshut, 7, 188–89, 215
Walpot, Peter, 182, 359, 381
Walser, Michael. *See* Schuster
Waltenhofen, Agnes von, 200, 395
Waltenhofen, George von, 250
Waltersdorf, 396
Walton, Robert, 325, 327
Wandl, Simon, 266
Wangen, 396
Wappler, Paul, 338–42
Watt, Tessa, 392
Weber, Georg, 180–81, 199, 373–74
Weber, Gregor, 177
Weber, Hans, 177, 181, 369–70
Weber, Jörg, widow of, 376
Weber, Max, 2
Wegscheid, 284
Weichsel (Vistula), 398
Weiden, Hans, 339
Weigelt, Horst, 343, 352–54, 399, 401

Weik, Bernhard, of Bruchsal, 347
Weil (der Stadt), 91
Weil (am Rhein), 91, 94
Weiler zum Stein, 350
Weinberger, Gabriel, 147–48, 362
Weischenfelder, Hans, 59
Weistritz River, 292
Weizenrode, 292
Wells, 58
Welsberg (Monguelfo), 162, 199, 366
Welser the Silesian (Schlesinger), 101
Wenger, John C., 332, 378
Werner, Bartel, 111
Werner, Hans, 340
Werner, John, 292
Wernitzer, Bonifacius, 348
Wernlin, Jerg. *See* Scherer
Westerburg, Gerhard, 291
Weyseyes, Blasius, 388
Widmann, Leonard, 362
Widmoser, Edward, 161, 170, 339, 364–65
Wiebe, Christoph, 327
Wiedemann, Hans, 339, 350, 355, 418
Wiedemann (Widemann), Jacob, 59–60, 64, 75, 78, 107, 136, 137, 215–20, 262, 283, 290, 340–41, 378–79
Wil, 31
Wilhelm, Count of Henneberg, 57, 342
Wilhelm IV, Count of Bavaria, 371
Williams, George, 1, 8, 36, 331, 337–38, 352, 355–56, 358, 360, 398–99
Wincklerin of Sal, 374
Windesheim, 85
Windorf, 276, 394
Wipp Valley, 164, 196
Wirt, Peter, 370
Wisternitz, 397
Wiswedel, Wilhelm, 120, 295, 344, 349, 352, 355–57, 360, 390, 398–400
Wittich, Joachim, 353
Wlodzimierz, 398
Wohlau, 107, 398
Wohlfeil, Rainer, 325
Wolff, Thomas, 329
Wolfgang of Burkhausen. *See* Brandhuber
Wolfgang of Moos, 370
Wölfl (Wolfgang), goatherd, 177–83, 199, 367–68, 370, 384
Wölfl of Götzenberg, 211–12, 377

Wolkan, Rudolph, 89, 170, 295, 348–50, 365, 381
Wolkenstein, Anton von, 179–81, 365, 384, 391
Wolkenstein, Elsbeth von, 179, 375
Wolkenstein, Sigmund von, 179, 375
Wolkenstein, Wilhelm von, 375
Worms, 27, 79–85, 94, 284, 329, 345, 352
Wratzow, 289
Württemberg, 135, 188, 284–86, 349
Würzlburger, Augustin, 339
Wycliff, John, 360

Yoder, John H., 36–39, 46, 303–15, 325–28, 330, 332–35, 337, 352

Zaisersweiher, 344
Zapolya, John, I, 67, 342
Zaunring (Zaunried), Jörg, 63, 87–88, 122, 169, 184, 200–203, 206, 209, 215–24, 230, 235, 291, 364–65, 374, 376, 379, 385, 400
Zaunring, Klärl (Klara), 376
Zellner, Erasmus, 147
Zeman, Jarold, 54–55, 69, 295, 337, 340–43, 347–48, 352, 356–62, 396–98, 400
Zeugerlin (Zugerin), Jacob, 393
Zieglschmid, A. Y. F., 334–35, 364, 376, 381, 383–84, 394
Zierotin, Johann of, 71
Ziller Valley, 259, 374
Zimmermann, Andre, 212, 373, 388, 391–92; wife Agnes, 391
Zimmermann, Christoff, 375
Zimmermann, Erhard, 391
Zirl, 367
Znaim (Znojmo), 67, 70, 87, 92–93, 147, 149, 221, 281, 289, 340, 382–83
Zoffingen, 335
Zollikon, 20, 22, 43–46, 49, 334
Zschäbitz, Gerhard, 10, 325
Zürcher, Isaac, 329–30, 335
Zurich, 9, 16–27, 44, 94, 177, 188, 215, 221, 328–29, 333–36, 352, 366, 376
Zweibrücken, 351
Zwingli, Ulrich (Huldrich), 2, 7, 9, 15–30, 32, 38–40, 46, 54, 181, 188–89, 274, 326–31, 333–34, 368, 400

About the Author

Werner O. Packull (b. 1941) is professor of history at Conrad Grebel College, University of Waterloo, Ontario. He was educated at Emmanuel Bible College in Kitchener (B.Th.) and the University of Guelf (B.A., with honors); he completed his M.A. at the University of Waterloo and his Ph.D. at Queen's University, Kingston. His books include *Mysticism and the Early South German-Austrian Anabaptist Movement, 1525–1531* (Herald Press, 1977), *The Anabaptists and Thomas Müntzer*, with James M. Stayer (Kendall/Hunt, 1980), and *Rereading Anabaptist Beginnings* (UMBC Publications, 1991). He has written chapters for more than a dozen books and numerous articles and reviews for publication in leading professional journals and encyclopedias.

The Library of Congress has cataloged the hardcover edition of this book as follows:

Packull, Werner O., 1941–
  Hutterite beginnings : communication experiments during the Reformation /
Werner O. Packull.
    p.   cm.
  Includes bibliographical references and index.
  ISBN 0-8018-5048-7 (alk. paper)
    1. Hutterite Brethren—History—16th century. 2. Anabaptists—History—16th
century. 3. Christian communities—Europe—History—16th century. I. Title.
Bx8129.H8P33   1995
289.7´3—dc20   95-41351
                                                                            CIP

ISBN 0-8018-6256-6 (pbk.)